The New Century Handbook

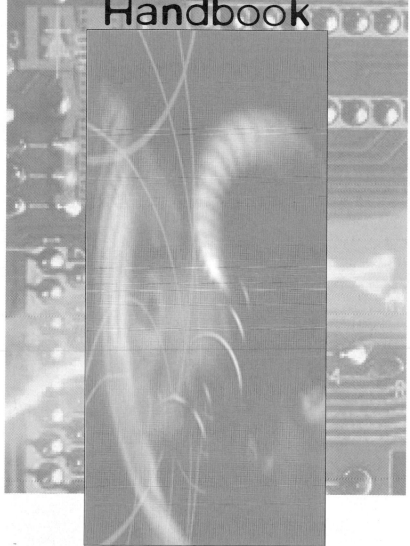

The New Century
Handbook

CHRISTINE A. HULT

Utah State University

THOMAS N. HUCKIN

University of Utah

ALLYN AND BACON

Boston   London   Toronto   Sydney   Tokyo   Singapore

Vice President and Editor in Chief, Humanities: *Joseph Opiela*
Development Editor: *Donna de la Perrière*
Editorial Assistant: *Mary Beth Varney*
Executive Marketing Manager: *Lisa Kimball*
Senior Editorial-Production Administrator: *Susan Brown*
Editorial Production Services: *Lifland et al., Bookmakers*
Interior Design: *The Davis Group, Inc.*
Cover Administrator: *Linda Knowles*
Cover Designer: *Susan Paradise*
Composition and Prepress: *Omegatype Typography, Inc.*
Composition Buyer: *Linda Cox*
Manufacturing Buyer: *Megan Cochran*

Copyright © 1999 by Allyn & Bacon
A Viacom Company
160 Gould St.
Needham, MA 02494
Internet: www.abacon.com

Between the time Website information is gathered and then published, it is not unusual for some sites to have closed. Also, the transcription of URLs can result in unintended typographical errors. The publisher would appreciate notification where these errors occur so that they may be corrected in subsequent editions.

Library of Congress Cataloging-in-Publication Data

Hult, Christine A.
    The new century handbook / Christine Hult, Thomas N. Huckin.
        p.   cm.
    Includes index.
    ISBN 0–205–27352–1 (hc.)
    1. English language—Rhetoric—Handbooks, manuals, etc.   2. Report writing—Data processing—Handbooks, manuals, etc.   3. English language—Grammar—Handbooks, manuals, etc.   I. Huckin, Thomas N. II. Title.
PE1408.H688   1999
808'.042'0285—DC21   98-43334
                                                                                        CIP

Printed in the United States of America
10 9 8 7 6 5 4 3 2 1   VHP   02 01 00 99

Contents

part two

Research

part three

Writing in the Disciplines

part four

Document Design

part seven

Correct Sentences

part nine

Effective Words

part eleven

Mechanics

Modal Auxiliary Verbs

Conditional Sentences

57   Tips on Word Order   790

58   Tips on Vocabulary   796

Preface

The New Century Handbook is a comprehensive resource for college writers. It shows students how to plan, compose, and revise; how to do research and formulate arguments; how to write for different disciplines and special purposes. At a time when many students arrive at college without adequate grounding in "the basics," this handbook provides thorough coverage of grammar, style, diction, and punctuation, as well as a special section on ESL problems. In an increasingly visual world, it shows students how to apply principles of document design. The handbook repeatedly emphasizes both the conventional and the rhetorical aspects of good writing, pointing out how even small details should reflect the writer's consideration of audience, persona, genre, field, and goals.

As we approach the new century, we find ourselves caught up in a technological revolution. Most students today do their writing on a computer, taking advantage of the unique features afforded by a word processor. Many use the Internet, gathering information on the World Wide Web and communicating via email with their peers. It is only logical that a handbook for writers should take these developments into account. We embarked on the writing of this handbook with the assumption that most of its users would be doing their writing on a computer. Consequently, *The New Century Handbook* is the first college handbook to be developed with computer users in mind, the first to integrate thoroughly the use of computer technology into instruction in the writing and research processes.

Content

Writing

While retaining a general focus on the rhetorical principles that underlie effective writing, this handbook is unique in that it shows students how to tap the power of computers to become more effective and more confident writers. The first part of the handbook shows students how to apply critical reading and writing processes to their own work. Accompanying boxes explain how computers can function as a powerful writing tool.

Part 1 opens with an overview of ways in which computers can help today's writers communicate better (Chapter 1). In the following chapters, student writers learn about critical thinking and the reading and writing processes (Chapter 2). They discover how to prepare for writing assignments (Chapter 3). They find out how to make the best use of the organizational possibilities computers offer for storing work in directories and folders. They also learn how to explore topics through Internet searches; how to brainstorm potential topics using email or newsgroups; and how to harness the power of computers to focus, develop, and organize ideas.

Chapter 4 introduces students to the many ways to compose. They learn techniques for combining prewriting and outlining documents, building a first draft from an electronic outline, and composing with documents in two separate windows. The chapter encourages students to collaborate online with other student writers, sharing drafts via computer networks and responding to each other's writing through document comments or email. Chapter 5 guides students through the steps in efficiently and effectively rewriting their work—from comparing and revising drafts of their texts to editing for more effective wording and sentence structure.

The next two chapters are devoted to two fundamental issues in writing academic papers: structuring paragraphs and formulating arguments. Chapter 6 explains how to devise an appropriate thesis, support it with compelling evidence, and construct paragraphs that guide readers through the text. Using a student essay on human cloning to illustrate its main points, Chapter 7 emphasizes the importance of audience analysis, sound reasoning, and considering alternative points of view.

Research

This handbook provides unparalleled coverage of the research process. The six chapters in Part 2 detail the steps in the research process; each chapter addresses the ways in which computers can facilitate researching and writing.

In addition to describing traditional library catalogs and print indexes, Chapter 8 covers such innovations as computerized notebooks and note cards, document comments and annotations, computerized footnote and bibliography programs, Boolean keyword searching, and online databases. Then, because the Internet is so radically changing the research process, two complete chapters explain using sources on the World Wide Web. Chapter 9 shows students how to use the Internet to find and explore topics, conduct background and focused research, and collaborate and exchange feedback with peers. It also illustrates the range of information available via the Internet and the use of search tools to find that information. Perhaps most importantly, Chapter 10 helps students assess the credibility and reliability of sources they find in print and on the Internet. Both Chapters 9 and 10 include model student searches.

An entire chapter (Chapter 11) covers using sources appropriately and effectively. The chapter offers helpful guidance on avoiding plagiarism and on quoting, summarizing, and paraphrasing source information. In Chapter 12, students learn to harness the power of computers as they plan and organize, draft, review and revise, and format research papers. Chapter 13 includes an overview of the MLA, APA, CMS, and CBE styles of documentation. In addition to supplying explanations and illustrations of how to document conventional sources, this handbook provides unprecedented coverage of how to document electronic sources. The latest information from the 1998 *MLA Style Manual* is included, as well as extensive and up-to-date tips on electronic citation formats across the disciplines.

Writing in the Disciplines

In Part 3, students get advice on writing papers for literature classes, as well as for other courses in the humanities, social sciences, and natural sciences. Each of these writing-across-the-curriculum chapters introduces students to the major types of writing in the disciplines and to the most important technological resources available. The extensive listings of Web sites were compiled by professors in the different disciplines and include only those sites they found most useful to themselves and their students.

Document Design

With the increase in the availability of computer graphics programs, the "look" of documents has become more important. Part 4 covers designing documents of all types.

Chapter 17 describes three basic design principles and then explains how various formatting tools (such as itemized lists, frames, and columns) can be used to put these principles into practice. The chapter also discusses common types of graphical displays. In all cases, students are encouraged to use design elements not simply for decoration but as a way to enhance their readers' engagement with and understanding of the document.

Because so many of today's writers are required to "publish" their work using the word-processing software available for personal computers, this handbook includes a chapter on desktop publishing. In Chapter 18, students learn how to write and publish both a brochure and a newsletter. Instructors may wish to suggest these types of desktop publishing as alternative ways to format traditional essays. The text of the "Global Warming" newsletter, which is used as a model in Chapter 18, is from the model research paper found in Chapter 12. By comparing these two pieces, students can see how the content found in a traditional research paper can be published as a newsletter.

Chapter 19 teaches students how to apply basic design principles when designing Web pages. In this chapter, students learn the important ways in which Web texts differ from print texts and proceed through the process of designing their own Web pages. In Chapter 20, students learn about writing for the Web. They are introduced to HyperText Markup Language (HTML) and receive step-by-step instruction in constructing a Web page. Once again, the "Global Warming" newsletter is used, this time to show students how they can publish a research paper as a Web document.

Special Purpose Writing

Part 5 covers special types of writing that students encounter, including writing email and writing résumés. Chapter 21 introduces the many ways students can use computer networks to enhance their writing. Students need to become familiar with all of these resources—email and listserv, bulletin boards and newsgroups, IRCs and MOOs, and collaborative software. In addition, the chapter explains how to use electronic media to write better papers. In particular, the chapter encourages students to become involved with online communities as a way to collaborate with other writers.

Writing in college offers an excellent opportunity to practice writing for the workplace. Chapter 22 provides basic instruction in writing letters, résumés, reports, memos, and other forms of business correspondence. With more and more business communication taking place electronically, the chapter devotes special attention to email, scannable résumés, and homepage résumés. Instructors may want to take advantage of the multiple links between this chapter and the report-writing sections of Chapter 16.

Chapter 23 covers essay exams. It includes both excellent and poor student responses for comparison.

Grammar and Style

Parts 6–12 of the handbook provide comprehensive coverage of grammar and style, including traditional topics such as sentence structure, pronoun case, agreement, consistency, conciseness, parallelism, word choice, spelling, and punctuation. Because students are likely to use this material selectively, discussions and explanations are concise and various devices (consistent formatting, FAQs at the beginning of each chapter, frequent cross-references, and a comprehensive index) make it easy for students to look up a particular topic. More than 100 exercise sets are sprinkled throughout these chapters, giving students hands-on practice in analyzing grammatical forms and correcting errors.

The handbook's unique emphasis on computers continues in this section. Warnings about the shortcomings of style/grammar checkers are accompanied by suggestions about special ways to make good use of these checkers. Help boxes explain how to customize a style/grammar checker, search for particular style/grammar problems, use an electronic thesaurus, customize and streamline spell checking, and identify punctuation problems. The text includes many references to helpful Web sites. Students who need basic instruction in using style/grammar checkers and other computerized word-processing tools can turn to Chapter 39 for help.

ESL students will benefit as much as native-speaking students from the material presented in this handbook. Four chapters address specific ESL problems: the use of definite and indefinite articles (Chapter 55), verb problems (Chapter 56), word order (Chapter 57), and vocabulary (Chapter 58).

Pedagogy

The New Century Handbook is an easy-to-use yet comprehensive reference. It contains both extensive writing instruction and a complete guide to grammar and style issues. The grammar coverage is authoritative. A leading linguist brings to these sections of the handbook an important understanding of grammatical systems. The examples, illustrations, and exercises that appear throughout the handbook will help students to write correctly and to understand the principles, both grammatical and rhetorical, on which good writing is based. The effectiveness of this handbook is extended via the Web links in the handbook and at the book's companion Web site. These Web links, designed to connect students to the many important writing resources found on the Internet, will be updated regularly to ensure their currency.

Help Boxes

A unique pedagogical feature throughout the handbook is the Help boxes. These boxes provide students with key computer-related information in an accessible, succinct form. Because the instructions are compartmentalized in Help boxes, they do not interrupt the flow of the text; instructors and students can use them as appropriate. The Help boxes are generic—the advice they provide will work across different operating systems and with a variety of computer software. An explanatory note points to any advice that is platform-specific.

FAQs and Other Informational Boxes

In addition to the Help boxes, other types of boxes highlight information throughout the handbook. FAQs, which introduce each chapter, cite frequently asked questions about the chapter's topic. Some boxes contain checklists, which guide students through a process or concept; other boxes summarize key information in a succinct format. All boxes work as reference aids for students, providing a concise representation of the information in the handbook.

Sample Student Papers

Student models and examples, which appear throughout the handbook, illustrate both the writing process and written products. Part 1 follows a student through the process of developing an essay on Net theft, from prewriting through revising. Chapter 7 uses a second student essay, on cloning, as its model for argumentation. Chapters 8–12 follow one student's research process, including Internet research. The resulting research paper on global warming appears first in Chapter 12 and then again in Chapter 18, reformatted as a newsletter, and in Chapter 20, reformatted as a Web site. A number of student models appear in Chapters 22 and 23. Finally, four model research papers from different disciplines appear in Chapters 14–17. All student models were chosen for their accessibility, their lively and interesting topics, and their usefulness to students as examples for their own work.

Engaging Exercises

The exercises in this handbook provide students with practice at every step in the writing process. The handbook includes individual, collaborative, and computer-based exercises, thus providing instructors and students with a number of helpful options. All exercises are designed with students in mind. The exercises are not busy work, but rather provide students with additional practice in important skills that they can put to use in their own writing.

Visuals and Artwork

This handbook was carefully designed to be visually appealing, colorful, and graphically intensive. Numerous computer screens are reproduced to show students and instructors the visual options available via desktop publishing and Web authoring. Screens illustrating computer software and Internet applications appear throughout the handbook.

Glossaries

Individual glossaries are provided for computer terms, grammatical and rhetorical terms, and usage.

Supplements for the Instructor

- *Instructor's Manual to Accompany the New Century Handbook*, written by the handbook's authors, presents a wealth of materials to help instructors, including chapter highlights, teaching suggestions, classroom activities, computer activities, usage notes, linguistic notes, computer novice notes, ESL notes, connections (cross-references to the handbook), additional exercises, and exercise answers.

- *The New Century Handbook Web Site* enables instructors to post and make changes to their syllabi; receive the scores of objective tests in the areas of grammar, punctuation, and mechanics; hold chat sessions with individual students or groups of students; and receive email and essay assignments directly from students.

- *Teaching Writing with Computers*, developed by Eric Hoffman and Carol Scheidenhelm, both of Northern Illinois University, offers a wealth of computer-related classroom activities. It also provides detailed guidance for both experienced and inexperienced instructors who wish to make creative use of technology in a composition environment.

- *The Allyn & Bacon Sourcebook for College Writing Teachers*, compiled by James C. McDonald of the University of Southwestern Louisiana, provides instructors with a varied selection of readings written by composition and rhetoric scholars on both theoretical and practical subjects.

- *Teaching College Writing*, an invaluable instructor's resource guide developed by Maggy Smith of the University of Texas at El Paso, is available to adopters who wish to explore additional teaching tips and resources.

- *Diagnostic Tests and Exercise Bank* includes two diagnostic tests, keyed to the relevant handbook sections, for analyzing common errors. The additional exercise sets on grammar, punctuation, and mechanics topics supplement those found in the handbook. (It is also available in computerized Windows and Macintosh formats.)

Supplements for the Student

- *Interactive Edition of the New Century Handbook* is a valuable resource and learning tool that brings instruction on writing, research, and grammar to a new and exciting level. This CD-ROM contains all pages from the text, with icons providing instant

Web links, audio and video explanations of key concepts, and interactive exercises.

- *The New Century Handbook Web Site* presents chapter summaries; the course syllabus; Web links keyed to specific text sections; the ability to chat with and email classmates and the instructor; and self-scoring tests in grammar, punctuation, and mechanics.

- *Writer's Toolkit CD-ROM* offers a complete writing environment for planning, drafting, and revising and presents a wealth of heuristic devices to assist students with a variety of computer activities. (It works on both Macintosh and IBM platforms.)

- *GrammarCoach Software* provides ten interactive modules, each containing 60 separate exercise items, on each of the ten most common student grammar, punctuation, and mechanics trouble spots.

- *CompSite Website* offers resources and instructional material for students, including helpful information on using computers for writing, techniques for using the Internet for research, and a forum for exchanging papers and writing ideas.

- *Exercise Book* puts forth seventy additional exercise sets that supplement and parallel the exercise sets found in the handbook.

Acknowledgments

We wish to acknowledge and thank the many people who helped to make *The New Century Handbook* a reality. In addition to those specifically mentioned below, we owe a debt of gratitude to the many researchers and writers in the fields of rhetoric, composition, and linguistics whose work informs our own. In particular, we are indebted to the following colleagues who have contributed in countless ways to the shaping of this handbook: Kenneth W. Brewer, Kathy Fitzgerald, Keith Grant-Davie, Joyce Kinkead, Lynn Meeks, Jeff Smitten, and William Strong, Utah State University; Barrett M. Briggs, University of Arizona; Louise Bown and Clint Gardner, Salt Lake Community College; Julie Simon, Southern Utah University; and Jeanette Harris, Texas Christian University. For their technical expertise and innovative ideas for online teaching and learning, we thank David Hailey, Chris Okelberry, and Adam Zamora, Utah State University. For the model papers, exercises, and assignments we thank Sonia Manuel-Dupont, Kristine Miller, and Anne Shifrer, Utah State University; Phil Sbaratta, North Shore Community College; Gail Forsyth; Daniela Liese, University of Utah; Kathryn Weeks, University of Utah; and Bumpy Johnson.

We owe a debt of gratitude to the entire team at Allyn & Bacon, who supported this handbook from the beginning. Specifically, we would like to thank Joseph Opiela, whose vision for this book both inspired its early beginnings and continued to shape it throughout its birthing process. If it weren't for Joe's constant support and encouragement, we doubt very much that this book would ever have been written. Many others of the Allyn & Bacon team also helped with both direct and indirect support. These include, among others too numerous to name individually, Sandi Kirshner, Lisa Kimball, and Doug Day. To our developmental editors, whose hands-on, in-the-trenches writing feedback made us write better and work harder, we owe our thanks as well: Marlene Ellin, Allen Workman, and Donna de la Perrière. And finally, to the production editors, Susan Brown and Sally Lifland, and their supporting staff, including many designers, copyeditors, and proofreaders, we are grateful for the careful attention to design and details that make this handbook unique.

Throughout the handbook, we stress the principle that writing is not a solitary act, but rather is collaborative in the best sense of the term. Writers need feedback from readers in order to communicate better. We benefited tremendously from the timely feedback of the many reviewers who read our manuscript. In particular, we would like to thank those reviewers who helped us to shape the early drafts of key chapters: John Clark, Bowling Green State University; Ray Dumont, University of Massachusetts, Dartmouth; Todd Lundberg, Cleveland State University; and Bill Newmiller, United States Air Force Academy. We are grateful to Kathy Fitzgerald, Utah State University, for help with a computer cross-platform review; Eric Hoffman, Northern Illinois University, for help with the Web links in the handbook; and Joe Law, Wright State University, for help with the documentation chapter.

We would also like to thank the other reviewers of various parts of the manuscript: H. Eric Branscomb, Salem State College; Susan Brant, Humboldt State University; Deborah Burns, Merrimack College; Joseph Colavito, Northwestern State University; Linda Daigle, Houston Community College; Carol David, Iowa State University; Kitty Chen Dean, Nassau Community College; Keith Dorwick, University of Illinois at Chicago; Scott Douglass, Chattanooga State College; John W. Ferstel, University of Southwestern Louisiana; Robert W. Funk, Eastern Illinois University; Casey Gilson, Broward Community College; Gordon Grant, Baylor University; Joseph Janangelo, Loyola University of Chicago; Michael Keller, South Dakota State University; Thomas P. Klammer, California State University at Fullerton; Richard Louth, Southeastern Louisiana University; Richard Marback, Wayne State University; Lawrence Millbourn, El Paso Community College; Kevin Parker, Orange Coast College; Donna Reiss, Tidewater Community College; Susan Romano, University of Texas at San Antonio; Jack Scanlon, Triton Community College; Allison Smith, Louisiana Technical University; Nancy Stegall, DeVry Institute of Technology; Nancy Trachsel, University of Iowa; Audrey Wick, University of Texas at Arlington; Christopher Wielgos, Northern Illinois University; Donnie Yielding, Central Texas College.

We were fortunate to have in our classes student writers who were willing to share their fine work with us—and with the larger readership of this handbook. Student writers whose work appears in these pages include the following: Brandy Blank, Heidi Blankenship, Jennifer Bodine, Ron Christensen, Janevieve Grabert, Eric Horne, Allan Johnson, Abbey Kennedy, Myndee McNeill, Wensdae Miller, Wyoma Proffit, Heather Radford, Kirsten Reynolds, Sarah Smith, DeLayna Stout, and Bryce Wilcox.

Lastly, we say thanks to our friends and families who supported us in our personal lives so that we could free up the time, and the energy, to work on this challenging project. Specifically, we wish to thank our respective spouses, Nathan Hult and Christiane Huckin, and our children, Jen and Justin Hult and Jed and Neil Huckin.

Christine A. Hult
Thomas N. Huckin

Welcome to the New Century Handbook

How to Use This Handbook

As we approach the new century, we are communicating ideas and information both more frequently and more quickly than ever before. Almost always, we communicate these ideas through language—either the spoken or the written word. Meeting the challenges of this new, technologically driven era involves communicating more clearly and concisely and making use of the most comprehensive and up-to-date resources available.

The New Century Handbook is one such resource. In it, you will find new ways to become a more effective and confident writer. In addition to learning about grammar and punctuation and usage, you will find tips on participating in online study groups, conducting Internet research, preparing for all kinds of writing assignments (for both school and the workplace), and even designing your own Web page. So that you can create the type of document that will best convey your ideas to your chosen audience, this handbook shows how to choose and use words and structure sentences and paragraphs. Put simply, you will learn to engage more fully (and more successfully) in the process of communicating with others.

With the advent of email and the Internet, writing became more important for both business and recreation. Today, we communicate with friends, colleagues, and customers by email and through Web pages. The written word matters—and what you have to say matters. *The New Century Handbook* is here to help you say what you want to say in a way that will get the message across.

What Is Here

On the inside front cover, you will find an overview of the handbook's contents. There are twelve sections:

- Part 1 (Chapters 1–7) will help you generate ideas, compose, and revise your writing assignments successfully. You will learn about the reading and writing processes in general, as well as specifics like how to create a workable thesis, how to construct solid paragraphs, and how to argue effectively. Part 1 also explains how to simply and successfully tap the power of computers throughout all the stages of the writing process to become a more effective writer.

- Part 2 (Chapters 8–13) will guide you through the process of completing a successful research project. Topics range from generating ideas to using the Internet for research, from organizing and formatting a research paper to documenting sources correctly. And, as in Part 1, you will learn how computers can facilitate both research and writing.

- Part 3 (Chapters 14–16) will show you how to write papers for literature classes, as well as for other courses in the humanities, social sciences, and natural sciences. You will be introduced to the major types of writing in various disciplines and to the most important technological resources available.

- Part 4 (Chapters 17–20) will teach you about document design. With the increase in the availability of computer graphics programs, the "look" of documents has become more important. These chapters describe basic design principles and explain how various formatting tools can make your document stand out from a crowd. You will learn about desktop publishing, Web texts, and using design elements to enhance reader engagement and understanding.

- Part 5 (Chapters 21–23) will help you with some special types of writing that you will encounter at school, in the workplace, and online. You will learn how to communicate via computer networks, making use of electronic media from email and listservs to bulletin boards and MOOs to write better papers. And you will discover how to write your best for essay exams. You also will find important information on writing letters, résumés, reports, memos, and other forms of business correspondence.

- Part 6 (Chapters 24–28), Part 7 (Chapters 29–33), and Part 8 (Chapters 34–39) will show you how to compose effective, grammatically correct sentences. After a review of the basics of standard English sentence structure, you will learn how to write sentences that are gramatically correct and see examples of some specific types of sentence errors you should avoid. Finally, you will get tips on writing sentences that are stylistically effective, clear, and precise.

- Part 9 (Chapters 40–44) will help you to choose the best words to convey your meaning—and to use the words you choose to best effect. This section will show you how to build a powerful vocabulary, as well as how to avoid biased language. You will receive helpful hints about using a thesaurus, a dictionary, and a computer spell-checking program to enhance your writing.

- Part 10 (Chapters 45–51) and Part 11 (Chapters 52–54) will help you with sentence punctuation and mechanics. You will learn how to use punctuation correctly to convey precise sentence meaning and how to eliminate punctuation errors. Special sections discuss correct use of capital letters, abbreviations, numbers, and hyphens.

- Part 12 (Chapters 55–58) provides tips that will be especially helpful if English is your second language. You will discover how to avoid common usage problems with nouns, articles, and verbs. You will learn how to navigate the conventions of English-language word order and how to avoid common vocabulary problems.

How to Find It

- The Brief Contents, on the book's inside front cover, provides a quick guide to the handbook's entire contents.

- The Contents gives a detailed outline of the handbook, with section and page numbers for all topics.

- The Index provides an alphabetical listing of every key term and topic in the handbook, as well as the precise pages on which it is covered.

- The list of Revision Symbols, on the inside back cover, is a guide to the marks that instructors commonly use when they suggest ways to revise essays.

Where to Look for More

Want more information?

Try our Web links. You will find over 100 World Wide Web links, which will provide you with the exact addresses of important writing resources on the Internet—from online writing centers with online tutors to powerful search engines that can help you find information on a particular topic. For additional writing help, visit The New Century Handbook's *companion Web site at*

http://www.abacon.com

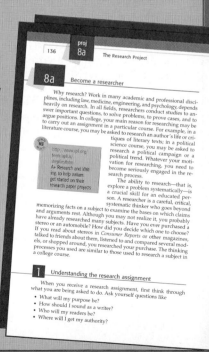

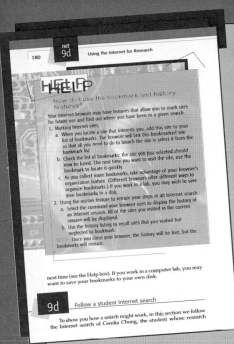

Need computer help?

Try the Help boxes. Throughout the handbook, you will find special boxes that provide clear, succinct computer advice and explanations—just what you need to make the most of your time at the keyboard and online. Within the text, you will find sample computer screens that clearly illustrate various computer and Internet activities.

Need a question answered?

Try the FAQs. The beginning of each chapter contains a list of the most frequently asked questions (FAQs) about the particular topic, as well as the section in which you will find the answer to each question.

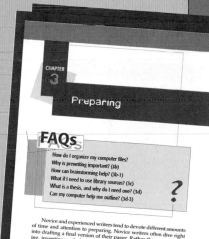

Need step-by-step guidance?

Try the checklists. Throughout the book, you will find boxes written specifically to guide you through a process or more fully explain a concept.

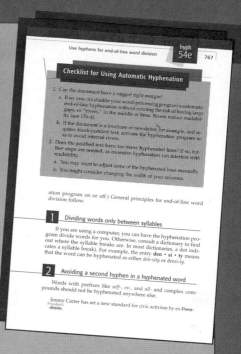

Want the quick version?

Try the summary boxes. In many chapters, you will find these helpful reference panels, which clearly and succinctly summarize key information on a variety of important topics.

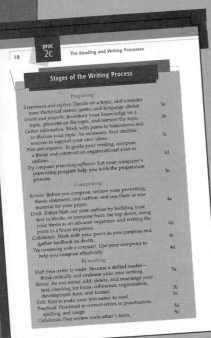

622 emph **37b** Emphasis

tence. If FDR had said "Fear itself is the only thing we have to fear," he would have missed out on a good opportunity to use this principle.

As you edit your writing, look for opportunities to give end-weight to key concepts. In this example, note how the writer made the phrase *better and wiser* more prominent by shifting it toward the end of the sentence:

FIRST DRAFT   We all muddle through life, falling along the way. But we will become better and wiser people if we pick ourselves up and keep moving on.

REVISION   We all muddle through life, falling along the way. But if we pick ourselves up and keep moving on, we will become better and wiser for it.

EXERCISE 37.1

The following are email tag lines, rewritten in a form less elegant than their original form. Using the end-weight principle, try to restore them to their original form. (Suggestion: First identify a key concept, then try to move the phrase related to that concept to the end of the sentence.)

1. Television is very educational: I go to the library and read a book the minute someone turns it on.
2. Recycled electrons were used to print this message.
3. The tree of liberty grows only when the blood of tyrants waters it.
4. Where ignorance is bliss, to be wise is folly.
5. The heart has its reasons which are not known by reason.
6. You risk even more if you do not risk anything is the trouble.
7. Life is nothing if it is not a daring adventure.
8. Time is the stuff life is made of. Do not squander time if you love life.
9. To gain your heart's desire and to lose it are the two tragedies in life.
10. Courage is the mastery of fear. It is not the absence of it.

37b   Create emphasis through selective repetition

Another powerful way of emphasizing important ideas is through repetition—especially combined with some form of grammatical par-allelism. Notice how Studs Terkel uses the repetition of the simple pronoun *my* to emphasize the personal significance of his work:

Need more practice?

Try the exercises. Throughout the book, you will find engaging tasks, questions, and problems that will help you practice your skills at every step in the writing process, from checking grammar to constructing paragraphs. The individual, collaborative, and computer-based exercises all will help you hone important skills you can use in your writing.

Wondering how other students approached an assignment?

Check out the sample student papers. In several chapters, you will find student models and examples that illustrate how real student writers engage in the writing process. As you follow the progress of students who are developing papers on topics ranging from Internet theft to human cloning, you will be able to observe the entire writing process—from brainstorming and prewriting through editing and revising.

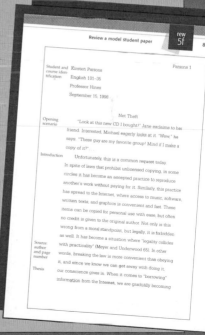

rew **5f** 83

Review a model student paper

Student and   Kirsten Parsons   Parsons 1
course iden-
tification   English 101-35

                    Professor Hines

                    September 15, 1998

                                      Net Theft

Opening   "Look at this new CD I bought!" Jane exclaims to her
scenario
                 friend. Interested, Michael eagerly looks at it. "Wow," he
                 says. "These guys are my favorite group! Mind if I make a
                 copy of it?"

Introduction   Unfortunately, this is a common request today.
                 In spite of laws that prohibit unlicensed copying, in some
                 circles it has become an accepted practice to reproduce
                 another's work without paying for it. Similarly, this practice
                 has spread to the Internet, where access to music, software,
                 written texts, and graphics is convenient and fast. These
                 items can be copied for personal use with ease, but often
                 no credit is given to the original author. Not only is this
                 wrong from a moral standpoint, but legally, it is forbidden

Source   as well. It has become a situation where "legality collides
author
and page   with practicality" (Meyer and Underwood 65). In other
number
                 words, breaking the law is more convenient than obeying

Thesis   it, and since we know we can get away with doing it,
                 our conscience gives in. When it comes to "borrowing"
                 information from the Internet, we are gradually becoming

WRITING

Writing and Computers

FAQs

Why is writing still a vital skill in today's high-tech
world? (1a)
In what ways can a computer help me write? (1b-1)
How do computers help with research? (1b-2)
How is technology changing communication? (1c)

Many college students feel a need for guidance in how to use computers effectively throughout every phase of the writing process. Obviously, computers have had an immense impact on all facets of life—at home, work, and school. But most students have had little direct help in learning how computers can improve their writing. Many students have discovered on their own that computers make it easier to think and compose at the same time. Some have found that computers also facilitate revising and editing, by making automatic spell checkers and style/grammar checkers available. And some students use desktop publishing techniques to produce professional-looking documents as final products.

If you are not one of the few students who are completely proficient at word processing, you will appreciate a chance to learn more about the basic processes of researching, composing, and rewriting with computer-based tools. This handbook looks at all the stages of writing in a way that recognizes how the computer influences and benefits every aspect of what writers do.

1a   Why write?

People are motivated to write for all sorts of reasons, but most writing falls into a few basic categories, each reflecting a different purpose. One important purpose for writing is to share information. Another is to clarify your own thinking on a topic. A third purpose is self-expression—writing to express what you think or feel about something meaningful to you. Whatever your specific purpose for writing, the ability to write well will help you succeed in college and in the workplace. Each purpose for writing assumes communication, sometimes just with oneself (as in some expressive writing that is never publicly shared), but more often with an audience of readers.

1   Writing to communicate

Every day you communicate with others using various channels or media. For example, in a typical day, you talk and listen to friends and acquaintances in person or over the telephone. You most likely also communicate with others through writing and reading. You may jot down a note to your roommate, compose a paper for a class assignment, read a novel or a magazine, write and send an email message, or read messages from friends. Like speech, writing helps you convey information and ideas to others. In many cases, writing is used to connect you with others who share some of your interests. Groups of writers who share a common set of interests and assumptions are sometimes called *discourse communities.* As you begin to use this book, reflect on how writing permeates your daily life. Even in this high-tech age, dominated by the telephone, talk shows, and chat lines, writing plays an important role in communication.

EXERCISE 1.1

In a journal or notebook, keep track of all the writing you do in one day. At the end of the day, look back and categorize the types of writing you found yourself involved in. How many different types of writing do you do in a typical day? What are your discourse communities?

2   Writing as a way of knowing

In addition to allowing you to communicate with others, both near and far, writing helps you get in touch with your own ideas. It is often said that people write what they know in order to know what they think. Writing about something can help you clarify your thinking about it. When beginning an essay for a course assignment, you probably have had the experience of not knowing exactly what you were going to say. As you wrote, you explored your ideas and in a sense "discovered" what you really thought (see Chapters 3 and 4). This discovery function is an important reason to write. However, sometimes writing not only reveals what you already know but also uncovers things you do not yet know but would like to learn. Thus, writing has an intimate connection with both reading (see Chapter 2) and research (see Part 2) because it encourages you to seek further knowledge by those means. In addition, through your writing, you can make the knowledge you have acquired available to others, thus completing the communication circle.

3   Writing to be creative

In addition to expanding knowledge, writing has an important creative dimension. Writing is an inherently creative act. In the process of writing, you explore what truly motivates you as you sort through your thoughts and impressions. As you generate ideas for writing, you may work from intensely personal notes in a journal to create a focused piece of writing that meets the goals of a particular course assignment (see Chapter 3). Writing an essay is essentially as creative as writing a story or poem, because any piece of writing shares the writer's vision of the world (see Chapter 4). Having written something that conveys your own personal vision or values is both emotionally and intellectually satisfying.

4   Writing to succeed in college

Much of the communication that occurs in an academic setting takes place through writing. Although you interact with your instructors to some degree through speech, by far the most prevalent way you convey your mastery of the subject matter to them is through writing. Think about the number and types of written assignments that are demanded of you each term. You are asked to write term papers, essays, and lab reports and to complete written exams of all types, from multiple choice to short essay. Clearly, knowing how to write well is one of the keys to success in college.

5 Writing to function in the workplace

Writing also plays a key role in success on the job. It is certainly true that technology has altered the workplace with the advent of such communication tools as email, voice mail, fax, and the Internet. However, all these technologies depend on the written word. In fact, the information explosion has increased the demand for good writing, not decreased it. When communicating on the job, you must be able to express your thoughts clearly and succinctly for them to be understood and acted on appropriately. The wide range of communication tools makes it essential that you make appropriate choices for your on-the-job writing. (Should I send my message via fax, email, or voice mail? Do I use a formal salutation or just say "Hi"?) The writing skills you will need in the workplace include the ability to analyze your audience and your purpose, called your *rhetorical stance* (see 3a-2). This handbook emphasizes the importance of adapting your style and tone to the needs of the writing task at hand.

1b Why write with a computer?

Most of the writing done today is produced on computers. Educators realize the importance of computers as writing tools. If you visited a kindergarten or first-grade classroom, you would be likely to see computers as part of the educational landscape. In addition to learning to read and handwrite, elementary school students are learning to keyboard and to use computers for writing. Similarly, many college writing classes are held in computer labs. This handbook assumes that you are already using computers to some degree and provides guidance in using them to the fullest at all stages of writing and for all types of writing.

EXERCISE 1.2

Look ahead to Stages of the Writing Process on page 18. Note that there are three major stages: preparing, composing, and rewriting.

In a notebook or a computer file, list the ways in which you think a computer could help you at each of these stages. Bring your list to class for discussion.

1 Getting help throughout the writing process

Chapter 2 of this handbook describes the three stages of the writing process, and Chapters 3, 4, and 5 guide you through them. Computers are intimately involved in every one of these stages. Word-processing programs help you keep your writing projects organized (see Chapter 3). They also are excellent tools for other aspects of preparation: experimenting and exploring (see 3a), inventing and prewriting (see 3b), and planning and organizing (see 3d). Anyone who has ever written papers by hand in pen or pencil is well aware that word processing has taken the drudgery out of composing (see Chapter 4) and has revolutionized revision (see Chapter 5).

Before computers, many writers had to retype page after page to eliminate typographical errors discovered during proofreading—only to introduce new errors while retyping! Now, with computers, corrections can be made instantly without redoing the rest of a page. In fact, because word processors have made it so easy to make changes, even the notion of a draft has changed. Before computers, a writer would often type a first draft, which would then be edited and proofread before being retyped as the second draft. With word processing, new drafts are created at the click of a mouse or the touch of a key. Each time a change is made on screen, a new draft essentially exists. The seamless way in which computers allow writers to edit, proofread, and revise their work has had a major impact on the writing process.

> http://www.cod.edu/ dept/kiesdan/engl_101/ computer.htm
> Information on computers and writing, from one of the best composition courses on the Web

Computers have made it far easier for writers to collaborate with others. For example, writers can quickly communicate with each other about works in progress by using email. The co-authors of this handbook used this method to collaborate—sending drafts of chapters back and forth electronically for review and feedback. You can use this process to share drafts with your peers (see Chapter 5).

2 Getting help with research

The use of computers for research is growing at a phenomenal rate, parallel with the growth of the Internet. Chapters 9 and 21 of this handbook show how computers can help you research for writing. You can find and explore research topics on the Internet (see 9a-1), and you can exchange information and discuss topics with interested individuals via networks and online bulletin boards and newsgroups (see 21a-1, 21a-2). The Internet contains current information on just about any topic (see 9b). And it is a relatively simple matter to download information found on the Internet to a computer drive or disk (see 8d-2). Furthermore, a word-processing program can help you store information in computerized note cards or notebooks (see 8c) and organize your notes (see 11a-2).

When you begin to draft a research paper, the power of word processing once again helps make the job much easier. Word processing allows you to view files simultaneously in dual windows and to combine information by using the COPY and PASTE functions (see 4a-2).

3 Gaining access to a wide audience

Yet another benefit of computers is that they give writers access to an unlimited number of readers. An ever-expanding readership extends the impact of a writer's work beyond immediate friends, classmates, and teachers. Work published on the Internet can reach highly specialized groups and broad segments of the public. When you participate in Internet conversations, including email, newsgroups, listservs, MOOs, and chat rooms (see Chapter 21), you can use writing to discuss topics of interest to you, sharing your own knowledge and receiving that of others.

You can use the Internet to experiment with writing for a wide range of rhetorical situations: from very informal (such as chat rooms) to highly formal (such as Web sites devoted to specific topics). Designing and writing Web pages allows you to communicate knowledge in a powerful way, using graphics and hypertext (see Chapters 19 and 20). Publishing your writing on the Internet makes it available to anyone who is connected to the Internet anywhere in the world. By including your email address on a Web site, you invite interested readers to share their thoughts with you.

1c   How have computers altered communication?

Computer technology has evolved and continues to evolve at a staggering pace. It is impossible for anyone to predict what the technological environment will look like in a few years. It is clear that the communication landscape has been dramatically altered by the advent of computers. Although all the consequences of the technological changes are not yet known, the information explosion has dramatically increased the demand for good writing, making learning to write effectively more crucial than ever.

Think about how the prevalence of email has changed communication practice. Many students are more likely to communicate with their parents and friends back home via email than through a phone call or letter. And many businesspeople are more likely to fire off an email memo than a printed one. Everyone who has come to rely on email knows that it is different in substantive ways from letters and phone calls. There is an immediacy to email that letters or memos do not have. But, at the same time, email is more distant than face-to-face or phone conversations. Because email cannot readily convey emotions through tone of voice, there is always the possibility that messages will be misunderstood. Email correspondents have invented "emoticons" to help fill in the missing intonations (see 21b-4), but these can go only so far in helping writers be understood appropriately.

> WWW
> WEB
>
> http://jefferson.village.
> virginia.edu/elab/
> hfl0276.html
> The Electronic Labyrinth,
> a great site devoted to
> computers and writing

Other aspects of the new communication landscape have had unsettling effects on efforts to communicate. Each of the many Internet communication forums that are now available—chat rooms, bulletin boards, newsgroups, MUDs, and MOOs (see Chapter 21)—has its own customs and protocols that writers need to know in order to communicate effectively. In some of these forums, it is possible to adopt a persona other than your own. And, since it may not always be clear who your audience is, it is especially important to avoid offending someone with a careless remark. Learning how to communicate effectively in these new forums is a tremendous challenge for writers in today's cyberculture.

In fact, in this ever-changing communication landscape, it is even more important that writers understand the basic principles of effective communication, also called the *principles of rhetoric*. If you understand these key rhetorical principles (which are covered extensively in this handbook), you will be a successful communicator, regardless of evolving technology.

This handbook will equip you with the basic skills you need to become a good writer for many different communication media. Because this handbook emphasizes the use of rhetorical analysis, regardless of the particular medium (from print to email to Web pages), you will learn how to adapt your writing to any situation you encounter. And, just as effective writing principles cross media, they also cross genres, or types of writing. As you write and experiment with computers, keep in mind that the lessons you learn about planning, drafting, and revising apply to any writing you do—from essays and research papers to business reports and memos to email messages and chat-room conversations.

The Reading and Writing Processes

FAQs

What is critical thinking? (2a)

How do I read critically? (2b)

Aren't good writers born rather than "made"? (2c)

What is involved in the writing process? (2c)

?

Throughout your life, you have been reading and writing—formally at school and work, informally with family and friends. The processes of reading and writing are closely interrelated. We read and write to understand our world, to communicate with others, and to share our thoughts and ideas. Everyone can improve both reading and writing abilities through practice.

As you read this chapter, notice that there are distinct parallels between the reading and writing processes. The reading process has three major stages: previewing, reading, and reviewing. Similarly, the writing process consists of three major stages: preparing, composing, and rewriting.

As a college student, you have a unique opportunity to practice your reading and writing skills. Much college work revolves around the processes of reading and writing. Academic knowledge is both created and shared through these processes. Whether your course of study is mathematics or sociology or engineering, reading and writing are intimately involved in learning. You read to understand what others think and say about a topic; you write to share what you learn or understand about a topic. This is how knowledge progresses.

2a   Think critically

A term often used to describe the way in which educated people approach knowledge building is *critical thinking*. To think critically is to make a conscious effort to delve beneath the surface of things. Much of the process of obtaining a college education is designed to help you become a more critical thinker. The term *critical* in this case does not mean the same as *criticize*. Critical thinking does not imply a negative attitude; rather, critical thinking involves the ability to contemplate, question, and explore ideas in depth without accepting easy answers. When you identify the political propaganda as you listen to a political speech on your campus, you exhibit critical thinking. When you recognize the overblown claims for a product in an advertisement in the local newspaper, you also exhibit critical thinking. The processes involved in thinking critically are the same for all aspects of communication—speaking and writing as well as listening and reading.

1   Analyzing

A critical thinker is able to analyze information. When you analyze something you have read or heard, you mentally divide it into its parts. Then, you look for any relationships there might be among the various parts. For example, if you had just finished reading a novel, you might analyze it by dividing the plot into segments that reflect phases in the action. Then, you might decide how the various parts of the plot contribute to the major theme or themes of the novel. Such literary analysis is often called *critical* analysis or literary *criticism* (see Chapter 14).

2   Summarizing

A critical thinker is able to abstract, or summarize, the "gist" of information read or heard. When you summarize something, you boil it down to its essence, picking out the major points or ideas and restating them in a succinct way. For example, if you had just attended a lecture by a history professor, you might summarize the lecture by writing down the three or four major points made by the speaker. The ability to summarize effectively is discussed at length in Chapter 11.

3 Synthesizing

Synthesizing involves approaching several sources of information with an eye to finding the relationships among them. When you synthesize, you seek to articulate the ways in which sources are related. Sources of information can be related in various ways. For example, several sources may provide different examples of a general topic, several sources may describe or define the same topic either similarly or differently, or several sources may present information or ideas that can be compared or contrasted. Rather than approaching the various sources of information as isolated entities, a critical thinker sees important relationships among them.

4 Making inferences

Another important critical thinking skill is the ability to make inferences, or "read between the lines." When you make inferences, you interpret what the author intended to say, even though the information may have been couched in neutral terms. For example, when you infer that the author of a Web page had a hidden agenda to promote a product or service, you are exhibiting an important kind of critical thinking. The ability to interpret the logic or faulty logic that underlies an argument (see 7g) is also an example of this critical thinking skill.

2b Engage critically and actively in the reading process

A good reader reads *critically;* that is, he or she reads with an open mind and a questioning attitude. To be a critical reader, you need to go beyond understanding what the author is saying; you need to challenge or question the author. You may question the validity of the author's main point or ask whether the text agrees or disagrees with other writings on the same topic.

A good reader also reads *actively.* As you read, you make meaning out of the letters and numbers you encounter in the text. Your mind must be actively engaged with what your eyes see on the page or the computer screen. You may have had the experience of dozing off while reading; when this happens, your mind is not actively engaged, even though your eyes might be following the lines. You need to pay close attention, to read *actively*, in order to understand what you are reading.

 1   Reading on three different levels

As you read critically and actively, you need to attend to three different levels of meaning in order to fully understand what you are reading. The three levels are literal meaning, inferred meaning, and evaluated meaning.

Literal Meaning

In reading for the literal meaning of a piece, the goal is to understand exactly what is being said by the author. Literal meaning does not include impressions you may take away from the piece, such as a hostile feeling or a sense that the author is displaying a negative attitude. Rather, the literal meaning includes the key facts or concepts and the plot or particular line of reasoning. It is important that you understand a piece thoroughly at the literal level, but it is also important that you not stop there.

Inferred Meaning

Once you have grasped the literal meaning, you should go beyond it to the realm of the inferred meaning. At this level, you are seeking clues to what the author has implied rather than overtly stated. Perhaps the language chosen by the author leads you to infer that he or she intends to be ironic or sarcastic. For example, a literal reading of Swift's *A Modest Proposal* would indicate that Swift was arguing for an inhumane solution to the hunger problem in Ireland—eating the children. However, reading between the lines, you can infer that Swift intends his "solution" to be highly ironic. You should always seek the inferred meaning of a piece, in addition to its literal meaning.

Evaluated Meaning

Finally, you want to read beyond the literal and inferred meanings to evaluate the significance of a piece's argument. At this level, you read for ways in which the author may have revealed his or her own prejudices or biases. It is important to detect where an author has presented opinions as though they were facts or displayed prejudices as if they were agreed-upon truths. You should never take anything you read strictly at face value. Rather, you should evaluate everything an author says and compare it to your own judgments and sensibilities. For example, you have every right to reject an argument by an author who displays racism or sexism. You also have a right to reject an argument that you judge to be weak or faulty. Reading for a work's evaluated meaning is the hallmark of a critical thinker (see Chapter 10).

2 Structuring your reading process

Reading thoroughly on all three levels is crucial to understanding a text well enough to discuss it intelligently and write about it knowledgeably. If you structure your reading process according to the three steps of previewing, reading, and reviewing, you will understand what you read more completely.

Previewing

Begin any reading session by previewing the material as a whole. By looking ahead, you will gain a general sense of what is to come. This sense will help you predict what to expect from the text as you read and will help you better understand what you are reading. Jot down in a journal or notebook any questions that occur to you during previewing.

As you approach a textbook for the first time, look closely at the table of contents to preview the book's main topics. You can also learn the relative importance of topics by scanning the table of contents. Next, preview one chapter. Page through the chapter, reading all chapter headings and subheadings in order to gain a sense of the chapter's organizational structure. Look also at words in boldface or italic print. These words are highlighted because the author considered them especially important. Finally, preview any graphs, charts, or illustrations. These visuals are included to reinforce or illustrate key ideas or concepts in the chapter. You will want to remember these key ideas.

> WEB
> http://www.dartmouth.edu/admin/acskills
> Help with reading and other academic skills, from Dartmouth College

You should also preview shorter works, such as magazine or journal articles, prior to reading them. An article may include subheadings, which provide an idea of the article's structure. Again, look for highlighted words or graphics in the article, since these can provide clues about key ideas. You should read any biographical information about the author, both to note his or her credentials and to determine whether he or she has a particular bias on the subject. For example, an author who is a leader in the National Rifle Association will probably express a particular bias about gun control. As the final step in previewing an article, read the opening and closing paragraphs to get an idea of the author's thesis and conclusion.

Reading

After you preview the text, read it carefully and closely. Pace your reading according to the difficulty of the material—the more difficult the material, the more slowly you should read it. You may find that you need to take frequent breaks if the text is especially dense or contains a lot of new information. You also may find that you need to reread some passages several times in order to understand their meaning. Material assigned for college classes often is packed with information and therefore requires not only slow reading but also rereading. As you read, pay attention to the three levels of meaning (see 2b-1). Do not be surprised if you find yourself having to go back over the text several times—that, too, is an essential part of the reading process.

Reviewing

Once you have completed a thorough reading, go back to the text and review it. Pay particular attention to those areas of the text that you previewed. Have the questions you had when previewing been answered? If not, reread the relevant passages. It may help to review the text with a classmate or a study group; discuss the text with your peers to be sure that your understanding conforms with theirs. Talking about the text with others also will help you communicate your understanding in a meaningful way. If your class has a computer bulletin board or online discussion group, post any questions that you still have about the reading. Like discussing the text in groups, writing about the text in such forums will help you articulate your ideas, which will serve you well when you are asked to write about the material more formally, in an essay or exam. To gain a thorough understanding from your reading, plan to review the material several times.

3   Annotating the text while reading

One way to ensure that you are reading critically and actively is to annotate the text as you read. **Annotating** a text means making summary notes in the margins, as well as underlining or highlighting important words and passages. Typically, it is best to preview material before annotating it. Annotating is important during the reading process. Your annotations should summarize the key ideas in the text. Take care, however, not to over-annotate. You need to be selective so that you do not highlight everything in the text. The following excerpt illustrates a student's annotation of a passage from an article on creativity in science and art:

> WWW WEB
>
> http://dlc.tri-c.cc.
> oh.us/wb/write/docs/
> process.htm
> A Web page that
> breaks the writing
> process down into a
> series of steps, one
> leading to the next

What is the relationship between science and art?

What is the kinship between these seemingly dissimilar species, science and art? Obviously there is some—if only because so often the same people are attracted to both. The image of Einstein playing his violin is only too familiar, or Leonardo with his inventions. It is a standing joke in some circles that all it takes to make a string quartet is four mathematicians sitting in the same room. Even Feynman plays the bongo drums. (He finds it curious that while he is almost always identified as the physicist who plays the bongo drums, the few times that he has been asked to play the drums, "the introducer never seems to find it necessary to mention that I also do theoretical physics.")

There must be a link, as so many scientists are also artists.

Art and science cover the same ground— several examples.

One commonality is that art and science often cover the same territory. A tree is fertile ground for both the poet and the botanist. The relationship between mother and child, the symmetry of snowflakes, the effects of light and color, and the structure of the human form are studied equally by painters and psychologists, sculptors and physicians. The origins of the universe, the nature of life, and the meaning of death are the subjects of physicists, philosophers, and composers.

—K. C. Cole, *The Scientific Aesthetic*

EXERCISE 2.1

Several more paragraphs from Cole's article are included below. Annotate these paragraphs, underlining important ideas and noting key points in the margin.

Yet when it comes to approach, the affinity breaks down completely. Artists approach nature with feeling; scientists rely on logic. Art elicits emotion; science makes sense. Artists are supposed to care; scientists are supposed to think.

At least one physicist I know rejects this distinction out of hand: "What a strange misconception has been taught to people," he says. "They have been taught that one cannot be disciplined enough to discover the truth unless one is indifferent to it. Actually, there is no point in looking for the truth unless what it is makes a difference."

The history of science bears him out. Darwin, while sorting out the clues he had gathered in the Galapagos Islands that eventually led to his theory of evolution, was hardly detached. "I am like a gambler and love a wild experiment," he wrote. "I am horribly afraid." "I trust to a sort of instinct and God knows can seldom give any reason for my remarks." "All nature is perverse and will not do as I wish it. I wish I had my old barnacles to work at, and nothing new." . . .

There are, of course, substantial differences between art and science. Science is written in the universal language of mathematics; it is, far more than art, a shared perception of the world. Scientific insights can be tested by the good old scientific method. And scientists have to try to be dispassionate about the conduct of their work—at least enough so that their passions do not disrupt the outcome of experiments. Of course, sometimes they do: "Great thinkers are never passive before the facts," says Stephen Jay Gould. "They have hopes and hunches, and they try hard to construct the world in their light. Hence, great thinkers also make great errors."

But in the end, the connections between art and science may be closer than we think, and they may be rooted most of all in a person's motivations to do art, or science, in the first place. MIT metallurgist Cyril Stanley Smith became interested in the history of his field and was surprised to find that the earliest knowledge about metals and their properties was provided by objects in art museums. "Slowly, I came to see that this was not a coincidence but a consequence of the very nature of discovery, for discovery derives from aesthetically motivated curiosity and is rarely a result of practical purposefulness."

—K. C. Cole, *The Scientific Aesthetic*

2c Engage critically and actively in the writing process

As well as reading, you will find yourself doing a great deal of writing in college. And many businesspeople and professionals list writing at the top of the skills they seek in those they hire. Thus, as a college student, you should be developing your writing skills. Although there are certainly writers who exhibit unique talent, everyone can improve his or her writing—and using this handbook will help.

Thinking critically is just as important to the writing process as it is to the reading process. To make sense out of the seeming jumble of ideas floating around in your head, you need to engage critically and actively with your own writing. The mental processes employed during writing are enormously complex. To even try to describe these processes is to oversimplify. However, we can make some generalizations about the writing process based on the accounts of experienced writers. To improve your own writing, you would do well to pay particular attention to the writing process described in this section of the chapter.

Stages of the Writing Process

Preparing

Experiment and explore. Decide on a topic, and consider your rhetorical stance, genre, and language choice.   3a

Invent and prewrite. Inventory your knowledge on a topic, prewrite on the topic, and narrow the topic.   3b

Gather information. Work with peers to brainstorm and to discuss your topic. As necessary, find credible sources to support your own ideas.   3c

Plan and organize. To guide your writing, compose a thesis and construct an organizational plan or outline.   3d

Try computer prewriting software. Let your computer's prewriting program help you with the preparation process.   3e

Composing

Review. Before you compose, review your prewriting, thesis statement, and outline, and use them as raw material for your paper.   4a

Draft. Either flesh out your outline by building your text in blocks, or compose from the top down, using your thesis as an advance organizer and writing the piece in a linear sequence.   4b

Collaborate. Work with your peers as you compose and gather feedback on drafts.   4c

Try composing with a computer. Use your computer to help you compose effectively.   4d

Rewriting

Shift from writer to reader. Become a skilled reader— think critically and evaluate your own writing.   5a

Revise. As you revise, add, delete, and rearrange your text, checking for focus, coherence, organization, development, tone, and format.   5b

Edit. Edit to make your text easier to read.   5c

Proofread. Proofread to correct errors in punctuation, spelling, and usage.   5d

Collaborate. Peer review each other's texts.   5e

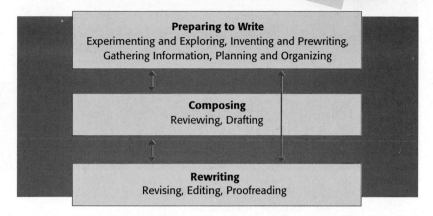

Figure 2.1   The Writing Process

Writing involves three stages, each of which includes a number of tasks. The diagram in Figure 2.1 will help you to envision what the writing process looks like. The preparing stage encompasses experimenting and exploring, inventing and prewriting, gathering information, and planning and organizing. The composing stage requires reviewing and then drafting. The rewriting stage incorporates revising, editing, and proofreading. These stages of writing are often described as *recursive,* as writers typically move freely among them as they plan, shape, compose, and revise their texts.

Thus, writing is often a messy process involving much cycling back and forth between stages: planning and drafting, and then revising and rewriting, and then more planning. If you slow down the process and really look at each stage, you will better understand what happens as you write. If you understand the process better, then you will also be able to control it better. It will seem less mysterious and more workable.

http://webster.
commnet.edu/HP/
pages/darling/
grammar/composition/
composition.html-ssi
A great introduction to
the writing process

The remaining chapters in Part 1 of this handbook discuss the stages of the writing process in more detail. They also suggest ways in which the computer can help you at every stage of writing, from preparing to write through proofreading a finished text.

Preparing

FAQs

How do I organize my computer files?
Why is prewriting important? (3b)
How can brainstorming help? (3b-1)
What if I need to use library sources? (3c)
What is a thesis, and why do I need one? (3d)
Can my computer help me outline? (3d-3)

?

Novice and experienced writers tend to devote different amounts of time and attention to preparing. Novice writers often dive right into drafting a final version of their paper. Rather than experimenting, inventing, and planning, they spend most of their time struggling with the writing itself. Many experienced writers, however, report that they spend a great deal of time thinking about what they want to say before they actually begin to write a piece. Learn from these experienced writers—take time to prepare prior to drafting.

Your computer can help you as you prepare for writing. You can designate directories or folders on your computer's hard drive or on a floppy disk to organize your work. Many operating systems permit you to create a tree-like hierarchy of directories, folders, and files. Using this capability, you can group related files in the same location on the hard drive or disk, much as you might store related papers within a folder in a file cabinet. Using the power of computers, you can store the following kinds of information, each in its own

How do I organize my files?

1. Using a file management program (such as Windows Explorer) or opening the FILE menu, create a directory or folder for each course in which you have written assignments (for example, English and history).
2. Within each directory or folder, create subdirectories or additional folders in which to store the work for each assignment.
3. Each time you begin a new writing assignment, save all the work in the appropriate assignment directory or folder.

folder: the experimental ideas you generate, the prewriting you do, and the preliminary information you gather. The screen in Figure 3.1 shows the structure one student selected for organizing files.

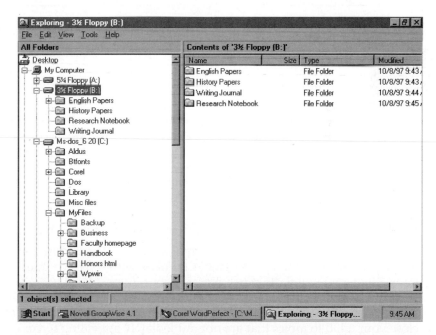

Figure 3.1   Screen Showing Directory Structure in Windows Explorer for PCs

How do I use the Internet to find a topic?

1. Use your Internet browser to access a search engine, such as Yahoo!, that has hierarchical subject categories.

2. On the subject tree, look for categories that interest you or that are related to the assignment you are working on (for example, "entertainment" or "politics").

3. Within each category, search for possible topics. (For example, under "society," you might find the topic "environment" interesting.)

4. Each time you go one level deeper in the subject tree, jot down other categories that might provide possible topics for you to write about.

NOTE: Not all search engines use subject trees. Some use only key word searching. (See Search Engines in Chapter 9.)

3a   Experiment and explore

During the first phase of the first stage of the writing process, you experiment and explore in preparation for writing. Writers have many ways of experimenting with language and exploring ideas.

1   Deciding what to write about

It is important that you choose a topic you are interested in, can develop an interest in, are somewhat familiar with, or have questions about. You will write much better if your interest level is high. If you choose a topic that you have absolutely no interest in, you may find yourself bored before you even begin. However, do not close your mind to topics that are not immediately appealing to you.

It is possible to develop interest in a topic once you know a bit more about it. Following are some ways to explore topic ideas:

- Watch educational programs on television (PBS or Discovery).
- Converse with friends, family members, or teachers.
- Think about your own hobbies and interests.
- Think about your employment experiences.
- Think about your college major or other courses you have taken.
- Surf the Net.
- Browse through current periodicals in the library.

When a person is writing at work, the topic is often predetermined: an engineer might write a report describing a new piece of computer hardware, a nurse might write a case history of a patient's illness, and so on. Often college writing assignments do not appear to have any inherent purpose, and thus you may feel that your writing is out of context. One of your major tasks when given a writing assignment is to assess what the instructor is asking you to do. Does your instructor want you to analyze or discuss something you have been reading about in class? Does she or he expect you to choose your own topic and write an argumentative essay? How the assignment is phrased will help you to determine how to approach the choice of a topic.

> http://www.
> colostate.edu/Depts/
> WritingCenter/
> references/
> processes.htm
> An introduction to
> the writing process,
> focusing on develop-
> ing ideas and writing
> strategies

EXERCISE 3.1

Using one of the search engines available on your Internet browser, explore possible topics of interest to you. Make use of the search engine's directory structure to search on topics in different categories (for example, "education," "entertainment," or "politics"). If you do not have access to the Internet, browse through the magazines in the current periodicals section of your library. Make a list of some topics that interest you. Share this list with your classmates.

2 Considering your rhetorical stance

Once you have selected a topic, you can begin to consider the approach that you will take toward your topic, called your **rhetorical stance.** The term *rhetoric* refers to written or spoken communication that seeks to inform or convince someone of something. The rhetorical stance you adopt for a particular writing assignment reflects the way you define the components of the rhetorical situation: your purpose for writing the piece, your persona (how you wish to come across as a writer), and your readers (audience). You can visualize the rhetorical stance in terms of a triangle, as shown in Figure 3.2. We will discuss each component of the rhetorical stance in turn.

Purpose

At the top of the rhetorical triangle is your paper's purpose. You need to decide on some general goals for the piece of writing and some strategies for accomplishing these goals. For example, for a newspaper reporter covering an automobile accident, the goal might be to describe the scene clearly for the newspaper's readers. For each writing task, you should determine your purpose. Is it to inform your readers of the current state of knowledge on a subject, to persuade them to accept a particular point of view, to illustrate or describe a scene?

Throughout the chapters in this part of the handbook, we will illustrate the writing process by following the progress of Kirsten Parsons, a college student assigned to write a paper on a computer topic that interests her. The teacher wants the piece to be written largely from the students' own experiences, from a brief Internet search, and from the class text. After thinking about several possible topics, Kirsten finally settled on the topic of Net theft. Her purpose in the

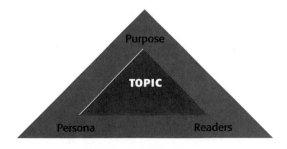

Figure 3.2 **Rhetorical Triangle**

Considering Your Rhetorical Stance

Considering Your Purpose
- Is a problem suggested by the topic?
- What are your writing goals?
- What is your intent—persuasive, argumentative, informative?

Considering Your Persona
- How do you want to sound to your readers?
- What kind of language will you use—formal or informal?
- What role or identity will you assume?

Considering Your Audience
- Who are your readers?
- Are your readers experts or novices on your topic?
- Are your readers likely to agree with you or not?

piece would be to persuade her fellow students that petty Net crimes were not much different from other petty crimes, such as shoplifting; they were simply easier to commit.

Persona

Next you need to consider your **persona**—how you will present yourself to those who will read your work. Do you want to sound objective and fair, heated and passionate, sincere and persuasive, informative and impartial? The term *persona* is used to describe the identity that a speaker or writer adopts and the credibility that the speaker or writer establishes. Just as you play many roles in life, depending on the situation in which you find yourself, you can be flexible about how you portray yourself in your writing, changing your persona with your purpose and readership. For example, a scholarly audience demands a rather formal persona, whereas an audience of your peers probably does not. The language you choose goes a long way toward establishing your persona.

Kirsten decided to take a somewhat light-hearted approach to her topic so as to maintain the interest of her peers. She would attempt to play the role of a knowledgeable student, but one with a sense of humor and an understanding of what other college students experience as they encounter the Internet.

Readers or Audience

Finally, try to identify as best you can your readers or audience. A piece of writing is often judged by how effectively it reaches its intended audience. Defining your potential audience will help you to make appropriate decisions about what to include in and exclude from your writing. Although your instructors are ultimately the audience for most writing you do in college, you may find yourself writing to others as well. Here are some questions about audience that you need to think through:

- Who are your readers likely to be? (Age, sex, income, belief systems, potential biases)
- Are your readers likely to be novices or experts on the subject you are writing about?
- Are they likely to agree with you, or will you need to persuade them of your point of view?
- What are your readers likely to know? (Educational level, prior knowledge)

After pondering this list of questions, Kirsten decided that her readers would probably be her peers—that is, other college students on her own campus. From talking with other students, she had learned that most seemed to think that it was acceptable to "borrow" material from the Internet. She wanted to alert students that this practice was unethical, if not illegal. She felt that it was important for her fellow students to realize that unattributed use of Internet sources was a form of plagiarism, not unlike stealing.

3   Considering genre and language choice

The **genre** of a piece of writing refers to the kind of writing, such as essay, poem, song lyrics, or report. Once you have identified a genre for a piece of writing, you can consider conventional ways in which that genre is typically written. For example, a convention of the fairy tale genre is to begin with "Once upon a time . . . ." Most of the writing you will do in college falls under the broad genre called *academic discourse.* The characteristics of academic discourse include the use of Standard Edited English; that is, academic writers pay close attention to the conventional uses of grammar, spelling, punctuation, and mechanics as described in later sections of this handbook. Other characteristics are a standard format (such as a report or essay format), clear presentation and organization of information, and a formal tone.

The tone of your writing is established through the language choices you make—the words you include in your sentences. A formal tone is conveyed by formal language; for example, you generally would not use contractions in formal writing. Similarly, you typically would not use jargon or slang in formal academic writing. You might, however, use technical terminology, if the particular terms would be known by your target audience.

Your tone contributes to your rhetorical stance by revealing the attitude you have adopted toward your topic and the audience you are writing to. In addition to a formal or informal tone, language can be used to convey an ironic tone, a scornful tone, or a distasteful tone. Take care that the tone you adopt reflects the rhetorical stance you have chosen.

EXERCISE 3.2

Using the guidelines given in Considering Your Rhetorical Stance, outline a rhetorical stance for one of the topics you listed in Exercise 3.1. Describe the rhetorical stance in a brief paragraph.

3b Invent and prewrite

Writing begins with thinking. The words that appear on your computer screen are the result of the thinking you do prior to and during the writing process. In the prewriting stage, you invent or discover what you want to say about your subject. As the words *invent* and *discover* imply, during this period you delve into your subject, come up with new ideas, connect these new ideas with prior experiences and knowledge, read about and research your subject, and generally allow your thoughts to take shape. All of these activities will help you to decide what you will write. In the prewriting stage, you retrieve from your memory the experiences

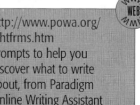

http://www.powa.org/
whtfrms.htm
Prompts to help you
discover what to write
about, from Paradigm
Online Writing Assistant

and information that will allow you to accomplish your writing task. Prewriting also helps you to decide what additional information you need to discover (through conversations, reading, and research) in order to write knowledgeably about your subject.

As you prewrite, you can use several techniques to tap your own inner resources and knowledge. Many of these techniques also work well when you begin writing with a partner or a small group. As we look at each technique, we will suggest ways to use it both on your own and with others.

1 Brainstorming

Brainstorming refers to generating random ideas or fragments of thought about a topic. You are probably familiar with brainstorming from writing classes you have taken in the past. It is possible to brainstorm as a group, calling out ideas to the instructor, who writes them on the blackboard. It is also possible to brainstorm at a computer, either individually or with another classmate. Or you may write brainstorming ideas in your writing journal.

KIRSTEN'S BRAINSTORMING

Taking information from the Net.

Is it legal? Can we swipe graphics?

People copying CDs from each other.

What is Net theft like? Maybe shoplifting?

Copyright laws.

Hackers and other Net criminals.

What is a criminal?

If I copied a graphic, was that a crime?

Who are hackers?

Do I know any?

Are they always criminals?

Maybe they're just having fun.

How do I brainstorm on a computer?

1. Open a new document in your word-processing program, and make a list of any ideas that occur to you about your topic.
2. Type what you know about your topic, what information you want to cover, and what you still need to find out about.
3. Review your list, and move items into logical groupings.
   a. Convert important items into headings, and group other items under them.
   b. CUT items that do not fit and PASTE them at the end of the list.
   c. Delete items that seem irrelevant.
   d. Expand ideas by moving your cursor to the appropriate position and inserting new phrases or sentences.
4. Save the brainstorming document on your hard drive or disk.
5. Update the brainstorming document as you come up with new ideas.

EXERCISE 3.3

Following the steps in the Help box, brainstorm at a computer on the topic you selected in Exercise 3.2. If you do not have a computer available, brainstorm in your writing journal instead.

2   Freewriting

Freewriting is related to brainstorming in that it involves writing down thoughts as they come to mind. However, unlike brainstorming, freewriting is typically formulated in connected sentences rather than lists. The idea is to write rapidly in an informal style without conscious regard to details of usage, spelling, and punctuation. It is possible to freewrite with pen and paper or at the computer. Using either your word-processing program or a writing journal, you can freewrite on a topic to generate ideas and to discover information stored in your mind. After freewriting on a particular topic for five or ten minutes without stopping, read over your freewriting. As you read it, you may see relationships between ideas that you had not seen before. If you were freewriting at the keyboard, you can CUT and PASTE in order to group related ideas. If you were freewriting with pen and paper, circle important ideas and use arrows to show relationships.

KIRSTEN'S FREEWRITING

I think that my topic will be about Net theft. Wondered about the legalities of copying stuff off the Net. A friend asked me the other day if he could copy my CD. Is that the same kind of crime? What about downloading a CD from the Net? Lots of people are worried about giving out their Visa number over the Internet. Is it really secure? Or I wondered, too, about when we use graphics in our other writing. It is so easy now to just go out on the Net, find a graphic, grab it, and paste it into your own paper. Can we do that? I'm concerned about copyright laws. Maybe that graphic is copyrighted, but I don't know that it is. I remember when I was little, I got caught shoplifting. Maybe stealing on the Net is the same kind of petty crime as shoplifting. But it's sure much easier to get caught in a store than on the Net. People can get away with a whole lot more in cyberspace.

MAIN IDEAS FROM KIRSTEN'S FREEWRITING

1. "Borrowing" information from the Internet: CDs, graphics, others? Is this legal? Are there copyright restrictions?
2. Comparisons of Net theft to other petty crimes: shoplifting, copying software, tapes, or CDs. Is it easier to steal on the Net?

E X E R C I S E   3 . 4

Using one of the ideas generated by your brainstorming session in Exercise 3.3, freewrite for ten minutes nonstop at the keyboard or in your writing journal. Print out your freewriting session for review, or read over your freewriting from your journal. Discuss the results with your group:
1. Identify what you consider to be the best ideas in your freewriting.
2. Pinpoint what you see as the logical connections among your ideas.

3 | Invisible writing

Invisible writing is a computer freewriting technique designed to release you from the inhibitions created by seeing your own words on the computer screen (see the Help box on writing invisibly). Compulsive revisers find it difficult to ignore the errors they see on the screen and so are unable to write freely at the computer. When you write invisibly, your words do not appear on the screen, so you are free to generate ideas without interruption. You can concentrate on the emerging thoughts rather than on the form those thoughts are taking. You may wish to alternate sessions of invisible writing and regular freewriting.

EXERCISE 3.5

After turning the computer monitor off or turning down the contrast, begin a ten-minute invisible freewriting session, either on the topic you selected in Exercise 3.2 or on another topic. Discuss the experience of invisible writing with your group:

1. How did it compare with regular freewriting?
2. Did you feel it freed you from editing constraints?
3. Was it more or less frustrating than regular freewriting?

How do I write invisibly?

You can reduce your anxiety about writing by turning off the computer's monitor.

1. On your computer, open a document in which to store your invisible freewriting.

2. Close down any other open windows or applications on your computer. (You do not want to lose valuable data if you should accidentally hit the wrong key.)

3. Turn down the contrast or turn your monitor off altogether, thus making your writing invisible.

4. When you have finished freewriting, turn the monitor back on and read what you have written.

4   Clustering

Clustering is a prewriting technique that can help you to see relationships among the ideas you have generated in brainstorming or freewriting exercises. You begin a clustering session by putting your topic, in the form of a word or a phrase, in the middle of a sheet of paper. Then, attach to the word or phrase other words or phrases that come to mind, linking and connecting related ideas or subtopics. When you cluster, you free associate from one word or phrase to another, allowing your mind to trigger related ideas that may not have occurred to you before. Because clustering helps you to see relationships among ideas, it is useful for planning the structure of a paper. When you have finished your clustering activity, look at the results closely for any new insights you might have uncovered. Perhaps a string of subtopics will indicate to you a line of argument on the topic. Through clustering, you can focus on one area of interest to pursue in your paper. Although it is possible to do clustering on a computer, it is easier to do it with pencil and paper. The results of a clustering session by Kirsten on her topic of Net theft are shown in Figure 3.3.

EXERCISE 3.6

> Try clustering your ideas on one of the topics you generated in Exercise 3.1. Make an effort to free associate rather than consciously thinking through the ideas and the relationships among them. This activity should free you for creative thinking rather than constrain your ideas.

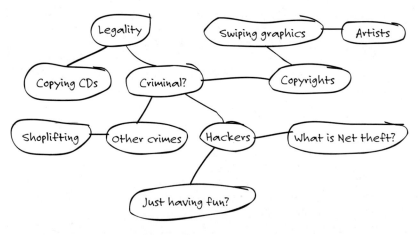

Figure 3.3   Clustering by Kirsten

5 Debating

Debating is a prewriting technique that can help you to explore a controversial issue from all sides. You might begin by writing down all the generalizations you can think of about the topic—either handwriting them in your journal or typing them into a computer file. Since Kirsten's Net theft topic has both pro and con arguments, she decided to write contrasting general statements that could then be supported through examples and evidence:

PRO

1. Using other people's work from the Net is just another form of sharing.

2. The Internet should be "free." To regulate it goes against its very nature.

3. When people put their ideas out on the Internet, they should just assume they're public.

CON

1. Authors and artists who publish on the Internet should not have their work "stolen."

2. "Borrowing" creative ideas, texts, and graphics from the Net is a form of stealing.

3. Net theft is the same thing as shoplifting.

Under each general heading or statement, you then can insert examples or evidence to support the generalization. In this way, you build your arguments and counterarguments. Once you have constructed a list of generalizations supported by evidence, look over the arguments with an eye to taking a side and defending it. Begin to think about how your arguments could be arranged to best advantage and how you could refute arguments on the other side. Examine areas where you need further evidence or additional information. Debate your pro and con lists with your classmates.

If you generate your lists using a word-processing program, you can add to, delete, replace, and rearrange the information. The general statements and evidence you accumulate while debating the topic can be used to start an outline or an exploratory draft of your paper.

EXERCISE 3.7

Pick one of the broad topics you listed in Exercise 3.1, and type into a document all the generalizations you can think of on the topic.

Order your generalizations, perhaps by pro and con positions. Then, for each generalization, list two or three specific examples or pieces of evidence. Save and print your prewriting. If you do not have access to a computer, complete this exercise in your writing journal. You may work individually or in a small group.

6   Narrowing your topic

Through prewriting, you develop an awareness of what you know and do not know about a topic. As you look back at your prewriting, think about ways in which you could narrow your topic to a manageable size. Think of any subdivisions there might be within the topic. You may have explored some of those subdivisions in your prewriting. Try to write down in one sentence what you take to be your specific, narrow topic.

Through brainstorming and clustering, Kirsten discovered that her broad topic of Net theft could be subdivided into legal issues, ethical issues, crimes on the Net, computer hackers, and so on. Out of all of the possible subtopics, Kirsten decided to narrow her focus to the practice of "borrowing" information from the Internet.

Once you have written down your narrow topic, try to state in one or two sentences the main point you want to make about that topic. This statement will be your *working thesis statement*. A thesis statement concisely identifies the topic and main point of a piece of writing. Many writers like to write a working thesis statement early in the writing process.

3c   Gather information

Particularly if your assignment is to write a research paper, you will need to supplement whatever prewriting techniques you use by gathering information from external sources. The first stage of your research may be informal and *ad hoc:* discussing the idea with friends and peers, talking to a professor, reading a few journal articles, or surfing the Net. The ideas you read about and formulate will lead you into a more systematic and extensive search that is focused on a specific topic. When searching in a focused way, you will likely consult library databases and the Internet and use CD-ROMs and online sources. Formal researching is discussed extensively in Part 2, particularly Chapters 9–11. If your writing task involves a significant research component, refer to those chapters for guidance.

1 Engaging in informal discussions

Informal discussions with classmates, friends, family members, and professors can provide valuable information on your topic. We suggest that you start with informal discussions before moving to more formal searching. Collaborating with your peers to brainstorm a topic is a good idea. Talking to others about your topic also may help you to pose the right questions before beginning a systematic search.

2 Browsing through periodicals

Your library most likely has a section devoted to current periodicals—that is, recently published magazines, newspapers, and journals. You can browse through these to see if your topic is one that currently is being discussed in the media. As you browse, look for articles related to your topic. If you find one, read it for background information.

3 Surfing the Net

A preliminary Internet search can serve much the same purpose as browsing through current periodicals. You can try out several Internet search tools, using a variety of key words, to see what kinds of information are available through the Internet. For more information on how to search the Internet, see Chapter 9.

4 Taking notes

As you begin your preliminary research on a topic, you will want to take notes. If you are reading, you should read actively and critically and annotate your readings (see 2b-3). If you are listening to a lecture, you should listen attentively and take accurate notes. Record the most important points the lecturer makes, rather than trying to write down everything. Be selective. Finally, always identify completely the source for the lecture notes (course, professor, date, and time of the lecture).

3d   Plan and organize

Once you have explored your topic, done some prewriting, and consulted a few sources, you are ready to begin thinking about a logical order in which to present the ideas you have developed. The structure of your paper will be influenced by all of the items shown in the rhetorical triangle in Figure 3.2 (purpose, persona, readers). For example, if your purpose is to report on a scientific experiment, the structure of your paper most likely will be the one conventionally used by scientists in professional journals (see 15a).

http://www.powa.org/
orgnfrms.htm
Several organizational
strategies, from Para-
digm Online Writing
Assistant

For most writers, formulating a working thesis is the first step in organizing a paper (see 3b-6). No matter how good your information, if your paper is not organized, your readers will not be able to understand what you are trying to say. Taking the time to organize your thoughts and ideas prior to drafting is one of the marks of a successful writer.

1   Revising your working thesis

As we mentioned earlier in this chapter, an effective thesis statement defines the specific topic and makes a strong point about it. At the same time, an effective thesis provides the reader with a blueprint for the direction the paper will take. In other words, the thesis not only states the writer's opinion on the topic but also indicates how the writer intends to support that opinion. You may need to revise your working thesis several times as you draft your paper. Allow your thesis to evolve as your understanding of the topic evolves.

EXERCISE 3.8

Draft a few potential thesis statements for one of the topics you identified in Exercise 3.1, either typing them into a computer document or writing them in your journal. Evaluate your potential thesis statements using the questions in Evaluating a Working Thesis. Discuss the thesis statements with a classmate or friend.

Evaluating a Working Thesis

Below are three important questions to ask regarding your working thesis:

1. Does the thesis define a specific topic?
2. Does the thesis make a strong point about the topic?
3. Does the thesis provide a blueprint for the paper's development?

Kirsten's Working Thesis: When it comes to "borrowing" information from the Internet, we are gradually becoming a people that can accept lawbreaking as long as we can participate, too.

Q1. The specific topic is borrowing information from the Internet.

Q2. The main point is that people accept lawbreaking if they can participate, too.

Q3. This thesis implies that the paper will explain how we have accepted lawbreaking in the Internet arena. We expect it to explain how easy it is for everyone to "participate" in this kind of lawbreaking.

Working Thesis 2:   Whatever the causes, males and females have different perspectives on computers and their uses.

Q1. The specific topic is computers and their uses.

Q2. The main point is that males and females have different perspectives on computers.

Q3. This thesis implies that the paper will list and describe the differences between male and female perspectives on computers and their uses.

Working Thesis 3:   Logging forests is a waste of resources.

Q1. This thesis is too broad and does not specify which forests are being discussed or in what ways they are being wasted. A broad thesis can be focused by using the journalists' questions: who, what, when, where, why, and how.

Q2. The main point of the thesis is not clear. The writer's opinion that logging is "a waste of resources" needs to be supported in the thesis; for example, "Logging is a waste of resources because . . . ."

Q3. It is not clear how the writer intends to develop this thesis.

2   Organizing your information

In addition to constructing an effective thesis, another step in coming up with a blueprint for your paper's structure is to revisit your rhetorical stance, since your persona, purpose, and readers will also influence how you arrange information in your text.

There is no one right way to organize material. However, since human beings habitually organize experience on the basis of time, space, and logic, these three factors often influence the organization of written work.

Organizing by *time* usually implies imposing a chronological order on information—that is, relating one thing after another in sequence. If you are telling a story in your paper, information most likely will be presented in the order in which events occurred. In Kirsten's essay on Net theft, for example, the section in which she tells the story of her own shoplifting experience is organized by time. Similarly, you would probably use a chronological organization when describing how to carry out a process.

Organizing by *space* implies providing a visual orientation for your readers. If you are describing something, you need to orient your readers spatially for them to be able to follow your writing. Spatial description most likely will proceed in an orderly fashion from a given vantage point. For example, if you are describing your college dorm room, you might begin at the far corner of the room and work your way across the room to the doorway.

By far the most frequently used principle of organization in college writing is *logic*. The typical patterns for logical organization are discussed at length in Chapter 6. With any logical organizational pattern, you are providing your reader with a familiar way of ordering experience, whether through causes and effects, problems and solutions, or some other logical pattern. Reviewing possible patterns at this point in your prewriting will help you construct an organizational plan.

EXERCISE 3.9

Consider what organizational principles might govern a paper on the topic you selected in Exercise 3.8. Type your ideas into a computer document or write them in your journal. Then, work together with your group to write a possible thesis statement that reflects the principle you have chosen.

3 Writing an outline

Once you have decided which organizational pattern best suits your working thesis, you may find it useful to construct an outline for your paper. You need not be overly concerned with formal outline structure at this point, unless your teacher stipulates a particular outline format. An outline should serve as a guide to you as you write—not a constraint that confines and limits your thinking. You may need to change your outline several times as you make new discoveries during drafting.

Formal Outlines

A formal outline is typically structured in a conventional hierarchy, with numbered and lettered headings and subheadings. A formal outline can be either a topic outline, in which words or phrases are used, or a sentence outline, in which complete sentences are used.

HELP

How do I use a word processor's outline feature?

1. With your word processor in OUTLINE mode, enter the outline.

2. Be sure to use your word processor's OUTLINE feature to set the levels within your outline, as well as the outline style (for example, bullets, numbers).

3. Use the outliner's COLLAPSE and EXPAND features to view your work at different levels of detail.

4. Rearrange major sections as needed. Your outliner will make sure that subpoints move automatically with the major headings.

5. When you have finished, end the OUTLINE feature and save your work.

NOTE: Programs differ in the ways they change levels and add text. Check your online HELP for details.

Formal Outline Pattern

Thesis Statement:

   I. First main idea

      A. First subordinate idea

         1. First example or illustration

         2. Second example or illustration

            a. First supporting detail

            b. Second supporting detail

      B. Second·subordinate idea

  II. Second main idea

Informal Outlines

Informal outlines are not structured as rigidly as formal outlines. For example, in a formal outline, you are not allowed to have a number one subheading unless there is also a number two subheading. Informal outlines allow you to create any hierarchies you like, without paying close attention to issues of format.

Informal Outline Pattern

Thesis Statement:

First main idea

    Subordinate idea

        Example or illustration 1

        Example or illustration 2

Second main idea

    Subordinate idea

Third main idea

    Example 1

In constructing an outline that would guide her through her paper, Kirsten used her thesis statement as a blueprint.

KIRSTEN'S NET THEFT OUTLINE

Thesis: When it comes to "borrowing" information from the Internet, we are gradually becoming a people that can accept lawbreaking as long as we can participate, too.

I. Introduction

   A. Scenario

   B. Definition of Net theft

II. Different medium, same crime

III. Standards of honor

   A. Describe what is legal

   B. Describe what is not legal

IV. Redefining a criminal

EXERCISE 3.10

If you have available a word-processing program with an OUTLINE feature, use it to generate a preliminary outline for a paper based on the working thesis and organizational plan you generated in Exercises 3.8 and 3.9. If you do not have a computer outlining program, outline on paper.

3e   Try computer prewriting software

As an alternative or a supplement to the prewriting suggestions provided for you in this chapter, you may find that your computer lab or writing center has prewriting software that can help you think through and prewrite on a topic. Such programs generally include a series of open-ended questions that allow you to generate ideas systematically. Your ideas are recorded in a computer file for later use. If you have access to commercial prewriting software, it is worth your while to give it a try. It may help you to come up with ideas that would not have occurred to you while prewriting on your own.

In this chapter, you have learned about the first stage in the writing process—preparing. We suggest that you try several of the prewriting techniques with various writing assignments from your courses. You may find that combining them in some unique way works best for you. Return to these prewriting techniques at different times during the writing process, whenever you need fresh ideas or feel that your writing is blocked in some way. Remember that all of the techniques we have discussed may be useful to you as you draft and revise your papers as well. Chapter 4 will focus on the activities that fall under the second major category in the stages of the writing process—composing.

FAQs

Why should I review my prewriting before I compose
a first draft? (4a)
How do I get over writer's block? (4b-3)
Can a computer help me collaborate? (4c)
Are there different ways to compose with
computers? (4d)

?

After paying conscious attention to prewriting and planning,
you are ready to begin composing—that is, writing a first draft of
your text. Of course, you already have
done considerable writing—through
your brainstorming and freewriting,
for example, and through your planning and outlining. But when we
talk about composing a draft, we are
speaking more specifically about the
stage in the writing process wherein
you put your ideas down in the form
of connected sentences and paragraphs. To write your first draft, you
may use pen and paper, a typewriter,
a word processor, or some combination of these tools. Your first
draft will be necessarily tentative and exploratory. It is important to

WWW
WEB
MMM

http://webserver.
maclab.comp.uvic.ca/
writersguide/Pages/
EssaysToc.html
An introduction to vari-
ous elements of the
writing process, from
one of the best writing
resources on the Net

understand that an effective piece of writing proceeds through a number of drafts, each of which is improved through revision. We discuss the revision process at length in Chapter 5.

4a Review

When you compose your first draft, you use the information and ideas you generated in your prewriting, as well as your working thesis and outline. In the composing stage of the writing process, your concern shifts from experimenting with ideas and gathering information to expanding on your ideas and structuring them into effective, coherent prose. Review that crucial prewriting information before you begin composing your first draft.

1 Reviewing prewriting, thesis, and outline

You can use your prewriting as the raw material for your first draft. If you recorded your prewriting in an electronic journal, begin by printing it out. Reading your prewriting in a printed format may spark fresh thoughts about the ideas you have generated. If your prewriting is in a handwritten journal or notebook, reread the journal entries. As you read, jot down notes in the notebook margin or enter notes at the bottom of the page in your computer journal. If one idea stands out, you may want to highlight it using a marker or the highlighting function on your computer.

Next, review your working thesis and outline. Add any new ideas you discovered while reading through your prewriting. If you think the main idea has shifted since you wrote your working thesis, rewrite it and adjust your outline. Finally, revisit your rhetorical stance—your purpose, persona, and readers—and make any needed adjustments to your plans.

When Kirsten read over her brainstorming and freewriting, she decided that her best topic ideas involved a focus on various kinds of "borrowing" from the Internet: copying files, graphics, CDs, and so on. She also found that she was interested in exploring why such Net crime seemed so accepted.

When Kirsten first wrote her working thesis, it reflected the focus she had decided on after her prewriting review:

ORIGINAL   Gradually, we are becoming a people that accept lawbreaking

as long as we can participate, too.

As she reviewed her thesis, she decided that it was too broad to give her a specific direction in the paper because it did not specify what kind of lawbreaking the paper would discuss. She revised it to more specifically describe the Net crimes she wanted to cover in the paper:

REVISED   When it comes to "borrowing" information from the Internet, we are gradually becoming a people that can accept lawbreaking as long as we can participate, too.

Kirsten's outline provided a broad plan for her paper. As she reviewed the outline, she added several more subheadings (in blue below) to make it more specific:

I. Introduction

   A. Scenario

   B. Definition of Net theft

   C. Thesis

II. Different medium, same crime

   A. Compare to shoplifting

   B. Compare difficulty of each crime

III. Standards of honor

   A. Describe what is legal

   B. Describe what is illegal

IV. Redefining a criminal

   A. Why Net theft is accepted

   B. What should we do about it?

EXERCISE 4.1

Review the brainstorming you did for Exercise 3.3. Think again about the rhetorical stance you adopted in Exercise 3.2. If you can, identify one main point, highlight it, and then review your working thesis statement and outline. Adjust your thesis and outline to reflect any new ideas you discover.

2 Copying prewriting and outline documents

It is a good idea to copy your prewriting and outline documents before you begin composing. Or, you can create a new document that contains both earlier documents (see the Help box). You can use this new document to manipulate the text and rewrite it into a finished product. If you change your mind about where your writing is headed, you will still have your original prewriting and outline documents to go back to.

If you prefer, you can use your prewriting and outline documents for reference and begin composing from scratch in a new

How do I combine my prewriting and outline documents?

Often word processors provide multiple ways to accomplish the same task. Here are two ways to combine documents.

1. Inserting the two documents into a blank document:
   a. Create a blank document.
   b. Insert the contents of your prewriting document.
   c. Insert the contents of your outline document.
   d. Move appropriate information from the prewriting document to the outline document (using CUT and PASTE).
   e. Save the combined document as a first draft with an appropriate new name.

2. Combining the two documents using multiple windows:
   a. Open your prewriting document and your outline document, each in its own window.
   b. Moving between the windows, COPY and PASTE appropriate information from the prewriting document to the outline document.
   c. Save the combined text to a new document with an appropriate name.

document. The WINDOW feature of many word-processing programs allows you to work on two or more documents simultaneously. Multiple windows are useful for keeping track of your ideas as you work—you can keep your prewriting and/or outline document in one window and your draft in another. Otherwise, because computer screens provide you with a limited view, it is easy to lose a sense of the flow of your document. With multiple windows, you can either switch back and forth from one window to the other or tile the windows so that they appear on the screen at once. Figure 4.1 shows three windows open simultaneously.

EXERCISE 4.2

Using the directions provided in the Help box, open a new document in one window (for your draft) and open your prewriting and outline documents (from Exercises 3.7 and 3.10) in two other windows. Arrange the three windows so that they will all be available on your screen when you begin composing.

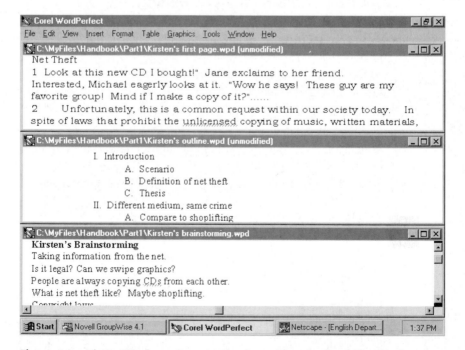

Figure 4.1   Three Windows Open at the Same Time in Corel WordPerfect for Windows

How do I open documents in separate windows?

If you want to work on more than one document at a time, you can do so by using separate windows.

1. Open a document containing a text you have written.
2. Open another document containing another text.
3. View your documents simultaneously by selecting the VIEW or WINDOW feature.
4. Arrange your documents on the screen for better viewing (select TILE or ARRANGE ALL, MINIMIZE, or click and drag).

TIP: It is also possible to use separate windows to display different parts of your document at the same time. For example, you could insert your thesis into one window and your draft into another.

NOTE: This feature requires that your operating system support windows.

4b   Draft

When you are ready to begin composing, you can choose from a number of different approaches. Two possible approaches are the building-block technique and the top-down method.

1   Using the building-block technique

One approach to composing is to create a group of building blocks that you can use to construct your text a piece at a time. Many writers first compose a skeleton of the finished text and then expand it by adding new arguments, supporting examples and evidence, or illustrative details, the "building blocks" of a text. Word processing is particularly effective for this approach. Some writers like to write their central paragraphs—the middle blocks of a text—first and add the introductory blocks and concluding paragraphs later. You can decide which blocks will be easiest and write those blocks first, saving the more difficult parts for last. Once you have a preliminary draft, you can return to your text to amplify sections, one block at a time. To create blocks, you can use the new document you made from copies of your prewriting and outline documents. Use the headings in your outline to expand and build your text. CUT and PASTE text from your prewriting to place under the headings; then rewrite and amplify the text to create blocks. You can also COPY information from your prewriting window and PASTE it into your document in the other window. In this way, you avoid having to retype information from your prewriting document as you compose.

Below is an illustration of how Kirsten built one section of her paper by copying and pasting information from her prewriting file into her outline file; the blocks are in blue.

COMPOSING FROM OUTLINE WITH BUILDING BLOCKS

I. Introduction

   A. Scenario

      "Look at this new CD I bought!" Jane exclaims to her friend.

      Interested, Michael eagerly looks at it. "Wow he says! These guys

      are my favorite group! Mind if I make a copy of it?" . . .

   B. Definition of Net theft

      In spite of laws that prohibit the unlicensed copying of music,

      written materials, and movies, it has become an accepted

      practice. Graphics, quotes, articles, and many other various things

      can be copied for personal use, but often no credit is given to the

      original author.

   C Thesis

      When it comes to "borrowing" information from the Internet, we

      are gradually becoming a people that can accept lawbreaking as

      long as we can participate, too.

2   Using the top-down method

As an alternative to composing from building blocks, you may prefer to work from the beginning of your paper straight through to the end, thus moving from the top down. You can use your working thesis statement and the corresponding organizational plan to compose in this way. Type or COPY and PASTE your working thesis statement into a new document. As we discuss in Chapter 3, your thesis statement can provide you with a blueprint for composing. With the thesis statement at the top of your screen, begin writing your draft, following the blueprint suggested by your thesis. Save your draft into the appropriate folder on your hard drive so that you can return to it for more work at a later time. Remember, your working thesis is just that—working. You can revise it at any time (see 7a). Be flexible as you write and open to new directions that may occur to you during composing.

3 Avoiding writer's block

Each writer develops his or her own writing rhythms. You need to discover what your rhythms are. If you find yourself "blocked" as a writer, set your work aside for a few days or even a few hours. Get up and stretch; make yourself a cup of coffee or grab a soft drink

Suggestions for Overcoming Writer's Block

- *Gain some distance.* Set your writing aside for a few days or hours. Take a coffee or snack break before coming back to your writing task.
- *Keep at it.* When your writing is flowing well, try to avoid interruptions so that you can keep the momentum going.
- *Try freewriting.* Often, the act of writing itself will stimulate those creative juices.
- *Use visualization.* Picture yourself writing or picture some aspect of the topic you are writing about. Then describe what you see.
- *Change your point of view.* Try writing from another person's point of view. Or try writing in a different genre, such as a letter or a memo.
- *Write what you know first.* Rather than beginning with an introductory paragraph, start by writing the portion of your paper that you know the most about.
- *Change your mode of writing.* If you normally type at a computer, try using pencil and paper, or vice versa.

before returning to your draft. Coming to it again fresh may give you renewed energy. If you find the writing is flowing well, try to keep at it—writing often takes on a life of its own and generates its own momentum. Finally, do not expect perfection from a first draft. Remember that writing is essentially rewriting: everything you write should undergo extensive revision in a continuous cycle of writing, revising, editing, and writing again.

EXERCISE 4.3

Using either the building-block technique or the top-down method, begin drafting in the new document you opened in Exercise 4.2. As you compose, refer often to your prewriting and outline documents. Remember to take advantage of the text-building capabilities of your word-processing program, including the WINDOW and CUT, COPY, and PASTE features.

4c   Collaborate

You might find it helpful to collaborate with others as you compose. In college classes, as in the work force, writers often work on projects in writing groups or writing teams. Your teammates can serve as a sounding board for your ideas and arguments. You can compose together at the keyboard, with one team member acting as the scribe. Or you can compose separately but then turn to each other for responses. Your peers can read early drafts and provide you with valuable feedback on your work. Take advantage of the help that can be found in such collaborative writing groups.

1   Working with a group

Working with a group may be something you enjoy or something you dread, depending on whether your prior experience with group projects was positive or negative. In some group projects, one or two students may end up feeling that they are doing all the work. In other group projects, a few students may be bossy or controlling rather than cooperative. But if you pay attention to group dynamics and role assignments from the start of your collaborative project, you all should get along just fine and together produce an outcome that none of you could have achieved alone.

When you first receive a collaborative assignment from your teacher, meet with your group to begin brainstorming the possibilities. One group member can act as the group's scribe, typing into the computer all of the ideas generated by the group. Do not cut off creative avenues; brainstorm in the spirit of both understanding and opening up the assignment for your group. Once you have a brainstorming list, begin to divide it into component parts, in an effort to outline a plan of action. You might want to "storyboard" your piece—that is, put the components of the overall piece onto 3" × 5" note cards and then work together to arrange the pieces to best advantage.

2 Writing collaboratively

Once you have come up with an overall plan of action for your writing project, you can assign specific tasks or roles to group

How do I collaborate on a computer?

If your teacher or lab supervisor has designated a common location on a local area network for your class, you can use it to share work with your classmates (step 1). Other ways to collaborate include using Web pages and email.

1. Post your work to the common drive by using the SAVE AS function in your word-processing program.

   a. Read and comment on the work that has been posted by your classmates (use all capital letters or your word processor's commenting feature).

   b. On a PC, use SAVE AS to save your classmates' work plus your comments in a new document under a new title.

2. If possible, post your work to a class Web site for others to read and review.

3. Use email to send your work to a peer.

(See also Chapter 21.)

members. One writing class was assigned the task of developing a group Web site on a topic related to cyberspace. The students in each group brainstormed together the possibilities for their site, first deciding on the nature of the content their Web site would present. They agreed to each write independently a two- to three-page piece that would be incorporated as a page at the site. Then, they assigned each person in the group one of the following roles: *group leader* (organized group meetings, set deadlines, reported progress to the teacher), *group librarian* (recorded relevant Web sites, produced a bibliography, ensured that all links in the site were operational), *group publisher* (took responsibility for the "look" of the site, importing graphics and deciding on appropriate fonts, colors, backgrounds), *group Webmaster* (took responsibility for placing all of the group's writing onto the server, making sure that the site was both functional and readable). Because each student in the group knew exactly what his or her contribution would be, group members were able to work together cooperatively.

EXERCISE 4.4

This exercise will provide you with practice in composing collaboratively in a computer classroom. First, exchange keyboards with the person sitting beside you so that your writing appears on the other person's screen. Next, decide who will be writer 1 and who will be writer 2. Writer 1 begins to freewrite on the topic "Why I chose my college major." Writer 2 begins to write when writer 1 types a series of question marks (???). When writer 2 runs out of ideas, she or he types a series of question marks. Continue to exchange ideas for about ten minutes.

4d   Try composing with a computer

Although some students who do not have computers readily available may still be writing out rough drafts by hand, most students (with computers of their own or liberal access to computer labs) now compose their papers directly at a computer keyboard. In this section, we will examine the ways in which computers have affected composing and suggest strategies for adapting to the changes.

1 Adapting your writing habits

If you are accustomed to writing with pen and paper, you may find that your old writing habits do not translate directly when you use a computer. Old habits are difficult to break, and some writers steadfastly resist the new technology. Others stick to their old habits because they are comforting. For example, one writer reports that before each writing session, he takes a dozen pencils and sharpens them to neat points. He then puts all the pencils in a pencil holder and sits down to type at the computer, not using the pencils at all! You too may find that it helps to observe some of the rituals you developed for writing with pen and paper. But the more familiar you become with writing at the computer, the more you will see its value to you as a writer. Most writers eventually move to composing at the keyboard once they get beyond the initial learning stages.

2 Changing your notion of text and draft

Changing to a new writing tool may subtly alter your relationship with your own words. At first, the words on the screen may seem distant to you—somehow foreign and strange—unlike the words you produced with paper and pencil. One of our students remarked that the words seemed like phantoms that could disappear at the touch of a key. However, this sense of distance that word processing creates also allows you to see your writing as more fluid and changeable. It will probably make you more willing to experiment and to abandon text that is not working. In fact, the very notion of a draft changes when you compose at a computer. Each time you open a document to make changes in the text, you are in essence creating a new draft, whether or not you print it out for review. Dozens of drafts may appear and disappear as you continue to revisit your text while composing.

3 Using the computer wisely

When you begin to use a computer for composing, do not get carried away. Some writing—such as a short note to a friend—is still better done with pen and paper. If you work in a computer lab where access is limited, you might want to write your first draft on paper,

How do I save my work in a series of drafts?

1. Each time you begin a new draft, use the SAVE AS feature and name your drafts in sequence: draft1, draft2, and so on. Then, if you decide that your revisions have not been successful, you can always return to your earlier draft.

2. When working on a draft, do not discard work too hastily by using the CUT function of your word-processing program.

3. Instead, use the COPY and PASTE functions. COPY any information you decide to cut out of your draft, and PASTE it at the end of the document so that you can retrieve it later if needed.

TIP: Because you may be revising frequently while you write, you need to be certain that you periodically save your work. You can set an AUTO-SAVE feature on your word processor that will automatically save at regular intervals.

saving your computer time for a later draft and for revisions. Even if you have a computer of your own, unless it is portable you may want to keep a notebook handy for on-the-spot composing. If you are fortunate enough to own a laptop computer, it probably has a NOTEPAD or SCRAPBOOK feature, which you can use to record notes and organize your ideas. Work on developing a writing system that uses the computer—and your time—to best advantage.

4   Working effectively in a lab environment

If your only access to a computer is in a lab, then you should strive to be flexible about your writing process. Try to schedule work at the time that best suits your own writing habits. However, if the lab is not open at 2:00 a.m., when you work best, you may need to write a draft on paper and then transfer it to the computer for revision later.

Most lab directors try to accommodate students by opening the lab some evenings or weekends, but during those times the lab may be overly busy or some computers may not be functioning. Plan ahead and leave time to compensate for these potential problems.

You can help your lab coordinator improve the environment by making suggestions and providing feedback on your lab experience. If a lab assistant is surly and unhelpful, say so. If other writers in the lab are noisy or disruptive, ask the lab assistant to quiet them down. In most cases, the lab coordinator and assistants will be genuinely interested in helping you write successfully, and your suggestions will help improve the lab environment for everyone.

EXERCISE 4.5

Write a brief paragraph describing your own writing process, paying particular attention to any composing habits that you have developed over the years. For example, do you have particular tools that you use or a special place where you are comfortable composing? Do you like to have music playing in the background, or is quiet better for you? Share your paragraph with your classmates and discuss the similarities and differences in composing habits.

4e   Review a student draft

Following is the first draft of a persuasive paper by Kirsten Parsons, the student introduced in Chapter 3. The assignment was to write an essay on a computer topic of interest. The piece was to be written largely from the students' own experiences, from a brief Internet search, and from the class text. Kirsten thought through several possible topics, but settled on Net theft.

There is much that is good about this draft. Kirsten has identified a real problem that many students experience—that is, being uncertain of the "rules" when it comes to using the Internet. The topic is compelling, and her comparisons to shoplifting are insightful. But there are things about the paper that can be improved. We have included the instructor's comments on this early draft (in green) to highlight some of the areas that need work. A revision of this paper is included at the end of Chapter 5.

Kirsten Parsons

English 101–35

Net Theft

"Look at this new CD I bought!" Jane exclaims to her

friend. Interested, Michael eagerly looks at it. "Wow he

says! These guy are my favorite group! Mind if I make a

copy of it?". . . .

Unfortunately, this is a common request within our

society today. In spite of laws that prohibit the unlicensed

copying of music, written materials, and movies, it has

become an accepted practice to reproduce another's work

without paying for it. Similarly, this has spread to the

Internet where access to software, phone cards, and other

products is convenient and fast. Graphics, quotes, articles

and many other various things can be copied for personal

use with ease, but often no credit is given to the original

author. Not only are these practices wrong from a moral

viewpoint, but legally, they are forbidden as well. It

has become a situation where "legality collides with

practicality" (Meyer and Underwood 65). In other words,

breaking the law is more convenient than keeping it

and since we know we can get away with doing it,

our conscience gives in. When it comes to "borrowing"

information from the Internet, we are gradually becoming

I'm not certain what the reference to phone cards and other products is in the above paragraph. There are many different kinds of computer thefts. It's not really clear what the focus of this paper will be because of all the different examples in this opening paragraph, although your thesis is quite good.

a people that accept lawbreaking as long as we can participate, too.

I'm sure all of us once glimpsed a tempting item in a store and after getting no for an answer from Mom or Dad, took matters into our own hands. Sneaking the treasure into a hidden pocket, it probably took only a few moments for your parents to notice something was up. I remember well a discussion about why taking the package was wrong. Then my Dad took me back to the store where an apology was made and my Strawberry Hubba Bubba Bubblegum was paid for. Walking into a store, and taking something without paying for it is obviously not encouraged in our society; ironically, this principle seems to break down where the Net is concerned. With available technology, Net theft is commonplace. Flowers, phone cards, magazines, books, and software all are vulnerable to cyber-shoplifting and plagiarism. Though its not encouraged per say, it is not discouraged either. Isn't this just stealing masked by softer adjectives such as "sharing"? Granted it is less noticeable, but that doesn't change the fact that you didn't pay for it.

Part of the problem is that the physical element involved in actually traveling to a store, and taking something is not necessary for these Net-crimes. Imagine walking down the aisle of the local Walmart with the intention of stealing a Hobbes Doll, your favorite cartoon

I really liked this comparison to other petty crimes, like shoplifting. Again, I wasn't sure about your Net comparison, however (flowers, phone cards, magazines, books—how are these vulnerable to Net theft?). Maybe it would be better to just focus on one kind of petty theft— like copying software or "borrowing" materials such as graphics from someone else's Web site.

character. Blood rushes to your hears and your heart begins to pound, as your body reacts to the rush of adrenalin. Casting a nervous glance around the nearby aisles, the coast is clear. Extending your arm, you grab the orange tiger, and place it in your backpack then walk nonchalantly towards the exit. This scenerio is only possible in a physical world. Because the Net is so unphysical, the risk of being caught, that may serve to deter many thieves in a store, is minimal. Theft is committed within the reach of the refrigerator! Besides, who has ever heard of someone being arrested for copying a graphic illegally, or copying a friend's WordPerfect program? Because Net-crimes often go ignored, and "everyone" is guilty, more and more people engage in them. The consequences seem to be less punitive and thus we give in to the influence of the Wild Net!

Information about copyright laws, what is legal and what isn't is available on the Net as well. Web Issues at the Copyright Website (www.benedict.com) provides information about what can be copied from the Net and how to do it properly. Another page specifically discusses using graphics (PageWorks available at http://www. snowcrest.net/kitty/hpages). Those who decide to break these "laws," run the risk of being ostracized by a group such as Netbusters! This vigilante group seeks to prevent

I think you are right about the ease of committing computer crimes. Good, vivid example of shoplifting the stuffed animal. Maybe you could finish this example with the store's alarm system sounding or the clerk spotting the theft to show how much easier it is to get caught.

what they call "bandwidth robbery" by informing Netusers about its devastating results. The Netbusters homepage has a place to report clandestine computer activities if you know of any perpetrators.

  If the definition of a criminal is one who has committed a crime, then in the world of the Net, perhaps we all need to serve some time.

I'm not certain of the relevance of the Netbusters example. It needs to be tied in with the rest of the paper. You seem to be going further astray here at the end. You need a strong conclusion that sums things up and returns you to your thesis.

Reference

Meyer, Michael, and Anne Underwood. "Crimes of the 'Net'." CyberReader. Ed. Victor Vitanza. Boston: Allyn, 1996. 63–65.

You will need to cite your Internet sources here as well as your print source. Please check MLA style for the correct format used with Internet sources.

Rewriting

Can I be an objective reader of my own writing? (5a)

How can the computer help me revise my writing? (5b)

What is the difference between revising and editing? (5b, 5c)

How do I proofread on screen? (5d)

How do I give effective feedback to my peers? (5e)

?

This chapter discusses three rewriting skills—revising, editing, and proofreading. As you think about rewriting, imagine that you are viewing your writing through the lens of a camera. The first view is panoramic (revising): you look globally at the entire piece of writing with the goal of revising its focus, coherence, organization, development, tone, and format. The second view is at normal range (editing): you look locally at specific sentence-level features with the goal of eliminating wordiness, repetition, and ineffective or awkward language. Finally, you zoom in for a close-up (proofreading): you look for any distracting errors that might interfere with a reader's understanding, including punctuation and mechanics.

5a Shift from writer to reader

To be skillful revisers, writers must put themselves in the place of their readers. When writers read their own work, however, they may have trouble seeing what they have actually written. Instead, they often see what they *intended* to write. This section offers some strategies to help you shift roles from writer to reader when you review your writing.

Allowing time to review your draft

If possible, allow at least a day between the time you finish a draft and the time you read it over to revise, edit, and proofread. You will be astonished at how much more clearly you can view your

How do I manipulate my text to make revising easier?

1. Change the way your text looks in any of these ways:
   a. Change the spacing of your text lines from double to triple.
   b. Change the font size from 12 point to 15 point.
   c. Insert a page break after each paragraph.
   d. Change the margin width from 1 inch to 2 inches.
2. Save the reformatted text under a different name.
3. Print out the reformatted text.
4. Read each paragraph of the printed text carefully, using the Critical Reading Questions for Revision (see page 63).
5. Write suggestions for revision in the margins.

writing if you take a break from working on it. If you are facing a tight deadline, even several hours are helpful. Also, try to schedule more than one session for revising. When your writing is stored electronically, it is much easier to revise because you do not need to retype or recopy the entire text after each change.

2   Reading critically

As you read your work critically, it will help if you pay attention to different major elements during each subsequent reading. These elements are focus, coherence, organization, development, tone, and format. (See page 63 for Critical Reading Questions for Revision.)

Focus

Focus refers to how well you adhere to your topic and your purpose throughout a piece of writing. As you reread a draft, check that each paragraph relates in some way to the thesis. Is each of your examples and supporting details needed for your argument? It is more important to maintain focus than to add length. Your readers expect you to fulfill the commitment promised by your thesis. If you go off on a tangent, they may lose interest.

Coherence

The various components of a piece of writing should "stick together," from sentence to sentence and from paragraph to paragraph. This writing glue is known as coherence. Make certain that your sentences and paragraphs are linked through transitional words and phrases. Your goal is to make your writing *cohere*— that is, form a unified whole. (See also Chapter 6 on structuring paragraphs.)

Organization

If your piece is well organized, it follows a direction set by the thesis and the opening paragraphs. If you have decided on a particular organizational pattern, check to be sure you followed through with that pattern. For example, if you decided to use the cause-and-effect pattern, make certain that you covered both causes and effects. You may find as you reread a draft that some paragraphs would be more effective in a different order or that your closing argument is not your most persuasive and so should not be the last one read by the reader. (See also Chapter 6.)

Critical Reading Questions for Revision

Focus

- Do I have a clearly stated or strongly implied thesis that controls the content of the entire piece?
- Do all the major points refer back to and support my thesis?
- Are all of the examples and illustrations relevant to my point?

Coherence

- Are individual sentences, paragraphs, and sections held together by transitions?
- Are the transitional words and phrases I have used the best, most accurate ones available?
- Have I avoided overusing any transitional word or phrase?

Organization

- Are the major points arranged in the most effective order, following the blueprint provided by my thesis?
- Are my strongest arguments placed near the end where readers will remember them?
- Are the supporting points arranged to best advantage?
- Have I followed through with the organizational pattern I selected?

Development

- Is my thesis adequately supported?
- Are my major points backed up by specific details and examples?
- Is there at least one paragraph for each major point?
- Are my paragraphs developed proportionately (none significantly longer or shorter than the others)?

Tone

- Is my tone appropriate to my rhetorical stance?
- Do my language choices reflect my intended tone?
- Have I eliminated contractions or first-person pronouns from a formal piece?
- Is my tone consistent throughout the text?

Format

- Does the "look" of my text help convey its meaning?
- Is the font I have used readable and appropriate to the topic?
- Are the headings descriptive and helpful in orienting the reader?
- Have I used graphics and illustrations appropriately?

Development

Development refers to the depth of coverage given key ideas. As you reread the text, you may identify places that are underdeveloped. Look particularly for ways in which you have supported your thesis and developed each part of your organizational pattern. For example, if you decided on a problem/solution pattern (see 6b-5), have you developed each alternative solution sufficiently, arriving at a best solution? Be certain that each of your main points is backed up within its own paragraph by supporting details, illustrations, or examples.

Tone

The language you chose to use conveys the **tone**—that is, your attitude toward your topic and your readers. Your tone may be formal or informal, perhaps even humorous. Revisit your rhetorical stance to determine whether the tone you adopted is appropriate to your persona, purpose, and readers (see 3a-2). If you are writing on a serious topic, you are likely to use a formal tone. Your sentences and paragraphs will be relatively long; your word choices may be abstract; you will use very few personal references and contractions—in general, you will establish a considerable distance between yourself and your readers. If, however, you are writing on a less solemn topic, you may wish to strike an informal tone. Your sentences and paragraphs will be shorter; you will use less abstract language; you may include contractions and perhaps first-person pronouns—your readers will feel a closeness to you, the writer. (See also 3a-3.)

Format

If your draft is more than a page or two in length, consider using formatting to help the reader navigate the text. By using headings to delineate the major parts, you can help the reader recognize the organizational structure. However, if a piece is relatively short, headings usually are more distracting than helpful. Note, too, that using headings is more common in some fields than in others. For example, papers written in APA format tend to have headings, while those in MLA format may not. Also, pay attention to the font (type style) you have used. It is important that the font be appropriate to the final product; that is, a font that is suitable for a brochure might not be appropriate for a research paper. Standard fonts for all types of writing include Times New Roman and Courier. (See Chapter 17 for more information on fonts.)

3 Outlining your draft

One technique that may help you evaluate a piece of writing is preparing a revision outline. When you have a first draft and perhaps some peer or teacher comments on it, you can create a revision outline by updating the original outline for the piece to reflect the weaknesses of the draft. To begin to plan for revising, add comments in brackets to the revision outline concerning items you need to change in your draft.

Kirsten used this revision outline to plan changes to her first draft on Net theft:

KIRSTEN'S REVISION OUTLINE

Net Theft

Thesis: When it comes to "borrowing" information from the Internet, we are gradually becoming a people that can accept lawbreaking as long as we can participate, too.

I. Introduction

   A. Scenario

   B. Definition of Net theft [I need to focus this better to correspond with my thesis.]

   C. Thesis

II. Different medium, same crime

   A. Compare to shoplifting

   B. Compare difficulty of each crime

III. Standards of honor

   A. Describe what is legal [I really didn't do this very well. Need to expand this section to show where the law stands now.]

   B. Ten commandments for computers [This section doesn't really fit the focus of the paper. Maybe just mention it.]

IV. Redefining a criminal

    A. Why Net theft is accepted [I need to eliminate examples that
don't fit the focus. Concentrate on why it's so widely accepted.]

    B. What should we do about it? [I need a strong conclusion that
restates the problem with Net theft and what—if anything—
should be done about it.]

EXERCISE 5.1

Reread the rough draft of a paper you are working on. Using the
Critical Reading Questions for Revision, come up with an overall
plan for revising your draft. Prepare a revision outline, and add
comments about those items you intend to revise.

5b   Revise

Critical reading can highlight problems of focus, coherence, organization, development, tone, and formatting in your paper. Revising involves the tasks of adding to the text, deleting from the text,
and rearranging information within the text to fix those problems.
Using a word-processing program makes these tasks easy. Knowing
what to add, to delete, and to rearrange is the tricky part.

1   Revising for focus

Revisit your working thesis, and revise it to more accurately reflect the overall point of your text. Then revise each paragraph, one by
one, to ensure that it is focused on only
one idea, which supports the thesis.
(Try changing the format of your text as
suggested on page 70 to help you revise each paragraph.) Delete any paragraphs that are not related to the thesis.

Kirsten revised her second paragraph to focus more clearly on the idea
of "borrowing" from the Internet. No-
tice how she eliminated references to phone cards and other products
and included music, software, written texts, and graphics instead.

http://www.rpi.edu/
dept/llc/writecenter/
web/text/prose1.html
A list of twelve revision
tips and strategies

How do I compare drafts of my text to track my changes?

Here are three ways you can use your word processor to track changes you have made to a draft:

1. When you begin to revise a document, turn on REVISION MARKING. This feature will mark any changes you make in the document. (Note: Not all word processors offer this feature.)

2. If you forgot to turn on REVISION MARKING, you may still be able to compare two versions of a document by selecting the DOCUMENT COMPARE or COMPARE VERSIONS feature of the word-processing program.

   a. Select the files that you want compared (for example, draft1 and draft2).

   b. Look closely at the changes you have made between the two documents. (Revisions will be indicated with markings in the text.)

   c. Check to see that your revisions were substantive; that is, you did not merely tinker with the text but actually added, deleted, and rearranged.

3. If your word processor does not have DOCUMENT COMPARE, open both files concurrently in two windows and scan for differences.

Unfortunately, this is a common request ~~within our society~~ today. In spite of laws that prohibit ~~the~~ unlicensed copying ~~of music, written materials~~ *in some circles* ~~and movies,~~ it has become an accepted practice to reproduce another's *practice* work without paying for it. Similarly, this has spread to the Internet *music,* *written texts, and graphics* where access to software, ~~phone cards, and other products~~ is convenient *These items* and fast. ~~Graphics, quotes, articles and many other various things~~ can be copied for personal use with ease, but often no credit is given to the original author.

2 Revising for coherence

Wherever you notice that sentences do not flow smoothly in your draft, add appropriate transitional words and phrases. Look particularly at the links between paragraphs. Insert transitions to help the reader follow the flow of the text. Such words or phrases as *however, on the one hand/on the other hand, but,* and *in addition* can help the reader see the relationships between ideas. Add these words to your text at appropriate places. If you are using one transitional word too frequently, check the thesaurus in your word-processing program for alternatives. (See also 6c-1.)

3 Revising for organization

If you have made a revision outline, you have already decided how to improve the organization of your text. Use the CUT, COPY, and PASTE commands to move parts of your text. Rearrange the words, sentences, and paragraphs that comprise your text into the most effective order. Be certain that you check for coherence after rearranging.

4 Revising for development

Your argument is stronger if you include many concrete examples or details. If you are writing an informal piece, do not hesitate to add anecdotes or narratives of personal experiences to give life and personality to your writing. If you are writing a formal paper, you can add information from sources that support your arguments. Using the INSERT command of your word-processing program, place the cursor where additional explanatory details, evidence, examples, or illustrations need to be added to your text.

While working on her revision outline, Kirsten discovered that she needed to focus and develop her discussion of the legalities of the Internet (item IIIA in her outline). She rewrote the paragraph as follows:

ORIGINAL PARAGRAPH

Information about copyright laws, what is legal and what isn't is available on the Net as well. Web Issues at the Copyright Website (www.benedict.com) provides information about what can be copied from the Net and how to do it properly. ~~Another page specifically discusses using graphics (PageWorks available at http://www.snowcrest.net/kitty/hpages).~~ ~~Those who decide to break these "laws," run the risk of being ostracized by a group such as Netbusters! This vigilante group seeks to prevent what they call "bandwidth robbery" by informing Netusers about its devastating results.~~ ~~The Netbusters homepage has a place to report clandestine computer activities if you know of any perpetrators.~~

REWRITTEN PARAGRAPH

Organizations and individuals have tried to establish standards of conduct for Internet use. For example, the Computer Ethics Institute wrote its Ten Commandments for Computer Ethics, which includes such obvious "rules" as "Thou shalt not use the computer to steal" (Roach). But what is stealing when it comes to materials found on the Internet? The Copyright Web site asserts that any texts or graphics that you find on the Internet are by their very nature published and thus are "copyrighted" (O'Mahoney). This means that in order to use anything from someone else's Web site, you need their permission. If you put a comic strip such as Calvin and Hobbes onto your home page, you run the risk of being sued for violation of copyright.

5 Revising for tone

In rereading, you may decide that your tone is either too formal or too informal. To revise your tone to be more formal, expand contractions into their full forms, combine some short sentences to make longer sentences, and change informal diction or slang into more formal wording. The Help box on page 70 offers guidance in using the SEARCH function of your word-processing program as you revise for tone.

> http://www.powa.org/revifrms.htm
> Extensive advice on revising the style and tone of your essay, from Paradigm Online Writing Assistant

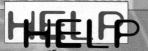

How do I use the search function to revise for tone?

1. Activate your word processor's SEARCH function. (Note: It may be called EDIT/REPLACE.)
2. Instruct the computer to search your document for a troublesome word, phrase, or punctuation mark (for example, the apostrophe in contractions).
3. As the computer moves to each case of the word, phrase, or punctuation mark in succession, you can decide whether to change it or not.
4. Revise any other troublesome words, phrases, or punctuation marks by initiating further searches.

6   Revising for format

To convey your information in a more visual way, you may want to add formatting more commonly found in a brochure or a newsletter (see 18a or 18b). You can import and insert graphics to illustrate your text at appropriate points. Try using different fonts by selecting them from the FORMAT menu. Remember, though, that readability of your text is the most important goal; choose fonts accordingly. (See Chapter 17 for more information on fonts.)

7   Writing effective openings, closings, and titles

Openings

Writers have very little time in which to grab the reader's attention—usually only a few seconds. That is why a piece's opening, or lead, is so important. But do not let concern over how you will begin become a stumbling block. Many writers find that leaving the opening for the last stages of revision works best.

Revision Checklist

Your response to each question should be "yes." If not, you need to go back and revise in that area.

Focus

- Do my thesis, paragraphs, and topic sentences all work together and deal with the same topic?

Coherence

- Have I used transitional words and phrases to provide the glue that holds various parts of the paper together?

Organization

- Does each part of the paper flow logically from the preceding part?
- Have I reserved my strongest arguments for last?

Development

- Have I used examples, facts, and source support to reinforce each major point in the paper?

Tone

- Is my tone consistent throughout the paper?

Format

- Is the format appropriate to the content?

If appropriate for a particular writing assignment, you can be inventive in your opening paragraph. To grab a reader's attention, try starting your lead with an anecdote or story, quotation, dialogue, or descriptive scene. For example, Kirsten decided to begin with dialogue:

"Look at this new CD I bought!" Jane exclaims to her friend. Interested,

Michael eagerly looks at it. "Wow," he says. "These guys are my favorite

group! Mind if I make a copy of it?"

Although some academic writing, by tradition, demands it, most experienced writers will not begin a piece with the thesis, or statement of purpose, such as "This paper will explore the pros and cons of drilling an auxiliary well in Smithfield Canyon." The following example illustrates a traditional academic lead:

> This essay examines issues of diversity and literacy education primarily in terms of the concept of *difference* via a new term: *non-negotiable difference*. It argues that networked classrooms provide writing instructors with unique extra-linguistic cues (body language) that can help teachers and students become more responsive to racial difference.
>
> —Todd Taylor, "The Persistence of *Difference* in Networked Classrooms: *Non-Negotiable Difference*"

Closings or Conclusions

A conclusion usually takes the form of a summary, which points the reader back to the text itself, or speculation, which points the reader outside of the text.

A SUMMARY CONCLUSION

> Few Interneters would disagree that stealing and reselling software or credit cards is wrong. But fewer still would feel guilty about copying the latest game version of Doom, or some such, rather than forking out $39.95. Unfortunately, that often admirable ethos makes it easier for genuine crooks to perpetrate—and justify—their crimes.
>
> —Michael Meyer and Anne Underwood, "Crimes of the 'Net' "

A SPECULATIVE CONCLUSION

> Nevertheless, in the litigations and political debates which are certain to follow, we will endeavor to assure that their electronic speech is protected as certainly as any opinions which are printed or, for that matter, screamed. We will make an effort to clarify issues surrounding the distribution of intellectual property. And we will help to create for America a future which is as blessed by the Bill of Rights as its past has been.
>
> —John Perry Barlow, "Crime and Puzzlement"

Do not feel obligated to limit yourself to a summary conclusion. Sometimes a speculative conclusion will work better. This type of conclusion is most appropriate for papers that point the reader in a new direction, that reflect on the implications of some topic, or that suggest the need for further research.

Titles

Because the title is the first thing a reader sees, it must make a good impression. The title also must help the reader anticipate the topic and perhaps the writer's particular point of view. Kirsten's title, "Net Theft," is descriptive and intriguing, if not particularly clever. It is more important that the title be related to the content than that it be cute or funny.

E X E R C I S E 5 . 2

Try out several titles and openings for your piece. Be inventive and playful. To catch your reader's attention, write an opening scene, describe a character, tell a story, give a startling fact or statistic, or make an outrageous claim. Then try out several possible conclusions for your piece. Write both a summary conclusion and a speculative conclusion. Share them with your peers. Which conclusion do they find more effective, and why?

5c Edit

When editing a text, the writer's goal is to make it easier to read. During revision, the writer concentrates on making the piece focused, organized, and well developed. During editing, the writer concentrates on refining words and sentences. Like a car buff putting the final finish on a classic automobile, an editor "finishes" a piece of writing—in general, refining what has been done and making it aesthetically pleasing as well as functional.

As with revising, it is important for writers to distance themselves from their words before editing and become objective readers of their own writing. Listening to the words as the text is read aloud helps writers to see where they need to clarify an idea or where they may have used too many words or expressed thoughts awkwardly. The Editing Checklist on page 74 refers to sections that can help you correct specific problems.

1 Checking sentence structure

As you edit your draft, make sure that your sentences are structured according to the conventions for academic writing. Over the years, scholars have developed a standard formal English used for academic writing. Following the conventions of Standard Edited English will mark you as an educated, careful writer.

Editing Checklist

Your response to each of the following questions should be "yes." If it is not, you need to go back and edit in that area, referring as necessary to the appropriate sections of this handbook.

Sentence Structure

- Are all of my sentences complete (see Chapter 29)?
- Have I avoided both comma splices and run-on sentences (see Chapter 30)?
- Do paired elements have parallel structures (see Chapter 36)?

Wordiness

- Have I avoided using unnecessary words, such as *in order to* instead of simply *to* (Chapter 34)?
- Have I replaced two-word and three-word phrases, such as *new innovation* and *repeating recurrence*, where one word is sufficient (see Chapter 38)?

Repetition

- Have I avoided excessive use of a single word (see Chapter 40)?
- Have I avoided repetition of a single idea that is not the thesis (see Chapter 38)?

Verb Usage

- Have I used primarily active rather than passive voice (see 26g)?
- Have I replaced overused, general verbs with more vivid specific verbs, where possible (see 40a)?

Other Errors

- Is my end punctuation correct (see Chapter 45)?
- Is my internal punctuation correct—commas (see Chapter 46), semicolons (see Chapter 47), and colons (see Chapter 48)?
- Have I used quotation marks appropriately (see Chapter 50)?
- Have I used other punctuation marks appropriately (see Chapter 51)?
- Is my spelling correct (see Chapter 44)?
- Are my mechanics correct—capitals and italics (see Chapter 52), abbreviations and numbers (see Chapter 53), and hyphens (see Chapter 54)?

How do I check sentence structure?

1. Scroll up from the end of the document, reading it backwards sentence by sentence.
2. Use the SEARCH function.
   a. Ask the computer to search for each period in the document (begin either at the start or at the end of the document).
   b. Each time you stop at a period, look carefully at the group of words that precedes it to be sure they form a complete sentence. If you are not sure, see Chapter 24 on sentence structure.
   c. Use the SEARCH function to review the other punctuation by locating first the commas and then the semicolons. See Chapters 45–51 for advice on punctuation.

Once you have checked sentence structure, you should look for sentence variety, making sure that you have not started most or all of your sentences in the same way or used the same sentence pattern over and over (see Chapter 38). The most effective writing contains sentences that are both clear and varied. Adding an introductory phrase to one sentence or moving a clause in another will help you achieve variety. Notice how Kirsten revised these sentences:

> http://www.powa.org/
> editfrms.htm
> Numerous suggestions for sentence-level editing, from Paradigm Online Writing Assistant

Blood rushes to your ~~hears~~ and your heart begins to pound, as your body reacts to the rush of adrenalin. Casting a nervous glance around the nearby aisles,ₐ*you decide that* the coast is clear.ₐ ~~Extending~~ *You extend* your arm, ~~you~~ grab the orange tiger, ~~and~~ place it in your backpackₐ*, and* then walk nonchalantly towards the exit.

2   Checking for wordiness

Many writers tend to overwrite their drafts, using a phrase or clause when a word will do. Unnecessary words can obscure the meaning or make the reader work harder than necessary to understand it. These three examples show how Kirsten edited sentences in her draft for wordiness:

> Unfortunately, this is a common request ~~within our society~~ today.
>
> [Kirsten omitted three words that convey no additional meaning.]
>
> Not only ~~are these practices~~ _is this_ wrong from a moral _standpoint_~~viewpoint~~, but legally,
> ~~they are~~ _it is_ forbidden as well. [By using pronouns to refer back to the
>
> previous sentence, Kirsten eliminated wordiness.]
>
> Walking into a store and taking something without paying for it is
> obviously not _legal._~~encouraged in our society~~. [Again, Kirsten omitted words
>
> that convey no additional meaning.]

3 Checking for repetition

Repeating words is not necessarily a bad thing. Using a key term more than once in a text may help you achieve coherence (see 6c-2). However, you do not want to use nonessential words repeatedly. Notice that Kirsten deleted the nonessential word _society_ twice as she edited her draft sentences (see 5c-2).

HELP

How do I check for overuse of specific words or terms?

1. Make a list of words that you suspect you may have overused.
2. Use the SEARCH function of your word-processing program to find each instance of each word in your document.
3. Use the THESAURUS function to help you think of alternative wording.
4. Be sure you are familiar with any word you decide to use from the thesaurus so that you use it appropriately for the context.

4 Checking for verb usage

Weak verbs can lead to ineffective writing. Review your verbs to be certain that they are used appropriately and effectively. Kirsten edited the verbs in one of her final paragraphs as follows:

> The problem, as Meyer and Underwood also point out, is that the "wild West culture of the Internet promotes an anything goes attitude in Net surfers" (p. 65). Most Internet users ~~think~~ *would agree* that stealing phone card numbers and selling them is wrong. However, many would not ~~think~~ *agree* that sharing a pirated copy of a game was illegal or even wrong. Similarly, many would not ~~think~~ *find* that using a cool graphic ~~found on~~ *from* someone else's page was unethical or illegal. The free-wheeling world of the Internet ~~finds~~ *considers* capitalist rules like "copyright" *to be* offensive.

5 Checking for other errors

In addition to editing for the *style* of your writing, you will also want to edit your text for usage, punctuation, spelling, and mechanics. For your writing to be acceptable in college courses as well as in most work settings, it must conform to the conventions of standard English. As the writer, you are responsible for making the text comprehensible as well as technically correct. Use the Editing Checklist to help you as you edit your work.

EXERCISE 5.3

Edit your text, using a combination of the strategies outlined in this section. Refer to the sections of the handbook referenced in the Editing Checklist for help; see also Chapter 39. When you have finished editing, run your word-processing program's grammar checker. Consider its advice carefully before making changes to your text.

5d Proofread

Proofreading is the final phase in rewriting. In this stage of the process, writers look closely for distracting punctuation and mechanical errors that will interfere with the reader's understanding. Proofreading prematurely, before there is a final, edited draft, may

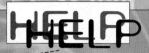

How do I use the computer to become a more effective proofreader?

1. When proofreading on screen, use the cursor arrow to scroll down one line at a time, forcing yourself to read each line slowly before reading the next one.
2. Use the VIEW menu to see the text one full page at a time by selecting the FULL PAGE option.
3. View the text two pages at a time, displayed side by side on the monitor.
4. Move the cursor to the end of the text, and read the sentences in reverse order.
5. Read the text aloud from the screen, slowing down as necessary to attend to the text more closely.
6. If you have a text-reading program, instruct the computer to do the reading aloud and listen for errors.

allow important revision and editing issues to be overlooked, in addition to wasting a lot of time. By proofreading after revising and editing, writers can concentrate on details related to manuscript preparation, such as typographical errors, missing words, and irregular spacing, as well as errors in punctuation that they may have missed in earlier stages.

WEB
http://www.ualr.edu/
~owl/proofrd.htm
Tips on proofreading,
including a useful list
of suggestions

Some writers prefer to proofread on the computer screen. However, recent studies have shown that writers who read their texts on screen may not see them as clearly or read them as carefully. Also, proofreading requires reading each word carefully, and doing so on a computer screen can be tiring to the eyes. Those who choose to proofread on screen should take frequent breaks. Experiment with your own proofreading technique, which may be a combination of on-screen and in-print proofreading.

Here are several strategies that may help you become a more effective proofreader:

1. Before printing the text, scroll rapidly through it to check for spacing, margins, indents, widows and orphans (single lines and words left alone at the top or bottom of a page), page numbering, and so on.

2. After printing the text, wait several hours, or longer if possible, before proofreading it.

3. When you proofread the printed text, use a pointer or ruler to force yourself to read slowly and deliberately.

4. Proofread the text several times; each time, you will pick up additional errors.

> **WWW WEB**
> gopher://gopher.
> bgsu.edu:70/00/
> Departments/
> write/Proofreading
> A good plain-text
> handout on proof-
> reading strategies

5. Be sure that you have changed your reading technique to a proofreading one. Normal reading involves skimming; a typical reader "reads" only two or three words per line. In contrast, proofreading requires that you look carefully at every word and punctuation mark.

6. Ask someone else—for example, a friend, a relative, or a classmate—to proofread the printed text as well.

EXERCISE 5.4

Proofread your text, using the strategies discussed in this section to read it both on screen and in print. Evaluate which method seems to work better for you. Were you able to identify more errors or different errors with either method?

5e   Give and receive feedback

In many writing classes, students work together in peer review groups, in which they exchange drafts for review, either electronically via a networked computer system (a local area network, or LAN) or in hard copy form. The instructor also may comment on early drafts and make revision suggestions. Or students may be asked to take their papers to a writing center, where a tutor will read them and offer suggestions. As a writer, you will find it helpful to receive feedback on your work from a variety of sources. Such feedback allows you to become increasingly sensitive to the needs of your readers.

1   Giving feedback

Peer review of one another's texts gives students in a writing class a sense of audience. A peer reviewer can tell a writer whether he or she understands the purpose, whether the thesis is clear, and whether the supporting evidence is sufficient. But a peer response is only as helpful as it is sincere. Just telling a peer that the writing is "good" is not particularly useful. A peer reviewer can be most helpful by showing interest in and enthusiasm for the work and by questioning and constructively commenting on the piece.

In order to respond appropriately, you should first read the entire draft, looking for global (general) features of organization and development. During a second reading, make your comments on the finer points (such as style and mechanics) specific. Comments should be phrased as praise, suggestions, and questions, not as barbed criticisms. Learning to be a sensitive peer reviewer will help you to be a better writer; to respond appropriately, you must put yourself in the writer's shoes.

The instructor may provide a list of questions or prompts to use as you read a peer's paper. If so, try to address each item completely and candidly. Here are some ways in which you can respond generally and specifically to a peer's writing.

Responding Globally

On the first reading, respond to the overall piece of writing, looking for global features of development and organization.

1. I identify with . . .
2. I like . . .
3. I wondered about . . .
4. I suggest . . .

Responding Locally

On the second reading, respond to specific features of the text.

1. Are the ideas understandable, and is the logic clear?
2. Is the writing style appropriate and the tone consistent?
3. Is the sentence structure correct?

4. Is the writing concise?
5. Are the verbs vigorous and active?
6. Are the sentences clear and easy to read?
7. Is the punctuation correct?
8. Is the format appropriate and the font readable?

2 Receiving feedback

Just as you need to criticize the work of peers with a generous spirit, you also need to receive criticism without becoming defensive. Read all comments with an open mind. Remember that you can learn a great deal from others who read your work. Try to get enough distance from your own writing so that you do not take comments personally. Your peer is reviewing your *writing*, not you personally. However, not all feedback you receive will be useful. Take it with a grain of salt—another's opinion may simply differ from yours.

Giving and Receiving Peer Feedback

Giving Feedback

1. Read the piece through carefully, taking note of strengths and weaknesses.
2. Phrase your comments as suggestions and questions, not as criticisms.
3. Give positive feedback and praise where appropriate.
4. Respond generally first and then specifically.
5. Respond completely to any prompts provided by the teacher.

Receiving Feedback

1. Read peer comments with an open mind, without becoming defensive.
2. Consider all comments seriously.
3. Accept those comments that help you improve your piece.
4. Reject those comments that seem to be leading you off in a direction you did not intend.
5. Ask for clarification if you do not understand a particular peer comment or suggestion.

How do I review a peer's work using a local area network?

1. Open a peer's document from the LAN.
2. Immediately save the document under a new name, using the SAVE AS command.
3. If your word-processing program has a commenting feature (called ANNOTATIONS or DOCUMENT COMMENTS), use it to insert your comments into the text. Otherwise, use italics or capital letters.
4. Refer to Giving and Receiving Peer Feedback to guide your comments.
5. Save the document back to the LAN so that your peer can read your comments.

EXERCISE 5.5

Exchange drafts with a peer, either on paper or via your class's LAN. Read your peer's work straight through once, with an eye toward global features such as purpose, audience, and tone. Then, read it again carefully before commenting. If you are reading on screen, use the word processor's commenting feature (see the Help box above).

5f　Review a model student paper

Let us consider a revised version of Kirsten's essay on Net theft. Kirsten followed her revision outline as she rewrote this piece (see pages 65–66). As you compare the first draft (in Chapter 4) with this draft, notice that Kirsten worked hard to organize and focus her piece better. She worked particularly hard on parts II and IV of her outline, where the paper had begun to fall apart in her earlier draft. She also edited sentences to make them clearer and proofread carefully to catch mechanical errors.

It is a truism in the writing field that there are no finished pieces of writing, only deadlines. Any piece can be revised and improved. In what ways do you think this draft is an improvement over Kirsten's first draft? Are there elements Kirsten could still work on to make them more effective?

Parsons 1

Student and
course iden-
tification

Kirsten Parsons

English 101–35

Professor Hines

September 15, 1998

Net Theft

Opening
scenario

"Look at this new CD I bought!" Jane exclaims to her

friend. Interested, Michael eagerly looks at it. "Wow," he

says. "These guy are my favorite group! Mind if I make a

copy of it?". . .

Introduction

Unfortunately, this is a common request today.

In spite of laws that prohibit unlicensed copying, in some

circles it has become an accepted practice to reproduce

another's work without paying for it. Similarly, this practice

has spread to the Internet, where access to music, software,

written texts, and graphics is convenient and fast. These

items can be copied for personal use with ease, but often

no credit is given to the original author. Not only is this

wrong from a moral standpoint, but legally, it is forbidden

as well. It has become a situation where "legality collides

Source:
author
and page
number

with practicality" (Meyer and Underwood 65). In other

words, breaking the law is more convenient than obeying

it, and since we know we can get away with doing it,

Thesis

our conscience gives in. When it comes to "borrowing"

information from the Internet, we are gradually becoming

Parsons 2

a people that accept lawbreaking as long as we can
participate, too.

**Compare to
shoplifting**   I'm sure all of us once glimpsed a tempting item in
a store and, after getting "no" for an answer from Mom
or Dad, took matters into our own hands, sneaking the
treasure into a hidden pocket. It probably took only a few
moments for your parents to notice something was up. I
remember well a discussion about why taking the package
was wrong. Then my Dad took me back to the store, where
an apology was made and my Strawberry Hubba Bubba
Bubblegum was paid for.

**Definition
of Net theft**   Walking into a store and taking something without
paying for it is obviously not legal; ironically, this principle
seems to break down where the Net is concerned. With
available technology, Net theft is commonplace. Written
texts, software, graphics, and music all are vulnerable to
cyber-shoplifting. Though it is not encouraged per se, it is
not really discouraged either. Isn't this just stealing masked
by softer adjectives such as "sharing" or "borrowing"?
Granted it is less noticeable, but that doesn't change the
fact that you didn't pay for it.

**Compare
difficulty of
each crime**   Part of the problem is that the physical element
involved in actually traveling to a store and taking
something is not necessary for these Net crimes. Imagine
walking down the aisle of the local Wal-Mart with the
intention of stealing a Hobbes doll, your favorite cartoon

Parsons 3

character. Blood rushes to your ears and your heart begins to pound, as your body reacts to the rush of adrenalin. Casting a nervous glance around the nearby aisles, you decide that the coast is clear. You extend your arm, grab the orange tiger, place it in your backpack, and then walk nonchalantly towards the exit. Then the alarm goes off and you are caught holding the goods!

This scenario is only possible in a physical world. Because the Net is so unphysical, the risk of being caught, which may serve to deter many thieves in a store, is minimal. Net theft is committed within the reach of the refrigerator! Imagine that while Net-surfing you find a cartoon of Calvin and Hobbes on a commercial Web site. You think it would look great on your home page. With a click of the mouse, you grab the graphic and paste it onto your own page. Who has ever heard of someone being arrested for copying a graphic? Because Net crimes often go ignored, and "everyone" is guilty, more and more people engage in them. The consequences seem to be less punitive, and thus we give in to the influence of the Wild Net.

Standards of conduct   Organizations and individuals have tried to establish standards of conduct for Internet use. For example, the Computer Ethics Institute wrote its Ten Commandments for Computer Ethics, which includes such obvious "rules" as

Online sources   "Thou shalt not use the computer to steal" (Roach). But

Parsons 4

what is stealing when it comes to materials found on the
Internet? The Copyright Web site asserts that any texts or
graphics that you find on the Internet are by their very
nature published and thus are "copyrighted" (O'Mahoney).
This means that in order to use anything from someone
else's Web site, you need their permission. If you put
a comic strip such as Calvin and Hobbes onto your
home page, you run the risk of being sued for violation
of copyright.

Summary of
the conflict

The problem, as Meyer and Underwood also point out,
is that the "wild West culture of the Internet promotes an
anything goes attitude in Net surfers" (65). Most Internet
users would agree that stealing phone card numbers and
selling them is wrong. However, many would not agree that
sharing a pirated copy of a game was illegal or even wrong.
Similarly, many would not find that using a cool graphic
from someone else's page was unethical or illegal. The free-
wheeling world of the Internet considers capitalist rules like
"copyright" to be offensive.

In the tangled world of the Internet, not all of the new
dilemmas that have surfaced will be solved immediately.
However, if the definition of a criminal is one who has
committed a crime, then in the world of the Net, perhaps
we all need to serve some time.

Parsons 5

References

Meyer, Michael, and Anne Underwood. "Crimes of the

'Net.' " CyberReader. Ed. Victor Vitanza. Boston: Allyn,

1996. 63–65.

O'Mahoney, Benedict. The Copyright Web Site. 1997.

1 Sept. 1998 <http://www.benedict.com>.

Roach, Kitty. PageWorks. 2 Jan. 1996. 1 Sept. 1998

<http://www.snowcrest.net/kitty/hpages>.

Structuring Paragraphs

Why do I need to learn how to structure paragraphs?
What is a topic sentence, and why is it important to my
   writing? (6a)
How long should my paragraphs be? (6f)
How should I link my paragraphs together? (6g)

?

A **paragraph** is a sentence or group of sentences that develops a main idea. Paragraphs serve as the primary building blocks of essays, reports, memos, and other forms of written composition.

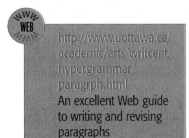

WWW
WEB

http://www.uottawa.ca/
academic/arts/writcent/
hypergrammar/
paragrph.html
An excellent Web guide
to writing and revising
paragraphs

In Shakespeare's time, a single paragraph could go on for pages, but English paragraphs have evolved into shorter and shorter units. This trend seems likely to continue, as it is now common to find paragraphs of only one or two sentences in news reports, advertisements, memos, and Internet communications.

Well-written paragraphs facilitate quick skimming and help readers stay focused on the main ideas so that they can understand and evaluate the text. To promote this kind of readability, paragraphs should be unified, coherent, and adequately developed, while flowing from one to the next as smoothly as possible.

6a Write unified paragraphs

A **unified paragraph** is one that focuses on and develops a single main idea. This idea is typically captured in a single sentence, called a *topic sentence*. The other sentences in the paragraph, the *supporting sentences*, should elaborate on the topic sentence in a logical fashion.

1 Using a topic sentence

A **topic sentence** serves the important purpose of giving readers a quick idea of what the paragraph as a whole is about. It is a good idea to place the topic sentence at the beginning of a paragraph, where it provides a preview of the rest of the paragraph. A topic sentence should, if possible, do four things: (1) provide a transition from the preceding paragraph, (2) introduce the topic of the paragraph, (3) make a main point about this topic, and (4) suggest how the rest of the paragraph will develop this point.

> During the past decade or two, children have slipped into poverty faster than any other age group. One of six white U.S. children, two of every five Latino children, and almost one of every two African-American children are poor. These figures translate into incredible numbers—approximately *18 million* children live in poverty: 9 million white children, 4 million Latino children, and 5 million African-American children.
>
> —James M. Henslin, *Sociology*

The opening sentence of this paragraph establishes the topic (child poverty in the United States), makes a main point about it (the percentage of individuals living in poverty is growing more quickly for children than any other age group), and allows the reader to guess that the rest of the paragraph will provide evidence supporting this point.

In a series of paragraphs, the first sentence of each paragraph should serve as a transition from the preceding paragraph. Often, you can make the first sentence both a topic sentence and a linking sentence, as it is in this example (a continuation of the preceding example):

> According to sociologist and U.S. Senator Daniel Moynihan, this high rate of child poverty is due primarily to a general breakdown of the U.S. family. He points his finger at the sharp increase in births outside marriage. In 1960, only 5 percent of U.S. children were born to unmarried mothers. Today that figure is *six times higher;* and single women now account for 30 percent of all U.S. births. The relationship to social class is striking, for births to unmarried mothers are not distributed evenly across the social classes. For women above the poverty line, only 6 percent of births are to single mothers, while for women below the poverty line this rate jumps to 44 percent.
>
> —James M. Henslin, *Sociology*

The expression "this high rate of child poverty" restates the main topic of the preceding paragraph and thus links the two paragraphs. The topic sentence immediately expresses a new idea ("is due primarily to a general breakdown of the U.S. family"), which represents the main point of this paragraph. The rest of the paragraph supports this point with relevant statistics.

2 Placing the topic sentence

The paragraph opening is not always the best location for a topic sentence. Sometimes writers use the first sentence of a paragraph to provide a transition, making the second sentence the topic sentence.

> Regardless of causes—and there are many—to say that millions of children live in poverty can be as cold and meaningless as saying that their shoes are brown. Easy to overlook is the significance of childhood poverty. Poor children are more likely to die in infancy, to go hungry and to be malnourished, to develop more slowly, and to have more health problems. They are more likely to drop out of school, to become involved in criminal activities, and to have children while still in their teens—thus perpetuating the cycle of poverty.
>
> —James M. Henslin, *Sociology*

The topic of this paragraph ("the significance of childhood poverty") is introduced not in the opening sentence but in the second sentence. The first sentence serves a transitional function, connecting this paragraph to the one preceding it. The goal here, as always with paragraphing, is to help the reader stay focused on the flow of the main ideas. This goal of preserving focus is as important in the brief paragraphs of a typical email message as it is in longer paragraphs like the examples above.

Occasionally a topic sentence falls at the end of a paragraph, either as a summary or as a restatement of a topic sentence appearing earlier in the paragraph. Sometimes no topic sentence is needed. If a paragraph continues the topic covered in the preceding paragraph or simply narrates a series of events or a set of details whose common theme is obvious, you may decide that an explicit topic statement is unnecessary. In Internet messages, especially email, short topic sentences and tightly linked paragraphs help avoid the conversational tendency to ramble on with an unfocused message.

EXERCISE 6.1

Open one of your textbooks to the beginning of a section, and examine the first five paragraphs. Do they all seem unified? Does each paragraph have a topic sentence? If so, where is it located?

EXERCISE 6.2

1. Examine the paragraphs in Kirsten Parsons's paper (pages 83–87). Do they all have topic sentences? Are the topic sentences properly positioned? Are they well worded? Could some of them be improved? If so, how?

2. See how paragraphs appear in Internet settings. Start by looking at how a topic that interests you is presented in listserv messages; then compare these messages with Usenet discussions on the same topic. Is the topic sentence or main idea more obvious in the Usenet discussions or the listserv messages?

6b Use clear organizational patterns

All paragraphs should be *coherent*: each sentence should connect logically with those preceding and following it. Readers are able to move smoothly from one idea to the next when the writer has constructed coherent paragraphs. One way writers create coherent paragraphs is through the use of organizational patterns.

HELP

How do I connect my ideas in a coherent way?

If you have problems connecting ideas and making paragraphs, try outlining the topics and subtopics within a section of your first draft (see 5a-3).

1. From within the first-draft document, open the function that provides numbered or lettered lists (usually called OUTLINE).

2. Find your first topic idea, and list it as main heading 1. If you have a second and third main idea following the first, list them as main headings 2 and 3.

3. Under each main heading, find ideas that support or expand on it. List these as subheads a, b, and so on. Ideas subordinate to these subtopics can be listed as (1), (2), and so on.

4. Survey the outline for connections between the main items. How can you use the subheads to build a phrase or sentence that will connect to the next main heading?

5. Finally, write full paragraphs based on your outline, constructing or combining sentences so that they flow in the order of the outline.

Among the countless ways to organize paragraphs, certain patterns are especially common: general to specific, cause and effect, comparison or contrast, definition, classification, problem and solution, narrative or process description, exemplification, and physical description. These organizational patterns mirror typical ways people categorize experience. Readers look for familiar patterns, so the more explicitly you signal those patterns, the easier it will be for readers to see the logic connecting your ideas.

1 Organizing by general to specific

The sample paragraphs in 6a-1 and 6a-2 both illustrate general-to-specific organization, in which a general statement is followed by specific supporting details. This is one of the most common of all paragraph patterns, and the general statement serves effectively as a topic sentence. Here is another example of general-to-specific ordering:

> Every society creates an idealized image of the future—a vision that serves as a beacon to direct the imagination and energy of its people. The ancient Jewish nation prayed for deliverance to a promised land of milk and honey. Later, Christian clerics held out the promise of eternal salvation in the heavenly kingdom. In the modern age, the idea of a future technological utopia has served as the guiding vision of industrial society. For more than a century utopian dreamers and men and women of science and letters have looked to a future world where machines would replace human labor, creating a near-workerless society of abundance and leisure.
>
> —Jeremy Rifkin, *The End of Work*

This paragraph leads off a chapter in Rifkin's book called "Visions of Techno-Paradise." Rifkin uses the general-to-specific pattern to first situate his discussion in universal terms ("every society") and then narrow his focus to the "near-workerless society" that will be the subject of the chapter.

It is possible to organize a paragraph in the reverse order—that is, from specific to general. Such a pattern is rarely used, however, even by professionals.

2 Organizing by cause and effect

Many pieces of writing link phenomena through cause-and-effect relationships. The cause-and-effect organizational pattern is especially appropriate for explaining why something happened the way it did or predicting some future sequence of events. Paragraphs organized with a cause-and-effect pattern usually include transitional words and phrases such as *therefore, thus, as a result, since, because, consequently, for this reason,* and *thereby.* Two of these are used in this example:

> Fetal alcohol syndrome (FAS) occurs when alcohol ingested by the mother passes through the placenta into the infant's bloodstream. *Because* the fetus is so small, its blood alcohol concentration will be much higher than that of its mother. *Thus,* consumption of alcohol during pregnancy can affect the infant far more seriously than it does the mother. Among the symptoms of FAS are mental retardation, small head, tremors, and abnormalities of the face, limbs, heart, and brain.
>
> —Rebecca J. Donatelle and Lorraine G. Davis, *Access to Health*

3 Organizing by comparison or contrast

Many writing situations call for comparing or contrasting two or more ideas, issues, items, or events. Comparison focuses on similarities; contrast focuses on differences. In either case, the writer evaluates two or more subjects on the basis of one or more criteria. Transitional words and phrases commonly found in comparison or contrast paragraphs include *however, on the one hand/on the other hand, similarly, in contrast, just as, while, but,* and *like.*

A paragraph based on the comparison or contrast pattern should be structured either (1) by evaluating one subject completely and then turning to the other or (2) by focusing on each criterion, one at a time. For example, in a comparison of the two sociological theories known as structural functionalism and conflict theory, arrangement by *subject* might look like this:

> *Subject A:* Structural functionalism
>   *Criterion 1:* How it views society
>   *Criterion 2:* What it emphasizes
> *Subject B:* Conflict theory
>   *Criterion 1:* How it views society
>   *Criterion 2:* What it emphasizes

Arrangement by *criteria,* on the other hand, would look like this:

> *Criterion 1:* How it views society
>   *Subject A:* Structural functionalism views society as . . .
>   *Subject B:* Conflict theory views society as . . .
> *Criterion 2:* What it emphasizes
>   *Subject A:* Structural functionalism emphasizes . . .
>   *Subject B:* Conflict theory emphasizes . . .

Which type of structural arrangement is better? It depends on where you want to focus the reader's attention—on the subjects or on the criteria.

The following paragraph is organized according to subject. The liberal view of affirmative action is contrasted to the conservative view, and the criteria used (such as group fairness and individual fairness) are secondary.

> The role of affirmative action in our multicultural society lies at the center of a national debate about how to steer a course in race and ethnic relations. In this policy, quotas based on race (and gender) are used in hiring and college admissions. Most liberals, both

white and minority, defend affirmative action, saying that it is the most direct way to level the playing field of economic opportunity. If white males are passed over, this is an unfortunate cost we must pay if we are to make up for past and present discrimination. Most conservatives, *in contrast*, both white and minority, agree that opportunity should be open to all, but say that putting race (or sex) ahead of people's ability to perform a job is reverse discrimination. They add that affirmative action stigmatizes the people who benefit from it because it suggests that they hold their jobs because of race (or sex), rather than merit.

—Adapted from James M. Henslin, *Sociology*

4 Organizing by definition

In academic writing, important new terms sometimes require a complete paragraph for their definition. The term is usually introduced in a topic sentence at the beginning of the paragraph and elaborated on in the sentences that follow. Here is a typical example of a paragraph organized by definition, from an educational psychology textbook:

Another tool for building a better understanding of the teaching and learning processes is *theory*. The common sense notion of theory (as in "Oh well, it was only a theory") is "a guess or hunch." But the scientific meaning of theory is quite different. "A theory in science is an interrelated set of concepts that is used to explain a body of data and to make predictions about the results of future experiments" (Stanovich, 1992). Given a number of established principles, educational psychologists have developed explanations for the relationships among many variables and even whole systems of relationships. There are theories to explain how language develops, how differences in intelligence occur, and, as noted earlier, how people learn.

—Anita E. Woolfolk, *Educational Psychology*

A paragraph organized by definition should include a formal definition—that is, a statement "X is a Y that _____," where X is the *term* being defined, Y is the *class* it belongs to, and _____ is a set of *distinguishing features*. In the above example, such a definition is found in the third sentence: "A theory in science is an interrelated set of concepts that is used to explain a body of data and to make predictions about the results of future experiments."

EXERCISE 6.3

Search the Web to find an interesting article of at least 300 words in a newspaper or other source. Download it. Then use the SEARCH function of your word processor to locate all instances of *however, on the one hand/on the other hand, similarly, in contrast, just as, while, but,* and *like.* In each case, identify the subjects that are being compared.

5 Organizing by classification

To make sense of the world, people routinely classify things according to their characteristic parts. Classification is an essential part of the analytic work you do in school. Whenever you search the Internet or a library, for example, you focus your quest by using a search system that classifies topics in helpful categories. In academic writing, an entire paragraph is often devoted to classifying some concept. Paragraphs organized by classification normally introduce the topic in the first sentence and the various subtopics in the following sentences. Using these subtopics as the grammatical subjects of their respective sentences, as in this example, creates grammatical parallelism (see 6e), which makes it easy for readers to see the structure of the paragraph:

> Human development can be divided into a number of different aspects. *Physical development,* as you might guess, deals with changes in the body. *Personal development* is the term generally used for changes in an individual's personality. *Social development* refers to changes in the way an individual relates to others. And *cognitive development* refers to changes in thinking.
>
> —Anita E. Woolfolk, *Educational Psychology*

6 Organizing by problem and solution

In the problem and solution organizational pattern, a particular problem is identified and one or more solutions are proposed. Usually the writer states the problem explicitly, though sometimes it is only implied. Posing the problem in the form of a question is especially attention-getting.

> What can be done about drug abuse among students? First, we should distinguish between experimentation and abuse. Many students try something at a party but do not become regular users. The best way to help students who have trouble saying no appears to be

through peer programs that teach how to say no assertively. The successful programs also teach general social skills and build self-esteem (Newcomb & Bentler, 1989). Also, the older students are when they experiment with drugs, the more likely they are to make responsible choices, so helping younger students say no is a clear benefit.

—Anita E. Woolfolk, *Educational Psychology*

E X E R C I S E   6 . 4

An Internet or library research project is frequently a search for a solution to a problem—specific information on an issue that the researcher wants to explore and clarify. Such a search often turns up key words and ideas that suggest an even more interesting issue.

Choose an issue to research. Write it down as the problem, and then list two or three "solutions," or pieces of information you hope or expect to find in your search. This list could be the outline for a descriptive paragraph with a problem and solution pattern.

Conduct the search, and list the information you actually discover in a second column. Do you need to revise your problem statement in light of what you found? Write a coherent problem and solution paragraph using the information.

7 Organizing by narrative or process description

Narratives and process descriptions present events in a time-ordered sequence. A **narrative** tells a story; a **process description** depicts a step-by-step procedure. In either case, the writer recounts events in chronological order, using verb tenses consistently and not jumping from one time frame to another.

When narrating the plot of a literary work, you normally use the present tense, as in this brief description of Ibsen's *Enemy of the People:*

The play is set in a little town which makes its living from the tourists who come to take its famous baths. Dr. Stockmann discovers that the waters have been contaminated by the local sewage system. He insists that the facts must be revealed, and expects that the city authorities will be grateful for his discovery. To his astonishment he finds that he has become an enemy of the people because he insists that the truth be known and the evil corrected. Doggedly he decides to fight on for truth even though the whole community is against him.

—Vincent F. Hopper and Bernard D. N. Grebanier, *Essentials of European Literature*

When writing a process description, keep the verb tenses consistent (see 26e), and use an occasional transitional word such as *first, second, finally, after, then,* or *while.* Notice the transitional words in this process description paragraph:

> Land reclamation is the careful burying and grading of refuse that is dumped into prepared sites, such as deep trenches, swamps, ponds, or abandoned quarries. *After* the refuse has been dumped, it is sprayed with chemicals to kill larvae and insects. *Then* it is compacted by heavy equipment, covered with a thick layer of clean earth, and graded so that it blends with surrounding land.
>
> —*The New Book of Knowledge*

8 Organizing by exemplification

Examples are a powerful way to make difficult concepts understandable. A paragraph organized by **exemplification** usually follows a general-to-specific pattern. The concept to be explained is introduced in general terms at the beginning, and then one or more specific examples are offered to make it meaningful, as in this paragraph:

> A general principle of human behavior is that we try to minimize our costs and maximize our rewards. Sociologist Richard Berk calls this a *minimax strategy.* The fewer costs and the more rewards we anticipate from something, the more likely we are to do it. For example, if we believe that others will approve an act, the likelihood that we will do it increases. Whether in yelling for the referee's blood at a bad call in football, or shouting for real blood as a member of a lynch mob, this principle applies. In short, whether people are playing cards with a few friends, or are part of a mob, the principles of human behavior remain the same.
>
> —James M. Henslin, *Sociology*

9 Organizing by physical description

A descriptive paragraph paints a picture of a person, place, or object by appealing to the reader's senses (sight, sound, touch, taste, or smell). It emphasizes details, which should be carefully selected so as to give the reader a vivid sense of what is being described. The following example brings to life something that most people can only imagine—the microscopic structure of ordinary soil.

The spaces between the soil grains offer a variety of habitats. The smaller pores and channels are filled with water, the larger ones mostly with air. Clay soils have narrow, threadlike channels that twist and taper downward; in sand, as might be imagined from seeing it on the beach, there are air pockets in the tiny spaces between the grains. Draped upon the skeleton of the soil are the sinews and flesh of a teeming life: each particle, even the finest, has a tight-fitting film of oxides, water, bits of organic matter. This skin is what gives life to the soil underfoot.

—Peter Farb, *Living Earth*

EXERCISE 6.5

Search the Web or peruse a magazine for a page that contains one or more descriptive paragraphs. Write a paragraph in which you describe the page as an example of an interesting way to organize material.

10 Organizing by mixing patterns

Although many paragraphs can be structured using one of the organizational patterns just described, you may sometimes want to express ideas in a way that does not conform to any one pattern. In such cases, do not be afraid to mix two or more organizational patterns. Just make it clear what pattern you are following at any one time. Here is an example of a paragraph that mixes patterns:

Popular music has never been a stranger to controversy or opposition. Herman Gray has noted three periods of particularly strong opposition: the response to jazz in the early part of the century, the reaction against rock 'n' roll in the 1950s and 1960s, and the most recent wave of controversy associated with heavy metal and rap. No matter what the genre, certain themes such as a fear of the connection between music and sexuality tend to run through all three periods. Such concerns may be expressed either as the fear that sensual rhythms can overcome rationality or that lyrics that push the boundaries of decorum can undermine moral values. Because of these fears, each genre has been linked at various times to drug abuse, lawless behavior, and general moral decline. In turn, all of these problems have been projected to some degree onto race.

—Reebee Garofalo, *Rockin' Out*

This paragraph basically follows the exemplification pattern, with sentences 2–6 exemplifying the generalization stated in the first sentence. But sentence 2, describing "three periods," is a classification statement. And sentences 5–6, marked by "Because . . . ," follow the cause-and-effect pattern. As long as pattern shifts are clearly marked, mixed paragraphs can be comprehensible and coherent.

EXERCISE 6.6

Examine the first four paragraphs in this chapter, and determine what patterns of organization they exemplify. (Remember that a paragraph may use more than one pattern.)

EXERCISE 6.7

The topic sentence often suggests the organizational pattern that governs the rest of a paragraph. Try to guess what pattern might follow each of these topic sentences.

1. **Self-disclosure** is the sharing of personal information with others. _____

2. Self-disclosure can be a double-edged sword, for there is risk in divulging personal insights and feelings. _____

3. Self-disclosure can affect our dealings within health-care settings. _____

4. Stores are exploiting your senses and sentimentality in order to make you comfortable, happy, and willing to spend more money. _____

5. In *Ties That Stress: The New Family Imbalance*, David Elkind writes that in today's post-modern family, the needs of hurried children have been sacrificed to the needs of their harried parents. _____

6. Reams of research have gone into what gets a shopper to buy. _____

7. There are three keys to conversations with children about difficult topics. _____

8. As a person living with HIV, he has had to struggle to understand the unique power this disease has to frighten people. _____

9. Wealth and income are sometimes confused with each other. _____

10. Unlike ordinary medicines, herbal remedies are not manufactured under the jurisdiction of the Food and Drug Administration. _____

6c   Use sentence-linking techniques

In addition to conforming to organizational patterns, writers increase the coherence of their paragraphs by developing connections between sentences through use of transitional expressions, repetition of words or phrases, or references to earlier information.

1 Using transitional words and phrases

Transitional words and phrases are useful for linking sentences. The various expressions listed under Common Transitional Words and Phrases (page 102) differ somewhat in degree of formality. For example, *furthermore* and *consequently* are more formal than *besides* and *so*. Being aware of these differences will help you strike a consistent tone in your writing (see 33c).

Notice how effective the transitional expressions are in making this paragraph more readable:

Many of us live in awe of statistics. Perhaps nowhere is our respect for statistics so evident—and so exploited—as in advertising. If three out of four doctors surveyed recommend Pain Away aspirin, it must be the best. If Sudsy Soap is 99.9 percent pure (whatever that means), surely it will help our complexions. *And* if nine out of ten people like Sloppy Catsup in the taste test, we will certainly buy some for this weekend's barbecue. How can the statistics be wrong? *On the other hand,* some people are suspicious of all statistics. They have witnessed too many erroneous weather forecasts and election predictions. *In reality,* the truth about statistics lies somewhere between unconditional faith in numbers and Mark Twain's wry observation that "there are three kinds of lies: lies, damned lies, and statistics."

—Adapted from Steven A. Beebe and Susan J. Beebe, *Public Speaking*

Common Transitional Words and Phrases

To show cause and effect	*therefore, thus, consequently, as a result, for this reason, so, so that*
To compare	*similarly, likewise, in like manner, also*
To contrast	*however, on the one hand/on the other hand, in contrast, conversely, but, yet, nevertheless, nonetheless, on the contrary, still*
To show addition	*and, in addition, also, furthermore, moreover, besides*
To indicate time	*before, now, after, afterwards, subsequently, later, earlier, meanwhile, in the meantime, while, as long as, so far*
To give examples	*for example, for instance, specifically, namely, to illustrate, that is*
To conclude or summarize	*in conclusion, to conclude, in summary, to summarize, in short, in other words, therefore, thus, in reality*
To generalize	*in general, for the most part, as a general rule, on the whole, usually, typically*
To emphasize a point	*indeed, in fact, as a matter of fact, even*
To signal concession	*of course, naturally, although it is true that, granted that*

2 Repeating key words

A paragraph almost always has key words. Repetition of these words helps the reader focus on the topic at hand. Exact repetition can become tiresome, however, so good writers use synonyms or paraphrases. (The THESAURUS feature of your word processor can help you choose synonyms.)

Notice how the writer of this paragraph about a teaching technique artfully uses repetition to maintain focus and coherence:

> *Modeling* has long been used to teach dance, sports, and crafts, as well as skills in subjects such as home economics, chemistry, and

shop. Modeling can also be applied deliberately in the classroom to teach mental skills and to broaden horizons—to teach new ways of thinking. Teachers serve as models for a vast range of behaviors, from pronouncing vocabulary words, to reacting to the seizure of an epileptic student, to being enthusiastic about learning. For example, a teacher might model sound critical thinking skills by thinking "out loud" about a student's question. Or a high school teacher concerned about girls who seem to have stereotyped ideas about careers might invite women with nontraditional jobs to speak to the class.

—Anita E. Woolfolk, *Educational Psychology*

After introducing the key word *modeling* in the first sentence, the writer repeats it three times (*modeling, models, model*) in the next three sentences. In each case, she links it to another key word, *teaching*. The reiteration of *modeling* and *teaching* keeps the reader's focus on the main topic of the paragraph and thus increases its coherence.

Pronouns allow for reference to the main topic without repetition. If one sentence after another has the same topic, you can often refer to it with a pronoun without confusing the reader. For example, the writer could have substituted *It* for *Modeling* at the start of the second sentence of the example paragraph. Using pronouns can also help reduce wordiness (see Chapter 34). Just make sure the pronouns always have clear referents (see Chapter 31).

3 Referring to old information

Another way to link sentences is to refer to "old information," something readers are already familiar with, at the beginning of the new sentence. These references to old information usually consist of repeated words, pronouns, or words marked by *the* or *this,* inserted into the subject position (see 24b). Here is an example from a textbook on public speaking:

In a classic study, Ralph Nichols asked both good and poor listeners what their listening strategies were. *The poor listeners* indicated that they listened for facts such as names and dates. *The good listeners* reported that they listened for major ideas and principles. *Facts* are useful only when you can connect them to a principle or concept. In speeches, *facts* as well as examples are used primarily to support major ideas. *You* should try to summarize mentally the major idea that the specific *facts* support.

—Steven A. Beebe and Susan J. Beebe, *Public Speaking*

Notice how the grammatical subjects of sentences 2–5 repeat concepts that are mentioned earlier and that two of these repetitions include the article *the*. The concepts "good [listeners] and poor listeners" are first mentioned in the first sentence. Both of these concepts are then referred to as old information in sentences 2 and 3. The concept "facts" is new information in sentence 2 but old information in sentences 4–6. In all cases, the reference to the old information occurs at the beginning of the sentence. Even the pronoun *you* starting off sentence 6 refers to old information; it acknowledges the ongoing existence of the reader and is preceded by the *you* in sentence 4.

Keeping the sentence subject fairly short makes it easier for readers to understand the sentence and see how it fits into the paragraph as a whole. Using repeated words or pronouns to refer back to old information should help you keep sentence subjects short. Notice how short the sentence subjects are in the preceding example paragraph: *Ralph Nichols, The poor listeners, The good listeners, Facts, facts, You.*

EXERCISE 6.8

Photocopy a page from one of your textbooks. Underline the grammatical subject of each sentence. (The subject is usually that part of the main clause that precedes the verb; see 24b if you need help.) What is the average length of the sentence subjects? How many of them refer to old information?

6d   Be consistent with verb tense, person, and number

Verb tenses help create a time frame for readers (see 26e). When writers jump from one verb tense to another within a paragraph, they disrupt the paragraph's coherence and risk confusing the reader. Conversely, maintaining a consistent point of view in the use of pronouns helps readers. After using the first-person plural (*we, us, our*), do not switch to the singular (*I, me, my*) or to second or third person (*you, they, . . .*) unless there is a good reason to do so (see Chapter 33).

Watching Monday Night Football on ABC has become a ritualistic practice for countless American sports lovers. Every Monday
                                                        millions of fans
night during the NFL season, ~~we would~~ gather to watch the "old
pigskin" being thrown around. This activity can be experienced in

the comfort of *one's* ~~your~~ own home, at parties, or in popular sports bars. ~~A typical viewer will~~ *Viewers* especially enjoy the opening segment of the program, with all its pyrotechnics and special effects. *The producers* ~~They~~ really know how to put on a show at ABC! *For those who* ~~If you~~ like football, MNF is not to be missed.

6e   Use parallelism to make paragraphs coherent

Many paragraphs contain embedded "lists"—that is, sets of sentences that have equivalent values and roles. In such cases, it is important to establish **parallelism** between the sentences by giving them the same grammatical structure. Such parallelism helps the reader easily see the relationship between sentences. (Chapter 36 discusses parallelism *within* sentences.) Notice how the two parallel sentences in this paragraph set off the contrast between poor and middle-class African Americans:

> Sociologist William Julius Wilson argues that there are two worlds of African-American experience. *Those who are stuck in the inner city live in poverty, confront violent crime daily, attend underfunded schools, face dead-end jobs or welfare, and are filled with hopelessness and despair, combined with apathy or hostility.* In contrast, *those who have moved up the social class ladder live in good housing in relatively crime-free neighborhoods, work at well-paid jobs that offer advancement, and send their children to good schools.* Their middle-class experiences and lifestyle have changed their views on life. Their aspirations and values have so altered that they no longer have much in common with African Americans who remain poor. According to Wilson, then, social class—not race—has become the most significant factor in the lives of African Americans today.
>
> —Adapted from James M. Henslin, *Sociology*

To make it easy for the reader to spot the "two worlds" that Wilson is talking about, the writer describes them in separate, grammatically parallel sentences (*Those who . . . , those who . . .*).

EXERCISE 6.9

1. Pick three paragraphs from one of your textbooks, and identify the techniques (such as use of an organizational pattern, sentence links, repetition, or parallelism) that give them coherence.

2. From a Web page, copy three interesting paragraphs that use repetition. Put them into a new document, and use the SEARCH function to locate all occurrences of key words. If there seems to be too much repetition or not enough, rewrite the paragraphs to better use repetition and other techniques that improve coherence.

6f   Decide on appropriate paragraph length

Each paragraph should be long enough to adequately develop its main point. Thus, paragraph length depends mainly on how complicated the topic is. The important thing is to make paragraphs complete and unified. A writer who does so is not likely to make them excessively long or excessively short.

Also, bear in mind that desirable paragraph length can vary from one type of writing to another. In college essays, most paragraphs are likely to be three to five sentences long. In contrast, email messages often have short paragraphs, sometimes with only one or two sentences, thereby capturing the flavor of conversational discourse. Likewise, newspaper reports usually have very short paragraphs (one to two sentences), in part to grab the reader's attention. But newspaper editorials aim for more reflective reading and so have somewhat longer paragraphs (two to three sentences). Paragraphs in the *Encyclopaedia Britannica* may contain twelve or more sentences.

6g   Link paragraphs with key words

In any series of paragraphs, a reader should be able to move easily from one paragraph to the next. If a paragraph picks up where the preceding one left off, provide at least one link in the first sentence of the new paragraph. Such links can be transitional words and phrases or expressions referring to old information and preceded by terms like *this, these,* or *such.* Notice that the first sentence of the second paragraph contains a phrase that continues a theme from the first paragraph:

One of the major forms of social stratification is caste. In a caste system, status is determined by birth and is lifelong. In sociological terms the basis of a caste system is ascribed status. Achieved status cannot change an individual's place in this system. People born into a low-status group will always have low status, no matter how much they personally may accomplish in life.

Societies with *this form of stratification* try to make certain that the boundaries between castes remain firm. They practice endogamy, marriage within their own group, and prohibit intermarriage. To prevent contact between castes, they even develop elaborate rules about ritual pollution, teaching that contact with inferior castes contaminates the superior caste.

—Adapted from James M. Henslin, *Sociology*

EXERCISE 6.10

1. Select an essay from a book you have used in one of your courses or an editorial from a daily newspaper, and choose one section of four or five paragraphs. In the first sentence of every paragraph except the first, identify all the words and phrases that help connect that paragraph to the one preceding it.

2. Look again at a single topic as presented in listserv messages and in Usenet discussions. What differences do you see in the way the two presentations make connecting links between paragraphs or parts?

6h Construct effective introductory and concluding paragraphs

The beginning and the end of a document are the two places where readers are most likely to give full attention to what they are reading. Thus, it is particularly important that you write effective opening and closing paragraphs (see 5b-7).

1 Writing an introductory paragraph that will draw the reader's attention

When readers start to read a piece of writing, they want to know what it will be about and whether it will be interesting—and they want to know these things quickly. Therefore, you should write an opening paragraph that is informative and interesting. The opening paragraph should always be appropriate to the genre: an academic essay requires a different sort of opening than does, say, a letter of complaint. In all genres, however, an introductory paragraph should accomplish four things:

1. Identify the topic of the piece
2. Stimulate reader interest
3. Establish a tone or style
4. Enable readers to anticipate what comes next

Here is an example of an effective introductory paragraph from an essay on gender differences in the electronic age:

> As a longtime *Star Trek* devotee, Janis Cortese was eager to be part of the Trekkie discussion group on the Internet. But when she first logged on, Cortese noticed that these fans of the final frontier devoted megabytes to such profound topics as whether Troi or Crusher had bigger breasts. In other words, the purveyors of this *Trek* dreck were all *guys*. Undeterred, Cortese, a physicist at California's Loma Linda University, figured she'd add perspective to the electronic gathering place with her own momentous questions. Why was the male cast racially diverse while almost all the females were

Some Effective Devices for Introductory Paragraphs

- *A personal anecdote.* Personal stories give readers a vivid sense of what a topic means.
- *A detailed description.* Another way of setting the scene is to describe the environment in detail.
- *A quotation.* If the relevance of the quotation to the rest of the writing is not entirely clear, add an accompanying explanation or comment.
- *A problem.* For most readers, stating the problem will pique interest in possible solutions.
- *An analogy.* If your topic is difficult to grasp, an analogy may clarify it. Note, however, that analogies are risky. For an analogy to work, there must be sufficient correspondence between the two things being compared (see 7g-7).
- *A provocative statement.* A statement that seems contradictory or nonsensical will certainly draw attention. Of course, for this strategy to be effective, you must be able to show that the statement is not contradictory or nonsensical at all.

young, white, and skinny? Then, she tossed in a few lustful thoughts about the male crew members.

—Barbara Kantrowitz, "Men, Women, Computers"

Because it relates a personal anecdote about a popular TV program, this paragraph is likely to interest many readers. The topic ("the purveyors . . . were all *guys*") is identified by the end of sentence 3. A jocular tone is established with words like *dreck, skinny,* and *lustful thoughts.* And the final sentence enables readers to guess what comes next (male Trekkies responded by flooding her email box with nasty flames).

While some types of writing, such as business letters and memos (see Chapter 22), have fairly conventional openings, other types of writing give you more latitude in ways to draw reader interest. For example, if you are writing an exploratory essay, such as the one by Kantrowitz, you have some freedom in how you construct your opening paragraph. You can adopt a relaxed style, and you can hint at your thesis instead of stating it explicitly. If you are writing an argumentative essay, your readers will expect you to use a more formal style and tighter structure, and they will look for an explicit thesis in the first paragraph.

2 Writing a concluding paragraph that creates a sense of completeness

The concluding paragraph of an extended piece of writing should not leave the reader hanging but, rather, should neatly tie things up. Except in a very short essay, the concluding paragraph should reiterate your main point, preferably not by simply restating it but by adding something to it. Ideally, it should also stimulate the reader to think beyond what you have already said. See Some Effective Devices for Concluding Paragraphs; sometimes two or more of these techniques work well together.

Some Effective Devices for Concluding Paragraphs

- Present an apt quotation.
- Tell a story that illustrates your main point.
- Pose a thought-provoking question.
- Pick up on a theme or idea that was mentioned at the beginning.
- Speculate about the future.

The following paragraph is the concluding paragraph of the Kantrowitz essay introduced in 6h-1. It includes a quotation, a story, and speculation about what the future may hold.

> Ironically, gender differences could help women. "We're at a cultural turning point," says MIT's Turkle. "There's an opportunity to remake the culture around the machine." Practicality is now as valued as invention. If the computer industry wants to put machines in the hands of the masses, that means women—along with the great many men who have no interest in hot-rod computing. An ad campaign for Compaq's popular Presario line emphasizes the machine's utility. After kissing her child goodnight, the mother in the ad sits down at her Presario to work. As people start to view their machines as creative tools, someday women may be just as comfortable with computers as men are.
>
> —Barbara Kantrowitz, "Men, Women, Computers"

E X E R C I S E 6 . 1 1

1. In light of the above discussion, evaluate the introductory paragraph and the concluding paragraph of Kirsten Parsons's essay on Net theft (pages 83–87). For practice, construct an alternative version of each paragraph, using one or more rhetorical devices not used by Kirsten.

2. Apply the same procedure to an essay found in one of your course readings, in a news magazine or newspaper, or on the Internet.

Formulating Arguments

How can I get people to understand my point of view?

How can I get people to respect what I am proposing?

What difference is there between a convincing argument
  and a personal opinion?

What makes a good, arguable thesis? (7a)

What's a "non sequitur"? (7g-3)

?

A natural outcome of the critical thinking you are expected to do in college (see 2a) is speaking or writing in which you formulate and defend your own point of view. This is called *argument*. Argument in this sense does not mean quarreling; rather, it means taking a position on an issue and supporting it with evidence and good reasoning.

Argument is essential to a democratic society. Unless people can discuss their differences in a rational, intelligent manner, they cannot make well-informed decisions about how to govern themselves. An important part of a college education is learning how to contribute, as a citizen, to the public discourse. Whether through writing a letter to

> http://cougar.vut.edu.
> au/~dalbj/argueweb/
> contents.htm
> An authorative guide
> to writing argumenta-
> tive essays

WEB

a legislator, attending a PTA meeting, discussing public issues with a neighbor, or participating in a newsgroup on the Internet, life beyond college will call on you to act as an informed member of the civic community. The ability to formulate coherent, well-supported arguments will enhance your ability to persuade people in your community or workplace to see your viewpoint or think and act in the ways you advocate. College courses are designed to give you the critical thinking and arguing skills you will need to achieve these goals.

7a   Formulate an arguable thesis

The first step in developing an argument is to formulate a good thesis, or claim (see 3d-1). In argument, as in exposition, a thesis is a statement in which the writer or speaker takes a supportable position on an issue—for example, "Voting rights can be extended safely to most of the mentally ill." In some college assignments, the thesis is given. For example, many standardized tests and final exams have essay questions on a preset thesis. In other cases, however, students are expected to formulate a thesis themselves. Many instructors give students complete freedom to select their own topics for course papers. The critical reading you do (see 2b) in preparation for an assignment may raise the kinds of questions that lead to an appropriate thesis, as may encounters with others' ideas on the Internet or exchanges with others in a network. (See Chapters 9 and 10 for help in finding and evaluating evidence from networks and the Internet.) Whether the thesis is one that has been assigned or one that you have created yourself, try to shape the thesis and develop the argument so that they become an expression of your own point of view.

WEB

http://csprit4.pinc.com/
ddgram/index.html
An excellent site on
argumentative writing
and grammar

1   What constitutes an appropriate thesis?

To have an influence on others, a thesis should be *open to debate*. That is, it should not make a claim that everyone would already agree

An Arguable Thesis or Claim

■ Is debatable. Not everyone will automatically agree with it.
■ Can be supported with evidence available to everyone.
■ Can be countered with arguments against it.
■ Is clearly stated. If it is of fact, value, or policy, with terms defined.
■ Is not based just on personal opinion or subjective feelings inaccessible to others.

with. "Smoking is harmful to your health" is not an effective argumentative thesis because almost no educated person would disagree with it. A more interesting, more arguable thesis would be "Smoking should be prohibited in all public places, including restaurants." It makes a better thesis because it would not meet with universal agreement or disagreement and thus would require argumentation.

Second, an appropriate thesis is *open to evidence and counterevidence*—you can gather and present evidence for and against this claim. For the smoking example, you could search the research literature, Web sites, or newsgroups for scientific evidence about the effects of second-hand smoke; you could look for health statistics on communities that have already enacted such a prohibition; or you could try to locate results of public opinion surveys. If a thesis merely expresses your own opinion about something ("I think smoking is cool"), without citing evidence beyond your own feelings, it offers no claim that can be objectively assessed by others.

Third, a thesis should be *clearly stated*. It should leave no confusion in the mind of the reader as to what you are claiming. Provide definitions or paraphrases of any terms that may be unclear. In the example about smoking in public places, readers would need to know exactly what is meant by the term *public places*. Indeed, the entire argument could hinge on how this term is defined.

A thesis can be either a claim of fact, a claim of value, or a claim of policy. A claim of fact asserts that something is true ("Smoking is harmful to your health"). A claim of value asserts that something is or is not worthwhile ("People should make efforts to protect their health by avoiding smoke"). A claim of policy argues for a course of action ("Smoking should be banned in all public places"). Your thesis should make clear to the audience which type of claim you are making (see 3d-1).

2 Working through a thesis

Not every claim, or thesis, ends up the way it began; most writers develop a thesis somewhat by trial and error, refining their ideas as they gather more information. For an essay in his composition class, Antonio Ramirez decided to write about cloning. There had been much reporting in the media about a sheep in England that had given birth to a lamb with identical genes—that is, a clone. Public discussion in the media focused on concern about potential abuses of cloning and whether the cloning of humans should be banned. In thinking about this topic, Antonio came to the conclusion that the public's anxiety about cloning was misplaced. He decided that the thesis for his essay would be something like "Cloning is nothing to worry about." But this was only his *working thesis*. As he explored the subject and worked through his ideas, he realized that he would have to make his thesis more specific, more open to evidence—that is, more arguable. To this end, Antonio decided to focus not on cloning itself but on the fact that people were talking about banning it. This resulted in a *revised thesis:* "Banning cloning of humans will do nothing except make people feel a little safer from the perceived misuse of cloning."

Antonio's thesis is a good one. First of all, it is not a statement that everyone would automatically agree with. In fact, animal cloning is a hot topic precisely because it could lead to human cloning, which many people fear. And even among those who fear it, there is disagreement over whether to ban it. In short, the thesis is arguable. Second, the thesis can be debated with evidence and counterevidence. Antonio could cite the effectiveness or ineffectiveness of other bans, the possible uses and misuses of cloning, and so on. Third, the thesis is clearly stated, alluding to several of the key subissues (the safety of cloning, people's anxieties, the possible misuses of cloning).

In writing a draft of his essay, Antonio wanted to make sure that his readers knew enough about the topic to appreciate the significance of his thesis. So before actually presenting this thesis, he devoted the entire first paragraph to background information. Here is how the beginning turned out:

In the past few weeks, the media have bombarded us with information about a Finn Dorset ewe named Dolly. Dolly is the first mammal to be cloned with a single surrogate. The process by which this occurred was by taking an arbitrary cell, which happened to be an udder cell, from the donor. The udder cell was then placed in a chemical bath that would ensure the DNA would keep working after being transplanted. The scientist then extracted an egg cell from another ewe and the nucleus was extracted. The two cells, the egg cell and udder cell, were then fused with a jolt of electricity which also caused the cell to begin dividing. Then after six days, the embryo was placed in the womb of another ewe. This embryo continued to develop to term and cloning was a reality. Since the first month when scientist Ian Wilmut announced that he had cloned the sheep, academicians and theologians have been in an uproar over whether we will be next. And editorial writers and national columnists have joined in. The fear of abuses, especially in possible cloning of humans, has led many to argue in favor of setting a legal ban against any cloning of humans.

Banning cloning of humans will do nothing except make people feel a little safer from the perceived misuse of cloning. . . .

Notice how Antonio's essay gently draws the reader into the issue before focusing on the main point he wants to make. Let this example serve as a reminder: although a thesis should be stated early, it should be preceded by any background information the reader needs to make sense of it. Delayed presentation of the thesis is especially appropriate if the audience is either ignorant of the subject or likely to disagree with or be skeptical about the thesis. Delaying the thesis encourages the reader to think that you are not "jumping to conclusions" but instead are thoughtfully and impartially working through the issue. Since readers in college are trained to be skeptical, you should not feel that you have to state your thesis up front (unless, of course, your instructor tells you to).

EXERCISE 7.1

Analyze each of the following claims to decide (a) whether or not it expresses a clear and arguable thesis and (b) what kinds of evidence and counterevidence would be relevant to it. In cases where the claim is not an arguable thesis, reformulate it into one.

1. The US military should clarify its regulations governing sexual activity between two consenting adults serving in the military.
2. Gun control should be improved in this country.
3. Smashing Pumpkins is the best group in the world.
4. The National Park System would be better off if it were privatized.
5. Overpopulation is threatening our quality of life.
6. "I Have a Dream" has become a comfortable poster slogan for white liberal Americans.
7. It is a bad idea for governments to attempt to regulate delivery of information via the Internet.
8. People should not drive drunk.
9. Within a decade, soccer will replace baseball as our national pastime.
10. Private charities will not be able to provide all of the services needed by those who will be cut from the welfare rolls.

7b   Generate good supporting evidence

Central to the strength of an argument is the evidence cited to support it. There are five main types of evidence: factual data, expert opinion, personal experience, examples, and statistics.

Factual data include any information presented as representing objective reality. Factual data most often consist of measurable, or quantitative, evidence such as distances, amounts, and ratios. But factual data can include historical events, longstanding assessments, and other widely attested observations about the world. Objectivity makes factual data difficult to refute. Therefore, in most academic disciplines, factual data are considered to be the most powerful form of evidence you can present.

Expert opinion also can be persuasive, because it represents the studied judgment of someone who knows a great deal about the subject at hand. If a famous literary critic said that *Twelfth Night* was one of Shakespeare's finest plays, quoting this expert's statement would strengthen any argument you made along those lines. But expert opinion has its limitations. First, a quotation taken out of context may not convey what the expert really meant. Second, experts sometimes fall prey to the influence of some special interest. Not long ago, experts employed by the tobacco industry testified that tobacco was not addictive. Finally, experts can simply be wrong in their judgments and predictions.

Personal experience is less objective than either factual data or expert opinion, but it can be highly compelling. Personal experience is especially effective when presented in the form of a narrative. The story you tell may represent only your own experience—and thus lack generalizability—but since it is coming directly from you it has a certain vividness that is missing from more detached accounts. Personal experience is not the same as personal opinion: the former is an account of an experience—something you have personally tested against reality—while the latter may be nothing more than a snap judgment. Arguments do not go far on opinion alone.

Examples are effective because, like personal experience, they are concrete, vivid, and therefore easy for readers to relate to. (Just think of how much you appreciate good examples in the textbooks and other instructional materials you read!) Unlike personal experience, examples are supposed to be generalizations about a larger category. That is, they are good only to the extent that they are typical of an entire class of phenomena. If you present an odd case as a "typical example," you may justifiably be criticized for giving a misleading example.

A collection of numerical data, statistics usually are compressed in a way that points to a certain interpretation. Because statistics typically represent a large body of data, they can be compelling as evidence. But they can also be manipulated in deceptive ways. If you gather your own statistics, be sure you know how to analyze them correctly. If you take statistics from other sources, try to use only sources that are considered reliable (for example, the US government or prestigious academic journals).

This is how Antonio chose to support his thesis about cloning:

Banning cloning of humans will do nothing except make people feel a little bit safer from the perceived misuse of cloning. Just as professor of bioethics Ruth Macklin stated, "While human cloning might not offer great benefits to humanity, no one has yet made a persuasive case that it would do any real harm, either." Many people are in such a tumult over the fact that an animal was cloned they lose sight of why this research is taking place. "The process is a quicker way to turn genetically altered cells into animals that could make disease-fighting drugs or donor organs for humans," says Alan Colman of PPL Therapeutics, which funded the program in which Dolly was created. In fact, the company's main mission is not cloning at all; it is genetically altering sheep so that human drugs are produced in their milk.

Many theologians argue that clones would violate human dignity, but as Ruth Macklin points out, this would only be true if society treated clones as "lesser beings," with fewer rights and lower status. "Twins are, in fact, nature's clones. They have the exact same genetic makeup, yet they do not lose dignity due to their repetitiveness," says Craig Turner, a professor of psychology from Yale. Twins grow up quite different from each other; clones would be quite different from their originals as well. In fact, since the clone will not share the womb as twins do and will live sometime after the donor, the clone will no doubt be quite different from the original. To put it simply: as Robert McFinn, a cellular biologist, stated, "Identical genes do not provide for identical individuals." Most theologians and scientists agree that the clone and the donor would be totally different and distinct persons.

Many people fear the fact that people will make clones in order to take the organs they need from them to survive life-threatening diseases. It is a well-known fact, though, that many parents have another child to save one of their other children suffering from a disease in which an organ or bone marrow must be matched. This is not often frowned upon because the child is cared for and loved just as the preceding sibling. The question that needs to be considered is how this would be different for a cloned child.

The banning of cloning will do nothing for society. Many mysteries abound in this world undiscovered. By banning cloning before even researching the potential contributions of this process, we may be limiting ourselves. Making cloning illegal by banning the process does not guarantee that all researchers will comply with the ban. Additionally it could increase the potential for misuse. We will have no control over the process and will gain no information about potential benefits. At least if it is legal, it can be regulated and watched. The question of whether cloning should be banned should be changed to how we should regulate and control cloning.

What kinds of evidence does Antonio use to support his argument? Mainly, he relies on the testimony of experts (Ruth Macklin, Alan Colman, Craig Turner, and Robert McFinn, plus "most theologians and scientists"). They, in turn, rely on scientific facts, such as McFinn's statement that "identical genes do not provide for identical individuals." Antonio offers other facts as well. (In the finished paper, Antonio will give source citations for the facts and quotations, from both print and electronic sources. See Chapter 13 on Documentation Formats.) And he uses a powerful example: the fact that identical twins are natural clones of each other.

EXERCISE 7.2

Of the different kinds of evidence that Antonio used, which—in your opinion—is most compelling? Why? Is there any other evidence he could have used?

7c   Take note of evidence for alternative views

In gathering evidence, do not go looking just for evidence that supports your case; take note of evidence supporting other positions as well, including evidence that argues directly against your case. On issues that are of any interest or value, the evidence will not be entirely one-sided; there will be evidence supporting alternative views. When you acknowledge the counterevidence, you gain credibility as a careful, conscientious thinker, thereby strengthening your argument rather than weakening it. (This is especially true in academia.) Conversely, failure to present a full spectrum of evidence will be interpreted by readers either as an indication of a less than full effort to address the issue or an attempt to hide negative evidence. Remember, you do not have to make an overwhelmingly lopsided argument in order to prevail; you simply have to show that there is more support *for* your thesis than against it. In most college writing, an awareness of the complexity of an issue is considered to be a sign of intellectual maturity. Do not be afraid to bring forth counterevidence. (See 7d for more information on how best to deal with such counterevidence.)

Another advantage of gathering counterevidence early on is that it enables you to review your thesis and, if necessary, modify it. In formulating your thesis, you may have overlooked some arguments against it. Maybe you overgeneralized, used either/or reasoning, or committed some other fallacy (see 7g). If so, this is a good time to reformulate your thesis and make it more defensible. (Getting your fellow students involved in this effort can be of great help; see 5e-1 for more on collaborating.)

Antonio's essay offers counterevidence in the form of two comments: first, that "many theologians argue that clones would violate human dignity," and second, that "many people fear the fact that people will make clones in order to take the organs they need from them to survive life-threatening diseases." He gives each of these counterarguments short shrift, though, immediately challenging and dismissing it. Thus, his essay comes off as a bit too one-sided. If Antonio had asked peers or collaborators on a student network to comment on his paper or if he had looked at more material in newsgroups, he might have collected some strong opposing viewpoints to deal with.

EXERCISE 7.3

Is there other counterevidence Antonio could have used? How could he have responded to it?

EXERCISE 7.4

Log on to a newsgroup, chat room, or other Web site where arguments are taking place (see 21a). (Some interesting newsgroups are *talk.politics, ab.politics, alt.society.resistance, alt.fan.rush-limbaugh,* and *alt.politics.radical-left.*) Print out two threads, each involving several exchanges: one in which the participants make some concessions to each other's point of view and another in which the participants do not make such concessions. Do the threads differ in tone, argumentative force, or intellectuality? Write a short paper describing the differences you find.

7d   Develop and test the main points

Once you have formulated an appropriate thesis and compiled enough information to make a case for it, you need to develop and test the main points you want to make. This is the heart of an argument, where you lay out your reasoning in step-by-step fashion.

1   Deciding what your strongest points are

In any argument, some points are stronger than others: they are more central to the issue at hand, they make more sense in terms of logical reasoning, they have more evidence supporting them, and they have less counterevidence opposing them. In constructing your argument, you need to try to identify those points that seem to be strongest. You might start by simply listing all the points you can think of to support your thesis. Then ask yourself this question: Which of these points are most central to the issue I am addressing? Any controversial topic will give rise to a hierarchy of concerns, which will vary from one person to another. If you ignore a concern that is of overriding importance to a particular reader, you will lose the argument with that reader. For example, in the debate over abortion, the stated overriding concern of most pro-life adherents is the sanctity of human life. No amount of arguing in terms of freedom of choice, population control, or women's rights is likely to sway such an audience if the sanctity-of-human-life issue is ignored. They will just say that you are missing the point. Thus, an important step at this stage is to analyze your audience and determine how they rank their concerns about the topic under discussion.

What do you do if your strongest points do not coincide with the main concerns of your audience? One strategy is to *re-define* their concerns and your points so that there is a closer fit. For example, if you were writing about abortion from the pro-choice side, you could argue that the sanctity of human life encompasses individual freedom, including the freedom of women to decide what happens to their own bodies. Another strategy is to accept the differences between yourself and your audience and prepare to make your argument anyway. Even a losing argument can have value, so long as it is a strong argument. It may gain the respect of your opponents, temper their views, resonate unexpectedly among disinterested parties, "plant a seed," or have other beneficial results. But for these good things to happen, you must at least acknowledge your opponents' point of view. Indeed, in some cases, your strongest points will be refutations of your opponents' strongest points.

2 Developing and checking your points using Toulmin logic

Starting with your strongest point, use careful step-by-step reasoning to develop each point. Your main goal is to make sure that your points are logically sound, by analyzing what the philosopher Stephen Toulmin calls their underlying warrants. A **warrant** is an explanation in the form of a general statement or rule (often unstated) that logically connects your evidence or data to the point you are making. For example, one of Antonio Ramirez's most powerful points is the one concerning identical twins. He makes this point in two steps, as follows:

http://powa.org/
argufrms.htm
Ideas for developing
your arguments, from
Paradigm Online Writing Assistant

STEP ONE

DATA	Identical twins, though having the same genetic makeup, differ in traits such as personality and interests. Thus, they are unique individuals.
WARRANT (UNSTATED)	Only if you are a unique individual can you have human dignity.
POINT OR CLAIM	Identical twins can have human dignity.

STEP TWO

DATA	Cloned humans would be like identical twins in having the same genes but different personalities. In short, they too would be unique individuals.
WARRANT (UNSTATED)	Only if you are a unique individual can you have human dignity.
POINT OR CLAIM	Like twins, cloned humans can have human dignity.

How do I decide if I have a strong argument or not?

1. Set up a table with your word processor, making three columns and a generous array of rows to handle your arguments. Title the first column "Pro," the second "Con," and the third "Audience Reactions."

2. Use the rows in the three parallel columns for brief summary statements of key points that must be balanced against each other in analyzing the strength of your overall argument.

   a. In the Pro column of each row, summarize each strong point.

   b. Balance each point in the Pro column with an actual or likely counterargument in the Con column.

   c. Use the Audience Reactions column to make brief notes about how your audience may stand in regard to either the Pro or the Con column's claims. Do they know a lot about the subject, or not much? If they favor one side or the other, why do they do so?

3. Compare the parallel columns and decide which are your most effective points and which are the ones that will give you the most difficulty. If the columns seem to show a deadlock or a strong opposing current, perhaps you should change your argument.

Notice that in both steps the validity of her point depends on the same unstated warrant. Is this warrant valid? Most people in our culture would say so.

When careful readers judge your arguments, they will be scrutinizing your chain of reasoning. Thus, be aware of the warrant you use for each point you make. Often, the warrant is assumed rather than actually stated. But if critical readers do not share your assumptions, they will say that your claims are *unwarranted*. Any assumptions that might not be shared by your readers should be stated explicitly.

Checking Your Argument for Sound Reasoning

1. Have I arrived at a clearly stated, arguable thesis (see 7a)?
2. Does my evidence support this thesis (see 7b)?
3. Do I need to revise my thesis based on evidence or counterarguments (see 7c)?
4. Can I locate a general rule or principle—a *warrant*—that logically connects my claim to my evidence?
5. If the warrant is unstated, will it be obvious to everybody in my audience? (If not, it should be stated specifically.)

EXERCISE 7.5

Identify a point in Antonio's essay other than the one analyzed above. Using the same data-warrant-claim structure, analyze this point.

7e   Build a compelling case

The primary goal of any argument is to make the best case you can. The three basic ways to make a case are by using logical reasoning, by asserting your and others' authority, and by appealing to the readers' emotions.

1   Appealing to logic

In college, certainly the most important type of support you can give to an argument is logical reasoning. Indeed, one of the main purposes of education is to promote the ability to communicate effectively with a broad, skeptical audience (in both professional and public life), and logical reasoning is the primary tool for doing so. In particular, you should avoid logical fallacies (see 7g). In whatever field of study you undertake—sociology, history, mathematics, or biology—your instructors will always be paying close attention to the logical reasoning you use (see Chapters 14–16). They will want to know that you can develop an argument step by step, laying out a chain of reasoning that compels skeptical readers to respect your thinking.

There are many effective patterns for developing an argument. They include linking cause and effect, making comparisons and contrasts, defining and classifying, narrating a series of events, generalizing from particulars (or *induction*), drawing particular inferences from general rules (or *deduction*), and providing relevant examples and analogies. (Some of these approaches underlie the paragraph patterns discussed in Chapter 6; see also 7f-6.)

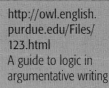

http://owl.english.
purdue.edu/Files/
123.html
A guide to logic in
argumentative writing

2 Appealing to authority

People usually are greatly influenced by the credibility or reputation of the person trying to persuade them. That is why advertisers like to use highly esteemed celebrities like Michael Jordan and Cindy Crawford to push their products. The appeal to authority takes advantage of a natural desire on the part of individuals to simplify their lives. If M.J. says that Nike shoes are the best, it is easier to take his word for it than to go to the local library and look up the research findings in *Consumer Reports*.

More discerning readers are not so likely to be influenced by celebrity endorsements, but they often are influenced by expert judgments. Thus, you can support an argument by invoking the authority of true experts. In doing so, it is important to (a) find experts who are addressing an issue within their field of expertise, (b) use actual quotes rather than paraphrasing, (c) include enough context to make the quote an accurate reflection of the expert's statement, and (d) provide a reference so that skeptical readers can look up the quote for themselves.

An even more important type of authority is your own. Since you are the person who has gathered the information and assembled the argument, your own credibility (or *ethos*) will be under scrutiny. If readers have any reason to doubt your honesty, fairness, or scholarly integrity, they will treat what you say with a good deal of skepticism. Here are some things you can do to safeguard and enhance your credibility:

1. Avoid making any exaggerated or distorted assertions.
2. Acknowledge opposing points of view and counterevidence.

3. If you use other people's ideas or words, give them explicit credit.
4. If appropriate, mention your credentials (without bragging).
5. Use good reasoning throughout.
6. Maintain a respectful, civil tone.
7. Pay attention to details of writing such as grammar, style, spelling, and punctuation.

3   Appealing to emotion

A third powerful way of supporting an argument is by enlisting the readers' emotions. Although this type of persuasion is generally not emphasized in academic and technical writing, it can be highly effective so long as it is used in conjunction with a more logical appeal. In many other kinds of writing (such as political discourse, journalism, and advertising), emotional appeals are used frequently.

Here are some things you can do to add emotional power to an argument:

1. Describe the issue in a way that relates it to the readers' values or needs.
2. Include examples that readers can identify with, such as stories featuring sympathetic human beings.
3. Occasionally use language that has emotive connotations (see Chapter 40).

EXERCISE 7.6

In your opinion, what type of support does Antonio's essay rely on most heavily? In his essay, identify examples of a logical appeal, an appeal to authority, and an emotional appeal, and evaluate, in writing, the effectiveness of each.

EXERCISE 7.7

Read the following letter to the editor, and point out the different types of support (logic, authority, emotion) it uses. Do you think some types are more effective than others? If so, why?

In detailing the painful story of a local family struggling to survive in the face of harsh welfare cuts (9.21.97), the *Tribune* has rendered an important public service. Tiffany Davis and her three children deserve our sympathy, and I applaud your reporter and the Davis family for giving us a glimpse of the grave impact that welfare "reform" is having on the lives of decent, hardworking citizens who happen to fall on hard times.

As a volunteer at a local homeless shelter, though, I would like to raise some questions: Why didn't you say something about the *father* of these three small children? Doesn't he bear some responsibility for their (and Tiffany's) plight? In an article of some 40 column inches, all we're told about him is that he gives the family "no support, financial or emotional." As taxpaying citizens, we deserve to know more. What is his name? What is his occupation? How comfortably does he live (while his family is barely hanging on)? Why doesn't he help support his own children? At a time when many men are abandoning their families yet politicians are slashing support programs, single mothers like Tiffany Davis are bearing increasingly difficult burdens. It's a nationwide problem, one that you only make worse by not exposing these deadbeats for what they are.

7f   Structure the argument

There are a number of ways to structure an argument. After looking at four of the most common ones, we will consider ways to decide which method to select and whether to use an inductive or a deductive arrangement.

1   Using the classic five-part method

The classic method, which dates back to antiquity, has five parts:

1. Introduce the topic, explain why it is important, and state or imply your thesis.

2. Provide enough background information so that readers will be able to follow your argument.

3. Develop your argument. If you did not state your thesis in step 1, state it here. Support it with appropriate evidence, compelling appeals, and sound reasoning.

4. Acknowledge and refute possible objections and counterarguments, using good evidence and reasoning. Various objections can be dealt with in different parts of the paper. For example, you may want to cite one or more counterarguments early in the paper in order to introduce some of your main points as refutations.

5. Conclude by re-emphasizing the importance of the issue and the main points of your argument.

2 Using the problem and solution method

The problem and solution method involves describing a problem and then proposing one or more solutions to it. This pattern is common in reports, memos, and other forms of business and technical writing. For example, a memo might state, "Some people can't get here in time for our 10:00 a.m. meetings. Do you think we could change the starting time to 10:10?" The key to this method is to clearly identify the problem before stating the solution. The problem and solution method is a good choice when (a) the audience agrees on the nature of the problem and (b) the possible solutions are few in number. In situations where these conditions do not exist, you are likely to have to spend too much time defining the problem and discussing the various solutions.

3 Using the Rogerian method

The aim of the Rogerian method is to defuse a hostile audience. The arguer begins by characterizing the opponent's position in terms the opponent can accept and then presents his or her own position in a form that respects both the opponent's and the arguer's views. Once a dialogue has been established, the differences between the two sides can be explored. For example, the letter to the editor in Exercise 7.7 starts out by applauding the reporter "for giving us a glimpse of the grave impact that welfare 'reform' is having on the lives of decent, hardworking citizens who happen to fall on hard times." Only after this common ground has been established does the writer launch into criticisms of the article.

4 Using the narrative method

Storytelling is a powerful and persuasive form of presentation, especially if the narrator has a lot of credibility with his or her audience.

But because a skeptical reader may not be willing to generalize from the experience of the narrator, the personal narrative is not effective in college writing unless it is backed up by other kinds of support.

Antonio's essay starts out with a narrative describing how scientists create a clone from an animal cell. With its concrete detail, this depiction is likely to engage the readers' interest. But then, in the remainder of his essay, Antonio shifts to a more traditional form of argument consisting of claims, points, warrants, and evidence.

5 Selecting a method

Which method works best? The answer depends mainly on how your audience is likely to react to what you have to say. In any argument, your readers are likely to agree with you on some issues and disagree on others. The usual strategy is to structure the argument so that the agreed-upon parts come first and the more contentious parts later. This way, you can establish common ground with your readers before going on to more difficult matters.

HELP

How do I keep track of my argument?

1. Analyze your audience and topic, and then select an appropriate argument structure.
2. Open the outlining feature.
3. List your main points from most important to least important, and plug them into the outline according to the argument structure you have selected.
4. Under each point, indicate your supporting evidence and basic line of reasoning.
5. Check the hierarchical structure of your outline. Make sure each point is distinct and independent. If two points say similar things, select one as a main point and make the other a supporting point under it.
6. Draft your paper as you normally would, but shift to your outline occasionally to make sure you are staying on track.

If you know, for example, that your readers are concerned about the same problem you are, the problem and solution method would be a good choice. If your readers know you personally and respect your experience and knowledge, you could start out with a personal narrative. If you and your readers have broadly divergent viewpoints, the Rogerian method is useful because you start out by stating the readers' position—something you know you can get agreement on. The classic method is popular in college writing because all it presumes about the readers is that they will take the time to read the entire paper carefully; thus, the first few paragraphs can be devoted to introducing the topic and providing whatever background information the readers need.

Although each of these four patterns can be used in its pure form, they also can be combined in different ways. For example, you could tell a personal narrative in the first part of the problem and solution method, or you could take a Rogerian approach in the first part of the classic method to establish common ground with a hostile reader. Indeed, one often sees expert writers combining techniques in interesting ways.

6 Deciding whether to use an inductive or a deductive arrangement

Tied to the selection of a method is the decision as to where to position your main claim. Again, an important consideration is the nature of your audience. A **deductive arrangement,** in which the main claim appears near the beginning of the piece, is appropriate when you have a basically supportive audience, which is likely to agree with your claim even before seeing much evidence. An **inductive arrangement,** in which the main claim comes later in the piece, is more appropriate for a skeptical audience, which will require substantial evidence before it will accept a claim. Since academic audiences are usually quite skeptical, academic writing employs inductive arguments more often than deductive ones.

EXERCISE 7.8

Reread the letter to the editor in Exercise 7.7. How is it structured? Why do you think the writer chose to structure it this way?

EXERCISE 7.9

Outline Antonio's essay, showing how it essentially follows the classic five-part structure.

7g   Avoid logical and emotional fallacies

As you work out your lines of reasoning, be sure to avoid any logical or emotional fallacies. Some of the most common ones are described in the following sections.

1   Overgeneralizing/oversimplifying

Overgeneralizing involves making a broad statement on the basis of too little evidence; oversimplifying is overlooking important differences. Usually the tipoff to the overgeneralization/oversimplification fallacy is the use of absolute qualifiers like *all, every, none, never,* and *completely,* as in "All Democrats are liberals" or "Corporations never look beyond quarterly profits." Examples are vulnerable to this fallacy because an example, by definition, makes a claim for generality. When you present an example of a broad category, make sure it truly represents that category. Otherwise, you will be guilty of overgeneralizing.

2   Begging the question

Making an argument at a superficial level and leaving the underlying issue or issues unaddressed is known as begging the question, assuming what needs to be proved, or engaging in *circular reasoning.* Consider this statement: "Sex education should be eliminated from the public schools. We should not be encouraging our young people to engage in sex." It implies that sex education encourages students to engage in sex, which is unproven. Often, as in this case, begging the question involves leaving controversial warrants unstated (see 7d-2).

3   Using a *non sequitur*

In Latin, *non sequitur* means literally "It does not follow." A *non sequitur* is a statement that does not logically follow from—or is irrelevant to—previous statements. Consider the statement "Senator Jones voted for the Flag Burning Amendment—she's a true patriot."

In a country that advertises freedom of speech as one of its basic values, prohibiting the burning of a political symbol does not necessarily count as true patriotism; indeed, some would say it is just the opposite! *Non sequiturs* often arise from faulty, unstated warrants. For example, if someone says, "I can tell he's an atheist, because he never goes to church," he or she is assuming, falsely, that only those who attend church believe in God. Such faulty assumptions are the basis of much stereotyped thinking.

4 Attacking the person instead of the evidence

Also called the *ad hominem* fallacy, the tactic of attacking the person instead of the evidence is common practice in public discourse. The speaker or writer, by discrediting his or her opponent, tries to divert attention from the real issue. An interesting variant of this fallacy is seen in much modern advertising (especially on TV), where the viewer's attention is directed to such diversions as a beautiful landscape, beautiful people, or funny dogs instead of to the merits of the product.

5 Using either/or reasoning

Assuming that there are only two possible solutions to a given problem leads to the fallacy of either/or (or "false dilemma") reasoning. This assumption is promoted heavily in the media, with its predilection for getting "both sides of the story"; in our adversarial system of justice; and in our two-party political system. But reality teaches us that there are typically *many* sides to a story. To be a good thinker, avoid falling into the either/or trap.

6 Using faulty cause-effect reasoning

The fact that two events occur closely spaced in time does not necessarily mean that one caused the other. As statisticians are careful to point out, correlation does not always imply causation. Here is an example of faulty cause-effect reasoning from a recent Internet posting: "Tax cuts can lead to higher economic growth. From 1990 to 1995, the ten states that raised taxes the most created zero net new jobs, while the ten states that cut taxes the most gained 1.84 million jobs, an increase of 10.8 percent." It could be that it was the lack of new jobs that caused the first group of states to raise taxes (to pay unemployment compensation, for example), not the other way around.

A special case of faulty cause-effect reasoning is the *post hoc* fallacy (from the Latin *post hoc, ergo propter hoc*, meaning "after this, therefore because of this"). The fallacy lies in assuming that because one event occurred after another, the first event caused the second. It could be, however, that the two events are unrelated.

http://calvin.
assiniboinec.mb.ca/
user/downes/fall
A guide to logical
fallacies

7 Making false analogies

False analogies arise when speakers and writers extend true analogies beyond reason, claiming similarities that do not exist. Here is an example of a false analogy: "Our Founding Fathers said that a well-regulated militia was necessary to the security of a free state. Similarly, modern-day militias like the Montana Freemen are the best guardians of our freedom."

8 Engaging in the bandwagon appeal

A common emotional ploy, the bandwagon appeal tries to pressure readers or listeners into going along with the crowd. Statements like "Everyone agrees that a free-market economy is best" or "The general consensus is that Pearl Buck was not as great a writer as Toni Morrison" suggest that, since "everyone agrees," there must be something wrong with you if you do not agree.

9 Using a red herring

Anything that draws attention away from the main issue under discussion is a "red herring." At one point in his essay on cloning, Antonio Ramirez states, "Many mysteries abound in this world undiscovered." Going on to talk about various mysteries would only have distracted the reader's attention from the point at hand. Wisely, he refrained from using such a red herring.

EXERCISE 7.10

The Internet, like other media, is fertile ground for logical and emotional fallacies. Log on to one of the political newsgroups (see 21a-2) and find two examples of fallacious reasoning. Analyze each according to the principles described in this chapter.

EXERCISE 7.11

The following argument was picked up from the Internet. Analyze it according to the principles suggested in this chapter.

A "Livable Minimum Wage" Is a Bad Idea

The only long-run solution for a truly higher real minimum wage is through higher productivity. There are no easy solutions; to earn more one must produce more. The minimum wage is essentially an unfunded mandate on business, as the government attempts to shift the responsibility of welfare to business. This may make good politics but very poor economics. In no way does raising the minimum wage increase the ability of a firm to pay a higher price for the product. It does nothing but put U.S. labor and capital at a cost/return disadvantage to foreign labor, and encourage people to turn to government, instead of themselves, for a higher wage. The minimum wage is an introductory, not a permanent wage. It allows firms to hire non-skilled workers and employ them through the unproductive portion of the learning curve. Very few people continue making the minimum wage for a period greater than one year. A livable minimum wage would also provide a huge incentive to drop out of high school, and likely drastically reduce the domestic competitiveness. Educate, don't legislate, a higher minimum wage. To earn more, one must learn more.

—"Internaut Capt. Jack"

PART 2

RESEARCH

CHAPTER

8

The Research Project

What does it mean to do research? (8a)
How will I ever get it all done? (8b)
Can I take notes on my computer? (8c)
What is a bibliography? (8d)
What are background sources? (8e)
How do I focus my search? (8f)

?

The process of writing a research paper does not differ markedly from the process of writing an essay, described in Part 1 of this handbook. The writing stages outlined in Chapter 2 (and discussed in Chapters 3, 4, and 5)—preparing, composing, and rewriting—still apply. The difference is one of scope. A research paper is longer than most essays and contains more information from external sources, found by doing research. It would be a good idea to review the stages of the writing process briefly before you begin a research project.

> **WEB**
> http://www.
> researchpaper.com
> Need we say more?
> An entire site devoted
> to helping writers of
> research papers

8a   Become a researcher

Why research? Work in many academic and professional disciplines, including law, medicine, engineering, and psychology, depends heavily on research. In all fields, researchers conduct studies to answer important questions, to solve problems, to prove cases, and to argue positions. In college, your main reason for researching may be to carry out an assignment in a particular course. For example, in a literature course, you may be asked to research an author's life or critiques of literary texts; in a political science course, you may be asked to research a political campaign or a political trend. Whatever your motivation for researching, you need to become seriously engaged in the research process.

http://www.ipl.org/
teen/aplus/
stepfirsthtm
A+ Research and Writing, to help writers get started on their research paper projects

The ability to research—that is, explore a problem systematically—is a crucial skill for an educated person. A researcher is a careful, critical, systematic thinker who goes beyond memorizing facts on a subject to examine the bases on which claims and arguments rest. Although you may not realize it, you probably have already researched many subjects. Have you ever purchased a stereo or an automobile? How did you decide which one to choose? If you read about stereos in *Consumer Reports* or other magazines, talked to friends about them, listened to and compared several models, or shopped around, you researched your purchase. The thinking processes you used are similar to those used to research a subject in a college course.

1   Understanding the research assignment

When you receive a research assignment, first think through what you are being asked to do. Ask yourself questions like

- What will my purpose be?
- How should I sound as a writer?
- Who will my readers be?
- Where will I get my authority?

Deciding on a rhetorical stance (see 3a-2) will help you to determine a general approach to the assignment. If a rhetorical stance has not been specified by the instructor, perhaps it would be a good idea to discuss it with him or her.

The two main types of research are primary research and secondary research. **Primary research** entails generating information or data through processes like interviewing, administering questionnaires, or observation (see 8f-6). **Secondary research** involves finding information in secondary, or published, sources. You need to decide which type or types of research your project demands. Can you find what you need in secondary sources, or will the research be primary in nature or some combination of the two? What kinds of sources does your instructor expect you to use? Today, secondary sources take a variety of forms: books in the library, articles in journals and magazines, newspapers and government documents, computerized hypertexts found on the Internet. Discuss with your instructor the kinds of sources that you should be locating and reading for your research project.

Does your assignment provide clues as to what your instructor expects from you? Look for key words, such as *analyze, discuss, explain, define, evaluate, compare,* and *persuade,* in the assignment. These words can help you decide how to approach your research project.

EXERCISE 8.1

Discuss the implications of the key words *analyze, discuss, explain, define, evaluate, compare,* and *persuade* with a small group of your peers. How might each word lead to a different research paper?

2   Finding a topic

Once you have a sense of the assignment, you can begin to think about possible topics for your research. If your instructor left the choice of topic up to you, you have an opportunity to research a question that interests you or a problem that intrigues you. It is important to find a topic that you already know something about or that you would like to become more knowledgeable about. Because you will be spending a great deal of time on the topic, it is helpful if the topic provokes some kind of response from you, even if that response is a questioning or skeptical one.

A good place to begin looking for a research topic is in the textbooks you are currently using. Scan the table of contents with an eye toward finding a topic that you would enjoy investigating. Or, begin by browsing through a specialized encyclopedia, such as the *Encyclopedia of Psychology* or the *Encyclopedia of Educational Research* (see 16d). These disciplinary encyclopedias, found in the reference section of the library, contain information that is generally considered to be "common knowledge" within the field. Looking through the topics covered in these reference books may give you some interesting ideas. For example, in the *Encyclopedia of Psychology*, you might find the entry on *childhood schizophrenia* intriguing. Another place to begin looking for a topic is on the Internet (see the Help box in Chapter 3, page 22). For additional information on Internet searching, see Chapter 9.

Once you have some preliminary ideas for a topic, discuss your ideas with a reference librarian, your instructor, and other students in your class. They may have suggestions about your topic or may be able to direct you to aspects of the topic that you had not considered. Listen particularly to your instructor's advice on the appropriateness of topics. Although there are no "bad" topics *per se*, there are topics that may prove difficult, given the constraints of the assignment. Your instructor will be able to tell you if topics are overused (for example, capital punishment and abortion), too trendy (for example, rock stars, fads, and fashions), or too trivial or specialized (for example, motorcycle maintenance and *The X-Files*). Take your instructor's advice so that you do not find yourself struggling with an unworkable topic.

EXERCISE 8.2

Investigate a few possible topics. Discuss the options with peers, classmates, a librarian, and your instructor. Narrow your choices down to one or two workable topics which you can later investigate more thoroughly.

3   Selecting a specific topic

Cecelia Chung, the student whose research paper serves as a model for this section of the handbook, was given the assignment of writing a research paper on an environmental topic. She was not sure what environmental issue she wanted to write about, so she decided to surf the Net as a way of generating some specific topics (see 9c-1). After browsing around for a while in the Yahoo! search engine looking for the subject "environment," she found "Environment and Nature" under "Society & Culture." There were numerous subtopics listed under the "Environment and Nature" heading, everything from disposal of nuclear waste to endangered species. In looking over the headings, she was intrigued by the topic "Climate Change Policy." She had read a little bit about global climate change in another course and wanted to find out more about it. In the "Climate Change Policy" subdirectory, Cecelia found many intriguing topics, including global warming.

4   Narrowing and focusing the topic

Search engines are useful not only for getting topic ideas but also for narrowing a general topic area or dividing a subject into several component parts, much as the subject trees on the Internet do. For example, under the broad topic of the environment, Cecelia selected the specific topic of climate change, passing over other possible environmental topics, such as nuclear waste and endangered species. Similarly, she narrowed the topic of climate change to the specific subtopic of global warming, choosing not to pursue other issues about climate changes, such as the effects of El Niño warming in the Pacific Ocean. (See also 3b-6 for more on narrowing topics.)

Asking Research Questions

Once you have identified a specific topic, the next step is to focus the topic by asking pertinent research questions that you will attempt to answer—your "starting questions." For the specific topic of global warming, Cecelia's starting questions were as follows:

Is global warming really happening?

What causes it?

What are the consequences of global warming?

What can we do about it?

Posing these questions allowed Cecelia to begin her background reading in search of an answer, rather than reading aimlessly in an unfocused way.

Developing a Hypothesis

As you work through the research process, attempting to answer your starting questions, you should come up with a hypothesis—a tentative statement of what you anticipate the research will reveal. A working hypothesis specifically describes a proposition that research evidence will either prove or disprove. As you begin to gather background information on your topic, you should develop a hypothesis that will help you to focus your research. Cecelia moved from her starting questions to a working hypothesis as follows:

TOPIC

Global warming

RESEARCH QUESTIONS

Is global warming really happening?

If so, what causes it?

What are its consequences?

What can we do about it?

WORKING HYPOTHESIS

Global warming is a real event with potential catastrophic

consequences that must be stopped.

A working hypothesis should be stated in such a way that it can be either supported or challenged by the research. Cecelia's research will either support or challenge her working hypothesis that global warming is a real event with potential catastrophic consequences that must be stopped. The hypothesis is called "working" because you may find that you need to change or revise it during the course of the research.

5 Developing a search strategy

A search strategy is a plan for proceeding systematically with research. Once you have decided on your starting questions and working hypothesis, you are ready to outline your search strategy. Your first decision will be about the nature of your research. Will you be relying mostly on secondary (library and Internet) research or on primary (field) research? Secondary research is discussed in 8f-1 through 8f-5. Primary research is discussed in 8f-6.

The goal of a search is to build a working bibliography—a list of possible sources that may or may not eventually be used in the final paper. A working bibliography is typically about twice as long as the final bibliography for a research paper (see 8d for more about working bibliographies), because many of the sources you identify will turn out not to be applicable to your paper or not to be available in time for you to use in your research. By searching for sources in a systematic way, you avoid aimlessly wandering around the library or surfing on the Internet. The diagram in Figure 8.1 shows possible steps in a search strategy.

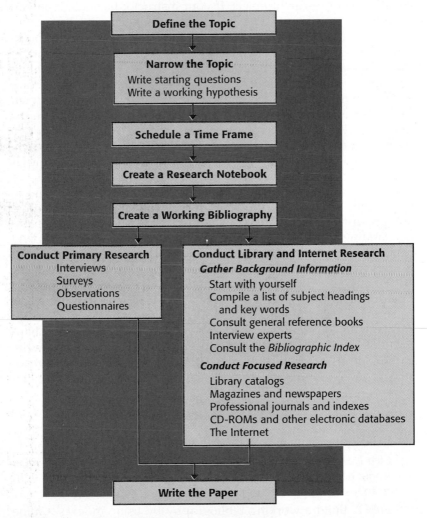

Figure 8.1   A Strategy for Writing a Research Paper

8b Schedule a time frame

If you have never done a research project before, you may be overwhelmed at the thought of such a large and complex task. If you break the job down into smaller parts, however, it will seem much more manageable. It will help to formulate a time frame in which to complete your research project. If your instructor has not given you deadlines, set your own dates for accomplishing specific tasks.

For a major project, allow at least three to four weeks for background research and a more focused search. As you begin to work in the library or on the Internet, you will see that searching and reading are time consuming. Plan to spend one or two hours in the library and/or on the Internet each day for the first month of your research project. After that, you may find that you can spend less time in the library. If your project involves primary research, allow one to two weeks for designing, conducting, and analyzing the primary research.

Schedule at least one to two weeks for preliminary writing. If you are a slow writer, you will need more time. To make sense of your subject and answer your starting questions, you will need to spend time studying and evaluating your sources, brainstorming, and prewriting. Eventually you should be able to express your understanding of the subject in a working thesis statement, which will control the shape and direction of the research paper and provide the readers with a sense of the paper's main idea or argument (see 3d-1).

Finally, give yourself enough time to plan, organize, and write a first draft and then several revisions. You need time to outline and construct your argument, using source information to reinforce or substantiate your findings in a clearly documented way (see Chapter 13). Most students need one to two weeks to organize and write a rough draft and an additional week to revise, edit, and proofread. As you can see from the following sample schedule, most research projects take an entire college term to complete.

Sample Schedule for Writing a Research Paper

(Allow approximately one week for each step.)

Step 1. Select a preliminary research topic; articulate starting questions; begin background research; schedule a time frame; begin to focus the topic (see 8e).

Step 2. Build a working bibliography by using indexes, online catalogs, databases, and the Internet (see Chapter 9); begin to locate sources in the library and on the Net (see 8f).

Step 3. Read and evaluate sources; take notes on relevant sources; in a research notebook, comment on the importance of sources to the topic and their relationship to other sources (see 10a); print out information from the Internet; write down complete bibliographical information for each source and make a note of Web site addresses, or URLs (see 8d-2).

Step 4. Arrange and conduct any primary research; complete the reading and evaluation of sources; identify gaps in the research and find more sources if necessary (see 8f).

Step 5. Begin preliminary writing in a research notebook—summarize key information; begin brainstorming on the topic; write a few possible thesis statements designed to answer the starting questions (see 12a).

Step 6. Write a thesis statement that will guide the direction of the piece; sketch a tentative outline or plan of the research paper (see 12a-2, 12b).

Step 7. Write a rough draft of the research paper; keep careful track of sources through accurate citations; take care to distinguish quotes and paraphrases and to document all source information appropriately (see Chapter 11); write a bibliography or references cited list (see Chapter 13).

Step 8. Revise and edit the rough draft; spell-check; check sentence structure and usage; check documentation of sources; solicit peer responses to the draft (see 5c).

Step 9. Print and proofread the final copy; have a friend or classmate proofread as well (see 5d, 5e).

EXERCISE 8.3

Using the sample time frame, draw up a time frame for your own research, with specific target dates for each step in the research process.

8C   Create a research notebook

It is important to create a notebook in which to record all the information relating to your research project. If you are using a word processor, you can take advantage of its storage capabilities to develop an electronic research notebook. Create a directory (see the Help box on page 21), and label it your research notebook directory. In this directory, you can create files to record your topic and your starting questions, notes from your background research and focused research, and your working bibliography (if you do not have bibliography software). In your electronic research notebook, you can also begin to articulate answers to your starting questions as your understanding evolves through research. As you investigate your topic, record not only what others have said on the subject, but also your own impressions and comments. You also can use research notebook files to develop your thesis statement and an informal outline or organizational plan for your paper, and to write all preliminary drafts of your paper.

If you do not have a computer, you might set up a ring binder with dividers for all of the files just described:

- Topic and starting questions
- Thesis statement and outline
- Research notes and comments
- Working bibliography
- Drafts 1, 2, 3, as needed

Many students like to record notes in their research notebooks, while others like to take notes on note cards.

1 Recording notes in a notebook

Whether the notebook in which you record your notes is handwritten or computer generated, be sure to keep your recorded notes separate from your comments. If your notebook is handwritten, you might use two columns when recording information: one for notes taken from the source and the other for comments, analyses, and queries. If your notebook is electronic, you can use your word-processing program's DOCUMENT COMMENTS (or ANNOTATIONS) feature to insert your comments and analyses into the notes taken from sources. Figure 8.2 shows a document comment on the screen.

2 Taking notes on note cards

Like notebooks, note cards can be either handwritten or computer generated. If you choose to handwrite notes on index cards, give each note card a descriptive title and take notes on only one side of each card to allow for easy sorting and scanning of information later on. Provide a page reference on your note card for all notes, both quoted and paraphrased (see Chapter 11). In the

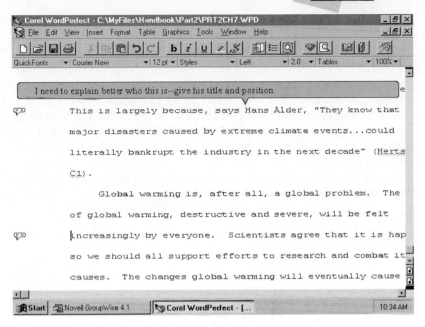

Figure 8.2   Example of a Document Comment in Corel WordPerfect

upper right-hand corner of the note card, include a control number that identifies the source. Then consecutively number your notes for each source. On the note card in Figure 8.3, the number 4.1 indicates that this note was the first one taken from source 4. It is im-

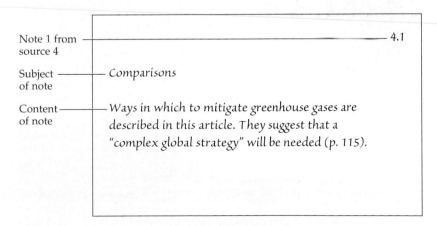

Figure 8.3   Note Card

portant to use this system consistently, since you will be relying on these cards later when you cite your sources in your final paper (see Chapter 13).

Some computer operating systems and Internet browsers offer computerized note card systems. Or you can purchase software for a note card system. Such a system can be particularly useful if you own a laptop computer that you can use while in the library taking notes. You can use the computer note cards just as you would use index cards: title each card by topic, and then type your notes onto the card provided by the computer. The computer note card system will sort the cards automatically by topic. The screen in Figure 8.4 contains five computerized note cards.

EXERCISE 8.4

Create a directory or folder to serve as your electronic research notebook. Divide it into subfolders to use as you pursue your search (a folder for your working bibliography, another for notes from sources, and so on).

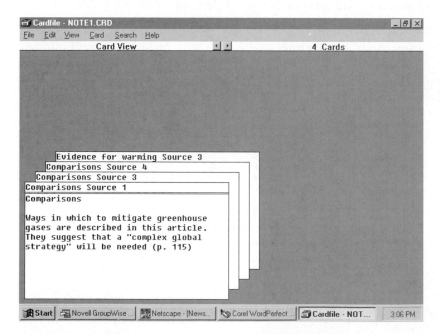

Figure 8.4   Example of Computerized Note Cards

8d Create a working bibliography

A **bibliography** is a listing of books and articles on a particular subject. When you submit a research paper, you include a bibliography to show readers what sources you consulted to find your information. As you begin your research, start a working bibliography, which will grow as your research progresses. This working bibliography likely will contain some sources that you ultimately will not use in your research paper, so entries need not be in final bibliographic form. However, it is important to record accurately all the information you will need to compose your final bibliography so that you do not have to track down sources twice. Include the author's full name, a complete title including subtitle and edition, the city and state where the work was published, the name of the publisher, and the date of publication.

1 Recording bibliographic information

You can prepare a working bibliography manually on index cards or electronically on a computer file. If you use index cards, record bibliographical information (author, title, and publication data) on one set of cards and content notes (see 11a-2) on a separate set. Figure 8.5 shows a sample bibliography card.

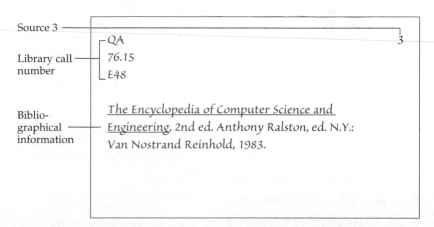

Source 3

Library call number

    QA
    76.15
    E48

Biblio-
graphical
information

The Encyclopedia of Computer Science and Engineering, 2nd ed. Anthony Ralston, ed. N.Y.: Van Nostrand Reinhold, 1983.

Figure 8.5   Bibliography Card

How do I use a computer bibliography program?

1. Open the bibliography software.

2. Follow the directions for entering data; usually you will be asked to enter information by category (author, title, publication data).

3. Wait for the bibliography program to generate your bibliography, based on the information you provide. It will format the information appropriately for a particular documentation style and place it in alphabetical order. Some bibliography programs will convert from one documentation style to another—for example, MLA (see 13a) to APA (see 13b) style.

4. Name and save your bibliography, as well as any works cited lists you may have generated from it.

NOTE: You still need to check your bibliography carefully to be certain the program has generated it in the correct format.

Using a computer to record bibliographic information is even more efficient because you can easily reformat the information later, when you prepare your final references or works cited list. Some word-processors are equipped with bibliographic software that automatically formats the information. (See the Help box.)

Here is Cecelia's working bibliography, which was generated electronically.

Britt, Robert. "The Heat Is On: Scientists Agree on Human Contribution to

Global Warming." Ion Science 1995. 13 Nov. 1998 <http://www.injersey.

com/Media/IonSci/features/gwarm/gwarm.html>.

Hertsgaard, Mark. "Who's Afraid of Global Warming?" Washington Post

21 Jan. 1996: C1. 13 Nov. 1998 <http://www.ji.org/jinews/newsline/

afraid2.htm>.

Hileman, Bette. "Climate Observations Substantiate Global Warming

   Models." Chemical and Engineering News 27 Nov. 1995. 13 Nov. 1998

   <http://jcbmac.chem.brown.edu/baird/Chem221/global/pg1.html>.

Krebs, Charles J. Ecology: The Experimental Analysis of Distribution and

   Abundance. 4th ed. New York: Harper, 1994.

Montague, Peter. "Global Warming--Part 1: How Global Warming Is Sneaking

   Up on Us." Rachel's Hazardous Waste News 26 Aug. 1992: 1. 22 Nov.

   1998 <http://www.envirolink.org/pubs/rachel/rhwn300.htm>.

Pate-Cornell, Elisabeth. "Uncertainties in Global Climate Change Estimates:

   An Editorial Essay." Climatic Change 33.2 (1996): 145.

Svitil, Kathy A. "Collapse of a Food Chain." Discover July 1995: 36-37.

2   Printing or saving online sources

If you are using sources from online databases, you may want to print out copies for later review or download them onto your own computer disk (see the Help box in 20b for how to download Internet sources). In either case, be sure that complete bibliographic information appears on the pages or files. If it does not, make a bibliography card for the source, in addition to the printout. If you print material from the World Wide Web, your browser may automatically include source information, but be sure to check. If you cannot find the complete address, or URL, on the printed copy, record it by hand.

EXERCISE 8.5

Establish a consistent format for entering the bibliographic information on your research, either as bibliography cards or as a computerized working bibliography. Meet with your peer group to discuss the sources in your working bibliography.

8e   Gather background information

Now is the time to gather background information, using your starting questions and working hypothesis as a guide. This information will help you conduct more focused research later on.

1 Starting with yourself

At the start of a research project, write down everything you already know about your topic. The list may be quite extensive or rather short. The important thing is to inventory your own knowledge first so that you can systematically build on that knowledge base. The more you know about your topic, the better you will be at judging the value of sources you read. Also check your biases and assumptions about the topic, asking yourself the following questions:

1. Do I already have a strong opinion about this topic?
2. Have I "rushed to judgment" about it without looking at all the facts?
3. Am I emotionally involved with the topic in some way that might bias my judgment?

If your answer to any of the above questions is "yes," think seriously about whether you will be able to keep an open mind as you read about the topic. If you will not, you might want to choose another topic.

2 Compiling a list of subject headings and key words

The cataloging system developed by the Library of Congress is the one most widely used for organizing library materials. In order to put information into related categories, the Library of Congress has developed a listing of subject headings. This listing is compiled in a multi-volume set, called the *Library of Congress Subject Headings* (or *LCSH*), available in both printed and computerized form. The *LCSH* is simply a listing of all of the subject headings used by libraries to classify source materials. Cecelia Chung, whose final research paper appears in Chapter 12, looked up the subject heading "Global warming" in the *LCSH*. Figure 8.6 shows what she found.

Notice that her topic was listed in the *LCSH* not as "Global warming" but as two related subjects, "Global temperature changes" and "Greenhouse effect, Atmospheric." Both of these subjects would prove to be important to her search. In addition to the main headings, the *LCSH* lists related subject headings that may lead to other potentially useful sources. Additional subjects are listed in the *LCSH* under RT (related term), BT (broader term), and NT (narrower term). The UF (used for) in Figure 8.6 means that the heading in bold is "used for" the other headings listed, which are *not* subject headings.

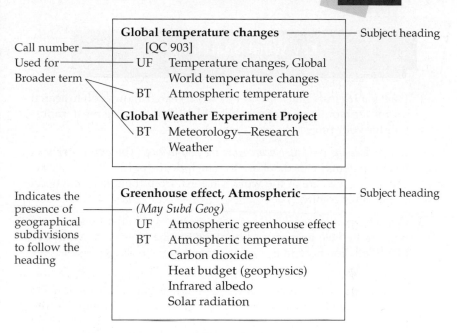

Global temperature changes ——————— Subject heading
Call number ———|— [QC 903]
Used for————|—— UF   Temperature changes, Global
Broader term ╲   World temperature changes
              ╲ BT   Atmospheric temperature

╲Global Weather Experiment Project
 ╲ BT   Meteorology—Research
          Weather

Indicates the   Greenhouse effect, Atmospheric———— Subject heading
presence of ———————— (May Subd Geog)
geographical   UF   Atmospheric greenhouse effect
subdivisions   BT   Atmospheric temperature
to follow the   Carbon dioxide
heading   Heat budget (geophysics)
                             Infrared albedo
                             Solar radiation

Figure 8.6   Library of Congress Subject Headings

Researchers use the subject headings in the *LCSH* to find both books and periodicals (magazines and journals) related to their topics. Whether you are using a regular library card catalog or a computerized catalog, the subject headings are the key to locating information on your topic. Searching a library's catalog is discussed in 8f.

Related to subject headings are **key words** (sometimes called descriptors or identifiers), which are used to identify the subjects found in electronic databases, including the Internet. The key words used to search for electronic sources may not be exactly the same terms that are used by the *LCSH* to categorize the subjects of books and periodicals. So, it is important at the outset of your research that you compile a comprehensive listing of both possible subject headings and possible key words for your topic. In an electronic database search, key words can be combined using what are known as **Boolean operators.** These operators, most commonly AND, OR, and NOT, tell the computer to combine key words in ways that it recognizes. (See Tips on Using Boolean Operators for Internet Searching, on page 174.)

Key Word Searching

1. *What is a key word search for?* A key word search allows you to search for the term or terms that you have identified as being most important for your project.

2. *Where does the computer search for the key words?* The computer will locate all items in the database that include the particular key words or terms anywhere in the work's record, from the title to the body to the bibliography.

3. *Can the computer supply other related words?* Typically the computer will not be able to supply synonyms for the key words you have identified. You need to think of as many key words as possible.

4. *What terms should I use as key words?* You will have to use your knowledge of the topic, gained through background reading, to come up with key words. For example, if you are searching the subject of UFOs, you might use *UFO* as a key word. But you also might want to try *flying saucers* or *paranormal events*.

5. *Can I do a key word search on the Internet?* The same kind of key word searching discussed here can be done on the Internet. (See Chapter 9 on Using the Internet for Research.)

3 Doing preliminary background reading in general reference books

We recommend that you begin your library search in the general reference section. Here you will find reference books that have condensed huge amounts of information into an accessible form. These sources can help you to define your subject area more clearly, to identify key words and important authors, and to gain a general understanding of your topic.

Most of the reference works listed on the following pages are available both in book versions and in computerized versions (either on CDs or on the Internet). Many libraries provide access to computer-based dictionaries, encyclopedias, thesauruses, bibliographies, almanacs, handbooks, and atlases. Such computerized reference sources often are more up-to-date and can be searched faster than the printed forms.

Dictionaries

Dictionaries typically provide concise information about words: definitions, pronunciations, usage, origin, and changes in meaning. It is essential to have a good desk dictionary to consult for all your writing. Some good ones include the following:

American Heritage Dictionary of the English Language. 3rd ed. Boston: Houghton, 1992.

Random House Dictionary of the English Language. 2nd ed. New York: Random, 1987.

Webster's Dictionary and *Roget's Thesaurus,* searchable through *My Virtual Reference Desk* <http://www.refdesk.com>.

Webster's Ninth New Collegiate Dictionary. Springfield, MA: Merriam, 1989.

Figure 8.7 shows the homepage for *My Virtual Reference Desk.*

Figure 8.7   My Virtual Reference Desk

Encyclopedias

Encyclopedias provide concise information on people, places, subjects, events, and ideas. Encyclopedias are particularly useful for locating general background information on a subject or person. Look in the encyclopedia's index for references to related subtopics and articles within the encyclopedia. Some general encyclopedias include the following:

Academic American Encyclopedia. Rev. ed. Danbury, CT: Grolier, 1995.
Encyberpedia: The Living Encyclopedia from Cyberspace <http://www.encyberpedia.com/ency.htm>.
Encyclopedia Americana. Rev. ed. New York: Grolier, 1998.
Encyclopaedia Britannica. Chicago: Encyclopaedia Britannica, 1992.

In addition to the general encyclopedias (print, CD, and online versions), there are also numerous specialized encyclopedias, such as the *Encyclopedia of American History* and the *Encyclopedia of World Art.* Listings of specialized encyclopedias by discipline can be found in Part 3 of this handbook.

Biographies

Biographies provide information on the lives and work of famous people. As with encyclopedias, there are both general and specialized biographies. General biographies include the following:

Current Biography: Who's News and Why. New York: Wilson, 1940 to present.
Dictionary of American Biography. New York: Scribner's, 1943 to present.

Bibliographies

Bibliographies are lists of books or articles about particular subjects. Some bibliographies appear at the end of an article or a book; others are entire books in themselves. General bibliographies include the following:

Guide to Reference Books. 10th ed. E. P. Sheehy. Chicago: American Library Association, 1986.
World Bibliography of Bibliographies. T. Besterman. Totowa, NJ: Rowman, 1963 (plus updates by A. F. Toomay).

Other Sources

The general reference section of a library contains many other sources that may be helpful in your research. Check with the reference librarian for the following types of sources, if they are relevant to your research: atlases, which contain maps; almanacs, which briefly present a year's events in government, sports, politics, and economics; yearbooks, which contain worldwide data; and handbooks, or fact books, which provide statistical data.

By reading about your topic in a number of general reference works, you can ascertain what is considered to be "common knowledge" about your topic. Common knowledge is information that is generally known and, therefore, need not be cited as the idea of one particular author. If you read the same information in three or more general sources, you can assume it is common knowledge. However, any facts or data found in general sources still need to be cited in your paper, and the reference source listed in your bibliography. (For information on citing sources, see Chapter 13; see also Chapter 11 on using sources.)

4 Interviewing experts or joining a discussion group

Even if your assignment does not specifically require primary research, it is a good idea to talk to experts in the field, if possible. You may know a professor or a family friend who is familiar with the topic. Make an appointment to talk to that person and get his or her advice on the topic. It is not necessary to conduct a formal interview—an informal conversation is generally sufficient. If there are online discussion groups or listservs on your topic, join in on the conversation or follow others' exchanges to gain a better understanding of your topic (see Chapter 21).

5 Consulting the *Bibliographic Index*

After surveying your own knowledge on a topic, reading background sources, and talking to experts, you should be able to narrow the focus of your topic. At this time, you may wish to consult the *Bibliographic Index*, an annual listing of bibliographies, arranged by subject. This index lists all the bibliographies on a particular subject in a given year (a bibliography of bibliographies). Browsing through this index for several recent years will give you a sense of the subject and its subtopics; in addition, you may find some pertinent sources on your topic.

EXERCISE 8.6

Using the suggestions outlined above, investigate background sources on your topic and begin to focus your research. Cast a wide net as you begin your research; you can always revise and refine your focus based on the information you locate. When you have completed your background reading and research, begin to search and read in a more focused way.

8f   Conduct focused research

Once background reading has helped you to understand your subject, narrow it to a manageable size, and formulate a hypothesis, you are ready to read in a more focused way on your topic. Conducting focused secondary research involves locating, through magazines, newspapers, journals, books, government documents, and the Internet, the specific information you need to write your paper. (For information on primary research, see 8f-6.)

1   Using library catalogs

Libraries have catalogs that list all the books and documents in the library. Library catalogs may be located in card files (which include cards for authors' names, subjects, and book titles), or they may be stored on computers. Although some libraries still use card files, either by themselves or in combination with computerized catalogs, most libraries today house their catalogs on computers. Computerized catalogs allow for ease of storage and ease of searching.

Card Catalogs

Information in a library's catalog will be organized alphabetically on three types of cards: author cards, subject cards, and title cards (see Figure 8.8). In some libraries, the author and title cards are kept in the same file. In other libraries, all three types of cards are stored in one alphabetical file.

Each card, regardless of type, contains basic information about the source it is cataloging. The *call number* may be the most important piece of information, because it tells you where the book is located in the li-

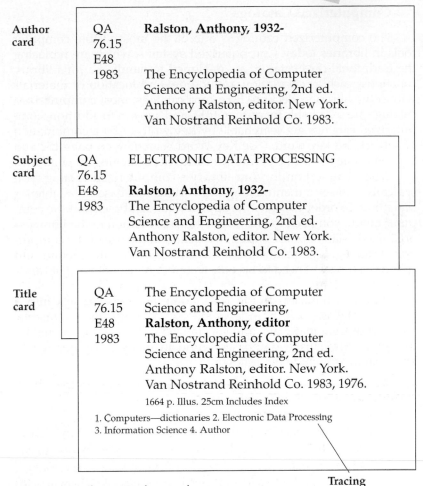

Author
card

QA
76.15
E48
1983

Ralston, Anthony, 1932-

The Encyclopedia of Computer
Science and Engineering, 2nd ed.
Anthony Ralston, editor. New York.
Van Nostrand Reinhold Co. 1983.

Subject
card

QA
76.15
E48
1983

ELECTRONIC DATA PROCESSING

Ralston, Anthony, 1932-
The Encyclopedia of Computer
Science and Engineering, 2nd ed.
Anthony Ralston, editor. New York.
Van Nostrand Reinhold Co. 1983.

Title
card

QA
76.15
E48
1983

The Encyclopedia of Computer
Science and Engineering,
Ralston, Anthony, editor
The Encyclopedia of Computer
Science and Engineering, 2nd ed.
Anthony Ralston, editor. New York.
Van Nostrand Reinhold Co. 1983, 1976.

1664 p. Illus. 25cm Includes Index

1. Computers—dictionaries 2. Electronic Data Processing
3. Information Science 4. Author

Tracing

Figure 8.8   Library Catalog Cards

brary. Most libraries use the Library of Congress system for their call numbers. In this system, a combination of letters and numbers is used to group sources by subject. Be sure to write down the call number of each source accurately, either on an index card or in your research notebook. Because books on the same subject are stored together, you may want to browse through the stacks for other related books after you find the one you were searching for. In Figure 8.8, notice the information in small print at the bottom of the card. This information is called the source's *tracing.* Using this information, you can find other subject headings under which the source is also cataloged.

Computerized Catalogs

The computerized catalog is one of the most visible computer tools in libraries today. Computerized systems, which are replacing the traditional card catalog, are designed to handle various library functions, such as circulation, cataloging, and location of materials within the library collection. Like card catalogs, most computerized catalogs are searchable by author, title, and subject; in addition, computerized catalogs are searchable by key word or by a combination of subject and key word. (See Key Word Searching on page 152 and Tips on Using Boolean Operators for Internet Searching on page 174.)

When you log on to your library's computerized catalog, you typically will see a menu listing the various databases available for searching. In order to select the appropriate database from the computer menu, you need to know how the information in the library is organized. Many libraries offer instruction in the use of the computerized catalog. If yours does, take advantage of such instruction, and spend the time you need to become a confident user of your library's computer system.

Typically, libraries divide their computerized catalogs into a general database, which indexes books, government documents, and audiovisual materials, and specialized databases, organized by discipline. Specialized databases found in many computerized library catalogs include the following:

Biological and Agricultural Sciences Index (lists articles from biology and agriculture journals)

Education Index (lists articles from education journals)

General Sciences Index (lists articles from journals related to science)

Humanities Index (lists articles from journals in the humanities)

Social Sciences Index (lists articles from social science journals)

Wilson Guide to Applied Science and Technology Index (lists articles from journals related to the applied sciences and technology)

Wilson Guide to Art Index (lists articles from art magazines and journals)

Wilson Guide to Business Periodicals (lists articles from business journals)

The articles that you find in a computerized catalog search may or may not be available to you in your own library, as most libraries can afford to subscribe to only a limited number of magazines, newspapers, and journals. Ask the librarian for a list of the periodicals your library subscribes to. Sometimes this information will appear right on the computer record when you locate the reference in the index. If your library does not own a particular magazine, newspaper, or journal, do not despair. Through interlibrary loan or the Internet, often you can locate an article and obtain it for your own use. Check with the librarian to find out about such reciprocal services.

When you are using computerized catalogs, it is important to be familiar with the *Library of Congress Subject Headings (LCSH)* (see 8e-2). To search a computerized database by subject, you must provide the computer with the official subject headings used by the Library of Congress, as listed in the *LCSH*. You also may want to search by title, author, or key word.

2 Using indexes to magazines and newspapers

The many specialized indexes, some of which are described in 8f-1, can be particularly helpful when you are searching in a focused way on a topic. In addition to being available through the library's computerized catalog, most also are available in print form.

Indexes are organized either by the type of publication they cover (the periodical indexes) or by the disciplines they cover (the discipline-specific indexes). We discuss discipline-specific indexes in 8f-3.

Magazines

Magazines and other publications that come out at regular intervals (usually longer than one day) are called periodicals. Articles in periodicals often can provide specific and up-to-date information on a topic. It is possible to locate magazine and newspaper articles both through computer searching and through print indexes. The most commonly used indexes to magazines are the *Readers' Guide to Periodical Literature* and the *Magazine Index*. In both sources, entries are arranged by subject and author. In looking at the *Readers' Guide,* Cecelia discovered that the subject headings "Global warming" and "Global climate change" both referred readers to the subject heading "Greenhouse effect" through a *See also* notation. Figure 8.9 on page 160 shows the beginning of the "Greenhouse effect" entry.

Newspapers

Libraries generally store back issues of newspapers on microfilm. You will need to use a newspaper index to locate relevant articles in newspapers. To gain access to articles in the *New York Times,* use the *New York Times Index,* which lists all major articles in the *Times* from 1913 to the present. The *Newspaper Index* lists articles from the *Chicago Tribune, Los Angeles Times, New Orleans Times–Picayune,* and *Washington Post.* Both indexes are arranged by subject.

Subject heading

Title of article

Illustrated

Author

GREENHOUSE EFFECT
See also
Framework Convention on Climate Change
Airborne particle analysis for climate studies [mass spectrometry] T. Peter. bibl f il *Science* v273 p1352-3 S 6 '96
Attacks on IPCC report heat controversy over global warming. T. Feder. il *Physics Today* v49 p55-7 Ag '96 pt 1
Ballooning over the Amazon [measurement of greenhouse gases and ozone; work of John Birks] *Science News* v150 p93 Ag 10 '96
Brave new world of Biosphere 2? [cover story] D. Vergano. il *Science News* v150 p312-13 N 16 '96
Butterfly displaced by climate change? [Edith's checkerspot; research by Camille Parmesan] J. Raloff. il *Science News* v150 p135 Ag 31 '96
Carbon debt: we all have one. A second look at global climate change [conclusions of the Intergovernmental Panel on Climate Change] G. J. Gray. *American Forests* v102 p22-3 Summ '96
Climate science and national interests. R. M. White. *Issues in Science and Technology* v13 p33-8 Fall '96
Controversy erupts over climate report [Intergovernmental Panel on Climate Change] *Science News* v150 p15 Jl 6 '96
Dirty climate. S. F. Singer. *National Review* v48 p62-3+ N 25 '96
Do disease cycles follow changes in weather? [global warming's effect on the carriers of human illness] K. S. Brown. il *BioScience* v46 p479-81 Jl/Ag '96
Farming and fishing in the wake of El Niño. J. Tibbetts. il *BioScience* v46 p566-9 S '96
Focus: plants of the future. J. Bower. il *Audubon* v98 p31 N/D '96

⋮

Hansen, James E. por *Current Biography* v57 p17-20 My '96
Human influence on the atmospheric vertical temperature structure: detection and observations. S. F. B. Tett and others. bibl f il *Science* v274 p170-3 N 15 '96
Mongolian tree rings and 20th-century warming. G. C. Jacoby, Jr. and others. bibl f il map *Science* v273 p771-3 Ag 9 '96
Oceanic carbon dioxide uptake in a model of century-scale global warming. J. L. Sarmiento and C. Le Quéré. bibl f il *Science* v274 p1346-50 N 22 '96
Plants: a secret weapon against global warming? [research by Walter Oechel] D. Graham. il *Technology Review* v99 p16–17 Jl '96
Reducing carbon by increasing trees [for greenhouse effect reduction] D. Hair and N. R. Sampson. il *American Forests* v102 p23-6+ Summ '96
Sky-high findings drop new hints of greenhouse warming [work of Benjamin Santer] R. A. Kerr. il *Science* v273 p34 Jl 5 '96
Stage set for curbing global warming gases. R. Monastersky. *Science News* v150 p54 Jl 27 '96
Urban trees and carbon. G. Moll and C. Kollin. il *American Forests* v102 p26+ Summ '96
Weathering Heights [extreme weather in Canada may be linked to greenhouse effect] D. Phillips. il *Canadian Geographic* v116 p25 My/Je '96
Economic aspects
Insurers: feeling the heat. P. L. Knox. il *World Press Review* v43 p38 D '96
Seasonal variations
Warming reaps earlier spring growth [study by Charles D. Keeling] R. Monastersky. *Science News* v150 p21 Jl 13 '96

Related subject heading
Periodical title

Volume 150, pages 312–313, November 16, 1996

Includes a portrait

Includes a bibliography

Figure 8.9   Listing from *Readers' Guide to Periodical Literature*

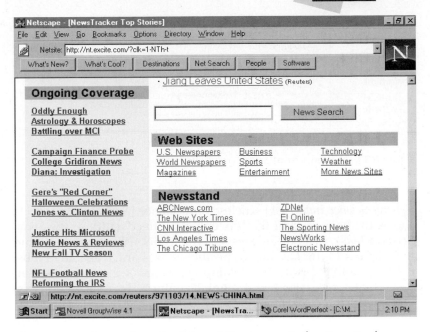

Figure 8.10   Screen from the Internet Newspaper Index NewsTracker

For business news, use the *Wall Street Journal Index*. Newspaper indexes are available in both print and computerized formats. Figure 8.10 shows a page from the Internet newspaper index NewsTracker, which can be used to access the many newspapers that are now available via the Internet. Using Excite's NewsTracker, you can read articles from many of the world's newspapers or you can search the news for specific articles about your topic. Excite's NewsTracker can be found at *http://nt.excite.com*.

3   Using indexes to professional journals

If you are researching a technical or academic subject, you will want to refer to articles written by professionals in the field. Professional journal articles are indexed in much the same way as magazine and newspaper articles. However, you will need to find a specialized index or database for professional articles in the particular discipline or subject area. For example, the *Social Sciences Index* lists articles from journals in the social sciences, and the

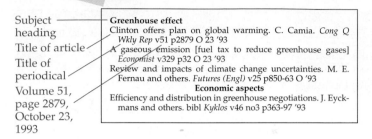

Subject heading
Title of article
Title of periodical
Volume 51, page 2879, October 23, 1993

Greenhouse effect
Clinton offers plan on global warming. C. Camia. *Cong Q Wkly Rep* v51 p2879 O 23 '93
A gaseous emission [fuel tax to reduce greenhouse gases] *Economist* v329 p32 O 23 '93
Review and impacts of climate change uncertainties. M. E. Fernau and others. *Futures (Engl)* v25 p850-63 O '93
Economic aspects
Efficiency and distribution in greenhouse negotiations. J. Eyckmans and others. bibl *Kyklos* v46 no3 p363-97 '93

Figure 8.11   Excerpt from *Social Sciences Index*

General Science Index lists articles from science journals. Figure 8.11 shows the beginning of the "Greenhouse effect" entry in the *Social Sciences Index*. Lists of indexes specific to disciplines can be found in Chapters 14–16. Discipline-specific indexes are available in most libraries, both in print and on computer. Some of the specialized indexes that can be searched through a computerized cataloging system are described in 8f-1.

4   Using CD-ROMs and other electronic databases

Locating specific information on a topic may require use of a variety of computerized search tools. In addition to your library's computerized catalog (8f-1) and computerized indexes to magazines, newspapers, and journals (8f-2 and 8f-3), investigate any CD-ROM databases available to you.

CD-ROM (compact disk—read only memory) databases make large amounts of information accessible by storing it digitally on compact disks. For example, the education index *ERIC* (Education Research Information Clearinghouse) is available in this format, as is the business index *ABI-INFORM*. CD-ROM databases are subject-specific, so you need to find out just which journals or subjects they cover. Most CD-ROM databases will provide an abstract of each work listed. By reading the abstract, you can gain a good sense of whether the article contains information useful for your research.

As with any computerized searching, it is important in using CD-ROMs to know your key words. Many CD-ROM databases use their own "controlled vocabulary," which may vary slightly from the subject headings used in the computerized catalog. Check with the librarian to discern whether there is a thesaurus or listing of subject headings for the particular database you are using. *ERIC* on disk, for example, uses the "ERIC Descriptors" as its method of cataloging by subject. To find the exact key word for your search, you need to look up your topic in the Descriptors volume.

Cecelia Chung, whose research on global warming we have been following in this chapter, looked up her topic in the CD-ROM database *Environmental Periodicals Bibliography*. Cecelia used these key words for a subject search: *global warming* and *global climate change*. One of the articles she found in her CD-ROM search is shown in Figure 8.12.

* *

NISC DISC REPORT
ENVIRONMENTAL PERIODICALS BIBLIOGRAPHY   June 1997

* *

TITLE: Uncertainties in global climate change
                      estimates. An editorial essay.
AUTHOR: Pate-Cornell, Elisabeth
SOURCE: Climatic Change; 1996 VOL. 33, NO. 2 (June),
                      page 145
KEY TERMS: Climate change; Uncertainty analysis;
                      Policymaking; Science role; Risk assessment;
                      Probability model
MAJOR TOPIC: AIR
NOTES: Assessing Uncertainty in Climate Change and
                      Impacts
RECORD ID: 1997-018516

TITLE: Evaluating the implementation of state-level
                      global climate change programs.
AUTHOR: Feldman, David L.; Wilt, Catherine A.
SOURCE: Journal of Environment and Development; 1996
                      VOL. 5, NO. 1 (March), page 46
KEY TERMS: Climate change, global; Environmental policy,
                      national and international; Government
                      compliance, state; Policy implementation
                      evaluation; Non-governmental organization
                      role; Evaluation criterion
MAJOR TOPIC: SOCIAL, POLITICAL AND PHILOSOPHICAL
                      ISSUES
RECORD ID: 1997-015217

Figure 8.12   **Listing from the *Environmental Periodicals Bibliography* CD-ROM**

5   Using Internet resources

The Internet is becoming an increasingly important research tool in all fields of study. A biologist observed that he can locate information crucial to his research in seconds or minutes via the Internet, when it used to take days or even weeks of searching through print sources. Since the Internet has become so crucial to research, we devote an entire chapter in this handbook to the topic. In Chapter 9, we follow Cecelia Chung's use of the Internet to research her topic of global warming. Cecelia discovered extensive information related to her topic on the Internet. For example, she discovered an Internet database called Envirolink, which led her to many other sources on her topic. You can find out more about how to use the Internet to enhance your research project by reading Chapter 9.

6   Doing primary, or field, research

In all disciplines, researchers use primary research methods to gather information and search for solutions to problems. (The researchers who read the printed reports generated from the primary research are using secondary research methods.) For example, when a chemist performs an experiment in the laboratory, that is primary research; when an archaeologist goes on a dig, that is also primary research. For our purposes, primary research will refer to the kind of field collection of data that you as a college undergraduate can do. Of course, there is a great deal to learn about the primary, or field, research methods commonly used in various disciplines; we will consider just a few field research techniques that can be adapted for use in a research project—observation, surveys, and interviews.

Observation

The general goal of observation is to describe and perhaps evaluate customary behaviors. Observation is best suited to the collection of nonverbal data. The observer watches people behave in customary ways in a particular environment or setting and takes notes. You might observe where people stand in an elevator, for example, or how they cross a street at an unmarked crosswalk. Through observation, you accumulate "field notes," which are used to analyze trends and discern customary behaviors. The disadvantages of observation include lack of control over the environment, lack of quantifiable data, and small sample size. Also, whenever an observer enters the environment to observe people, the participants' behaviors may cease to be natural. For example, if you stand for hours in an elevator taking notes about people's behavior, eventually they will notice you, and they may no longer behave the way they ordinarily would. As you think about your research project, consider whether observational data would enhance your report.

Surveys

Ideally, an entire population would be studied to gain insights into its society. However, polling an entire population is seldom feasible, so surveys are used to sample small segments of the population selected at random. The most frequently used sampling technique is random-digit-dialing of the telephone. Researchers have refined sampling techniques to be extremely accurate. One common kind of survey is the questionnaire, a form that asks for responses to a set of questions. Designing questions is a science that has been developed over the years. Although the details are beyond the scope of this book, the basic principles are to be sure that the questions you write are clear and understandable and written in such a way that the responses will be easy to tabulate. Researchers generally agree that closed questions, which require checking a box or answering yes or no, yield more usable data, but open-ended questions, which require a short written response, can provide valuable insights (though they are harder to interpret). Think through your research topic to see if a questionnaire might yield useful data. For an example of a paper that uses data from a student-generated questionnaire, see the social science paper in Chapter 16.

Interviews

Interviews are one particular type of survey. The advantages of the interview include flexibility (the questioner can interact with the respondent), speed of response (the questioner immediately knows the responses), and nonverbal behavior (the questioner can gather nonverbal as well as verbal clues). However, because interviews take time, fewer responses can be gathered. Another disadvantage is that the character of the interviewer himself or herself can influence the outcome of the interview. Here are some considerations in designing an interview:

1. Be certain that the questions are written down in advance and asked exactly as worded.

2. Be certain that you probe any unclear or incomplete answers.

3. Be certain that inadequate or brief answers are not probed in a biasing (directive) way.

If you decide that an interview would enhance your research, be sure that you conduct the interview professionally. Be prompt, have your questions ready, ask permission before taping responses, and be careful not to take up more of the person's time than you indicated when setting up the interview. A follow-up letter thanking the person for the interview is a polite gesture. After the interview, take time to review your notes and to clarify or supplement them as needed while the information is still fresh in your mind.

EXERCISE 8.7

Using the suggestions and resources given in this section, conduct focused research on your topic. Include both secondary (print and Internet) sources and primary (field) sources, as appropriate to your topic.

CHAPTER
9

Using the Internet
for Research

How can the Internet help me with my research? (9a)

What kind of information is available on the Internet?
(9b)

How can I find anything on the Web? (9c)

What is a search engine? (9c-1)

What does an Internet search look like? (9d)

?

One of the primary benefits of the Internet is that it connects computer users to information on computer networks around the world. People use the Internet for a variety of purposes, such as communicating with each other, playing games, sharing information, and selling products. We discuss the uses of computer networks for communication in Chapter 21. The Internet also has many educational uses. Much information published by educational institutions, libraries and service organizations, commercial and corporate providers, the public press, and the government can be located through an Internet search. This chapter introduces the ways in which the Internet can help with a research project.

9a   Use Internet sources throughout the research process

As mentioned in Chapter 8, the Internet is becoming increasingly important for research. Searching the Internet for information on a topic is similar in many respects to researching in the library. When beginning to research on the Internet, you should follow a search strategy, as outlined in 8a-5. Use the Internet for finding and exploring research topics, for background and focused searching, and even for collaboration with your peers and feedback from your instructor.

http://www.lib.
berkeley.edu/
TeachingLib/
Guides/Internet/
FindInfo.html

Current information on
Internet searching, from
UC Berkeley librarians

1   Finding and exploring topics

You do not need to wait until you are well into your research to turn to the Internet. In fact, you can use the Internet in the preparing stage of the writing process, to help you find a topic. The Help box in 3a-1 explains how to use the Internet to explore topic choices. Because Internet search tools (see 9c) are often organized by topic and subtopic in subject trees, you can use them to explore topic options. For an example of how one student used the Internet to explore research topics, see 8a-3.

2   Conducting background and focused research

Once you have decided on a topic, you can use the Internet to find background information and to search in a more focused way. Many of the reference materials used in the library for background information (such as dictionaries, encyclopedias, and handbooks) are also available through the Internet. Internet libraries and online collections are discussed in 9c-2. In particular, you will want to consult the list of Internet libraries in that section. Other sources of information available via the Internet include journals and magazines, newspapers, and government documents.

3   Collaborating and exchanging feedback

Email and online discussion forums are ideal for trying out your topic ideas on your instructor and your peers. These Internet tools are discussed in Chapter 21. As you research and write your paper, take advantage of the forums the Internet provides for sharing information—trade ideas, drafts, research sources, and revision feedback. For more information on collaboration, see also 3c-1, 4c, and 5e.

9b   Get to know the Internet and the Web

The many helpful research tools on the Internet include communication tools (email and mailing lists, bulletin boards and Usenet discussion groups, real-time writing with Internet Relay Chat or MOO) and collaboration tools (such as Microsoft's Netmeeting or Netscape's Collaborator). All of these tools are discussed in Chapter 21 on Communicating via Computer Networks.

But no doubt the main Internet tool that you will be using for research is the World Wide Web.

> http://magi.com/
> ~mmelick/it96jan.htm
> Beyond Surfing—tools
> and techniques for
> searching the Web

The World Wide Web, or the Web for short, is by far the easiest and most popular way of accessing information from the Internet. The Web provides a hypertext interface for "reading" Internet information. This means that information is presented in the form of a series of **hyperlinks,** each leading to another document or another location on the Internet. Documents structured as a series of links are called **hypertexts.** One simply uses a mouse to click on the link (usually a graphic or a word or phrase in blue type with blue underlining) to connect with the hyperlinked document. Researchers navigate the Web through the use of an Internet browser. Two of the most popular browsers today are Netscape Navigator and Internet Explorer.

1   Looking at Web documents: homepages and beyond

The World Wide Web, a huge spider web–like structure that encompasses computer networks throughout the world, seems to have been woven overnight. No one spider wove this web; anyone and everyone can contribute (see Chapters 19 and 20 for information on designing and writing for the Web). This is probably the Web's greatest strength as well as its greatest weakness. It is a strength because no single organization could have compiled the varied and vast amounts of information placed on the Web for anyone to access. It is a weakness because the lack of control creates an information hodge-podge, with the trivial alongside the profound. When looking for information on the Web, you may find everything from vanity homepages to the latest scientific information from a NASA space probe.

Though no entity controls the Web, the organization that establishes common standards for Web technology is the World Wide Web Consortium, or W3C. The Consortium consists of CERN, the organization in Geneva, Switzerland, that originated the Web; the Laboratory for Computer Science at MIT (Massachusetts Institute of Technology); and INRIA, the European W3C center. The Consortium does not regulate information on the Web. Rather, the Consortium establishes technical standards that ensure that the Web will be accessible to people around the world.

2 Respecting copyright protection for Internet material

The unprecedented growth of the Internet has spawned numerous debates about censorship and freedom of information. At issue is the amount of control that governments should be able to exercise with regard to information found on the Internet. Because information that you access electronically is in the form of pixels and not print, everything from the Internet that you see on your screen is a copy of a file located on someone else's computer. Electronic sharing of information via the Internet is predicated on the copying of files—including files of digitized music, art, graphics, or films—from one computer to another. This ability to copy the work of others has led people to ask legislators to place restrictions on copying, or "borrowing," information from the Internet.

Current legal interpretation of copyright law indicates that anything (such as text, graphics, or music) placed on the Internet by an individual or group is presumed to be copyrighted by its authors. This interpretation is based on the fact that any information found on the Web has in a sense been published; that is, it has been placed where thousands of people can read it. However, the ease with which information can be copied and distributed via the Internet makes it nearly impossible to enforce such a rigid interpretation of copyright law. The debate over rights is likely to continue to rage, as commercial authors and publishers seek to receive just compensation for their work and Internet boosters try to preserve the free flow of Internet information. The Copyright Website at *http://www.benedict. com* provides detailed information on the copyright controversy.

Although as a student you probably will not be reproducing source material in any form that would require you to procure permission from the copyright holder, be sure to document in your research paper any and all information found on a Web site. To learn about how to document information from the Internet, see Chapter 13.

9c   Search the Internet and the Web

Many corporations, nonprofit organizations, and special interest groups maintain information-rich Web sites. The purposes of these sites vary from disseminating information to peddling propaganda to luring customers into spending money. When you use information from an Internet source, remember that it probably has not been reviewed by anyone other than members of the organization that maintains the site. For example, a review of computers on Gateway Computer's Web site is likely to be biased in favor of Gateway products, and a discussion of gun control at the National Rifle Association's site will reflect that organization's views. (See Chapter 10 for guidelines on evaluating Internet sources.)

1   Using search engines to locate information

How do you go about finding specific information on a particular topic? The most reliable way is to use one of the **search engines,** such as Yahoo! or WebCrawler, designed to help users locate information on the Internet. Many of these search engines automatically find and catalog new sites as they are added to the Web, indexing information by title or key words.

http://www.onlineinc. com/onlinemag/ MayOL/zorn5.html Tips for advanced searching, from ONLINE magazine

However, this indexing system has become inefficient as the Internet has continued to grow at a phenomenal rate. When you enter a key word for a search, you may receive a list of thousands of sites that include that key word. So, to narrow the search parameters, many search engines have **subject trees**—hierarchical listings that lead more and more specifically toward the topic of interest. The combination of subject trees and key word searching is enormously powerful.

Searching via Subject Trees

A subject tree is basically an organized index of topics and subtopics. The Infoseek guide to information on the World Wide Web, for example, starts with the following subject areas on the opening screen: Arts & Entertainment, Business & Finance, Computers & Internet, Education, Government & Politics, Health & Medicine, Living, News, and Reference. Using this subject tree, you can narrow the scope of your search. For example, if you were interested in finding out about Brazil's form of government, you could select the "Government & Politics" subject list. Then, once you were in that subtopic, you could type in the key word *Brazil*.

AltaVista is a popular search engine because it is both fast and comprehensive, including listings from newsgroups in addition to links to thousands of Web pages. Other search engines that offer both subject trees and key word searching include Lycos, Yahoo!, and Excite. Use several different search engines to look for information on your topic. Each search engine is organized slightly differently, so each may yield different results. Or you can use a search engine that searches many databases simultaneously, such as ProFusion or WebCrawler.

A few search engines are organized by academic subject areas. These include Yanoff's Internet Services List and the Clearinghouse for Subject-Oriented Internet Resource Guides. The lists in such search engines are prepared by individuals or groups that have evaluated and screened entries for their usefulness to academic researchers. Most subjects of interest to academics are covered, including sciences, social sciences, technology, humanities, government, and health.

Searching with Key Words

Once you have selected a search engine and narrowed your way down a subject tree, you need to determine what search terms to try. If you searched your library's collection (see 8e-2), you may already have identified subject headings and key words that you can use. Enter a key word that identifies your topic and ask the engine to search for **hits** of that key word—Web pages on which the word appears. Many search engines also permit more sophisticated, customized searches, but the options differ from one search engine to another. Check the search engine's HELP screen to discover ways in which you can customize your search, particularly if you are getting hundreds or even thousands of hits for your search term.

Search Engines

AltaVista
http://altavista.digital.com

Large, comprehensive database. Key word searching only. Supports Boolean searching (see Tips on Using Boolean Operators for Internet Searching).

Clearinghouse for Subject-Oriented Internet Resource Guides
http://www.clearinghouse.net

Selective collection of topical guides to academic subjects.

Excite
http://www.excite.com

Subject tree and key word searching available. Supports Boolean searching.

Infoseek
http://guide.infoseek.com

Subject tree and key word searching available. Does not support Boolean searching.

Lycos
http://lycos.com

Subject tree and key word searching available. Supports Boolean searching.

ProFusion
http://profusion.ittc.ukans.edu

Searches multiple engines simultaneously, using key words (includes most search engines in this table). Supports Boolean searching.

WebCrawler
http://webcrawler.com

Subject tree and key word searching available. Includes newsgroups and email. Supports Boolean searching.

Yahoo!
http://yahoo.com

Subject tree and key word searching available. Includes news, chat, and email. Does not support Boolean searching.

Yanoff's Internet Services List
http://www.spectracom.com/islist

Selective collection of guides to academic subjects.

Using Boolean Operators

One of the ways in which search engines allow you to focus is by means of Boolean operators—for example, AND and NOT (see Tips on Using Boolean Operators for Internet Searching). The same principles used to search by key word in a library database also apply to searching on the Internet. For example, if you type *childcare in Utah,* you may get all of the hits for *childcare* in addition to all of the hits for *Utah,* yielding thousands of sources. But if you combine the terms using the Boolean operator AND, you ask the search engine to find only those sources that include both *childcare AND Utah* in the same source (the AND limits the search). To limit the search

Tips on Using Boolean Operators for Internet Searching

Online databases use what are termed Boolean operators to combine two or more terms in ways that the computer recognizes. The Boolean operators most commonly used are AND, OR, and NOT.

1. Be sure to use the appropriate Boolean operator.
   a. AND (&) limits the search, because both key words must be found in the search. For example, if you wanted to find information only on cats as pets, you could limit your search with the AND operator, typing in *pets AND felines.* The search would then be limited to those sources that included both words.
   b. OR (|) expands the search, because any text with either key word will be included in the search results. For example, if you wanted to expand your search to include both dogs and cats, you would use the OR operator, typing in *dogs OR felines.* Both groups would then be included in your search.
   c. NOT (!) limits the search by excluding any text containing the key word after the operator. For example, if you wanted to exclude dogs from your search of pets, you could do so with the NOT operator, typing in *pets NOT dogs.*
2. Enter Boolean operators in UPPERCASE letters (unless you use the symbols).
3. Leave a white space before and after each Boolean operator.
4. If your phrase is complex, involving several Boolean operators, use parentheses: *(pets AND felines) AND (NOT dogs).* The same search can be indicated using symbols: *(pets & felines) & (! dogs).*

even more, you could add the Boolean operator NOT: *childcare AND Utah NOT preschool.* Then, any sources mentioning preschool would be eliminated from the list.

Using Quotation Marks

Another way to focus the search in some search engines is by using quotation marks, which indicate that the words must appear in a particular order in the text. For example, *"global warming"* would tell the search engine that you are not interested in *global* or *warming* by itself; you want only the two terms in combination, exactly as written inside the quotation marks. In her search on global warming (see 9d), Cecelia found that Yahoo! yielded over 1,000 hits for *global warming* without quotation marks and 37 hits for *"global warming."*

The only way to see if your search is yielding the results you are after is to browse through the listing of sites found by the search engine. Most search engines provide a brief description of the site, so you can quickly ascertain whether or not the search is finding relevant sources. If it is not, try again with new search terms, subject areas, or delimiters (such as Boolean operators). Make use of the search engine's HELP screen if you are not achieving the results you desire.

Using Internet library and periodical collections

If you are working in a particular academic subject area, it may be more efficient to use virtual library collections instead of (or in addition to) search engines. Virtual libraries are often organized in much the same way as traditional libraries—with separate listings for periodicals, dictionaries, government documents, and so on. But they are generally more limited than regular libraries, so you should not rely on them exclusively. Rather, use a virtual library search as a supplement to a traditional library search.

Searching Virtual Libraries

Many libraries make some of the information from their collections available via the Internet. For example, the online collection of the University of California is available at the site listed in Internet Libraries and Collections. You can also use LibCat, which provides links to hundreds of libraries with Web access, or LibWeb, which provides links to online document and image collections of libraries around the world. Once you connect with these sources, you will need to browse through an index much like the online catalog in your own library, using key word and subject searches to locate specific information.

Internet Libraries and Collections

AskERIC Virtual Library http://ericir.syr.edu	Includes the ERIC database and materials
Internet Public Library http://www.ipl.org	Reference site built by the University of Michigan
LibCat http://www.metronet.lib.mn.us/lc/lc1.html	Links to hundreds of online libraries
My Virtual Reference Desk http://www.refdesk.com	Good starting point for locating online reference materials
Online Reference Tools http://www.library.cmu.edu/bySubject/CS+ECE/lib/reftools.html	Links to reference sites in many academic subjects
Purdue's Virtual Library http://thorplus.lib.purdue.edu/olibrary/index.html	Lists many online journals by academic subject
University of California–Berkeley, LibWeb http://sunsite.berkeley.edu/cgi-bin/welcome.pl	Links to online documents and image collections around the world
University of California–Riverside, Infomine http://lib-www.ucr.edu	Lists many online sources by academic subject
Virtual Information Center http://www.lib.berkeley.edu/Collections	Links to reference sites in many academic subjects
Virtual Reference Collection http://www.lib.uci.edu/home/virtual/virtual.html	Reference site built by the University of California–Irvine
Virtual Reference Desk http://www2.lib.udel.edu/ref/docs/virtref.htm	Reference site built by the University of Delaware

Some libraries have special online directories that link researchers to resources in specific subject areas. For example, the University of California at Riverside sponsors the Infomine Internet Library. Its resources are divided topically into major subject disciplines, such as scientific and medical sources, government sources, and social sciences and humanities sources.

Searching Government Documents

The federal government maintains numerous sites that you may want to use for research. The White House Web site offers an online photographic tour of the White House and provides links to important information about the federal government, including pending legislation, recently produced government documents, and Cabinet activities and reports. At the site produced by NASA, you can find information on space flights, space research, and aeronautics. By using a search engine, you can locate specific information on hundreds of other government Web sites, including city and state sites.

Searching Online Periodicals

Journals and magazines that are published on the Web can be a good source for a research paper. Several publishers now offer online versions of their publications to consumers. Often you can access the full texts of articles that appear in the print version. For example, the *New York Times* is available online, as is *Time* magazine. Once again, there is no one quick and easy way to locate online periodicals. If you know the name of the publication, you can search for it by name, using one of the search engines described in 9c-1. In addition, some Web sites will link you to major journals, newspapers, and magazines. For example, Ecola's 24-hour Newsstand provides links to thousands of magazines and newspapers from around the world, catalogued by region and organized by topic (business, health, religion, sports, travel, social issues, and so on). Time Warner provides an extensive site for its online magazines, searchable through Pathfinder. Using Pathfinder, you can locate information by key word as well as major subject area. Finally, you can use a search engine such as Excite or Yahoo! to search for news in magazines and newspapers by selecting "NewsTracker" or "Today's News" from the subject index.

Use Internet sources in combination with indexes in other media—print or CD (see 8f-4). Note that URLs change often. If the URL we have listed does not work, try shortening the address or searching by title. Also, go to *http://www.abacon.com* and click on the Web site for this handbook to get updates on URLs and additional sites to search.

Internet Sites for Government Documents

Bureau of the Census
http://www.census.gov

Social, demographic, and economic information; index a–z; searchable by place, location, and word

Bureau of Justice Statistics
http://www.ojp.usdoj.gov/bjs

Statistics on all criminal justice topics—law enforcement, drugs, crime, and so on

Bureau of Labor Statistics
http://stats.bls.gov

Statistics by region, searchable by key word; economy at a glance

Department of Education
http://www.ed.gov

Educational initiatives; news; publications; programs

Fish & Wildlife Service
http://www.fws.gov

Information related to fish and wildlife

Library of Congress
http://lcweb.loc.gov

Centralized guide to information services provided by the Library of Congress

National Institutes of Health
http://www.nih.gov

Health information, grants, health news; database searchable by key word

National Library of Medicine
http://www.nlm.nih.gov

Free Medline searches; other medical databases

NASA
http://www.nasa.gov

Tracking of current space flights and missions, including Pathfinder on Mars

Statistical Abstract of the U.S.
http://www.census.gov/stat_abstract

Collection of statistics on social, economic, and international subjects

Thomas (congressional legislation)
http://thomas.loc.gov

Full text of current bills under consideration by US House and Senate

White House
http://www.whitehouse.gov

Information on federal government initiatives, tours, and the President, Vice President, and First Lady; includes a help desk

Internet Sites for Online Periodicals

CNN Interactive *http://www.cnn.com*	CNN news from around the world; includes audio and video clips
Ecola Newsstand *http://www.ecola.com/news*	Links to newspapers and magazines in the United States and around the world; searchable by subject
Electronic Library *http://www.elibrary.com*	Key word searching of online magazines and newspapers; subject tree
Excite NewsTracker *http://nt.excite.com*	News headlines from Excite (includes Reuters and UPI)
Lycos News *http://www.Lycos.com/news*	News headlines from Lycos news service (includes CNN, ABC, Reuters, and others)
New York Times *http://www.nytimes.com*	Daily contents of the *New York Times*
Time/Warner Publications *http://pathfinder.com*	Articles and top stories from periodicals such as *Time, People, Money,* and *Fortune*
Yahoo! Today's News *http://yahoo.com/headlines*	News headlines from Yahoo! news service (includes CNN, ABC, Reuters, and others)

EXERCISE 9.1

Open your Internet browser and explore several of the search tools described above, including library links, government links, and newspaper links. Take an online tour of the White House, try searching the *New York Times* database, or find an online version of a local or regional newspaper. (Search for the newspaper by title, using any available search engine.)

3   Bookmarking important sites

When you find a site that you plan to return to frequently, use your browser's BOOKMARK feature to mark the site for easy access the

HELP

How do I use the bookmark and history features?

Your Internet browser may have features that allow you to mark sites for future use and find out where you have been in a given search.

1. Marking Internet sites:
   a. When you locate a site that interests you, add this site to your list of bookmarks. The browser will link this bookmarked site so that all you need to do to launch the site is select it from the bookmark list.
   b. Check the list of bookmarks: the site you just selected should now be listed. The next time you want to visit the site, use the bookmark to locate it quickly.
   c. As you collect more bookmarks, take advantage of your browser's organization feature. (Different browsers offer different ways to organize bookmarks.) If you work in a lab, you may wish to save your bookmarks to a disk.

2. Using the HISTORY feature to retrace your steps in an Internet search:
   a. Select the command your browser uses to display the history of an Internet session. All of the sites you visited in the current session will be displayed.
   b. Use the history listing to recall sites that you visited but neglected to bookmark.

NOTE: Once you close your browser, the history will be lost, but the bookmarks will remain.

next time (see the Help box). If you work in a computer lab, you may want to save your bookmarks to your own disk.

9d   Follow a student Internet search

To show you how a search might work, in this section we follow the Internet search of Cecelia Chung, the student whose research paper appears in Chapter 12. Cecelia was interested in global warming. Her starting questions were

Is global warming really happening?

What causes it?

What are the consequences of global warming?

What can we do about it?

Her search strategy included looking for current sources on the Internet. She used the Yahoo! database as a launching point for her Internet search.

When Cecelia opened the Yahoo! guide to information on the World Wide Web, she saw several potentially interesting subject categories listed (see Figure 9.1). Noticing that the word "Environment" was listed under the "Society & Culture" subject heading, she clicked on "Society & Culture," where she discovered a subcategory called "Environment and Nature." She typed the words *global warming* into the search screen and asked Yahoo! to search just the "Environment and Nature" category.

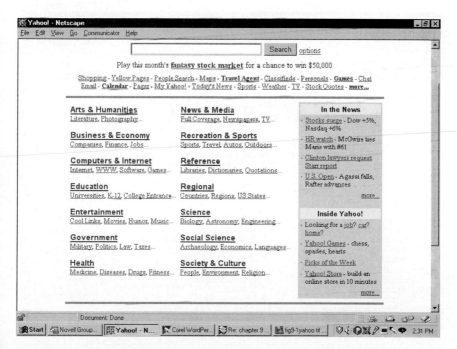

Figure 9.1 Yahoo! Subject Tree

That search yielded more than 1,000 hits on Web sources that contained either the word *global* or the word *warming*. Cecelia realized at this point that she needed to narrow the search further, especially since many of the links listed appeared to be irrelevant to her research topic. For example, one listing was "Record dengue fever cases in Singapore." She could have looked at the links under a specific subcategory within "Environment and Nature," such as "Climate Change Policy," which had 48 hits. (The number in parentheses in the Yahoo! listing indicates the number of Web links found within that particular subcategory; see Figure 9.2.) But she decided instead to focus her search by putting the search terms in quotation marks so that Yahoo! would look for the key words together in sequence rather than separately. When she typed *"global warming"* in quotation marks and clicked SEARCH, Yahoo! informed her that there were now 37 hits, a much more focused result (see Figure 9.3). As she browsed through the list, she found that the sources seemed to be exactly on the topic of interest. One that caught her attention was Envirolink, "the largest online environmental information resource on the planet." She followed the link to the Envirolink library and

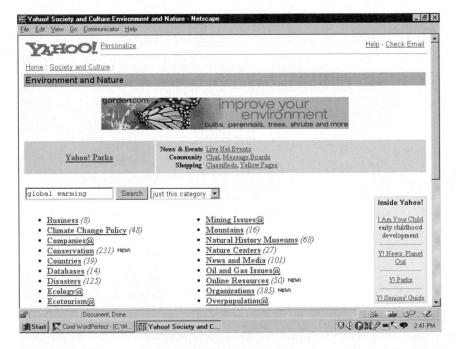

Figure 9.2   Hits on *global warming*

Figure 9.3   Hits on *"global warming"*

searched there for information on global warming, finding several government and organization sources that were helpful.

After reading through the 37 sources and evaluating them for their relevance to her research questions, she printed out a few for later use. Two of the sources appeared to be biased in their approach (see 10a)—particularly one site, sponsored by a large labor organization, that argued against taking a stronger stance on auto emissions for economic reasons. Tighter emissions standards would obviously affect the jobs of the organization's members.

Cecelia then went to the Infoseek Directory to search for newspaper and magazine sources available online. She used both Premier News (news stories from several major journals and magazines), which yielded 82 hits for *"global warming"*, and Top News (news stories currently in the headlines), which produced 17 hits for *"global warming"*. Of all these links, three were of particular interest to her: one article from *Chemical and Engineering News*, another from *Ion Science*, and a third from the *Washington Post*.

In addition to searching for information on the Internet, Cecelia also searched her library's database for books and journals. She found one book and one journal article that proved useful. As you can see, following the suggestions in Chapter 8 and in this chapter for searching the Internet yielded the kind of focused information that Cecelia needed.

EXERCISE 9.2

Pick a topic that interests you and begin a search. First use a search engine with a subject tree to work your way down the database; then type in a key word and see what results you achieve. Check out some of the links. Are you finding relevant sources? If not, try narrowing your search using AND or NOT; you can also combine terms in quotation marks. Record your results, including the URLs of the sites, and report to your classmates.

Evaluating Electronic and Print Sources

How can I tell if a Web site has reliable information? (10a)
What makes a source worth reading? (10a-1)
What makes a source worth using? (10a-2)
How important is the date something was published? (10a)
Are there ways to evaluate an author's credibility when
   conducting an Internet search? (10a)

As a researcher in today's information environment, one of your most important tasks is to evaluate what you read. The tendency to believe everything one reads is dangerous, especially with respect to Internet sources. Print sources typically undergo a rigorous process of peer review and evaluation before they are published. (Peer review refers to the practice of sending written material out to experts in the field for evaluation before it is actually published.) In contrast, the screening process for Internet materials is usually determined by the author. Many people who create Web sites have a sense of personal integrity, but others are less than forthright in the ways

http://www.science.
widener.edu/~withers/
webeval.htm
A fabulous collection
of materials to help
you evaluate all kinds
of electronic and
print texts

How do I find a site's homepage?

To locate a site's homepage, you can travel up the URL's directory path.

1. Open your browser and locate the site that interests you.
2. Look at the URL, listed on the LOCATION line of your browser.
3. Back your way up the URL by deleting the last section of the address, following the last slash. Hit ENTER to retrieve the new page.
4. Look at the URL of the page you have now located.
5. Continue backing up in the URL until you reach the site's homepage.

NOTE: A well-designed Web page contains a link to the site's homepage.

they use the medium to promote themselves or their viewpoints. Reading with a critical eye is always important, but it is particularly crucial in dealing with Internet information (see 2b).

10a   Choose legitimate sources

Because you will be relying on your sources to provide the evidence and authority to support your hypothesis, it is crucial that you choose legitimate sources. Your reputation as a researcher may be at stake. Choosing a legitimate source is a two-step process. First decide whether or not the source is worth reading. Then decide whether or not the source is worth using in the research paper.

http://www.library.
cornell.edu/okuref/
research/skill26.htm
Another excellent
source-evaluation page

1   Deciding whether the source is worth reading

To save yourself a great deal of time, quickly assess a source by skimming for a few key elements.

Relevance

Is the source relevant to your research? That is, does it address the topic you are researching? Sometimes a title will mislead you; a source will turn out to be on another topic entirely or on an aspect of the topic that does not interest you. If a source is not relevant, quickly move on.

Publisher or Sponsor

Who is the sponsoring organization or publisher? Is the article in a popular magazine, such as *Ladies' Home Journal*, or a professional journal, such as *Journal of Behavioral Sciences*? Depending on the nature of the research project, it may or may not be appropriate to use information from the popular press, which tends to be less scholarly than information found, for example, in a professional journal. For many college papers, however, the popular press—including major newspapers like the *New York Times* and magazines like *Time* and *Newsweek*—can certainly be useful. The publishers of newspapers and popular magazines are typically commercial publishers. The publishers or sponsoring organizations for professional journals are usually academic societies, such as the Modern Language Association or the Society for Engineering Educators. Generally you can rely on the information found in publications produced by these academic entities. But no information, regardless of its publisher or sponsoring agency, should be accepted at face value without critical evaluation (see 2a).

Although determining the sponsoring organization or individual is no less important for an Internet site than for a print source, it may not be as easy to accomplish. One clue to the nature of the sponsoring organization is the URL itself. Internet conventions have been established to identify domains for Web sites. These domains tell you something about the nature of the sponsoring organization. Looking at the domain of a Web site will help you to understand the purpose behind the page—whether educational or commercial, for example. Common domains include

- Education (.edu)
- Government (.gov)
- Nonprofit organization (.org)
- Commercial (.com)
- Network (.net)
- Military (.mil)
- Other countries (.ca for Canada; .uk for United Kingdom)

How do I find out about an author through an Internet search?

1. Open a search engine such as AltaVista or Infoseek.
2. In the search box, type the name of an author about whom you want information.
3. Choose phrase searching if it is available. If not, put the name in quotation marks.

NOTE: By typing *"Nicholas Negroponte"* into the AltaVista search engine, we found hundreds of columns in *Wired* magazine written by Negroponte. In addition, we found biographies, book reviews, speeches, interviews, and photographs. We learned that Negroponte is the director and founder of MIT's MediaLab.

Author

In addition to a sponsoring organization, is an individual author listed? Look carefully at both print and online sources to evaluate the author's credentials. Does he or she work for a government agency, a political group, a commercial industry, or an educational institution? Often the author's professional affiliation will be noted at the bottom of a journal or magazine article. A Web site may have an "About the author" page. Of course, the sponsoring organization itself may provide the author with credibility. We assume, for example, that anyone who writes for *Time* or *Newsweek* magazine must have appropriate credentials. National magazines are selective about their writers and extremely careful to provide authoritative information to their readers. Of course, this does not mean that sources written by authors in magazines should not be read critically (see 2b).

Timeliness

Be sure that you check the date of any piece you encounter. In many fields, the timeliness of the information is as important as the information itself. For example, if you are researching a medical topic, you want to be certain that your sources include the most up-to-date research. One of the many benefits of the Internet is that it allows information to be updated continually, but unfortunately not all Web sites list the dates on which they were first posted and last updated. With print sources, you need to be especially careful about when a piece was written. Months or even years may go by between when something is discovered and when it finally appears in print. Thus, research conducted many months or years ago may just now be appearing in print. In fields where information is changing rapidly, such as medicine, access to current information can be crucial.

Although the instant access of the Internet compares favorably with the lag time often associated with print sources, the down side of the Internet is that it is sometimes difficult to know what information is reliable. Many ideas presented on the Internet have not stood the test of time or endured the rigors of peer review. Typically, information that appears in printed sources, in contrast, has been rigorously reviewed by peers, editors, and professional reviewers before it appears in print. Of course, there are exceptions. You need look no further than your local supermarket counter to find printed sources, such as the *National Enquirer* or the *Star,* that are not appropriate sources of reliable information for a research paper.

Cross References

Is the source cited in other works? You can sometimes make decisions about a work's credibility by considering how it is cited by other sources. When you are researching a topic, sometimes one author's name will come up repeatedly in references and in discussions. This author is probably an expert on the topic; it would be worth your while to check into sources written by that person.

2 Deciding whether the source is worth using

Once you have decided that a source is worth reading, read and evaluate the source to determine whether or not you want to use it in your paper. First look at the author's rhetorical stance (see 3a-2). Then evaluate the content of the piece itself.

Rhetorical Stance

Who is the intended audience for the piece? Does the title help you to understand which readers it is targeting? Is there evidence that the author has taken a particular stance in a controversy on his or her subject? Journals and magazines typically write for particular target audiences, who they assume share certain biases and opinions.

Elements to Examine to Assess a Potential Source's Appropriateness

Print Sources	Electronic Sources
Title and Subtitle: Check both the title and the subtitle for relevance to your topic. For example, you could not be sure that a book entitled *Wishes, Lies, and Dreams* was appropriate without reading the subtitle: *Teaching Children to Write Poetry.*	**Title and Subtitle:** Check the Web page title (found on the top line of your screen, above the browser window) and the title on the page itself for their relevance to your topic.
Copyright Page: Check this page, just after the title page, to find out who published the book, where it was published, and when.	**Copyright Information:** At the bottom of the homepage, you should find information about who sponsors the site.
Table of Contents: Check the titles of parts, chapters, and sections. The outline of a book can show you the topics covered and the detail of that coverage.	**Major Links to Secondary Pages:** Check to see if the site includes links to secondary pages that elaborate on subtopics.
Abstract: Read the abstract, if included. It will provide you with a concise summary.	**Abstract:** Read the abstract, if included. It will provide you with a concise summary.
Preface: Read the preface. This is where the authors generally set out their purpose.	**Introduction:** Read any introductory material on the homepage. It should tell you about the site's purpose.
Chapter Headings and Subheadings: Check the headings and subheadings to find out what specific subtopics will be discussed.	**Headings and Subheadings:** Look closely at the major divisions on the homepage. They may tell you how detailed the site is.

(continued)

Print Sources	Electronic Sources
Conclusion: Read any conclusion or afterword. It may give you another sense of the authors' stance.	**Conclusion:** Read any concluding material on the final page of the site. It may give you another sense of the authors' stance.
Author Note: To evaluate credibility, read anything provided about the author.	**Author Page:** To evaluate credibility, read any "About the author" or "About our site" pages or information. Conduct a search on the author's name, using a search engine.
Index: If available, check the index for a listing of topics included in the book.	**Glossary:** If the Web site includes a glossary of terms, use it to help you understand the topics covered.
Bibliography: Look at the list of references at the end of the article or book. It can tell you how carefully an author researched and also lead you to other related information.	**Links to References or Related Sites:** Look at the links to related sites or to sources referenced. They can tell you about the site's research and also lead you to other related information.

If you are aware of that bias before you read a piece, you will be able to keep the information in context. As well as considering the audience, think about the purposes for writing and publishing the piece. What are the author and sponsoring organization trying to accomplish? Are they trying to sell a product or market an idea? Are they trying to persuade you to accept a particular point of view? If the source is a magazine or newspaper, turn to the opening pages and read the editorial policy to get an idea of the publication's purpose. If the source is on the Internet, you need to exercise caution as an information "consumer." Check to see if the site includes an "About our site" page, which describes the site's purpose or agenda. Knowing this purpose will help you to evaluate the credibility of the information.

Content

Pay close attention to the content itself. Does the language seem moderate and reasonable, or are there terms that might be considered inflammatory or prejudiced? Does the writer seem overly emotional? Is the tone strident or preachy? Other factors to consider as you read closely include how the piece uses source evidence, how logically the argument is developed, and how the content matches (or contradicts) what others have said on the subject.

Special Criteria for Internet Sources

As we have discussed, some Internet sources are more reliable than others. When evaluating a Web site, look to see what other sources are linked to it and what sites it links to. How useful and/or legitimate are the linked sites? If the Internet source is an online bulletin board or newsgroup, you should question its reliability. Because the online discussion medium is by nature freeform, it is difficult to evaluate the credibility of the information found there. Those who enter into newsgroup discussions are ordinarily people who have some kind of interest in the topic. Occasionally you will find an expert on the topic with professional credentials, but usually you will just find others like yourself, with a variety of opinions to share. Newsgroup discussions can be helpful in pointing out interesting areas for further research. But they will not help much with the actual information you need for a research paper. When evaluating a newsgroup posting, you should be asking the same questions about the author, audience, and purpose that were discussed above. As a general rule, verify with another source any information you find in a newsgroup posting.

EXERCISE 10.1

Select for evaluation four of the Web sites you found in your search in Exercise 9.2. For each site, make note of the sponsoring organization, the author (if known), the target audience, the purpose, any apparent bias, and the timeliness of the information. Rank the sites in order of trustworthiness, from the most trustworthy to the least trustworthy. Share the information and your evaluation with your peer group.

10b Follow a student's evaluation of Web links

To give you a sense of how you might go about evaluating information you find via an Internet search, we will follow a student's

Checklist for Evaluating Information

The Sponsoring Organization

1. Where does the information appear—in the popular press, in a scholarly report, on a Web site?
2. Who is the sponsor of the source—an academic society, a publishing house, an organization?
3. For a Web site, what is the domain of the URL—educational, governmental, commercial?

The Author

1. Who is the author? Have you ever heard of this person? Have you run across the name in other sources?
2. What are the author's credentials?
3. What kind of language does the author use?
4. What kind of tone has the author adopted?

The Audience

1. Who is the intended audience for the publication?
2. Does the publication target obvious biases in its audience?
3. What are the characteristics of the audience members?

The Purpose

1. What are the author and sponsoring organization trying to accomplish?
2. Is an idea or product being marketed?
3. Are you being urged to adopt a particular point of view?

The Timeliness

1. When was the piece published?
2. When was the Web site posted and/or updated?
3. How important is it that your information be current?

search for information related to smoking. Mark Robb had been reading about the debate on smoking and addiction. He wanted to find out about both sides of the debate, in an effort to answer the question "Is smoking addictive?" Mark knew that the tobacco industry had argued recently that smoking was not addictive, but rather habit-forming.

Mark began by turning to the Lycos search engine, located at *http://www.lycos.com* Browsing through the subject tree, Mark noted a category "Health" (see Figure 10.1). He clicked on "Health" and found the subcategory "smoking and health." On the search line, Mark typed *nicotine AND addiction* to find out what kinds of sources would be listed. By using the AND operator, Mark limited the search to sites that included both "nicotine" and "addiction." (See Tips on Using Boolean Operators for Internet Searching, page 174.)

He found 14 hits for his search terms. These were mainly sites to help smokers quit (see Figure 10.2). He wanted to find information on both sides of the question. One link caught his eye:

Smoking from All Sides   I've tried to include links about all perspectives of smoking: Health Aspects Statistics Tobacco News Anti-Smoking Groups Smoking Cessation Tobacco History Commentary http://www.cs.brown.edu/people/lsh/smoking.html (Size 1.6K)

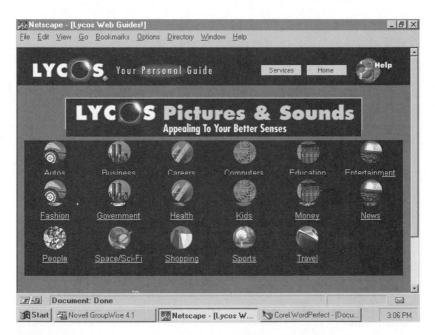

Figure 10.1   Homepage for Lycos Search Engine

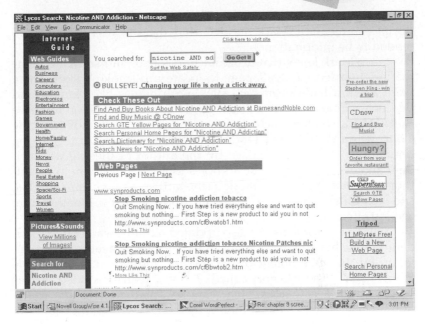

Figure 10.2   Boolean Search for *nicotine AND addiction*

Mark clicked on the link to find out what this site was all about. He found page links to newsgroups, articles, and homepages that discussed smoking. The introductory material on the page stated

> I've tried to include links about all perspectives of smoking. Unfortunately for my quest for a balanced page, the anti-smoking position seems to be overwhelmingly more prevalent than the pro-smoking position on the net.

Mark wondered about the author of this page. He wanted to find out if the person who had collected the links at this site was reliable. He followed the link to the author's page and discovered that the author, Loring Holden, was a software engineer in the Brown University Computer Science Department. Although Mark was not sure that these credentials related in any way to expertise on the to-bacco industry, he decided to give the author the benefit of the doubt and read the site. He could not figure out from reading Holden's résumé why he was interested in tobacco issues or what rhetorical purpose was behind the creation of the "Smoking from

All Sides" page. But since the site provided links without much editorial commentary, Mark decided that the site was probably intended to be informational.

Since Mark knew that he could find lots of anti-smoking information, he used Holden's page to locate pro-smoking sites. There were about a half-dozen such sites, with names like "Smoke and Be Cool," "Smoker's Home Page," and "Tobacco Litigation Information." Mark went to each of these links in turn. "Smoke and Be Cool" was a diatribe by an individual smoker against anti-smoking regulation. The language used by the author of the site was strident and even offensive. The author's tone clued Mark in to the author's agenda of irritating those in the anti-smoking campaign. The site was timely, though; it had been updated just a month before Mark visited.

"Smoker's Home Page," also updated recently, was a bit less strident in tone but equally militant in its arguments against any regulation by the government of the tobacco industry. On "Smoker's Home Page" was a category called "Issues," which included articles with such titles as "Second Hand Smoke: The Big Lie" and "Addiction." These articles were authored by Joe Dawson. Mark could not find any information at the site about Joe Dawson, but it was obvious from his arguments that he was extremely suspicious of all government-sponsored studies having to do with smoking. The main thrust of his arguments was to keep the government out of the lives of individuals.

Mark read the addiction article with interest. The argument focused on making a distinction between a substance that was "habit-forming" and a substance that was "addictive." The article concluded that smoking was habit-forming rather than addictive and that the efforts to have nicotine classified as an addictive drug were part of the government's attempts to control smoking and infringe on smokers' rights. Mark printed out this article for later reference. It was the only article he found that explicitly argued that nicotine was not addictive.

Next Mark turned to the link for "Tobacco Litigation Information," also found on Holden's page. That link brought him to a page titled "Tobacco Litigation Information" at *http://www.rbb.com/tobaclaw*. The explanatory preface included the following:

> As a service to the news media, the tobacco industry has created a library of reference materials to serve as background for stories on tobacco litigation. The library contains legal documents, news stories, broadcast transcripts, discussion papers and other literature from various sources.

You may conduct a free search by date, author, publication, or title or simply browse an index of the entire database by topic. Full-text copies of your search results can be obtained for free by submitting a request as instructed on the screen or by calling our toll-free number . . .

Mark wondered who exactly the sponsor for this site was. The first sentence, "As a service to the news media, the tobacco industry has created . . . ," led him to wonder about the motives for producing this site. Was it really altruism on the part of the tobacco industry? Did they sincerely have the desire to help out the news media with information related to tobacco? Mark wanted to find out what the purpose behind this site might be. Backing up through the URL to the first level, by deleting everything that followed the slash (see the Help box on page 186), brought him to the site at *http://www.rbb. com*. The address rbb.com (which he knew was commercial because of the domain .com) turned out to stand for Rubin, Barney, and Birger, Public Relations Counselors. So the real sponsor of the tobacco industry's page was a public relations firm, which undoubtedly was hired by the tobacco industry to produce the "Tobacco Litigation Information" site. Knowing that the PR firm had an agenda that included enhancing the reputation of the tobacco industry helped Mark to read materials found there with a critical eye.

Mark now had information from both sides of the smoking and addiction issue. He proceeded to read the relevant sources carefully, taking notes in his electronic notebook file. In addition to taking notes, Mark wrote down evaluative information about each source's sponsor, author, purpose, and so on, to remind himself of the source's credibility.

Mark's brief researching tour through the Internet illustrates the importance of evaluating everything you read. In thinking critically about the sites he encountered in his search, Mark posed all of the questions on the Checklist for Evaluating Information (page 193). He considered the sponsoring organization, the rhetorical stance of the site (including author, audience, and purpose), and the timeliness of the site. By using these evaluative questions, Mark was able to get a sense of the reliability of the information he encountered.

EXERCISE 10.2

Make a chart in which you compare the sites you labeled "most trustworthy" and "least trustworthy" in Exercise 10.1. Use the questions in the Checklist for Evaluating Information to help you construct your chart. Bring a copy of your chart to class for discussion.

CHAPTER

11

Using Sources

What should I put in my notes? (11a)
How many quotes do I need? (11b)
What is plagiarism and how do I avoid it? (11a-3)
What is the difference between paraphrasing and
summarizing? (11c, 11d)

?

Writers gain credibility through the use of information from experts. It is the responsibility of research authors to be certain that any information from another author, whether paraphrased, summarized, or quoted, is accurately relayed and clearly acknowledged. Integrating source information into one's own writing is a skill that takes practice. Previous chapters discussed ways to locate sources, organize a notetaking system, and evaluate sources. This chapter discusses how to record information from sources and how to incorporate source information into a paper in a responsible way.

11a   Use sources responsibly

When writing a research paper, you must acknowledge any original information, ideas, and illustrations that you find in another author's work, whether it is in print or on the Internet. Acknowledging the work of other authors is called documenting sources. (The appropriate forms for documentation are discussed in Chapter 13.) When incorporating information from other authors into a research paper, you can present the source information in the form of a direct quote (see 11b); a paraphrase, in which you restate the ideas in your own words (see 11c); or a summary, in which you condense the information (see 11d). By incorporating source information appropriately, you will avoid plagiarism (see 11a-3).

http://www.wisc.edu/
writing/Handbook/
QuoSuccessfulSummary.
html
Detailed explanations
and examples of using
quotes, paraphrases,
and summaries

1   Reading critically

Your main task as a researcher is to make sense of the subject you have chosen to research. To understand the subject and come to some conclusions of your own about it, you need to read widely and critically. If you rely on only one source throughout your paper, you immediately lose credibility with your readers. Readers will question the depth of your research and the level of your knowledge; your competence as a researcher will be called into question. On the other hand, if you use a number of authors to provide supporting evidence, you gain credibility with your readers. So, it is important to read and evaluate several sources.

Chapter 2 describes the process of reading critically, which involves previewing, reading, and then reviewing. When you read sources for your research paper, pay special attention to reading with a critical eye. It would be a good idea at this time to review the Checklist for Evaluating Information in Chapter 10.

Previewing

Preview the source first. As you preview, pay attention to key words or phrases and try to get a general idea of the work's purpose and structure.

Reading

Read the work a first time at a relatively rapid pace, either a section or a chapter at a time. This first reading should be more than skimming, however, as the goal is to understand in general what you have read. Then read the work again, carefully and slowly. When you are reading your own books or photocopied articles, use a highlighter or a pencil to underline key ideas. Stop frequently to take notes, either in your research notebook or on index cards (see 8c).

As you read, keep your hypothesis in mind (see 8a-4). By providing you with a focus, your starting questions and hypothesis will prevent you from reading aimlessly. If you focus your research by stating a hypothesis that you seek to prove or disprove, you can avoid the pitfall of switching from one source to another without direction. As you read various sources, decide both how the sources relate to your hypothesis and how they relate to each other. Read each one with your purpose clearly in mind—using the sources to reinforce your own opinion, as stated in your hypothesis.

Reviewing

As part of your review, assess and evaluate each source, including those you find as you search the Internet. As discussed in Chapter 10, assessment is a two-step process of deciding whether or not the source is worth reading and whether or not the source is worth using in your paper. Evaluating involves thinking carefully about key elements in the work.

2 Taking accurate, usable notes

If you do not take good notes while you read, you may have to retrace your steps in an attempt to relocate a particular source. In the worst-case scenario, the source you need to reference will have been checked out by another library patron or the Internet site will be gone. So, it is important to take accurate, usable notes when you first encounter a source.

Taking Content Notes and Bibliographical Notes

Chapter 8 describes taking content notes and bibliographical notes. Content notes include source information; bibliographical notes provide documentation information (see 8d). Be sure to take both kinds of notes, either on note cards or in a research notebook.

Recording Substantive and Interpretive Information

The most successful research papers incorporate information from several sources into the flow of the paper. The least successful papers tend to make one of the following major mistakes. Either they rely too heavily on just one source for support of the argument or they cobble together the opinions of three or four authors, one right after the other, without interpreting their meanings or relationships. To avoid these mistakes, make your notes both substantive and interpretive. That is, record in your notes both what the source author is saying and what you think about it (see 8c).

Deciding Whether to Quote, Paraphrase, or Summarize

When you record content notes from a source, you typically either paraphrase or summarize what you have read. If the information seems especially significant to your research topic or if it provides new insights or ideas that you have not encountered before in your research, you will probably want to paraphrase it. Paraphrasing is an almost line-by-line rewording of the source information. (See 11c for examples of appropriate paraphrasing.) If the information seems less crucial to your topic or if you need little detail to make your point, you may wish to summarize instead. A summary, in contrast to a paraphrase, condenses information. (See 11d for examples of appropriate summarizing.) Record information in the form of a direct quote if it is impossible to put the information into your own words—for example, if the author expressed a thought so memorably that you could not possible say it otherwise. (See 11b for examples of appropriate quoting.)

3 Avoiding plagiarism

If you use source information carefully and accurately, you will avoid any charges of plagiarism. **Plagiarism** is defined as the unauthorized or misleading use of the language and thoughts of another author. By following the guidelines in this chapter when you paraphrase, summarize, and quote, you can avoid plagiarism.

Sources That Require Acknowledgment

Any word, phrase, or sentence that you copied directly from a source must be placed in quotation marks, and complete bibliographic information must be given, including the page reference for the quotation. Similarly, you must acknowledge paraphrases and summary restatements of ideas taken from a source, even though you have cast them in your own words. (See Chapter 13 on Documentation Formats.)

If you find information on a Web site, it is a relatively simple matter to download it onto a disk or into your computer's hard drive. However, you need to be careful to use the information fairly. When you summarize, paraphrase, or quote from a Web site, you must give proper acknowledgment to the source. It is not acceptable to CUT and PASTE text or graphics from the Internet without acknowledging the source. The same general principles about paraphrasing, summarizing, and quoting apply to other online sources found through the Internet.

Many online databases provide abstracts rather than complete works (see 8f-4). For example, when searching the ERIC database on CD-ROM, you will find abstracts that tell what an article or document is about, in addition to showing its location and source. What if you use information from the abstract, but do not actually read the original? You need to acknowledge the abstract when paraphrasing, summarizing, or quoting information it contains. Note in your bibliography that you are quoting the abstract rather than the source itself.

Sources That Do Not Require Acknowledgment

You need not document "common knowledge." This term refers to information that is generally known or accepted by educated people. Information that you can find readily in general reference works such as encyclopedias or in the popular media is probably common knowledge and need not be documented. But common knowledge should be verified. Be certain that several sources provide the same information before assuming that it is common knowledge. Well-proven historical facts and dates need not be documented. As a general rule, it is better to over-document than to under-document and be accused of plagiarizing. When in doubt, document.

Separating Your Thoughts from Those of Others in Your Notes

Your notes should accurately record source information in your own words, when possible. You should be able to tell at a glance from your notes when information is from a source and when it is your own commentary or thoughts on a source. If you record your notes by hand in a research notebook, you can divide each page into two columns, one for notes and one for your comments. If you use note cards, you can label the cards, indicating which are notes from a source and which are your own commentary. If you use a computerized research notebook, you can use the ANNOTATIONS or DOCU-

MENT COMMENTS feature of the word-processing program to separate source notes from your own thoughts (see 8c-1).

Unintentional versus Intentional Plagiarism

Students taking notes from a source sometimes commit *unintentional* plagiarism by carelessly copying words and phrases from a source into their notes and then using these words and phrases without acknowledgment in a paper. One way to avoid this problem is to read a piece carefully and then set it aside while you write your notes. If you follow the reading and notetaking procedures outlined above, paraphrasing and summarizing in your own words what you have read, you are unlikely to use the author's exact wording inappropriately in a research paper.

Sometimes plagiarism is *intentional;* that is, a writer knowingly copies the work of another without proper acknowledgment of the source. A *Newsweek* article reported on a Stanford University business school lecturer who used several pages from an article by Greg Easterbrook in his book, word for word, without acknowledging the original author (G. Easterbrook, "The sincerest flattery: Thanks, but I'd rather you not plagiarize my work," *Newsweek,* 19 July 1991, pp. 45–46). When the plagiarism came to light, the Stanford author apologized to Easterbrook, but insisted that he had not plagiarized because he had included Easterbrook's name in the book's footnotes. Easterbrook's response explains an important distinction: "Footnotes my foot. Footnotes mean the place a fact can be found; they do not confer the right to present someone else's words as your own work" (p. 46).

The distinction being made here is that whenever you use words from a source, this must be indicated clearly through the use of quotation marks and documentation at the point in the text where the source information is used. It is not enough to list the author in the footnotes or bibliography. Readers must be able to tell as they are reading your paper exactly what information came from which source and what information is your contribution to the paper.

11b   Quote sources sparingly

Quotations are exact wordings taken from sources. Use direct quotes sparingly in a research paper. A string of quotes can be confusing for readers, especially if each quote presents information in a different writing style. By paraphrasing and summarizing instead of quoting, you can more smoothly incorporate the ideas from sources into your own writing. However, if an author uses unique language or an interesting image, a brief quote may be an effective addition to a paper. Generally, you should limit each quote to a sentence or two so that it does not interrupt the flow of your paper. Enclose it in quotation marks (see 50a) and include documentation (see Chapter 13).

1 Using quoted material

When you quote from a source, it is important to be accurate. Unless you download text from the Internet, you are most likely copying from a source into your notes and then into your paper, so it is easy to make a transcription error. Making photocopies of a source can help you to quote exactly because you can recheck the wording from the photocopy.

Every time you copy information from a source, indicate through quotation marks on your note card that you have taken the exact wording from the original. Figure 11.1 shows a note card with information that a student intends to use as a direct quote. The student decided to quote this information because she felt that the author expressed a key idea in forceful language. The quote helps the student

> Quote on Climate Change   3.1
>
> According to researchers at Carnegie Mellon University, "Scientists disagree about whether climate change will be a serious problem in the next 50 to 100 years. The main reason for this disagreement is that nobody knows for sure whether climate changes caused by human actions will be large enough and fast enough to cause serious damage" (U.S. Global Change Research Information Office).

Figure 11.1   Note Card with Direct Quote

to validate the point made in her hypothesis—that there is still disagreement about global climate change—thus giving her some authoritative backing. This particular quotation came from an article found on the Internet. Note that since Internet sources typically do not provide page numbers, the student could not indicate a specific page on the note card. The student also created a corresponding bibliography card for this source (see 8d-1). The number 3.1 in the upper right-hand corner of the note card indicates that this is the first note card from source number 3.

2 Integrating quotations into a paper

When you use a direct quote, you must integrate it smoothly into the flow of your ideas. Many teachers report that students have trouble with this skill. You need to use signal phrases to alert your reader that a quote is coming. You also need to attribute the source appropriately (see Chapter 13 on Documentation Formats) and punctuate it correctly (see Chapter 50 on Quotation Marks). The quotes that you use should be relatively short to minimize interruption. If you decide to use a long quote in your paper, you are obliged to explain your choice to the readers. Otherwise, they are likely to just skim over the long quote. (For instructions on how to format a long quotation appropriately, see 50a-2.)

Techniques for Incorporating Quotes

Observing the three suggestions outlined below for incorporating quotes will help you to avoid choppy or incoherent sentences.

1. Integrate the quote smoothly into the grammatical flow of your sentence.

NO   Carnegie Mellon researchers, "Scientists disagree about whether climate change will be a serious problem in the next 50 to 100 years" (U.S. Global Change). [Grammar problem—fused sentence]

YES   According to researchers at Carnegie Mellon University, "Scientists disagree about whether climate change will be a serious problem in the next 50 to 100 years" (U.S. Global Change).

2. Provide an explanation as to why you are using a particular quote.

NO   "The main reason for this disagreement is that nobody knows for sure whether climate changes caused by human actions will be large enough and fast enough to cause serious damage" (U.S. Global Change). [No introductory explanation]

YES   Researchers at Carnegie Mellon University note that there is no agreement among scientists as to the seriousness of global warming. They state, "The main reason for this disagreement is that nobody knows for sure whether climate changes caused by human actions will be large enough and fast enough to cause serious damage" (U.S. Global Change).

3. Cite the author's name or, if the author is unknown, the title or sponsor of the work as you introduce the quote.

YES   The U.S. Global Change Research Information Office wrote an informational newsletter on global warming, which they shared with interested readers via a Web site. The newsletter reports that Carnegie Mellon researchers found "scientists disagree about whether climate change will be a serious problem in the next 50 to 100 years."

Deletions Using Ellipses and Brackets

Indicate with **ellipses,** or three spaced periods (see Chapter 51), when you delete any words or phrases within quoted information. If you use ellipses, you need to make certain that what remains is still readable and coherent. Put brackets around any words that you have changed from the original.

YES   According to researchers at Carnegie Mellon University, "Scientists disagree about whether climate change will be a serious problem . . . [since] nobody knows for sure whether climate changes caused by human actions will be large enough and fast enough to cause serious damage" (U.S. Global Change).

EXERCISE 11.1

Select a short article on a topic of interest to you, and print or photocopy it. Choose a sentence or two from the article in which the author states an important idea in memorable words. Imagine that you will be using the quote in a research paper. Introduce the quote by providing a context, and then write the quote, using correct grammar and punctuation. Share and discuss your quote with your peers.

Guidelines for Effective Quoting

1. Use direct quotes sparingly as support for your own ideas.
2. Use primarily short quotes (one or two sentences).
3. Be extremely careful to be accurate when copying a quote.
4. Attribute quotes to their sources and punctuate them correctly (see 50a).
5. Integrate quotes smoothly into the stylistic flow of the paper.
6. Incorporate quotes in a way that is grammatically correct (see 50e).
7. Provide an explanation to place the quote in context.
8. Use the author's name or the work's title to introduce the quote.
9. Use ellipses when words or phrases are omitted from the quote (see 51k).

11c   Paraphrase sources accurately

Instead of directly quoting from sources, writers have the option of paraphrasing source information. The objective of paraphrasing is to present an author's ideas clearly, using your own words and phrases instead of the author's. This important skill not only deepens your understanding of the author's ideas but also helps you to avoid plagiarism (see 11a-3). Here are some suggestions to help you paraphrase.

1. *Place the information in a new order.* When paraphrasing, you must rework a passage. One way to do this is to reorder the information. In the following example, the good paraphrase inverts the sentence structure of the original, whereas the poor paraphrase copies both words and sentence structure from the source.

DIRECT QUOTATION FROM ORIGINAL SOURCE

"If you're coping with an illness or want to exchange views about a medical topic, you'll want to find your way to a newsgroup. Despite the name, these are not collections of news items. They are, in effect, virtual bulletin boards open to anyone who cares to participate. The messages generally consist of plain text" (Schwartz 28).

GOOD PARAPHRASE [WITH INVERTED SENTENCE STRUCTURE AND DIFFERENT WORDS]

In a recent *Consumer Reports* article, the author suggests finding a relevant newsgroup if you have a particular medical problem or if you want to talk with others about a medical subject. Newsgroups are online bulletin boards that are available to anyone; in spite of their name, they are not news reports. Anyone who wishes to may join in a newsgroup discussion (Schwartz 28).

POOR PARAPHRASE [COPIES WORDS AND SENTENCE STRUCTURE DIRECTLY FROM SOURCE]

If you're faced with an illness or want to exchange views about a medical topic, you'll want to find your way to a newsgroup. Despite the name, these are not news items. They are virtual bulletin boards open to anyone. The messages generally consist of ordinary text (Schwartz 28).

2. *Break the complex ideas into small units.* If the author has expressed himself or herself in a rather complicated way, paraphrasing gives you the opportunity to state the complex ideas of the source more simply:

DIRECT QUOTATION FROM ORIGINAL SOURCE

"The 'perfect' search engine would guide users to every relevant location, ranked in order of usefulness, without leaving anything out and without including anything irrelevant. That engine doesn't yet exist" (Schwartz 29).

PARAPHRASE [WITH SIMPLIFIED SENTENCE STRUCTURE]

Schwartz states that no Internet searching tool is yet able to be "perfect." If it were, it would lead you to all the appropriate locations on your topic. It would rank all the Web sites by how useful they were. It would never leave something out that was relevant. It would never include anything that was irrelevant (29).

3. *Use concrete, direct vocabulary in place of technical jargon.* If the author has used technical vocabulary, you can replace some of the technical jargon with more direct, familiar words as you paraphrase. Here are some examples of jargon from these examples that might be changed in a paraphrase:

newsgroup = online bulletin board

search engine = Internet searching tool

users = those who are using the Internet

location = Web site found at a unique Internet address

4. *Use synonyms for words in the source.* Just as you can replace jargon with more familiar terms, you can use synonyms (words that mean roughly the same thing) in the place of words from the source. Here are some of the synonyms used in the paraphrases above:

illness = medical problem

exchange views = talk to others

medical topic = medical subject

available to = open to

despite = in spite of

news items = news reports

5. *Accompany each important fact or idea in your notes with the source page number.* With paraphrases, as with quotes, you must indicate exactly on what page in the source you found the information. Ideally, anyone else reading your work should be able to locate the exact wording from which your paraphrase was taken. If the source has no pages, as is true of many Internet documents, you might wish to use a screen number or a paragraph number instead. (See Chapter 13 for more information on documenting electronic sources.)

1   Recording paraphrases in notes

As you take notes on sources, you will mostly be recording these notes in the form of paraphrases (or summaries). The example below shows a passage from an Internet newsletter and a student's paraphrased notes. In the student paraphrase, notice how the words have been changed or reordered and the sentence patterns altered from the original. Notice also that the information is fairly complete, with most of the ideas from the original source retained in the paraphrased version.

DIRECT QUOTATION FROM ORIGINAL SOURCE

"Part 2: If climate changes what might happen? Why do scientists disagree about possible impacts of climate change? Scientists disagree about whether climate change will be a serious problem in the next 50 to 100 years. The main reason for this disagreement is that nobody knows for sure whether climate changes caused by human actions will be large enough and fast enough to cause serious damage. Many scientists believe that they may be. Others argue that if changes occur, the problems they cause will be minor compared with problems caused by today's storms and droughts" (U.S. Global Change Research Information Office).

PARAPHRASE [FROM STUDENT COMPUTERIZED NOTEBOOK]

"Why Do Scientists Disagree About Possible Impacts of Climate Change?"

There is no agreement among scientists as to whether or not global climate change will become a serious problem in the next century. The lack of agreement stems from the impossibility of predicting exactly how much or how quickly human actions will impact global climate change. Although many scientists think the effects will be great, others argue that the effects will be relatively minor when compared to other climate problems like water shortages, hurricanes, or tornados.

From U.S. Global Change Research Information Office (http://www.gcrio.org/gwcc) (1994)

2   Integrating paraphrases into a paper

Paraphrases from notes should be integrated into a paper in much the same way as direct quotes. You should introduce them with signal phrases, place them in context for the readers, or perhaps use the author or title in the introduction. As with quoting, you need to provide documentation indicating the source of the information (see Chapter 13).

EXERCISE 11.2

Select a short paragraph from the article you printed or photocopied in Exercise 11.1. Following the guidelines in this section, paraphrase that paragraph. Provide appropriate documentation for the source, as if you were using the paraphrase in a research paper. Bring your paraphrase, plus the original source, with you to class. Discuss it with your peers.

11d   Summarize sources briefly

Summaries condense the information found in sources. Like paraphrasing, summarizing involves restating the author's ideas or information in your own words, but summaries are typically much briefer than the original information. To be sure that your summary accurately reflects the author's most important ideas, you first must read the source carefully in order to understand it thoroughly. Summaries typically leave out extended examples, illustrations, and long expla-

Guidelines for Effective Paraphrasing

1. Place the information in a new order.
2. Break the complex ideas into small units.
3. Use concrete, direct vocabulary in place of technical jargon.
4. Use synonyms for words in the source.
5. Accompany each important fact or idea in your notes with the source page number.
6. Incorporate the paraphrase smoothly into the grammar and style of your own writing.

nations. The goal of a summary is to record the gist of the piece—its primary line of argument—without tangential arguments, examples, and other departures from the main ideas. As with paraphrasing, you need to be sure that the summary is stated in your own words.

 Recording summaries in notes

When you first preview a source to determine its relevance to your research, you can also decide how much of the source you are likely to use in your paper. You would not want to paraphrase an entire article, for example, if only the introduction related to your topic. Rather, you could simply summarize the relevant portion. On note cards or in a research notebook, record summary information in the form that will be most useful to you later on. As with paraphrasing, you should keep track of the page numbers covered by the summary, when they are available. Summarizing is the technique you will probably use most when recording information in your notes. A student summarized the original wording from Part 2 of the U.S. Global Change newsletter (quoted on page 209) as follows:

STUDENT SUMMARY IN RESEARCH NOTEBOOK

Researchers at Carnegie Mellon University discuss the impacts of climate changes. They point out that scientists disagree about the impacts because it is impossible to know for sure the extent to which human actions will affect global climate (U.S. Global Change Research Information Office).

Here are some additional suggestions to help you summarize effectively:

1. *Identify key points.* A summary must reflect the main ideas of the source accurately, so you need to read carefully before you write a summary. As you read your own books or photocopied articles, underline or highlight key ideas, words, or phrases. Ask yourself, "What is the central idea of this passage?" Try to articulate that idea in your own words, using just a sentence or two.

2. *Record information.* As you record the key ideas, be certain that you separate your own interpretive comments from the source information itself. You can do this by using a two-column notebook or document comments (see 8c-1).

3. *Create lists and tables.* When you are condensing ideas, sometimes it helps to write them down in the form of a list or a table. In this way, you can capture the most important ideas in the simplest form possible and present them to readers as a listing of key ideas. In the following example, the student has summarized an entire article in the form of a table of key ideas. Notice that the article headings, taken directly from the source, are placed in quotation marks to indicate a direct quote.

STUDENT SUMMARY OF THE ARTICLE "FINDING MEDICAL HELP ONLINE"

In a recent <u>Consumer Reports</u> article titled "Finding Medical Help Online," Schwartz explains how to find the "good stuff" (27). The major parts of the article are summarized in the table below:

"Basic Information about the Internet" (27–28)	Discusses terminology, equipment, hardware and software issues.
"Newsgroups" (28)	Explains how newsgroups work and how they can provide forums for like-minded individuals to discuss issues.

"Search Engines" (29)	Describes some general search engines and explains how they work.
"Health Web Sites" (29)	Outlines general and specific medical sites that might be useful.
"Strategies for Searching" (30–31)	Walks through a model search, explaining what one is likely to find and how useful it is likely to be.

Source: Consumer Reports (Feb. 1997): 27–31.

4. *Check for accuracy.* Just as you did when quoting or paraphrasing from a source, you need to check your summaries to ensure their accuracy. Check to make sure that the words and phrases are your own. Place any of the author's unique words or phrases in quotation marks and include a page reference. Check to be sure that you have not been interpretive or judgmental about anything the author has said. When summarizing, you should restate the author's main ideas objectively in your own words, without interpretation. Record any interpretive judgments as document comments or clearly distinguish them in a two-column notebook. It is a good idea to reread the source after you have summarized it, just to be certain that you have not inadvertently altered the author's meaning.

2   Integrating summaries into a paper

Summaries are incorporated into a paper in much the same way as direct quotes and paraphrases. Introduce a summary with a signal phrase, place it in a context for the readers, or perhaps use the author's name or article title in the introduction. As with quoting and paraphrasing, you need to provide documentation indicating the source of the summarized information (see Chapter 13).

Guidelines for Effective Summarizing

1. Identify the main points as you read the source.
2. Put those main points into your own words.
3. Condense the original, keeping the summary short.
4. Use a table or a list, when appropriate, to summarize the information.
5. Be objective rather than interpreting or judging source ideas.
6. Integrate the summarized ideas into the flow of your prose.
7. Provide proper documentation for the source.

EXERCISE 11.3

Using the same article as in Exercises 11.1 and 11.2, choose one brief section or page to summarize. Remember that a summary is a condensed version of the original source. Write up your summary and turn it in to your teacher. Be sure to include a printout or photocopy of the original source, with the relevant sections marked to indicate the key ideas.

Writing the Research Paper

FAQs

Is it OK to use "I" in my paper? (12a-3)

How do I arrange all the information? (12b)

How do I write a draft? (12c)

How do I revise? (12d)

Should I use footnotes? (12e-1)

?

Now that you have gathered and evaluated your information, you need to step back and assess just where all this research has taken you. Although the writing process that you will follow in writing your research paper is not radically different from the writing process outlined in Part 1 of this handbook, there are some important differences. As mentioned in Chapter 8, the first difference is one of scope; a research paper is longer than most essays. Sometimes students find themselves overwhelmed by the sheer volume of information they have collected. It is indeed an enormous challenge to organize and present research. Another major difference between a research paper and most essays is that you will be using information from sources, rather than your own ideas, as support for your

> **WEB**
> http://www.
> researchpaper.com
> The perfect starting
> point for all researchers
> with questions

thesis. The suggestions in this chapter will help you to write a successful research paper.

12a   Review the rhetorical stance and thesis

http://www.ipl.org/
teen/aplus/
Internet Public Library's
excellent guide to writing research papers

Chapter 3 suggests that you decide on a rhetorical stance, which will help you determine the direction of your research. It would be a good idea to review your rhetorical stance at this time, reassessing your topic, purpose, audience, and hypothesis.

1   Reassessing purpose, persona, and audience

Remind yourself of your intended purpose for writing the research paper and your persona (see 3a-2, 8a). Ask yourself, "Who is my audience?" You may not be able to determine for certain who your readers will be, but you can assume that they will be intelligent people who have an interest in the topic you are writing about. It is unlikely that they will be experts in the field you are discussing; therefore, you should define any terms carefully and avoid using jargon or technical vocabulary.

2   Refining your topic

Your starting questions and working hypothesis helped you to focus your research. Reassess your working hypothesis at this time. Does it still reflect the position you wish to take in your paper? If not, revise the hypothesis. Remember that a hypothesis usually takes a side on a debatable issue.

Testing Your Hypothesis

Cecelia Chung's starting questions about global warming had to do with its seriousness, its causes, and its possible prevention (see 8a for a description of Cecelia's starting process). As she looked over the material gathered in her research, she was convinced that global warming was a serious problem that needed the immediate attention of the world community. In other words, she confirmed that her research had supported her working hypothesis:

> Global warming is a real event with potential catastrophic consequences that must be stopped. [Yes, Cecelia determined that this hypothesis was supported by the research.]

Writing a Thesis Statement

A thesis statement for a research paper is similar to a thesis statement for an essay (see 3b-6). That is, it states for readers the central idea that the paper will argue. Many times, the preliminary thesis statement is revised during the actual writing process. Cecelia decided to write a thesis that stated in strong language her concern about the global warming problem:

> Working thesis: We cannot afford to disregard the problem of global warming because of its potential for devastation.

Revising the Thesis

Most research papers argue a position. However, some research papers are informational; that is, they report on information without taking a position. Your teacher may require that your thesis (and thus your research paper) have an argumentative edge. If so, make sure that you have taken a stand that can be supported through arguments in the paper (see Chapter 7). If your research paper is informational rather than argumentative, your thesis should reflect the fact that you are reporting information rather than taking a stand on an issue. Neither type of research paper is inherently better; the two types are simply different. Your thesis statement should tell readers clearly what direction your paper will take. Readers should not be surprised at the end by a position that was not acknowledged up front in the introduction to the paper.

AN ARGUMENTATIVE THESIS

> Whatever the causes, males and females have different perspectives on computers and their uses.

AN INFORMATIONAL THESIS

This paper will trace the evolution of computers from the first room-sized mainframes to the current hand-held notebooks.

After Cecelia reread her research notebook, she decided to tone down her specific thesis statement so that it would better reflect the sources she intended to cite in support of her argument.

Revised thesis: While I agree that some caution is warranted when predicting the final outcome of this warming trend, I feel that to disregard the problem altogether is extremely short-sighted, because the effects of even a temporary, "normal" warming trend are potentially devastating for earth and its inhabitants.

3 Deciding on a voice and tone

Academic papers should be informative and serious, but they need not be dull or dry. You can still put your own personality into a piece (as Cecelia did by inserting the first person "I" in the excerpt above, for example). Although it is generally not appropriate to adopt too informal a tone for an academic research paper, taking yourself out of the piece entirely may leave readers with the impression that the piece is lifeless and uninteresting. Try to strike a balance in your tone, making it pleasing to readers (see 3a-3).

Before you begin to draft your research paper, answer the following questions about voice: "Do I want to sound forceful and authoritative? Do I want to sound reasonable and moderate? Or perhaps passionate and concerned?" Notice the voice in this passage, taken from Kirsten's paper on Net theft found in Chapter 4:

I'm sure all of us once glimpsed a tempting item in a store and, after getting "no" for an answer from Mom or Dad, took matters into our own hands, sneaking the treasure into a hidden pocket. It probably took only a few moments for your parents to notice something was up. I remember well a discussion about why taking the package was wrong. Then my Dad took me back to the store where an apology was made and my Strawberry Hubba Bubba Bubblegum was paid for.

The voice in this passage is light and friendly. Kirsten seems to be speaking directly to her readers. Contrast that voice to Cecelia's:

> Alternatively, some say that extinctions due to climate change will be limited because populations will migrate to cooler climates, avoiding the effects of climate change. To a point, I agree. However, rates at which warming will continue are unknown, and successful migrations are dependent upon populations being able to move faster than the rate of change. If warming is gradual, some species may be able to outpace the change.

In this passage, Cecelia sounds authoritative and knowledgeable. The much more serious voice is appropriate for a research paper.

12b   Plan a structure

Some writers like to work from an organizational plan or outline, fleshing out the skeleton by incorporating additional information under each of the major points and subpoints. Others prefer to begin writing and have the structure evolve more organically. You need not be overly concerned about formal structure at this point, unless your teacher stipulates a particular outline format. An outline or plan should be a guide as you write, not a constraint that confines and limits your thinking. You may need to change your organizational plan several times as you make new discoveries while writing. Whatever structure you select must include a format for incorporating opposing viewpoints.

1   Developing an organizational plan or outline

As you write your outline (see 3d-3), remember that you are trying to make the information or argument accessible to readers as well as clear and comprehensive. If you used note cards, sort them by heading and subheading into related ideas and information. If you used a computer research notebook, sort your materials by using the CUT, COPY, and PASTE features of your word-processing program.

Once you have sorted your source materials, you should be able to produce an outline or plan from the headings and subheadings in your notes. For example, after Cecelia decided on the stand she would take in her paper, as articulated in her thesis, she outlined an organizational structure in which she systematically answered each of her starting questions so that her argument would be easy for a reader to follow and understand. In order to explain global warming to her readers, Cecelia decided on the following plan:

Global warming: Is it really happening?

What is global warming and how does it work?

Why are global temperatures increasing?

What are possible effects of global warming?

What will happen to life on earth?

What can be done about global warming?

Why care?

She entered these headings into her electronic notebook, stored in a computer file in her hard drive. (For more information on planning and outlining, see 3d.)

2 Including opposing viewpoints

In an argumentative research paper, it is crucial to present the counterarguments—that is, the arguments on the side opposite the position you are taking. In Cecelia's paper, it was important to acknowledge that some scientists do not believe that global warming is a dramatic problem. In her revised thesis, she acknowledges that position in the opening clause, calling for caution. Then, in the first section of her paper, she systematically refutes the opposition by showing that there is considerable evidence that global warming is in fact happening. As she wrote the rest of her paper, Cecelia was conscious throughout of the opposing viewpoint and was careful to counter that view with her own arguments.

12c Write a draft

Now you should be ready to begin drafting your research paper. Remind yourself of your general understanding of the topic, of your starting questions and hypothesis, and of the answers to the questions as stated in your thesis. When writing your first draft, use concrete and simple language to explain in your own words your research conclusions. Ideally, you should type your draft on a computer to make revisions easier. Be certain to back up your computer files and save to a disk frequently so as not to lose any of your hard work.

1 Choosing a drafting strategy

You will need to establish your own strategy for writing a first draft, one that fits your writing style. Here are a few different ways in which writers of research projects proceed:

- Write a draft systematically from a plan, using the building block technique (see 4b-1).
- Write a draft from piles of notes arranged according to a blueprint from the thesis (see 4b-2).
- Write a sketchy first draft without looking at the notes—just writing down everything remembered from the research; follow up by fleshing out the partial draft with a more complete version while referring to the notes.
- Write a rough first draft and then write a revision outline that suggests ways in which the draft needs to be changed (see 5a-3).
- Write a draft by cutting and pasting information from an electronic research notebook (see 8c).
- Write a draft while viewing electronic note cards in a second window (see 8c-2).

2 Applying the drafting strategy to blend material

As you draft, you blend your own knowledge and material from sources. In writing a first draft, it is best to put down your own understanding of the topic first, rather than relying too heavily on your sources. After you have written your draft, you can go back and add specific sources to support your arguments. Readers want to know what *you* think about the subject. They do not want to read a string of quotes loosely joined by transitions. Studying the topic and reading the source materials should have given you a general understanding of your topic. Writing a working thesis should have provided you with the main point you wish to make. Once you have drafted your paper, important data, facts, illustrations, and supporting evidence gleaned from your sources can be added to your arguments to give them authority and force (see 11b-2, 11c-2, 11d-2).

Cecelia kept all her information in an electronic notebook. After making a backup copy of the notebook file, Cecelia began manipulating information (using CUT, COPY, and PASTE) to put related ideas under the relevant subheadings of her plan. She moved to the end of the file all of the information that did not seem immediately related to her thesis statement. Once the material was in the categories, it was easy for Cecelia to see which areas needed additional information. She could then return to her sources or even find new sources if necessary, in order to present a balanced view of the issues. In this way, she wrote the first draft of the research paper, using the building-block technique discussed in 4b-1.

3 Writing a working title

Writing effective titles is discussed in 5b-7; it would be helpful to review that section of the handbook at this time. Writing a title can help you to state succinctly the topic your research paper will cover. Try out a few titles before deciding on one. It should be brief yet descriptive.

4 Writing an introduction and conclusion

Composing introductions and conclusions is discussed in 5b-7 and 6h. Because a research paper typically covers more information than an essay, it may take a couple of paragraphs to introduce the topic effectively. Cecelia used two opening paragraphs for her research paper; the first paragraph provides data on global warming, and the second, leading up to her thesis, discusses the controversy. In Cecelia's conclusion, she clearly sums up the global warming debate and her stance on the topic. You should make certain that both your introduction and your conclusion help readers to understand your research paper's main point.

EXERCISE 12.1

Write an introductory paragraph for a research paper. First, write a straightforward, academic paragraph with a serious tone. Then, write a second version of the opening paragraph that is light in tone and perhaps even humorous. You might tell a story or describe a scene. Discuss these two opening paragraphs with your classmates. Which do you like better? Which seems more appropriate for your research paper?

12d   Review and revise the draft

A great deal of important work remains to be done on your paper once you complete a rough draft. You must revise the paper to make the most effective possible presentation of the research. Readers expect you to be clear and correct; they should not be distracted by ambiguous source references, confusing language, or incorrect punctuation. It is a good idea to set your draft aside for a day or two, if time allows, so that you can look at it with a fresh eye. It is also a good idea to gather as much feedback as you can from peers. Plan to exchange drafts with a classmate or two for their suggestions (see 5e for more on giving and receiving feedback).

You need to reread your rough draft several times, both on the computer screen and in hard copy (see the Help box on page 78). Each time you read it, pay attention to a different aspect of the paper. The first time, think about the overall structure and style of the paper (see 5b). The second time through, check grammar and punctuation (see 5c, 5d). The third time, make sure source materials are incorporated smoothly and accurately into the text (see 11b, 11c, 11d).

How do I automatically number my pages?

1. Almost all word processors will automatically number pages, but because the commands vary, you will have to check the HELP menu or documentation for specifics. Words to look for include "pages," "page numbers," "headers," and "footers."

2. Other commands you should look for include the one that controls the position of the page numbers on the pages (and allows you to include running heads with the page numbers) and the one that suppresses page numbers on particular pages (such as the title page and the works cited page).

Checklist for Revising a Research Paper

1. Does the paper fulfill the promise made by the thesis (see 3d-1, 12a)?
2. Do the arguments flow smoothly and logically (see 12b)?
3. Is sufficient attention paid to counterarguments (see 12b-2)?
4. Does the introduction lead effectively into the paper (see 5b-7, 6h)?
5. Does the conclusion either summarize or describe implications (see 5b-7, 6h)?
6. Is the paper focused, adequately developed, and coherent (see 5a-2)?
7. Are the sources integrated smoothly into the flow of the paper (see 11b, 11c, 11d)?
8. Is information in quotes, paraphrases, and summaries accurately related and clearly acknowledged (see Chapter 11)?
9. Are the parenthetical citations clear and accurately tied to the works cited (see Chapter 13)?
10. Are the works cited in the proper format (see Chapter 13)?
11. Is the format of the piece appropriate for a research paper (see 12e)?
12. Has the paper been edited and proofread to eliminate errors (see 5c, 5d)?

Finally, consider formal details such as conventions of documentation and format (see Chapter 13). After your paper has been typed and spell-checked, proofread it several times to catch and correct all typographical and mechanical errors. For more information on rewriting your draft, refer to Chapter 5.

12e   Follow formatting conventions

Research paper formatting conventions are those customary ways of presenting information that have developed in various disciplines. The documentation and format conventions common to different disciplines are described in detail in Chapter 13. The main systems are the MLA (Modern Language Association) system, typically used in the humanities and fine arts; the APA (American Psychological Association) system, used in the social sciences; the CMS (*Chicago Manual of Style*) system, used in business; and the CBE (Council of Biology Editors) system, most often used in the sciences. Ask your teacher if there is a particular format you should use. If not, select the format from the discipline most closely related to your research topic.

Preparing footnotes, endnotes, and reference lists

Once you have determined a particular format for your paper, follow that format closely for all sources used in the research paper. Depending on the conventions of the particular discipline, your paper may or may not have footnotes or endnotes. All research papers are required to provide readers with a listing of the sources used in the paper. Again, the way this listing is formatted will depend on the particular discipline.

Footnotes and Endnotes

Footnotes or endnotes are used most often in the humanities. For information on using them appropriately, see 13a-3. In research papers in the sciences, citations generally appear in parentheses within the text. However, there may be times when you need to use explanatory notes, in the form of footnotes or endnotes. Your word-processing program probably includes an automatic footnote/endnote feature (see the Help box on page 226). This feature puts the superscript number in the appropriate location (where the cursor is) and then generates the note, placing it either at the bottom of the page or at the end of the text, whichever you specify. The advantage of using the automatic footnote/endnote feature is that the computer will automatically place the note in the appropriate place as the rest of the text changes during revisions. Check your word-processing program's HELP menu to discover how to activate this feature.

Works Cited and Reference Lists

A works cited list or a reference list is an alphabetical listing of sources at the end of a paper. For information on formatting a works

How do I use a computer footnote program?

1. Place the cursor at the point in the text where you want the number to appear.

2. Find the FOOTNOTE command (typically on the INSERT menu). Select either a footnote or an endnote.

3. Type in the text of the footnote.

4. Close the FOOTNOTE command.

5. The computer will automatically generate the footnote and place it at the bottom of the appropriate page or generate an endnote and place it in a consecutive list at the end of the paper.

NOTE: Most word-processing programs offer considerable control over the appearance of footnotes, but to take advantage of these features, you will need to read the program documentation.

cited or reference list, see the section in Chapter 13 for the appropriate discipline. Your word-processing program may have a feature that will alphabetize references automatically. However, you need to enter the data in a certain fashion in order for the computer to sort appropriately. Once again, check your word-processing program's HELP menu to ascertain whether this feature is available and to learn how to use it (see 8d).

2 Understanding formatting conventions

In addition to helping you as a writer, word processing can help you create a text that is professional in appearance. If you are to communicate effectively with readers, in the end you must attend to both form and content. However, be sure to make attention to format your last consideration. Too often, writers using word processors spend an excessive amount of time playing with the appearance of the text—varying the fonts, for example—rather than concentrating on content.

HELP

How do I use my word-processing program to set margins?

1. Locate your word processor's command for setting margins. Usually you can find it by looking up the word "margin" in the program's documentation or the online HELP menu.
2. Once you have found the margin feature, follow its directions for setting up margins.
3. Choose margins consistent with the formatting style you are using in the paper (MLA, APA, CMS, or CBE); see Chapter 13.

These margins will apply to the entire paper unless you change them.

NOTE: Some word processors let you set the margins and tabs by moving controls on the document's ruler bar. Your program's documentation will also explain how to use this feature.

Most word-processing programs offer formatting features such as underlining, boldface, and italics, with which you can vary the appearance of the text and highlight important information. (See also Chapter 17.) However, you should check with your instructor about his or her preferences before you spend a lot of time playing with the format of your paper. Your goal should be to make the paper look professional. An English Gothic typeface with scrolling capital letters is not appropriate for a formal research paper, nor are margins that are justified (even) on the right side of the page. It is best to be conservative and justify left margins only. The preferred format for each documentation style is described in Chapter 13.

12f   Review an annotated student research paper

The following research paper, written by Cecelia Chung, is formatted following the MLA system of documentation. Annotations are included on facing pages to explain the various conventions. See Chapter 13 for additional information on MLA documentation.

Global Warming:

Is It Really Happening?

by

Cecelia Chung

English 204, Section 01

Professor Hult

November 14, 1998

The *MLA Handbook for Writers of Research Papers* says that a research paper does not need a title page. However, if your instructor requires a title page, use the format illustrated opposite. Double-space all material on the title page. Then, on the first page of your paper, put your last name, a space, and the number 1 in the upper right-hand corner. The title page is not numbered. If you do not use a title page, follow the first-page format illustrated in Chapter 14.

Title

Student Identification

Course Identification

Chung 1

Global Warming: Is It Really Happening?

Global warming, at least as measured by climate experts, is   1
really happening. Over the last 100 years, it has been estimated
that the average global air temperature has risen between 0.3 and
0.6 degree Celsius (Hileman). Though there is debate over other
aspects of global warming, scientists generally agree that global
temperatures have risen.

However, a big source of disagreement is whether this is a   2
normal or an abnormal warming. Too little is known about long-
term global temperature cycles, some say, to determine if this is
abnormal. Reliable weather data, it is true, have only been kept
for the last century or so (Montague 1). As a result, some question
whether there is significant cause for alarm about global warming
as a real problem. While I agree that some caution is warranted
when predicting the final outcome of this warming trend, I
feel that to disregard the problem altogether is extremely short-
sighted, because the effects of even a temporary, normal warming
trend are potentially devastating for earth and its inhabitants.
Most people would agree. It is in our best interests to know as
much as possible about global warming, its causes and potential
effects. Before we discuss the true nature of the controversy, let's
look at how global warming works.

Global warming is an increase in average air temperature on   3
earth's surface, as measured from many points across the globe.
Global warming, in its simplest form, is a product of two factors: so-
called greenhouse gases and radiation from our local star, the Sun.

Page Number. Cecelia numbered the pages automatically by using the page numbering command. The numbers are located ½ inch from the top of the page and flush with the right margin. She included her last name along with the page number.

Title. The title of Cecelia's research paper is intriguing and yet simple and direct (see 5b-7). She uses a question to grab the readers' interest. The title is centered 1 inch from the top margin.

Introductory Data. Cecelia begins with an introduction that provides data on global warming, the topic of her research paper (see 5b-7, 6h). Everything is double-spaced.

Describing the Controversy. In paragraph 2, Cecelia describes the current controversy over global warming. Is it a normal or abnormal event?

An In-Text Citation. In citing Montague, Cecelia follows the MLA format of using the author's last name plus the page number of the quote or paraphrase in parentheses (see 13a).

Thesis. After her introductory sentences, Cecelia states her thesis (see 7a, 12a-2). In the thesis statement, she takes a position on the issue, which she will argue for in her paper.

Topic Sentence. The first sentence in paragraph 3 is an example of a topic sentence (see 6a). It tells us what the topic of the paragraph will be—the causes of global warming.

Chung 2

The idea is that sunlight enters earth's atmosphere, hits molecules
of atmospheric gas on earth's surface, and is converted to other
forms of energy such as heat. Sometimes this energy is prevented
from escaping back into space by a "blanket" of gases such as
carbon dioxide, and a net gain of heat occurs (Britt). Without
these gases, our planet would be about 60 degrees Fahrenheit
colder than it is today (Montague 1), too cold for many terrestrial
life forms that now thrive here. But there is concern that too much
heat buildup caused by unnatural levels of so-called greenhouse
gases will be dangerous for our planet.

    Now that scientists have established that global warming   4
is taking place, the next question is why? Is this, as before
stated, a normal trend for our planet? Or is this something
that is occurring because of human interference with earth's
natural systems?

    Most likely, our planet does experience warming and cooling   5
cycles, and it is possible that the current warming trend is one of
them. However, the normal warming trend may be compounded
by human practices that increase atmospheric levels of the four
principal greenhouse gases: carbon dioxide, methane, nitrous
oxide, and chlorofluorocarbons (CFC's) (Montague 1). Many of our
activities could lead to a buildup of these gases and a resulting
increase in global temperatures.

    Carbon dioxide makes up the majority of the atmospheric   6
gases. Therefore its emission is of the most concern. The greatest
source of increase in atmospheric carbon dioxide is suspected to

Internet Source Paraphrased. These two sentences are paraphrased (that is, reworded and reordered) from a section of a source (see 11c). We can tell from the in-text citation that the author of the source is Britt. Because Britt is an Internet source and, like many such sources, has no page numbering, the author's name is cited without the page number.

Transition. Notice the effective transitional sentence that Cecelia uses at the beginning of paragraph 4 to lead the readers into the next major section of her paper (see 5b-2, 6c). She tells us through this transitional sentence that her paper, having established that global warming is a real event, will now turn to the question of why it is happening.

Why Global Warming? In paragraph 5, Cecelia begins to answer the question of why global warming is happening. Cecelia says that not only does earth experience periodic warming and cooling trends, but humans have contributed to the warming trend. She will go on to show the ways in which the activities of humans have resulted in accelerating temperatures.

Development of the Topic. In paragraph 6, Cecelia elaborates on the topic introduced in the prior paragraph (see 5b-4, 7b). She discusses one of the significant ways in which humans are affecting the atmosphere: increasing the amount of carbon dioxide through burning fossil fuels. Her source, Montague, helps her to make this argument.

Chung 3

be the burning of fossil fuels such as coal and oil. Since the beginning of the Industrial Age, burning of fossil fuels has increased dramatically, resulting in an increase of atmospheric carbon dioxide of almost 55% (Montague 1). According to current theory, this is a major cause of the current warming trend, and the whole effect of this has yet to be seen.

Already, increased temperatures have had many effects, including weather pattern changes, increased rates of glacial melting, subsequent sea-level increases, and air and sea-surface temperature increases, sometimes with resulting shifts in plant and animal species.   7

Models predict that, if current theories hold true, temperatures will rise between 1 and 3.5 degrees Celsius by 2100 (Hileman). Temperature increases are expected to be highest over land, changing climates and affecting habitat suitability for terrestrial species, which may be forced to migrate or go extinct. These temperature increases are also expected to result in a sea-level rise of 15 to 95 cm (Hileman) due to increased glacial melting. This would result in flooding in low-lying coastal regions. Changes in ocean circulation will result in rising local sea temperatures, causing unforeseeable effects for species in these areas.   8

The biggest immediate effect of global warming is changes in weather, especially greater variability in temperatures and precipitation. Extreme seasonal temperatures can contribute to formation of hurricanes and tornados. Hurricanes are encouraged by high air temperatures, which lead to increased   9

Discussion of the Effects. In paragraph 7, Cecelia begins to discuss what the effects of the rising temperatures are likely to be (see 6b-1).

Summary of an Internet Source. Cecelia relies on an Internet source, Hileman, for the information in paragraph 8. In the online journal article, Hileman argues that direct climate observations support the theory that there is a global climate change in progress. Cecelia summarizes the parts of the article that reinforce her argument (see 11d).

Topic Sentence. In this topic sentence for paragraph 9, Cecelia introduces a new topic: the effect of global warming on the weather—particularly, changes in temperature and precipitation.

Chung 4

water temperatures over the oceans. A current increase in US tornados within the last four decades is thought to be associated with temperature increases, as well. Will global warming lead to mass extinctions, or will species migrate to the cooler poles and adapt to life there? Both are likely, but extinctions are inevitable if, as predicted, global temperature increases continue far into the future.

But even without these continued increases, minor 10 temperature changes can have huge effects on habitats, simultaneously affecting populations of many species. For instance, a long-term study of coastal waters off southern California, conducted by John McGowan and Dean Roemmich of the Scripps Institution of Oceanography, has shown a 2–3 degrees Fahrenheit temperature increase in the sea-surface temperature in the last fifty years (Svitil 36). This has led to density changes in the surface waters, which have had broad implications for the suitability of the habitat for the species living there.

Changes in habitat naturally lead to changes in energy 11 resources as species unable to cope with change die out or disperse to other areas. As one population shrinks, other dependent species populations are stressed for food resources, in turn stressing the populations dependent upon them. In the study previously mentioned, changes in density stratification of the water altered the amount of chemical nutrients carried up from the bacterial beds in the depths of the ocean. As nutrient levels declined near the surface, plants dependent upon these nutrients

Posing a Question. Within paragraph 9, Cecelia poses the question of what will happen to life on earth if global temperatures continue to rise. She goes on to describe predictions of what might happen.

Introducing a Source within a Source. From reading Svitil's article in *Discover* magazine, Cecelia learned about an experimental study conducted by researchers of the Scripps Institution of Oceanography. Notice how Cecelia cites these researchers' study, as reported in the Svitil article (see 13a). Because of the information Cecelia provides, we can tell just who the source of this information is.

Describing What Happens. In paragraph 11, Cecelia describes another result of global warming—the impacts on various species.

Chung 5

suffered declines in population, which in turn reduced populations of plant-dependent phytoplankton. The population-reducing effects moved up the food chain reducing populations, from phytoplankton to zooplankton to fish to seabirds (Svitil 36). Clearly, even minor temperature changes have the capacity to significantly alter population numbers, and, as the scale of climate change increases, extinctions are inevitable.

Alternatively, some say that extinctions due to climate   12 change will be limited because populations will migrate to cooler climates, avoiding the effects of climate change. To a point, I agree. However, rates at which warming will continue are unknown, and successful migrations are dependent upon populations being able to move faster than the rate of change. If warming is gradual, some species may be able to outpace the change.

However, some predictions state that temperatures will   13 rise exponentially as compounding factors come into play. As temperatures rise, rates of successful migration will be affected by individual mobility (locomotion), energy resource mobility, reproductive rate, habitat dispersal, and geography. Since a population can only migrate as quickly as its slowest-moving resource, and only to places with suitable habitat unblocked by barriers beyond their capacity to overcome (such as deserts, mountains, oceans), many species will be unable to migrate quickly enough to keep up with rates of climate change.

Counterarguments. Notice here how Cecelia introduces arguments that run counter to her own thesis that global warming is a significant problem (see 7c, 12b-2). In paragraph 12, she acknowledges the opposition's point of view, but goes on to refute it. She concedes that some populations may be able to outrun the rate of change. However, she says that many will not be so fortunate.

Transition to Next Argument. Paragraph 13 leads us into a discussion supporting her own position that many species may not survive global climate changes. She uses the transition word "however" to lead into this paragraph from the previous one.

Writing the Research Paper

Chung 6

For example, historical models have shown that the   14

geographic range of American beech has moved just 0.2 km

per year since the last Ice Age. However, to keep pace with

current predictions of climate change, beech will have to move

7–9 km per year to the north (Krebs 113). Thus, the beech is

destined to extinction unless we intervene. I predict that many

species, both plant and animal, will be unable to move quickly

enough to keep up with change and will become extinct.

What does this mean for human life on earth? The answer   15

to this question is unknown. If this warming trend continues to

escalate, then it is possible that even humanity as we know it will

eventually reach its capacity for adaptation and become extinct,

perhaps replaced by another, revolutionarily advanced species. If

the trend does not continue but the earth begins to cool, then the

effects for human populations will be less drastic. Regardless of

the duration of this warming trend, humans cannot fail to feel

the effects of a warming trend, as we already are to some degree.

Oceans are rising and may eventually encroach upon beaches

and sea-side homes. Ocean microorganisms are shifting in

abundances and will affect conditions in many economies. It is

impossible for humanity to escape entirely unaffected by even

a minor warming trend.

Already, many groups and individuals are concerned and   16

taking action about global warming and the problems it may

bring. The cooperative effort of local, national, and international

entities is necessary, because the potential effects of global

Transitional Phrase. Here again, Cecelia leads into the paragraph with a transition, "for example." We know that paragraph 14 will give an example of how certain species have not survived climate changes (see 6b-7). Information in this paragraph is summarized from Krebs's book on ecology.

Summary of Main Arguments So Far. In paragraph 15, Cecelia steps back to summarize her arguments up to this point. She begins this section of the paper with the question "What does this mean for human life on earth?" She acknowledges the uncertainty about the answer to this question.

Final Topic. Finally, Cecelia comes to the question of action (see 6b-5). Her topic sentence for paragraph 16 lets us know that others are concerned and are taking action, too.

Chung 7

warming are so huge. Global warming will affect not only individuals but businesses and governments as well.

    Businesses dependent upon world conditions are especially   17 concerned about global warming, for economical if not environmental reasons. Two of these are the global insurance and banking industries. These industries are working with the United Nations to reduce environmentally damaging activities. This is largely because, says UN Environment Program director Hans Alder, "They know that a few major disasters caused by extreme climate events . . . could literally bankrupt the industry in the next decade" (Hertsgaard C1).

    Global warming is, after all, a global problem. The effects of   18 global warming, destructive and severe, will be felt increasingly by everyone. Scientists agree that it is happening, so we should all support efforts to research and combat its causes. The changes global warming will eventually cause are unknown in their severity and scope but already we can feel some of them. Let's take action to prevent further escalation of global warming.

Integrating a Quotation. Cecelia quotes Hans Alder, United Nations Environment Program Director, regarding industry's concern over global warming. Notice that Alder's quote appeared in Hertsgaard's article. Cecelia has used ellipses to show that the quote is an excerpt with some words and phrases missing (see 11b).

Conclusion. In her conclusion, Cecelia goes back to her central arguments and repeats them (see 5b-7, 6h). In this way, she reinforces them in her readers' minds. She ends with a final call to action—asking everyone to get involved to help solve the problem of global warming.

Chung 8

Works Cited

Britt, Robert. "The Heat Is On: Scientists Agree on Human
Contribution to Global Warming." Ion Science 1995. 13 Nov.
1998 <http://www.injersey.com/Media/IonSci/features/
gwarm/gwarm.html>.

Hertsgaard, Mark. "Who's Afraid of Global Warming?" Washington
Post 21 Jan. 1996: C1. 13 Nov. 1998 <http://www.ji.org/
jinews/newsline/afraid2.htm>.

Hileman, Bette. "Climate Observations Substantiate Global
Warming Models." Chemical and Engineering News 27 Nov.
1995. 13 Nov. 1998 <http://jcbmac.chem.brown.edu/baird/
Chem221/global/pg1.html>.

Krebs, Charles J. Ecology: The Experimental Analysis of Distribution
and Abundance. 4th ed. New York: Harper, 1994.

Montague, Peter. "Global Warming--Part 1: How Global Warming
Is Sneaking Up on Us." Rachel's Hazardous Waste News 26
Aug. 1992: 1. 22 Nov. 1998 <http://www.envirolink.org/pubs/
rachel/rhwn300.htm>.

Svitil, Kathy A. "Collapse of a Food Chain." Discover July 1995:
36-37.

Works Cited. The works cited page is an alphabetical listing of all the sources used by Cecelia in her research paper. It is double-spaced throughout. The title is centered 1 inch from the top margin. Notice that the first line of each source is even with the margin, but the rest of the information is indented. In this way, the author's name is made to stand out. For more information about the MLA style of documentation, see 13a.

Internet Journal. The first source is an online journal. The title of the article is "The Heat Is On . . . ." The journal name is *Ion Science*. The first date listed is the date of publication. The second date listed is the date of access (when Cecelia read the work). The complete URL is included in angle brackets so that readers can find the source.

Internet Newspaper. The second source is a newspaper that was read on the Internet.

Internet Journal. The third source is another online journal, from the field of engineering.

Book. The fourth source provides an example of a book citation.

Internet Newsletter. There are many types of Internet publications, some of which do not have print counterparts. The newsletter in the fifth source citation exists only online.

Journal Article. The sixth source provides an example of a printed journal article citation.

Documentation Formats

FAQs

What is the purpose of documentation?

How does documentation differ from one discipline to
  another? (13a, 13b, 13c, 13d)

How do I cite electronic sources (13a, 13b, 13c, 13d)?

What are some other style manuals for the disciplines?
  (13e)

You may have noticed that some of the publications you read are
careful to provide detailed documentation to show you exactly
where the information used in the articles was found, while others
are not as thorough. Providing a documentation trail that leads back
to the original sources is a feature of scholarly writing that distinguishes it from writing found in the popular press. Scholars and researchers in all disciplines base their own work on the work that
others have done in the past. The thread of knowledge can be traced
from one scholar to another. In scholarly writing, it is essential to
provide readers with evidence of that thread of knowledge, not only
so that readers can trace the thread if they so desire, but also to let
them know that the information is from reliable sources.

Scholars and researchers in various academic disciplines have
developed different documentation systems—conventional ways of
showing the sources of the scholarship on which their work is built.

Although they differ in the details, all these systems have the same purpose: to help readers locate the sources used in the piece of writing. Thus, the writer needs to alert the reader within the text, by means of an in-text citation, whenever information comes from an outside source. The in-text citation is a kind of shorthand, signaling to readers that source information has been used. The in-text citation provides readers with just enough information to locate the source's complete bibliographic citation, which generally is found at the end of the text in the Bibliography or Works Cited list.

The system of documentation commonly employed in the humanities and fine arts was developed by the Modern Language Association (MLA). It is detailed in two books: *MLA Handbook for Writers of Research Papers*, 4th ed. (New York: MLA, 1995), by Joseph Gibaldi, is designed for undergraduate students, and *MLA Style Manual and Guide to Scholarly Publishing*, 2nd ed. (New York: MLA, 1998), also by Joseph Gibaldi, is geared to graduate students.

The system of documentation commonly employed in the social sciences was developed by the American Psychological Association (APA). The APA system is set forth in *Publication Manual of the American Psychological Association,* 4th ed. (Washington, DC: APA, 1994).

The system of documentation commonly used in business and economics, as well as in art history, history, philosophy, political science, and communications, is based on *The Chicago Manual of Style,* 14th ed. (Chicago: University of Chicago Press, 1993).

The system most widely used in the sciences is outlined in a book published by the Council of Biology Editors (CBE): *Scientific Style and Format: The CBE Manual for Authors, Editors, and Publishers,* 6th ed. (New York: Cambridge University Press, 1994).

This chapter provides an overview of these four systems of documentation. It is not necessary for you to memorize the information found here or in any of the documentation style guides. Rather, refer to these formatting guides as you write your research papers for courses in various disciplines. If you are not sure which system to use, ask your instructor which one he or she prefers. As you document your sources, follow the guidelines for your chosen system closely. Documentation styles, though alike in purpose, vary greatly in their details.

You might wonder why you or anyone else should care whether a period or a comma is used in any given style of documentation. You need to pay attention to these details as a courtesy to your readers, who are expecting you to observe the codified conventions in their field. Observing the conventions expected by your readers is comparable to following the conventions expected at a social gathering. Just as you would be violating social conventions by arriving at a formal dinner party dressed in blue jeans and a T-shirt, you would be violating the conventions of good scholarship by failing to observe standards for documentation.

13a   Document by using the MLA system

The Modern Language Association (MLA) system of documentation has been adopted by many scholarly writers in the fields of language and literature. The MLA system of documentation consists of in-text citations (found in parentheses) and an alphabetical listing of works cited (found at the end of the paper). For humanities researchers, specific sources and the pages on which information can be found are more important than the date on which the source was published. Thus, in-text citations in the MLA system include the author's last name and the page number of the source information.

http://www.english.
uiuc.edu/cws/
wworkshop/
mlamenu.htm
MLA style citation
guides

1   In-text citations in MLA style

In the MLA documentation system, citations within the body of the paper are linked to the Works Cited list at the end. The in-text citations are sometimes called *parenthetical references,* because the documentation is placed within parentheses. Both the author who is being cited and the page number of the source (when known) are included in the in-text citation in the MLA system. Following are some guidelines for incorporating parenthetical citations in the text of your research paper.

Author Named in the Narrative

If a paraphrase or direct quote is introduced with the name of the author, simply indicate the page number of the source in parentheses at the end of the cited material.

Attempting to define ethnic stereotyping, Gordon Allport states that "much

prejudice is a matter of blind conformity with prevailing folkways" (12).

A Directory to the MLA System

(continued)

(continued)

No page number is necessary when an entire work is cited. (Note that titles of independently published works are underlined.)

Conrad's book <u>Lord Jim</u> tells the story of an idealistic young Englishman.

The World Wildlife Federation Web site has links to many helpful sites about the environment.

Author Not Named in the Narrative

If the author's name is not used to introduce the paraphrased or quoted material, place the author's last name along with the specific page number in parentheses at the end of the cited material. Do not separate author and page number with a comma. Note that the parenthetical material precedes the sentence's end punctuation.

When Mitford and Peter Rodd were first engaged, "they even bought black shirts and went to some Fascist meetings" (Guinness 304).

Multiple Sentences Borrowed

Indicate every instance of borrowed material. If an entire paragraph is taken from a single source, mention the author's name at the beginning of the paragraph and cite the page number where appropriate.

As Endelman shows, the turbulence of the interwar years--"political agitation, social discrimination, street hooliganism" (191)--culminated in the formation of the British Union of Fascists. He states that anti-Semitism "was common enough that few Jews could have avoided it altogether or been unaware of its existence" (194).

Work by Two or Three Authors

Include the last names of all the authors (the last two connected by *and*) either in the text or in the parenthetical reference. Because the following reference is to the entire work, no page number is necessary:

Goodsell, Maher, and Tinto write about how the theory of collaborative learning may be applied to the administration of a college or university.

Work by Four or More Authors

In citing a work by four or more authors, either provide the names of all the authors or provide the name of the first author followed by the abbreviation *et al.* ("and others").

In The Development of Writing Abilities, the authors call writing that is close to the self "expressive," writing that gets things done "transactional," and writing that calls attention to itself "poetic" (Britton, Burgess, Martin, McLeod, and Rosen).

or

In The Development of Writing Abilities, the authors present a theory of writing based upon whether a writer assumes a participant or a spectator role (Britton et al.).

Work by a Corporate Author

When the author is an organization or corporation, treat the group's name the same way as the name of an individual author. If the name is long, try to incorporate it into the text rather than including it in a parenthetical note.

In the book <u>The Downsizing of America</u>, by the New York Times, a report is quoted as showing "that 131,209 workers had been cast out of their jobs in just the first quarter of 1996" (220).

Work in More than One Volume

If the work consists of more than one volume, provide the volume number, followed by a colon, just before the page number. When referring to an entire volume of a multivolume work, add a comma after the author's name, followed by *vol.* and the volume number.

In Ward's introduction to the collected works of Sir John Vanbrugh, he states that "the Vanbrugh family seems to have been both ancient and honorable" (1: x).

The collected plays of Vanbrugh show the range of his talent (Ward, vol. 2).

Different Works by the Same Author

When the Works Cited list refers to two works by the same author, include in the parenthetical reference the title (which may be abbreviated), as well as the author and the page number of the source. If the author's name is included in the text, cite only the title and page number in parentheses.

Her first volume of memoirs, published in 1975, tells the story of her brother's friend, whom her mother would not allow her to choose for games at parties (Mitchison, <u>All Change Here</u> 85). In her pre-war novel, Mitchison, who was the housebound wife of an Oxford don, derives a strange solution to England's economic problems (<u>We Have Been Warned</u> 441).

Different Page Numbers in the Same Work

When it is apparent that two citations refer to the same work, there is no need to repeat the author's name. Identifying the appropriate page number will suffice.

In <u>We Have Been Warned</u>, Mitchison's pre-war novel, she states that "these commercial ideas have crept into all our morality, art and science" (441). She continues in this vein when she asks, "How could he with that racial inheritance and that education--even if he saw through the education very young?" (444).

Work Cited Indirectly

If possible, take information directly from the original source. However, sometimes it is necessary to cite someone indirectly—particularly in the case of a published account of someone's spoken words. To indicate an indirect quote, use the abbreviation *qtd. in* (for "quoted in") before listing the source.

High school teacher Ruth Gerrard finds that "certain Shakespearean

characters have definite potential as student role models" (qtd. in

Davis and Salomone 24).

Two or More Sources within the Same Citation

When referring to two or more sources within the same parenthetical reference, use semicolons to separate the citations. For the sake of readability, however, take care not to list too many sources in a single citation.

The works of several authors in the post-war years tend to focus on racial

themes (Mitchison 440; Mosley 198).

If students are allowed to freely exchange ideas about a work of literature,

they will come to examine their own sense of the work in light of the

opinions of others (Bleich 45; Rosenblatt, Literature as Exploration 110).

Anonymous Work

Sources such as magazine articles, Web sites, and reports by commissions may not list an author. Such works are listed by their title on the Works Cited page. For the in-text citation of an anonymous work listed by title, use an abbreviated version of the title, in parentheses.

The article points out the miscommunications that can occur between men

and women because of differences in communication styles ("It Started").

In many Native-American cultures, the feather often symbolizes a prayer

("Feather").

Work of Literature

Classic works of literature are often available in different editions. It is therefore helpful to include location information, such as chapter number, section number, act number, and scene number, in the parenthetical reference so that the reader can locate the reference in any edition of the work. Include this location information after a page reference, where appropriate. When citing classic poetry or plays, use the line numbers instead of page numbers. Generally, use arabic numbers rather than roman numerals.

In the novel Lord Jim, Conrad describes the village of Patusan and its

inhabitants (242; ch. 24).

In Paradise Lost, Satan's descent to earth is described in graphic detail

(Milton 4.9-31).

As Laertes leaves for France, Polonius gives the young man trite and

unhelpful advice such as "Beware/Of entrance to a quarrel, but being

in,/Bear't that th' opposed may beware of thee" (Hamlet 1.3.65-67).

Long Quote

When a quote is lengthy (takes up more than four lines), indent the quote ten spaces from the left-hand margin (or 1 inch, if you are using a word processor). Lines remain double-spaced throughout the indented quote. Note that the end punctuation is different for indented quotes than for internal citations that are run into the text— the period comes before the parenthetical citation for indented quotes. Also note that no quotation marks are used and generally a colon introduces the quotation.

McMurtry's novel chronicles the growing-up years of a young man in rural

Texas. In this passage, we see the alienation that Lonnie feels as his family

falls apart around him:

> The next day was the last of the rodeo, and I didn't much care.
>
> The whole crazy circle of things got so it tired me out. When I
>
> woke up that morning I could see Jesse down in the lots, moving
>
> around, and I got up to go talk to him. I had looked for him the
>
> night before, after the dance, but he wasn't around . . . . There
>
> was nobody to cook my breakfast, and I didn't feel like cooking
>
> it myself. (112)

Electronic Source

When information is from an electronic medium, usually the entire work is referenced. In such cases, incorporate the reference to the work within the sentence by naming the author of the source (or the title, if no author is listed) just as it is listed on the Works Cited page. No parentheses are needed when an entire work is cited.

One of the features of The Encyclopedia Mythica Web site is its archive of cultural myths, such as those prevalent in Native-American society.

Andy Packer's homepage lists a number of links to Star Wars Web sites.

When citing a Web site with secondary pages, list separately each secondary page used in the research paper. Be sure that the Works Cited list includes the correct URL for each secondary page and lists each page independently by its title.

According to Britannica Online, in Native-American mythology, a feather often symbolizes a prayer ("Feather").

Britannica Online shows that mythology has developed in all societies ("Mythology").

When quoting or paraphrasing directly from an electronic source, either give the section title in quotation marks (as in the example above) or cite the paragraph number (with the abbreviation *par.*) or screen number, if provided, so that a reader will be able to find the section used in the paper.

The writer discusses his reasons for calling Xerox's online site "a great place to visit" (Gomes, par. 5).

The balance sheet for 1997 showed a significant upturn in sales (Gateway Computers, screen 2).

2 Bibliographic footnotes in MLA style

Generally, footnotes and endnotes are not used in the MLA system of documentation. However, notes may be included to refer the reader to sources that contain information different from the content of the paper. In the text, indicate a note with a superscript number typed immediately after the source that is referred to. Number notes consecutively throughout the text.

Use a note to cite sources that have additional information on topics covered in the paper.

[1]For further information on this point, see Barbera (168), McBrien (56), and Kristeva (29).

[2]For an additional study of Smith's fictional characters, see Barbera's Me Again.

Use a note to cite sources that contain information related to that included in the paper.

[3]Although outside the scope of this paper, major themes in the novel are discussed by Kristeva and Barbera.

Use a note to cite sources containing information that a reader might want to compare with that in the paper.

[4]On this point, see also Rosenblatt's Literature as Exploration, in which she discusses reader response theory.

For the endnote format, start a new page following the end of the text, before the Works Cited list. Type the title "Notes," centered horizontally one inch from the top of the page. Double-space to the first note. Indent the first line five spaces (or ½ inch) from the left margin, and type the note number slightly above the line (or use the superscript format on a word processor). Then follow, without any space, to the text of the note. Double-space between and within all notes.

For the footnote format, position the text of the note at the bottom of the page on which the reference occurs. Begin the footnote four lines below the text. Single-space within a footnote, but double-space between footnotes if more than one note appears on a page.

On the Works Cited page, include all the sources mentioned in the notes.

3 Works Cited page in MLA style

The listing of all the sources used in a paper, usually entitled Works Cited, comes at the end of the paper. Other names for this listing include Bibliography, Literature Cited, Works Consulted (which includes works not directly cited), and Annotated Bibliography (which includes brief summaries of sources). Check with your instructor to determine which format she or he prefers. The purpose of this listing is to help readers find the information used in the paper, so the entries must be complete and accurate.

List sources alphabetically by the last name of the author, using the letter-by-letter system of alphabetization. When no author is given, alphabetize by the first word of the title (excluding *A, An,* or *The*). Type the first word of each entry at the left margin. Indent subsequent lines of the same entry five spaces (or ½ inch). Double-space the entire reference page, both between and within entries.

WWW
WEB

http://www.mla.org/
main_stl.htm#sources
Straight from the
horse's mouth—the
MLA's guide to citing
electronic resources

When you have more than one work by the same author, arrange the titles alphabetically. Give the author's name for the first entry only. For subsequent works by the same author, substitute three hyphens (followed by a period) for the author's name.

Books

A citation for a book has three basic parts:

Author's name. <u>Book title</u>. Publication information.

For books, monographs, and other complete works, include the author's full name as given on the title page—start with the last name first, followed by a comma; then put the first name and middle name or initial, followed by a period. After the author's name, give the complete title of the work as it appears on the title page (underlined), followed by a period. Important words in the title should be capitalized. Include the subtitle, if there is one, separated from the title by a colon. Next, include (if appropriate) the name of the editor, compiler, or translator; the edition of the book; the number of volumes; and the name of the series. Finally, indicate the place of publication, followed by a colon (if several cities are listed, include only the first one); the publisher's name as it appears on the title page, followed by a comma; and the date of publication from the copyright page, followed by a period.

In MLA style, the publication information is abbreviated as much as is possible in the bibliographic entry. The city where the book was published is given without a state abbreviation, unless the city may be unfamiliar (*Redmond, WA*) or confused with another city (*Springfield, MA*). A country abbreviation may be needed for clarity for some foreign publications (for example, *Ulster, Ire.; Bergen, Norw.*). But if a foreign city is well known (such as London or Paris), a country abbreviation is unnecessary. Abbreviate the publisher's name to one word wherever possible (for example, McGraw-Hill, Inc. to *McGraw*; Houghton Mifflin Co. to *Houghton*). Similarly, abbreviate the names of university and government presses: *Columbia UP* stands for Columbia University Press; the letters *GPO* for Government Printing Office. (For guidelines on citing electronic books, see pages 272–273.)

Note: Unless your instructor directs you differently, show the title of a complete work or a journal in underlined form, even though such titles appear in italics in most printed documents. If the titles you cite were initially in italics (perhaps because you used citations from an electronic file source), remember to run the SEARCH/FIND AND REPLACE routine on your Works Cited document. Set the search to find italic type (it may be under FONT) and replace it with underlined type.

Book by One Author

Author's name   Book title   Publication information

Allport, Gordon W. The Nature of Prejudice. Palo Alto: Addison, 1954.

Haire-Sargeant, Lin. H. New York: Pocket, 1992.

Manguel, Alberto. A History of Reading. New York: Viking, 1996.

Book by Two or Three Authors

Write multiple authors' names in the order in which they are given on the book's title page. Note that this order may not be alphabetical. Reverse the name of the first author only, putting the last name first; separate the authors' names with commas.

Goodsell, Anne S., Michelle R. Maher, and Vincent Tinto. Collaborative

     Learning: A Sourcebook for Higher Education. University Park, PA:

     National Center on Postsecondary Teaching, Learning, and Assessment,

     1992.

Guinness, Jonathan, and Catherine Guinness. The House of Mitford. New

     York: Viking, 1985.

Book by More than Three Authors

For a book with more than three authors, either write out the names of all the authors listed on the book's title page or write only the first author's name, followed by a comma and the Latin phrase *et al.* (for "and others").

Britton, James, Tony Burgess, Nancy Martin, Alex McLeod, and Harold

Rosen. The Development of Writing Abilities. London: Macmillan, 1975.

or

Britton, James, et al. The Development of Writing Abilities. London:

Macmillan, 1975.

Book by a Corporate Author

A book by a corporate author is any book whose title page lists as the author a group, rather than individuals. Start with the name of the corporate author, even if it is also the publisher.

Conference on College Composition and Communication. The National

Language Policy. Urbana: NCTE, 1992.

New York Times, Inc. The Downsizing of America. New York: Random, 1996.

Book with an Editor

For books with editors rather than authors, start with the editor or editors, followed by a comma and the abbreviation *ed.* (for "editor") or *eds.* (for "editors").

Barbera, Jack, and William McBrien, eds. Me Again: The Uncollected

Writings of Stevie Smith. New York: Farrar, 1982.

Cooper, Jane Roberta, ed. Reading Adrienne Rich: Reviews and Re-Visions,

1951-1981. Ann Arbor: U of Michigan P, 1984.

Gates, Henry Louis, Jr., and Nellie Y. McKay, eds. The Norton Anthology of

African American Literature. New York: Norton, 1997.

Selection from an Edited Work

In addition to the information provided for an edited book, an entry for a particular selection needs to have the author's name and the title of the work. The title is underlined if the work is a book or a play; it is enclosed in quotation marks if the work is a poem, short story, chapter, or essay. Note that the name of the editor or editors follows the book title and is preceded by the abbreviation *Ed.* (for

"Edited by"). The inclusive page numbers of the work follow the publication information.

Bambara, Toni Cade. "Raymond's Run." The Norton Anthology of African

American Literature. Ed. Henry Louis Gates, Jr. and Nellie Y. McKay.

New York: Norton, 1997. 2307-13.

Spivak, Gayatri. "Feminism and Deconstruction, Again: Negotiating

with Unacknowledged Masculinism." Between Feminism and

Psychoanalysis. Ed. Teresa Brennan. London: Routledge, 1989. 206-23.

Two or More Books by the Same Author

Alphabetize entries by the first word in the title. Include the author's name in the first entry only. In subsequent entries, type three hyphens in place of the author's name, followed by a period.

Rose, Mike. Lives on the Boundary: A Moving Account of the Struggles and

Achievements of America's Educationally Underprepared. New York:

Penguin, 1989.

---. Possible Lives: The Promise of Education in America. Boston: Houghton,

1995.

Article in a Reference Book

An entry for an article in a reference book follows the same pattern as an entry for a work in an anthology. Note, however, that the editor's name and full publication information need not be provided; it is sufficient to provide the edition (if known) and the year of publication. If the article is signed, provide the author's name. (Often the author's name is given in abbreviated form at the end of the article and included in full form elsewhere.)

Robins, Robert Henry. "Language." Encyclopaedia Britannica. 1980 ed.

If the article is unsigned, start with the title of the article:

"Lochinvar." Merriam-Webster's Encyclopedia of Literature. 1995 ed.

Introduction, Preface, Foreword, or Afterword

Start with the name of the author of the specific part being cited, followed by the name of the part, capitalized but not underlined or enclosed in quotation marks. If the writer of the specific part is the same as the author of the book, give the author's last name, preceded by the word *By*. If the writer of the specific part is different from the author of the book, give the book author's complete name after *By*. Provide complete publication information and inclusive page numbers (even if they are given as Roman numerals) of the part being cited.

Tompkins, Jane. Preface. A Life in School: What the Teacher Learned. By

Tompkins. Reading: Addison, 1996. xi-xix.

Book with an Author and an Editor

Start with the author's name and the title of the author's work; then provide the editor or editors, preceded by the abbreviation *Ed.* (for "Edited by").

Bishop, Elizabeth. The Complete Poems 1927-1979. Ed. Alice Helen

Methfessel. New York: Farrar, 1983.

Book in Translation

Begin the entry with the author's name and the title of the book. After the book's title, insert the abbreviation *Trans.* (for "Translated by") and give the translator's name. If the book also has an editor, give the names of the editor and the translator in the order in which they are listed on the title page.

Kristeva, Julia. Powers of Horror: An Essay on Abjection. Trans. Leon S.

Roudiez. New York: Columbia UP, 1982.

Second or Subsequent Edition of a Book

If a book is not a first edition, identify the edition in the way that it is identified on the book's title page: by year (*1993 ed.*), by name (*Rev. ed.* for "Revised edition"), or by number (*2nd ed., 3rd ed.*).

Freire, Paulo. Pedagogy of the Oppressed. Trans. Myra Bergman Ramos. New

rev. 20th anniversary ed. New York: Continuum, 1993.

Work in More than One Volume

When citing more than one volume of a multivolume work, insert the total number of volumes in the work before the publication material. When citing one volume of a multivolume work, include only the particular volume number before the publication information.

Doyle, Arthur Conan. The Complete Sherlock Holmes. 2 vols. Garden City:

Doubleday, 1930.

Poe, Edgar Allan. The Complete Poems and Stories of Edgar Allan Poe. Illus.

E. McKnight Kauffer. Vol. 2. New York: Knopf, 1982.

Book in a Series

If the title page indicates that the book is part of a series, insert the series name (do not underline it or enclose it in quotation marks) and the series number, if any, before the publication material.

Berlin, James A. Rhetorics, Poetics, and Cultures. Refiguring College English

Studies. Urbana: NCTE, 1996.

Jameson, Frederic. Foreword. The Postmodern Condition: A Report on

Knowledge. By Jean-François Lyotard. Trans. Geoff Bennington and

Brian Massumi. Theory and History of Lit. 10. Minneapolis: U of

Minnesota P, 1989. vii-xxi.

Republished Book

Insert the original publication date, followed by a period, before the publication material of the work being cited.

Dewey, John. Experience and Education. 1938. New York: Collier, 1963.

Government Document

If the author of a government document is unknown, start with the name of the government, followed by the name of the agency that issued the document, abbreviated. The title of the publication, underlined, follows, and the usual publication material completes the entry.

United States. FBI. Uniform Crime Reports for the United States: 1995.

Washington: GPO, 1995.

(*GPO* stands for Government Printing Office.)

Published Proceedings of a Conference

Write an entry for proceedings in the same way as for a book. Provide information about the conference after the title of the proceedings.

Kelder, Richard, ed. Interdisciplinary Curricula, General Education, and

Liberal Learning. Selected Papers from the Third Annual Conference

of the Institute for the Study of Postsecondary Pedagogy, Oct. 1992.

New Paltz, NY: SUNY New Paltz, 1993.

Book in a Language Other than English

Provide the author's name, title, and publication material as they are given in the book. Note that this information may appear on a page other than the title or copyright page.

Habermas, Jürgen. Erkenntnis und Interesse. Frankfurt: Suhrkamp, 1968.

Book Published before 1900

Do not provide the publisher's name when writing an entry for a work published before 1900. Use a comma after the place of publication.

Bacon, Francis. The Essays, or Councils, Civil and Moral, of Sir Francis

Bacon. London, 1706.

Periodicals

A citation for an article in a periodical follows a format similar to that for a book:

Author's name. "Title of the article." Publication information.

In the publication information, the title of the journal, as it appears on the journal's title page (without introductory articles such as *A* and *The*), is underlined. The volume and issue numbers, if provided, go after the journal title and are followed by the publication date, in parentheses. A colon follows the parentheses. Then, inclusive page numbers are provided for the entire article.

When citing magazines and newspapers, list the day and month (abbreviated except for May, June, and July) of publication, with the day before the month and the month before the year (*19 Dec. 1997*). Provide page numbers for the entire article. Note that if the article is not printed on consecutive pages, you need to provide only the first page number and a plus sign, with no space between them. (For guidelines on citing articles in online periodicals, see page 273.)

Article in a Journal Paginated by Volume

Many professional journals are numbered continuously, from the first page of the first issue to the final page of the last issue within a volume. Do not include an issue number when citing this kind of journal.

Author	Article title	Journal title

Bloom, Lynn Z. "Why I (Used to) Hate to Give Grades." Conference on College

Composition and Communication 48 (1997): 360-71.

Volume	Year of	Consecutive
number	publication	pages

Holbrook, Sue Ellen. "Women's Work: The Feminizing of Composition."

Rhetoric Review 9 (1991): 201-19.

When there are two or more authors, write the authors' names in the order in which they are given on the first page of the article. Note that this order may not be alphabetical. Reverse the name of the first author only (putting the last name first); write the other names in normal order. Write the rest of the entry in the same way that you would an entry for a journal article with one author.

Kidda, Michael, Joseph Turner, and Frank E. Parker. "There Is an Alternative

to Remedial Education." Metropolitan Universities 3 (1993): 16-25.

Shamoon, Linda K., and Deborah H. Burns. "A Critique of Pure Tutoring."

Writing Center Journal 15 (1995): 134-51.

Article in a Journal Paginated by Issue

If each issue of the journal is numbered separately, starting with page 1, include both volume and issue numbers. Put a period after the volume number, and write the issue number after the period—for example, 12.1 signifies volume 12, issue 1.

Kogen, Myra. "The Conventions of Expository Writing." Journal of Basic

Writing 5.1 (1986): 24-37.

Mohanty, S. P. "Us and Them: On the Philosophical Bases of Political

Criticism." Yale Journal of Criticism 2.2 (1989): 1-31.

Magazine Article

If the article is unsigned, begin with the title. For a weekly or bi-weekly magazine, provide the day, the month (abbreviated, except for May, June, and July), and the year, followed by a colon and the inclusive page numbers.

"It Started in a Garden." Time 22 Sept. 1952: 110-11.

For a monthly or quarterly magazine, give only the month or quarter and the year before the inclusive page numbers. (If the article is not printed on consecutive pages, give the first page number followed by a plus sign.)

MacDonald, Heather. "Downward Mobility: The Failure of Open Admissions

at City University." City Journal Summer 1994: 10-20.

Newspaper Article

Provide the name of the newspaper, but do not use the article (*The, An, A*) that precedes it (*Boston Globe*, not *The Boston Globe*). If it is not included in the newspaper's title, add the city of publication in brackets following the title. Nationally published newspapers, such as *USA Today*, do not need a city of publication in the reference. Next, provide the day, month (abbreviated, except for May, June, and July), and year. (Do not list volume or issue numbers; however, if the edition is given on the newspaper's masthead, do include it, followed by a colon.) Conclude the entry by providing the page numbers, preceded by the section number or letter if each section is separately paginated.

Doherty, William F. "Woodward Jury Seeks Definitions." Boston Globe 29 Oct.

1997: B1+.

"Twenty Percent Biased Against Jews." New York Times 22 Nov. 1992: A1.

Editorial

Provide the name of the editorial writer (last name first), if known, and then the title of the editorial (in quotation marks). Next, write the word *Editorial*, but do not underline it or enclose it in quotation marks. End the entry with the name of the newspaper, magazine, or journal and the standard publication information.

Paglia, Camille. "More Mush from the NEA." Editorial. Wall Street Journal

24 Oct. 1997: A22.

"Six Who Serve Their Council Districts." Editorial. Boston Globe 31 Oct.

1997: A22.

Letter to the Editor

Include the designation *Letter* after the name of the letter writer, but do not underline it or enclose it in quotation marks. End the entry with the name of the newspaper, magazine, or journal and the standard publication information.

Schack, Steven. Letter. New York Times 1 Dec. 1997, late ed.: A20.

Review

Start with the name of the reviewer and the title of the review. Then insert *Rev. of* (for "Review of"), but do not underline it or enclose it in quotation marks. Next, provide the title of the piece reviewed, followed by a comma, the word *by*, and the name of the author of the piece being reviewed. If the name of the reviewer is not given, start with the title of the review; if no title is given either, start with *Rev. of.* End the entry with the name of the newspaper, magazine, or journal and the standard publication information.

Ribadeneira, Diego. "The Secret Lives of Seminarians." Rev. of The New

Men: Inside the Vatican's Elite School for American Priests, by Brian

Murphy. Boston Globe 31 Oct. 1997: C6.

Abstract from an Abstracts Journal

Begin by providing publication information on the original work. Then provide material on the journal in which you found the abstract: the title (underlined), the volume number, and the year (in parentheses), followed by a colon and the page or item number.

Johnson, Nancy Kay. "Cultural and Psychosocial Determinants of Health and

Illness." Diss. U of Washington, 1980. DAI 40 (1980): 425B.

(*Diss.* means "Dissertation," and *DAI* is the abbreviation for *Dissertation Abstracts International.*)

Juliebo, Moira, et al. "Metacognition of Young Readers in an Early

Intervention Reading Programme." Journal of Research in Reading 21.1

(1998): 24-35. Psychological Abstracts 85.7 (1998): item 22380.

Other Sources

Film or Video Recording

Begin with the film's title (underlined), followed by the director, distributor, and year of release; also provide other pertinent material, such as the names of the performers, writers, and producers, between the title and the name of the distributor.

Indiana Jones and the Temple of Doom. Dir. Steven Spielberg. Paramount,

1984.

Wayne's World. Dir. Penelope Spheeris. Prod. Lorne Michaels. Perf. Mike

Myers, Dana Carvey, and Rob Lowe. Paramount, 1992.

If citing an individual's work on the film, begin the entry with that person's name and title.

Spielberg, Steven, dir. Indiana Jones and the Temple of Doom. Paramount, 1984.

Television or Radio Program

Provide the title of the episode (enclosed in quotation marks), if known; the title of the program (underlined); the title of the series (not underlined or enclosed in quotation marks), if any; the network; the call numbers and local city, if any; and the date of broadcast.

"Commercializing Christians." All Things Considered. Natl. Public Radio.

WBUR, Boston. 8 Dec. 1997.

"The Great Apes." National Geographic Special. PBS. WGBH, Boston. 12 July

1984.

Sound Recording

For a sound recording that is available commercially, provide the name of the artist, the title of the recording (underlined, unless the piece is identified only by form, number, and key), the manufacturer, and the year of issue. Indicate the medium, if other than a compact disc, before the manufacturer's name.

Ball, Marcia. Blue House. Rounder, 1994.

Ormandy, Eugene, cond. Symphony no. 3 in C minor, op. 78. By Camille Saint-

Saëns. Perf. E. Power Biggs, organ. Philadelphia Orch. Sony, 1991.

Raitt, Bonnie. "Something to Talk About." Luck of the Draw. Audiocassette.

Capitol, 1991.

Performance

An entry for a play, concert, opera, or dance begins with the title (underlined), includes information similar to that given for a film, and ends with the performance site (for example, the theatre and city) and the date of the performance.

Blues for an Alabama Sky. By Pearl Cleage. Dir. Kenny Leon. Perf.

 Phylicia Rashad, Tyrone Mitchell Henderson, Sean C. Squire, Deidre

 N. Henry, and John Henry Redwood. Huntington Theatre, Boston.

 5 Feb. 1997.

Riverdance. Dance Capt. Kevin McCormack. Perf. Colin Dunne, Eileen

 Martin, Maria Pagés, and the Riverdance Irish Dance Troupe. Wang

 Center, Boston. 18 Jan. 1997.

Work of Art

Provide the name of the artist, the title of the work (underlined), the name of the site that houses the work, and the city. If it is available, include the date the work was created immediately after the title. If the work is part of a private collection, provide the collector's name.

Cassatt, Mary. Breakfast in Bed. 1886. Private collection of Dr. and Mrs. John

 J. McDonough,Youngstown, OH.

---. Five O'Clock Tea. Museum of Fine Arts, Boston.

Published Interview

Provide the name of the person being interviewed; the title of the interview (enclosed in quotation marks), if any; the title of the source in which the interview is published; and any other pertinent bibliographic material.

Faulkner, William. "The Meaning of 'A Rose for Emily.'" Interview. 1959. The

 Story and Its Writer: An Introduction to Short Fiction. Ed. Ann Charters.

 Compact 4th ed. Boston: Bedford-St. Martin's, 1995. 772-73.

Unpublished Interview

Provide the name of the person being interviewed, the designation *Personal interview* (not underlined or in quotation marks), and the date.

Jensen, Steven. Personal interview. 12 Apr. 1997.

Published Letter

Provide the name of the letter writer; information about the letter (enclosed in quotation marks), if given; and the date of the letter. Conclude with remaining pertinent bibliographic material.

Faulkner, William. "To Malcolm Cowley." 1 Nov. 1948. The Faulkner-Cowley

File: Letters and Memories, 1944-1962. Ed. Malcolm Cowley. New York:

Viking, 1966. 114-18.

Personal Letter to the Author

Bush, George. Letter to the author. 8 Sept. 1995.

Dissertation

Enclose the title of the dissertation in quotation marks, followed by the abbreviation *Diss.* (for "Dissertation"), the name of the degree-granting institution, a comma, and the year written.

UNPUBLISHED

Balkema, Sandra. "The Composing Activities of Computer Literate Writers."

Diss. U of Michigan, 1984.

Cite a published dissertation as a book, but add dissertation information before the publication data.

PUBLISHED

Deatherage, Cynthia. A Way of Seeing: The Anglo-Saxons and the Primal

World View. Diss. Purdue U, 1997. Ann Arbor: UMI, 1997. 9821728.

UMI stands for University Microfilms International. (For examples of dissertation abstracts, see page 267.)

Unpublished Manuscript

Provide the name of the author, the title of the piece being cited (in quotation marks), the phrase *Unpublished essay* or *Unpublished manuscript,* and the date.

Welter, William. "Word Processing in Freshman English: Does It Compute?"

Unpublished essay, 1985.

Speech or Lecture

Provide the name of the speaker; the title of the presentation (in quotation marks), if known; the meeting and sponsoring organization, if applicable; the place where the speech or lecture was given; and the date.

Booth, Wayne. "Ethics and the Teaching of Literature." College Forum. NCTE
Convention. Cobo Center, Detroit. 21 Nov. 1997.

Electronic Media

As electronic media continue to evolve, the details of citations
will change to reflect new formats. However, the basic rationale for
citing references will remain the same: researchers using electronic
material need to provide information identifing each source, and
they must give clear directions for locating it. Because electronic
sources tend to be less permanent and subject to fewer standards
than printed works, their citations need more information than is
required for print sources. Coverage of electronic references in MLA
format is given in the second edition of the *MLA Style Manual and
Guide to Scholarly Publishing*, by Joseph Gibaldi (New York: MLA,
1998).

Because electronic information can be changed quickly, easily,
and often, the version available to your readers may be different
from the one you accessed during your research. MLA recommends
listing two dates—the date of posting or updating and the date of access (that is, the date the source was read)—and printing out the
electronic source on the day of access. MLA also recommends including the electronic address (URL) within angle brackets to distinguish it from the surrounding punctuation of the citation. Be
accurate when recording URLs and other identifying information
(such as the author's name or the title of the Web page) so that readers can use a search tool to find the source if the URL becomes outdated. Begin the URL with the access-mode identifier (*http, ftp, gopher,
telnet, news*), followed by the complete address.

Tips on citing some of the most commonly used electronic sources
follow. In its 1998 guidelines for electronic citation style, the MLA
acknowledges that not all of the information recommended for a
citation may be available. Cite whatever information is available. It
might be wise to consult your instructor before finalizing your
Works Cited list to ensure that you are conforming to his or her requirements for electronic citations.

Online Professional or Personal Site

Reference information on the Internet varies. Include the information available at the site, in the following sequence:

1. The creator of the site (not the editor or compiler)
2. The title of the site, project, or database (underlined) or, if there
   is no title, a brief description of the site (such as *Homepage*)

3. The editor or compiler of the project or database

4. The version number, the date of electronic publication or latest update, the name of the sponsoring organization or institution

5. The date of access

6. The electronic address (URL), placed within angle brackets

Dye, Sylvania. <u>Victoriana On-Line</u>. 12 Jan. 1998 <http://www.geocities.com/

Athens/Delphi/9613>.

<u>The Encyclopedia Mythica</u>. Ed. Micha F. Lindemans. 1995-98. 14 May 1998

<http://www2.cc.gc.ca/climate/index.html>.

<u>Global Climate Change</u>. 1 May 1998. Environment Canada. 15 May 1998

<http://www.eg.gc.ca>.

Packer, Andy. Homepage. 1 Apr. 1998 <http://www.suu.edu/~students/

Packer.htm>.

To cite a poem, short story, or other short work within a scholarly project, begin with the author's name, followed by the title of the work (in quotation marks). Continue with the relevant information on the project, such as the access date and the URL.

Conrad, Joseph. "<u>Typhoon</u>" and Other Stories. Garden City: Doubleday, 1921.

<u>The Electronic Text Center</u>, U of Virginia. 23 Apr. 1998 <http://www.lib.

virginia.edu/ecenters.html>.

To cite an anonymous article from a reference database, start with the title of the article (in quotation marks). Continue with the electronic publication information from the reference work. Be sure to give the unique address of the article you are citing if it is different from the URL for the database itself.

"Feather." <u>Britannica Online</u>. Vers. 98.1.1. May 1998. Encyclopaedia

Britannica. 12 Aug. 1998 <http://www.eb.com:175>.

Online Book

The complete texts of many books are now available online as well as in print. Provide the following items when citing such works:

1. The name of the author (if only an editor, compiler, or translator is mentioned, give that person's name first, followed by *ed.*, *comp.*, or *trans.*)

2. The title of the work, underlined

3. The name of any editor, compiler, or translator (if not given earlier)
4. Publication information from the printed work if the work has been printed
5. The date of electronic publication and the name of any sponsoring organization
6. The access date and the electronic address, in angle brackets

Woolf, Virginia. The Voyage Out. London: Faber, 1914. The English Server,

Carnegie Mellon U. 9 Mar. 1997 <http://eserver.org/fiction/voyage-out.txt>.

When citing a part (chapter or section) of an online book, place the title or name of the part in quotation marks after the author's name. Be sure to give the URL of the specific part of the book if it is different from the complete book's URL.

Einstein, Albert. "Relativity." Relativity: The Special and General Theory.

Trans. Robert W. Lawson. New York: Bonanza, 1961. 3 Apr. 1997 <http://

ourworld.compuserve.com/homepages/eric-baird/ein-home.htm>.

Article in an Online Periodical

Many magazines, newspapers, and scholarly journals are now available in online formats. Generally, citations for online periodicals follow the same sequence as citations for print periodicals. They should include the following:

1. The author's name, if provided
2. The title of the work, in quotation marks
3. The name of the journal, magazine, or newspaper, underlined
4. The volume and issue number (or other identifying number)
5. The date of publication
6. The range or total number of pages, paragraphs, or sections, if they are numbered
7. The publication medium, such as CD-ROM
8. The name of the online service, if provided
9. The date of access and the electronic address, in angle brackets

A GOPHER SITE

Caplan, R. "General Agreement on a New Economy: A New Website on

Sustainable Economics." Economics Working Group/Project of the Tides

Foundation 19 Mar. 1996: 17 pars. 29 Oct. 1996 <gopher://gopher.igc.

apc.org/00/environment/forests/western.lands/current/55>.

AN FTP SITE

Deutsch, Pater, "archie--An Electronic Directory Service for the Internet."

Mar. 1993. 15 Apr. 1995 <ftp://ftp.sura.net/pub/archie/docs/whatis.

archie>.

A TELNET SITE

Gomes, Lee. "Xerox's On-Line Neighborhood: A Great Place to Visit."

Mercury News 3 May 1992. 5 Dec. 1996 <telnet://lambda.parc.xerox.

com_8888>.

AN ARTICLE IN AN ONLINE NEWSPAPER OR ON A NEWSWIRE

Dedman, Bill. "Racial Bias Seen in U.S. Housing Loan Program." New York

Times on the Web 13 May 1998. 13 May 1998 <http://www.nytimes.com/

archives>.

O'Brien, John. "Chicago at Heart of Heroin Case." Chicago Tribune Online 15

Oct. 1996. 29 Oct. 1996 <http://www.chicagotribune.com>.

AN ARTICLE IN AN ONLINE MAGAZINE

Ricks, Delthia. "Sickle Cell: New Hope." Newsday 12 May 1998. 13 May 1998

<http://www.newsday.com/homepage.htm>.

Sanchez, Robert. "The Digital Press." Internet World Sept. 1995. 20 Feb. 1996

<http://www.internet.com/>.

AN ONLINE REVIEW

Bast, Joseph L. Rev. of Our Stolen Future, by Theo Colborn et al. Heartland

Institute 18 Apr. 1996: 27 pars. 25 June 1997 <http://www.heartland.

org/stolen1.htm>.

AN ONLINE ABSTRACT

Reid, Joy. "Computer-Assisted Text-Analysis for ESL Students." Calico

Journal 1.3 (1983): 40-42. Abstract. DIALOG. 14 Jan. 1990. Item: EJ29870.

AN ONLINE EDITORIAL

"A Nuclear Threat from India." Editorial. New York Times on the Web 13 May

1998. 14 May 1998 <http://www.nytimes.com/archives>.

AN ONLINE LETTER TO THE EDITOR

Lowry, Heath. Letter. <u>Deseret News Online</u> 23 Mar. 1998. 25 Mar. 1998

    <http://www.desnews.com/archst.html>.

AN ARTICLE IN AN ONLINE SCHOLARLY JOURNAL

Reinhardt, Leslie Kaye. "British and Indian Identities in a Picture by

    Benjamin West." <u>Eighteenth Century Studies</u> 31.3 (1998). 12 July

    1998 <http://muse.jhu.edu/journals/eighteenth-century_studies>.

Nonperiodical Publication on CD-ROM, Magnetic Tape, or Diskette

Often, works on CDs, disks, or magnetic tape are published in a single edition, much as books are. To cite such publications, use a format similar to that used to cite books, with the addition of a description of the publication medium.

<u>Corel WordPerfect Suite 8</u>. CD-ROM. Ottawa, CA: Corel, 1998.

DeLorme Mapping. "Paris." <u>Global Explorer</u>. CD-ROM. Freeport, ME:

    DeLorme, 1993.

(Note that DeLorme Mapping is the corporate author of this CD.)

Halio, Marcia. <u>Exercise Disks for Writing with WordPerfect</u>. Diskette. 4 discs.

    New York: Harper, 1997.

Database Periodically Published on CD-ROM

Periodicals and periodically published reference works (such as bibliographies and collections of abstracts) are commonly distributed on CD-ROM, with updated CDs issued regularly. When citing such works, include the information on the printed source, plus the publication medium, the name of the vendor (if relevant), and the electronic publication date.

Arms, Valerie M. "A Dyslexic Can Compose on a Computer." <u>Educational</u>

    <u>Technology</u> 24.1 (1984): 39-41. Abstract. <u>ERIC</u>. CD-ROM. SilverPlatter.

    Sept. 1984.

Levi Strauss. "The Levi Strauss Co.: Balance Sheet, 1/1/95-12/31/95."

    <u>Compact Disclosure</u>. CD-ROM. Digital Library Systems. Jan. 1996.

Multidisc Publication

To cite a CD-ROM publication on multiple discs, list the number of discs or the specific number of the disc you used.

Great Literature Plus. CD-ROM. 4 discs. Parsippany: Bureau of Electronic

Publishing, 1993.

The History of European Literature. CD-ROM. Vol. 2. Chicago: ClearVue,

1995.

Work in More than One Medium

When a work is published in more than one medium (for example, both as a book and as a CD or both as a CD and as a diskette), you may specifiy all the media or only the medium you used.

Hult, Christine A., and Thomas N. Huckin. The New Century Handbook.

Book, CD-ROM. Boston: Allyn, 1999.

Work in an Indeterminate Electronic Medium

If you cannot determine the medium of a source (perhaps you accessed the work from a library's Web site and are unsure whether it is on CD-ROM or stored on the library's Internet server), use the designation *Electronic* for the medium.

Delk, Cheryl L. Discovering American Culture. Ann Arbor: U of Michigan

P, 1997. Electronic. Berkeley Public Lib. 20 June 1998.

Electronic Television or Radio Program

Lifson, Edward. "Clinton Meets Kohl." Morning Edition. Natl. Public Radio.

13 May 1998. 20 June 1998 <http://www.npr.org/programs/morning/

archives/1998/>.

Electronic Sound Recording or Sound Clip

Beethoven, Ludwig van. Symphony no. 5 in C, op. 67. New City Media Audio

Programs, June 1998. 20 July 1998 <http://newcitymedia.com/radiostar/

audio.htm>.

Electronic Film or Film Clip

Anderson, Paul Thomas, dir. <u>Boogie Nights</u>. Trailer. New Line, 1997. 13 May

1998 <http://hollywood.com>.

Online Work of Art

van Gogh, Vincent. <u>The Starry Night</u>. 1889. Museum of Modern Art, New

York. 20 Mar. 1998 <http://www.moma.org/paintsculpt/index.html>.

Online Interview

Gregson-Wagner, Natasha. Interview. <u>Hollywood Online</u> May 1998. 15 May

1998 <http://hollywood.com/pressroom/interviews/>.

Online Advertisement or Cartoon

3D RealAudio. Advertisement. 20 Aug. 1998 <http://www.real.com>.

Trudeau, Gary. "Doonesbury." Cartoon. <u>New York Times on the Web</u> 13 May

1998. 13 May 1998 <http://www.nytimes.com/archives>.

Online Manuscript

Hendrickson, Heather. "Art: Impractical but Essential." Working paper, n.d.

28 Aug. 1998 <http://english.usu.edu/W98/204honors/index.html>.

(Note that n.d. stands for "no date.")

Email Communication

Provide the writer's name (or alias or screen name); the subject (title) of the communication, if any (in quotation marks); the designation *Email to;* the name of the person to whom the email is addressed; and the date of the message.

Gardner, Susan. "Help with Citations." Email to the author. 20 Mar. 1995.

Gillespie, Paula. "Members of the NWCA Board." Email to Michael Pemberton.

1 Aug. 1997.

Online Posting

In addition to the information provided for an email citation, a citation for an online posting should include the description *Online posting* and the date of the posting. Provide the name of the discussion forum, if known. Then give the date of access. Last, provide the URL, if known, or the email address of the list's moderator or supervisor (in angle brackets).

Glennon, Sara. "Documenting Sessions." Online posting. 11 Dec.

  1997. NWCA Discussion List. 12 Dec. 1997 <wcenter@ttacs6.

  ttu.edu>.

When possible, cite an archival version of the posting so that readers can more easily find and read the source:

White, Edward. "Texts as Scholarship: Reply to Bob Schwegler." Online

  posting. 11 Apr. 1997. WPA Discussion List. 12 Apr. 1997 <http://gcinfo.

  gc.maricopa.edu/~wpa>.

Citation of a posting to a World Wide Web forum follows the style for an online posting.

Hochman, Will. "Attention Paid This Sunday Morning." Online posting.

  5 Apr. 1998. Response to Selfe. 7 May 1998 <http://www.ncte.org/

  forums/selfe/#forums>.

Citation of a posting to a Usenet newsgroup also follows the style for an online posting. Be sure to include the name of the newsgroup in angle brackets.

Shaumann, Thomas Michael. "Technical German." Online posting. 5 Aug.

  1994. 7 Sept. 1994 <news:comp.edu.languages.natural>.

Online Synchronous Communication

To cite an online synchronous communication, begin with the name (or alias or screen name) of the speaker, if available and if you are citing only one. Include a description of the event, the date of the event, the forum (for example, the name of the MOO), the access date, and the electronic address, preceded by *telnet://*.

Pine_Guest. Personal interview. 12 Dec. 1994. MediaMOO. 12 Dec. 1994

  <telnet://moo.mediaMOO.com_7777>.

WorldMOO Christmas Party. 24 Dec. 1994. WorldMOO. 24 Dec. 1994 <telnet://

  world.sensemedia.net_1234>.

Downloaded Computer Software

Fusion. Vers. 1.1. 30 June 1998 <http://www.allaire.com>.

13b   Document by using the APA system

The documentation system commonly employed in the social sciences was developed by the American Psychological Association (APA). Detailed documentation guidelines for the APA system are included in the *Publication Manual of the American Psychological Association*, 4th ed. (Washington, DC: APA, 1994). The social sciences use an author/date method of documentation. In-text citations identify the source by the author's name and the date of publication so that the reader knows immediately whether the research cited is current. The date of publication is also emphasized in the References list, which appears at the end of the paper.

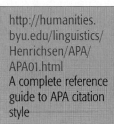
http://humanities.
byu.edu/linguistics/
Henrichsen/APA/
APA01.html
A complete reference
guide to APA citation
style

1   In-text citations in APA style

In the APA documentation system, reference citations found in the body of the paper are linked to the References list at the end. Both the author's last name and the year of publication are included in the in-text citation.

Author Named in the Narrative

If the author is mentioned in the narrative, provide the year of publication in parentheses just after the name.

Hacking (1995) covers much that is on public record about multiple personality

disorder.

Author Not Named in the Narrative

If the author is not mentioned in the narrative, provide the author's last name and the year of publication in parentheses at an appropriate place. Include a comma between the author's name and the date of publication.

In antiquity and through the middle ages, memory was a valued skill

(Hacking, 1995).

A Directory to the APA System

(continued)

Specific Page or Paragraph Quoted

When quoting or directly paraphrasing the author's words, provide a page number (or a paragraph number if the electronic source includes one). Precede the page reference with the abbreviation *p.* (to cite one page) or *pp.* (to cite more than one page).

There may be a causal explanation for multiple personality disorder, because "multiplicity is strongly associated with early and repeated child abuse, especially sexual abuse" (Hacking, 1995, p. 73).

If the direct quotation is taken from an electronic source that does not have pages but does provide specific paragraph numbers, include that information.

Vault Reports makes the following request on its Web site: "If you work (or have worked) for a company we write about, or you have recently gone through a job interview, please fill out our Survey and tell us about your experience" (1998, paragraph 7).

Work by Two Authors

In citing a work by two authors, provide the last names of both authors. Use the word *and* to separate their names in the narrative, but use an ampersand (&) to separate their names in an in-text parenthetical citation.

As Sullivan and Qualley (1994) point out, many recent publications take the politics of writing instruction as their central concern.

The explanation for recent turmoil in the academy may be found in politics (Sullivan & Qualley, 1994).

Work by More than Two Authors

In the first reference to a work by three, four, or five authors, provide the last names for all authors. In subsequent citations, use the first author's last name and the Latin phrase *et al.* (for "and others"). When a work has six or more authors, include only the name of the first author, followed by *et al.,* in the first and in all following citations.

Writing becomes less egocentric as the child matures (Britton, Burgess, Martin, McLeod, & Rosen, 1975).

According to Britton et al. (1975), mature writers consider their readers more than themselves.

Anonymous Work

If no author's name is provided, use either the title or an abbreviated form of the title (usually the first few words) for the in-text citation. Underline the title of a book, periodical, brochure, or report; use quotation marks around the title of an article or chapter.

Public schools have become overly dependent on the IQ test as an indication of academic potential (Human Abilities in Cultural Contexts, 1988).

An individual's success in life depends in large measure on the cultural context in which he or she was raised ("Beyond IQ in Preschool Programs," 1994).

Work by a Corporate Author

Generally, provide the full name of a corporate author in in-text parenthetical citations.

Recently published statistics show the gap between the rich and poor to be widening (New York Times, Inc., 1996).

If the name of the corporate author is long (such as United Cerebral Palsy Association) or if its abbreviation is easily recognized (such as APA), use the abbreviation after including both the complete name and the abbreviation in the first text reference.

FIRST TEXT REFERENCE

There is a Web site that explains citing information from the Internet (American Psychological Association [APA], 1998).

SECOND AND SUBSEQUENT TEXT REFERENCES

The documentation system commonly employed in the social sciences is presented in great detail (APA, 1994).

Different Works by the Same Author

To distinguish citations of two or more works by the same author published in the same year, add a lowercase letter after the date of publication in the parenthetical reference: (1995a), (1995b).

Assign the lowercase letter after alphabetizing the entries in the References list.

The Art of Wondering: A Revisionist Return to the History of Rhetoric

focuses on historical rhetoric in general (Covino, 1988a), while "Defining

Advanced Composition: Contributions from the History of Rhetoric"

concentrates on advanced composition (Covino, 1988b).

Works by Authors with the Same Last Name

When the reference list includes two or more primary authors with the same last name, provide those authors' initials in all citations, even if the publication dates are different.

G. A. Fraser (1990) writes about abuse as the cause of multiple personality

disorder.

S. Fraser (1987) has written a memoir about incest and its effect on multiplicity.

Two or More Sources

To cite several different sources within the same parenthetical citation, list the sources in alphabetical order by the authors' names and use a semicolon to separate the entries.

Several studies (Prinsky & Rosenbaum, 1987; Record Labeling, 1985; Thigpen,

1993) show concern about songs with themes of drugs and violence.

Personal Communication

Personal correspondence, such as letters, telephone conversations, lecture notes, and email, should be cited only in the text itself. Do not list the communications on the References page because readers cannot access them. Provide the initials and the last name of the correspondent, the designation *personal communication*, and the date.

J. Tompkins suggests that fear and authority prevent true learning in

elementary, secondary, college, and university classrooms (personal

communication, August 7, 1997).

The misinterpretation of Herrnstein's study is widespread (H. J. Miller,

personal communication, April, 1989).

2   Content notes in APA style

The APA discourages use of content notes—they can distract readers from the flow of the text. Content notes should be included only if they enhance or strengthen the discussion. Each note should make a single point. Number notes consecutively throughout the text, using a superscript number. List the notes on a separate Notes page at the end of the text.

3   References page in APA style

The research paper's References page (the equivalent of the Works Cited listing in MLA style) contains an alphabetical listing of all the works used as sources. The purpose of the References list is to help readers find the materials used in writing the paper, so the entries must be complete and accurate. List sources alphabetically by the last name of the author, using the letter-by-letter system of alphabetization. When no author is given, alphabetize by the first word of the title (excluding *A, An,* or *The*). Format the References list in a paper according to the APA style for a final text: type the first word of each entry at the left margin, and indent subsequent lines of the same entry five spaces (or ½ inch). Double-space the entire References page, both between and within entries.

Books

A citation for a book has four basic parts:

Author's name. (Publication date). <u>Title.</u> Publication information.

Begin a book citation with the author's last name, followed by a comma and the first and middle initials. Include the year of publication, enclosed in parentheses, next. Underline the title and subtitle of the book. Capitalize the first word of the title, the first word of the subtitle, and any proper nouns. Follow the title with publication information: the city of publication and the publisher, separated from each other with a colon. If more than one location is listed for the publisher, give the site that is listed first on the title page or the site of the publisher's home office. If the city is not known or could be confused with another city, include a state or country abbreviation. Omit the word *Publisher* and abbreviations such as *Inc.* and *Co.* from the publisher's name. Include the complete names of university presses and associations. (For guidelines on citing books in electronic format, see page 293.)

Book by One Author

```
          Year of
Author    publication                    Title
┌──────┐ ┌──────────┐ ┌────────────────────────────────────┐
```

Bolick, C. (1988). Changing course: Civil rights at the crossroads.

New Brunswick, NJ: Transaction Books.
```
└────────────────────────────────────┘
```
                 Publication information

Hacking, I. (1995). Rewriting the soul: Multiple personality and the sciences

of memory. Princeton, NJ: Princeton University Press.

Book by Two or More Authors

When a book has multiple authors, provide all the authors' names (last name first, followed by initials) in the order in which they appear on the title page. Note that this order may not be alphabetical. Connect the final two names with an ampersand (&).

Britton, J., Burgess, T., Martin, N., McLeod, A., & Rosen, H. (1975). The

development of writing abilities. London: Macmillan.

Hindelang, M. J., Hirschi, T., & Weis, J. G. (1981). Measuring delinquency.

Beverly Hills, CA: Sage.

Book by a Corporate Author

Begin the entry with the full name of the group; alphabetize the entry by the first important word in the name. Should the same group be listed as author and publisher, include the word *Author* at the end of the entry in place of the publisher's name.

American Psychological Association. (1994). Publication manual of the

American Psychological Association (4th ed.). Washington, DC: Author.

National Commission on Excellence in Education. (1984). A nation at risk:

The full account. Cambridge, MA: USA Research.

Book with an Editor

For an edited book, provide the editor's name in place of an author's name. Include the abbreviation *Ed.* (for "Editor") or *Eds.* (for "Editors") in parentheses immediately following the editor's name.

Dilts, S. W. (Ed.). (1991). <u>Peterson's guide to four-year colleges</u> (21st ed.).

Princeton, NJ: Peterson's Guides.

Selection from an Edited Book

To cite a particular selection in an edited work, start with the author's name, the year of publication, and the title of the selection. Do not underline the title or enclose it in quotation marks. Next, provide the names of the editors in normal order as they appear on the title page, preceded by the word *In* and followed by the abbreviation *Ed.* or *Eds.* (in parentheses). End the entry with the book's title (underlined), the inclusive page numbers for the selection (in parentheses), and the publication information.

Kadushin, A. (1988). Neglect in families. In E. W. Nunnally, C. S. Chilman, &

F. M. Cox (Eds.), <u>Mental illness, delinquency, addiction, and neglect</u> (pp.

147-166). Newbury Park, CA: Sage.

Two or More Books by the Same Author

When two or more entries have the same author, arrange the entries by the date of publication, with the earliest first. If you have two or more works by the same author published in the same year, alphabetize by title and distinguish the entries by adding a lowercase letter immediately after the year: (1991a), (1991b).

Flynn, J. R. (1980). <u>Race, IQ, and Jensen.</u> London: Routledge.

Flynn, J. R. (1991). <u>Asian Americans: Achievement beyond IQ.</u> Hillsdale, NJ:

Erlbaum.

Article in a Reference Book

If an encyclopedia entry is signed, start with the author's name; if it is unsigned, start with the title of the article. In either case, follow with the publication date. Provide the volume number and page numbers of the article (in parentheses) after the title of the reference book.

Davidoff, L. (1984). Childhood psychosis. In <u>The encyclopedia of psychology</u>

(Vol. 10, pp. 156-157). New York: Wiley.

Schizophrenia. (1983). In <u>The encyclopedic dictionary of psychology</u> (Vol. 8,

pp. 501-502). Cambridge, MA: MIT Press.

Book in Translation

Indicate the name of the translator in parentheses immediately after the book's title, with the abbreviation *Trans.*

Freire, P. (1993). <u>Pedagogy of the oppressed</u> (New rev. 20th anniv. ed.). (M. B.

     Ramos, Trans.). New York: Continuum.

Subsequent Edition of a Book

If a book is not a first edition, indicate the relevant edition in parentheses immediately following the title of the book. Use abbreviations to specify the type of edition: for example, *2nd ed.* stands for "Second edition" and *Rev. ed.* stands for "Revised edition."

Lindeman, E. (1987). <u>A rhetoric for writing teachers</u> (2nd ed.). New York:

     Oxford University Press.

Republished Book

Provide the original date of publication in parentheses at the end of the entry, with the words *Original work published.*

Dewey, J. (1963). <u>Experience and education.</u> New York: Collier. (Original work

     published 1938).

Government Document

Unless an author's name is given, begin an entry for a government document with the name of the agency that issued the publication.

National Center for Educational Statistics. (1996). <u>The condition of</u>

     <u>education 1996.</u> Washington, DC: U.S. Department of Education,

     Office of Educational Research and Improvement.

Periodicals

A citation of an article in a periodical or a journal follows a format similar to that for a book:

     Author's name. (Publication date). Article title. Publication information.

When citing magazines and newpapers, include the month and date of publication. The article title and subtitle appear neither set in quotation marks nor underlined. The publication information begins with the name of the publication as it appears on the publication's title page, with all major words capitalized. Underline the title. Include the volume number (underlined and not preceded by the abbreviation *vol.*) and the issue number (in parentheses and not underlined). End with the inclusive page numbers for the article. (Use the abbreviation *p.* or *pp.* with articles in newspapers but not with articles in journals or magazines.) (For guidelines on citing articles in online periodicals, see pages 294–295.)

Article in a Journal Paginated by Volume

        Publication
Author   date   Article title   Article subtitle

Popenoe, D. (1993). American family decline, 1960-1990: A review and

appraisal. Journal of Marriage and Family, 55, 527-555.

                        Publication information

Shotter, J. (1997). The social construction of our inner selves. Journal of

Constructivist Psychology, 10, 7-24.

Article in a Journal Paginated by Issue

If each issue of a journal begins with page 1, provide the issue number (in parentheses) immediately following the volume number.

Alma, C. (1994). A strategy for the acquisition of problem-solving expertise in

humans: The category-as-analogy approach. Inquiry, 14(2), 17-28.

Article in a Monthly Magazine

Include the month, not abbreviated, in the publication date.

Katz, L. G. (1994, November). Perspectives on the quality of early childhood

programs. Phi Delta Kappan, 76(3), 200-205.

Article in a Weekly Magazine

Provide the year, month, and day of publication.

Ives, D. (1994, August 14). Endpaper: The theory of anything. The New York

Times Magazine, 58.

If the article has no known author, start the entry with the title of the article, and alphabetize by the first important word in the title (usually the word that follows the introductory article).

The blood business. (1972, September 7). Time, 47-48.

(In the References list, this entry would appear in the B's.)

Newspaper Article

Provide the complete name of the newspaper (including any introductory articles) after the title of the article. List all discontinuous page numbers, preceded by *p.* or *pp.*

Fritz, M. (1992, November 7). Hard-liners to boycott German anti-racism rally.

The Dallas Morning News, pp. 1, 25.

Twenty percent biased against Jews. (1992, November 22). The New York

Times, p. A1.

Editorial

Add the word *Editorial*, in brackets, after the title of the editorial.

Paglia, C. (1997, October 24). More mush from the NEA [Editorial]. The Wall

Street Journal, p. A22.

Six who serve their council districts [Editorial]. (1997, October 31). The

Boston Globe, p. A22.

Letter to the Editor

Add the designation *Letter to the editor*, in brackets, after the title of the letter or after the date if there is no title.

Schack, S. (1997, December 1). [Letter to the editor]. The New York Times,

p. A20.

Review

Provide the name of the reviewer, the date of publication (in parentheses), and the title of the review, if given. Then, in brackets, write the designation *Review of* and the title of the piece that was reviewed.

Ribadeneira, D. (1997, October 31). The secret lives of seminarians [Review of

the book The new men: Inside the Vatican's elite school for American

priests]. The Boston Globe, p. C6.

Other Sources

Film or Video Recording

Begin with the names of those responsible for the film and, in parentheses, their titles, such as *Producer* and *Director*. Give the title (underlined), and then designate the medium in brackets. Provide the location and the name of the distributor.

Michaels, L. (Producer), & Spheeris, P. (Director). (1992). <u>Wayne's world</u>

[Film]. Hollywood: Paramount.

Television or Radio Program

Identify those who created the program, and give their titles— for example, *Producer, Director,* and *Anchor*. Give the date the program was broadcast. Provide the program's title (underlined), as well as the city and the station where the program aired.

Miller, R. (Producer). (1982, May 21). <u>Problems of freedom.</u> New York: NBC-TV.

Technical Report

Write an entry for a technical report in a format similar to that for a book. If an individual author is named, provide that information; place any other identifying information (such as a report number) after the title of the report.

Vaughn Hansen Associates, in association with CH2M Hill and Water

Research Laboratory, Utah State University. (1995). <u>Identification and</u>

<u>assessment of certain water management options for the Wasatch</u>

<u>Front: Prepared for Utah State Division of Water Resources.</u> Salt Lake

City, UT: Author.

Published Interview

For a published interview, start with the name of the interviewer and the date. In brackets, give the name (and title, if necessary) of the person interviewed. End with the publication information, including the page number(s), in parentheses, after the title of the work in which the interview is published.

Davidson, P. (1992). [Interview with Donald Hall]. In P. Davidson, <u>The fading</u>

<u>smile</u> (p. 25). New York: Knopf.

Unpublished Interview

Follow the format for a published interview.

Hult, C. (1997, March). [Interview with Dr. Stanford Cazier, past President,

Utah State University].

Unpublished Dissertation

Provide the author's name, the date, and then the title of the dissertation, underlined and followed by a period. Add the phrase *Unpublished doctoral dissertation,* a comma, and the name of the degree-granting institution.

Johnson, N. K. (1980). <u>Cultural and psychological determinants of health and</u>

<u>illness.</u> Unpublished doctoral dissertation, University of Washington.

Unpublished Manuscript

Write an entry for an unpublished manuscript in the same format as a book entry. In place of the publication information, write *Unpublished manuscript.*

Speech or Lecture

For an oral presentation, provide the name of the presenter, the year and month of the presentation, and the title of the presentation (underlined). Then give any useful location information.

Meeks, L. (1997, March). <u>Feminism and the WPA.</u> Paper presented at the

Conference on College Composition and Communication, Phoenix, AZ.

Electronic Media

The electronic documentation formats found in *Publication Manual of the American Psychological Association,* 4th ed., are based on X. Li and N. B. Crane's *Electronic Style: A Guide to Citing Electronic Information* (Westport, CT: Meckler, 1993). For material with a print equivalent, the APA has updated some of its formats at the Web site *http://www.apa.org/journals/webref.html.* Li and Crane have continued to update their book at the Web site *http://www.uvm.edu/~ncrane/estyles/apa.html.* The formats discussed in this section are based both on available APA models and on models provided by Li and Crane at their Web site.

When citing electronic media, use the standard APA format to identify authorship, date of origin (if known), and title, much as for print material; then add a clear indication of the path or address for the electronic source. (In case your instructor has a distinct preference as to how to list source data from online computer networks, confirm the details of electronic citation forms before submitting a final paper.)

Online Professional or Personal Site

To comply with APA style, present information in the following general sequence when citing on-line sources:

1. The author's or editor's last name and initial(s)
2. The creation date of the work, in parentheses (write *No date* if the electronic publication date is not available)
3. The title of the complete work, underlined or italicized
4. The type of electronic medium, in brackets—for example, [Online]
5. The producer of the database or Web site (optional)
6. The designation *Available:*, followed by the access protocol or path or URL
7. The date of access or visit in the order year, month, day, in brackets

Jarvis, P. (No date). <u>My Homepage.</u> [Online]. Available: http://www.mtu.edu/ ~students [1997, December 3].

<u>Victoriana--Resources for Victorian Living.</u> (1996-1997). [Online]. Reflections of the past--Antiques. Available: http://www.victoriana.com [1998, January 20].

Online Book

Provide any data on the print publication before details on where the electronic version may be located.

Aristotle. (1954). <u>Rhetoric</u> (W. R. Roberts, Trans.). [Online]. The English Server at Carnegie Mellon University. Available: http://www.rpi.edu/~honeyl/ Rhetoric/index.html [1997, April 8].

Article in an Online Work

Generally, citations for articles in online works follow the same sequence as citations for their print counterparts.

Women in American History. (1998). In <u>Encyclopaedia Britannica</u> [Online]. Available: http://www.women.eb.com [1998, May 25].

AN ARTICLE IN AN ONLINE NEWSPAPER OR ON A NEWSWIRE

Schmitt, E. (1998, February 4). Cohen promises "significant" military
campaign against Iraq if diplomacy fails. The New York Times on
the Web [Online], 6 paragraphs. Available: http://www.nytimes.com/
archives [1998, February 4].

Wright, R. (1998, February 4). U.S. wins support but no mandate against Iraq.
The Los Angeles Times [Online], p. A1. Available: http://www.latimes.
com/home/archives [1998, February 4].

AN ARTICLE IN AN ONLINE MAGAZINE

Thakker, S. (1998, May). Avoiding automobile theft. Ontario Police
Crime Prevention Magazine [Online], 3 paragraphs. Available:
http://www.opcpm.com/inside/avoidingautomobile.html [1998,
May 26].

AN ONLINE REVIEW

Spiers, S. (1998). [Review of the report "Blood poisoning" by Prevention/
NBCToday.] OBGYN.net [Online], 10 paragraphs. Available:
http://www.obgyn.net/women/articles [1998, August 3].

AN ONLINE ABSTRACT

Reid, Joy. (1983). Computer-assisted text-analysis for ESL students [CD-
ROM]. Calico Journal, 1(3), 40-42. Abstract from: DIALOG File: ERIC
Item: EJ29870 [1998, August 2].

AN ONLINE EDITORIAL

Spilner, M. (1998, May). Walking club welcome [Editorial]. Prevention
[Online], 5 paragraphs. Available: http://www.prevention.com/walking/
welcome.html [1998, June 20].

AN ONLINE LETTER TO THE EDITOR

Rivel, D. (1998, May 6). Art in the schools [Letter to editor]. The New York
Times on the Web [Online], 4 paragraphs. Available: http://www.nytimes.
com/yr/mo/day/letters [1998, May 6].

AN ARTICLE IN AN ONLINE SCHOLARLY JOURNAL

Britt, R. (1995). The heat is on: Scientists agree on human contribution to

global warming. Ion Science [Online]. Available: http://www.injersey.

com/Media/IonSci/features/gwarm [1996, November 13].

Nonperiodical Publication on CD-ROM, Magnetic Tape, or Diskette

To cite works distributed on CDs, disks, or magnetic tape, give the authors, publication date, title, and publication information in standard APA format. After the title, identify the type of electronic medium in brackets—for example, [CD-ROM].

ClearVue, Inc. (1995). The history of European Literature [CD-ROM]. Chicago:

Author.

Online Work of Art

Seurat, G. (1884). A Sunday Afternoon on the Island of La Grande Jatte

[Online]. Art Institute of Chicago. Available: http://www.artic.edu/

aic/collections [1998, August 3].

Online Interview

Jorgenson, L. (1998, May 26). For a change, Jazz feel bullish [Interview

with Jeff Hornacek]. Deseret News [Online], 15 paragraphs. Available:

http://www.desnews.com/playoffs [1998, May 26].

Online Posting

Although unretrievable communication such as email is not included in APA References, somewhat more public or accessible Internet postings from newsgroups or listservs may be included.

Heilke, J. (1996, May 3). Webfolios. Alliance for Computers and Writing

Discussion List [Online]. Available: http://www.ttu.edu/lists/acw-l/

9605/0040.html [1996, December 31].

Shaumann, T. (1994, August 5). Technical German. Technical German

Discussion List [Online]. Available E-mail: USENET@comp.edu.

languages.natural [1994, September 7].

Online Synchronous Communication

WorldMOO Computer Club. (1998, February 3). Monthly meeting. Available:

telnet:world.sensemedia.net1234 [1998, February 3].

13c   Document by using the Chicago Manual of Style (CMS) system

The documentation system used most commonly in business, communications, economics, and the humanities and fine arts (other than languages and literature) is outlined in *The Chicago Manual of Style,* 14th ed. (Chicago: The University of Chicago Press, 1993). This two-part system uses footnotes or endnotes and a bibliography to provide publication information about sources quoted, paraphrased, summarized, or otherwise referred to in the text of a paper. Footnotes appear at the bottom of the page; endnotes appear on a separate page at the end of paper. The Bibliography, like the Works Cited page in the MLA documentation style, is an alphabetical list of all works cited in the paper.

http://www.press.
uchicago.edu/Misc/
Chicago/cmosfaq.html
Answers to frequently
asked questions about
Chicago style

1   In-text citations in CMS

In the text, indicate a note with a superscript number typed immediately after the information that is being referenced. Number notes consecutively throughout the text.

In A History of Reading, Alberto Manguel asserts that "we, today's readers, have yet to learn what reading is."[1] As a result, one of his conclusions is that while readers have incredible powers, not all of them are enlightening.[2]

2   Notes in CMS

For footnotes, position the text of the note at the bottom of the page on which the reference occurs. Separate the footnotes from the text by skipping four lines from the last line of text. Single-space

A Directory to the CMS System

Notes

within a note, but double-space between notes if more than one note appears on a page.

For endnotes, type all of the notes at the end of the paper, in a section entitled Notes. The title, centered but not in quotation marks, should appear at the top of the first page of the notes. List the notes in consecutive order, as they occur in the text. Double-space the entire endnote section—between and within entries.

The other details of formatting are the same for both footnotes and endnotes. Indent the first line of each note five spaces (or ½ inch). Use a number that is the same size as and is aligned in the same way as the note text (do not use a superscript); follow the number with a period and a word space to the note itself. Begin with the author's name (first name first), followed by a comma. Then provide the title of the book (underlined or italicized) or article (enclosed in quotation marks). Finally, provide the publication information. For books, include (in parentheses) the place of publication, followed by a colon; the publisher, followed by a comma; and the date of publication. Conclude with the page number of the source, preceded by a comma. For articles, include the title of the periodical (underlined or italicized), followed by the volume or issue number. Then add the date of publication (in parentheses), followed by a colon and the page number.

1. Alberto Manguel, <u>A History of Reading</u> (New York: Viking, 1996), 23.

2. Steven Brachlow, "John Robinson and the Lure of Separatism in Pre-Revolutionary England," <u>Church History</u> 50 (1983): 288-301.

In subsequent references to the same source, it is acceptable to use only the author's last name and a page number:

3. Manguel, 289.

Where there are two or more works by the same author, include a shortened version of each work's title:

4. Merton, <u>Mystics</u>, 68.

5. Merton, <u>Buddhism</u>, 18.

Books

Book by One Author

6. Iris Murdoch, <u>The Sovereignty of Good</u> (New York: Schocken Books, 1971), 32-33.

Book by Two or Three Authors

List the authors' names in the same order as on the title page of the book.

7. John Sabini and Maury Silver, <u>Moralities of Everyday Life</u> (New York: Oxford University Press, 1982), 91.

8. Anne S. Goodsell, Michelle R. Maher, and Vincent Tinto, <u>Collaborative Learning: A Sourcebook for Higher Education</u> (University Park, Pa.: National Center on Postsecondary Teaching, Learning, and Assessment, 1992), 78.

Book by More than Three Authors

Use the abbreviation *et al.* after the first author's name; list all authors in the accompanying bibliography.

9. James Britton et al., <u>The Development of Writing Abilities</u> (London: Macmillan, 1975), 43.

Book by a Corporate Author

10. American Association of Colleges and Universities, <u>American Pluralism and the College Curriculum: Higher Education in a Diverse Democracy</u> (Washington, D.C.: American Association of Higher Education, 1995), 27.

Book with an Editor

11. Jane Roberta Cooper, ed., <u>Reading Adrienne Rich: Review and Re-Visions, 1951-1981</u> (Ann Arbor: University of Michigan Press, 1984), 51.

12. Robert F. Goodman and Aaron Ben-Ze'ev, eds., <u>Good Gossip</u> (Lawrence: Kansas University Press, 1994), 13.

Book with an Editor and an Author

13. Albert Schweitzer, <u>Albert Schweitzer: An Anthology</u>, ed. Charles R. Joy (New York: Harper & Row, 1947), 107.

Selection from an Edited Work

14. Gabriele Taylor, "Gossip as Moral Talk," in <u>Good Gossip</u>, ed. Robert F. Goodman and Aaron Ben-Ze'ev (Lawrence: Kansas University Press, 1994), 35-37.

15. Langston Hughes, "Harlem," in The Norton Anthology of African American Literature, ed. Henry Louis Gates, Jr., and Nellie Y. McKay (New York: Norton, 1997), 1267.

Article in a Reference Book

The publication information (city of publication, publisher, publication year) is usually omitted from citations of well-known reference books. Include the abbreviation *s. v.* (*sub verbo,* or "under the word") before the article title, rather than page numbers.

16. Frank E. Reynolds, World Book Encyclopedia, 1983 ed., s. v. "Buddhism."

17. Encyclopedia Americana, 1976 ed., s. v. "Buddhism."

Introduction, Preface, Foreword, or Afterword

18. Jane Tompkins, preface to A Life in School: What the Teacher Learned (Reading, Mass.: Addison-Wesley, 1996), xix.

Work in More than One Volume

19. Arthur Conan Doyle, The Complete Sherlock Holmes, vol. 2 (Garden City, N.Y.: Doubleday, 1930), 728.

Government Document

20. United States Federal Bureau of Investigation, Uniform Crime Reports for the United States: 1995 (Washington, D.C.: GPO, 1995), 48.

Periodicals

Article in a Journal Paginated by Volume

21. Mike Rose, "The Language of Exclusion: Writing Instruction at the University," College English 47 (1985): 343.

Article in a Journal Paginated by Issue

22. Joy S. Ritchie, "Confronting the 'Essential' Problem: Reconnecting Feminist Theory and Pedagogy," Journal of Advanced Composition 10, no. 2 (1989): 160.

Article in a Monthly Magazine

23. Douglas H. Lamb and Glen D. Reeder, "Reliving Golden Days," Psychology Today, June 1986, 22.

Article in a Weekly Magazine

24. Steven Levy, "Blaming the Web," Newsweek, 7 April 1997, 46-47.

Newspaper Article

25. P. Ray Baker, "The Diagonal Walk," Ann Arbor News, 16 June 1928, sec. A, p. 2.

Abstract from an Abstracts Journal

26. Nancy K. Johnson, "Cultural and Psychological Determinants of Health and Illness" (Ph.D. diss., University of Washington, 1980), abstract in Dissertation Abstracts International 40 (1980): 425B.

Other Sources

Speech or Lecture

27. Wayne Booth, "Ethics and the Teaching of Literature" (paper presented to the College Forum at the 87th Annual Convention of the National Council of Teachers of English, Detroit, Mich., 21 November 1997).

Personal Letter to the Author

28. George Bush, letter to author, 8 September 1995.

Electronic Media

Because *The Chicago Manual of Style*, 14th ed., primarily covers citation formats for electronic journals with a print equivalent, researchers continue to adapt to new electronic formats by modifying some of the basic CMS conventions. Melvin E. Page of East Tennessee State University has developed a CMS-based style sheet for citing Web sources and other online material, available at *http://h-net.msu.edu/~africa/citation.html*. This section reflects features of that style sheet, which has been recommended by H-Net, a consortium of email lists aimed at historians. One feature of Page's proposed style is the convention of enclosing URLs within angle brackets. Another is the provision of any publicly recorded email addresses (but not privately recorded ones) as part of the author's identification. The date of posting, if available, follows the Internet address without parentheses; a date of access is provided when no date of posting is available.

Online Professional or Personal Site

29. Joy Reid, "Computer-Assisted Text-Analysis for ESL Students," in Calico Journal [database online], accession no. EJ298270; available from DIALOG Information Services, Inc., Palo Alto, Calif.

30. Michelle Traylor, "Michelle Traylor Data Services," <http://www.mtdsnet.com>, 1989-1998.

31. John C. Herz, "Surfing on the Internet: A Nethead's Adventures Online," Urban Desires 1.3, <http://www.desires.com>, March/April 1995.

Online Posting

Archived source addresses are given separately from any other addresses in citing listserv messages. The date of posting is the only date given.

32. James Heilke, "Webfolios," <acw-l@ttacs.ttu.edu>, 3 May 1996, archived at <http://www.ttu.edu/lists/acw-l/9605>.

33. Peter Ellsworth, "WWW Devalues Writing," <news:alt.prose>, 7 November 1997.

Computer Software

To cite computer software, start with the title and then include the edition or version, if any. Next, give the name and location of the organization or person with rights to the software.

34. A.D.A.M: Animated Dissection of Anatomy for Medicine, Benjamin Cummings/Addison-Wesley and A.D.A.M. Software, Inc., Reading, Mass.

3   Bibliography entries in CMS

The style for Bibliography entries is generally the same as that for Works Cited entries in MLA style. Follow the formatting conventions outlined in 13a-3 when creating a Bibliography page.

13d   Document by using the CBE system

Although source citations in the sciences are generally similar to those recommended by the APA, there is no uniform system of citation in the sciences. Various disciplines follow either the style of a particular journal or that of a style guide, such as the guide produced by the Council of Biology Editors: *Scientific Style and Format: The CBE Manual for Authors, Editors, and Publishers*, 6th ed. (New York: Cambridge University Press, 1994).

http://www.jasperweb.com/online/cite8.html
CBE style on-line documentation reference

1   In-text citations in CBE style

The CBE system of documentation offers two alternative formats for in-text citations: the author-year (or name-year) system and the number system.

Author-Year System

The basic outline of the CBE's author-year system for in-text citation can be found at *http://www.wisc.edu/writing/Handbook/DocCBENameYear.html*.

Author Named in the Narrative

If the author's name is used to introduce the source material, include only the publication date in the citation.

According to Allen (1997), frequency of interactions and context of occurrence were unknown.

A Directory to the CBE System

(continued)

Author Not Named in the Narrative

If the author is not mentioned in the narrative, the source material is followed, in parentheses, by the last name of the author and the publication date of the source.

Frequency of interactions and context of occurrence were unknown (Allen 1997).

Specific Page or Paragraph Quoted

If the source material is paraphrased or directly quoted, include the page numbers after the source material, in parentheses and preceded by *p* or *pp*.

Allen (1997) reported "only one encounter that described defensive behavior by a fox toward a coyote" (p 125).

Work by Two Authors

If the work has two authors, join their last names with *and*.

Categories of behavior included traveling, resting, hunting small mammals, and feeding on a carcass (Bekoff and Wells 1981).

Work by Three or More Authors

To cite a work with three or more authors, give the first author's name, followed by *and others* and the publication year.

Social status was categorized as alpha, beta, or young (Rabbet and others 1967).

Different Works by the Same Author

To differentiate between two or more works published by the same author in the same year, add a lowercase letter following the year:

Sargeant and Allen (1989a, 1989b) noted only a single encounter of defensive behavior by a fox toward a coyote.

Work Cited Indirectly

When information comes from work cited in another work, the in-text citation should mention both works.

Deterrence was recorded when coyotes caused foxes to avoid the area (Mech 1970, cited in Bekoff and Wells 1981).

Two or More Sources within the Same Citation

When two or more sources are cited, arrange the sources in chronological sequence from earliest publication to latest. Sources published in the same year should be arranged alphabetically.

Separate hierarchies of dominance for males and females were observed within each resident pack (Rabbet and others 1967; Schenkel 1967; Mech 1970).

Number System

In the number system, numbers are assigned to the various sources, according to the sequence in which the sources are initially cited in the text. Then the sources are listed by number on the References page. Set citation numbers within the text as superscripts.

Temperature plays a major role in the rate of gastric juice secretion.[3]

Multiple sources are cited together:

Recent studies[3,5,8-10] show that antibodies may also bind to microbes and prevent their attachment to epithelial surfaces.

2   References page in CBE style

Like the MLA's Works Cited page, the CBE's listing of references contains all the sources cited in the paper. The title of this page may be References or Cited References. Since the purpose of this list is to help readers find the materials used in writing the paper, information must be complete and accurate.

The format of the References page will depend on whether the author-year system or the number system is used. Since the References page for the CBE author-year system basically resembles the APA References page discussed in 13b-2, we will consider only the

References page for the number system. For an example of a student paper using the author-year system, see 15c. (Note that initial numerals accompany citations in the list *only* when the number system is used. The citations appear in alphabetical order when the author-year system is used.)

> http://www.wisc.edu/
> writetest/Handbook/
> DocCBE6.html
> A complete CBE
> citation style manual

Double-space the entire References list, both between and within entries. Type the citation number, followed by a period, flush left on the margin. Leave two word spaces to the first letter of the entry. Align any turn lines on the first letter of the entry. List the citations in order of appearance in the text.

List authors with last names first, followed by initials. Capitalize only the first word of a title and any proper nouns. Do not enclose titles of articles in quotation marks, and do not underline titles of books. Abbreviate names of journals, where possible. Include the year of publication. Cite volume and page numbers when appropriate.

Books

Book by One Author

1. Kruuk H. The spotted hyena: a study of predation and social behavior. Chicago: University of Chicago Pr; 1972.

2. Abercrombie MLJ. The anatomy of judgment. Harmondsworth (Eng.): Penguin; 1969.

Book by Two or More Authors

3. Hersch RH, Paolitto DP, Reimer J. Promoting moral growth. New York: Longman; 1979.

Book by a Corporate Author

4. Carnegie Council on Policy Studies in Higher Education. Fair practices in higher education: rights and responsibilities of students and their colleges in a period of intensified competition for enrollment. San Francisco: Jossey-Bass; 1979.

Book with Two or More Editors

5. Buchanan RE, Gibbons NE, editors. Bergey's manual of determinative bacteriology. 8th ed. Baltimore: Williams & Wilkins; 1974.

Selection from an Edited Work

6. Kleiman DG, Brady CA. Coyote behavior in the context of recent canid research: problems and perspectives. In: Bekoff M, editor. Coyotes: biology, behavior, and management. New York: Academic Pr; 1978. pp 163-88.

Government Document

7. Mech D. The wolves of Isle Royal. National Parks fauna series. Available from: United States GPO, Washington; 1966.

Periodicals

Journal Article by One Author

8. Schenkel R. Expression studies of wolves. Behavior 1947; 1:81-129.

Journal Article by Two or More Authors

9. Sargeant AB, Allen SH. Observed interactions between coyotes and red foxes. J. Mamm. 1989; 70:631-3.

Article with No Identified Author

10. Anonymous. Frustrated hamsters run on their wheels. Nat. Sci. 1981; 91:407.

Newspaper Article

11. Rensberger B, Specter B. CFCs may be destroyed by natural process. Washington Post 1989 Aug 7; Sect 1A: 2 (col 5).

Magazine Article

12. Aveni AF. Emissaries to the stars: the astronomers of ancient Maya. Mercury 1995 May: 15-8.

Other Sources

Unpublished Interview

13. Quarnberg T. [Interview with Dr. Andy Anderson, Professor of Biology, Utah State University, 1988 Apr 15].

Dissertation

14. Gese EM. Foraging ecology of coyotes in Yellowstone National Park [dissertation]. Madison (WI): University of Wisconsin; 1995. 124p.

Unpublished Manuscript

15. Pegg J, Russo C, Valent J. College cheating survey at Drexel University. [Unpublished manuscript, 1986].

Personal Letter

16. Fife A. [Letter to President Calvin Coolidge, 1930]. Located at: Archives and Special Collections, Utah State University, Logan, UT.

Electronic Media

Internet formats are covered briefly in *Scientific Style and Format: The CBE Manual for Authors, Editors, and Publishers,* 6th ed., on pages 665–669. The Vancouver style for electronic citations, a set of conventions observed by the American Medical Association, the American College of Physicians, and the World Association of Medical Editors, expands basic CBE citation conventions to encompass electronic journals and print-based Internet sources. A Web site summarizing this style is at *http://www.ama-assn.org/public/peer/wame/ uniform.htm.*

Online Professional or Personal Site

17. Gelt J. Home use of greywater: rainwater conserves water--and money [online]. 1993 [cited 1996 Nov 8]. Available from: URL: www.ag.arizona. edu/AZWATER/arroyo/071.rain.html

Online Book

18. Merck. The Merck index on-line [monograph online]. 10th ed. Rahway
    (NJ): Merck; 1972 [cited 1990 Dec 7]. Available from: BRS Information
    Technologies, McLean, VA.

Article in an Online Periodical

20. Lechner DE, Bradbury SF, Bradley LA. Phys Ther J [serial online]. 1998
    Aug [cited 1998 Sept 15]. Available from: URL: http://www.apta.org/
    pt_journal/Aug98/Toc.htm

13e   Consult the style manual for the appropriate discipline

Following is a listing of style manuals for the systems of documentation most commonly used in the disciplines. Consult the style manual appropriate to the discipline for which you are writing a research paper. Remember: If you are unsure as to which style to adopt, ask your instructor for help.

Biology

Council of Biology Editors. *Scientific Style and Format: The CBE Manual for Authors, Editors, and Publishers.* 6th ed. New York: Cambridge UP, 1994.

Chemistry

Dodd, Janet S., ed. *The American Chemical Society Style Guide: A Manual for Authors and Editors.* Washington: ACS, 1985.

Education

National Education Association. *NEA Style Manual for Writers and Editors.* Rev. ed. Washington: NEA, 1974.

Engineering

Michaelson, Herbert B. *How to Write and Publish Engineering Papers and Reports.* 3rd ed. Phoenix: Oryx, 1990.

English and the Humanities

Gibaldi, Joseph. *MLA Handbook for Writers of Research Papers*. 4th ed. New York: MLA, 1995.

Gibaldi, Joseph. *MLA Style Manual and Guide to Scholarly Publishing*. 2nd ed. New York: MLA, 1998.

General

The Chicago Manual of Style. 14th ed. Chicago: U of Chicago P, 1993.

Turabian, Kate. *A Manual for Writers of Term Papers, Theses, and Dissertations*. 5th ed. Chicago: U of Chicago P, 1987.

Geology

United States Geological Survey. *Suggestions to Authors of the Reports of the United States Geological Survey*. 7th ed. Washington: GPO, 1991.

Law

Editors of Columbia Law Review, comp. *The Bluebook: A Uniform System of Citation*. 15th ed. Cambridge, MA: Harvard Law Review, 1991.

Garner, Diane L., and Diane H. Smith. *The Complete Guide to Citing Government Information Resources: A Manual for Writers and Librarians*. Bethesda: Cong. Info. Serv., 1993.

Linguistics

Linguistic Society of America. *LSA Bulletin*, Dec. issue, annually.

Mathematics

American Mathematical Society. *A Manual for Authors of Mathematical Papers*. Rev. 8th ed. Providence: AMS, 1990.

Medicine

Iverson, Cheryl, et al. *American Medical Association Manual of Style*. 8th ed. Baltimore: Williams, 1989.

Music

Holoman, D. Kern, ed. *Writing about Music: A Style Sheet from the Editors of 19th Century Music*. Berkeley: U of California P, 1988.

Physics

American Institute of Physics. *AIP Style Manual*. 4th ed. New York: AIP, 1990.

Political Science

Kelley, Jean P., et al., eds. *Style Manual for Political Science*. Rev. ed. Washington: American Political Science Association, 1985.

Psychology

American Psychological Association. *Publication Manual of the American Psychological Association*. 4th ed. Washington: APA, 1994.

PART 3

WRITING IN THE DISCIPLINES

CHAPTER
14

Writing in the Humanities

FAQs

What are the humanities, and why do people study them?

I have to write a paper about a poem we read in class. Where should I start? (14b)

How is a literary analysis paper formatted? (14c)

How can I find information in the library or on the Internet for a humanities research paper? (14d)

The humanities, which include classical and modern languages and literature, history, and philosophy, have as an overall goal the exploration and explanation of the human experience. Sometimes the fine arts and performance arts (music, art, dance, and drama) are classified as part of the humanities, but more often they are viewed as a separate category. In this handbook, we will treat fine arts and performance arts as though they were the embodiment of a "text" that could be interpreted and analyzed. Scholars and students in the humanities are interested in exploring difficult questions about humankind. Humanists deal in significance, insight, imagination, and the meaning of human experience. They write to express their understanding of some aspect of the world. In John Steinbeck's *The Grapes of Wrath,* for example, the focus is California during the Depression.

In general, humanists inquire into consciousness, values, ideas, and ideals as they seek to describe how experience shapes understanding of the human condition.

14a   Know the different types of writing in the humanities

In history, philosophy, and literature, written texts are extremely important. Historians document and analyze past events, usually focusing on a particular group of people, country, or period. Philosophers examine human ideas, constructing logical systems to explain our thoughts and interactions and our relationships with each other and the rest of nature. Literary authors attempt to capture in writing their own experiences or, through their imaginations, the experiences of other people in other settings. Through stories, they convey their understanding of the world.

Written texts in the humanities fall into three broad categories: (1) creative writing, such as fiction, poetry, and drama; (2) interpretive and analytical writing, such as literary and art criticism; and (3) theoretical writing, such as historical, philosophical, and social theories of literature and art.

1   Creative writing

Human beings have always been tellers of stories. The impulse to create works of literature, whether in the form of oral folk narratives or formal written sonnets, is as old as humankind. Creative writing, or literature, provides readers with an aesthetic experience. Readers expect a literary work to mean something to them—to show them new ways of looking at themselves and the world.

The major **literary genres,** or types of literature, are poetry, fiction, and drama. Biography and autobiography are also sometimes considered literary genres.

2   Interpretive and analytical writing

Readers of literary works ask interpretive or analytical questions: What sort of work is it? Does it have a message? How powerful or meaningful is the message? Critical writing in the humanities is usually either interpretive, analytical, or some combination of the two. **Interpretive writing** discusses the author's intended meaning or the impact of the work on an audience. For example, an interpretive writer might try to explain a novelist's attitude toward the heroine of her or his book or weigh the aesthetic impact of a dance. Interpretive writers support their claims by using evidence from the work itself. A book report that summarizes the plot and discusses the significance of a work is an example of interpretive writing. **Analytical writing** takes interpretation one step further, examining the whole of the work in relationship to its component parts. For example, an analytical writer might try to understand how the plot of a play is reinforced by its setting or how a ballet's musical score contributes to its theme. A critical essay that argues for a particular position with respect to a literary work is an example of analytical writing.

When you read a piece of literature or view a work of art, you are not a neutral observer; you allow the work to speak to you on many levels. As you absorb its meaning, you question and probe. Assignments that call for interpretation and analysis require you to set down in words the results of this questioning and probing process.

3 Theoretical writing

The third type of humanistic writing is **theoretical writing.** Theorists look beyond individual works of literature and art to see how they exemplify broader social and historical trends. For example, a theorist might use the characters in a Dickens novel to speculate about shifts in class structure in 19th-century England. Or he or she might look at the use of perspective in a medieval fresco to theorize about the origins of Renaissance painting. Theorists provide links among art, literature, and other disciplines such as history, sociology, and psychology. Their writing involves interpretation and analysis, but their goal is to *synthesize*—to present interpretations in a larger context. Many of the articles published in professional humanities journals exemplify theoretical writing.

14b Write interpretively or analytically about literature

Much of the writing done in college literature courses is interpretive or analytical. Instructors generally expect students to make a claim about a literary work and then support that claim

http://www.crayne.com/
victory/howcrit.html
"How to Critique
Fiction"—an excellent
introduction to literary
analysis

through reasoned arguments and evidence from the work itself (see Chapter 7). Your goal in writing interpretively or analytically is to shed light on an aspect of the work that the reader might not otherwise see.

1   Reading literature critically

Begin by reading the work critically (see 2b). Using the following critical reading process when you read a piece of literature will start you on the way to writing an interpretive or analytical essay.

First, read the work straight through, with an eye toward understanding the text and noting its impressions on you as a reader. Does the work make you feel happy or sad? Is there a character, event, or scene that is particularly moving or striking? Does anything in the text confuse or puzzle you? Keep a journal (either on a computer disk or in a notebook) in which you jot down impressions as you read.

Once you have finished reading the work, skim it in its entirety to highlight important passages, such as scenes that are pivotal to the plot, revealing character descriptions, and vivid descriptive passages. Then try writing a brief plot outline for the work to be sure that you have a clear sense of the chronology. You might also list key characters and their relationships to each other.

Finally, review your marginal notes, outline, and lists to determine what aspects of the work interested you most. Try freewriting at your computer or in your journal for ten minutes (see 3b-2), recalling your overall impressions and any important points you may have overlooked earlier.

2   Determining purpose, persona, and audience

Once you have completed your critical reading, you should establish a rhetorical stance for your paper (see 3a-2). In determining your rhetorical stance, you will make decisions about your purpose for writing, your persona, and your intended audience. If you are writing to complete an assignment, begin by carefully studying the assignment itself.

To decide on your purpose for writing, look for key terms in the assignment, such as *analyze* or *discuss*. Both of these terms imply an interpretive or analytical purpose for writing (see 23a-3). Your instructor may have specified some aspect of the work that you should write about, or he or she may have left the topic open-ended. In most cases, your instructor will expect you to write a piece with an argumentative edge that makes a point about the work and supports that point with examples and illustrations from the text. Examples of some typical assignments follow.

Writing Assignments Calling for Interpretation

- Discuss the key ideas or themes that the author of the poem "One Art" is trying to convey. Connect the poem to your own experiences of loss.
- Explain how the setting of *Regeneration* affects its major themes.

Writing Assignments Calling for Character Analysis

- Analyze the relationship between Cathy and Adam Trask in *East of Eden*.
- Explore the character of Lady Macbeth in the play *Macbeth*.

General Assignments That Allow the Writer to Decide the Purpose

- Discuss in depth some aspect of one of the novels we read this term.
- Explain how one of the authors we read this term used imagery.

Next, think about your persona for the paper. How do you wish to come across as a writer? Will you be objective and fair or heated and passionate? Your persona is revealed in the paper through the words and sentence structures you choose (see 26g, 26h).

Finally, ask yourself who the audience for the paper will be. Most often the audience, in addition to your teacher, will be intelligent readers who are interested in literature but who may not be acquainted with the particular text you are writing about. Your paper should provide your readers with background information about the text so that they will be able to follow your argument.

3 Developing a claim and writing a thesis

How you interpret or analyze a work of literature will depend on what you have read, your interests, your prior knowledge, the information presented in class, and your general understanding of the work in question. If you have a choice, you should write about something that interests or intrigues you about the work. You will need to come up with your own critical interpretation or analysis of the work and then write a thesis statement that articulates your claim.

Literary works are typically analyzed with respect to some major aspect such as characters or plot. Following are various questions you can use in arriving at a thesis related to one of the major aspects of literary works. The list does not cover every possible topic, but it should help you get started.

Characters (major actors)

- How convincing are the characters?
- Does a particular character's behavior seem consistent throughout the work?
- Does the author reveal the thoughts of the narrator?

Plot (what happens)

- How effective is the plot?
- Does it hold your interest and build to an effective climax?
- Does the plot line seem well connected or is it disjointed and hard to follow? What difference might this make to an interpretation of the work?

Theme (major idea or main message)

- What is the overall theme or point that the work is trying to make?
- Is the point one that you agree with?
- Does the author convince you that the point is well taken?
- Is the theme used consistently throughout the work or are there contradictions?

Structure (organization)

- What is the structure, or overall design, of the text itself?
- Does it skip around chronologically or geographically?
- Does one chapter lead logically to the next?
- What is the author trying to accomplish with the particular structure he or she chose?

Setting (where and when the events take place)

- How has the author used setting?
- Are descriptions of people and places particularly vivid?
- Did you feel as though you were in the place being described?
- How well did the author re-create a sense of place?

Point of View (perspective of whoever presents the ideas)

- What is the point of view adopted by the writer?
- Who is the narrator?
- Did the narrator color the way you reacted to the work?
- Does the point of view remain consistent?

Rhythm (meter or beat) and Rhyme (correspondence in the sounds of words)

- Are there striking rhythmic patterns or rhyme schemes?
- What is the impact of the work's language?

Imagery (visual impressions created) and Figures of Speech (metaphors and similes)

- Did the author use imagery and figures of speech effectively?
- Is a particular image repeated throughout the work?

Symbolism (use of familiar ideas to represent something else) and Archetypes (traditional models after which others are patterned)

- How have symbols and archetypes been used in the work?
- Does the author repeat a certain key symbol? To what purpose?
- Is there a mythical archetype at work? How effective is it?

Tone and Voice (persona of the author as reflected through word choice and style)

- What tone or voice has the writer adopted?
- Is the tone appropriate to the theme? To the characters?
- How does the writer's tone affect you as a reader?

4 Using the appropriate person and tense

In writing interpretively about literature, it is generally appropriate to use the first person (*I, we, our*) to express your own point of view: "*I* was greatly moved by the character's predicament." However, in academic papers, the third person (*he, she, it, they*) is typically used to discuss information found in sources.

Also, in writing about a work of literature, the commonly accepted practice is to use the present tense (sometimes called the *literary present*) when describing events that happened in the work: "Adam Trask *learns* about his wife's true character slowly." Similarly, use the present tense when discussing what an author has done in a specific literary work: "Steinbeck *uses* Cathy and Adam Trask to illustrate his point about the pure evil that *exists* in human nature."

5 Writing your literature paper

Once you have articulated a thesis, you can proceed to write your paper, following the advice in Part 1 of this handbook. In particular, it would be wise to review the Stages of the Writing Process (see 2c). If your assignment specifies that you support your thesis through research, follow the advice in Part 2 of this handbook on researching your topic. See the list in 14d of reference materials commonly used in the humanities.

14c Review some model student papers

Let us now look at how two students approached the task of writing about literature, one to produce a literary interpretation and the other to produce a literary analysis.

1 An example of literary interpretation

In a first-year course on understanding literature, students were asked to interpret the poem "One Art" and discuss the impact on readers of its major theme—loss. Wayne Proffitt began his task by rereading the poem, circling and annotating words relating to its major theme (see Figure 14.1). He then listed those items he had high-lighted in outline form. For his rhetorical stance, he decided on an interpretive purpose, an objective persona, and a novice audience. Next, Wayne wrote his working thesis, which articulated the claim he would make in his paper: "Bishop wrote one poem specifically about loss and accepting it." This thesis makes an interpretive claim about the meaning of the poem. Wayne then went on to write the paper, using the poem itself as his source as he explained and justi-fied his claim.

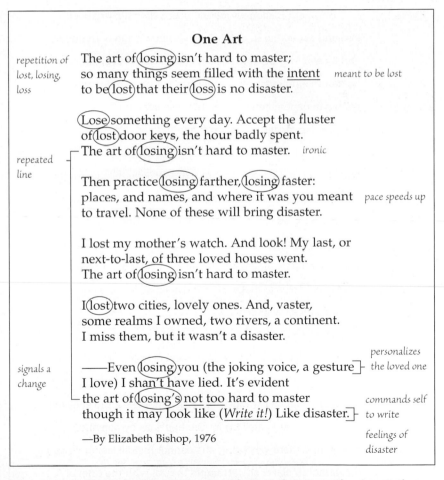

One Art

repetition of   The art of losing isn't hard to master;
lost, losing,   so many things seem filled with the intent   *meant to be lost*
loss   to be lost that their loss is no disaster.

  Lose something every day. Accept the fluster
  of lost door keys, the hour badly spent.
repeated   The art of losing isn't hard to master.   *ironic*
line

  Then practice losing farther, losing faster:
  places, and names, and where it was you meant   *pace speeds up*
  to travel. None of these will bring disaster.

  I lost my mother's watch. And look! My last, or
  next-to-last, of three loved houses went.
  The art of losing isn't hard to master.

  I lost two cities, lovely ones. And, vaster,
  some realms I owned, two rivers, a continent.
  I miss them, but it wasn't a disaster.

                                      personalizes
signals a   ——Even losing you (the joking voice, a gesture   *the loved one*
change   I love) I shan't have lied. It's evident
  the art of losing's not too hard to master   *commands self*
  though it may look like (*Write it!*) Like disaster.   *to write*

  —By Elizabeth Bishop, 1976   *feelings of*
                                        disaster

Figure 14.1   **Elizabeth Bishop's Poem with Wayne's Interpretive Annotations**

No title page. For a model with
a title page, see Chapter 11.

Proffitt 1

Student
and course
number

Wayne Proffitt

English 1116–03

Last name and page
number in upper
right-hand corner

Double-
spaced

May 15, 1998

Emotional Distance and Loss in a Poem

by Elizabeth Bishop

Thesis   Elizabeth Bishop wrote one poem specifically about

loss and accepting it. She offers her knowledge with humor

and a casual air in "One Art." It seems that this poem may

be autobiographical, as it describes not only things that

people in general tend to lose but also specific items that

the poet herself has lost during her lifetime. The reader is

led through a list of lost objects that the speaker claims

Words of
the author
in quota-
tion marks
were meant to be lost. "So many things seem filled with the

intent" that when they finally do get lost it "is no disaster."

The reader is advised--in a casual way--to get used to

losing things and to practice getting better at letting go.

The ironic encouragement of "the art of losing isn't hard

to master" helps to make clear the speaker's real emotions

and attitudes towards losing.

Interpreta-
tion of the
change in
voice
The humorous and casual voice of the speaker

becomes quite forced towards the end of the poem, however,

and we suspect that the loss of her loved one was not really

one that could be shrugged off. It is almost as if the speaker

is trying to gear herself up for the final loss by convincing

herself that there is nothing she cannot handle losing. With

this armor in place, she attempts to deal with the grief of

Proffitt 2

losing one well-loved, but finds that in the end she cannot

hold her nonchalance and indifference steadily enough.

At this point, perhaps both the speaker and the reader

suddenly feel the art of losing for what it really is--an

inevitable task--and that it can truly be "disaster" for

Interpreta-
tion of the
meaning
of loss in
the poem

the one who has lost. The remembered "joking voice, a

gesture I love" bring a real beloved person into the poem

and emphasize the enormity of the loss. The speaker has

difficulty completing the closing sentence and must goad

herself to "write it" and be done.

Emotional
impact of
the poem

    The ability to create such distance between the

speaker and the object being discussed increases the

impact of the submerged emotion when it is finally

allowed to surface. The very distance of this poem's

opening stanzas is one of the reasons that the emotional

loss at the end of the poem contains so much power.

Personal suffering and loss is not openly exposed in this

poem, and because of this, careful reading is necessary

to see past the distance crafted into the poem. The effort

of seeing more than is directly stated contributes to the

reader's eventual understanding and even sharing of the

sense of loss.

Work Cited

Source

Bishop, Elizabeth. "One Art." <u>The Complete Poems 1927-</u>

<u>1979 by Elizabeth Bishop</u>. New York: Farrar, 1983. 215.

2   An example of literary analysis in MLA format

For a sophomore-level course on the British novel, students were asked to analyze a significant theme in one of the novels they read for the course. Heidi Blankley decided to write about the novel *Regeneration*. She was fascinated by the theme of gender stereotypes, which had been discussed in class and also in a conversation she had with her professor during office hours. She found the theme compelling, especially in light of her own interest in the changing roles of men and women in contemporary society. Her essay illustrates literary analysis —an analytical argument about a work of literature.

http://home1.gte.net/
turner24/critcont.htm
An extensive introduction to advanced literary analysis techniques and schools of thought

In her first two sentences, she articulates her critical stance. Notice how she begins with a quote stating the general topic of the book (the treatment of shell-shock victims after World War I), followed by her own claim that the book is even more profoundly about the theme of gender stereotypes. This claim, or thesis, provides the reader with a clear understanding of the analysis Heidi plans to make in her paper. As the writer, she must prove to her readers, using examples from the text, that the novel *does* explore the theme of gender stereotyping.

The paper exemplifies the MLA documentation and formatting conventions (see 13-a). The list of works cited shows that Heidi read secondary sources about the novel and used information from her class, from a journal article, from a book, and from the Internet as support for her essay.

Student,
professor,
and course
identifica-
tion

Heidi Blankley

Professor Kristine Miller

British Novel

2 April 1997

Ending the Violence

Pat Barker, a contemporary British author and winner

In MLA
style, source
citations
include the
author and
the page
number,
with no
comma

of the prestigious Booker Prize, writes novels about England

during the war years (Middlemiss). In <u>Regeneration</u>, Pat

Barker "examines the treatment of shell-shock victims at

Edinburgh's Craiglockhart hospital during World War I"

(Perry 44). Although Barker's novel is mainly about the

acculturation of shell-shock victims from World War I, it is

Thesis

more concerned with the larger issue that lurks behind the

battle scenes: gender stereotypes. Barker suggests that the

violence created by adhering to the masculine stereotype--

that men are brave warriors and not nurturers--is not

merely a social problem, but a mythical, psychological

obstacle, the effects of which are seeping into all facets

of life. If humans are ever to recover from the violence,

Barker thinks we must analyze the root of the violence

and come to terms with our destructive behavior toward

the environment, other species, and one another.

First
example
of coming
to terms
with
violence

In chapter fifteen, a relatively bizarre scene occurs

which forces the patient, David Burns, to realize he can

exert influence on the violence surrounding him. Burns

Blankley 2

leaves Craiglockhart and comes into contact with a tree

that reeks of death, "laden with animals . . . [which are tied

to it] like fruit" (Barker 138). Burns's first impulse is to give

in to fear and run from the grotesque tree, but Barker has a

different plan in mind for Burns. Instead, Burns faces his

fear head-on and unties the animals:

Long quote from the novel is indented ——————▶ 10 spaces

> When all the corpses were on the ground, he
> arranged them in a circle round the tree and sat
> down within it, his back against the trunk. He
> felt the roughness of the bark against his knobby
> spine. He pressed his hands between his knees
> and looked around the circle of his companions.
> Now they could dissolve into the earth as they
> were meant to do. (Barker 139)

Punctuation precedes the citation for indented quotes only

This scene is so strange and so grotesque that it forces

the reader to question Barker's motives for including it.

When the naked Burns surrounds himself with the corpses,

the scene becomes a reflection of the war; the animals

represent the hundreds of decaying soldiers. The inhumane

placement of the animals suggests that the soldiers are

dying for an inhumane and unnatural purpose. Just as this

scene is unnatural in its placement of the animals, so are

the massive murders involved with the war.

Furthermore, the circle Burns makes with the decaying

animals resembles the cyclical pattern of history; humanity

has spawned war after war, apparently without learning

Blankley 3

anything from its own violence. As the creator of the

circle and also the one who sits within it, Burns recognizes

that he is both a physical perpetrator of violence and a

The example is related to the theme of gender stereotypes

psychological victim of it. He copes with this paradoxical

situation simply by revising gender stereotypes. As he

steps into the circle and returns the animals to the earth,

he takes on the qualities of a nurturer, a role contradictory

to the masculine stereotype, and hence, his genitals

look somehow out of place. However, although Burns

might wish to remove himself from the situation, from his

contributions to the war and violence in general, he is still

a part of it, the "white root" of it.

Critical analysis of the scene described

What Barker is trying to accomplish with this scene is

to show that no matter what gender, we are a part of the

recurring historical pattern of violence, whether it is toward

humans or other creatures. The only way to get out of the

circle, as Burns does in his dream, is to see ourselves inside

the circle (Barker 140).

Second example of coming to terms with violence

Another character, Rivers, also displays his sensitivity

to the destruction around him. Rivers, modeled after a

real-life doctor, is shown by Barker to be a humane and

sensitive man (Perry 44). In chapter thirteen, a bumble bee

is trapped inside a room where Craiglockhart officials are

holding a meeting. Rivers is unable to concentrate on the

meeting and keeps scanning the windows, trying to find

the bee because "the noise was unreasonably disturbing"

Brackets
show letters
changed
from the
original
to fit the
sentence

Blankley 4

(Barker 132). When he finally finds the insect, he "fetch[es]
a file from the desk and, using it as a barrier, guide[s] the
insect into the open air" (Barker 132). When he turns back
into the room, he finds "everybody, Burns included, staring
at him in some surprise" (Barker 132-33); judging from
this reaction, one can assume that Rivers's response to
the bee is an abnormal one. Perhaps the others in the
room were unaware of the bee's presence, or if they were
aware, maybe they would have acted like "bloodthirsty little
horrors" (Barker 172), smacking the bee with the file instead
of rescuing it.

The second
example is
is related to
the theme
of gender
stereotypes

    Through his action, Rivers transcends the masculine
stereotype, which is why his action is met by surprise from
the other men. The release of the bee might simply be
symbolic of Rivers's escape from Craiglockhart--for at the
end of this chapter, he takes some time off for sick leave.
But this connection seems too obvious. Barker is once more
forcing the reader to question gender stereotypes. By
releasing the bee instead of smashing it, Rivers becomes
Barker's ideal human. He is a man with the capacity to
nurture not only other men but nature as well. In this
instance, he represents the balance, a human being acting
on natural instinct to save another creature, without
questioning his own motives.

The myth of
regeneration
is related to
the theme
of violence

    Throughout her novel, Barker plays with the myth of
regeneration. Typically (in American mythology), the myth

Blankley 5

of regeneration involves a male character who seeks to

escape the bonds of his old life. To do so, he retires from

civilization into the purity of wilderness and, after a while,

is reborn a newer, wiser man who is more in tune with

himself and his surroundings. Although the wilderness in

Regeneration is civilized, Burns and Rivers try to use the

wilderness in the same way. Burns returns to his native

home in Suffolk hoping to rejuvenate himself from the

psychological trauma he experienced in the war. Burns

invites Rivers to join him there, hoping Suffolk will have the

same invigorating effect on Rivers.

The theme of violence is analyzed   Barker's idea of regeneration appears to apply to

violence in general, to the war, and to gender roles. Early

in the novel, Rivers has an insightful revelation about

gender roles:

> He distrusted the implication that nurturing, even
>
> when done by a man, remains female, as if the

Ellipses indicate omissions

> ability were in some way borrowed, or even stolen
>
> from women. . . . If that were true, then there was
>
> really very little hope. (Barker 107)

The two themes of violence and gender stereotypes are connected   If women are the only ones who can be considered

nurturers, if men are permanently locked into the role

of brave warriors, and if neither females nor males have

the capacity to extend the boundaries of these roles, then

there is little hope that the psychological trauma of war

can be overcome. There is also little hope that the cycle of

Blankley 6

violence will ever cease, because the masculine gender
stereotype depends on war and violence for the man to
prove himself as a brave warrior, while the female
stereotype depends on wounded soldiers to nurture.

The result of clinging to these stereotypes is a perpetual
cycle of violence that extends past the war and into the
physical qualities of the environment. If the stereotypes
are left unquestioned, the cycle of violence will continue,
and neither men nor women will be able to recover from
the violence.

Analyzes
the use of
metaphor

However, in chapter fifteen, Barker illustrates a remedy
for the destructive cycle of violence with a brilliant metaphor:

> Rivers knew only too well how often the early
> stages of change or cure may mimic deterioration.
> Cut a chrysalis open, and you will find a rotting
> caterpillar. What you will never find is that
> mythical creature, half caterpillar, half butterfly, a
> fit emblem of the human soul. . . . No, the process
> of transformation consists almost entirely of decay.
> (Barker 184)

Barker reveals that the only way to abolish war and all the
violent behavior equivalent to war is to internalize those
traits which are perceived as inherently masculine and
inherently feminine--to view the soul as a combination of
butterfly and caterpillar, enclosed in the delicate chrysalis
of the earth. War is a transition period, a devastating event

Blankley 7

which can lead to the positive transformation of social roles,

if we let it.

Introduces
the quote
with the
author's
name in
a signal
phrase

In her article on women's fiction, Lyn Pykett suggests

that "Pat Barker, like a number of other recent women

writers, does not interrogate or deconstruct history . . . but

rather she seeks to recover and reclaim the past on behalf

of those who have been silenced and marginalized by

Conclusion
returns to
thesis idea

history" (Pykett 75). In this novel, the shell-shock victims

are those who have historically been silenced. Barker gives

them a voice in <u>Regeneration</u>. Through them, she suggests

that it is possible to heal society if we cease adhering to the

stereotypical male and female gender roles. What we need

in order to solve the trauma of war and to prevent future

violence are not heroes or warriors, but a reconsideration of

gender, a restructuring of the rules so that men may reveal

their "feminine" sensitivity without being typecast as

effeminate, homosexual, or motherly.

Blankley 8

Works Cited   MLA citation style

Novel   Barker, Pat. <u>Regeneration</u>. New York: Plume, 1993.

Internet   Middlemiss, Perry. Homepage. 1 Jan. 1997. 15 May 1997

<http://ncc1701.apana.org.au/~/arrikin/lit/prizes/

booker.html>.

Class notes   Miller, Kristine. Class notes and personal interview.
and
interview   10 May 1997.

Nonfiction   Perry, Donna. <u>Backtalk: Women Writers Speak Out</u>. New
book   Book title is underlined
              Brunswick, NJ: Rutgers UP, 1993.
                                            Second line is indented
Journal   Pykett, Lyn. "The Century's Daughters: Recent Women's

Initial   Fiction and History." <u>Critical Quarterly</u> 29.3 (1987): 71-77.
capitals are
used in   Journal name
article titles,   is underlined
which are
also put in
quotation
marks

14d Look to the Internet and traditional materials for resources

Scholars in the humanities are beginning to use technology in their research and their writing. Students of the humanities, too, should familiarize themselves with available resources, particularly those on the Internet. (Chapter 9 discusses the types of Internet resources and how to locate and evaluate them.) Take a look at some of the Internet sources in the following list, such as the Project Gutenberg Web site, which contains numerous full texts of important works of literature, or the Classics Resources site, which has links to sites on classical languages and literature. There are also numerous discussion groups, bulletin boards, and newsgroups related to the humanities. You can find these discussion sites through an Internet search (see Chapter 21 for information on using computer networks).

Web Sites for the Humanities

Art

The Center for Creative Photography *(http://www.ccp.arizona.edu/ccp.html)*
The Parthenet *(http://home.mtholyoke.edu/~klconner/parthenet.html)*
World Wide Arts Resources *(http://wwar.world-arts-resources.com)*

Classics

Ancient World Web *(http://julen.net/aw)*
Classics Resources on the Internet *(http://www.usask.ca/classics/resourcesurls.html)*
Perseus Project *(http://www.perseus.tufts.edu)*

English Literature and Language

Elements of Style by William Strunk, Jr. *(http://www.columbia.edu/acis/bartleby/strunk)*
English Server—Carnegie Mellon *(http://english-www.hss.cmu.edu)*
Literary Resources on the Net *(http://dept.english.upenn.edu/~jlynch/Lit)*
Project Bartleby *(http://www.columbia.edu/acis/bartleby/index.html)*
Project Gutenberg *(http://promo.net/pg)*
The Victorian Web *(http://www.stg.brown.edu/projects/hypertext/landow/victorian/victov.html)*
Voice of the Shuttle: English Literature *(http://humanitas.ucsb.edu/shuttle/english.html)*

Folklore

Handilinks to Folklore (*http://ahandyguide.com/cat1/f/f321.htm*)

History

Archiving Early America (*http://earlyamerica.com*)
19th Century Scientific American (*http://www.history.rochester.edu/ Scientific_American*)

Humanities (General)

Humanities Hub (*http://www.gu.edu.au/gwis/hub/hub.home.html*)
The Humbul Gateway (*http://users.ox.ac.uk/~humbul*)
Voice of the Shuttle (*http://humanitas.ucsb.edu*)

Journalism and News

CNN (*http://www.cnn.com*)
New York Times on the Web (*http://www.nytimes.com*)
Trib.Com—The Internet Newspaper (*http://www.trib.com*)
USA Today (*http://www.usatoday.com*)
Wall Street Journal (*http://www.wsj.com*)

Landscape Architecture

American Society of Landscape Architecture (*http://www.asla.org/asla*)
Landscape Architecture (*http://www.clr.utoronto.ca*)
Lincoln Institute for Land Policy (*http://www.lincolninst.edu/home.html*)

Motion Pictures and Film

Cinema (*http://cinemania.msn.com/cinemania/home.asp*)
Hollywood Online (*http://www.hollywood.com*)
Movie Web (*http://www.movieweb.com*)

Music

Music Education Links (*http://www.geocities.com/Athens/2405/resources. html*)
MusicLink: Music on the Internet (*http://toltec.lib.utk.edu/~music/www. html*)

Philosophy

The American Philosophical Association (*http://www.udel.edu/apa/index. html*)
Handilinks to Philosophy (*http://ahandyguide.com/cat1/p/p95.htm*)

Religion

Comparative Religion (*http://www.academicinfo.net/religindex.html*)

Theatre

The Theatre Links Page *(http://www.theatre-link.com)*

Women's Studies

The Women's Resource Project *(http://sunsite.unc.edu/cheryb/women)*
Women's Studies Resources *(http://www.inform.umd.edu:8080/EdRes/Topic/WomensStudies)*

Writing

Allyn and Bacon's Compsite *(http://www.abacon.com/compsite)*
Rensselaer Writing Center Handouts *(http://www.rpi.edu/dept/llc/writecenter/web/handouts.html)*
Writing Centers Online *(http://departments.colgate.edu/diw/NWCAOWLS.html)*

General Sources and Guides to Literature

Field Guide to the Study of American Literature. Kolb, H. Charlottesville: U of Virginia P, 1976. (Paperback Rpt. Ann Arbor: Books on Demand, 1996.) A guide to selected sources in American literature.
Harvard Guide to American History. Rev. ed. Freidel, F., and Showman, R., eds. Cambridge: Harvard UP, 1979. A guide to sources in American history; contains an introduction to the discipline.
Information Sources in Architecture. Bradfield, V. J. Stoneham: Butterworth, 1983. A general guide to sources.
Literary History of America. Wendell, B., ed. New York: Macmillan, 1992. A history of US literature from colonial times to the 1960s.
New Cambridge Medieval History. Cambridge, Eng.: Cambridge UP, 1995. An introduction to medieval history.
Oxford History of English Music. Caldwell, J., ed. Oxford, Eng.: Oxford UP, 1992. A comprehensive, historical overview.
Reader's Guide to American History. Parish, P. J., ed. Dearborn: Fitzroy, 1996. An introduction to major sources for American history.
Reference Sources in English and American Literature: An Annotated Bibliography. Schweik, R. C., and Riesner, D., eds. New York: Norton, 1977. A good starting source.

Dictionaries

Dictionary of Architecture. Meikleham, R., ed. New York: Gordon, 1980. 3 vols. General information.
Dictionary of Comparative Religions. Brandon, S. G., ed. New York: Scribner's, 1978. Information on world religions.

Dictionary of Composers and Their Music. Gilder, E. New York: Random, 1993. Useful background information.

Dictionary of Contemporary American Artists. 5th ed. Cummings, P. New York: St. Martin's, 1988. Concise information on living American artists.

Dictionary of Literature in the English Language. Meyers, R. New York: Pergamon, 1978. 2 vols. Useful background information on classical English literary works.

Dictionary of Philosophy. Mautner, T. London: Blackwell, 1995. General information and definitions.

Encyclopedic Dictionary of American History. 4th ed. Faragher, J. M., ed. Guilford: Dushkin, 1991. Complete background information on American history.

Funk & Wagnalls' Standard Dictionary of Folklore, Mythology, and Legend. Leach, M., and Fried, J., eds. New York: Funk, 1984. Concise information on myths and legends.

The New Grove Dictionary of Music and Musicians. Sadie, S., ed. London: Macmillan, 1980. 20 vols. Information on musical topics from ancient to modern times.

Encyclopedias

Encyclopaedia of Architecture. Yarwood, D., ed. London: Batsford, 1994. Concise information on all facets of architecture.

Encyclopedia of American History. 7th ed. Morris, R. B., and Morris, J. B., eds. New York: Harper, 1996. Valuable overview of American history; contains brief biographies of famous Americans.

Encyclopedia of Bioethics. 2nd ed. Reich, W. T., ed. New York: Macmillan, 1995. Information on philosophy and religion.

Encyclopedia of Philosophy. Edwards, P., ed. New York: Free, 1973. Complete reference work on both Eastern and Western philosophical thought.

Encyclopedia of Religion. Eliade, M., ed. New York: Macmillan, 1993. 14 vols. Concise articles on world religions.

Encyclopedia of Science Fiction and Fantasy. Tuck, D., ed. Berkeley: Adventure, 1983. 3 vols. Concise articles on works of science fiction.

Encyclopedia of World Art. Eggenberger, D., ed. New York: McGraw, 1987. 16 vols. Information on world art and artists.

Encyclopedia of World History: Ancient, Medieval, and Modern. Langer, W. L., ed. Boston: Houghton, 1973. Major world events from earliest times to 1970. (The *New Illustrated Encyclopedia of World History* is essentially the same work with illustrations.)

The New College Encyclopedia of Music. Westrop, J. A., and Harrison, F. L., eds. New York: Norton, 1981. Concise information on all aspects of music.

Princeton Encyclopedia of Poetry and Poetics. Preminger, A., ed. Princeton: Princeton UP, 1974. Concise information on poetry and poetics through time; covers history, theory, technique, and criticism of poetry.

Biographies

American Novelists Since WWII. Helterman, J., and Layman, R., eds. Dictionary of Literary Biography Series, vol. 2. Detroit: Gale, 1980. Illustrated biographical entries on recent American novelists.

American Poets Since WWII. Greiner, D., ed. Dictionary of Literary Biography Series, vol. 5. Detroit: Gale, 1980. Illustrated biographical entries on recent American poets.

Contemporary Authors: A Biographical Guide to Current Authors and Their Works. Detroit: Gale, annual (1962–present). Information on current American authors.

Contemporary Musicians. Detroit: Gale, 1995. Information on current musicians.

Directory of American Scholars. 8th ed. New York: Bowker, 1982. Biographical directory of notable scholars still active in their fields.

Indexes, Bibliographies, and Abstracts

(An asterisk indicates that the source can be accessed through a computer search.)

Art and Architecture

Architectural Index
*Art Index
Ceramics Abstracts

English and Language Studies

Abstracts of English Studies
American Literature Abstracts
Annual Bibliography of English Language and Literature
Articles on American Literature
Cambridge Bibliography of English Literature
Essay and General Literature Index

Granger's Index to Poetry
International Guide to Classical Studies
Language and Language Behavior Abstracts
*MLA (Modern Language Association) International Bibliography
Short Story Index
Year's Work in English Studies

Folklore

Abstracts of Folklore Studies
Index to Fairytales, Myths and Legends

History

*America: History and Life
Combined Retrospective Index to Journals in History
*Historical Abstracts
Writings on American History

Humanities (General)

*Arts and Humanities Citation Index
*Humanities Index
Index to Book Reviews in the Humanities
Social Science and Humanities Index

Journalism

Journalism Abstracts

Motion Pictures and Film

Film Literature Index
International Index of Film Periodicals
Landers Film Reviews
New York Times Film Reviews
*New York Times Index

Music

Music Article Guide
Music Index
*RILM Abstracts

Philosophy

Philosopher's Index

Religion

Religion One Index
Religious and Theological Abstracts

Theater

New York Times Theater Reviews
Play Index

Women's Studies

Women's Studies Abstracts

EXERCISE 14.1

Investigate the Internet resources available for one of the disciplines
within the humanities. Search by topic for a newsgroup or a bulletin
board (see 21a-2). Bring to class a printout of a Web site or discussion that you found in your search. Share the information with your
classmates.

Writing in the Natural Sciences

FAQs

What kinds of writing assignments can I expect in science courses? (15a)

What makes scientific writing different from other kinds of writing? (15b)

Should I use headings in a scientific report? (15c)

How can I find information in the library or on the Internet for a science research paper? (15d)

The natural sciences hold an authoritative position in society and thus are a dominant force in our lives. Using a widely accepted methodology, scientists formulate and test theories about the natural and physical world, and their findings are used to solve problems in medicine, industry, and agriculture. Typically, the natural sciences are classified into two categories: pure and applied. The pure sciences include the life sciences (such as biology and botany), the physical sciences (such as physics and chemistry), and the earth sciences (such as geology and geography). The applied sciences include the medical sciences (such as forensics, pathology, surgery, and

http://mspiggy.etl.
noaa.gov/write/
An online course in
analytical writing in
science and technology

ophthalmology), engineering (mechanical, environmental, aerospace, and electrical), and computer science.

15a Know the different types of writing in the natural sciences

To solve problems in a systematic way, scientists use the scientific method. Writing plays a critical role in each step of the scientific method. The first step is to express the problem in writing, clearly and objectively, in the form of a statement, usually called a *problem statement*. The second step is to gather all relevant information needed to solve the problem, including information found in library sources such as books and journals. The third step is to analyze that information and formulate a hypothesis. A *hypothesis* is a statement that predicts what the scientist expects to find by conducting controlled experiments related to the problem under investigation. The fourth step is to design and conduct controlled experiments to test the hypothesis. The scientist must keep a detailed record of each experiment and its outcome. The fifth step is to analyze these records to determine how well they support the hypothesis or predicted results. Finally, the sixth step is to restate the hypothesis as a conclusion that explains how the experimental data supported, refuted, or modified the initial hypothesis. Whether you are writing up your own work in the form of a research report or summarizing and evaluating other people's work in the form of a review of literature, you need to be familiar with the scientific method.

1 Research report

The majority of scientific writing is in the form of research reports, which are found in all branches of the sciences and technology. Research reports are based on primary research conducted by scientists. The motivation for much primary research in the natural sciences is an event or experience that challenges existing ideas and promotes inquiry. In general, the aim is to improve the congruency between theories and concepts about the world and actual experiences or experimental results.

It is through primary research that great breakthroughs in the advancement of knowledge occur, and it is through research reports that these developments are announced to the scientific community. One famous example of primary research is the studies conducted by the English biologist Sir Alexander Fleming. When he noticed that one of his cultures of *Staphylococcus* bacteria had been contaminated by a microorganism from the air outside, Fleming examined the contaminated plate in detail and noticed a surprising phenomenon: where the colonies of bacteria had been attacked by microscopic fungi, a large region had become transparent. Fleming hypothesized that the effect could be due to an antibacterial substance secreted by the foreign microorganism and then spread into the culture. Fortunately, Fleming proceeded to research the phenomenon at length, and the secretion he hypothesized turned out to be a variety of the fungus *Penicillium,* from which the antibiotic penicillin is now made.

Whether a research report announces the discovery of penicillin or the results of a student lab experiment, the basic outline is the same, as it parallels the steps in the scientific method. The standard format used to report scientific findings is as follows:

- *Abstract,* which summarizes the report in one compact paragraph
- *Introduction,* which states the problem, background information, and the hypothesis
- *Literature review,* which summarizes related research
- *Research methods,* which outlines the processes used in the experiments
- *Research results,* which describes the outcomes and findings of the experiments
- *Discussion and conclusion,* which relates the research back to the problem and hypothesis and speculates on the implications of the research
- *Endmatter,* which may include notes, references, and appendixes

Individual scientists use many variations on this standard format, depending on the audience they are addressing. Less formal reports may not include an abstract or a literature review, for example. An abbreviated version of the research report may serve as a laboratory report or a progress report.

2 Review of literature

The second major category of scientific writing is the review of literature. In this type of writing, based on secondary research, the writer discusses literature found in the library rather than his or her own original research. Only by analyzing and synthesizing the findings of other scientists, reported in journal articles and other relevant sources, can students, scholars, and researchers keep up on developments in their field.

WWW
WEB

http://darkstar.engr.
wisc.edu/alley/
students.html
An excellent writing
workbook for students of
science and engineering

A literature review may be a brief summary of the literature on a specific topic; it may be a lengthy critical review of a single work or an extended critical review of several works on the same topic. A literature review may even take the form of annotations—critical or explanatory notes added to another text.

15b Write objectively about science

Because it is used to inform audiences about scientific findings and data, scientific writing needs to be objective, exact, and complete. In most cases, it describes scientific problems and their solutions.

As a student, when you are writing about the natural sciences, generally you are responding to an assignment. The assignment may specify whether you are to write a research report or a review of literature. If it does not, you are probably better off reviewing the literature on a particular topic, unless you are already involved in a scientific experiment. If the assignment calls for primary research, you will probably need your instructor's help in designing an appropriate method for collecting data. (For information on how to report your research, see 15a-1.)

If your instructor has not assigned a particular topic, you can turn to the media—television, radio, magazines, and the Internet—for ideas. Look for controversies or new discoveries in the natural sciences and begin to ask questions about them. For example, a television documentary on some of the newest findings about the planet Mars might lead you to wonder if there really is evidence of life on Mars. What exactly did the scientists working on the Pathfinder mission discover?

1 Determining purpose and audience

Once you have a topic, you can establish a rhetorical stance (see 3a-2). To decide on your purpose for writing, begin by carefully studying the assignment itself. Look for key terms, such as *analyze* or *discuss*. Both of these terms imply an interpretive or critical purpose for writing. Your instructor will expect you to write a piece that makes a point, supported by secondary sources.

Next, ask yourself who your audience will be. Usually you can assume that you are writing for intelligent readers who are interested in the subject but may not know many details about the topic. You should provide enough background information so that such readers will be able to follow your argument. (Because of the focus on objectivity, the writer's persona is less of an issue in scientific writing.)

2   Writing a thesis

To write a thesis, you need to refine your topic. For example, if you decided to write about life on Mars, you could use print sources and the Internet to find out more about the Pathfinder mission and then write an informative thesis describing what you found out. If your instructor wanted your report to have an argumentative edge, your thesis could argue for or against the claim that life exists on Mars.

3   Completing the research and writing your paper

In any writing assignment, regardless of the discipline for which you are writing, you should follow the writing process described in Part 1 of this handbook. Refer to Chapters 3, 4, and 5 for advice on prewriting, drafting, revising, and editing. If your paper consists of or includes a literature review, refer to Part 2 of this handbook for information on library research. See the list in 15d of reference materials commonly used in the sciences, including Internet resources.

15c   Review a sample research report in CBE format

In a sophomore-level engineering course, the students were allowed to work with their peers on a primary research project. Following is a report produced by one group of four students. Notice how the students' report begins with a cover memorandum, which includes an executive summary outlining the study and its recommendations. Then, in the body of the report, the students describe their own research, which was designed to determine the method that would best solve the water shortages anticipated in a neighboring community.

The report illustrates an adapted scientific report format. It begins with a cover memo to introduce the problem and proposed solutions. The cover memo also serves as an abstract. Next comes a title page. The sections have headings that parallel the research itself. However, not all of the sections typically found in a research report are included. The students did not include a formal literature review, choosing instead to integrate references within the body of the report. They followed the CBE citation style (see 13d), electing to use the author-year system rather than the number system. Notice that the sections of the report are numbered; this practice is common in scientific and engineering reports, as it helps readers find relevant information quickly and easily.

Cover memo

TO: Brent Adams, CEE Professor

FROM: Group 4: David Hunter, Carl Jones, Lee Duong, Rhonda Peterson

SUBJECT: RECOMMENDATION FOR CHOOSING AN ALTERNATIVE WATER SOURCE/SYSTEM

REF.: Your letter of request, September 10, 1996

DATE: January 5, 1997

DIST.: Sonia Manuel-Dupont, Project Supervisor

Smithfield City will not have an adequate supply of culinary water in the future. Their current supply is only adequate for another 5 years (Gass 1996). We were asked by you to research and derive a solution for this problem. After discussing as a group the various alternatives that could be implemented, we decided on 4 alternatives that would be the most effective. Each of us in the group researched articles and made personal interviews to determine the most appropriate solution. From our findings we have gathered that the most effective alternative is installing a new well that will have enough supply to meet future demand.

Executive Summary used
in place of abstract

Executive Summary

The population of Smithfield City is growing rapidly. The current water supply for Smithfield is not adequate to meet the needs of the city over the next 25 years. We need to find a source to provide an additional 70 million gallons of water per month to Smithfield City in order to have an adequate water supply for the next 25 years. We have researched the problem in scientific journals and books and also have spoken with the Smithfield City Engineer and also others who deal directly with water supply.

Our purpose of communication is to inform you of our 4 researched alternatives: 1) development of a new well, 2) no action, 3) installation of a dual system, and 4) water reuse. Only the development of a new well will supply enough water for Smithfield City over the next 25 years. Development of a new well was ranked best on cost, feasibility, and adequacy, and average on maintenance and impact on the environment. Therefore, we recommend the development of a new well to provide the necessary water for Smithfield City.

Title page

RECOMMENDATION FOR INSTALLING A WELL FOR SMITHFIELD CITY

TO:
Brent Adams
CEE 361 Professor

FROM:
GROUP 4

DIST:
Dr. Sonia Manuel-Dupont
Project Supervisor

DATE:
January 5, 1997

Sections
numbered

1.0 Introduction and Problem Statement

Introduction   The City of Smithfield currently receives most of its culinary water from springs in Smithfield Canyon. There are 8 springs near the top of the canyon and 3 springs located further down the canyon. These springs produce an estimated flow rate that varies seasonally from 1800 gallons per minute in the spring to 1100 gallons per minute in the winter (Gass 1996). In addition to the springs, Smithfield has a secondary water supply provided by a 12 inch diameter, 40 foot deep well located at Forrester Acres, west of the city. Water is pumped from this well during 3 or 4 months out of the year, only as a secondary water source to provide for residential summer irrigation. This well was recently modified to be able to supply up to 1500 gallons per minute but rarely runs at such capacity (Forsgren 1995). With full use of the springs and supplementation from the well, there can be a minimum of 77 million gallons of water per month supplied to Smithfield at all times.

Problem
statement   The current water supply is enough to sustain the residents of Smithfield. However, the population of Smithfield City is growing rapidly; therefore, additional water must be found to supply the future residents of Smithfield. The population, as of now, is about 6800 people (Gass 1996). The average water use per service is 36,862 gallons per month. Our predictions show that 14,346 people will be living in Smithfield City by the year 2021 and the amount of water they

Page
number
centered at
the bottom
of each page

will use will average approximately 144.52 million gallons per month, assuming the amount of water use per service remains constant. Appendix B contains the equation used to predict the population growth and a yearly prediction of population for the next 25 years. Appendix C contains information on the current and projected water use.

The difference between the minimum current water supply for Smithfield (77 million gallons per month) and the predicted water use in 25 years (144.52 million gallons per month) is 67.52 million gallons per month. We used 70 million gallons per month as the amount of water that Smithfield needs to meet the water demand in the year 2021.

Literature review included in discussion of proposed solutions

2.0 Four Proposed Alternative Solutions

Given the problem of finding an additional water supply, we researched Smithfield's current population and water supply to make predictions for the next 25 years. We also researched 4 different alternatives to find out what would be the best option to meet the expected demand. The alternatives considered were 1) drill a new well, 2) take no action, 3) implement a dual water irrigation system, and 4) recycle greywater.

Subsection

2.1 Drill a New Well

The 1st alternative is to drill a new well for culinary water. This new well will be located on the north end of the Smithfield City golf course. There is a large protected aquifer in that area (Gass 1996). The well will be

Sources cited by author and year, with no comma

4

about 400 feet deep, and it will use a 16 inch diameter pipe. After the water leaves the well, it will pass through a chlorine gas chlorinator. The chlorine mixes with the water to disinfect it. Time is required for the chlorine to treat the water, so the water will enter an 18 inch pipe to slow down the velocity of the water. The water will then travel 2500 feet to connect with the existing water lines (Gass 1996). The system will be run automatically. Monitors in the storage tank and water lines will inform a computer when the storage supply is low. The computer will then activate the well to supplement the water demand. When the storage water is sufficiently recharged, the computer will shut down the well, thus conserving energy and the water in the aquifer.

2.2 Take No Action

The 2nd alternative is that of no action. This means that Smithfield's water system would remain the same and run at present capacity.

2.3 Implement a Dual Water Irrigation System

The 3rd alternative that was considered is the implementation of a dual water irrigation system. A dual water system consists of 2 parts: 1) a culinary distribution system to provide potable water for residential use, and 2) a distribution system to provide untreated, "raw" water for irrigation purposes (Vaughn 1995). Approximately 65 percent of the households in Smithfield are currently using some type of dual water irrigation system. Almost all of those using the current

5

dual system are supplied water by Smithfield Irrigation Company (Gass 1996). Implementation of a dual system would consist of routing canals and irrigation lines to those residences that are not using dual water and also to any new homes in the city. Under this alternative, irrigation would be provided separately for everyone, and the strain on the culinary supply would be reduced.

2.4 Recycle Greywater

The 4th alternative that was considered is recycling greywater. Recycling greywater is a relatively inexpensive and effective way to reuse waste water. Greywater is defined as "untreated household wastewater which has not come into contact with toilet waste. Greywater includes used water from bathtubs, showers, bathroom wash basins, and water from clothes washing machines and laundry tubs. It shall not include wastewater from kitchen sinks or dishwashers" (Pope 1995, p 2). A schematic of greywater reuse for a typical residential home is listed in Appendix D, Figure D-1. After clear water has been used in a home, it becomes greywater. The water then goes through a settling and filtration process; it then can be reused in some areas of the home. Greywater is most suitably reused for subsurface irrigation such as that of non-edible landscape plants. This cuts down on the amount of culinary water used for lawn irrigation. All of the information (including values) given under this alternative is given under the assumption that, as with the dual system, only 35

Direct quote requires page number

percent of the present homes in Smithfield City would be affected by a greywater system. A greywater system will be useless to the people who receive irrigation water separately from their culinary supply. We assumed that the number of connections that currently use water from the canal irrigation system will remain relatively constant through the next 25 years.

3.0 Research Methods

3.1 Five Evaluative Criteria

Each of the alternatives we have described has been examined with respect to 5 criteria. The criteria we have selected, in order of significance, are 1) cost of implementation, 2) feasibility, 3) adequacy of supply, 4) maintenance required, and 5) impact on the environment. Table 1 shows the alternatives and the criteria. The alternatives are ranked on a scale from 0 to 2, 2 being the most favorable and 0 being the least favorable. The rankings are multiplied by a weighting factor of 1, 2, or 3, depending on the importance of the criterion involved. A description of our criteria is as follows:

1. Cost—The complete cost of installation and implementation of the alternative
2. Feasibility—The ease of implemention and whether it is allowable
3. Adequacy—Whether or not it will supply a sufficient amount of water
4. Maintenance—The person hours and cost for upkeep

7

5. Impact on the Environment—How the alternative affects land usage and habitat

Table used to report data

Table 1. Weighted Selection Criteria for Water Supply Alternatives

| | | ALTERNATIVES | | | |
| | | | No | Dual | |
Multiplier	Criterion	Well	Action	Water	Reuse
3	Cost	2	2	1	0
2	Feasibility	2	2	1	0
2	Adequacy	2	0	0	0
2	Maintenance	1	1	2	1
1	Environment	1	2	1	2
	TOTALS	17	14	10	4

Based on our findings and the rankings provided by Table 1, our recommendation to the City of Smithfield is to construct a new well to provide water for its domestic supply. In sections 3.2–3.5, students analyze the four alternatives in detail, in light of their criteria.

4.0 Results and Discussion

With the increasing population, the City of Smithfield has concerns over water demand. Our research shows that with the increasing population, Smithfield will need to provide more water for its citizens. We developed alternatives to help Smithfield meet demands.

8

Statement of suggested solution to the problem

Given the 4 alternatives—groundwater well, no action, dual water system, and water reuse—we believe constructing a groundwater well is the best choice for the City of Smithfield. For a reasonable price, an efficient well can be built to meet the predicted needs of Smithfield with low maintenance and minimal impact to the environment. The well could carry Smithfield into the next century and beyond.

9

CBE citation
style

Personal
communi-
cation

Journal
article

Internet
source

Technical
report

Appendix A

References

Burgess M, Distributor, Fairbanks Morse Pump Corp. 1996 Dec 3. [Personal communication].

Carter R. 1994. Trickle-down economy. Sierra 79: 18–19. —— Page nos.   Title   Journal   Volume

[DWR] Division of Water Resources. 1992. State water plan—Bear River Basin executive summary [online]. [Cited 1996 Nov 8]. Available from: www.nr.state.ut. us/WTRRESC/WTRRESC.htm

[Forsgren] Forsgren Association, Inc. 1995. Computer simulation and master plan for domestic water system: prepared for the Smithfield City Corporation. Salt Lake City: Forsgren Assoc., Inc.

Gass J, Smithfield City Engineer. 1996 Nov 8. [Personal communication].

Gelt J. 1993. Home use of greywater: rainwater conserves water--and may save money [online]. [Cited 1996 Nov 8]. Available from: www.ag.arizona.edu/ AZWATER/arroyo/071.rain.html

[IAPMO] International Association of Plumbing and Mechanical Officials. 1996. Uniform plumbing code. Los Angeles: Plumbing Assoc.

Pope T. 1995. Greywater, a recyclable resource [online]. [Cited 1996 Nov 8]. Available from: www.waterstore.com/article1.html

10

[Roscoe] Roscoe Moss Co. 1995. The engineers' manual for water well design. Los Angeles: Roscoe Moss Co.

Rowland P, Assistant City Engineer. 1996 Nov 17. [Personal communication].

[Vaughn] Vaughn Hansen Associates, in association with CH2M Hill and Water Research Laboratory, State University. 1995. Identification and assessment of certain water management options for the Wasatch Front: prepared for the State Division of Water Resources.

Wilding D, Water Department Head. 1996 Dec 2. [Personal communication].

In addition to Appendix A (References), students included the following appendixes.

Appendix B: Population Projections
Appendix C: Projection of Water Flow Rates
Appendix D: Schematic of Greywater Reuse System
Appendix E: Individual Cost of Water Well Construction
Appendix F: Discussion of Cost of Implementation of a
        Dual System
Appendix G: Calculations for Percent of Water Use

11

15d   Look to the Internet and traditional materials for resources

Scientists were quick to see that technology could help them with their research and their writing. Students of the natural sciences, too, should familiarize themselves with the available resources, particularly those on the Internet. (Chapter 9 discusses the types of Internet resources and how to use them.) An extended listing of useful Internet sites for the natural sciences follows. Take a look, for example, at the Discovery Channel site, which has many links to general science information on the Internet. There are also numerous discussion groups, bulletin boards, and newsgroups related to the natural sciences. You can find these discussion sites through an Internet search (see Chapter 21 for information on using computer networks).

http://interserver.
miyazaki-med.ac.jp/
~kimball/w/logo.htm
"Exercises in Science:
A Writing Course"–a
superb writing-for-the-
sciences page, focusing
on ESL

Web Sites for the Sciences and Technology

Aerospace

Applied Aerodynamics: A Digital Textbook *(http://aero.stanford.edu/ OnLineAero)*
Jet Propulsion Laboratory *(http://www.jpl.nasa.gov)*
Pathfinder Mission, Ames Research Center *(http://www.arc.nasa.gov)*

Agriculture

Future Farmers of America *(http://www.ffa.org)*
U.S. Department of Agriculture *(http://www.usda.gov)*

Animal Science

American Society of Animal Science *(http://www.asas.org)*

Astronomy

American Astronomical Society *(http://www.aas.org)*
Handilinks to Astronomy *(http://www.ahandyguide.com/cat1/a/a166.htm)*

Botany and Plant Genetics

Genetics *(http://www.biology.arizona.edu/mendelian_genetics/mendelian_ genetics.html)*

Plant Genetics *(http://vflylab.calstatela.edu/edesktop/VirtApps/VflyLab/ IntroVflyLab.html)*

Chemistry

American Chemical Society *(http://www.acs.org)*

The Learning Matters of Chemistry *(http://www.knowledgebydesign. com)*

Computers and Robotics

Byte Magazine *(http://www.byte.com)*

Electronic Frontier Foundation *(http://www.eff.org)*

Internet Society *(http://www.isoc.org/indextxt.html)*

Iworld *(http://www.iworld.com)*

MIT Laboratory for Computer Science *(http://www.lcs.mit.edu)*

Virtual Computer Library *(http://www.utexas.edu/computer)*

Engineering

Cornell's Engineering Library *(http://www.englib.cornell.edu)*

ICARIS for Civil Engineering *(http://www.fagg.uni-Lj.si/ICARIS)*

Environment and Ecology

ATSDR Science Center (Agency for Toxic Substances and Disease Registry) *(http://atsdr1.atsdr.cdc.gov:8080/cx.html)*

Envirolink *(http://envirolink.org)*

International Institute for Sustainable Development *(http://iisd1.iisd.ca)*

Forestry

Pacific Forestry Center *(http://www.pfc.forestry.ca)*

Geography, Geology, and Mining

American Geological Institute *(http://www.agiweb.org)*

Geological Surveys and Natural Resources *(http://www.lib.berkeley. edu/EART/surveys.html)*

The WWW Virtual Library: Geography *(http://www.icomos.org/WWW_ VL_Geography.html)*

Mathematics and Statistics

American Mathematical Society (*http://www.ams.org*)
Electronic Journal of Undergraduate Mathematics (*http://math.furman. edu/~mwoodard/fuejum/grafv/title2.html*)
E-Math (*http://e-math.ams.org*)
Math Archives (*http://archives.math.utk.edu*)
National Council of Teachers of Mathematics (*http://www.nctm.org*)

Medicine, Nursing, and Health

Doctor's Guide to the Internet (*http://www.pslgroup.com/docguide.htm*)
The Global Health Network (*http://www.pitt.edu/HOME/GHNet/ GHNet.html*)
HyperDoc (National Library of Medicine) (*http://www.nlm.nih.gov*)
Medicine and Global Survival (*http://www.healthnet.org/MGS/MGS. html*)
Medscape (*http://www.medscape.com*)
Medweb (*http://www.emory.edu/WHSCL/medweb.html*)
National Institutes of Health (*http://www.nih.gov*)
SatelLife (*http://www.healthnet.org*)
World Health Organization (*http://www.who.ch*)

Natural Sciences (General)

Discover Magazine (*http://www.dc.enews.com/magazines/discover*)
Discovery Channel Online (*http://www.discovery.com*)
National Academy of Sciences (*http://www.nas.edu*)
Network Science (*http://www.netsci.org*)
Science Hypermedia (*http://www.scimedia.com/index.htm*)

Physics

American Institute of Physics (*http://www.aip.org*)
American Physical Society (*http://www.aps.org*)
Physics Information (*http://www.desy.de*)

Wildlife and Fisheries

National Audubon Society (*http://www.audubon.org*)
National Fish and Wildlife Foundation (*http://www.nfwf.org*)
U.S. Fish and Wildlife Service (*http://www.fws.gov*)

General Sources and Guides to Literature

Guide to Sources for Agricultural and Biological Research. Blanchard, J., and Farrell, L., eds. Los Angeles: U of California P, 1981.
Information Sources in Engineering. 3rd ed. Mildren, K., and Hicks, P., eds. New Providence: Bowker-Saur, 1996.

Information Sources in Physics. 3rd ed. Shaw, D., ed. New Providence: Bowker-Saur, 1994.

Information Sources in the Life Sciences. 4th ed. Wyatt, H. V., ed. New Providence: Bowker-Saur, 1996.

Information Sources in the Medical Sciences. 4th ed. Morton, L. T., and Godbolt, S., eds. New Providence: Bowker-Saur, 1992. A useful reference guide for all medical fields.

> **WEB**
> http://www.library.ucla.edu/libraries/college/instruct/discp.htm
> Thinking critically about discipline-based World Wide Web resources

Information Sources in Science and Technology. 2nd ed. Hurt, C. D. Littleton: Libraries Unltd., 1994. A general reference guide for the sciences.

Science and Engineering Sourcebook. Lewart, C. R. Littleton: Libraries Unltd., 1982. Annotated lists of reference works in various scientific fields.

Dictionaries

Chambers Dictionary of Earth Science. Walker, P., ed. Edinburgh, Scot.: Chambers, 1992. Concise source for definitions of terms.

Dictionary of Artificial Intelligence. Mercadel, D., ed. New York: Van Nostrand, 1990.

Dictionary of Biology. 3rd ed. Martin, E., ed. New York: Oxford UP, 1996.

Dictionary of Chemistry. Parker, S. P., ed. New York: McGraw, 1996.

Dictionary of Computing. 3rd ed. New York: Oxford UP, 1991. Over 4,000 terms used in computing and associated fields of electronics, mathematics, and logic.

Dictionary of Electrical and Electronics Engineering. Schwenkhagen, H., ed. New York: McGraw, 1992. Comprehensive guide to terms.

Dictionary of Geology and Geophysics. Lapidus, D. F., ed. New York: Facts on File, 1987. Definitions of many terms in the context of modern geological theories.

Dictionary of Mathematics. Lincolnwood: NTC, 1996.

Dictionary of Physics. New York: McGraw, 1996. Comprehensive dictionary of terms.

McGraw-Hill Dictionary of Scientific and Technical Terms. 5th ed. Parker, S. New York: McGraw, 1994. Clear definitions of terminology.

A Modern Dictionary of Geography. 3rd ed. Small, J., and Witherick, M. New York: Halsted, 1994. Definitions accessible to college students.

Handbooks

Handbook of Chemistry and Physics. 68th ed. Weast, R. C., ed. Cleveland: Chemical, 1987. Facts and data on chemistry and physics.

Materials Handbook. 14th ed. Brady, G. S., et al., eds. New York: McGraw, 1996. Descriptions of properties of naturally available and commercially available materials.

Medical and Health Information Directory. 7th ed. Detroit: Gale, 1996. 3 vols. Comprehensive guidebook.

Physician's Handbook. 21st ed. Krupp, M. A., et al., eds. E. Norwalk: Appleton and Lange, 1986. Useful, quick reference book for all medical questions.

Standard Handbook for Civil Engineers. 4th ed. Merritt, F. S., ed. New York: McGraw, 1996. Basic information in an easy reference format.

Standard Handbook for Electrical Engineers. 13th ed. Fink, D. G., and Beaty, H. W., eds. New York: McGraw, 1996. Basic information in an easy reference format.

Encyclopedias

The Encyclopedia of Astronomy and Astrophysics. Maran, S. P., ed. New York: Van Nostrand, 1992. Concise summaries geared for a nontechnical audience.

The Encyclopedia of Bioethics. 2nd ed. Reich, W., ed. New York: Macmillan, 1995.

Encyclopedia of Computer Science. Rev. ed. Ralston, A., ed. New York: Van Nostrand, 1997. Concise information in the fields of computer science and engineering.

Encyclopedia of Computer Science and Technology. Belzer, J., ed. New York: Dekker, 1997. 37 vols. Short articles on subjects in computer science.

Encyclopedia of Physical Science and Technology. Meyers, R. A., ed. Orlando: Academic, 1987. 15 vols. A comprehensive encyclopedia on the status of knowledge across the entire field of physical science and related technologies.

The Encyclopedia of Physics. Lerner, R. G., and Trigg, G. L., eds. Reading: Addison, 1990. Background information on major principles and problems in physics.

Grzimek's Encyclopedia of Mammals. 2nd ed. Grzimek, B., ed. New York: McGraw, 1996. General information on the study of mammals.

McGraw-Hill Encyclopedia of Engineering. 2nd ed. New York: McGraw, 1993. Short articles about all fields of engineering.

McGraw-Hill Encyclopedia of Environmental Science. 3rd ed. Parker, S. P., ed. New York: McGraw, 1993. Information on the earth's resources and how they have been used.

McGraw-Hill Encyclopedia of Science and Technology. 7th ed. New York: McGraw, 1992. 15 vols. Concise, current background information on scientific and technical topics; an excellent place to begin a science research project, since the articles are not written for specialists.

McGraw-Hill Yearbook of Science and Technology. New York: McGraw, annual. Yearly updates on the encyclopedia listed above; consult the yearbook for the most recent developments in a particular field.

Van Nostrand's Scientific Encyclopedia. 8th ed. New York: Van Nostrand, 1995. Concise background information on a variety of scientific disciplines.

VNR Concise Encyclopedia of Mathematics. Gellert, W., et al., eds. New York: Van Nostrand, 1989. Short articles on all areas of mathematics.

Biographies

American Men and Women of Science. 19th ed. Cattell, J., ed. New York: Bowker, 1996. Information on living, active scientists in the fields of economics, sociology, political science, statistics, psychology, geography, and anthropology.

Dictionary of Scientific Biography. Gillispie, C., ed. New York: Scribner's, 1981. 8 vols. Information on scientists from classical to modern times; covers only scientists who are no longer living.

National Academy of Sciences: The First Hundred Years. Washington: Natl. Acad. of Sciences, 1978. Information on American scientists.

Who's Who in Science in Europe. 8th ed. Detroit: Gale, 1997.

Indexes, Bibliographies, and Abstracts

(An asterisk indicates that the source can be accessed through a computer search.)

Aerospace

Aerospace Medicine and Biology
*International Aerospace Abstracts
*Scientific and Technical Aerospace Reports
*U.S. Government Reports, Announcements and Index (NTIS)

Agriculture

*Agricola
*Agricultural Engineering Abstracts
 Agritrop
*Agronomy Abstracts
*Bibliography of Agriculture
*Biological and Agricultural Index
 FAO Documentation, Government Documents Index
 Farm and Garden Index
*Fertilizer Abstracts
*Field Crop Abstracts
*Herbage Abstracts
*Seed Abstracts
*Soils and Fertilizers
*World Agricultural Economics and Rural Sociology Abstracts

Animal Science

*Animal Behavior Abstracts
*Animal Breeding Abstracts
 Bibliography of Reproduction
*Dairy Science Abstracts
*Index Veterinarius
*Veterinary Bulletin

Astronomy

*Astronomy and Astrophysics Abstracts
*Meteorological and Geoastrophysical Abstracts

Biology, Botany, Entomology, and Zoology

 Asher's Guide to Botanical Periodicals
*Biological Abstracts
*Biological and Agricultural Index
 Biology Digest
 Botanical Abstracts
 Current Advances in Plant Science
*Entomology Abstracts
*Genetics Abstracts
*Horticultural Abstracts
 International Abstracts of Biological Science
*Plant Breeding Abstracts
*Review of Applied Entomology
*Review of Medical and Veterinary Entomology

Review of Plant Pathology
Torrey Botanical Club Bulletin
*Weed Abstracts
*Zoological Record

Chemistry

Analytical Abstracts
*Chemical Abstracts

Computers and Robotics

*Artificial Intelligence Abstracts
*CAD/CAM Abstracts Index
*Computer Abstracts
*Computer and Control Abstracts
Computing Reviews
Data Processing Digest
*Electrical and Electronic Abstracts
*Microcomputer Index
Robomatix Reporter

Energy and Physics

Energy Abstracts for Policy Analysis
*Energy Information Abstracts
*Energy Research Abstracts
INS Atomindex
Nuclear Science Abstracts
*Physics Abstracts

Engineering

Applied Mechanical Reviews
Civil Engineering Hydraulics Abstracts
*Electrical and Electronics Abstracts
*Engineering Index
*ISMEC Bulletin (mechanical engineering)

Environment and Ecology

Abstracts on Health Effects of Environmental Pollutants
Air Pollution Abstracts
Current Advances in Ecological Sciences
Ecological Abstracts
Ecology Abstracts

*Environment Abstracts
*Environment Index
Environment Information Access
*Environmental Periodicals Bibliography
*Pollution Abstracts
*Selected Water Resource Abstracts
*Water Resources Abstracts

Food Science and Nutrition

*Food Science and Technology Abstracts
*Foods Adlibra
*Nutrition Abstracts and Reviews
Nutrition Planning

Forestry

Fire Technology Abstracts
*Forestry Abstracts

Geography, Geology, and Mining

*Bibliography and Index of Geology
*Bibliography of North American Geology
Current Geographical Publications
Deep Sea Research Part B
*GEO Abstracts
*Geographical Abstracts
Geophysical Abstracts
*Oceanic Abstracts
Population Index

Mathematics and Statistics

*American Statistics Index
Current Mathematical Publications
Demographic Yearbook
*Mathematical Reviews
Statistical Abstract of the United States
Statistical Reference Index
Statistical Theory and Method Abstracts
Statistical Yearbook

Medicine, Nursing, and Allied Health Fields

*Ageline
AIDS Bibliography

Bibliography of Reproduction
*Cumulated Index Medicus
*Cumulative Index to Nursing and Allied Health Literature
Endocrinology Index
*International Nursing Index
*Medline Clinical Collection
MEDOC
*Physical Fitness/Sports Medicine
*Virology Abstracts

Natural Sciences (General)

*Applied Science and Technology Index
Current Bibliographic Directory of the Arts and Sciences
*General Science Index
Index to Scientific and Technical Proceedings
*Science Citation Index

Textiles

Clothing and Textile Arts Index
Clothing Index
Textile Technology Digest
World Textile Abstracts

Wildlife and Fisheries

*Aquatic Science and Fisheries Abstracts
Commercial Fisheries Abstracts
Fisheries Review
Marine Fisheries Abstracts
Ocean Abstracts
Sport Fishery Abstracts
Wildlife Abstracts
Wildlife Research
Wildlife Reviews
World Fisheries Abstracts

EXERCISE 15.1

Investigate the Internet resources available for one of the disciplines within the natural sciences. Search by topic for a newsgroup or a bulletin board (see 21a-2). Bring to class a printout of a Web site or discussion that you found in your search. Share the information with your classmates.

Writing in the Social Sciences

What makes writing in the social sciences different from
  writing in other sciences? (16a)
What kinds of writing assignments can I expect in social
  science courses? (16a)
How should I use the scientific method in a social science
  report? (16a-1)
How can I find information in the library or on the
  Internet for a social science research paper? (16d)

?

The social sciences—psychology, anthropology, political science,
sociology, and education—have as their overall goal the systematic
study of human behavior and human
societies. The social sciences are com-
paratively young disciplines; most
came into their own in the early part
of this century. To establish their credibility as academic disciplines, they
adopted methods used in the natural
sciences. Today, many social scientists use the scientific method to study
people: they develop hypotheses and then design and conduct controlled experiments or observations to test those hypotheses (see 15a).

WWW
WEB
MMM

http://www.ipl.org/
teen/aplus/
The Internet Public
Library's excellent
guide to writing
research papers

16a   Know the different types of writing in the social sciences

The goal of any science is the systematic, objective study of phenomena. Thus, social scientists study the only objectively observable aspect of people—behavior. They cannot observe human emotions and consciousness directly, but they can observe the behaviors that result from feelings and thoughts in human consciousness. Social scientists write to convey research findings discovered by observing human behavior. Writing in the social sciences often begins with the careful recording of field or observation notes. From the notes, the social scientist formulates a hypothesis, and then he or she seeks to test that hypothesis through further systematic experiments or observations. Notes from these experiments are then analyzed and compared to the hypothesis. Finally, the social scientist writes a conclusion explaining how the experimental and observational data supported, refuted, or modified the initial hypothesis. The entire process is typically recounted by the social scientist in a research report. Then that research report and others are typically summarized and evaluated by other social scientists in a review of literature.

1   Research or case study report

The majority of social science writing, like natural science writing, is in the form of research reports and case study reports. Research reports are based on primary research conducted by social scientists using interviews, surveys, questionnaires, and the like.

Because much of what social scientists study has not been examined before, they often collect and analyze their own data, announcing their results in research reports. One well-known example is Stanley Milgram's book-length research report, *Obedience to Authority: An Experimental View* (New York: Harper, 1974). Milgram, a Yale psychologist, sought to determine to what extent ordinary individuals would obey the orders of an authority figure. Through his experiment, he hoped to probe the psychological processes that allowed the Germans to carry out mass human extermination during World War II. The research process used by Milgram closely followed that of other scientific researchers. He began with a question: How could Hitler have succeeded in marshaling so much support from those who were called on to carry out his inhuman orders? After much preparation, Milgram designed and conducted an experiment to test his hypothesis. Using simulated shock experiments, which he admitted were controversial, Milgram showed that an alarming proportion of adults (65 percent of those tested) were willing to inflict severe and, as far as they knew, permanent damage on strangers simply because they were instructed to do so by an authority figure—in this case the experimenter. From the results of these tests, Milgram concluded that, indeed, many people will follow immoral orders, particularly when acting out of a sense of duty and obligation to someone in command.

Whether it summarizes years of laboratory experiments on human motivation or presents the results of a survey conducted in class, a research report in the social sciences typically follows the same pattern as a research report in the natural sciences. (The structure of a typical research report is detailed in 15a-1.) Many research reports begin with a brief review of the literature, to set the current study in context.

2   Review of literature

The second major category of social science writing is the review of literature. In this type of writing, based on secondary research, the writer discusses literature found in the library rather than his or her own original research. Primary researchers, students, and scholars all must keep up with current research in their fields. Researchers need to know what other researchers have found so that they can replicate the experiments, either to confirm or to disprove the hypotheses. Students and scholars should be aware of controversies in their fields so that they can present balanced reports and make observations and contributions of their own. Scholars in a field often publish reviews of literature, in which they analyze, critique, and discuss journal articles. These literature reviews, or summaries, can take a variety of forms—the same forms found in the natural sciences. (For a description of the forms of literature reviews, see 15a-2.)

16b   Write persuasively about social science

Most writing in the social sciences is argumentative in nature. You need to take a stand or make a claim about a particular issue and then argue for that position. You can support your argument with primary research and/or secondary sources.

As a student, when you write about the social sciences generally you are responding to an assignment. If the assignment calls for primary research, you will probably need your instructor's help in designing an appropriate method for collecting data. (For information on how to report primary research, see 15a-1.)

If your instructor has not assigned a particular topic, you can turn to the media—television, radio, magazines, and the Internet—for ideas. Look for controversies about human behavior and begin to ask questions about them. For example, a magazine article on the influence parents have on their children's use of alcohol or drugs might lead you to wonder if there really is a connection between parenting and drug use. If so, who researched the connection and what exactly did they discover?

1 Determining purpose and audience

Once you have a topic, you can establish a rhetorical stance (see 3a-2). To decide on your purpose for writing, begin by carefully studying the assignment itself. Look for key terms, such as *analyze* or *discuss*. Both of these terms imply an interpretive or critical purpose for writing. Your instructor will expect you to write a piece that makes a point, supported by secondary sources.

Next, ask yourself who your audience will be. Usually you can assume that you are writing for intelligent readers who are interested in the subject but may not know much about the topic. You should provide enough background information so that such readers will be able to follow your argument. Because social science writing attempts to be objective, the writer's persona is less of an issue than in other forms of writing. You should attempt to sound reasonable and informed on your topic.

2 Writing a thesis

The variety in human behavior is tremendous. The thesis of a social science paper will generally relate to a claim about a particular kind of observed behavior. With regard to children and drugs, for example, you might claim (based on a literature review and/or observational or survey data) that, indeed, parents are the most important determining factor in whether their children ever experiment with alcohol and drugs.

3 Completing the research and writing your paper

In any writing assignment, regardless of the discipline for which you are writing, you should follow the writing process described in Part 1 of this handbook. Refer to Chapters 3, 4, and 5 for advice on prewriting, drafting, revising, and editing. The writing habits that you have developed in English courses will serve you well in social science courses; try keeping a journal, outlining the information you are reading, exploring through brainstorming or clustering, or working collaboratively with peers (see Chapter 3). If your paper consists of or includes a literature review, refer to Part 2 of this handbook for information on library research. See the list in 16d of reference materials commonly used in the social sciences.

16c Review a sample research report in APA format

In a first-year liberal arts and sciences course, students worked with partners on a primary research project that included a brief review of literature. In the following paper, notice how the student authors begin with an overview of the current research on the study habits of introverts and extroverts. Then, they report the results of their own research, which tested the findings in the literature review against the experiences of their fellow students. Brandy and Sarah used a typical research report format for their paper, following the conventions of the American Psychological Association (APA) (see 13b).

Title page

Shortened title appears with   Introverts & Extroverts 1
page number on every page

Running Head: INTROVERTS AND EXTROVERTS

If the paper is being submitted for publication, include the
shortened title to be used as a header on every page of the
printed version

Title   A Study of the Study Habits of

Introverts and Extroverts

Student   Group: True Colors
and course
identifica-   Brandy Black
tion
Sarah Summers

Liberal Arts & Sciences 124

Professor Long

October 30, 1998

Introverts & Extroverts 2

An abstract is a brief summary of the paper, often included in social science papers

Abstract

The purpose of this research report is to review the literature on student study habits and to present information from our own research about ways in which students on our campus study. We reviewed several articles on study habits in journals such as <u>Psychological Reports,</u> <u>Personality and Individual Differences,</u> and <u>The Journal of Research in Personality.</u> We also investigated the study habits of two student personality types on our campus: introverts and extroverts. Our research included a four-page survey about academic success and study habits (which we asked fifteen students to answer) and a six-day study log to chart the length of study time, duration of breaks, and type of studying. This report shows that our own research, for the most part, replicated the findings of many of the national studies.

Introverts & Extroverts 3

Title   A Study of the Study Habits of Introverts and Extroverts

Double-   Research about personality types and their study
spaced text
habits has become increasingly important. In particular,

psychologists have studied how to recognize personality

types of students and how to teach different kinds of

students. Because of this national interest, we decided

to investigate the study habits of two personality types,

introverts and extroverts. We began this study with two

general assumptions. First, we thought that introverts

would be less socially active in their study habits, spend

Hypothesis more time studying, and have a higher degree of academic

success. Second, we thought that extroverts would study

in groups, study less, and have slightly lower grades.

In order to investigate our assumptions, we read several

Background articles in journals such as <u>Psychological Reports,</u>
information <u>Personality and Individual Differences,</u> and <u>The Journal</u>
<u>of Research in Personality.</u>

We constructed a four-page survey about academic

success and study habits which we asked fifteen students

to answer. In addition, we also created a six-day study log

to chart the length of study time, duration of breaks, and

type of studying done by the students. The purpose of this

research report is to review the literature and to present

information from our own research. This report shows that

Thesis   our own research, for the most part, replicated the findings

of many of the national studies. Information in this paper

Introverts & Extroverts 4

will be presented in two sections. First, findings from the

larger, national studies will be summarized. Then, findings

First-level from our study will follow.
heading is
centered Literature Review

Others' According to national studies, there are three major
research is
reviewed trends used in tracing the academic life of extroverts and
and sum-
marized introverts. The first trend is the academic success of the

student, classified into self-rated academic success and

actual degree of success. The second trend is preferred

study locations and situations. The third trend is the

number of study breaks taken by extroverts and introverts,

Second-level measured by frequency and duration.
heading is
set flush on Academic Success
left margin
and under- Several studies chart the success of extroverted and
lined
introverted students. These have divided academic success
In APA
style, source into two categories: self-rated academic success (Irfani, 1978)
citations
include and the actual degree of success (Furnham & Medhurst,
last name
and date, 1995; Olympia et al., 1994). One study showed that more
with a
comma extroverts rated themselves as academically successful

than introverts (Irfani, 1978). So, according to this study,
Brackets
show word- "the possibility [that] a student will rate himself academically
ing change
successful is likely to be greater when the student is

extroverted rather than introverted" (Irfani, 1978, p. 505).
Direct
quotes In contrast, another national study found that "stable
require a
page num- introverts [are] the highest academic performers" (Furnham
ber in the
citation & Medhurst, 1995, p. 197). This study charted the actual

Introverts & Extroverts 5

degree of academic success and concluded that "introverts

predominate among outstanding students" (Furnham &

Medhurst, 1995, p. 207). It was also noted that although

introverts are frequently among the top students, the GPA

of introverts and extroverts differs only slightly.

The relevant literature under each topic is reviewed   Preferred Study Locations and Situations

Several studies addressed preferred study locations

and discussed whether students favored working in

groups or alone. One report concluded that introverts

choose to study where the number of people and amount

of stimulation is minimized (Campbell & Hawley,

1982, p. 141). Group study is usually minimal because

introverts study better when they are not being distracted.

Introverts tend to select study environments that have

few or no people, such as their bedroom. When they

study in libraries, they prefer locations that allow them to

be alone.

When we look at preferred study environments

and study groups for extroverts, the results are nearly

the opposite. Campbell and Hawley's study found

that "extroverts . . . prefer locations where socializing

opportunities abound and the level of external stimulation

is high" (1982, p. 141). Extroverts typically spend more time

studying in groups and choose "busier" locations to study

in, such as student centers and dining halls. Campbell and

Hawley stated that "the typical extrovert is sociable, . . .

Introverts & Extroverts 6

needs to have people to talk to, and does not like reading or studying by himself" (1982, p.139). If extroverts do study at the library, they "occupy library study locations which maximize external stimulation" (Campbell, 1983, p. 308). These reports suggest that introverts and extroverts differ in regard to study location and studying in groups.

Number of Study Breaks

In a study by Campbell and Hawley (1982) it was discovered that there were differences in the frequency of breaks and the reason for taking these breaks between introverts and extroverts. Introverts prefer study locations without a lot of external stimuli so they are not distracted or influenced to take breaks. Consequently, they study for longer periods of time before they take a break. On the other hand, because extroverts are sociable and prefer to study in areas where there is a great deal of external stimulation, they are more easily distracted, leading to a higher frequency of breaks.

The hypothesis to be tested is stated

According to the national research reports, we expected to find differences in the study habits of introverts and extroverts in our own research as follows: extroverts should rate themselves higher than introverts for academic success; the average GPA should be fairly similar between the two groups; introverts should prefer to study alone in quiet places while extroverts should prefer groups in busier places; introverts should take fewer study breaks.

Introverts & Extroverts 7

The primary research study is described and the results discussed

Methods: The State University Study

To determine how State University students would compare to reports found in our literature review, we administered a four-page questionnaire to fifteen students. We also asked the students to keep a six-day study log. The methodology used to create this questionnaire follows.

Developing the Research Questions

We designed a questionnaire to learn about the academic life of introverts and extroverts. The main areas we wanted this questionnaire to address were:

1. How do students view themselves? as introverts or extroverts? as successful academically?

2. Do introverts or extroverts do better in school?

3. Do introverts and extroverts study differently?

By writing these research questions, we were then able to design the actual questionnaire. We randomly selected fifteen students in the library who agreed to answer the questionnaire. The students were given a brief personality survey to determine if they were introverted or extroverted. The subjects were divided into two groups: 8 introverts and 7 extroverts. Thirteen of the students also agreed to keep a six-day study log.

Results and Discussion

Demographic Information

The following demographic information was obtained in order to categorize our subjects. Students were asked to

Introverts & Extroverts 8

check off their age from a range of ages 18 through 26.

From Table 1 it can be seen that the majority of the

students that we surveyed fell in the 18-20 range.

Table is
used to
report data

Age	<18	18-20	21-23	24-26
Introvert	0	63%	25%	12%
Extrovert	0	71%	29%	0%

Table 1: Age of Subjects

Students analyzed other demographics as well—years in school, gender,
marital status, number of roommates, and number of children. Then,
they analyzed the academic success, time management skills, study
habits, and preferred study situations and locations of their subjects
by using the questionnaire and study log data.

Results of
the study
are com-
pared to the
hypothesis

Conclusions

In comparing the national studies with our State

University study, we made several observations about the

three major trends we had intended to address. Our first

trend dealt with academic success. Both studies agreed

that the GPA is only slightly different between introverts

and extroverts. In the national studies, more extroverts

rated themselves as academically successful. In contrast,

our study showed more introverts rated themselves as

academically successful.

In one area,
results run
counter to
hypothesis

The second trend dealt with the preferred study

locations and situations of introverts and extroverts. The

national studies concluded that introverts liked quiet

environments; however, our study showed that the majority

of introverts preferred to listen to music while studying.

Both the national studies and our study concluded that

Introverts & Extroverts 9

introverts like to be alone while studying and that

extroverts prefer group study. Our final trend dealt

with the frequency of study breaks. Our study showed

that introverts took fewer study breaks than extroverts,

which agreed with the national studies.

APA citation style   Introverts & Extroverts 10

References

Initials — Campbell, J. B. (1983). Differential relationships of

Date — extroversion, impassivity, and sociability to study

Only first word and proper nouns are capitalized in article or book title

habits. Journal of Research in Personality, 17, 308-313.—Page numbers

Campbell, J. B., & Hawley, C. W. (1982). Study habits and

Eysenck's theory of extroversion-introversion. Journal of

Journal name, in capital and lowercase letters, is italicized or underlined — Research in Personality, 16, 139-146.

No quotation marks around title

Furnham, A., & Medhurst, S. (1995). Personality correlates of

academic seminar behavior: A study of four instruments.

Personality and Individual Differences, 19, 197-208.

Volume number is italicized or underlined

Irfani, S. (1978). Extroversion-introversion and self-rated

academic success. Psychological Reports, 43, 505-510.

Olympia, D. E., Sheridan, S. M., Jenson, W. R., & Andrews, D.

(1994). Using student-managed interventions to increase

homework completion and accuracy. Journal of Applied

Behavior Analysis, 27, 88-99 [Online]. Available: http://

www.envmed.rochester.edu/www.rap/behavior/jaba.htm

[1998, September 25].   Following the References was Appendix A, which included Tables 3–7.

16d   Look to the Internet and traditional materials for resources

Social scientists were among the first to realize that technology could help them with their research and their writing. Students of the social sciences, too, should familiarize themselves with the available resources, particularly those on the Internet. (Chapter 9 discusses types of Internet resources and how to use them.) An extended listing of useful Internet sites for the social sciences follows. Take a look, for example, at the Social Research site, which has many links to general social science information on the Internet. There are also numerous discussion groups, bulletin boards, and newsgroups related to the social sciences. You can find these discussion sites through an Internet search (see Chapter 21 for information on using computer networks).

http://www.clas.ufl.edu/users/gthursby/socsci/subjects.htm
The WWW Virtual Library guide to social science links

Web Sites for the Social Sciences

African American Studies

University of Texas Center for African and African American Studies (*http://www.utexas.edu/depts/caaas*)
University of Georgia Institute for African American Studies (*http://www.uga.edu/~iaas*)

Anthropology

American Anthropology Association (*http://www.ameranthassn.org*)
Anthropology Institute—University of Oxford (*http://www.rsl.ox.ac.uk/isca/index.html*)
Anthropology Resources on the Internet (*http://www.nitehawk.com/alleycat/anth-faq.html*)
Applied Anthropology Network (*http://anthap.oakland.edu*)

Asian Studies

Asian Studies Resources (*http://sunsite.unc.edu/ucis/Asian.html*)
University of Texas Asian Studies Network Information Center (*http://asnic.utexas.edu/asnic/index.html*)

Education

AskERIC (*http://ericir.syr.edu*)
Council for Exceptional Children (*http://www.cec.sped.org/home.htm*)
Department of Education (*http://www.ed.gov*)
Educom (*http://educom.edu*)
EdWeb (*http://edweb.gsn.org*)
National Association for the Education of Young Children (*http://www. naeyc.org*)
Online Educational Resources (*http://quest.arc.nasa.gov/OER*)
Online Education WWW Server (*http://www.online.edu/index.htm*)
The World Lecture Hall (*http://www.utexas.edu/world/lecture*)

Law

Internet Legal Resource Guide (*http://www.ilrg.com*)

Political Science

Political Science Resources on the Web (*http://www.lib.umich.edu/ libhome/Documents.center/polisci.html*)

Psychology

Clinical Psychology Resources (*http://www.psychologie.uni-bonn.de/kap/ links_20.htm*)

Social Sciences (General)

Social Science Information Gateway (*http://sosig.esrc.bris.ac.uk/welcome. html*)

Sociology and Social Work

ACLU Freedom Network (*http://www.aclu.org*)
American Sociological Association (*http://asanet.org*)
Bureau of Justice Statistics (*http://www.ojp.usdoj.gov/bjs*)
Bureau of Labor Statistics (*http://stats.bls.gov*)
Inter-University Consortium for Political and Social Research (*http:// www.icpsr.umich.edu*)
Research Resources for the Social Sciences (*http://www.socsciresearch. com*)
Sociological Research Online (*http://kennedy.soc.surrey.ac.uk/ socresonline*)
Statistical Abstract of the United States (*http://www.census.gov/statab/ www*)

Sports

CBS Sportsline USA (*http://www.sportsline.com/index.html*)
ESPNET Sports Zone (*http://espn.sportszone.com*)
Outside Online (*http://outside.starwave.com:80*)

United Nations

United Nations (*http://www.un.org*)

US Government

Bureau of the Census (*http://www.census.gov*)
FedWorld (*http://www.fedworld.gov*)

http://www.library.ucla.
edu/libraries/college/
instruct/critical.htm
Thinking critically
about World Wide
Web resources

Government Information Sharing
Project (*http://govinfo.kerr.orst.edu*)
Government Servers (*http://www.eff.org/govt.html*)
The IRS Digital Daily (*http://www.irs.ustreas.gov/basic/cover.html*)
Library of Congress (*http://lcweb.loc.gov*)
Population Index (*http://popindex.princeton.edu*)

STAT-USA (*http://www.stat-usa.gov/stat-usa.html*)
Thomas (congressional legislation) (*http://thomas.loc.gov*)
Vote Smart (*http://www.vote-smart.org/ce/c-index.html*)

General Sources and Guides to Literature

The Annual Register: A Record of World Events. Hodson, H. G., ed. Detroit: Gale, annual (1980–present). Record of major events worldwide over the year.
A Bibliographic Guide to Education. New York Public Library Staff, eds. New York: Hall, annual (1985–present). An annual guide to sources for education topics.
Family Facts at Your Fingertips. Thacher, C. A., ed. Salt Lake City: Hawkes, 1987. Useful, up-to-date statistics about families.

Dictionaries and Almanacs

Almanac of American Politics. Barone, M., and Ujifusa, G., eds. Washington: Natl. Journal, annual. Facts and data on American politics for each year.
Congressional Quarterly Almanac. Washington: Cong. Quar., annual (1945–present). Summary of the activities of Congress, including voting records and major legislation.

Dictionary of Anthropology. Barfield, T. London: Blackwell, 1997. Information on anthropological topics.

Dictionary of Behavioral Sciences. 2nd ed. Wolman, B., ed. New York: Van Nostrand, 1989. Simple and concise definitions of terms in psychology and related fields.

Dictionary of Education. Passow, A., ed. Phoenix: Oryx, 1998. Concise definitions of terminology in education.

Dictionary of Political Thought. Scrutin, R., ed. New York: Hill & Wang, 1984.

Dictionary of Psychology. 2nd ed. Chaplin, J. New York: Dell, 1985. Concise definitions of psychological terms.

Handbooks

Handbook of Developmental Family Psychology. L'Abate, L., ed. New York: Wiley, 1993. Guide to issues and information in human development and family relationships.

Handbook of Educational Technology: A Practical Guide for Teachers. 3rd ed. Percival, F., and Ellington, H. New York: Nichols, 1993. Guide to terms in educational technology.

International Yearbook of Education. Lanham: Bernan, annual (1979–present). Each year, a new topic in education is covered; for example, the 1984 yearbook theme was "Education for Life."

Political Handbook of the World. Banker, A. S., et al., eds. Binghamton: CSA, annual (1982–present). Summaries of world political events.

United States Government Manual. Washington: GPO, annual (1934–present). Current information on all aspects of the federal government.

Encyclopedias

Encyclopedia of Educational Research. 6th ed. Alkin, M., ed. New York: Macmillan, 1992. Excellent summaries of research in education.

Encyclopedia of Human Development and Education. Thomas, R., ed. New York: Pergamon, 1990. Terms, theories, and information related to development and education.

Encyclopedia of Policy Studies. Nagel, S., ed. Public Administration and Public Policy Services. New York: Dekker, 1994. Information about public policy issues.

Encyclopedia of Psychology. 2nd ed. Corsini, R., ed. New York: Wiley, 1994. An overview of important terms and concepts in psychology.

Encyclopedia of Social Work. 19th expanded ed. Edwards, R. L., ed. New York: Natl. Assn. of Social Workers, 1995. General information on a variety of topics related to social work; includes both articles and biographies.

Encyclopedia of Sociology. Borgata, E. F., and Borgata, M. L., eds. New York: Macmillan, 1991. Terms, concepts, major ideas, major theorists in sociology.

International Encyclopedia of Education. Husen, T., and Postlethwaite, T. N., eds. New York: Pergamon, 1994. Background information on topics related to education beyond high school.

International Encyclopedia of Politics and Law. State Mutual Book and Periodicals Services. New York: Archives, 1987.

International Encyclopedia of Psychiatry, Psychology, Psychoanalysis, and Neurology. Wolman, B. B., ed. New York: Van Nostrand, 1997. 12 vols. Concise information on psychology and related fields.

International Encyclopedia of the Social Sciences. Sills, D. L., ed. New York: Macmillan, 1996. 8 vols. plus annual supplements. Analyses of current topics and issues in social science; a biographical supplement was published in 1979.

Man, Myth, and Magic. Cavendish, R., ed. New York: Marshall Cavendish, 1994. An illustrated encyclopedia of mythology, religion, and the unknown.

Biographies

Biographical Dictionary of American Educators. Ohles, J. F., ed. Westport: Greenwood, 1978. 3 vols.

Biographical Dictionary of Modern Peace Leaders. Jacobsen, H., et al., eds. Westport: Greenwood, 1985. Concise biographies of important figures in the peace movement around the world.

Biographical Dictionary of Psychology. Zusne, L. Westport: Greenwood, 1984. Concise biographies of important psychologists.

Statesman's Yearbook. New York: St. Martin's, annual (1975–present). Concise information about the important political leaders of the year.

Who's Who in American Politics. Cattell, J., comp. New York: Bowker, annual (1985–present). Discussion of important figures in American politics each year.

Indexes, Bibliographies, and Abstracts

(An asterisk indicates that the source can be accessed through a computer search.)

Anthropology

Abstracts in Anthropology

Asian Studies

Bibliography of Asian Studies

Black Studies

Black Index: Afro-Americans in Selected Periodicals
Index to Periodical Articles by and about Negroes

Crime

Abstracts on Criminology and Penology

Education

Child Development Abstracts and Bibliography
*Current Index to Journals in Education
Deaf, Speech, Hearing Abstracts
*Education Index
Educational Administration Abstracts
*ERIC on Disc
*Exceptional Child Education Resources
Physical Education Index
Physical Fitness/Sports Medicine
*Resources in Education
*Resources in Vocational Education
State Education Journal Index

Family Studies

Inventory of Marriage and Family Literature
Sage Family Studies Abstracts

Law

Current Law Index
Index to Legal Periodicals

Library Science

*Library and Information Science Abstracts
*Library Literature
Library Science Abstracts
Library Technology Report

Political Science

ABC Political Science
Combined Retrospective Index to Journals in Political Science
Congressional Quarterly Weekly Reports
International Political Science Abstracts
*Public Affairs Information Service Bulletin

Psychology

*Psychological Abstracts

Social Sciences (General)

Consumer's Index
*Social Science Citation Index
*Social Science Index

Sociology and Social Work

Combined Retrospective Index to Journals in Sociology
Index to Current Urban Documents
Rehabilitation Literature
Social Work Research and Abstracts
*Sociological Abstracts
Women's Studies Abstracts
*World Agricultural Economics and Rural Sociology Abstracts

Transportation

Highway Research Abstracts
Highway Safety Literature
Transportation Research Abstracts

United Nations

Specialized Agency Catalogs
United Nations Documents Index

US Government

*American Statistics Index (ASI)
CIS Annual Index to Congressional Publications of Legislative Histories
CIS U.S. Congressional Committee Prints Index
Commerce Clearing House Congressional Index
*Congressional Information Service
Congressional Quarterly Almanac
Index to U.S. Government Periodicals
*Monthly Catalog of U.S. Government Publications
*U.S. Government Reports, Announcements and Index (NTIS)

EXERCISE 16.1

Investigate the Internet resources available for one of the disciplines within the social sciences. Search by topic for a newsgroup or a bulletin board (see 21a-2). Bring to class a printout of a Web site or discussion that you found in your search. Share the information with your classmates.

PART 4

DOCUMENT DESIGN

CHAPTER 17

Design Principles and Graphics

FAQs

How should I format a paper? (17b)
What is the best font to use? (17b-7)
How can I best use graphics? (17c)
When is one type of graphic better than another? (17d)

?

In today's consumer-oriented, message-dense society, people are inundated with advertisements, solicitations, entertainment, news reports, and all other manner of electronic and print documents. In this environment, people tend to read selectively, focusing only on documents that are interesting, inviting, and clear.

This is where *document design* comes in. By using headings, itemized lists, graphics, white space, effective layouts, and special typefaces, you can increase the chances that people will read your writing. These design elements also can help you emphasize the most important parts of your writing.

WEB

http://itrc.uwaterloo.ca/
~engl210e/BookShelf/
Recommended/Design/
toc.htm
A great site devoted
to issues in document
design

The key to good document design is to keep your reading experience in mind as you compose. In other words, as in every other aspect of writing, always try to put yourself in the reader's shoes. In particular, ask yourself these questions:

- Who will be reading this document?
- If these readers only skim the document, what parts do I want them to focus on?
- How can I get them to focus on these parts?
- How can I make these parts especially clear?

Underlying these questions is an important guideline: *Do not use design elements just for decoration. Use design elements to enhance your readers' understanding of the document.*

17a   Follow the three basic design principles

Adhering to the three basic principles of graphic design will make your documents more meaningful and more readable. These principles, which we will refer to as "the three C's," are clustering, contrasting, and connecting.

Clustering: grouping closely related items

Ideas or concepts that are closely related in meaning or communicative value should be clustered together visually. Consider the title page from a student paper shown on page 389 in the upper left. The layout is neat and centered, but there appear to be five separate pieces of information, none of them having anything to do with any of the others.

Logically, the title and subtitle go together, as do the title of the course and the name of the instructor. Grouping them, as shown in the revised version in the lower right, produces a better layout, because the reader can now see at a glance that there are three main pieces of information instead of five. In addition, the writer's name (Devon Johnson) stands out more.

An example of clustering is found at the beginning of this chapter, where the FAQs are grouped together in a box. These questions have a similar origin and a similar purpose, so it makes sense to present them together.

Nature and the
Poetic Imagination

Death and Rebirth in
"Ode to the West Wind"

Devon Johnson

English 202

Professor Baker

Nature and the
Poetic Imagination

Death and Rebirth in
"Ode to the West Wind"

Devon Johnson

English 202

Professor Baker

2 Contrasting: highlighting differences

A second way of using design to make documents more meaningful and readable is to create visual contrasts that mirror important differences in content. For example, the heading for this section is set in boldface over a gold line so as to distinguish it from the rest of the paragraph. This makes it easy for readers to see that the words *Contrasting: highlighting differences* represent an introductory guideline (in contrast to the rest of the paragraph, which is an explanation).

Contrast can also be seen in Devon Johnson's title page, where the main title is set larger and in bolder type. This formal difference makes it immediately clear to the reader that, although these two lines have something in common (and thus should be clustered together), they differ in content and purpose.

3 Connecting: relating every part to some other part

The third way of employing design to make text more coherent is to repeat important graphical or typographical elements—that is, visually connect different parts of a document so that no single element is left stranded. These connections should not be made haphazardly but, rather, in a way that underscores connections in meaning, value, or purpose. In this handbook, for example, the headings and subheadings are set off in different colors, to make it easier for readers to skim through the chapters and see how sections are related. Notice the colons in the three subheadings in this section; by reinforcing the grammatical parallelism (see Chapter 36) of these subheadings, the colons emphasize the fact that these three guidelines relate to a single concept.

EXERCISE 17.1

Design your own business card or greeting card, adhering to the principles in this section. Feel free to use the document design program on your computer, if it has one.

EXERCISE 17.2

Analyze a few short to medium-size advertisements on the Internet or in your local newspaper to get a clear sense of the genre (including both good and bad examples). Then design an ad of your own (say, to offer a service).

17b   Use formatting tools

Formatting is another powerful way of using visual representation to make a document easier to read and more emphatic in its message. Formatting can be done for decorative reasons only, but it is more effective if it also helps readers understand the text. Today's word-processing programs provide all the formatting tools you are likely to need, from boldface type to hanging indents. Familiarize yourself with the common formatting tools, discussed in this section.

1   Headings

Headings (and subheadings and titles) are useful for several reasons. They draw attention, they mark off parts of a text, and they give the reader a quick sense of what those parts are about. Headings are especially beneficial for readers who only skim a text instead of reading it closely. Such readers are common in business and the professions (see Chapter 22). College instructors, who are expected to read all student papers thoroughly, may not have the same need or appreciation for headings. (To be on the safe side, ask your instructors whether they want headings.)

Headings should always be informative; that is, they should give the reader an idea of what the paper, section, or illustration is about. If this chapter had been labeled simply "Chapter 17," you would have had no clue as to what it covered. Yet a long descriptive label can be distracting. We suggest that you strive for informative headings that are no longer than four or five words.

Headings also are useful during the writing process, to help you keep track of your overall writing plan. If you write an outline before composing, you can often convert the main points of the outline into headings and subheadings for your paper, especially if you are using a word processor (see 3e, 4a). Always check to make sure that your headings promote the kind of connectedness discussed in 17a. Do they form a list? If so, are they in grammatically parallel form (see Chapter 36)? If one heading is less important than another, is this relationship clear? Are numbers and letters used accurately and consistently?

Writers generally use from one to five levels of headings, depending on how complex the document is. In this chapter, we have used three levels:

1. The chapter heading, or title (Chapter 17 Design Principles and Graphics)
2. Section headings (for example, 17b Use formatting tools)
3. Subsection headings (for example, 17b-2 Itemized lists)

To create a consistent and distinctive formatting scheme, we have used typography (see 17b-7), color, numbering, white space, and parallelism. Using the same format for all of the headings at a particular level helps readers to see how the chapter is constructed and, thus, to get a better grasp of the subject itself.

2 Itemized lists

One of the most effective ways of organizing and drawing attention to details in a text is to put them in an **itemized list.** Itemized lists are a powerful form of visual clustering, as they show how several things form a closely related set. There are two main types of list formats. A **numbered list** or **lettered list** has ordered numbers or letters, suggesting either a ranking of the items or a stepwise procedure, as in the Help box. The main headings in each chapter of this book

HELP

How do I create an itemized list?

1. Introduce the list with a title or brief sentence describing the topic covered.
2. Set off each item with a number, letter, bullet, dash, asterisk, or other marker, and align the markers. Most word-processing programs will automatically do this formatting for you—check the user's manual or online HELP to make sure you are taking full advantage of the LIST feature.
3. Put all of the items in the same grammatical form (see Chapter 36). You will have to do this yourself, as no computer can do it for you.

(including this one) constitute a numbered list, in most cases reflecting our ranking of the sections. A **bulleted list,** which uses bullets (•), diamonds (♦), dashes (−), or some other symbol, is useful for an unordered set of items, such as the list of questions in the third paragraph of this chapter.

Since itemized lists attract a lot of attention, be careful not to overuse them. If you have too many lists too close together, their effectiveness will be lost. Try to have no more than one itemized list per manuscript page or computer screen. Remember: Use lists only when you want to draw special attention to a set of items.

3   Indentation and spacing

In academic papers, the first line of each paragraph is customarily indented five spaces or ½ inch. This indentation provides contrast with the other lines, indicating that a new idea or point is about to be introduced (see Chapter 6). With a word processor, you can set this indentation automatically, using either the ruler or the PARAGRAPH feature on the FORMAT menu. Quotations longer than four lines of prose or three lines of poetry are set off as a block, with each line indented ten spaces (see Chapter 50). In bibliographies, résumés, bulleted lists, and certain other types of writing, you may want to use **hanging indents,** where the first line begins at the left margin and following lines are indented. Hanging indents can usually be set on the PARAGRAPH menu.

Normally, your instructor will want you to use double-spacing throughout your paper (except perhaps in footnotes). You should leave a space after all end punctuation, such as periods, question marks, and exclamation points, and after commas, semicolons, colons, and each dot in ellipses. (See the sample student papers in sections 5f, 12f, 14c, 15c, and 16c.)

4   Margins

For academic papers, the standard margin is 1 inch all around, to give the instructor space in which to write comments. These are also the default margins used by most word-processing programs. Such margins leave a line length of about 6 inches, or sixty to seventy characters. Longer lines will make your writing less readable. Word processors are normally set to **left-justify** your text—that is, start lines at the left margin and leave the right margin ragged, thus avoiding the need to hyphenate at the end of a line (see Chapter 54). Academic papers are usually written with left justification.

If you prefer the formal look of a commercial publication, you can **block-justify** your text, starting lines at the left and ending them evenly at the right; just click the appropriate icon in the toolbar. Block justification sometimes looks more elegant (especially in documents with columns, such as newspapers or brochures), but bear in mind that it can leave unsightly gaps in lines unless you use appropriate hyphenation. A word processor can resolve this problem by automatically hyphenating lines, but the result may be another problem—too many hyphens. You will have to use your best judgment in such cases, either making manual adjustments in hyphenation or reverting to a ragged right margin. (See 54e for further discussion.)

5 Frames and boxes

An effective way to highlight a paragraph, graphic, or other part of a document is by putting a rectangular frame or box around it. Frames and boxes are especially useful for summarizing main points or procedural steps, because they simultaneously cluster these points or steps and set them off, through contrast, from the rest of the text. Frames and boxes are commonly found in textbooks, handbooks, user manuals, and other instructional documents (including this one). They are rarely found in academic writing and can be tricky to position, so you should use them only with caution. (You may want to check with your instructor to see whether he or she finds them acceptable.)

A **frame** is more dynamic and flexible than a box, as most word processors will automatically adjust a frame to fit on the page and will allow text to flow around it. You can anchor a frame to a paragraph, thereby ensuring that if you move the paragraph, the framed object will move with it. Its placement still requires care, however. By contrast, a **box** is a ruled element of fixed size, which is simply placed around a text or graphic. In many word processors, you can also use boxes to put imported graphics behind text, as "watermarks" for special effects. Be aware that when frames and boxes are converted to another medium, they may not appear in the same form as in your application.

Aligning text within boxes and frames can sometimes be tricky. If you are new at it, avoid complications by using simple spacing, tab commands, and hanging indents.

6 Columns

Putting text into columns is a useful way of clustering information in documents like brochures, newsletters, résumés, and Web pages. (See Chapter 18 for a sample brochure and newsletter and Chapter 22 for a sample résumé.)

There are basically two kinds of columns: newspaper and tabular. In **newspaper columns,** the text starts on the left, flows down the first column, and then continues at the top of the next column to the right. In other words, the text is continuous. Newspaper columns are created with the COLUMNS feature on the FORMAT menu. Most word processors will create this kind of column when the COLUMNS setting is chosen.

Tabular columns consist of independent texts side by side. They are useful if you want to have text in one column and numerical data in another, as in a table, or different kinds of corresponding entries, as in a résumé. Tabular columns are created by using the TABLE feature on a word processor.

Whenever you set up columns, either newspaper or tabular, be sure to leave a reasonable amount of space between the columns. If the space is too narrow or too wide, you can adjust it in either the COLUMNS menu or the TABLE menu.

7 Typography

Since readers will be focusing their eyes on your words, the typographical appearance of your text will have an effect on them. **Typography** refers to all the features associated with individual letters, numbers, and other symbols: font type, font style, font size, color, and case.

Font type refers to the distinctive design of the typeface; some of the most common font types are Courier, Times New Roman, Garamond, and **Arial**. Font types typically occur in families, so you have several variants to choose from. For example, the Arial family includes standard Arial, **Arial MT Black**, Arial Narrow, and **Arial Rounded MT Bold**. Font types that have little extra lines (*serifs*) at the ends of the letter strokes are called *serif fonts*. The font used for the main text of this book (Palatino) is a serif type. *Sans serif* (literally, "without serif") *fonts* lack such extra lines. The font used for the FAQs at the start of each chapter in this book (Formata) is a sans serif type.

This sentence is written in a serif font.

This sentence is written in a sans serif font.

Because the extra lines help the eye move from letter to letter, serif fonts are often considered better for extended prose; the extra lines create a visual connectedness between the letters. Sans serif fonts have a more contemporary look and are often preferred for short texts like advertisements, signs, and instructions. More creative fonts like Whimsy, Figaro, and *Brush Script* should be avoided in academic writing.

Font style (or **font weight**) refers to the particular variant of a single typeface: regular, *italic,* **bold,** or *bold italic.* Italic, bold, and bold italic typefaces can all be used for emphasis, but they have other uses as well. Italic typeface, for example, is commonly used for book titles (see 52e) and for words that are set off as vocabulary items (see examples in Chapter 40). Bold typeface is often used for introducing new terms, as in this handbook, and for headings. It is important to be consistent in your use of these font styles so as to avoid confusing the reader. Also, overuse of italic and bold typefaces for emphasis, like use of all capital letters in email, will give readers the impression that you are shouting at them.

Font sizes range from 4 to 144 points, although most word-processing programs offer sizes from about 6 to 72 points. The standard size range for academic papers is 10 to 12 points, with section headings often set in 14-point type and the title of the paper in 20- or even 24-point type. More specialized bulletins or reports may use a wider range of heading sizes and styles to distinguish sections and subsections.

Color is another option that has become available with the widespread use of computers. Like bold and italic type, however, color should be used sparingly—and systematically. As has been done with the headings and subheadings in this book, try to establish a color theme that promotes connections within your document. If your final product is to be hard copy, do not forget that only color printers and color copiers will be able to produce and reproduce, respectively, the colors you have chosen.

One other typographical variable is case. Academic writers normally use the standard combination of lowercase (small) and uppercase (capital) letters, except for acronyms and other abbreviations (see Chapter 52). In rare cases, all uppercase letters may be used for emphasis or for special categories of headings.

8 Page numbering

In a multipage document, it is a good idea to number the pages. This helps you keep track of the pages as you scroll through the document and as you staple the pages together after printing. Page numbering also makes it easier for an instructor to refer to a particular page in end comments. Consult your word processor's documentation on how to operate the PAGE NUMBERING feature, as well as how to adjust numbering if you create section breaks in your document. Headers and footers can be used to put other interesting types of information—such as your name, a filename, the date and time, or even a company logo—at the top or bottom of the page along with the page number.

9   Document review

Before you print out a document, review it to be sure that the page numbers and headers or footers are set up as you want them to be. Reviewing the document is particularly important if you change from one printer to another, as you may need to adjust the formatting of the document to accommodate the fonts, spacing, and different graphics of the new printer.

The best way to review a document on a computer is by selecting either PAGE LAYOUT (VIEW menu) or PRINT PREVIEW (FILE menu) and then scrolling through to simulate a reader leafing through the document. A two-page view is especially useful with newsletters and brochures.

In reviewing a document, check for the following features:

- *Widowed or orphaned lines.* Single lines left stranded at the top and bottom of a page are known as widowed and orphaned lines, respectively. Particularly irritating to readers are orphaned headings. Although you should still inspect your document, you can avoid having to make a lot of manual adjustments by using the automatic features found on many word processors.

- *Interrupted lists.* Like widowed or orphaned lines, short lists that start on one page and end on another have an adverse effect on readability. You will have to visually check all short lists for this problem, as the computer will not do it for you.

- *Misplaced graphics or boxes.* Graphics and boxes should appear on the same page as their text reference, and generally they should be centered on the page. Your word-processing program will prevent such elements from being placed on a different page from their reference, provided you anchor the graphic or box properly to the reference. Otherwise, you will have to make manual adjustments. Centering a graphic is best done by positioning it at the left margin, highlighting it, and then clicking on the CENTER button in the toolbar. Alternatively, you can either position the graphic manually using the ruler or use the PAGE SETUP menu to input the numbers for the placement desired.

- *Errors in page or section numbering.* Numbering errors are likely to annoy and even confuse readers. You can avoid page numbering errors by having the word-processing program do the page numbering automatically. Using outlining and templates consistently through the development of your paper will prevent section numbering problems as well. Still, you should visually survey your paper to make sure all sections are properly numbered.

- *White space.* Unused space is important because it makes different elements of a text (such as graphics, lists, and titles) stand out. By surveying your document in the PAGE LAYOUT or PRINT PREVIEW mode, you can decide whether specific elements are getting proper emphasis. White space also is important simply for aesthetic reasons. As readers leaf through your document, they should find its look appealing—neither too crowded nor too empty. Many readers will appreciate the "breathing space" afforded by white space.

E X E R C I S E   1 7 . 3

Find a poorly formatted page from a user manual, junk mail, or the Internet. Referring to the principles discussed in this section, write a two-page critique of it.

E X E R C I S E   1 7 . 4

Reformat the document you critiqued in Exercise 17.3. If the document is from the Internet, you may be able to copy it with its original format features and then edit and reformat it on your computer.

17c   Use graphics

Graphics include tables, line graphs, bar graphs, pie charts, clip art, photographs, cartoons, drawings, maps, and other forms of visual art. Each type of graphic has its own special uses and features. In our increasingly visually oriented culture, graphics add a lot of power to a document. This power, however, should be used judiciously to emphasize or clarify an important point. The use of too many graphics dilutes their effectiveness.

Tables

Tables are the best type of graphic for presenting a lot of data in compressed form. Although tables are not as visual as other types of

Guidelines for Using Graphics

1. Place the graphic near the text to which it relates.
2. Introduce each graphic with a text reference. For example, precede the graphic with a sentence ending in a colon or a brief parenthetical comment like "(see Figure 2)."
3. Use a caption that makes the graphic self-explanatory.
4. Keep the graphic as simple and uncluttered as possible.

graphics in that they require readers to compare numbers rather than look at direct visual representations, they provide a convenient way to organize data, and they do draw readers' attention. Table 17.1 illustrates how information-rich a table can be.

Country	1992	1993	1994	1995
United States	82.2	83.9	85.6	88.3
China	29.2	31.7	33.9	35.7
Russia	32.7	30.9	27.9	26.8
Japan	19.0	19.0	20.7	21.4
Germany	14.1	13.9	13.9	13.7
Canada	11.0	11.4	11.6	11.7
India	8.6	9.1	9.5	10.5
United Kingdom	9.7	9.3	9.3	9.8
France	9.7	9.4	9.2	9.4
Italy	7.0	6.9	7.0	7.4
Other	119.3	123.5	123.3	127.5

Table 17.1   Annual World Energy Consumption
(in quadrillion Btu)
Source: U.S. Energy Information Administration, *International Energy Annual*, 1992–1995.

Notice how Table 17.1 adheres to the four guidelines for using graphics:

1. It immediately follows the text to which it relates.
2. It is introduced by the phrase "Table 17.1 illustrates . . . ."
3. The caption, "Annual World Energy Consumption (in quadrillion Btu)," makes the table self-explanatory.
4. It is maximally simple and uncluttered.

Notice, in particular, how the designer has "factored out" the units of measurement (quadrillion Btu), putting them in the caption instead of alongside each entry.

Current word-processing programs offer a variety of table formats to choose from. Just click on TABLE and explore the options it gives you.

Once you have the data laid out in a table, you can convert to other formats (such as line graphs and bar graphs) by selecting certain cells to import into whatever graphics program you have on your computer.

2 Line graphs

Line graphs generally do not contain as much data as tables do. But they can make data more understandable and are especially effective for showing changes over time. Figure 17.1 is a line graph

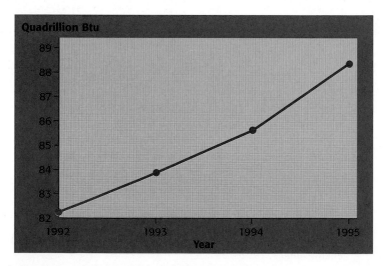

Figure 17.1   US Energy Consumption 1992–1995

representing the top row of data in Table 17.1. The line graph visually depicts the steady growth in US energy consumption from 1992 to 1995. It focuses the viewer's attention on just one aspect of Table 17.1, thereby giving it more prominence. The graph is uncluttered and properly labeled.

As shown in Figure 17.1, highlight the line on your line graph by using color or a heavy-weight line. If your graph has more than one line, be sure to distinguish the various lines clearly (for example, by having one solid, another dotted, and a third dashed). Do not use more than three lines in a graph, as too many lines will produce a cluttered effect.

3 Bar graphs

Bar graphs emphasize discrete points rather than continuity, but they can also show changes over time, sometimes more dramatically than line graphs. For example, the bar graph in Figure 17.2 emphasizes the overall pattern of rising US energy consumption even more strongly than does the line graph in Figure 17.1.

The sheer weight of the bars makes this graph more powerful than the line graph. Like the line graph, the bar graph is maximally simple and uncluttered. The caption makes it self-explanatory, and the units of measurement are mentioned only once.

When is a line graph better than a bar graph? Because they do not emphasize discrete points, line graphs are better for showing

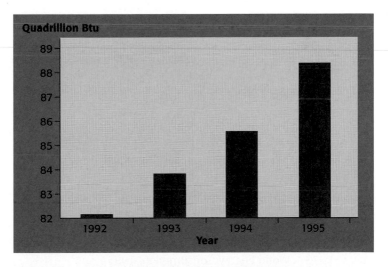

Figure 17.2   US Energy Consumption, 1992–1995

continuous variation over time. Thus, if many points in time can be plotted (for example, forty-eight months instead of four years), a line graph may be preferable. Also, line graphs are better for tracking several variables at once. If you wanted to compare the 1992–1995 energy consumption of two other countries with that of the United States, a line graph, with three lines running approximately in parallel, would be more manageable and more useful than a bar graph, with twelve different bars.

> **WEB**
> http://www.
> colostate.edu/
> Depts/WritingCenter/
> references/
> graphics.htm
> An excellent guide to
> using illustrations, graph-
> ics, tables, and figures in
> document design

4   Pie charts

Pie charts are effective in showing how a fixed quantity of something is divided into fractions. Generally, the "pie" as a whole should represent 100 percent. Figure 17.3 shows the energy consumption data for a single year (1995) for the entire world.

The pie chart vividly depicts the energy-guzzling ways of the United States. It is relatively simple, in part because it contains no

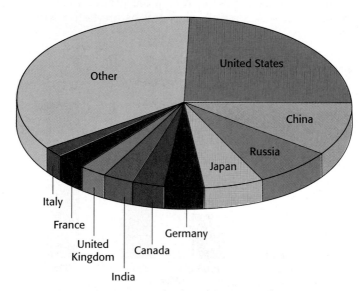

Figure 17.3   **World Energy Consumption, 1995**

units of measurement. Since pie charts depict ratios rather than absolute quantities, units of measurement are unnecessary. (Some word
processors offer the option of including percentages in a pie chart.)

The pie chart shown in Figure 17.3 leaves something to be desired, however: it has too many small pieces. The pieces representing Germany, Canada, India, the United Kingdom, France, and Italy
are so tiny that it is difficult to label them. As a result, the graph
seems slightly cluttered. In general, use a pie chart only when most
of the pieces are large enough to be labeled without pointers.

5 | Clip art

Clip art, or ready-made images, can add a decorative touch to a
document. A well-chosen image can enhance the appeal of a newsletter, brochure, business card, or advertisement. Do not get carried away,
though; too much of a good thing may only distract or annoy readers.
Be especially cautious about using clip art in academic papers. Professionals in most academic fields take
their work very seriously and may not
appreciate decorative artwork.

You can find a gallery of computer clip art in MS Works, Corel/
WordPerfect Office, and other programs like Windows 98. Clip art is
also available commercially on disk,
as well as in traditional print form
(for example, Clip Books) from com-
panies such as Dynamic Graphics. Whatever the source, be sure to
determine whether the owner has authorized republication of the art
and whether there are restrictions on its use.

> **WEB**
>
> http://lcweb.loc.gov/
> global/internet/html.
> html#graphics
> A great list of links to
> free graphics, icons,
> and other stuff on
> the Web

The major drawback of purchasing commercial clip art is the
cost. In general, good-quality reproducible clip art—in print or digital form—is expensive. If you have to choose between poor-quality
clip art and no clip art at all, choose none; poor-quality clip art will
make your documents look amateurish. Here are some principles to
keep in mind when using clip art:

- *Select art by its theme.* Sticking to one theme or one type of art in
  a document will help unify the document—that is, give it more
  connectedness.

- *Reconfigure any clip art you use.* Change the size, shape, crop,
  background, and other features of the art as necessary to adapt
  it to your document.

- *Use a contrasting color.* If available, a contrasting color will make the clip art stand out from the rest of the document.

6 Photographs, cartoons, drawings, and maps

You may find that you want to use other types of art besides clip art in your documents. The advent of graphical scanners and Internet downloading has made it easy to incorporate photographs and other images (such as cartoons, drawings, and maps) into documents. But remember that you cannot use copyrighted materials, such as cartoons or photographs created by someone else, without that person's permission.

If you have access to a scanner, follow this process to include your own photographs in a document:

1. Start with a good original, and align it on the scanner plate.
2. Open a scanning program, such as Hewlett Packard's DeskScan.
3. Preview the document. The scanner will reproduce the image on screen for your review.
4. Adjust the image as needed. Most scanners will allow you, for example, to crop the image, zoom in or out to make it larger or smaller, and change its resolution (contrast and brightness).
5. Check the size of the file. You do not want the file to be too large to include in your document. If necessary, adjust the size, colors, and resolution of the image until the size of the file becomes reasonable. Usually 30 K, or **kilobytes,** is about right.
6. Choose an image format, such as bitmap, gif, or jpeg.
7. Save the image in an appropriate location on your disk or hard drive.

Once you have saved a graphical image, you can insert it into your document at the appropriate location by using INSERT on the FILE menu. Then, you can adjust the image to the appropriate size for your document. (With specialized software, you can edit, focus, or clarify the image as well.) For an example of the use of photographs in a document, see Felicia Alvarez's brochure in Chapter 18.

EXERCISE 17.5

Use information from the following table to create (a) a line graph, (b) a bar graph, and (c) a pie graph. In each case, write a caption that describes what the graph illustrates.

How Households Divided the Nation's Income: 1975 and 1995

	1975		1995	
	Segment Average	Share of All Income	Segment Average	Share of All Income
Top 20%	$80,834	43.2%	$109,411	48.7%
Second 20%	$46,417	24.8%	$52,429	23.3%
Middle 20%	$31,963	17.1%	$34,106	15.2%
Fourth 20%	$19,535	10.5%	$20,397	9.1%
Bottom 20%	$8,227	4.4%	$8,350	3.7%
Total population	$37,365	100.0%	$44,938	100.0%

Source: Data from U.S. Census Bureau. Cited in A. Hacker, *Money* (New York: Scribner, 1997), p. 11.

17d   Respect different norms and preferences

Headings, lists, and graphics are more common in some fields and genres than in others. For example, a business professor may expect your reports to have frequent headings and subheadings, lists, and graphics, while an English professor may expect your literary essays to have only a title. Be sensitive to these differences, and respect the norms of the field. If your field of study does not typically employ certain document design features, you may be able to achieve the same effects in other ways. In literary essays, for example, you can emphasize main points by putting well-crafted topic sentences at the beginnings of paragraphs and by using parallelism, contrast, and the other techniques discussed in Chapter 37.

Desktop Publishing

How do I design and produce a brochure? (18a)

How can using a brochure or newsletter template help me? (18a-1)

How do I decide what to include in my newsletter? (18b-1)

How can I use white space and color effectively? (18a-2, 18b-2)

Desktop publishing refers to the process of producing printed documents on a personal computer. Although special publishing programs such as QuarkXpress and Pagemaker offer many more design options, word-processing programs can produce a variety of exciting designs. This chapter discusses ways to produce attractive, professional-looking brochures and newsletters. **Templates,** which are preformatted files available in word-processing programs, allow you to desktop publish a first project with ease. You may also want to refer to Chapter 17 on design principles and graphics as you work on your desktop publishing projects. If you cannot find

http://desktopPublishing. com/
An awesome collection of desktop publishing resources, collected in one place for one-stop shopping

a template that suits your needs, search for a printed model to follow. Brochures suitable for use as models may be found in libraries, in doctors' offices, and in local promotional outlets such as the Chamber of Commerce.

18a   Produce a simple brochure

A brochure is a particular type of document with the following characteristics:

- An informative or persuasive purpose
- An uncommitted audience
- Text and/or graphics focused on a single objective
- A direct or indirect persuasive style
- Limited space
- Layout designed for quick and easy readability
- A physical design that typically uses a single sheet of folded paper

—Jeri Cassity, *Brochure Writing*

How do I use a document template?

1. Write the text of your document and save it.
2. Select the desired template (for example, brochure, newsletter, memo, or report) and style.
3. Follow the instructions within the template to begin formatting your document; for example, select the number of columns or select a border.
4. Insert your document into the template, using the INSERT command. Your document will be "poured" into the columns of the template.
5. Revise your document, observing the design principles described in this chapter and in Chapter 17.

NOTE: These steps apply to Word for Windows and WordPerfect. For other word processors, check your documentation.

1 Making decisions about content

The content decisions you make when you produce a brochure should be based on a rhetorical analysis (see 3a-2). Notice that the list of brochure characteristics addresses not only topic, but also purpose, persona, and audience. A brochure is focused on a specific topic, and its purpose is clearly persuasive. Designed to reflect a knowledgeable and convincing persona, it is targeted toward readers who have not yet committed to a point of view on the topic and might be swayed by the brochure's message.

Most word processors have templates that can help you organize the content. Felicia Alvarez set out to produce a brochure inviting her father's friends and relatives to a retirement party and family reunion. The topic of the brochure was the reunion; the purpose was to inform family members of the event and persuade them to come; the persona was that of a caring daughter who wants to honor her father and celebrate his life's achievements; and the readers were family and friends of Ricardo (Ricky) Alvarez.

Since Felicia was new to brochure writing, she turned to her word-processing program for help. By searching for "brochures" under the HELP menu, she discovered that she could access two brochure templates through the FILE menu: the elegant brochure template and the traditional brochure template. When she opened the elegant brochure template, she was asked to supply a brochure title and a descriptive subtitle. She decided to use a teaser for the brochure title: "Do You Know This Young Man?" For the subtitle, she chose "Ricardo Alvarez's Retirement and 70th Birthday."

When Felicia entered that information, the six panels that represent the two sides of a tri-fold brochure appeared on the screen. Instructions in the template told her where to type in specific kinds of information:

Panel 1: Features (of the product, service, or company)

Panel 2: Benefits (to the clients or audience)

Panel 3: Action (what you want people to do)

Panel 4: People (behind the product or service)

Panel 5: Return address

Her title and subtitle appeared on the sixth panel, centered, in large type.

Though her purpose was not to sell a product or service, Felicia was able to adapt these instructions to her purpose: to persuade friends and family to attend the reunion. Here are the headings that she entered for the first four panels:

> Panel 1 (Features): "He's About to Retire. We Hope You Can Join Us for the Big Celebration."
> Panel 2 (Benefits): "Included in the Celebration Will Be . . . "
> Panel 3 (Action): "Let Us Know If You Can Come . . . "
> Panel 4 (People): "Who Is Coming?"

2 Making decisions about layout and design

Chapter 17 discusses three basic design principles, called the three C's: clustering, contrasting, and connecting. When you design a brochure, you must attend to all of these principles, paying particular attention to the following considerations:

- *An enticing cover.* The first thing a brochure needs to do is entice someone to read it. Use a combination of lively copy and strategically placed graphical images to draw readers' interest. To spark interest, Felicia decided to use a question and a photograph of her father as a young man on the cover panel.

  http://www.
  graphic-design.com/
  The graphics and
  design homepage,
  featuring an impressive
  collection of desktop
  publishing resources

- *A cohesive story.* Once you have enticed readers to open the brochure, lead them through the text in a logical way. The text should tell a story; that is, each panel should relate to the previous one and to those that follow. The template instructions helped Felicia construct a logical story line for her brochure.

- *Coherent graphics.* In a brochure, graphics often play as important a role as copy in telling the story. Like the copy, the graphics should be logical and consistent. Several design features were incorporated into the brochure template Felicia used, including a graphical icon in the form of a fleur-de-lis at the bottom of each panel (which Felicia later decided to delete; see 18a-3), a capital letter in a large font size for the start of each panel's heading (called a special initial), and an elegant, readable font. Such features help provide visual coherence throughout a brochure. Felicia added family photographs to maintain readers' interest and to provide additional coherence throughout the brochure. She used a graphical scanner to digitize family photos (see 17c-6). Then, using the INSERT feature, she inserted the graphics at the appropriate locations in the brochure. Finally, around each photo she placed a double-ruled box.

- *Adequate white space.* Because the space available in a brochure is extremely limited, you should include only essential information. You can always provide readers with a method for obtaining more information, as Felicia did by including her phone number. Leave plenty of white space to maintain readability. Small chunks of text broken up by white space and informative headings, plus simple and direct language, help make a brochure readable. Aim for a 3:2 ratio between text and white space—that is, three parts of text for every two parts of white space. If the text seems dense, try reducing the font size and adding space between paragraphs. But be sure that you do not make the type too small to be read easily.

3   Refining the brochure

Once you have prepared the first draft of your brochure with all of the text you intend to include, print it out and evaluate it, keeping in mind the three C's of design. When Felicia printed her draft, she discovered that it did not make good use of the clustering principle—everything was too spread out, and the photographs were too small and too far from the related text. She revised by clustering related text together and by enlarging and moving the photographs. She liked the contrast provided by the drop caps in the headings and decided to repeat that design element (contrasting upper- and lowercase lettering) in the list on panel 2. Then, Felicia looked for coherence in her brochure. Did all of the elements connect to each other? After experimenting with various combinations of justifications (right, left, block), she decided that left justification would best show how each of the panels was connected to the others. So she changed the justification on the title, which the word-processing program had centered. And she deleted the subtitle, which made the cover too cluttered. She checked to make sure that all the fonts were the same, with the exception of the title (for contrast). She added captions to the pictures and deleted the fleur-de-lis graphic, which did not seem to fit with the style of the rest of the brochure. Finally, she opened

The Brochure Writing Process

1. Deciding on the content and writing the text:
   a. Conduct a rhetorical analysis.
   b. Choose a template.
   c. Write and insert the text.
2. Deciding on the layout and design:
   a. Design an enticing cover.
   b. Tell a cohesive story.
   c. Add coherent graphics.
   d. Include adequate white space.
3. Refining the brochure:
   a. Check for clustering.
   b. Check for contrast.
   c. Check for connectedness.

the brochure in the two-page view window to verify that the alignment was consistent throughout. The finished brochure appears in Figure 18.1 on pages 412–413.

EXERCISE 18.1

Write a brochure to announce a party or other event. First, decide who your readers will be, why they should attend the event, what special information will convince them to attend, and what action you would like them to take. Then, select a brochure template from your word-processing program. See the Help box on page 407 for instructions. Enter text for the cover and for the other panels. If you want to write the text first on your word processor, the Help box explains how to transfer the contents of the document to your template. When you have completed the brochure, print it out, and ask a few friends or classmates to respond to these questions:

1. What clues does the cover provide about the brochure's contents, and what emotional effects does it create?
2. What story does the brochure tell?
3. How well do the graphics help to convey the story?
4. Is the brochure easy to read? Why or why not?

Revise your brochure based on the feedback you gather.

Text clustered
together

He's About to Retire. We Hope You Can Join Us for the Big Celebration.

On Labor Day weekend, August 31, 1997, friends and family of Ricardo Alvarez will gather in celebration of his retirement and birthday.

◆ **Retirement** (Ricky is finally retiring after 50 years of work for the same company)

◆ **Birthday** (Ricky is also about to celebrate his 70th birthday)

Ricardo Alvarez, Sr. Family, 1940 (Ricky, Maria, José)

Picture captions

Panel 1

Included in the Celebration Will Be:

Dinner at the Terrazza del Sol Restaurant in downtown Tampa

A barbeque the following afternoon at Felicia's house

Dancing under the stars on the restaurant's famous terrace

'

Swimming, fishing, and windsurfing on Tampa Bay

Special **D**ay!

Good use of white space

Panel 2

Let Us Know If You Can Come . . .

We need to make reservations for the Tampa Hilton as soon as possible. Please let Felicia know if you will be attending the reunion. Also, please indicate on the form below how many of your family members will be attending and how many rooms you will need reserved for you.

_____ **Yes,** we plan to attend the reunion

_____ **Number** of family members attending

_____ **Number** of rooms needed at the hotel

Alvarez Children and Frisky, 1956

Picture border

Panel 3

Figure 18.1   Felicia's Brochure

Special
initial

Who is Coming?

All of Ricky's children are
planning to attend and all
his brothers and sisters.
We are not certain yet
how many grandchildren
or other relatives will be
coming.

We hope you can come too.
But don't tell Ricky.

IT'S A SURPRISE

**For more information,
contact Felicia at
555-1313.**

Address:

Felicia Alvarez
17 First Street
Tampa, Florida 33602

*Do You
Know
This
Young
Man?*

Alvarez Children, 1960

Panel 4   Panel 5   Panel 6

Figure 18.1 (cont.)

18b Produce a simple newsletter

Newsletters are extremely versatile print publications that deliver timely information to a target audience with similar interests, such as business customers or employees of an organization. Many newsletters use an 8½" × 11" page size and are four pages long, printed front and back. Sometimes they include an additional one-page, two-sided insert, for a total of six pages. The design and production decisions you must make for a newsletter are similar to those for a brochure. However, in a newsletter you have more space to work with.

1 Making decisions about content

As always, you first need to consider your rhetorical stance, looking at the topic in terms of purpose, persona, and audience (see 3a-2). Articles should both enlighten and entertain the newsletter's audience; they should be informative rather than overtly persuasive. Since readers already have some stake in the organization, business, product, or service that sponsors the newsletter, you can assume they will be interested in the subject matter. But you still want to make your writing lively and engaging. If the newsletter will be published at regular intervals, plan ahead to stay on top of new developments in the field, to ensure that you have timely information for each issue.

2 Making decisions about layout and design

Be sensitive to the needs of busy, selective newsletter readers by including a table of contents on the first page and providing headings, subheadings, lists, and graphics to help readers find information quickly and easily. Observing the three C's—clustering, contrasting, and connecting—is particularly important in newsletter design. Available design elements include different type fonts, pull-out quotes (quotes that are set off from the regular text and printed in larger type), special initials, rules (lines), boxes, color, and graphics.

Newsletters are typically printed in columns, with a masthead, or banner, at the top of the first page, followed by text arranged in either two or three columns per page. Think of white space as an element of contrast—it does not emphasize itself but rather draws attention to something else. It also provides a place for readers to pause. Do not "trap" white space in the fold area of a two-page spread; the only white space down the center of the spread should be the space between the text columns. Instead, use white space creatively to draw the reader's eye toward important information. This will give the spread a coherence that it otherwise might not have.

Graphical elements such as color, pictures, and text art are used in a newsletter for emphasis. Generally, the banner will be the first graphic a reader will see in a newsletter. Other graphics should coordinate with the banner, in accordance with the design principle of connectedness. Pick up and repeat colors or visual elements from the banner, for example, elsewhere in the newsletter. (For some ideas on using text art, see 17c-5, 17c-6.) Graphics can occupy either one, two, or three columns in a newsletter. Of course, the larger the graphic, the stronger the emphasis. You might consider using a small graphic in the lower right-hand corner of the first page, to balance the banner at the top of the page.

To set off headings and subheadings in a newsletter, use a larger type font and/or color. Such graphic cues will help readers locate the major sections of your newsletter.

3 Refining the newsletter

Most word processors have newsletter templates. Cecelia Chung, who wrote the research paper in Chapter 12, decided to publish her paper in newsletter format. In the FILE menu on her word-processing program, she found a newsletter template. The template first asked her to select a title, subtitle, volume number, issue number, and date. It next asked her to decide on the number of columns she wished to use and whether she wanted those columns divided by a rule (vertical line). The program then created a template for the first page of the newsletter.

The template left space for a table of contents, which would be generated automatically as Cecelia supplied the copy for headings and subheadings. Once she had the various elements in place, Cecelia inserted her research paper file into the template by choosing INSERT. The template arranged the text automatically into columns. Cecelia then began the job of formatting the newsletter to make it reader-friendly and visually appealing. She chose a blue border for subsequent pages, to match the gold and blue banner. In the lower right-hand corner of the first page, she inserted a graphic to balance the banner. She opted for block justification and consequently centered the image of the sun on the fourth page. She used the same font throughout; only the banner was set in a different font.

The finished newsletter appears in Figure 18.2 on pages 416–419. Notice how the larger font size and added line spaces set off the headings and how the white space around the sun image draws the reader's eye out toward the text itself.

Global Climate Change

Cecelia Chung ⟍Banner November 14, 1998

Global Warming: What, How, Why Care?
⎯⎯Larger bold font for headings

Global Warming: Is It Really Happening?

Global warming, at least as measured by climate experts, *is* really happening. Over the last 100 years, it has been estimated that the average global air temperature has risen between 0.3 and 0.6 degree Celsius (Hileman). Though there is debate over other aspects of global warming, scientists generally agree that global temperatures have risen.

However, a big source of disagreement is whether this is a normal or an abnormal warming. Too little is known about long-term global temperature cycles, some say, to determine if this is abnormal. Reliable weather data, it is true, have only been kept for the last century or so (Montague 1). As a result, some question whether there is significant cause for alarm about global warming as a real problem. While I agree that some caution is warranted when predicting the final outcome of this warming trend, I feel that to disregard the problem altogether is extremely short-sighted, because the effects of even a temporary, normal warming trend are potentially devastating for earth and its inhabitants. Most people would agree. It is in our best interests to know as much as possible about global warming, its causes and potential effects. Before we discuss the true nature of the controversy, let's look at how global warming works.

Table of contents ⟋

What Is Global Warming and How Does It Work?

Global warming is an increase in average air temperature on earth's surface, as measured from many points across the globe. Global warming, in its simplest form, is a product of two factors: so-called greenhouse gases and radiation from our local star, the Sun. The idea is that sunlight enters earth's atmosphere, hits molecules of atmospheric gas on earth's surface, and is converted to other forms of energy such as heat. Sometimes this energy is prevented from escaping back into space by a "blanket" of gases such as carbon dioxide, and a net gain of heat occurs (Britt). Without

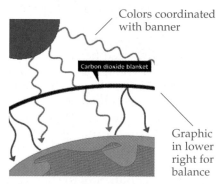

Colors coordinated with banner

Carbon dioxide blanket

Graphic in lower right for balance

Figure 18.2　Cecelia's Newsletter

2 Global Climate Change — Running head — November 14, 1998

Two-column format

these gases, our planet would be about 60 degrees Fahrenheit colder than it is today (Montague 1), too cold for many terrestrial life forms that now thrive here. But there is concern that too much heat buildup caused by unnatural levels of so-called greenhouse gases will be dangerous for our planet.

White space

Why Are Global Temperatures Increasing?

Now that scientists have established that global warming is taking place, the next question is *why*? Is this, as before stated, a normal trend for our planet? Or is this something that is occurring because of human interference with earth's natural systems?

Most likely, our planet does experience warming and cooling cycles, and it is possible that the current warming trend is one of them. However, the normal warming trend may be compounded by human practices that increase atmospheric levels of the four principal greenhouse gases: carbon dioxide, methane, nitrous oxide, and chlorofluorocarbons (CFC's) (Montague 1). Many of our activities could potentially lead to a buildup of these gases and a resulting increase in global temperatures.

Carbon dioxide makes up the majority of the atmospheric gases. Therefore its emission is of the most concern. The greatest source of increase in atmospheric carbon dioxide is suspected to be the burning of fossil fuels such as coal and oil. Since the beginning of the Industrial Age, burning of fossil fuels has increased dramatically, resulting in an increase of atmospheric carbon dioxide of almost 55% (Montague 1). According to current theory, this is a major cause of the current warming trend, and the whole effect of this has yet to be seen.

What Are Possible Effects of Global Warming?

Already, increased temperatures have had many effects, including weather pattern changes, increased rates of glacial melting, subsequent sea-level increases, and air and sea-surface temperature increases, sometimes with resulting shifts in plant and animal species.

Models predict that, if current theories hold true, temperatures will rise between 1 and 3.5 degrees Celsius by 2100 (Hileman). Temperature increases are expected to be highest over land, changing climates and affecting habitat suitability for terrestrial species, which may be forced to migrate or go extinct. These temperature increases are also expected to result in a sea-level rise of 15 to 95 cm (Hileman) due to increased glacial melting. This would result in flooding in low-lying coastal regions. Changes in ocean circulation will result in warmer local sea temperatures, causing unforeseeable effects for species in these areas.

The biggest immediate effect of global warming is changes in weather, especially greater variability in temperatures and precipitation. Extreme seasonal temperatures can contribute to formation of hurricanes and tornados. Hurricanes are encouraged by high air temperatures, which lead to increased water temperatures over the oceans. A current increase in US tornados within the last four decades is thought to be associated with temperature increases, as well.

What Will Happen to Life on Earth?

Will global warming lead to mass extinctions, or will species migrate to the cooler poles and adapt to life there? Both are likely, but extinctions are inevitable if, as predicted, global temperature increases continue far into the future.

But even without these continued increases, minor temperature changes can have huge effects on habitats, simultaneously affecting populations of many species. For instance, a long-term study of coastal waters off

Figure 18.2 (cont.)

3 Global Climate Change

Matching colors

White space around graphic draws eye outward to the text

November 14, 1998

southern California, conducted by John Mc-Gowan and Dean Roemmich of the Scripps Institute of Oceanography, has shown a 2–3 degrees Fahrenheit temperature increase in the sea-surface temperature in the last fifty years (Svitil 36). This has led to density changes in the surface waters, which have had broad implications for the suitability of the habitat for the species living there.

Changes in habitat naturally lead to changes in energy resources as species unable to cope with change die out or disperse to other areas. As one population shrinks, other dependent species populations are stressed for food resources, in turn stressing the populations dependent upon them. In the study previously mentioned, changes in density stratification of the water altered the amount of chemical nutrients carried up from the bacterial beds in the depths of the ocean. As nutrient levels declined near the surface, plants dependent upon these nutrients suffered declines in population, which in turn reduced populations of plant-dependent phytoplankton. The population-reducing effects moved up the food chain reducing populations, from phytoplankton to zooplankton to fish to seabirds (Svitil 36). Clearly, even minor temperature changes have the capacity to significantly alter population numbers, and, as the scale of climate change increases, extinctions are inevitable.

Alternatively, some say that extinctions due to climate change will be limited because populations will migrate to cooler climates, avoiding the effects of climate change. To a point, I agree. However, rates at which warming will continue are unknown, and successful migrations are dependent upon populations being able to move faster than the rate of change. If warming is gradual, some species may be able to outpace the change.

However, some predictions state that temperatures will rise exponentially as compounding factors come into play. As temperatures rise, rates of successful migration will be affected by individual mobility (locomotion), energy resource mobility, reproductive rate, habitat dispersal, and geography. Since a population can only migrate as quickly as its slowest-moving resource, and only to places with suitable habitat unblocked by barriers beyond their capacity to overcome (such as deserts, mountains, oceans), many species will be unable to migrate quickly enough to keep up with rates of climate change.

For example, historical models have shown that the geographic range of American beech has moved just 0.2 km per year since the last Ice Age. However, to keep pace with current predictions of climate change, beech will have to move 7–9 km per year to the north (Krebs 113). Thus, the beech is destined to extinction unless we intervene. I predict that many species, both plant and animal, will be unable to move quickly enough to keep up with change and will become extinct.

What does this mean for human life on earth? The answer to this question is unknown. If this warming trend continues to escalate, then it is possible that even humanity as we know it will eventually reach its capacity for adaptation and become extinct, perhaps replaced by another, revolutionarily advanced species. If the trend does not continue but the earth begins to cool, then the effects for human populations will be less drastic. Regardless of the duration of this warming trend, humans cannot fail to feel the effects of a warming trend, as we already are to some degree. Oceans are rising and may eventually encroach upon beaches and seaside homes. Ocean microorganisms are shift-

Figure 18.2   (cont.)

ing in abundances and will affect conditions in many economies. It is impossible for humanity to escape entirely unaffected by even a minor warming trend.

What Can Be Done about Global Warming?

Already, many groups and individuals are concerned and taking action about global warming and the problems it may bring. The cooperative effort of local, national, and international entities is necessary, because the potential effects of global warming are so huge. Global warming will affect not only individuals but businesses and governments as well.

Businesses dependent upon world conditions are especially concerned about global warming, for economical if not environmental reasons. Two of these are the global insurance and banking industries. These industries are working with the United Nations to reduce environmentally damaging activities. This is largely because, says UN Environment Program director Hans Alder, "They know that a few major disasters caused by extreme climate events . . . could literally bankrupt the industry in the next decade" (Hertsgaard C1).

Why Care?

Global warming is, after all, a global problem. The effects of global warming, destructive and severe, will be felt increasingly by everyone. Scientists agree that it is happening, so we should all support efforts to research and combat its causes. The changes global warming will eventually cause are unknown in their severity and scope but al-

ready we can feel some of them. Let's take action to prevent further escalation of global warming.

Works Cited

Britt, Robert. "The Heat Is On: Scientists Agree on Human Contribution to Global Warming." *Ion Science* 1995. 13 Nov. 1998 <http://www.injersey.com/Media/IonSci/features/gwarm/gwarm.html>.

Hertsgaard, Mark. "Who's Afraid of Global Warming?" *Washington Post* 21 Jan. 1996: C1. 13 Nov. 1998 <http://www.ji.org/jinews/newsline/afraid2.htm>.

Hileman, Bette. "Climate Observations Substantiate Global Warming Models." *Chemical and Engineering News* 27 Nov. 1995. 13 Nov. 1998 <http://jcbmac.chem.brown.edu/baird/Chem221/global/pg1.html>.

Krebs, Charles J. *Ecology: The Experimental Analysis of Distribution and Abundance.* 4th ed. New York: Harper, 1994.

Montague, Peter. "Global Warming—Part 1: How Global Warming Is Sneaking Up on Us." *Rachel's Hazardous Waste News* 26 Aug. 1992: 1. 22 Nov. 1998 <http://www.envirolink.org/pubs/rachel/rhwn300.htm>.

Svitil, Kathy A. "Collapse of a Food Chain." *Discover* July 1995: 36–37.

Graphics Sources

Carbon dioxide blanket. 13 Nov. 1998 <http://www.injersey.com/Media/IonSci/features/gwarm/gwarm.html>.

Friendly sun. 13 Nov. 1998 <cuisun9.unige.ch/eao/www/gif/New_Sun.color.gif>.

Figure 18.2   (cont.)

The Newsletter Writing Process

1. Deciding on the content and writing the text:
   a. Conduct a rhetorical analysis.
   b. Choose a template.
   c. Write and insert the text.

2. Deciding on the layout and design:
   a. Choose a banner.
   b. Select a color scheme.
   c. Include white space.
   d. Place graphics.
   e. Select fonts for the text, and add headings and a table of contents.

3. Refining the newsletter:
   a. Check for clustering.
   b. Check for contrast.
   c. Check for connectedness.

EXERCISE 18.2

Analyze the design of Cecelia's newsletter with respect to the three C's. Write your evaluation of Cecelia's application of each design principle.

EXERCISE 18.3

Design your own newsletter, using a template found on your word-processing program. Or, design a class newsletter as a collaborative project.

Designing for the Web

FAQs

What does it mean to "design" a Web site? (19a, 19b-5)
What is hypertext? (19a-2)
How can I get my Web files to appear on the Internet?
(19b-1)
What is a storyboard? (19b-3)
How can I help readers navigate through my Web site?
(19b-4)

As you begin to think about designing Web documents, it is important to remember that writing for the Web is not all that different from writing for other purposes. The basic rhetorical principles outlined in Part 1 of this handbook still apply. Web authors need to consider carefully their rhetorical stance (purpose, persona, and audience) and let it dictate the content and structure of their Web sites. However, Web documents differ from print documents in two important ways: they tend to include more graphics than print documents do, and they are hypertextual (that is, they have electronic

WEB

http://www.w3.org/
Provider/Style/
Introduction.html
A hypertextually or-
ganized manual on
Web design from the
creator of the WWW,
Tim Berners-Lee

links). This chapter discusses these differences and what they mean to writers.

You may not associate design with writing. Perhaps you think of design in terms of designing graphics or designing page layouts (discussed in Chapters 17 and 18). But designing is something that happens during any writing process. We will use the term *design* to refer broadly to the ongoing planning involved in developing and writing for a complicated project such as a Web site. We discuss the broad design issues in this chapter. Chapter 20 provides more specific guidance on constructing Web pages.

19a   Generate a basic design for the Web

A third grader in Huntsville, Alabama, and a research scientist in Osaka, Japan, have equal access to a worldwide audience on the Web. And, like anyone else who authors a Web site, both proceed through a design planning process in which they generate ideas and then plan, draft, revise, and publish the Web site. When a Web page is well designed, the author's message is successfully conveyed to readers, and the look and content of the page match the purposes of the author. Thus, effectively designed Web sites make good use of both graphics and hypertext.

1   Using graphics effectively

In print media, the printed words convey most of the text's meaning. But even printed texts contain other meaningful visual cues in addition to the words themselves—for example, by indenting five spaces at the beginning of a paragraph, using italics for titles of books, and using boldface for chapter titles, we also convey meaning. When Web authors consider document design, formatting, and graphics, they make decisions similar to those made by writers of print documents. However, the role of visual features in conveying meaning is greater in Web documents than in print documents.

> **WWW WEB MMM**
>
> http://www.glover.com/ss.html
> A great site with great advice in the form of Web design tips and warnings

Background

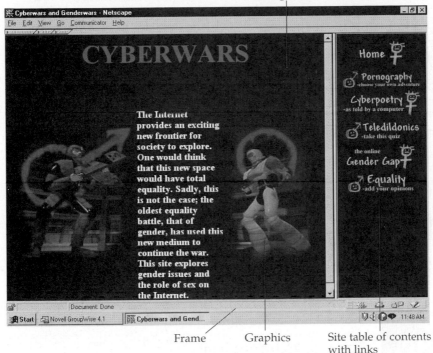

Frame | Graphics | Site table of contents with links

Figure 19.1   Web Page Illustrating Several Design Features

Web authors typically use images instead of words to show readers how to find information and to help them understand concepts. They employ such visual tools as color, background images, typographical distinctions, spacing, graphics and icons, lists, and tables and frames (see Figure 19.1). Increasingly, Web sites are becoming multimedia; they use sound and even movement to convey their message to readers.

2   Using hypertext effectively

Effective writers accommodate the busy, selective reader through the use of headings, itemized lists, and graphics (see Chapter 17). Hypertext goes a logical step beyond print by allowing busy readers to choose among short chunks of text on specific topics, deciding what to read and what to ignore. **Hypertext** is text that is broken down into discrete pieces, which are then connected through electronic links. The first page of a Web site appears to be a flat, one-dimensional document, but it is not. It is hypertext, linked to other pages that will pop open at the click of the mouse. These links are embedded in "hot" words, phrases, and graphics, which lead the reader to related texts within the same Web site (relative links), graphics and other media (hypermedia), and other related Web sites (remote links). One of the greatest challenges in writing hypertext is to make it easy for readers to navigate through the links. Careful design is the key to constructing a successful Web site.

E X E R C I S E   1 9 . 1

Find two Web sites that you think are visually appealing. Describe what makes them interesting. How has each site's author used color, graphics, and other media? Bookmark the sites (see the Help box on page 434). Print copies for your classmates, or post them to your class's common directory. Discuss the sites with your classmates.

19b Plan your Web document

As you think about how you want your Web site to look, you should keep in mind the basic strengths and limitations of this medium. Although the Web allows you to be extremely creative in using graphics, photos, colors, and even video and sound, the Web authoring language HTML (HyperText Markup Language) is not as versatile as many desktop publishing programs. For example, constructing columns for a Web page is more difficult than producing a newsletter in columns using a word-processing program. In addition, the number of fonts available is limited.

1 Learning about design technology

You do not compose a Web site directly on the World Wide Web. Instead, you create the text and graphics in files on your computer's hard drive or on disk. When the files are complete, you transfer them from your computer or the lab's server to your college's Internet server or to an Internet service provider. Typically, this is accomplished using **FTP** (file transfer protocol) software. There are several versions of FTP software. Ask your instructor or lab supervisor for help in using FTP.

Before you begin your Web project, you should understand how Web files are stored on your college's or service provider's computer system. If your college provides Internet access for students and faculty, it will have dedicated storage space on a large computer that is used as the campus Internet server. You need to learn to save files using correct names, formats, and locations so that the Internet server can interpret them properly. Many servers require that filenames be written in all lowercase characters without any spaces or nonstandard symbols. Filenames should be simple and short. Your instructor or lab supervisor can help you learn the requirements of the server you will be using.

It is a good idea to create a project directory on your hard drive or disk in which to store all documents and graphics related to a particular writing project. As you construct your Web site, you will probably create a number of separate files that will later be connected to each other with hypertext links. If you keep them all in the same location on your disk or hard drive, you will find it easier to organize your Web site and you will be able to transfer all of the related files at once, using FTP, to your Internet server.

2 Deciding on a rhetorical stance

The kinds of writing decisions you must make in determining a rhetorical stance for your Web site are similar to those you confront in writing a paper (see 3a-2). If you are creating a Web site as a class assignment, analyze the requirements of the assignment. Think about what knowledge and information you will need in order to write a successful Web site. If you are to choose your own topic, think through what topics might be appropriate (see 8a).

Purpose

You should have a clear purpose in mind before you start. What specific goals do you want to accomplish with your Web site?

- Do you want to share your own creative work—such as poetry, fiction, music, or art—with others?
- Do you want to educate your audience about a topic that concerns you—such as the plight of the African elephant or the health dangers of nuclear waste?
- Do you want to provide a service to readers, such as a link to materials about a particular topic?

The Web has thousands of sites that focus on specific topics, such as individual authors, musicians, health and environmental concerns, and political causes.

Persona

If you look at various Web sites, you will notice that they convey distinctive impressions. Some are whimsical and humorous, while others are professional and serious. As you consider your own Web site, think about how you want to portray yourself.

- What kind of background would be most suitable for the site?
- What colors would be appropriate?
- Which images would enhance the site?
- What text would reflect best on you as an author?

Audience

Most readers want a balance between graphics and text. And they like a hypertext structure that allows them to choose their own path through the site. Finally, they appreciate helpful elements such as navigational buttons, which guide them through the site (see 19b-4). In thinking about your audience, consider the following questions:

- Is the text so dense that it is difficult to read on screen?
- Will the text be interesting to readers?
- Are there too many graphics?
- Does the site allow readers to skim and read selectively?
- Are there enough navigational tools and icons (see 19b-4, 19b-5)?

3 Storyboarding your Web presentation

Storyboarding—that is, making a drawing of a work's component parts—is a technique developed by journalists and graphic artists to plan newspapers, magazines, TV commercials, movies, and other media that mix text with graphics. One way to storyboard a Web site is to outline the text and sketch the graphics for each page on a 3" × 5" index card. Pin the cards to a bulletin board, and then move them around until you have a unified story. You can show the links between the cards by stretching a piece of string from one card to another. You also can storyboard by doing small, "thumbnail" page plans on a sheet of paper. Figure 19.2 illustrates the two major types of organizational structures used for Web sites: linear and hierarchical.

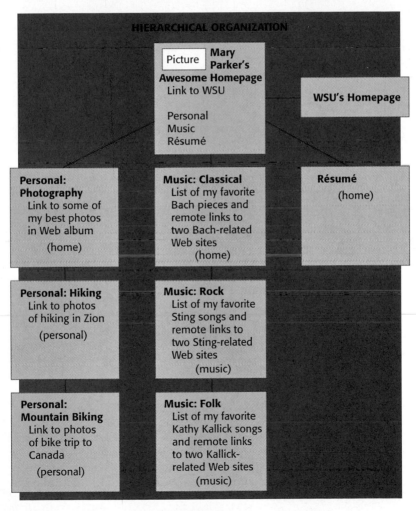

Figure 19.2   Two Storyboards for a Web Site

Planning a Web Site

Purpose

The general purpose of my Web site is

The specific objectives of my Web site are

1.

2.

3.

Persona

The persona I want my Web site to reflect is

The specific ways in which I will reveal my persona are

1.

2.

3.

Audience

The readers I want to address in my Web site are

The specific ways in which I will help my readers are

1.

2.

3.

In a simple Web site with a straightforward story, the pages can be linked in a linear sequence, with one leading to the next in a straight line. The pages of a more complicated Web site should be linked in a hierarchical structure.

4   Planning navigation

As Figure 19.2 shows, a Web site begins with a homepage (the first page), which also serves as an introduction to the site. It often includes several secondary pages (relative links), which are accessed from the homepage. Each page (designated by a different filename) should be no more than two or three screens long. For high-impact pages, try limiting the length to what will fit on one screen so that readers can see the entire page at a glance without scrolling.

Links are highlighted words and phrases within a document that allow readers to get from one page to another. **Navigational buttons** are graphical icons, such as arrows, symbols, buttons, or pictures, that will take readers in a particular direction or to a particular location. You may need to include text in addition to the graphic, as on the "Previous," "Contents," and "Next" buttons in Figure 19.3, if the purpose of the graphic is not readily apparent. Navigational buttons

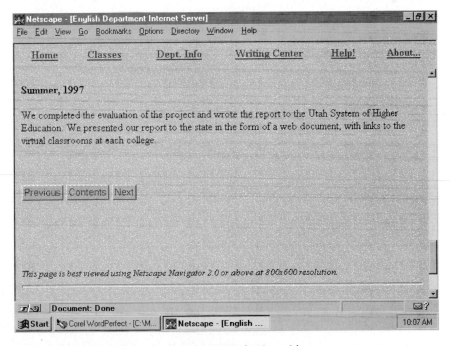

Figure 19.3   One Page of a Multipage Web Site with Navigational Buttons

may be included at the top, bottom, or one side of each page within a multipage Web site.

5   Applying the basic design principles to a Web site

Given the vast quantity of information on the World Wide Web, accommodating the busy, selective reader is imperative. The homepage is the first page readers will see when they access your site, so it should introduce your site concisely, providing an overview of the content and the organization of the site. Do not waste readers' time with decorative design elements; rather, include elements that will enhance readers' understanding of your message. Observing the basic design principles (see Chapter 17) exemplified by the three C's—clustering, contrasting, and connecting—may be even more critical to Web design than to print design. Note that some Web sites offer the reader a choice between two versions: one that is intensively graphical and one that is text-based. This option allows viewers to read the page even if they do not have a graphics-capable browser. You may want to consider text alternatives for your viewers (see 20b-5).

http://techwriting.
miningco.com
Yet another fantastic
Web design resource

Clustering: Grouping Closely Related Items

When designing Web pages, position chunks of information that are related in meaning close to one another. Emphasize clusters of information by placing white space around them. Group important elements at the top left and lower right of the screen, as readers of the English language are trained to move their eyes from left to right. Use numbered and bulleted lists to show relationships among items in a group.

Contrasting: Highlighting Differences

Use contrasting fonts or font sizes to highlight basic elements. For example, you might use the largest HTML headings (H1) for titles and smaller HTML headings (H3) for any subtitles (see 20b-2). Use colors or patterns to contrast other elements on the page.

Connecting: Relating Every Part to Some Other Part

Adhering to the principle of connectedness is especially important for Web authors. Since readers can access the pages within a site in any sequence, use a design template (see 18a, 18b-3) and a consistent graphic, title, or logo to foster visual connectedness. Furthermore, because readers can easily become lost when reading hypertext, it is important to include navigational aids to connect all pieces of the Web site. One way to do so is to provide a "home" link on every secondary page that takes readers back to the homepage (see Figure 19.3). You might also supply a site map on the homepage, showing how all of the pieces are connected (see Figure 19.4).

Figure 19.4   A Site Map

Some Dos and Don'ts of Web Design

Do organize your information before designing your site.

Do aim for pages that are no more than two or three screens long.

Do accommodate text-only browsers.

Do use a template and repeat visual elements.

Do use other Web pages to learn new code (see 20b).

Don't include unnecessary design elements.

Don't use graphics files of over 30 K (kilobytes).

Don't use copyrighted text or graphics without permission and acknowledgment.

It is a good idea to provide readers with alternative routes through the site's pages so that they are not forced along a single path. Busy, selective readers will appreciate the optional routes.

EXERCISE 19.2

Begin planning and designing a Web site. Set goals for your Web site by filling in the blanks in the box on Planning a Web Site. Then storyboard your Web site on 3" × 5" cards or by making a sketch in a notebook. Pay careful attention to planning the navigation through the various linked pages within your site. What pages need to be linked to each other? Draw arrows on your storyboard to indicate links. To ensure that readers are not left stranded on a page, plan to provide icons or buttons that lead them home or on to the next page.

FAQs

How do I save a word-processing document into
   HTML? (20a)
What is HTML code? (20b-2)
How do I add a link to another site? (20b-3)
Where can I find images to use? (20b-4)
How should I refine my Web site? (20c)

?

This chapter addresses some of the basics of writing for the Web—
how to use HyperText Markup Language (HTML) to construct basic
Web pages and how to add links that attach graphical images and
other documents to pages in a hypertextual "web."

The homepage of your Web site is the first page that readers
will come to when they locate your Web site by using its URL (uniform resource locator). From the homepage, you can provide **relative links** to secondary pages that you have written. You also can
include on your pages **remote links** to other Web sites located elsewhere on the Internet. Although one chapter cannot possibly discuss everything there is to know about writing for the Web, you will
be off to a good start if you work your way through the information
provided here.

20a Construct the individual Web pages

Once you have an overall plan for your Web site (see Chapter 19), you can begin to write the text for your Web pages. The text of a Web site—what it "says" to the reader—is as important as how it looks; Web pages communicate through both text and graphics. If you are familiar with HTML, you may decide to write directly in an HTML editor (see 20b-1). However, if you are new to Web authoring, you may wish to write the content in your word-processing program first. Once you have written the text, many word-processing programs will allow you to save it in the HTML format that is used on the World Wide Web (see the Help box). Saving the text as an HTML document will remove the word-processing codes that might interfere with reading the text in a Web browser; these codes will be replaced by HTML codes.

To illustrate writing for the Web, we will once again use Cecelia Chung's research paper. Cecelia first wrote her research paper, shown in Chapter 12, using a word-processing program. After she completed the paper, she decided to desktop publish it as a newsletter, shown in Chapter 18. Then, her instructor provided her with the opportunity to publish her research paper on the World Wide Web. To do so, she first saved the paper as an HTML document, causing her word-processing program to automatically convert the text

HELP

How do I save a word-processing document into HTML?

1. If your word processor allows you to save a document as HTML, just use its SAVE AS feature and specify HTML.

2. If your word processor will not save a file as HTML, then you must follow these steps:
   a. Highlight the text you want to convert to HTML, and copy it.
   b. Open your HTML editor, and paste the copied text into it.
   c. Use the HTML editor's features to format the text for the Web.

into an HTML document by adding important codes. This HTML document would form the basis for Cecelia's Web site.

20b   Use HTML to embed codes

HyperText Markup Language (HTML) is not really a language but rather a system for embedding codes into text. These codes tell a Web browser how to display the text in the browser window. To introduce yourself to HTML, surf the Web until you find a site that you think is lively and well designed. Then view the source code by following the instructions in the Help box. In writing the code for your own pages, you can analyze the code from other Web sites and use it as a model, as long as your

http://www.ncsa.
uiuc.edu/General/
Internet/WWW/
HTMLPrimer.html
One of the best intro-
ductory HTML tutorials
on the Web

HELP

How do I view the source code of a Web page?

1. On many browsers, you can view the HTML source code of a document by selecting the appropriate menu item. Often, the command VIEW or VIEW DOCUMENT SOURCE will bring the source code onto the screen. (See Figure 20.1 on page 436 for an example of HTML source code.)

2. If you cannot find a VIEW command, you can save the document to a file and then view the source code in a text editor (such as Windows Notepad) or word-processing program:

   a. On the FILE menu of your browser, select the SAVE or SAVE AS command to save the document to a file. (Remembering where you saved the file will be helpful when you want to view it.)

   b. Start your text editor or word-processing program.

   c. Open the file and display the code.

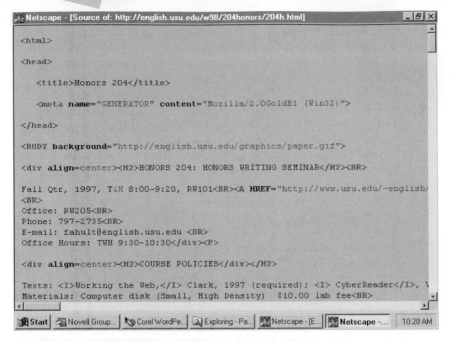

Figure 20.1   View of Source Code

pages are for educational and not commercial purposes. However, if you rely heavily on another Web page's design, be sure to credit the original site.

EXERCISE 20.1

Following the steps outlined in the Help box, look at the source code of a Web site you like. Notice how the author has coded various items on the page, including the graphics, the background, and the links. Save and print the source code. Bring a copy of the source code to class to share with your classmates.

1   Using an HTML editor

In order to work with the HTML document that was saved by your word-processing program, modifying it to suit your own purposes, you will need to know how to use an **HTML editor**—a software program designed to help writers insert the appropriate HTML codes into their documents. Although it is possible to insert all of the necessary HTML codes by typing them into your document in a word-processing program, HTML editors provide tools that greatly simplify the process. The screen in Figure 20.2 shows some of the HTML authoring tools that are provided by an HTML editor.

Many popular HTML editors are available in shareware versions that can be downloaded from the Internet. To find these HTML editors, consult the Shareware Directory, which is located at *http://www.sharewaredirectory.com*. Or, you can type "HTML Editors" as a search term in a search engine (see 9c-1). The various Internet browsers also include their own HTML editors, along with much useful advice and several tutorials on writing Web pages.

Many HTML editors provide two windows into your document—an editing window in which you edit the HTML code and a browser window (as shown in Figure 20.3 on page 438) in which you see how that code will be translated by an Internet browser. You can move between the editing window and the browser window as you work on your document. If the editor you are using does not provide

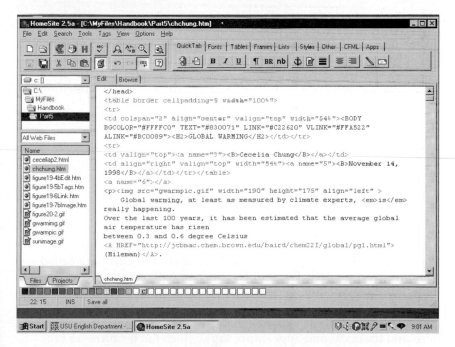

Figure 20.2   View from HTML Editor

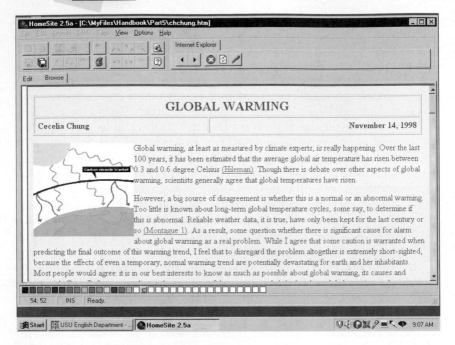

Figure 20.3   View from Browser Window

a browser window, you can view your Web document by launching your Internet browser and selecting OPEN PAGE IN BROWSER.

2   Using basic HTML codes

Most HTML codes, called **tags,** come in pairs: the first tag turns on the feature and the second turns it off. The second tag includes a slash, which the browser reads as signaling the end of that feature:

```
<B>Bold this sentence</B>
```

The pairs of HTML tags that bracket the text they affect are called **containers.** Any text between the containers will be affected by the code. It does not matter whether the tag is in lower- or uppercase letters. Tags fall into two basic categories: **document tags,** which tell the browser how to handle major elements of the document such as the head and the body, and **appearance tags,** which tell the browser how to handle the appearance of the text.

Document Tags

The major document tags are html, head, title, body, background, and comment.

1. *Creating a head, title, and body.* All HTML documents begin with the tag <html> and end with the tag </html>. Within these containers, the information is divided into two major categories: head and body. The head of the document contains the document's title, which appears at the top of the browser, outside the browser window. The body of the document includes the Web page's content—that is, everything that is seen within the browser window.

Your first task in composing a page is to enter the basic codes for these major document components. (If you save your word-processed document as an HTML file, these codes will be entered for you during the conversion process. However, you will need to type your title at the appropriate location in the HTML document.)

Go to the editing window of your HTML editor, and type the following tags exactly as they appear:

```
<html>

<head>

<title>Global Warming</title>

</head>

<body>

</body>

</html>
```

When you finish, you will not see anything in the browser window except a title on the top line of the screen, above the navigational buttons. This is because no actual text has been added to the body of the document.

2. *Creating a body background.* Frequently, Web authors include a background color or graphic that shows up behind the text on the page. Using backgrounds can greatly enhance the look of a page, provided they are light enough that the text shows through clearly. The background tag needs to be added within the first body tag (which immediately follows the second head tag) to tell the browser what background to include. The background color is specified with a color code. For example, the code for white is "#FFFFFF" and the code for black is "#000000." Most HTML editors will insert the appropriate code for you after you select a color. The code for the pale yellow color Cecelia selected for her on-screen background is

```
<BODY BGCOLOR="#FFFFC0">
```

If Cecelia had wanted to include the graphics file named "sunpic.gif" as a background instead of a color, the code would have read as follows:

```
<BODY BACKGROUND="sunpic.gif">
```

3. *Creating a document comment.* If you wish to insert a comment into your HTML document, you can do so by using a comment tag. Writers use comments to remind themselves of information or instructions they may want for future work on the document. Comments will not be read by the Web browser. Document comments like

```
<!--Remember to add the link here-->
```

can be included anywhere in an HTML document.

Here is what Cecelia's file looked like after she added text and more instructional tags for interpreting that text:

```
<html>
<head>
<title>Global Warming</title>
</head>
<BODY BGCOLOR="#FFFFC0" TEXT="#000000">
<H2>Cecelia's Global Warming Newsletter</H2>
<B>Global Warming: What, How, Why Care?</B>
<p>
Global warming, at least as measured by climate experts, is really happening.
Over the last 100 years, it has been estimated that the average global air
temperature has risen between 0.3 and 0.6 degree Celsius (Hileman). Though
there is debate over other aspects of global warming, scientists generally
agree that global temperatures have risen.
<!--Remember to add the link here-->
</body>
</html>
```

As you can see by looking at Figure 20.4, the view from the browser window looks quite different from the coded file, which would appear in the editing window. By moving back and forth between the two windows, you will be able to see how the tags you have inserted into the document are being read by the browser. In this way, you can make corrections as you work.

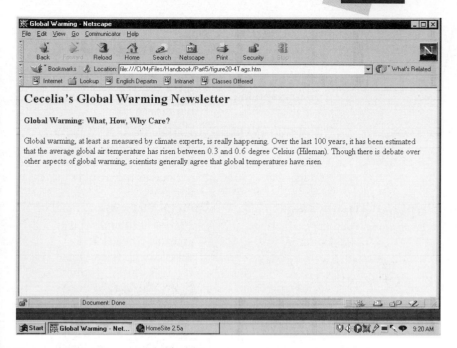

Figure 20.4   Browser Window After Document Tags Were Added

Appearance Tags

HTML documents do not include embedded codes for typographical distinctions such as boldface, underlining, and highlighting in the same way that word processors do. To create these typographical distinctions, you must use formatting, or appearance, tags. In the code that produced Figure 20.4, the <H2> and </H2> appearance tags tell the browser to create a standard heading that is large and bold, and the <B> and </B> appearance tags tell the browser to boldface the words contained between the tags.

An appearance tag also must be inserted to begin a new line. The <br> tag instructs the browser to break, or begin a new line. Because the HTML system of coding assumes blocks of texts, blank lines (rather than indents) are typically used to distinguish one paragraph from the next. The <p> tag instructs the browser to insert a blank line to designate a new paragraph. Most HTML editors allow you to insert the major appearance tags (which tell the browser how to format text) with a click of your mouse.

Major HTML Appearance Tags

<p>	Paragraph tag	Skip a line to start a new paragraph.
 	Line break tag	Start a new line (without leaving a blank line).
<hr>	Horizontal rule tag	Insert a long line stretching across the display window.
<H> and </H>	Heading tags	Put the information in a larger font and set it apart as a heading or subheading. (Headings can be numbered from <H1>, the largest heading, to <H5>, the smallest heading. The browser automatically skips a line following any heading.)
<blockquote> and </blockquote>	Block quote tags	Set the information apart as an indented quote.
<ul> and </ul>	Unordered list tags	Create a list of bulleted items. (Each item in the list must also be tagged. <L1> signals the first item in the list, which is automatically preceded by a bullet; <L2> signals the second item in the list, which is automatically preceded by a bullet; and so on.)
<ol> and </ol>	Ordered list tags	Create a numbered list rather than a bulleted list. (Items in the list must be tagged <L1>, <L2>, and so on, the same as for an unordered list.)

(continued)

`<em>` and `</em>`	Emphasis tags	Emphasize a word or phrase with italics or some other typographical distinction specified under STYLE.
`<strong>` and `</strong>`	Stronger emphasis tags	Strongly emphasize a word or phrase, usually through boldface.
`<cite>` and `</cite>`	Citation tags	Format the bracketed text as a citation line, usually in a different font.
`<B>` and `</B>`	Boldface tags	**Boldface the bracketed text.**
`<I>` and `</I>`	Italics tags	*Italicize the bracketed text.*
`<U>` and `</U>`	Underline tags	<u>Underline the bracketed text.</u>
`<tt>` and `</tt>`	Typewriter text tags	`Show the bracketed text in a monotype font, as a typewriter would.`

NOTE: The style for the `<em>`, `<strong>`, and `<cite>` tags can be adjusted by using the browser's STYLE feature in the OPTION menu. Be sure to insert a container tag with a slash where you want the feature turned off.

Here is Cecelia's code after she added more appearance tags; the view from the browser window is shown in Figure 20.5 on page 444.

```
<html>

<head>

<title>Figure 20.5 Cecelia's Page With Formatting Tags</title>

</head>

<BODY BGCOLOR="#FFFFC0" TEXT="#830071">
<center><H2>GLOBAL WARMING</H2>

</center>

<center><H4>Global warming: is it really happening?</H4>
</center>

<p>
```

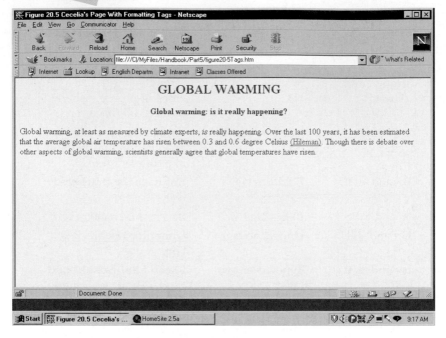

Figure 20.5   Browser Window After Appearance Tags Were Added

Global warming, at least as measured by climate experts, <I>is</I> really happening. Over the last 100 years, it has been estimated that the average global air temperature has risen between 0.3 and 0.6 degree Celsius <A HREF="http://jcbmac.chem.brown.edu/baird/chem22I/global/pg1.html">(Hileman)</A>.

<!--This is an example of an anchor, discussed in 20b-3, Creating Links-->

Though there is debate over other aspects of global warming, scientists generally agree that global temperatures have risen.

</body>

</html>

EXERCISE 20.2

Open your HTML editor and type in the basic codes used by Cecelia to create her homepage. Then change the text information to create a homepage of your own. Try out a number of the appearance tags

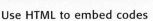
listed under Major HTML Appearance Tags. View your homepage in the browser window.

3 Creating links

To provide readers with links to other documents on the World Wide Web, to other locations within the same document, or to related documents within the same Web site, you use an anchor.

Basic Anchor

All links are coded with an **anchor** that includes anchor tags. The basic format of an anchor is as follows:

```
<A HREF="Web address">highlighted text</A>
  |        |         |          |          |
Anchor  Reference  URL      Hot text    Anchor
 tag      tag                            tag
```

The <A tag indicates the start of an anchor. HREF, which stands for Hypertext REFerence, refers to the address of the Web page with which you want to establish a link. In actual code, you would supply the Web address (URL) inside the quotation marks. The highlighted text becomes the **hot text,** linked to the referenced address. When the user clicks on the highlighted text, the browser will retrieve the document indicated in the hypertext reference. The </A> tag at the end closes the anchor.

In Figure 20.5, an anchor links Cecelia's homepage to the URL of her reference source. When a reader points to the highlighted words using a mouse, a small hand appears, indicating a link, and the URL for the link appears in the lower left-hand portion of the browser's screen. When the reader clicks on the highlighted words, the browser links to the URL indicated.

Jump-to Anchor

Anchors can link to destinations on the same Web page, allowing the reader to jump quickly from one part of the document to another. To jump within a single Web page, insert a jump-to tag instead of the URL inside the quotation marks:

```
              Anchor   Reference  Jump-to
               tag        tag       tag
You may wish to read my resume in the <A HREF="#JUMP-to-Resume">
resume</A> folder found later in this document.
  |          |
Hot link   Anchor tag
```

To show the browser where the linked text begins, you also need to include a destination tag (NAME), indicating the point to which the browser should jump:

```
<A NAME="JUMP-to-Resume"></A>
```
Anchor Name Jump-to   Anchor
 tag   tag   tag   tag

Anchor to Another Document in the Same Web Site

Often Web sites are made up of a series of documents that are linked to each other. When the documents all reside at the same location (in the same directory or folder) within the Web server, the links are called relative links and you do not need to include the entire URL. Simply supply the appropriate filename inside the quotation marks and then, in your highlighted text, describe the page you want linked.

```
<A HREF="ceceliap2.html">next page</A>
```
Anchor Reference Filename Hot text Anchor
 tag   tag   tag

Figure 20.6 shows relative links to subsequent pages of Cecelia's Web site.

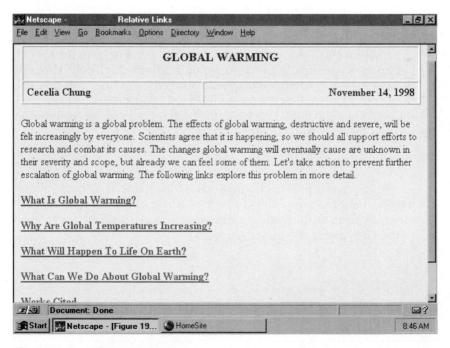

Figure 20.6   Relative Links

4 Locating images

Many wonderful images can be found on the Web. However, you need to be aware that all graphics, by virtue of their publication on the Web, are automatically copyrighted by the author. To use another person's graphics from a Web site, you must secure that person's permission. If an email address is included at a site, you can email the person and ask his or her permission to replicate the graphic on your site. Or, you may find a statement on the page permitting certain limited, noncommercial uses of the graphics. Remember: Using someone else's graphic on your own site without prior permission is a form of plagiarism (see 11a-3).

Many sites on the Web were created specifically to make images available for use by others. A search engine will help you locate these images. For example, the InfoSeek search engine includes an ImageSeek directory. Or, you can search by name for the image you are looking for. For example, if you are looking for a picture of a tiger, you can instruct the search engine to search for "tiger image." For more information on graphics, go to the PageWorks homepage at *http://www.snowcrest.net/kitty/hpages*, which discusses fair use of

How do I save an image from the Internet to my computer?

1. Locate an image on the Internet that is not protected by copyright.
2. Click your mouse button (in the case of PC users, the right mouse button) over the image.
3. Select SAVE IMAGE AS on the menu that comes up.
4. Name the graphic. (It will be in a gif or jpg format, since these are the graphical formats that can be read by Internet browsers.)
5. Choose an appropriate directory or folder on your hard drive or disk for the graphics file.

You can now insert your graphics file into an HTML document by using the image source tag (see 20b-5).

NOTE: Some operating systems and browsers will not provide a menu in response to a mouse click.

graphics and has links to numerous image directories on the Web. Other useful sites include the Clip Art Connection, at *http://www. clipartconnection.com/index.html*, and Barry's Clip Art Home Page, at *http://www.barrysclipart.com*. In addition to clip art, these sites include numerous backgrounds and animated graphics.

5 Inserting images

To include graphical images in a Web document, you need to in-sert a code, called an **image source tag,** in the body of the page telling the browser where to locate the image. Image source tags allow you to incorporate into your document many kinds of graph-ical images, such as photographs, clip art, drawings, icons, charts and graphs, and animations. The basic format for the image source tag is as follows:

```
<IMG SRC="gwarmpic.gif">
```

Image source tag   Filename

Include within the quotation marks the name of the image file you wish to use. The graphical image itself is not located within the HTML document; rather, it is linked to the document. The image source code tells the browser to retrieve the appropriate graphics file. You must use FTP (file transfer protocol) to transfer the image file to your Internet server at the same time you transfer your HTML document. And you must indicate the exact directory path in your image source tag so that the browser can locate the image's source. You may need to ask your instructor or lab supervisor for help with the transfer.

Here's Cecelia's code with the image source tags added; the view from the browser window is shown in Figure 20.7.

```
<html>

<head>

<title>Figure 20.7 Example of image source</title>

</head>

<--!What follows is a table definition, creating the table used for the banner.
See 20b-8-->

<table border cellpadding=5 width="100%">

<tr>

<td colspan="2" align="center" valign="top" width="54%">
<BODY BGCOLOR="#FFFFC0" TEXT="#830071">
```

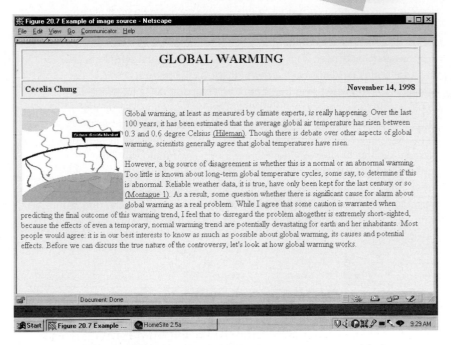

Figure 20.7   Browser Window After Image Source Tags Were Added

```
<H2>GLOBAL WARMING</H2></td></tr>

<tr>

<td valign="top"><B>Cecelia Chung</B></td>

<td align="right" valign="top" width="54%">
<B>November 14, 1998</B></td>

</tr>

</table>

<p><IMG SRC="gwarmpic.gif" width="190" height="175" align="left">
```

Global warming, at least as measured by climate experts, is
really happening. Over the last 100 years, it has been estimated that the
average global air temperature has risen between 0.3 and 0.6 degree
Celsius <A HREF="http://jcbmac.chem.brown.edu/baird/chem22I/global/
pg1.html">(Hileman)</A>. Though there is debate over other aspects
of global warming, scientists generally agree that global temperatures
have risen.

```
<p>
```

However, a big source of disagreement is whether this is a normal or an abnormal warming. Too little is known about long-term global temperature cycles, some say, to determine if this is abnormal. Reliable weather data, it is true, have only been kept for the last century or so <A HREF="http://www.envirolink.org/pubs/rachel/rhwn300.htm">(Montague 1)</A>. As a result, some question whether there is significant cause for alarm about global warming as a real problem. While I agree that some caution is warranted when predicting the final outcome of this warming trend, I feel that to disregard the problem altogether is extremely short-sighted, because the effects of even a temporary, normal warming trend are potentially devastating for earth and its inhabitants. Most people would agree. It is in our best interests to know as much as possible about global warming, its causes and potential effects. Before we discuss the true nature of the controversy, let's look at how global warming works.

</body>

</html>

Providing Text Alternatives to Images

Some Internet browsers, such as LYNX, cannot display images. These browsers will automatically display the word IMAGE in place of a graphic. If you would prefer that visitors to your site see descriptive text in place of an image, simply add an ALT tag within the image source tag:

<IMG SRC="sunpic.gif" ALT="Sun Graphic">

Image source tag   Filename   ALT tag   Alternative description
for text browsers

Aligning Images and Text

When you insert an image into a document, the written text that follows the image tag will normally be aligned with the bottom of the graphic. If you want the text to appear somewhere else, you need to include the appropriate instructions in your image source tag:

<IMG SRC="sunpic.gif" ALIGN="left" ALT="Sun Graphic">

Image source tag   Filename   Graphic alignment   Alternative description
for text browsers

The ALIGN="left" code tells the browser to put the graphic to the left of the text. The text will wrap around the graphic. Other possible alignments include "right," which puts the graphic to the right of the text, and "center," which centers the graphic. If you do not want the words to wrap around the graphic, use the <BR CLEAR="left"> or the <BR CLEAR="right"> code. If you just want the text to drop down below the graphic before it resumes, include the break tag <br> as the next command following the image source tag.

Sizing Your Images

Notice that the image source code that produced Figure 20.7 includes a size command (width="190" height="175"). This code tells the browser how many pixels wide and high the picture should be when displayed on the screen. To avoid distorting the image, it is better to size the graphic before you save it rather than using the size codes in your image source tag. However, size code can be used to make minor adjustments to the width and height of the image after it has been saved as a file.

6 Scanning pictures

You may wish to scan your own photographs or graphics and save them as graphics files. To use a scanner, you will need basic instructions from your lab supervisor or instructor. Remember that graphics files should not exceed 30–50 K (kilobytes) in size. For advice on how to size your graphic appropriately, see the Help box.

HELP

How do I resize an image?

1. Launch your graphics program, such as PhotoShop, and open the graphics file you wish to resize.
2. Find the menu item that allows you to resize images. You may be able to use either pixels or inches to adjust width and height.
3. Change any other aspects of the graphic that need revising, such as shading, contrast, and sharpness.
4. Check the size of the graphics file to make sure that you have not made the file too large to load easily on the Web (30–50 K is a reasonable size).
5. Resave the graphic. Be sure it is still in a gif or jpg format, since these are the graphical formats that can be read by Internet browsers.

7   Inserting your address

You should include your name, address, and the date of posting on any Web site you author (preferably at the bottom of the home-page). To do so, enclose your name, the dates on which the site was posted and updated, your email address, plus any copyright or ac-knowledgment information within a pair of address tags, <address> and </address>. In order to link your email address, use the fol-lowing code, entering the appropriate information within the ad-dress containers.

Address tag

<address> Cecelia Chung

Established: 14 November 1998, Last Updated: 25 January 1999

Anchor tag   Reference tag   Mail tag and address   Hot text   Close anchor tag

<A HREF=mailto:cecelia@cc.usu.edu>cecelia@cc.usu.edu</A>

</address>

Address tag

This coding follows the typical pattern of anchors: the first part after HREF tells the browser what email address should be linked, and the second part indicates the text to be highlighted on the page. When readers click on the highlighted text, they will be provided with an email screen that includes space to type an email message.

8   Using tables and frames

To place information appropriately on a page, you can use a table, which divides the page both vertically and horizontally into cells. The individual cells can vary in size, have borders of various types (either visible or invisible), and contain text or graphics. Tables allow Web authors to display information in vertical columns, for ex-ample. Look at the code used to produce the banner in Figure 20.7. Notice that the table code begins with the table command, including the border definition (5 pixels wide). Each new table row is indicated with the <tr> command; each table cell is defined with the table de-finition <td> command. Remember to close the code with the slash command (</td> or </tr>) once each cell is completed. Most HTML editors will help you create a table. Or, you can create a table in your word-processing program; then the table will be converted into HTML code automatically when you save the document as an HTML file. This is how Cecelia created the table for her banner.

Another way Web authors divide information is by using frames to put the information into different windows on the page. It is beyond the scope of this handbook to describe writing in frames. However, most HTML editors provide such instruction, as do guidebooks on HTML authoring.

9   Creating a template

Once you have created your homepage, you may want to design a template. It is easier for readers if all the pages at your site have the same look. The template should include elements such as background information, fonts, colors, headers, navigational buttons, author information, and your email address, if it will appear on all secondary pages at your site as well as your homepage. Save the template as a separate document, and title it template.htm. Then, each time you begin a new page for your site, you can open the template and use the SAVE AS option to save it under that page's designated filename.

Here is a sample template:

```
<html>

<head>

<title>Your site's name</title>

</head>

<BODY BGCOLOR="red">

<H2>The page's title as a number 2 heading</H2>

<!--Place the page's text here, including all relative and remote links.-->

<p>

<A HREF="http:URL of your homepage">Home</A>

<!--This link will return to homepage-->

<Address>

Created by (Your Name)<br>

Established: (date), Last Updated: (date)<br>

<AHREF=mailto:yourlogin@yourschool.edu>yourlogin@yourschool.edu</A>

</address>

<!--This links to your email address-->

</body>

</html>
```

EXERCISE 20.3

Using your homepage as a starting point, create a template. The template should include all features that will be consistent through-out your Web site. Delete the text of the homepage, leaving only the necessary codes. Your template should look something like the sample template in this section. Save the template as a document in an appropriate directory or folder.

20c   Refine your Web site

Once you have created your homepage and secondary pages, review them carefully to ensure that the text is correct, the links are accurate, the graphics are well located, and the overall look of the site is pleasing. Refine your Web site, using the HTML editor of your choice. Switch from the editing window to the browser window from time to time to see how the site is shaping up. It would be a good idea to review the design principles in Chapter 19 at this time.

WWW WEB

http://lcweb.loc.gov/global/html.html
The Library of Congress HTML resource page

1   Checking the text

Be sure that the text of your page is absolutely correct—there should be no spelling or punctuation errors. Some HTML editors do not have spell checkers, so you should carefully spell-check the text through your word-processing program prior to saving it as an HTML file. Proofreading is more difficult on screen than on paper, so you might want to print out a copy of your Web site for proof-reading. (See also the editing and proofreading advice in Chapter 5.) When you post your work to the Web, it will be published in a forum that can be read by anyone anyplace in the world. You want your site to reflect well on you and to highlight your abilities as a writer. In addition to being correct, information must be properly attributed; be certain that you give credit for anything that you have taken from other sources—whether the material is graphics or text, and whether the sources are on the Internet or in print.

2   Checking the relative links

The relative links—to other pages on the same site and to other sections of the same page—should all work in the HTML editor's browser window. If they do not, go back to the editing window and check your codes. Internet browsers are extremely literal—if a period or a quotation mark is missing in the code, the link will not work.

3 Checking the remote links

The remote links—to Web sites other than your own—also can be checked with the HTML editor's browser. However, first you need to launch your Internet browser and minimize it so that it is running in the background while you are working in the editor. If the Internet browser is open and running, your links from the HTML editor should work. If they do not, you need to go back to the HTML editing window to check your codes. The URL for the link must be typed *exactly* as it is listed at the site or the link will not work.

4 Checking the graphics

When you view your document in the HTML editor's browser window, the graphics that you have included should appear. If something is wrong, the browser will display an icon instead of the graphic. When an icon appears, first check the code for image source tags. Each graphics filename needs to be listed in the image source tag in exactly the same way as it is in your folder. Second, check the location of your graphics file. Either the graphics file must be in the same folder on your disk or hard drive as the HTML document file or you must provide the exact path, including all subfolders. If the graphics file is in a different folder (perhaps an image folder), the browser will not be able to locate it without such a path. When you uncover a problem, the easiest thing to do—rather than changing the path in all your image source links—is to move or copy the graphic into the appropriate folder.

5 Checking the overall look

As a final check, open your Web site in your Internet browser (using the OPEN FILE IN BROWSER option from the FILE menu). Try to read the site as an objective reader might. Does the rhetorical stance you wish to portray (persona, purpose, audience) come across? Ask a friend, a classmate, or your instructor to view your site and give you feedback. Did he or she have any trouble with navigation? What impression did your site leave?

20d Transfer your site to an Internet server

Prior to sending the Web files to your Internet server, be certain that your site is exactly as you want it to be. Once the files are on the server, they will stay there until you send them again. You cannot edit your Web site from the server. Rather, you have to edit the files in the HTML editor and transfer them again, overwriting the original files. Use FTP (file transfer protocol) to send your Web files to the Internet server.

E X E R C I S E   2 0 . 4

Check your Web documents carefully. Open the documents in your Internet browser and have readers give you feedback. Finally, FTP all of the files in your Web site directory, including the graphics files and secondary page files, over to your Internet server.

PART 5

SPECIAL PURPOSE WRITING

Communicating via Computer Networks

Is email the same thing as the Internet? (21a-1)
What is a newsgroup? (21a-2)
How can I find a friend's email address? (21b-2)
What is netiquette? (21b-3)

The Internet—or the Net, as it is affectionately called—is a system of interconnected computer networks. It allows users to communicate with each other through a variety of forums:

- Electronic mailing lists
- Bulletin boards and newsgroups
- Real-time writing
- Collaborative writing via networks
- Personal email

21a   Log on to networks

The most common ways of logging on to a network are through a direct link and through a telephone link. To connect to a network through a telephone line, many people use a modem. To use a modem,

How do I find a mailing list about a particular topic?

1. To check via the Web, go to one of the following addresses: *http://tile.net/lists* or *http://www.liszt.com.*
2. To check via email:
   a. Address a message to listserv@listserv.net, leaving the subject line blank. (When using listserv software, you do not need a subject.)
   b. As your message, type "list global" or "list global/[your subject]." For example, if you were interested in lists having to do with the subject of writing, you would type "list global/writing." The listserv will respond with a listing via email.
3. When you identify a list you would like to join, follow the instructions in the next Help box.

you first need an Internet service provider that will supply you with a connection to the Internet. Many such providers exist; investigate several to find the provider that works best for you. Often, colleges and universities provide the academic community with direct Internet access from campus labs, faculty offices, classrooms, and dorm rooms. At some schools, students are given an electronic mailing address during orientation when they first arrive on campus.

1 Electronic mailing lists

If you are a computer user, you probably are already familiar with electronic mail, or **email,** which is the most basic form of Internet communication. Corresponding via email is an excellent way to keep in touch with friends, classmates, and instructors. Personal email is discussed in more detail in 21b. In this section, we discuss the use of **mailing lists,** which are special-interest email lists that distribute messages simultaneously to their many participants, or subscribers.

There are thousands of mailing lists on the Internet. Mailing lists are begun by people with a common interest, who want a forum in which to talk to each other. Lists can facilitate committee meetings,

How do I subscribe to a mailing list?

1. Enter the listserv's address on the "to" line of your email form, leaving the subject line blank.

2. Type the following as your message: "subscribe [listname Firstname Lastname]." For example, if John Doe were subscribing to the WPA-L list, he would type this message: "subscribe WPA-L John Doe."

3. Send your email message. The mailing list will contact you with further instructions.

4. Save these instructions, since they will also tell you how to "unsubscribe."

fan club meetings, scholarly discussions, and even class discussions and research projects. For example, first-year writing students might want to find a mailing list that will help them better understand a research paper topic. (See the Help box on page 458 for details on finding relevant mailing lists.)

One subscriber or group "hosts" the list, providing the software necessary to start and maintain it. The most commonly used software is called listserv. **Listserv** software facilitates group discussions and stores and indexes those discussions for later access by participants. When listserv is working well, you will not notice its operation.

Many lists allow anyone who wishes to subscribe to do so. Other lists are selective about their participants and limit the number who can join. In either case, you must subscribe to the list in order to join the discussion or access its archives. (See the Help box for instructions on subscribing to a mailing list.)

http://www.catalog.com/vivian/interest-group-search.html
A searchable list of listservs

Some lists are moderated; that is, an individual designated as the list's moderator evaluates the appropriateness of messages before they are sent out to everyone on the list. Other lists are unmoderated; that is, anyone can send any message to the others on the list. You should realize, however, that sometimes mailing lists entail a considerable investment of time. Once you subscribe, all of the group's messages will appear in your electronic mailbox. If the group is large and active, your mailbox will quickly fill up with messages. For this reason, you should be selective about the number of mailing lists that you subscribe to. When you first join a list, it is a good idea to spend a few days just reading the messages of others—an activity called **lurking**. In this way, you will get a sense of the discussions and the subscribers.

Mailing lists can help you become informed about topics currently under discussion in a particular field, as you prepare for a research paper project. For example, joining a mailing list of psychologists would provide you with information on the hot topics in psychology. You also can use mailing lists to do preliminary background research on a topic. However, take care not to request information that you could easily find in books or journals, as this will certainly annoy the other subscribers. (See 21b-3 for more on netiquette, and see 21b-4 for information on email formatting.)

If you use information from a mailing list in a research paper, the posting must be cited either in the text itself or in your list of works cited (see Chapter 13). Do not quote anyone's mailing list posting without his or her permission. Here is an example of a listserv posting, reprinted with permission of Barrett M. Briggs.

From: IN%"WPA-L@ASUVM.INRE.ASU.EDU" "Writing Program Administration"

1-DEC-1997 09:20:43.95

To: IN%"WPA-L@ASUVM.INRE.ASU.EDU"

CC:

Subj: Resuscitating Trigger

Return-path: <owner-wpa-l@ASUVM.INRE.ASU.EDU>

Date: Mon, 01 Dec 1997 09:08:27-0700

From: BMB <bmbriggs@CCIT.ARIZONA.EDU>

Howdy,

To the extent that we can discern the elective from the required: Are students required to attend this university at this time and in this place? No, they elect to register. Do they elect to commit to a program of instruction? Yes, they elect to accept program requirements. They elect whether to attend class or not. They elect the extent to which they participate in instructional activities. They elect ways in which to reap the rewards of having accepted and fulfilled program requirements.

In what sense, sphere or context are students required to take first year composition? Don't we all (fairly often) elect to put ourselves into situations where, once there, we are required to behave in certain ways? Also, I suggest to my students, vigorously and often, that no class is more important than one such as first year composition (fyc) that helps them understand how to manipulate, consciously, the world for their benefit, and how people will try to manipulate them ("manipulate" in the neutral sense, that is, meaning: "to manage and handle skillfully"). Even if "required" meant something akin to being arbitrarily forced, I'd say fyc should be required, if only to give students a dawning sense of the value and power of language consciously manipulated and consciously interpreted.

Barrett M. Briggs

Tucson

EXERCISE 21.1

Following the directions found in the Help boxes in this section, find and join a mailing list on a topic that interests you. Read the conversation for a few days—that is, lurk on the list without posting any messages yourself. What is the thrust of the discussion? Does it surround a controversy? Write a brief summary of the discussion to share with your classmates.

2   Bulletin boards and newsgroups

Like mailing lists, bulletin boards provide a forum for discussion. However, instead of sending email messages to subscribers, **bulletin boards** post messages electronically for anyone to access and read. There is no need to subscribe individually to a bulletin board.

A **newsgroup** is a type of bulletin board consisting of a collection of email messages tied to a specific topic. Usenet has the most extensive array of public newsgroups. In order for you to access Usenet newsgroups from campus labs, your college must subscribe to them. Newsgroups are organized by topic under several umbrella categories, indicated by a prefix.

Umbrella category	Topics covered	Example
talk	discussion of issues	talk.politics.gun
alt	alternative topics	alt.smokers
comp	computer topics	comp.sys.mac
rec	recreational topics	rec.sport.golf
soc	social topics	soc.culture.Kurdish

cnet
21a

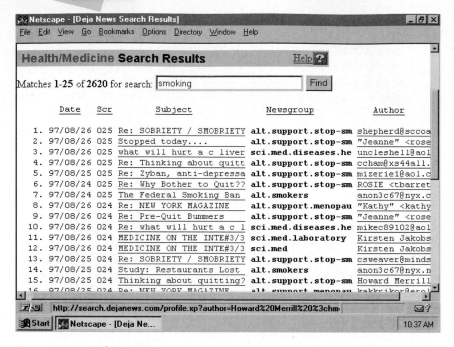

Figure 21.1   Deja News Screen

One way to access newsgroups is through an Internet browser.
You may need to configure the Internet browser to allow you to
read the newsgroups. Once your system is appropriately config-
ured, you might choose NETSCAPE NEWS from the WINDOW menu, for
example, to get a listing of the news-
groups to which your college subscribes. There are literally thousands
of Usenet newsgroups to choose from.
For a directory of Usenet newsgroups,
see Liszt (the mailing list directory) at
http://www.liszt.com. Like mailing lists,
newsgroups can be especially useful as you begin to think about topics for essays and research papers. To search Usenet groups by subject, you can use a search engine such as Lycos, at *http://www.lycos.
com*, or Deja News, at *http://www.dejanews.com*. Figure 21.1 shows a
sample Deja News screen.

WWW
WEB
MMM

http://www.webcom.
com/impulse/list.html
All-in-one resource for
email and listserv

EXERCISE 21.2

If your college subscribes to Usenet newsgroups, choose one on a
topic that interests you and read a few of the postings. What is being

discussed? Who are the participants in the newsgroup? Print out a few postings to discuss with your classmates, and then brainstorm as to how you might use bulletin boards in a research project (see Chapter 10).

3   Real-time writing

The communication tools discussed thus far (email, mailing lists, bulletin boards, and newsgroups) are lacking in one respect: they do not allow for conversations in real time. With mailing lists and newsgroups, users post their messages, and others access those messages at their convenience. However, Internet users sometimes like to exchange messages more rapidly, as if they were conversing face to face. To provide a more conversational forum, a variety of real-time Internet tools have been developed. One such tool is **IRC** (Internet relay chat). To use IRC, you need to know the Internet address and port number of an IRC server. Once connected to IRC or a similar chat program, each participant opens a "chat" window on his or her computer. An IRC chat directory can be found at the following address: *http://www.liszt.com*.

Anyone who has his or her chat window open can read what the participants on the same IRC channel are saying. The words that are typed

> WWW WEB
>
> http://www.du.org/
> cybercomp.html
> Associated with Diversity U, a site on composition in cyberspace, with a focus on MOOs and MUDs

scroll onto the screen for others to read and respond to. In this way, Internet users can chat with each other. The only delay is the time it takes for a message to travel through phone lines to the participants' computers. However, depending on how many participants are in a given chat room, the delay can be considerable—and result in a strange conversation in which participants have to wait several seconds or even minutes between replies. Figure 21.2 on page 464 shows a sample Internet chat window.

Another type of real-time writing tool used on the Internet is provided by MUDs and MOOs. Both a **MUD** (Multi-User Dimension) and a **MOO** (MUD Object Oriented) define a space on the Internet where users can interact with each other simultaneously (hence the name *Multi-User Dimension*). Those who wish to participate in a MUD or a MOO need to establish a remote connection between their own computer and the computer that controls the MUD's or MOO's Internet space. Such a connection can be established by using telnet or other Internet software that provides an interface, such as Pueblo.

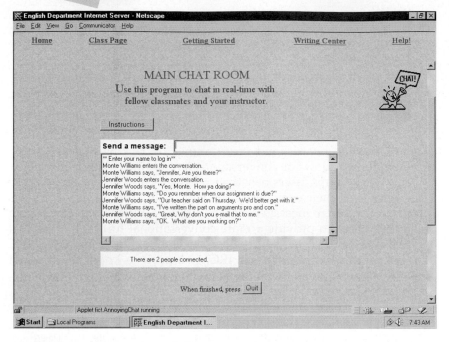

Figure 21.2   Internet Chat Window

You need to know the Internet address and port number of the MUD/MOO server. Instructions for connecting to a MUD or a MOO vary considerably from site to site. You can use an Internet search engine to find out more about the MUDs and MOOs that are currently available.

MUDs and MOOs were originally developed to allow users in different locations to play computer games with each other. Increasingly, these forums are being used for educational and business purposes. For example, some colleges, such as Salt Lake Community College, have created MOO spaces in which students can meet to access class assignments or discuss course readings. As shown in Figure 21.3, the Online Writing Center at Salt Lake Community College provides students with a MOO for getting assistance with writing and attending writing classes taught at a distance.

EXERCISE 21.3

Access the Salt Lake Community College Writing Center MOO at its Web site *http://www.slcc.englab.wc.edu*. Log on to the site as a guest. Move around in the site's various rooms and read the conversations you find there. What are the students and instructors talking about?

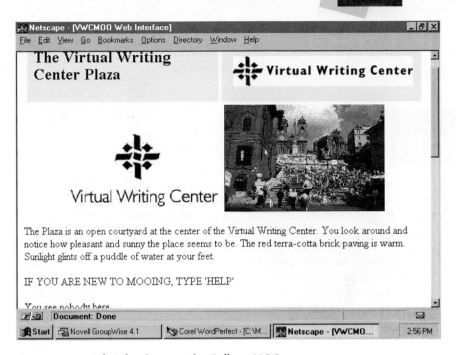

Figure 21.3   Salt Lake Community College MOO

Join in the discussion, if you would like. Discuss your experience with classmates. How might this medium be used to enhance class discussions or peer reviews?

4   Collaborative writing via networks

Increasingly, Internet users are taking advantage of software designed to help writers work collaboratively via networks. Using collaborative writing software, several writers can work simultaneously on the same document. For example, suppose a writer wants advice from an editor on a chapter of her book. Both the author and the editor can open up the chapter in a collaborative writing program. Then, in a chat window, they can discuss changes that might be made. When the writer makes a change on the document, it shows up on both screens at the same time. Each person's cursor becomes a unique symbol so that it is clear who is doing what with the text. The editor need not even possess the particular software in which the chapter was written; the collaborative writing software will display pages from any other application. Although few colleges are currently using this software, it is gaining acceptance in the workplace.

EXERCISE 21.4

If collaborative writing software is available to you, try revising a paper together with a friend. Discuss the experience with your classmates.

21b   Build community through electronic mail

Using electronic mail, you can communicate with others around the world, much faster than through traditional "snail mail." Because it is fast, easy, and relatively inexpensive, email is enormously popular.

There may be several options available to you for accessing your email. Through its email program (called a **mail client**), your college may provide you with access to an email account on its Internet server. Or, you may use your Web browser's email program to read your mail. Finally, you may have access to a local mail client that resides on your own computer, such as Eudora or GroupWise.

1   Collaborative work or study groups

Email is a great way to maintain contact with classmates in a work or study group. Email addresses have two parts: the user name and the domain name. These parts are separated by the @ sign, as in mparker@cc.mtu.edu. Collect your classmates' email addresses just as you might their phone numbers. Store these addresses in the address book on your mail client so that you do not have to retype them each time you want to send a message. Most mail clients allow you to store multiple addresses in an address book under one heading, such as "study group." Each time you select the group name, all of the addresses will appear in the "to" slot of your SEND MAIL dialogue box.

If you are involved in a joint writing project, forming an email discussion group can facilitate collaboration with others in the group. Suppose you were assigned a project that involved working with a group of other students to write and build a Web site. Using a study group address, you could email to your entire study group the first draft of your Web page for their review. Your mail client probably offers the option INCLUDE EMAIL MESSAGE IN REPLY. That option would place the entire message, in this case the draft of your Web page, into the reply window. Members of your study group could add their comments and suggestions in ALL CAPS to make them stand out

How do I send an email message?

1. Open the email program (mail client) that you wish to use. Some common ones are Pine, Eudora, Pegasus, and GroupWise.

2. Select NEW MESSAGE, and type the recipient's address in the "to" or "send" slot. (To reply to a message, click your mouse on the REPLY option rather than NEW MESSAGE. Your mail client will supply the address automatically.)

3. Type the subject on the "subject" line (for example, "Your question about our paper" or "Responding to Sara's point").

4. Type the full address of any other recipients on the "cc" line.

5. Type your email message, and then send it.

NOTE: If the program notifies you that the message has been returned, check the address in one of the directories listed in 21b-2.

from the draft itself before sending their replies back to you. By selecting the REPLY TO ALL option, they could send the reply message to everyone in the group, not just to you. Or, by selecting the REPLY TO SENDER option, they could choose to send their replies to you.

EXERCISE 21.5

Using your mail client, set up a study group with a group address that includes the addresses of all members of the group. Mail a few test messages to each other, and use the REPLY function to reply to everyone in the group. Discuss the ways in which this email study group could help you with your class work.

2 Email addresses

To find the address of a student on your own campus, go to your college's homepage on the Web and look for an email directory of students. To search for the address of someone on another campus, go to one of the Web search engines and type in the name of the college as the search term. For example, if you wanted to contact a friend at Washington University, you would type "Washington University" as the search term. Once you found and opened the university's home-page, you could look for your friend's address in the student email directory. Note, however, that not all schools allow outside access to their student directories.

Here are some other Internet sites that offer help in locating email addresses:

Bigfoot	*http://www.bigfoot.com*
WhoWhere	*http://www.whowhere.com*
Four 11	*http://www.four11.com*
Internet Address Finder	*http://www.iaf.net*
Usenet Addresses Database	*http://usenet-addresses.mit.edu*
Lycos PeopleFind	*http://www.lycos.com/emailfind.html*
World Email Directory	*http://www.worldemail.com*

Such email directories are not always comprehensive. If you cannot find someone's email address by using directories, contact that person directly via regular mail or telephone and ask for his or her email address.

EXERCISE 21.6

Look in several email directories for the email address of a friend or acquaintance in another state. Discuss your results with classmates. How successful were you? What problems, if any, did you have? Brainstorm about other similar searches you might want to conduct. Describe what you learned, in the course of this exercise, that might be useful in the future.

3 Email etiquette

Internet users have developed a set of rules to help keep the medium friendly and courteous. These rules have been nicknamed **netiquette.**

http://www.albion.com/netiquette/
A great netiquette homepage

If your class is using email for collaborative work, familiarize yourself with any rules your college may have about email use. Behaviors that are not acceptable in other settings, such as verbal or sexual harassment, will not be tolerated on the Internet. It is not appropriate to use your class-mates' email addresses for chain letters, advertising, or other similar purposes. Nor is it appropriate to use those addresses to ask someone out on a date. Also, be sensitive about "flaming"—writing angry or abusive messages. If you are flamed, do not reply in kind. Either ignore the message or respond calmly.

Netiquette

- Always type a subject heading for your email that describes the message's content. Use the REPLY function to maintain continuity on a topic.

- Use an appropriate salutation. For informal messages, you can just begin with the person's name. For business messages, use the standard business salutation and form of address (for example, "Dear Ms. Smith:").

- Keep messages brief and to the point.

- End messages with your name and email address. Keep this information in your AUTOTEXT file or store it as a macro or the equivalent in your word processor. Alternatively, if your email program allows you to create and store a signature file, you can insert it at the end of your message with a click of the mouse. (Note: Some mail clients automatically attach the signature file, once it has been established.)

- Do not forward a message you received unless you have a compelling reason to do so. When people send you an email message, they are communicating with *you*, not with some undetermined person to whom you might forward the message.

- Do not quote from an email message unless the writer has given you explicit permission to do so.

- Be careful about punctuation and spelling—but also be tolerant of others' errors. Email is less formal than many other types of writing, and many people neglect to proofread their messages because of the conversational nature of the medium.

- Avoid using all capital letters in email messages because it is the electronic equivalent of shouting. Do not overuse punctuation—especially exclamation points.

- Carefully consider the potential effect of your message before you send it. If there is any chance that the message could be misinterpreted by the reader, take time to revise it.

4 Email shortcuts

Because email is conversational, users have evolved a kind of shorthand to get their meanings across. You may encounter some of the following acronyms:

BTW   by the way
FWIW   for what it's worth
FYI   for your information
IMHO   in my humble opinion
TIA   thanks in advance
TTFN   ta ta for now
TTYL   talk to you later

Email diacritics are the asterisks, emoticons, and other characters used to add emphasis or other flavoring to email messages. Creativity is the rule here, so we will only mention some common practices.

In lieu of underlining or italicizing, putting asterisks before and after a word or phrase is the most common way to indicate emphatic or contrastive intonation.

That exam was *way too hard*, if you ask me!

(Notice that the final asterisk precedes the comma.) To increase the force of the emphasis, you can put asterisks around *each* of the words in the phrase.

That exam was *way* *too* *hard*, if you ask me!

You also can surround the words you want to emphasize with other unusual characters, as in "#way too hard#" or "_way_too_hard_." Some people use UPPERCASE LETTERING for emphasis, but many people consider uppercase lettering to be too much like shouting.

Emoticons are those combinations of standard keyboard characters that look like faces when they are turned sideways. They are appropriate only in informal messages to friends. Some word-processing programs will automatically convert :-) to ☺ and :-(to ☹. Check your FORMAT menu.

Some Common Emoticons

:-)	smile	;-)	wink	:-(	chagrin
:-o	shock	:-/	sarcasm	>:D	demonic laugh

As always, be conscious of your audience when using acronyms and emoticons. Include them only when the situation is appropriately informal.

5   File attachments

Many email systems allow you to attach files or documents to your messages. Check your mailing system for an ATTACHMENT option. Using attachments is a convenient way to send your work to a classmate for peer review. One of the advantages of using attachments over the copy-and-paste method of incorporating text into an email message is that much of your word-processing format can be preserved. Instructors may ask that assignments be turned in as attachments so that they can see the exact formatting of your bibliography, for example, or the way in which you have formatted subheadings in your paper.

Sending attachments can pose problems, however. Compatibility between email systems is often an issue. For an attachment to be read by an email recipient, the sender's and the recipient's mailing systems must be compatible. Some experimenting may be needed before you can send attachments successfully. But it is worth the effort to investigate this feature because of the ease with which you can then share your writing (see 4c).

EXERCISE 21.7

Using the ATTACHMENT feature of your email program, send a classmate a paper you are currently working on. In the email message itself, specify the kind of advice you would find helpful. Discuss in person the success you had sending the attachment. Describe how you could use attachments to help you write and revise your papers.

CHAPTER

22

Business Correspondence and Reports

FAQs

How do I write a good business letter? (22a)

How do I prepare an electronic résumé? (22c-3)

What's the difference between a memo and a report? (22e)

How do I use a document template? (22e)

?

Writing at work differs significantly from writing in school. Instead of writing for a single reader (the instructor) who is obligated to read and evaluate your entire written document, you often must write for multiple readers who are under no such obligation. These readers may choose to only glance at your writing, rather than read it thoroughly. Thus, when writing letters, memos, reports, proposals, and other forms of business correspondence, you must get to the point quickly and convey your message clearly and concisely.

http://owl.english.
purdue.edu/writers/
by-topic.html#job

A collection of useful handouts from Purdue's OWL

22a   Write concise and professional business letters

People write business letters for a variety of purposes: to make an inquiry or a request, to complain, to apply for a job, to issue an announcement, to sell something, to respond to a previous letter. Letters typically are addressed to a specific person, but they may be circulated to other readers as well. Thus, you should make the purpose of your letter clear at the outset, and you should anticipate the possibility that people other than the addressee (an assistant, for example) might read it. Be sure to provide whatever background information these readers might need. Be clear and concise (see Chapter 34), and try to strike a friendly, courteous, and professional tone (see 40c).

The appropriate format and style depend on the medium. Letters sent by post or by fax tend to be more formal and have a more traditional format than letters sent by email. (See Chapter 21 for a discussion of email.)

The traditional business letter is printed on white or light-colored 8½" × 11" stationery, with every line starting at the left margin (this is known as the **full block format**). If you do not have letterhead stationery, put your return address at the top of the page, also on the left margin. Before typing the name and address of the recipient, put the date. Be sure to spell the recipient's name correctly. If you are not sure how to spell it, call his or her office and ask someone there rather than relying on a spell checker. For the salutation, use *Dear Mr. ___* or *Dear Ms. ___* or an appropriate title. Avoid using either a first name (unless you know the recipient personally) or a generic term like *Dear Sir.* If you are unsure of the recipient's gender, use the full name: *Dear Terry Norman.* If you do not know the recipient's name, use an institutional title or position: *Dear Service Department.* The body of the letter should be divided into block paragraphs, though you may want to use an indented list to draw the reader's attention to special information. Use a conventional closing like *Sincerely, Sincerely yours,* or *Yours truly.* After leaving enough space for your signature, type your name and any other pertinent information, such as your email address, your phone number, and the word *enclosure* if any items are enclosed. A sample business letter in the traditional format appears in Figure 22.1 on page 474.

2222 Stockton Street
Austin, TX 78701

January 10, 1999

Margaret Weston, Owner
Cliffside Climbing Gym
3345 S. Laurel Street
Waco, TX 76712

Dear Ms. Weston:

I am a senior in Communication at the University of Texas. For my class project in market research, I am studying the recent proliferation of climbing gyms in the United States. I would like to conduct several case studies of climbing gyms and am writing to see if I may include your gym among them.

I became aware of your gym while searching the Internet. You have an excellent Web site, but I need more information than any Web site can provide, hence this request for an on-site visit.

To conduct my research, I would like to interview you, your assistants, and several of your regular clients. This interviewing would be done at a convenient time for all and would be as nonintrusive as possible. Any information I gather would be held in strict confidentiality.

I sincerely hope you can help me with this research. Unless I hear from you first, I will call next week to see if you can accommodate my request.

Yours truly,

Lorinda Brown
lorinda.brown@emx.cc.utexas.edu
Tel. (555) 580-5625

Figure 22.1   Sample Business Letter

Guidelines for Email Letters

1. Use the subject line to orient the reader.
2. Provide any necessary background information in the first sentence; if appropriate, reference previous correspondence.
3. Quickly establish your purpose.
4. Focus on the main point, and repeat it at least once.
5. Use simple sentences and short paragraphs.
6. Use personal pronouns and active verbs.
7. Keep it short.

Business letters sent by email should satisfy the same general requirements as other business letters: a clear purpose, sufficient background information, correct grammar and spelling, a friendly yet professional tone. But email business letters usually are less formal than traditional ones and have a different format. Since email readers are likely to scroll quickly through a long message and may miss key items if they are buried in the text, email letters should focus on a single topic and be short enough, if possible, to fit on one screen. Always remember to observe proper netiquette and to consider your audience's reaction to the message (see Chapter 21).

http://www.colostate.edu/Depts/WritingCenter/references/documents/bletter/page2.htm
A great guide to writing business letters

22b   Write specifically tailored letters of application

Knowing how to write a good application letter is crucial to the job-seeking process. An application letter is a kind of sales pitch, where the product you are selling is yourself. It usually is the first thing a prospective employer sees from you, and, of course, you want to make a good first impression. There is no room for error in a letter of application—no room for beating around the bush, shyness, misrepresentations, or misspellings.

Usually, a letter of application is accompanied by a résumé and includes some of the same information. But unlike the résumé, the letter should be tailored to one specific job. Whereas a résumé contains a full summary of your past accomplishments, the letter includes only those accomplishments that are relevant to the job you are applying for. The tone of the letter should be polite, confident, and enthusiastic, but not pushy.

WEB

http://www.io.com/
~hcexres/tcm1603/
acchtml/lettov.html
All about business correspondence and résumés

A letter of application has the same general format as a business letter. It should be brief (no more than one page). The first paragraph should state clearly what position you are applying for. The next paragraph or two should describe your primary credentials for the position. The closing paragraph should express your desire for an interview and give the reader information about your availability. A sample letter of application is shown in Figure 22.2.

22c   Write densely but appropriately packed résumés

A **résumé** is a concise summary of an individual's accomplishments, skills, experience, and personal interests. It is more complete and inclusive than a letter of application; the same résumé can be sent to more than one potential employer, whereas each letter of application should be different.

ESL Note: In some countries, a résumé may include an individual's age, marital status, religious affiliation, and other highly personal information. In the United States, such information is considered too personal and so should not be included.

A résumé should be densely packed with appropriate information. You should neither pad a résumé with irrelevant information nor include any information that is not true. Most résumés use five standard categories of information: (1) Position Desired or Objective, (2) Education, (3) Experience or Employment, (4) Related Activities, and (5) References, in that order. If you think your experience or employment history is more impressive than your educational achievements, you may want to reverse the position of those two categories. The entries within any one category normally are listed in reverse chronological order (that is, the most recent achievement is listed first). For most students and other workers just starting out, a résumé should be no longer than a single full page.

2222 Stockton Street
Austin, TX 78701

February 4, 1999

Mr. Jeffrey Lee
Director of Marketing Training
Future Consumer, Inc.
4444 North Sycamore Avenue
Los Angeles, CA 90009

Dear Mr. Lee:

I am writing to apply for acceptance into your marketing training program. I am especially impressed with the program's emphasis on market research, product planning, and catalog sales. As a marketing major at the University of Texas, I believe I am ready to undertake this challenge and would welcome the opportunity to prove myself.

Marketing has been a major focus of my college and work experience. My studies have provided a strong foundation in communication and business. I have also had experience in product testing and merchandising through my jobs in market research and retailing and have been on the "receiving end" of customer indecision and anxiety. My ability to handle difficult customers earned me a promotion from direct sales to sales management.

My résumé is attached. I will be graduating in early June and would be available for training immediately thereafter. I look forward to hearing from you.

Sincerely yours,

Lorinda Brown
lorinda.brown@emx.cc.utexas.edu
Tel. (555) 580-5625

enclosure

Figure 22.2   Sample Letter of Application

An alternative to the standard résumé just described is the **functional résumé,** in which certain skills are emphasized through categories like Computer Skills, Management Skills, and Language Skills or Ability to Solve Problems, Ability to Motivate Others, and Ability to Maintain Diverse Interests. If you do not have a long employment history but have been doing volunteer work or internships or want to emphasize your coursework, the functional résumé may be a better format for you to use. Keep in mind, though, that the functional résumé is somewhat unconventional; some employers may not care for it.

Today, résumés may be submitted and inspected in a variety of ways:

1. A traditional hard-copy résumé, sent by post or fax or delivered by hand, may be reviewed personally by one or more people at the receiving company.
2. A hard-copy résumé, sent by post or fax or delivered by hand, may be scanned into the receiving company's computer for review on screen.
3. An electronic résumé, sent by email, may be reviewed as is by one or more people at the receiving company.
4. An electronic résumé, sent by email, may be converted by the receiving company into its own database format for review on screen.
5. An electronic résumé, posted to a Web site, may be available for prospective employers to locate through a key word search.

Also, it is becoming increasingly common for companies to have job applicants log on to their Web site and fill out electronic application forms, or **e-forms,** the information from which is then added to the company's résumé databank.

Given all this variety, you may want to prepare several different versions of your résumé. In the next few pages, we will show you how. Many Internet sites can help you, too (see the Help box on page 483).

1 Formatting a traditional résumé

A traditional hard-copy résumé should be designed to be pleasing to the eye. It should be centered on the page, and it should approximately fill the page. A skimpy résumé suggests that you have not accomplished much, while an overcrowded one puts too much pressure on the reader to absorb all the information provided. Use suitable margins (about 1 inch all around), and use white space to set off the major categories and groupings. Use boldface type for your name and for major headings and subheadings. (See Chapter 17 for a more complete discussion of document design principles.) Use verb phrases instead of full sentences to describe your various activities

Lorinda Brown
2222 Stockton Street
Austin, TX 78701
(555) 580-5625

OBJECTIVE

Marketing/management trainee in the retail industry.
Am willing to relocate if necessary.

EDUCATION

Bachelor of Science, University of Texas at Austin, June 1999
(present GPA: 3.4)

Major: Communication. Minor: Marketing. Completed 25
credit hours in marketing and management.

BUSINESS EXPERIENCE

Retail sales, Stevens Brown Sports, Austin, since September
1997. Started with floor sales; promoted to assistant manager
of weekend operations. Designed the company's Web site,
which features links to local bike trails, golf courses, and
other sites of recreational interest. Drew up new marketing
plan that increased sales by 15%.

Intern, Frito-Lay, Inc., Austin, June–August 1997. Completed
10-week marketing internship, which included product testing
and merchandising. Handled accounts during 6 weeks'
absence of local representative.

Server, Tony Roma's Restaurant, Austin, September 1996–May
1997. Responsible for five-table section. Used sales and public
relations techniques in a high-volume environment.

OTHER EXPERIENCE

Vice-President, University of Texas Black Student Association,
September 1997 to present. Represented the Association at the
1997 Southwest meeting.

Counselor-Tutor, Upward Bound, Austin, January–May 1996.

AWARDS

Employee of the Month, Stevens Brown, November 1997.

REFERENCES

Available upon request from the University of Texas
Placement and Career Information Center, 350 SSB, Austin,
TX 78704. Tel. (555) 581-6186.

Figure 22.3   Sample Traditional Résumé

and achievements; consistent use of such phrases will produce an elegant parallelism (see Chapter 36). Using active-voice verbs will give you a dynamic image (see 26g). Always use white or light-colored paper. Avoid printing in color, as it will not reproduce on black-and-white copiers. A sample traditional résumé is shown on page 479. Note that the applicant added a category for Awards.

2 Formatting a scannable résumé

Many companies are now using computer technology to quickly scan large numbers of hard-copy résumés and insert the results into a databank. Later, a key word search can be used to select only those applicants whose self-descriptors fit a certain profile. If you are applying to technologically oriented organizations, you should format your résumé to take advantage of this technology. Some significant differences exist between the traditional résumé and the scannable résumé.

Since computer scanning of résumés is based mainly on key word searches and key words usually are nouns or noun phrases, use a noun-heavy style instead of the verb-heavy style favored in traditional résumés. Rather than verb phrases like "Performed maintenance on . . . ," try noun phrases like "Maintenance mechanic for . . . " *Maintenance mechanic* is more likely to be a key phrase than *performed maintenance* is. Do not shy away from using technical jargon. Many computer programs use technical jargon as a way of sorting out candidates. Since some computer programs process only the first 50 or 75 words of a résumé, it is a good idea to list your key word self-descriptors in a separate section at the beginning of your résumé.

Computer scanners are not entirely reliable when it comes to distinguishing letters and other marks on paper. So, in putting together a scannable résumé, do everything you can to make things easy for the scanner:

1. Use white or light-colored, standard-size (8½" × 11") paper.
2. Use a clean original, not a photocopy.
3. Use laser or inkjet printing, not dot matrix.
4. Use a standard typeface, such as Palatino, Futura, Optima, or Helvetica.
5. Use 10- to 14-point font sizes.
6. Do not use italics, underlining, or fancy type styles.
7. Do not use lines, graphics, boxes, or color.
8. Keep normal spacing between letters; do not use kerning.
9. Start every line from the left margin; do not use columns.
10. Do not fold or staple the résumé.

A scannable version of Lorinda Brown's résumé is shown in Figure 22.4.

Lorinda Brown
2222 Stockton Street
Austin, TX 78701
(555) 580-5625

KEY WORDS: Marketing/management trainee, retail sales, Web site designer, communication major, management experience, marketing planner, recreation industry, product testing, merchandising.

OBJECTIVE: Marketing/management trainee in the retail industry. Am willing to relocate, if necessary.

EDUCATION: Bachelor of Science, University of Texas at Austin, June 1999 (present GPA: 3.4). Major: Communication. Minor: Marketing. Completed 25 credit hours in marketing and management.

BUSINESS EXPERIENCE: Retail sales, Stevens Brown Sports, Austin, since September 1997. Assistant manager, Web site designer, marketing planner. Management of weekend operations after promotion from floor sales. Web site design features links to local bike trails, golf courses, and other sites of recreational interest. New marketing plan has increased sales by 15%.

Intern, Frito-Lay, Inc., Austin, June–August 1997. Completed 10-week marketing internship which included product testing and merchandising. Did accounting during 6 weeks' absence of local representative.

Server, Tony Roma's Restaurant, Austin, September 1996–May 1997. Was responsible for five-table section. Used sales and public relations techniques in a high-volume environment.

OTHER EXPERIENCE: Vice-President, University of Texas Black Student Association, September 1997 to present. Represented the Association at the 1997 Southwest meeting.

Counselor-Tutor, Upward Bound, Austin, January–May 1996.

AWARDS: Employee of the Month, Stevens Brown, November 1997.

REFERENCES: Available upon request from the University of Texas Placement and Career Information Center, 350 SSB, Austin, TX 78704. Tel. (555) 581-6186.

Figure 22.4   Sample Scannable Résumé

Using Key Words

Instead of	Write
performed maintenance	maintenance mechanic
designed a Web site	Web site designer
tested products	product tester
worked in a laboratory	laboratory technician
developed software	software developer
wrote grant proposals	grant proposal writer

3 Formatting an electronic résumé

It is becoming increasingly common for companies to solicit résumés via email or the Internet. In such cases, you should format your résumé so that it conforms to the company's specifications.

Email Résumés

Given the variety of word-processing programs, text editors, and email programs available, if you plan to send your résumé by email to several different companies you should put it into as simple and universal a format as possible. This means (1) using a simplified layout with a prominent key words section, like that of the scannable résumé, and (2) putting the résumé in ASCII, Text Only, or Simple Text format. Most companies prefer that you embed the résumé in the email message itself, after the cover letter, rather than as an attached file. You would be wise to first send a test copy to a friend who has a different system than you do. If the look of the résumé is of great importance to you, you might try using RTF (Rich Text Format) and sending your résumé as an attachment to your email message.

Homepage Résumés

Although designing your own homepage résumé can be fun, it is generally not the most effective way to go about searching for a job. Most potential employers will not go to the trouble of logging on to your Web site. You would make better use of your time logging on to *their* Web sites and submitting your résumé according to *their* specifications.

If, however, you are determined to have your own homepage résumé, we suggest that you follow these guidelines:

1. Make sure that you are familiar with the principles of good Web page design (see Chapter 19).
2. Put your key word self-descriptors up front, as in the scannable résumé.
3. Use key words in your page's title and URL. Companies' search engines will not recognize your name, but they will recognize certain key words.
4. Consider creating an additional page containing an ASCII version of your résumé, with all HTML tags removed, in case employers want to copy it into their database.
5. Surf the Web and look at some other homepage résumés. If you look at enough of them, you will get a sense of what works and what does not.

HELP

Where can I get online information about writing and posting a résumé?

Try these Web sites:

- Rebecca Smith's eRésumés and Resources
  http://www.eresumes.com

- Archeus: Guide to WWW Résumé Writing Resources
  http://www.golden.net/~archeus/reswri.htm

- Proven Resumes.com Career Center
  http://www.provenresumes.com

- Riley Guide: Online Résumé Databases
  http//www.dbm.com/jobguide/resumes.html

- Preparing the Ideal Scannable Résumé
  http://www.resumix.com/resume/resume_tips.html

- Resumania On-Line
  http://www.umn.edu/ohr/ecep/resume/

EXERCISE 22.1

On the Internet, on a campus bulletin board, or in your local newspaper, find an advertisement for a job that you would want, and write a letter of application for the job.

EXERCISE 22.2

Prepare two versions of your résumé—traditional and scannable.

22d Write clearly organized reports

A report, as the name implies, is a document that describes the results of an activity. If you do experiments in a chemistry lab, you will be expected to write them up in a lab report. If you research a topic for your composition class in the library, you may be asked to write a library report. Company employees who go on a business trip usually are asked to submit a trip report. Scientists and engineers conducting research projects are expected to submit ongoing progress reports and then, at the end, a final report. There are many other kinds of reports as well, including feasibility reports, environmental impact statements, and activity reports. A report can be as short as one or two pages or as long as a thousand pages. Short reports (for example, lab reports and trip reports) usually have a small, local readership; longer reports often are circulated to a variety of readers both inside and outside the organization in which they are written.

1 Making decisions about content, layout, and design

Designing reports generally is easier than designing brochures or newsletters, because most instructors and businesses have specific formats or conventions that they expect you to follow. For example, the report in 15c follows a format commonly used in engineering courses. It is important to find out what format your instructor expects you to use for a report.

2 Dividing the report into four basic parts

There are four basic parts to a report: a header, an introduction, a body, and a conclusion. Reports may have additional components as well, such as a title page, an abstract, attachments, a table of contents, and a cover letter or memo. If you do not have a specified format to follow, many word processors provide document templates that can help get you started.

Header. The first part of a report is called the header. It provides basic information about the document, such as for whom it is intended, who wrote it, when it was written, and what it is about. If you are writing a report in memo form, the header should contain four standard lines: TO, FROM, SUBJECT (or RE), and DATE. Fill in each of these lines with the appropriate information. In a more formal report, you may want to use a title page instead of a header (see 22d-3).

Headers can include other information, such as a distribution list (recipients other than the person named on the TO line may be listed under DIST or CC), a list of enclosures or attachments (indicated by ENCL or ATTACHMENT), and a reference to previous correspondence (indicated by REF). (In their header in 15c, the engineering students used TO, FROM, SUBJECT, REF, DATE, and DIST.)

Introduction. The introduction serves the vitally important purpose of orienting and informing busy readers. Like brochures and newsletters, reports often are distributed to a variety of readers both inside and outside the organization in which they originate. Many of these readers may be unfamiliar with the report's subject matter. Furthermore, unlike college instructors, who are obligated to read entire student papers, readers in the "real world" often skim reports. In your introduction, you should tell readers quickly (1) what problem you are addressing, (2) how you have addressed it, and (3) what your findings and recommendations are. Begin with a brief problem statement, usually only one paragraph long, and then follow it with a separate summary, also only one paragraph long. (The engineering students in 15c stated the problem and their recommended solutions in a two-paragraph "Executive Summary" that preceded the report itself.)

Body. The main part of the report should contain your claim(s), present your evidence, lay out your reasoning, acknowledge counterarguments, and cite references—in short, provide a good, solid argument (see Chapter 7). If the problem statement on the first page of your report needs elaboration, elaborate at the beginning of the body. Visual aids, including typographical distinctions, itemized lists, graphs, and tables (see Chapter 17), should be used throughout to distinguish and clarify important information. If your report is two or more pages, divide the body into sections, using informative headings such as Introduction, Method, Results, and Discussion. (The engineering students in 15c used the following headings for the body of their report: Introduction and Problem Statement, Four

Proposed Alternative Solutions, Research Methods, and Results and Discussion.)

Conclusion. Conclude the report with a summary of your main points, a recommendation, a proposal for action, and/or an expression of appreciation. You can repeat information from the summary section of the introduction for emphasis. (The engineering students in 15c did this in the conclusion of their report.)

3   Adding optional parts

Title Page. Formal reports of more than five pages often have a title page instead of a header. The title page should include the name of the person or group to whom the report is addressed, the names of any other recipients, the names of the writers, the date, the subject (that is, the title), and references to any funding sources.

Abstract. An **abstract** is a concise synopsis (100–150 words) of the report that (1) introduces the topic, (2) briefly describes the method of investigation, (3) details the main findings, and (4) states the general conclusions and implications of these findings. If your report is published, the abstract may be separated from the report and entered into a computerized database; therefore, it should be comprehensible on its own.

Attachments. Many reports are based on detailed information—lengthy calculations, drawings, published articles, and other secondary matter—that not every reader will need or want to see. Rather than including such materials in the report, append them either as a formal appendix or as attachments. If you have multiple attachments, include a separate table of contents prior to the attachments. (In addition to listing their references in Appendix A, the engineering students in 15c presented much of their supporting data in Appendixes B through G.)

Table of Contents. A table of contents helps readers get a sense of the overall structure of the report and allows busy readers to skip directly to those parts that interest them. If your report is fairly long and complex, with a title page, abstract, and attachments, you should include a table of contents just after the abstract.

Cover Letter or Memo. A cover letter (also called a letter of transmittal) or a memo often accompanies a long report sent to specific readers. This letter gives the writer an opportunity to (1) introduce the report to readers who are not expecting it and (2) draw readers' attention to specific parts of the report. Writers often send different cover letters to different readers. (The engineering students in 15c included a memo to introduce their report to readers.)

4 Formatting for the selective reader

Some readers will want to read the entire report, while others will want to read only parts of it. Thus, it is important that reports—especially long reports—be formatted so as to accommodate selective reading behavior.

EXERCISE 22.3

Write a two-page report evaluating the engineering students' report in 15c for ease of skimming. Use the guidelines given in How to Make It Easy for Readers to Skim a Report.

How to Make It Easy for Readers to Skim a Report

1. Use an informative *title.*
2. Provide a short *abstract.*
3. At the very beginning, define the *problem* the report is addressing.
4. Provide an *executive summary* on the first page of the report.
5. Provide good *visual aids* to accompany appropriate text (see Chapter 17).
6. Divide the report into logical sections, with informative *section headings.*
7. Provide informative *subheadings* as well.
8. Begin each paragraph with a good *topic sentence* (see 6a).
9. Give *typographical prominence* to key points (without overdoing it).
10. Relegate supporting information (such as calculations and reference materials) to *appendixes,* making sure to reference such information in the body of the report.
11. For a long report, include a *table of contents.*

22e Write focused memos

One of the most important types of documents in business and professional contexts is the memorandum, or memo. People write memos for a variety of purposes: to inform, to summarize, to recommend, to make a request. Memos usually are quite short, informal in tone, and focused on a single topic. Unlike reports (see 22d), memos typically are written to only a local audience, such as supervisors, colleagues, or employees internal to a company or department.

Structurally, a memo has the same four basic parts as a report: a header, an introduction, a body, and a conclusion (see 15c and 16c for example reports; see 22d for an explanation of these parts). In addition, like a report, a memo may have attachments. But all of these components are typically much shorter in a memo than in a report, and the document as a whole seldom exceeds two pages. The opening component usually is compressed into a background description or problem statement of only one to three sentences, and it has no summary. The body may be only a few sentences long, and the conclusion may be only a sentence or two.

With most word-processing programs, you can create a document template (a preset form). If your department or company has a standard format for memos, you can create a template that conforms to this standard.

The sample memo in Figure 22.5 was written by two students to their writing instructor. The instructor, Professor Gilbert, had asked all the students in the class to form two-person teams, call local nonprofit

HELP

How do I use a memo template?

1. On the FILE menu, select NEW.
2. When a screen pops up, select the desired option (for example, MEMO).
3. Select the desired style (for example, PROFESSIONAL MEMO).
4. Fill in the blanks or type over the text that is already there.
5. To customize the memo, follow the on-screen instructions.

Header containing basic information	To:	Prof. Gilbert
	From:	Mona Kitab and Fernando Marquez
	Date:	4 June 1999
	Subject:	Proposal for a service-learning project

Introduction, describing the problem and proposed solution

After telephoning five agencies, we have decided that the project we would most like to work on is an information brochure for the city's homeless shelter. Although about 150 homeless people use the shelter on a regular basis, the shelter is badly underfunded and needs more volunteers to help out. Miriam Hatcher, the shelter director, told us she thought that more university students would volunteer to help if they only knew more about it. She said that a well-written brochure answering students' questions about the shelter might be the answer, because it could be easily distributed all around campus.

We plan to create a six-panel, folded brochure that will answer the following questions:

Body of memo giving details

- What is the homeless shelter?
- How many people does it serve, and in what way?
- Why does it need volunteer help? Why doesn't the government pay for it?
- If I volunteered, what would I be doing? How much time would it take?
- How do I sign up?

According to Ms. Hatcher, these are the questions that students are most likely to ask. The brochure will be well written, nicely illustrated, and elegantly formatted.

Conclusion, summarizing the main point of the memo

We are enthusiastic about this project, as it seems to address an important need in our community, and we hope that it meets your approval. We look forward to getting your feedback on this.

Figure 22.5   Sample Memo

agencies to find a suitable service-learning project, and then submit to her a one-page memo describing their proposed project.

EXERCISE 22.4

Write a short memo to your instructor on a topic of your own choosing. For example, you might request special help on an upcoming writing project, pose some questions about English grammar, or describe a new Web site you recently discovered. If your computer has a document template program, use it to write your memo.

Essay Exams

In college and on the job, much of the writing you do will be "on demand"—that is, you will have a limited time in which to complete it. In college, such writing often takes the form of a timed essay exam or an in-class writing assignment. This chapter discusses some ways you can prepare for this type of writing.

23a Prepare for an essay exam

You can use a number of strategies to prepare for on-demand writing in general and essay exams in particular. These strategies include keeping up on your reading and notetaking, studying and reviewing your notes, and analyzing the exam question.

HELP

How do I use a key word search to find important information in lecture notes?

If you keep your lecture notes in an electronic notebook, you can search for key information by doing the following:

1. Use your word processor's WORD COUNT feature to find out how many times a particular key word appears in your notes.
2. Use your word processor's SEARCH function to search for each occurrence of the key word.
3. Highlight the word by using italics or a contrasting color.
4. For review purposes, make a hard copy of pages that contain the key words.

1 Keeping up on your reading and notetaking

Many instructors judge your success in a course by how well you are able to analyze and apply course material in a timed essay exam. In order to do a good job on such exams, you must be well prepared. Few essay exams are open-book, so you must learn the material well enough to be able to remember and write about it without access to your notes or textbooks.

http://www.english.uiuc.
edu/cws/wworkshop/
essayexams.htm
Tips on writing
essay exams

You can prepare by keeping up with course assignments and discussions on a daily basis throughout the term. Attend every class and read your textbooks carefully, looking for key ideas and arguments. Pay close attention to chapter summaries, subheadings, and key terminology. Write the key ideas and terms down in a notebook for later review. When your instructor lectures, do not write down everything he or she says; rather, listen for and record main points and ideas that show relationships.

2 Studying and reviewing your notes

As the exam date approaches, you will want to study more systematically. Ask the instructor if he or she is willing to provide models of previous exam questions or some general guidelines about the kinds of questions that might be included on the exam. Organize a study group to discuss and review the course materials. If possible, the study group should meet regularly during the term, either in person or through an email discussion group (see 21b-1). Practice responding to course readings by taking a stance opposite that of the authors or by questioning the authors' position. Review your class notes, paying particular attention to your lists of key ideas and terms. For each key idea, develop a practice thesis statement that you could explore and support in an essay.

Avoid the last-minute cram session. Cramming for several hours prior to the exam will not give you enough depth of knowledge to succeed on an essay exam. And if you stay up all night before an exam studying, you will be in no condition to take it the next day. Instead, pace your studying over several days and try to get a good night's sleep so that you will be fresh for the exam itself.

3 Analyzing the exam question

When you receive the exam question, the first step is to analyze it carefully. The question itself will guide the organization of your response. An essay question will ask you to focus on a specific issue, and you should address it rather than cataloging everything you learned from the course. Try to minimize your anxiety by taking a deep breath and focusing your thinking on the structure of your response. If the exam contains more than one question, determine how much time you have to devote to each question, so that you do not run out of time before you complete your writing. Table 23.1 shows appropriate responses to some of the organizational cue words that typically appear in essay questions.

EXERCISE 23.1

Reread Chapter 2 of this handbook, and follow the suggestions outlined in 2b-2 and 2b-3 on taking and reviewing notes. Formulate a set of essay exam questions based on what you take to be the key ideas in Chapter 2. Bring your questions to class for discussion.

Example question	Cue word	Organizational scheme of response
Analyze Shakespeare's use of dreams in *Macbeth*.	**Analyze:** Divide something into parts and discuss the parts in relationship to the whole.	1. State your thesis. 2. Discuss the play's major themes. 3. Identify places where dreams occur, and explain each instance in relation to the play's major themes. 4. State your conclusion.
Argue either for or against caps on political spending in presidential campaigns.	**Argue:** Take a position or stand and support it with reasoned arguments and evidence.	1. Choose a side—either for or against such caps—and state that position in a thesis sentence. 2. List each point that supports your side, with evidence. 3. Conclude by restating your side.
Classify street people into types based on their sociological characteristics.	**Classify:** Divide some larger whole into groups on the basis of shared traits.	1. State your thesis, pointing out the number of types of street people. 2. Identify one type and describe its characteristics. 3. Continue identifying types and describing their characteristics. 4. State your conclusion.
Describe the mechanism of the transmission of the disease typhus.	**Describe:** Systematically explain something's features, sometimes visually or sequentially.	1. State your thesis—that typhus is transmitted by parasites. 2. Describe the disease carrier—lice. 3. Explain how lice spread typhus. 4. State your conclusion.
Discuss the structure of US society in terms of its economic relationships.	**Discuss:** Consider as many important elements related to an issue as you can.	1. State your thesis, outlining what you take to be the important relationships. 2. Consider as many key elements of US society and economics as you can, such as monetary policy, agricultural policy, and political policy. 3. Conclude by restating your thesis.

Table 23.1 Cue Words in Essay Exam Questions

Example question	Cue word	Organizational scheme of response
Evaluate the effectiveness of the performance of Handel's *Water Music* by the San Francisco Symphony.	**Evaluate:** Give your opinion about something's value and provide the reasons on which your judgment is based.	1. State your opinion about the effectiveness of the performance in the form of a thesis. 2. Briefly summarize the performance. 3. List the reasons on which your opinion is based, with supporting evidence from the performance itself. 4. Conclude by restating your opinion.
Explain why an object thrown up into the air falls to the ground.	**Explain:** Tell about something that is complex in a way that makes it clear.	1. State the physical principle in the form of a thesis. 2. Tell about the nature of gravity that causes the object to fall. 3. Tell about the physical principles that determine how objects are affected by gravity, including the scientific formula for gravitational pull. 4. State your conclusion.
Illustrate the importance of color in Duchamp's *Nude Descending a Staircase.*	**Illustrate:** Provide examples and detail about something.	1. State in your thesis why color is important in the painting. 2. Provide an example relating to color. 3. Provide additional examples relating to color. 4. State your conclusion.
Summarize the major advantages of mainstreaming handicapped children in school.	**Summarize:** Repeat the main points in abbreviated form.	1. State your thesis. 2. List the advantages, one after another, along with reasons that support each point. 3. State your conclusion.

Table 23.1 (cont.)

HELP

How do I write an essay exam in a computer lab?

If your instructor allows you to write your timed response to an essay exam in a computer classroom or lab, do the following:

1. Briefly attend to the stages of the writing process, as described in 23b.
2. Budget your time carefully. Check your watch or the clock periodically.
3. Save your work frequently—to your disk or hard drive—so that you do not inadvertently lose your essay because of a computer glitch or power failure.
4. Run the spell checker before turning in your exam.

23b   Attend to the writing process

When you write an essay exam, you should briefly attend to each stage of the writing process (see also 2c).

1   Preparing an outline

When taking an essay exam, you will not have much time for prewriting, but you should take a few minutes to jot down in an informal outline (see 3d-3) some of the key concepts you want to cover in your answer. Begin your response with a thesis statement and a short introductory paragraph that captures the main thrust of your response. Then, in subsequent paragraphs, you can elaborate with examples and details until you run out of time. As you outline, try to cover the most important points first, leaving the less important ones for last. If you have less than an hour to respond to the question, do not spend more than about five minutes planning and outlining your response.

2 Drafting your response

Try to remain focused as you draft your response. Your instructor will have many essays to read and will not want to plow through a lot of extraneous information. If you know a great deal about the question, resist the temptation to write down everything. Rather, stick to your thesis, and plan your writing so that your response is coherent and organized. The easier it is for the instructor to follow your line of argument, the better.

3 Analyzing and evaluating your response

As you draft your response, allow time to ensure that you have satisfied the demands of the assignment. When you read over your essay, you may find that you have overlooked the second part of a two-part question, for example, or that you have concentrated on defining terms when the question asked you to analyze information. Do not panic. If possible, write a new final paragraph that addresses the issues you missed. If you do not have time for that, write your instructor a brief message explaining where you went wrong and outlining how you would correct your essay if you had the time. Many instructors will give at least partial credit for such a response.

Also, look carefully at your thesis statement. Does it reflect accurately the direction of your essay? If not, then revise it. Check your organization. Does your essay read smoothly and flow logically? If not, then perhaps you can insert transitional words or phrases that will help your instructor follow your argument. Have you included enough examples to support your thesis? If you need more, write a new paragraph and use an arrow to indicate where it should be inserted. Finally, does your conclusion provide a clear understanding of the main point of your essay? If not, then add a sentence or two to sum up your argument.

4 Proofreading and editing your response

Your instructor will not expect your writing to be grammatically and structurally perfect in a timed-writing situation. However, he or she will expect your exam response to be readable and clear. If possible, write your response in pencil so that you can easily erase and correct errors. Take a few minutes to proofread and also to check your penmanship. If your response is unreadable, your instructor cannot evaluate it fairly.

Checklist for Writing Successful Essay Exam Responses

- Have I shown my understanding of the question by including a thesis statement at the beginning of my response?
- Have I organized my response so as to present my ideas in a logical progression that supports my thesis?
- Have I used the specific details, facts, or analyses called for in the question?
- Have I shown my own independent thoughts and insights in my response?
- Have I concluded with a brief sentence that sums up the gist of my response?
- Have I evaluated and edited my response as time allowed?

23c Review sample student responses to an essay exam question

To help you write better exam responses, we include here two student responses to the following exam question, which appeared on the midterm for a course in twentieth-century British literature.

Below you will find a quotation from a novel we read this term. Spend 15 minutes writing a short essay that performs a close reading of the passage. Pick out specific details from the quotation that illustrate some of the central themes or ideas of the novel. Your response should demonstrate both an ability to read closely and a general understanding of the novel.

From Henry James's *The Turn of the Screw:* "I remember feeling with Miles in especial as if he had had, as it were, nothing to call even an infinitesimal history. We expect of a small child scant enough 'antecedents', but there was in this beautiful little boy something extraordinarily sensitive, yet extraordinarily happy, that, more than in any creature of his age I have seen, struck me as beginning anew each day. . . . I could reconstitute nothing at all, and he was therefore an angel."

The instructor considered the first response to be a good response and the second one to be a poor response.

GOOD STUDENT RESPONSE

This quotation expresses the governess's naivete regarding the innocence of the children she is looking after. She assumes that just because they are children, they have had little experience and are, thus, pure "angels." Her perception of this, however, is erroneous and detrimental to Miles. Assuming that he is pure, she takes all measures to protect him from any horrors that may have happened in the past, not realizing that the past is part of Miles's history. His past takes the form of ghosts which haunt the governess, although they do not seem to frighten the children. In fact, the children are drawn to the ghosts and want the governess to go away. Her lack of experience and her innocence are actually greater than the children's, who no longer have parents and have experienced the death of two servants. Her inability to see this truth ends up killing Miles. Caught between the image of the governess and Peter Quint, Miles finally has to make evident to her what is so obvious to everyone else—Peter Quint exists, the past is a part of his present. Not willing to let Miles exist outside of her perceptions, the governess ironically reassures him, "I caught you." She strips him of his history, his identity, and he dies a young boy "dispossessed."

POOR STUDENT RESPONSE

The governess here is expressing how she feels about the child Miles vs. the Miles she knew once upon a time. The use of the run-on sentence is a radical change from the accepted format of the past. The form represents thought put on paper and not interpreted through writing. The effect that the child had on her doesn't seem realistic. It seems more mystic and of fantasy.

The instructor wanted the exam responses to demonstrate both an ability to read closely and a general understanding of the novel. In the first response, the student shows a clear understanding of the major themes of the novel, using specific details from the quotation to illustrate that understanding and connect the passage to the larger themes of innocence and history. In contrast, the second response does not draw any specific connections between the quote and the major issues or themes of the novel. It appears from the second response that this student did not really understand the novel. Furthermore, the second response does not answer the question posed. As reading these responses makes clear, you must understand both the subject and the examination question in order to answer well.

http://webserver.
maclab.comp.uvic.ca/
writersguide/Pages/
ExamEssays.html
More on essay exams

EXERCISE 23.2

Using the Checklist for Writing Successful Essay Exam Responses, analyze the two student essay exam responses. In each of the responses, which of the guidelines were observed? Which were not? How could each response have been improved?

SENTENCE GRAMMAR

CHAPTER 24

Sentence Structure

FAQs

What is an adverb? (24a-5)

What is the difference between a participle and a gerund? (24a-8)

What is a sentence subject? (24b-1)

What is a predicate? (24b-2)

?

Parts 6–12 of this handbook will help you improve your grammar and writing style so that you will be able to express your thoughts more precisely and make your writing more readable and interesting. To get the most from this section, you will need to know the basic elements of sentence structure. This chapter provides that information.

Most word processors include a style/grammar checker. Many writers use this feature to improve their writing (see the Help box). However, computerized style/grammar checkers are far from perfect. In fact, they have so many shortcomings that you should use one only with caution (see 39a).

24a   Learn to identify parts of speech

In writing a sentence, you put words together in certain combinations. These combinations depend, in part, on the different kinds

How do I use a style/grammar checker?

1. Start the checker. (It may be on the TOOLS menu.)
2. Position your cursor on the IGNORE (or SKIP) command, and be prepared to click on it often.
3. Consider each suggestion the checker makes, but do not automatically follow its advice. In most cases, you will decide to click IGNORE.
4. If you are not sure whether to accept the checker's suggestion, use the EXPLANATION feature (if there is one).
5. If you are still in doubt, read the relevant discussions in this handbook (see 39a or the index). Use the book's advice to help you decide whether or not to revise.

of words, or **parts of speech,** you use: nouns, pronouns, adjectives, verbs, adverbs, prepositions, conjunctions, verbals, and expletives.

1 Nouns

A **noun** (n) is the name of a person, place, thing, quality, idea, or action. Some examples of nouns are

Picasso   Mexico   printer
honesty   democracy   stamp-collecting

Nouns are often preceded by *a, an,* or *the;* these words are called **articles.** Use *a* before nouns beginning with consonant sounds; use *an* before nouns beginning with vowel sounds; use *the* to identify a specific noun:

a printer   *an* insult   *the* river

ESL Note: The indefinite article (*a* or *an*) is used with a nonspecific count noun (see below), while the definite article (*the*) is used with a count or noncount noun that refers to something specific. (See Chapter 55 for further discussion.)

Common nouns refer to general persons, places, things, concepts, or qualities.

man   city   mouse   philosophy   generosity

Proper nouns, which are almost always capitalized, name particular persons, places, institutions, organizations, months, and days.

Tom Cruise   Salt Lake City   the World Court
Duke University   Buddhism   Monday

Concrete nouns specifically refer to things that can be sensed through sight, hearing, touch, taste, and smell.

bookshelf   fork   billboard   hamburger

Abstract nouns refer to ideas, emotions, qualities, or other intangible concepts.

beauty   sadness   truth   love

Count nouns name things that can be counted and thus can have a plural form.

lake(s)   violin(s)   baseball(s)   goose (geese)

Noncount nouns, or **mass nouns,** name things that typically are not counted in English and thus cannot be made plural.

water   snow   hatred   health   news

Collective nouns name groups; they are plural in sense but singular in form.

committee   team   class   crowd

2   Pronouns

Pronouns (pron), such as *she, they,* and *it,* are words that substitute for nouns and always refer to a noun. The noun a pronoun substitutes for and refers to is called the **antecedent** of the pronoun. The noun antecedent often precedes the pronoun in a sentence:

Lucinda said *she* was not feeling well.

Sometimes the noun antedecent follows the pronoun:

Saying *she* was not feeling well, *Lucinda* left the room.

Types of Pronouns and Their Roles

Type	Role
Personal pronouns Singular: *I, you, he, she, it;* *me, you, him, her, it;* *mine, yours, his, hers, its* Plural: *we, you, they;* *us, you, them;* *ours, yours, theirs*	Refer to specific persons, places, or things: "I borrowed *his* book."
Demonstrative pronouns *this, that, these, those*	Point to their antecedent nouns: "*That* was an interesting idea!"
Indefinite pronouns *all, any, anybody, anyone,* *anything, both, everybody,* *everyone, everything,* *few, many, one, no one,* *nothing, somebody, someone,* *something, several, some*	Refer to nonspecific persons, places, or things and do not require an antecedent: "*Nothing* could be done."
Relative pronouns *that, what, which, who,* *whom, whose, whoever,* *whichever, whatever*	Introduce dependent clauses: "She is the teacher *who* runs marathons."
Interrogative pronouns *who, whom, which, what, whose*	Introduce questions: "*Whose* bike is this?"
Reflexive and **intensive pronouns** (consist of a personal pronoun plus *-self* or *-selves*) Singular: *myself, yourself, himself,* *herself, itself* Plural: *ourselves, yourselves, themselves*	A reflexive pronoun refers back to the subject to show that the subject itself is the object of an action: "She saw *herself* in the mirror." An intensive pronoun is used for emphasis: "They did it *themselves.*"
Reciprocal pronouns *one another, each other*	Refer to the separate parts of a plural antecedent: "They gave presents to *each other.*"

Pronouns can be singular or plural, and their case can vary depending on how they are used in a sentence. The change from *he* to *him* or *his* reflects pronoun use according to case—subjective, objective, or possessive. (See Chapter 25 for a discussion of pronoun case and Chapter 27 for a discussion of pronoun-antecedent agreement.)

3   Adjectives

An **adjective** (adj) is a word that modifies a noun or pronoun by qualifying or describing it. In English, the adjective usually precedes the noun it modifies (an *old* tree, the *other* day), but in literary usage an adjective occasionally follows the noun (a woman *scorned*). In sentences such as "The program was *challenging*," the adjective falls on the other side of a verb linking it to the noun it modifies. An adjective used in this way is called a **predicate adjective.**

Many adjectives have comparative and superlative forms created by the addition of *-er* and *-est* (*small, smaller, smallest*). (See Chapter 28.) Many other adjectives have the same form as the present or past participle of a verb (a *roaring* lion, a *deserted* island).

ESL Note: If you use two or more adjectives before a noun, you often must put them in a certain order (see 57a).

Finally, many pronoun-like adjectives are related in function to some of the pronouns discussed in 24a-2. These adjectives are called **possessive adjectives** (*our* school), **demonstrative adjectives** (*this* page), **interrogative adjectives** (*Which* button do I push?), and **indefinite adjectives** (*some* money).

See Chapter 28 for a more detailed discussion of adjectives.

4   Verbs

A **verb** (v) is a key word that expresses an action (*swim, read*) or a state of being (*is, seemed*). Main verbs are often accompanied by **auxiliary verbs** (also called **helping verbs**), which include forms of the verbs *be, have,* and *do,* and/or by **modal verbs,** such as *may, might, can, could, will, would, shall, should,* and *must.* Auxiliary and modal verbs are critical parts of special verb forms that express questions, future tenses, past tenses, and various degrees of doubt about or qualification of the main verb's action. (See Chapter 26 for more on verbs.)

Transitive verbs (VT) transfer action from an agent (usually the subject of the sentence) to an object or recipient (usually the direct object of the sentence): "Michael *fumbled* the ball." Some common transitive verbs are *carry, reject, show, build,* and *destroy* (see 24b-2, 24b-3). **Intransitive verbs** (VI) may express action, but they do not transfer it to an object or recipient: "The bridge *collapsed*." Some common intransitive verbs are *sleep, fall, die, erupt,* and *disappear.* Many verbs can be used either intransitively or transitively: "Frank *eats* often, but he does not *eat* red meat."

The five major forms a verb takes are usually referred to as its **principal parts.** They are the **base form** (or **infinitive form**), **present tense, past tense, past participle,** and **present participle.**

Base form	Present tense	Past tense	Past participle	Present participle
(to) erase	erases	erased	(have) erased	(am) erasing
(to) run	runs	ran	(have) run	(am) running

These different forms of a verb serve different functions. For **regular verbs,** the past tense and the past participle are formed by adding *d* or *ed* to the base form (*erased*). For **irregular verbs,** the past tense and past participle are formed differently (*ran/run*). (See 26b for more on irregular verb forms.)

Verbs also have an **active form,** called the **active voice** ("He *committed* the crime"), as well as a **passive form,** called the **passive voice,** consisting of a form of the verb *be* and a past participle ("The crime *was committed* by him"). In addition, verbs may take on alternative forms to reflect different **moods.** Normally they are in the **indicative mood,** used to make assertions, state opinions, and ask questions. But they can take past-tense forms to express unreal conditions or wishes, in the **subjunctive mood:** "I wish I *were* in Hawaii." They can appear in the base form, usually with no apparent subject, to issue a command, in the **imperative mood:** "Don't *do* that again!" or, occasionally, "Don't you *do* that again!" Finally, verb forms become verbals when they change their function and are used as nouns, adverbs, or adjectives (see 24a-8). See Chapters 26 and 56 for a more complete discussion of verbs.

5   Adverbs

An **adverb** (adv) modifies a verb, an adjective, another adverb, or an entire clause or sentence. Adverbs usually answer one of the following questions: when? where? how? how often? to what extent?

The mayor lives *alone* in a downtown apartment.   [*Alone* modifies the verb *lives*.]

She has a *very* busy schedule.   [*Very* modifies the adjective *busy*.]

She *almost* never takes a vacation.   [*Almost* modifies the adverb *never*.]

Apparently, she doesn't seem to need one.   [*Apparently* modifies the entire sentence.]

Many adverbs (*quickly, hopefully*) are formed by adding *-ly* to an adjective, but many others (*very, not, always, tomorrow, inside, therefore*) are not.

ESL Note: Adverbs must be positioned properly within a sentence (see 57c).

Conjunctive adverbs, such as *however, thus,* and *consequently,* modify an entire sentence or clause while linking it to the preceding sentence or clause. (See Chapter 35.)

Today's weather will be beautiful. *However,* we expect rain tomorrow.

See Chapter 28 for a more detailed discussion of adverbs.

6   Prepositions

A **preposition** (prep) is a word such as *in, on, of, for,* or *by* that comes before a noun or pronoun and its modifiers to form a **prepositional phrase.** Some examples of prepositional phrases are *in the water, off the deep end,* and *toward them.* The noun or pronoun in such phrases (*water, end, them*) is called the **object of the preposition.** Here are some of the most common prepositions used in English:

about	beneath	into	through
above	beside	like	to
across	between	near	toward
after	by	of	under
along	despite	off	underneath
among	down	on	unlike
around	during	onto	until
at	except	out	up
before	for	outside	upon
behind	from	over	with
below	in	past	without

Prepositions also occur in multiword combinations: *according to, along with, because of, in case of, in spite of, on account of,* and *with respect to.*

Prepositions can be linked to certain verbs to form **phrasal verbs,** such as *do without, put up with,* and *look over.* In phrasal verbs, the preposition is called a **particle.** Compare the following sentences:

> She *came across* a dead animal.   [*Came across* is a phrasal verb meaning "discovered."]

> She *came* across the bridge.   [*Came* is a simple verb; *across* is part of the adverbial phrase *across the bridge.*]

ESL Note: Phrasal verbs are common in idiomatic English. (See Chapters 56 and 58.)

7 Conjunctions

A **conjunction** (conj) joins two sentences, clauses, phrases, or words. The relationship between the two parts may be an equal, or coordinate, one; it may be an unequal, or subordinate, one.

Coordinating conjunctions (*and, but, or, nor, yet, so, for*) connect sentences, clauses, phrases, or words that are parallel in meaning and grammatical structure. **Correlative conjunctions** (*both/and, neither/nor, either/or, not/but, whether/or, not only/but also*) are pairs of conjunctions that give extra emphasis to the two parts of a coordinated construction. **Subordinating conjunctions** introduce dependent clauses and connect them to main clauses. Some common subordinating conjunctions are *although, because, if, since, unless,* and *while.*

See Chapter 35 for further discussion of conjunctions.

8 Verbals

A **verbal** is a verb form that functions in a sentence as a noun, an adverb, or an adjective. There are three types of verbals: participles, gerunds, and infinitives.

Participles are words such as *sweeping* and *swept,* the present and past participles of a verb (*sweep*) that function as adjectives and can modify nouns or pronouns.

Beware of *sweeping* generalizations.

Swept floors make a house seem more livable.

Gerunds are verb forms that end in *ing* and function as nouns.

Sweeping the floors is something I do not enjoy.

An **infinitive** is the base form of a verb preceded by *to* (*to read, to fly, to ponder*). Infinitives can function as nouns, adjectives, or adverbs.

NOUN *To quit* would be a mistake.

ADJECTIVE Her desire *to quit* is understandable.

ADVERB He is eager *to quit*.

9 Expletives

An **expletive** (*there, here, it*) is an introductory, "empty" word that opens a sentence. Expletives are usually followed by a form of *to be*. The expletive *there* serves to introduce a new topic into a discussion:

There once was a pharaoh named Sosistris I.

The expletive *it* adds emphasis to a sentence:

It is disgraceful that the United States has so many homeless people.

Expletives are sometimes overused (see 34c). Also, an expletive can cause an error in subject-verb agreement because of its position as an apparent "false" subject (see 27a-8).

H HELP

How do I locate expletives in my writing?

1. Open the SEARCH (or FIND) feature of your word-processing program.
2. Enter the word *it* or *there* in the SEARCH field.
3. Run the search.

NOTE: Not every *there* or *it* is an expletive.

24b Learn to identify basic sentence patterns

Sentences are the basic units for expressing assertions, questions, commands, wishes, and exclamations. All grammatically complete sentences have a subject and a predicate. In a sentence fragment, one of these elements may be missing. (See Chapter 29 for more on fragments.)

1 Sentence subjects

The **subject** (sub) of a sentence is a noun, a pronoun, or a noun phrase that identifies what the sentence is about. Usually it directly precedes the main verb.

You probably have a pointing device (or PD) connected to your computer.

Many PDs have a ball that rolls against wheels.

The rubber ball found inside most PDs oxidizes over time and begins to slip.

The preference settings for double-click speed and for the ratio of hand or finger travel to pointer travel are set in the OPTIONS menu.

The **simple subject** is always a noun or pronoun. In the example sentences, the simple subjects are *you, PDs, ball,* and *settings.* The **complete subject** is the simple subject plus all its modifiers; the complete subjects are italicized in the example sentences. Some sentences have a **compound subject** including two or more simple subjects.

http://owl.english.
purdue.edu/writers/
by-topic.html
Comprehensive
coverage of parts
of speech and sen-
tence construction

Tips and techniques can be found in the HELP menu.

In imperative sentences, which express a command or a request, the subject is understood to be *you,* even though it is not usually stated.

[*You*] Use macros to automate repetitive tasks.

The subject of a sentence always agrees in number with the main verb. That is, a singular subject takes a singular verb, and a plural subject takes a plural verb.

SINGULAR   The rubber ball . . . oxidizes

PLURAL   The preference settings . . . are set

Subject-verb agreement is discussed further in Chapter 27.

EXERCISE 24.1

Put brackets around the complete subject in each of the following
sentences. The first one has been done for you.

1. After its Industrial Revolution, [England] led the world as the
    most advanced nation in mechanization and mass production.
2. The Arts and Crafts Movement in Victorian England started
    as a mild rebellion by a group of artists, designers, and
    architects.
3. These artisans were concerned about the poor standard of
    design in English building and furnishings.
4. One of the most influential leaders of the Arts and Crafts
    Movement was William Morris (1834–1896).
5. Unable to find the fabrics he wanted for his home, Morris set
    up his own textile design firm in London in 1861.
6. Each year, the students at MIT compete to execute ever more
    creative pranks.
7. One year, they managed to park a car on top of a building.
8. In the winter, people need to be alert for signs that their
    heating systems are malfunctioning and emitting carbon
    monoxide gas.
9. The light breeze was welcome on that hot summer afternoon.
10. Most of us look forward to the hamburgers and potato salad
    served at summer cookouts.

2   Predicates

The **predicate** is the part of a sentence that contains the verb and
makes a statement about the subject. The **simple predicate** is the verb
plus any auxiliary (helping) verbs.

The World Wide Web *offers* information, graphics, music, movies,
and much more.

With a Web browser, you *can locate* information efficiently.

The **complete predicate** consists of the simple predicate plus any objects, complements, or adverbial modifiers.

The World Wide Web *offers information, graphics, music, movies, and
much more.*

A **compound predicate** has two or more verbs that have the same subject.

A Web page *informs and entertains.*

A **direct object** (DO) is a noun, a pronoun, or a noun phrase that completes the action of a transitive verb (see 24a-4)—one that is capable of transmitting action. In this sentence, *information* is the direct object of the verb *locate:*

Sub   V   DO
You can locate *information.*

An **indirect object** (IO) is a noun, a pronoun, or a noun phrase that is affected indirectly by the action of a verb. It usually refers to the recipient or beneficiary of the action described by the verb and the direct object. The verbs *give, buy, bring, teach, tell,* and *offer* commonly take indirect objects.

Sub   V   IO   DO
The teacher told *us* a story.

Most indirect objects can be presented instead as the object of the preposition *to* or *for.*

The teacher told *us* a story.

OR

The teacher told a story *to us.*

I bought *my mother* a plant.

OR

I bought a plant *for my mother.*

An **object complement** (OC) is a noun, a noun phrase, an adjective, or an adjective phrase that elaborates on or describes the direct object.

Sub   V   DO   OC
The news made us *depressed.*

Sub   V   DO   OC
They appointed Laurie *head of the task force.*

A **subject complement** (SC) is a noun, a noun phrase, an adjective, or an adjective phrase that follows a linking verb (such as *is, was,* or *seems*) and elaborates on the subject.

Sub LV   SC
She was *pleased.*

Sub LV   SC
Laurie is *the new head of the task force.*

3 | Basic sentence patterns

The complete predicate is usually structured according to one of five basic sentence patterns:

Pattern 1: A sentence may have an intransitive verb and no object.

Pred
Sub   V
Time flies.

Pattern 2: A sentence may have a transitive verb with a direct object.

Pred
Sub   VT   DO
Time heals all wounds.

Pattern 3: A sentence may have a transitive verb with a direct object and an indirect object.

Pred
Sub   VT IO   DO
Free time gave us an opportunity.

Pattern 4: A sentence may have a transitive verb with a direct object and an object complement.

Pred
Sub   VT DO OC
Time pressures made us tense.

Pattern 5: A sentence may use a **linking verb,** which connects the subject to a subject complement, indicating a condition, quality, or state of being.

Pred
Sub LV   SC
Time is precious.

EXERCISE 24.2

Insert a slash (/) between the subject and the predicate in each sentence.

1. I was in college at Albany State in the early 1960s.
2. My major interests were music and biology.
3. I was a soloist with the choir.
4. The black music I sang was of three types.
5. The choir specialized in spirituals.
6. They had major injections of European musical harmony and composition.
7. Gospel music was also a major part of black church music at the time.
8. Black choral singing was full, powerful, and richly ornate.
9. The hymns were offset by upbeat call-and-response songs.
10. I saw people in church sing and pray until they shouted.

24c Learn to expand sentences

The five basic sentence patterns can be expanded using words, phrases, or clauses to modify the subject or predicate.

1 Modifying with single words

Any simple sentence part can be modified, qualified, or described by appropriate single words. Verbs, adverbs, and adjectives can be modified by adverbs, and nouns can be modified by adjectives.

http://www.uottawa.ca/
academic/arts/writcent/
hypergrammar/bldsent.
html
All about sentence structure and options—even includes review exercises

Sub V Adv
Time flies *quickly.*

Adj Sub V Adv Adv
Spare time flies *very quickly.*

Adjectives usually are placed before the noun or pronoun they modify (*terrible* burden). Adverbs are placed near the verb, adjective, or other adverb they modify. Adverbs that modify an entire sentence can be placed at the beginning, the middle, or the end of a sentence.

Frantically, Martha crammed for the exam.

Martha *frantically* crammed for the exam.

Martha crammed for the exam *frantically.*

See Chapters 28 and 57 for more on placing adjectives and adverbs.

2   Modifying with phrases

Sentence parts can also be modified by phrases. A **phrase** is a group of words consisting of (1) a noun and its related words or (2) a verbal and its related words. Phrases add detail to any of the subjects, verbs, objects, or complements used in the five basic sentence patterns.

Adding Prepositional Phrases

A preposition and its object (a noun or a pronoun) form a **prepositional phrase:** *in the dark, on time, outside Dallas.* Prepositional phrases can be used to modify nouns, verbs, or adjectives.

Sub   Prep phr   V   Prep phr
The TV *in the corner* does not work *without an antenna.*

Sub   V   Adj   Prep phr
Juan was jealous *beyond reason.*

Adding Verbal Phrases

A **verbal** is a verb form that functions as a noun, an adverb, or an adjective (see 24a-8). The three kinds of verbals—infinitives, gerunds, and participles—can be combined with other words to form infinitive phrases, gerund phrases, and participial phrases.

An **infinitive phrase** consists of the *to* form of a verb plus modifiers, objects, and/or complements. Such a phrase can function as a noun, an adjective, or an adverb.

He wanted *to plant the garden.*   [The infinitive phrase functions as a noun and is the object of *wanted.*]

Free time gave us an opportunity *to reflect.*   [The infinitive phrase functions as an adjective modifying *opportunity.*]

The company was eager *to expand its operations.*   [The infinitive phrase functions as an adverb modifying *eager.*]

A **gerund phrase** consists of the *-ing* form of a verb plus modifiers, objects, and/or complements. Gerund phrases function as nouns and thus can be used as sentence subjects, objects, or complements.

> Sub
> *Lifting boxes all day* made Stan tired.

> DO
> Rebecca hates *cooking*.

> SC
> Her favorite activity is *watching old movies*.

ESL Note: Some English verbs can take only one kind of verbal as a complement—an infinitive ("I want *to go*") or a gerund ("I enjoy *biking*"); other verbs can take either ("Rebecca hates *cooking*" or "Rebecca hates *to cook*"). For further discussion, see Chapter 56.

A **participial phrase** consists of a present participle (the *-ing* form of a verb) or a past participle (the *-ed* or *-en* form of a verb) plus modifiers, objects, and/or complements. Participal phrases function as adjectives, modifying subjects and objects of sentences.

> *Having decided to quit his job,* Roberto began looking for another one.   [The participial phrase modifies the sentence subject, *Roberto*.]

> I caught someone *trying to break into my car.*   [The participial phrase modifies the object *someone*.]

As these examples illustrate, participial phrases should be placed next to the words they modify. Failure to do so may produce dangling modifiers or other modification problems. (See Chapter 32.)

Adding Appositive Phrases

An **appositive phrase** is a noun phrase that describes or defines another noun. Appositive phrases directly follow or precede the nouns they modify and are usually set off by commas.

> *One of the world's most famous celebrities,* Muhammad Ali draws crowds wherever he goes.

> The Ford Mustang, *a car originally designed by Lee Iacocca,* has been an enduring icon of the US automotive industry.

Adding Absolute Phrases

An **absolute phrase** consists of a subject and an adjective phrase (most commonly a participial phrase). Unlike other kinds of phrases, which modify single words, absolute phrases are used to modify entire clauses or sentences.

Maria could not wait to start writing another book,

Abs phr

| Sub | Part phr |

her first book *having been well received by critics.*

Abs phr

| Sub | Part phr |

His curiosity *satisfied*, Marco decided to move on to other topics.

Abs phr

| Sub | Part phr |

Her face *white as a sheet*, Sue put down the phone and slowly stood up.

EXERCISE 24.3

Download several paragraphs from an Internet site or photocopy a newspaper or magazine article. In the text, find (1) three prepositional phrases, (2) two gerund phrases, (3) two participial phrases, and (4) an appositive phrase or an absolute phrase.

3 Modifying with clauses

A **clause** is a group of words that has a subject and a predicate. If a clause can stand alone as a sentence, it is an **independent clause,** (or **main clause**); if it cannot, it is a **dependent clause** (or **subordinate clause**). There are three major types of dependent clauses: adjective, adverb, and noun.

Adjective clauses (also called **relative clauses**) modify nouns and pronouns. An adjective clause usually begins with a relative pronoun (*which, that, who, whose, whom*) or a subordinating conjunction (*where, when, how*) and immediately follows the noun or pronoun it modifies.

The student *who is best prepared* is most likely to succeed.

The place *where I work best* is in my basement.

If the relative pronoun is the direct or indirect object in the adjective clause, it can be omitted.

The person *[whom] I gave the money to* has disappeared.

Chapter 31 discusses the correct use of relative pronouns; Chapter 35 describes how to use adjective clauses to subordinate ideas.

Noun clauses function in a sentence the way simple nouns do—as subjects, objects, complements, or appositives (see 25c). A noun clause begins with a relative pronoun (*who, that, whom, whoever*) or a subordinate conjunction (*whatever, wherever, how, why*).

Sub
Whoever leaked the news should be punished.

Ob
No one seems to know *how the rumor got started.*

Adverb clauses modify verbs, adjectives, clauses, or other adverbs, answering questions such as the following: when? where? why? how? An adverb clause begins with a subordinating conjunction (*if, although, because, whenever, while*).

If you cannot find the topic you want, double-click on the HELP button.

Although I have been late for work three times in the past two weeks, my boss has not said anything to me.   [The adverb clause modifies the entire main clause.]

EXERCISE 24.4

Combine each of the following pairs of sentences to form a single sentence. In so doing, turn one of the sentences into a dependent clause attached to the main clause.

1. Some people live in a cold climate. They should anticipate car-battery problems.
2. Your car will not start. You reach for some jumper cables.
3. You attach the cables to your battery. You should consider the possibility of explosion or injury.
4. Hydrogen gas in the battery case combines with air. It becomes a very explosive material.
5. There is a risk that an explosion will hurt your eyes. You should carry a pair of safety goggles with your cables.
6. Some drivers do not know how to use battery cables. They should not try to do it on their own.
7. You want to attempt a jump start. It is a good idea to read the owner's manual.
8. Car computers can lose memory when batteries fail. You will have to reset some things.
9. Prevent battery drain. Be certain to shut the car doors tightly.
10. It is easy to forget your headlights are on when you leave your car. Be sure to double-check.

24d Learn how to classify sentences

Good writers vary the types of sentences they use in order to make their writing more interesting. The two main categories of sentence types are functional and structural.

1 Functional classifications

Sentences can be categorized functionally, or rhetorically, according to their role. A **declarative sentence**, for example, makes a direct assertion about something.

Our political system is heavily influenced by corporate interests.

An **interrogative sentence** asks a question and ends with a question mark.

Have you ever traveled overseas?

An **imperative sentence** makes a request, gives a command, or offers advice. Although it is always addressed to *you*, the pronoun is usually omitted.

Use the TOOLBAR buttons to align or indent text.

Please send me a short reply.

An **exclamatory sentence** expresses strong emotion and ends with an exclamation point. Sometimes an exclamatory sentence is written in a form that is not a complete sentence.

We're finally connected!

What a show [it was]!   [Although not part of the sentence, *it was* is understood.]

2 Structural classifications

Sentences can also be categorized structurally according to their overall grammatical construction. A **simple sentence** has a single independent clause and no dependent clauses. Though a simple sentence has only one clause, it may have many phrases and thus be quite long.

I walk.

The high plateau of western Bolivia, called the *altiplano,* is one of the world's highest-elevation populated regions, with several towns at over 12,000 feet above sea level.

A **compound sentence** has two or more independent clauses and no dependent clauses. A compound sentence is created when two or more independent clauses are connected with a comma and a coordinating conjunction (*and, or, but, nor, for, so, yet*), with a semi-colon and a conjunctive adverb (*therefore, however, otherwise, indeed*), with a semicolon alone, or with a correlative conjunction (*either/or, neither/nor, both/and, not only/but also*).

Ind cl   Ind cl
An eagle once flew past our house, *but* I got only a brief glimpse of it.

Ind cl
Personal computers are becoming more user-friendly; *therefore,*

Ind cl
more people are buying them.

Ind cl   Ind cl
Feinstein voted for the bill; Boxer voted against it.

Ind cl   Ind cl
Either we go to the movie *or* we stay home.

A **complex sentence** contains one independent clause and one or more dependent clauses.

Sub   LV   SC
The sentence you are reading is a complex sentence.

A **compound-complex sentence,** as the name implies, consists of two or more independent clauses and one or more dependent clauses.

Dep cl
Millions upon millions of years before civilization had risen upon earth,

Ind cl
the central areas of this tremendous ocean were empty; *and*

Dep cl   Ind cl
where famous islands now exist, nothing rose above the rolling waves.

—James Michener, *Hawaii*

EXERCISE 24.5

Mark each sentence as declarative (D), imperative (Im), interrogative (In), or exclamatory (E) *and* as simple (S), compound (Cd), complex (Cx), or compound-complex (CC). The first one has been done for you.

1. Modern American Indian women are deeply engaged in the struggle to redefine themselves. (D, S)

2. They must reconcile traditional tribal definitions of women's roles with industrial society's definitions of these roles.

3. How does society define the role a woman should play?

4. If women are told they are powerless, they will believe it!

5. In the West, few images of women form part of the cultural mythos, and those that do are usually sexually charged.

6. The Native American tribes see women variously, but they do not question the power of femininity, which has always been a strong force.

7. Go cook the food.

8. Would you be friends with someone you couldn't trust?

9. The Indian women I have known have shown a wide range of personal styles and demeanors.

10. We must celebrate cultural differences!

EXERCISE 24.6

Log on to an Internet site of your choice, and download into a file a block of text of at least five sentences. (Alternatively, photocopy a block of text from a book or magazine.) Then classify each of the sentences according to the functional and structural classifications in this section.

Pronoun Case

FAQs

Is it correct to say "This is her"? (25a)

How do I know when to use *who* or *whom*? (25d)

What is wrong with "Mark likes school more than me"? (25f)

?

Case refers to the form a pronoun takes to indicate its grammatical relation to other words in a sentence. For example, the difference between *he, him,* and *his* is a matter of case: *he* is the **subjective case,** indicating its use as a grammatical subject, whereas *him* is the **objective case,** indicating its use as a grammatical object, and *his* is the **possessive case,** indicating its use as a grammatical possessive.

	Subjective	*Objective*	*Possessive*
First-person singular	I	me	my, mine
Second-person singular	you	you	your, yours
Third-person singular	he, she, it	him, her, it	his, her, hers, its
First-person plural	we	us	our, ours
Second-person plural	you	you	your, yours
Third-person plural	they	them	their, theirs
Relative and interrogative	who, whoever	whom, whomever	whose

Writers and speakers familiar with English seldom have a problem using the correct case when a single pronoun occupies the position of subject, object, or possessive in a sentence.

SUBJECT	*She* hoped that *they* would do well. [Subjects in both clauses.]
OBJECT	The crew helped *her*. [Direct object] Sarah gave *him* timely help. [Indirect object]
OBJECT OF A PREPOSITION	Help came for *them* immediately, thanks to *her*.
POSSESSIVE	Two of *my* friends have recently quit *their* jobs.

In some special situations, however, choosing the correct pronoun form can be confusing.

25a   Use the subjective case when a pronoun functions as a sentence subject, clause subject, or subject complement

The subjective case (*I, you, he, she, it, we, they, who, whoever*) is required for all pronouns used as subjects, including pronouns that are paired with a noun to form a compound subject or to rename the noun (see 25c).

> *She* and Octavio are good friends.   [Sentence subject]

> It seems that only Harrison and *I* were not invited.   [Clause subject]

A common problem with the subjective case pronouns occurs in a distinctive kind of subject-complement construction (see 24b-2). The verb *be* is used to set up an "equation" between a noun subject or a pronoun subject such as *it, that, this* and a personal pronoun such as *he, she, it,* or *they*.

> Who deserves to get the award ? It is ~~them~~ ^{they}, the actors.

> "Hello, is Carol there?" "Yes, this is ~~her~~ ^{she}."

> Who will be the lead actor—~~him~~ ^{he} or ~~me~~ ^I?

In casual conversation, many people would say "It is them" or "this is her" or "him or me." But standard English grammar requires the subjective forms, as is clear from these related versions of the examples: "*They* deserve to get the reward" or "*She* is here" or "Will *he* or will *I* be the lead actor?" (See 40c for a discussion of levels of formality.)

25b — Use the objective case when a pronoun functions as an object

The objective case (*me, you, him, her, it, us, them, whom, whomever*) is required for all pronouns used as objects, indirect objects, and objects of prepositions, including any pronoun paired with a noun or another pronoun to form a compound object. (See 25c for more on compound objects and 24b-2 for more on objects.)

Deborah called *us* as soon as she heard the good news.   [Pronoun as direct object]

The boss invited Janice and *him* to lunch.   [Pronoun as indirect object]

Just between *you* and *me,* don't you think Marty's been a little out of line lately?   [Pronoun as object of a preposition]

25c — Test for pronoun case in compound constructions by using the pronoun alone

Most problems with pronoun case arise in compound constructions, when a pronoun is paired with a noun:

The instructor gave Natasha and [*me, I*] an extra project to do.

In such sentences, the case of the pronoun—subjective or objective—depends on its function in the sentence. If you are unsure about which case to use, the best way to find out is to try the sentence without the noun:

The instructor gave [*me, I*] an extra project to do.

Seeing it in this form makes it easier to decide what the correct form is:

The instructor gave Natasha and *me* an extra project to do.

A special type of pronoun-noun pairing, called an **appositive,** occurs when a pronoun is conjoined with a noun.

We Americans tend to be patriotic.

Sometimes people from other countries complain about *us Americans.*

The sorority members chose to send *one person—me*—to the national convention.

How do I customize a style/grammar checker to search for pronoun case problems?

1. Open the style/grammar checker.
2. Click on the OPTIONS feature.
3. Instead of one of the standard rule sets (such as FORMAL or CASUAL), select a CUSTOM file.
4. Open the customization feature.
5. Deselect all the grammar and style features except the one for pronoun case problems, which should be called something like PRONOUN ERRORS.
6. Run the program on your document. *Remember:* It may not catch all your errors!

NOTE: You can use the customization feature for many similar purposes. For example, if you want to check for run-on sentences (Chapter 30), turn off PRONOUN ERRORS and select CLAUSE ERRORS instead.

Again, if you are unsure about which case to use in such situations, just omit the noun and see which pronoun form is correct.

We tend to be patriotic.

Sometimes people from other countries complain about *us.*

The sorority members chose to send *me* to the national convention.

EXERCISE 25.1

Circle the correct pronoun in each of the following sentences.

1. Are you going to invite her and [I, me] to your party?
2. It is unfair to make Paul and [I, me] do all the extra work by ourselves.
3. The coach asked Chris and [I, me] to design a new team logo.
4. Neither Paco nor [she, her] wants to go to Alaska to study.
5. It is unfair to stereotype [we, us] Asians as people who do nothing but study all the time.

6. She is not willing to give up her ticket, and neither are Luis and [he, him].
7. [We, us] New Yorkers love the city life.
8. The neighborhood council has asked [we, us] club members to keep the sidewalk clean.
9. Tokashi and [I, me] do not always see eye to eye, but we are generally good friends.
10. She read the manuscript to Eiko and [I, me].

25d Choose the form for an interrogative or relative pronoun based on how it functions in its clause

The *wh-* pronouns *who, whom, whoever, whomever,* and *whose* are used in questions and relative clauses (see 24c-3). In questions, they are called **interrogative pronouns;** in clauses, they are called **relative pronouns.**

Who reserved this book?   [Interrogative pronoun]

I'd like to find the person *who* reserved this book.   [Relative pronoun]

When you ask a question and reverse normal sentence word order, choosing the correct interrogative pronoun is often puzzling:

[*Who, Whom*] are you going to invite to the wedding?

In conversational English, many speakers would use *Who* in this sentence. But, according to the rules of English grammar, the correct form is *Whom.* To understand why, rearrange the question into a statement, using a personal pronoun: "You are going to invite [*he, him*] to the wedding." After rewording, you will have no trouble recognizing the correct personal pronoun—in this case, *him.* The rewording clearly points to the objective case and the choice of the objective form *whom.*

> http://www.edunet.
> com/english/grammar/
> pronoun.html
> A complete guide
> to pronouns

As a writer, you must decide whether the *wh-* pronoun functions as a subject or an object in the clause in which it is used. Because independent and dependent clauses are often tightly linked, the choice can be unclear. If you are uncertain about which form to use, try this test: (1) isolate and, if necessary, transpose the clause in which the *wh-* pronoun occurs, (2) substitute different personal pronouns (such as *she, her, he,* or *him*) for the *wh-* pronoun and see which case sounds best, and then (3) select the corresponding *wh-* pronoun. For example, consider this sentence:

> One fellow playwright [*who, whom*] Shakespeare admired was Marlowe.

1. The *wh-* pronoun occurs in the relative clause *wh___ Shakespeare admired;* transposed, the clause becomes *Shakespeare admired wh___.*

2. Of the different personal pronouns substituted in the *wh___* slot, the one that sounds best is *him: Shakespeare admired him.*

3. The *wh-* pronoun that corresponds in case to *him* is *whom.* So the grammatically correct form of the sentence is

> One fellow playwright *whom* Shakespeare admired was Marlowe.

The same process can be used for the pronouns *whoever* and *whomever:*

> The place is open to [*whoever, whomever*] wants to go there.

1. The *wh-* pronoun occurs in the relative clause *wh___ wants to go there.*

2. Of the different personal pronouns substituted in the *wh___* slot, the ones that sound best are *she* and *he: She (or he) wants to go there.*

3. The *wh-* pronoun that corresponds in case to *she* or *he* is *whoever.* So the grammatically correct form of the sentence is

> The place is open to *whoever* wants to go there.

EXERCISE 25.2

Select the correct form of the pronoun in each sentence.

1. How can someone [who, whom] makes the minimum wage invest in the stock market?

2. My financial adviser, [who, whom] most of the business community trusts, has recently moved to New York.

3. [Who, Whom] does she wish to contact at the law firm?

4. She made it perfectly clear that [whoever, whomever] wants to come is welcome.

5. Judge Reynolds is a man in [who, whom] the community has placed great trust.

6. Barbara Ehrenreich is someone [who, whom] I have long admired.

7. He addressed his remarks to [whoever, whomever] would listen.

8. Fortune sometimes comes to those [who, whom] seek it.
9. Richard, [who, whom] updated his investment portfolio last week, decided against purchasing the no-load mutual fund.
10. We will support [whoever, whomever] the people elect.

25e   Use possessive pronouns to show ownership

There are two different types of possessive pronouns. **Attributive possessive pronouns** (*my, your, her, his, its, our, their*) are used directly before a noun, while **nominal possessive pronouns** (*mine, yours, hers, his, its, ours, theirs*) are used with a linking verb (*is, was*).

This is *my* car.

This car is *mine.*

Note that the possessive forms ending in *s* (*yours, hers, ours, its, theirs*) do not take an apostrophe (see 49a).

Gerunds require an attributive possessive pronoun:

His wanting to do extra work was what impressed me.

In this sentence, *wanting to do extra work* is a gerund phrase. Since gerunds act as nouns, the possessive pronoun modifying this phrase should be an adjectival one (*his*). Be sure not to make the mistake of using the objective case pronoun (*him*) in this kind of construction.

His
~~Him~~ wanting to do extra work was what impressed me.

25f   Choose the case for a pronoun in a comparison based on how it would function in its own clause

What is the meaning of this sentence?

Mark likes school more than me.

Technically, it means that Mark has a greater liking for school than he does for the speaker of the sentence. It does not mean that Mark has a greater liking for school than the speaker does. The latter meaning is correctly expressed with this construction:

Mark likes school more than I.

Many writers fail to make this distinction, thereby potentially confusing their readers.

How can you avoid this problem? You can avoid it by recognizing that the second part of the comparison (the part after *than*) is an incomplete clause. The complete versions of the two sentences make the distinction clear:

> Mark likes school more than [he likes] me.

> Mark likes school more than I [like school].

A similar procedure can be used with *as . . . as* constructions:

> President Clinton's wife is as much a Democrat as *he*.

He is the correct pronoun here (not *him*) because the complete sentence actually is

> President Clinton's wife is as much a Democrat as *he is a Democrat*.

The writer has simply dropped *is a Democrat* from the end of the sentence. Alternatively, you can write

> President Clinton's wife is as much a Democrat as *he is*.

WEB

http://owl.english.
purdue.edu/Files/
80.html
A discussion of pronoun case problems in compound structures, comparisons, and formal vs. semiformal writing

EXERCISE 25.3

Circle the correct pronoun in each sentence.

1. My brother is as conservative as [me, I].
2. The recruiter rated Susan higher than [me, I].
3. Trang claims that she enjoys the opera as much as [him, he].
4. Mark went to Paris this summer and liked it as much as [we, us].
5. Without even realizing it, Pia hurt Kelly's feelings today as much as she hurt [my, mine] last week.
6. Ronaldo does not play volleyball as well as [her, she].
7. I think it was Martin who said that Stacy is taller than [him, he].
8. Are you going to talk to [he, him] about the controversy created by the proposal?
9. He is as much to blame for the tension in the office as [her, she].
10. Ahmad felt that Jerry was better suited for the position than [me, I].

Verbs

What is wrong with the sentence "He believed that his
thesis is credible"? (26e-2)

How can I decide when to use *sit* or *set*? (26f)

When I make an "if" statement, where should I put the
would? (26h-1)

Using verbs correctly can help make writing lively and precise.
This chapter explains some of the major aspects of verb usage: form,
tense, voice, and mood. (Two other aspects, gender and number, are
discussed in 27a and 33a.)

26a   Learn the regular verb forms

All verbs in English, except *be,* have five possible forms or **principal parts.**

Base form	Present tense (-s form)	Past tense	Past participle	Present participle
jump	jumps	jumped	jumped	jumping
erase	erases	erased	erased	erasing
add	adds	added	added	adding
veto	vetoes	vetoed	vetoed	vetoing

Most English verbs are **regular verbs.** That is, starting with the base form, their forms follow the pattern of the preceding examples: adding *s* (or *es*) to the base form to make the third-person singular present tense, adding *d* (or *ed*) to make the past tense and past participle, and adding *ing* to the base form (and sometimes dropping the final *e*) to make the present participle.

The **base form,** or **simple form,** of a verb is the form listed in a dictionary. It is the form normally used with subjects that are plural nouns or the pronouns *I, you, we,* or *they* to make statements in the present tense.

Hummingbirds *migrate* south in winter.

I *walk* two miles every day.

When the subject of a sentence is *he, she, it,* or some other third-person singular subject, the **present tense** of the verb has an *s* added to it.

She *visits* New York every month.

My neighbor *walks* laps around our block.

Sometimes a slight change is required in the spelling of the base form (*fly/flies, veto/vetoes*).

The **past tense** of a verb is used to describe action that occurred in the past. For a regular verb, add *d* or *ed* to the base form to get the past tense:

Fox TV *televised* Super Bowl XXXI.

We *wanted* to see the game.

The **past participle** of a regular verb is similar in form to the past tense. The past participle can be used (1) with *has* or *have* in the present perfect tense, (2) with *had* in the past perfect tense, (3) with some form of *be* to create a passive-voice construction, and (4) by itself, as an adjective, to modify a noun.

We *have petitioned* the school board for a new crosswalk.
[Present perfect]

Before last night's meeting, we *had talked* about going directly to the mayor.   [Past perfect]

Last year, two students *were injured* trying to cross this street.
[Passive voice]

The parents of the *injured* students are supporting our cause.
[Adjective]

The **present participle** is created by adding *ing* to the base form of a verb. It is used (1) with some form of *be* to indicate ongoing action (the progressive tense), (2) as a gerund, and (3) as an adjective.

Joaquin *is working* on a new project.   [Progressive tense]

He enjoys *working*.   [Gerund]

This is a *working* draft of my paper.   [Adjective]

EXERCISE 26.1

What are the principal parts of the following regular verbs?

1. print
2. drown
3. compile

26b   Learn common irregular verb forms

An **irregular verb** is one whose past tense and past participle do not follow the standard pattern of being created by adding *d* or *ed* to the base form. Instead, these forms often have different internal vowels than in the base form (base form: *find*; past tense: *found*; past participle: *found*). Other variations are possible as well; for example, the past tense and past participle may be the same as the base form (*set/set/set*) or may be radically different (*go/went/gone*). (Note: *Be* and *have* also have irregular present-tense forms.)

Base form	Past tense	Past participle
beat	beat	beaten
become	became	become
begin	began	begun
bite	bit	bit, bitten
blow	blew	blown
break	broke	broken
bring	brought	brought
build	built	built
burn	burned, burnt	burned, burnt
buy	bought	bought
catch	caught	caught
choose	chose	chosen
come	came	come
cost	cost	cost
cut	cut	cut
dig	dug	dug

Base form	Past tense	Past participle
dive	dove, dived	dived
do	did	done
draw	drew	drawn
drink	drank	drunk
drive	drove	driven
eat	ate	eaten
fall	fell	fallen
feel	felt	felt
fight	fought	fought
find	found	found
fly	flew	flown
forget	forgot	forgotten, forgot
freeze	froze	frozen
get	got	gotten, got
give	gave	given
go	went	gone
grow	grew	grown
hang	hung	hung
have	had	had
hear	heard	heard
hide	hid	hidden
hit	hit	hit
keep	kept	kept
know	knew	known
lay	laid	laid
lead	led	led
leave	left	left
lend	lent	lent
lie	lay	lain
lose	lost	lost
make	made	made
mean	meant	meant
pay	paid	paid
prove	proved	proved, proven
read	read	read
ride	rode	ridden
run	ran	run
say	said	said
see	saw	seen
send	sent	sent
set	set	set

Base form	Past tense	Past participle
shake	shook	shaken
shoot	shot	shot
show	showed	shown, showed
shrink	shrank	shrunk
sing	sang	sung
sink	sank	sunk
sit	sat	sat
sleep	slept	slept
speak	spoke	spoken
steal	stole	stolen
stick	stuck	stuck
strike	struck	struck, stricken
swear	swore	sworn
swim	swam	swum
swing	swung	swung
take	took	taken
teach	taught	taught
tear	tore	torn
think	thought	thought
throw	threw	thrown
wake	woke, waked	woken, waked
wear	wore	worn
win	won	won
write	wrote	written

As you can see, many of the most common verbs in the English language are irregular. Therefore, it is important that you learn their forms.

The two most common verbs in English, *be* and *have,* are also two of the most irregular. The third-person singular present tense of *have* is not *haves* but *has.* See the chart Forms of *be* on page 535 for a complete outline of the forms of this irregular verb.

EXERCISE 26.2

What are the principal parts of each of the following irregular verbs? (Answer first by thinking about how you would use the forms when speaking; then consult a dictionary.)

1. arise
2. dream
3. ring
4. stand
5. sweep

Forms of *be*

Present Tense

	Singular	*Plural*
First person	I *am*	we *are*
Second person	you *are*	you *are*
Third person	he/she/it *is*	they *are*
	Michael *is*	people *are*

Past Tense

	Singular	*Plural*
First person	I *was*	we *were*
Second person	you *were*	you *were*
Third person	he/she/it *was*	they *were*
	Michael *was*	people *were*

26c   Know how to use auxiliary verbs

An **auxiliary verb** (or **helping verb**) is one that is used with a main verb to indicate tense (see 26d), mood (see 26h), or voice (see 26g). The most common auxiliary verbs are *be, have,* and *do.* Some form of one of these helping verbs is frequently used with a base form, present participle, or past participle of a main verb to create a more complex **verb phrase.**

She *is finishing* her paper.   [Progressive tense, indicating ongoing action]

The college *has adopted* a new honor code.   [Present perfect tense, indicating past action with ongoing effects]

We *do need* to get going.   [Emphasis]

My roommate *has been asked* to run for the student senate.   [Passive voice, present perfect tense]

Does he *know* what's involved?   [Question]

Other important helping verbs are the **modal auxiliary verbs** (*may/might, can/could, will/would, shall/should, must, ought to,* and *have to*). These verbs communicate degrees of probability, necessity, or obligation. A modal auxiliary verb is used only with the base form of another verb:

> The concert *might be* sold out.

> We *should get* tickets before it is too late.

Most of the modal auxiliaries do not have a third-person present *-s* form or a participle form; *have to* is the only exception.

> Sandra *has to* write a paper.

> Yesterday she *had to* spend all afternoon in science lab.

> Earlier she *had had to* prepare for a math test.

Modal auxiliaries can be used with forms of *be, have,* or *do,* but not with other modal auxiliaries. For example, "We might could do that" is ungrammatical in standard English. You can often create a standard English version of such a double-modal expression by substituting a synonymous verb phrase for one of the modal auxiliaries:

NONSTANDARD   We might *could* do that.

REVISED   We might *be able to* do that.

In some cases, you can simply eliminate one of the modal auxiliaries:

NONSTANDARD   Sally *should ought to* cancel her appointment.

REVISED   Sally *should* cancel her appointment.

OR

Sally *ought to* cancel her appointment.

EXERCISE 26.3

In the following sentences, underline the verb phrases, circle the modal auxiliary verbs, and correct any double modals.

1. Joey is working on his chemistry assignment tonight.
2. Li-Ping wanted Michael to have lunch with her, but he told her that he might ought to work.
3. Angelica must should go with us to see the soccer match.
4. I heard that the company has adopted a new policy with regard to employee absences.
5. Does she know that he might not come to the play with us?
6. Fernando is staying home tonight.
7. He must not leave the house while he is recovering from knee surgery.

8. School uniforms should ought to be the standard in the public schools.
9. Ikuto may be walking over to our house right now.
10. My neighbor has been accused of stealing company office supplies.

26d Learn the verb tenses

Verb tense expresses the time of the action or the state of being indicated by a verb. English has three basic tenses: past, present, and future. Each tense can also take on a **verbal aspect,** indicating duration or completion of the verb's action or state of being. The three verbal aspects in English are progressive, perfect, and perfect progressive. With all possible combinations of tenses and aspects, English has twelve verb tenses.

SIMPLE PRESENT TENSE	we wonder
PRESENT PROGRESSIVE TENSE	we are wondering
PRESENT PERFECT TENSE	we have wondered
PRESENT PERFECT PROGRESSIVE TENSE	we have been wondering
SIMPLE PAST TENSE	we wondered
PAST PROGRESSIVE TENSE	we were wondering
PAST PERFECT TENSE	we had wondered
PAST PERFECT PROGRESSIVE TENSE	we had been wondering
FUTURE TENSE	we will wonder
FUTURE PROGRESSIVE TENSE	we will be wondering
FUTURE PERFECT TENSE	we will have wondered
FUTURE PERFECT PROGRESSIVE TENSE	we will have been wondering

Present tenses

The **simple present tense** is used to express a general truth, to make an observation, or to describe an habitual activity.

A rolling stone *gathers* no moss.

Oates's stories *depress* me.

My father *mows* the lawn every week.

With an appropriate time expression, the simple present can be used to refer to a scheduled future event.

The show *begins* in five minutes.

The simple present is used in stage directions and in critical discussions of literary works.

Max suddenly *appears* at the door.

In *The Tempest,* all the action *occurs* in one place during one day.

The simple present also is used to express a scientific fact or law.

Water *boils* at 100° Celsius.

Gravity *causes* objects to fall.

The **present progressive tense** is formed of the auxiliary verb *am, are,* or *is* and the present participle (*-ing* form) of a main verb. The present progressive is used to indicate action occurring at the present time.

Jennifer *is preparing* for the MCAT exam.

With an appropriate time expression, the present progressive can be used to announce future events.

A new supermarket *is opening* next week.

ESL Note: Certain verbs, called **stative verbs,** do not have any progressive tenses. These verbs include *know, believe, need, consist,* and *exist.* Thus, it is incorrect to say "I am needing a new computer" (see 56f).

The **present perfect tense** is formed with the auxiliary verb *have* or *has* and the past participle of a main verb. The present perfect is used to indicate action that began in the past and either is continuing or has continuing effects in the present.

Many people *have expressed* alarm about environmental degradation.

ESL Note: The present perfect tense and the simple past tense cannot be used interchangeably. The present perfect implies *duration* of past action; the simple past tense expresses *completed* past action. The sentence "She was at the university since 1996" is incorrect, because the *since* phrase refers to a continuous time period. The grammatically correct version of this sentence is "She *has been* at the university since 1996."

The **present perfect progressive tense** is formed by combining *have been* or *has been* with the present participle of a main verb. The present perfect progressive is used similarly to the present perfect but emphasizes the ongoing nature of the activity.

Eric *has been studying* German for two years.

This sentence means that Eric is still studying German, whereas the sentence "Eric *has studied* German for two years" could mean that he is not currently studying it (although he might again study it someday).

E X E R C I S E   2 6 . 4

Correct any errors in verb tense in the following sentences.

1. Lily walking to the supermarket every day.
2. The concert beginning in only ten minutes.
3. I am knowing that Jay was not telling me the truth last night.
4. The nail kit is consisting of a buffer, a file, and three shades of polish.
5. Jonathan lived in Oakland since 1992.
6. He knew her since the beginning of the 1980s.
7. Jenny prepares for the SAT examination this week.
8. During the play, the protagonist entering from the left in the final scene.
9. He is understanding that there is very little he can do to avoid bankruptcy this year.
10. Since the 1970s, women were guaranteed equal opportunity in federally funded school sports programs.

2 | Past tenses

The **simple past tense** is used to describe actions or conditions that occurred or applied entirely in the past.

Jonas Salk *invented* the polio vaccine.

In 1950, the United States *consisted* of only forty-eight states.

The **past progressive tense** is formed by combining the auxiliary verb *was* or *were* with the present participle of a main verb. The past progressive describes action continuing over a period of time in the past. It is often used to set the stage for another action of shorter duration.

He *was cleaning* the living room when the phone rang.

The **past perfect tense** is created by combining the auxiliary verb *had* with the past participle of a main verb. The past perfect is used to describe a past action that preceded another past action.

Amanda *had thought* of volunteering for the job, but then she got sick.

The **past perfect progressive tense** functions like the past perfect tense but puts more emphasis on the continuing or repetitive nature of the past action. The past perfect progressive is formed by combining *had been* with the present participle of a main verb.

Amanda *had been thinking* of volunteering for the job, but then she got sick.

EXERCISE 26.5

Correct the verb tense errors in the following sentences.

1. Eli Whitney has invented the cotton gin in 1793.
2. She divulged the secret, even though she promised not to.
3. It was five years since I last saw Aihua.
4. Three years ago, I had visited China.
5. The United States first was consisting of thirteen colonies.
6. Joseph Conrad was writing *The Heart of Darkness* in English, his third language.
7. She waited for the phone to ring when her brother came into the bedroom.
8. Miguel did well in the course until last week, when he unexpectedly received a D on an important quiz.
9. Tim has learned the results of his preliminary examinations two weeks after he took them.
10. He was my best friend, even though he had been two years older.

3 Future tenses

The **simple future tense,** as its name implies, expresses actions or conditions that will occur in the future. The simple future consists of the modal auxiliary verb *will* and the base form of a main verb.

Ames *will be* a half hour late.

ESL Note: In casual English, future conditions are often expressed using the modal auxiliary *is going to* instead of *will*, as in "Ames *is going to* be a half hour late." It is best to avoid this usage in formal English.

The **future progressive tense** is formed by combining *will be* with the present participle of a main verb. The future progressive expresses action that will be continuing or repeated in the future.

Right now my son is working, but next year he *will be going* to college.

The **future perfect tense** consists of *will have* and the past participle of a main verb. The future perfect is used to describe an action that will occur in the future but before some specified time.

By the end of this year, gun-related violence *will have taken* the lives of more than 2,000 American teenagers.

The **future perfect progressive tense** is similar to the future perfect but emphasizes the continuous or repetitive nature of the action. The future perfect progressive consists of *will have been* plus the present participle of a main verb.

By tomorrow morning, I *will have been working* on this paper for eighteen hours.

26e Observe sequence of tenses

Good writing presents a coherent framework of time. Since time is indicated in part by verb tense, it is important to select verb tenses carefully and logically. The relationship between two or more verbs in the same sentence or in adjacent sentences is called the **sequence of tenses.**

1 Sequence of verb tenses in compound or adjacent sentences

Two or more independent clauses about closely related events or situations may be connected by a coordinating conjunction (*and, or, but*) to form a compound sentence. Alternatively, two related independent clauses may be presented as consecutive sentences. Typically, the main verbs in each clause or sentence have the same tense.

Joe *wants* to go to the game, but Lori *does* not.

He *likes* baseball. She *dislikes* the game.

Sometimes, however, one event or action may logically precede or follow the other, requiring different verb tenses to indicate which of the two came first.

Joe *could* not *go* to the game, because he *had* not *done* his homework.

2 Sequence of verb tenses in complex sentences

A complex sentence has one independent clause and one or more dependent clauses (see 24d-2). Each clause has its own main verb. The appropriate tense for each main verb depends on the context and the intended meaning. If the actions expressed by these verbs occur at approximately the same time, the verbs should be in the same tense.

When the conductor *gives* the signal, the musicians *start* playing.

Before you *sit* down, *adjust* the height of your chair.

When you need to make it clear that one past action or event preceded another, use the past perfect or past perfect progressive tense in one clause and the simple past tense in the other clause.

Although Amanda *had thought* of volunteering for the job, she *was* now no longer interested.

When you need to show that a past action or event preceded a present or future one, use the present perfect or present perfect progressive tense to express the past action or event.

Since the Pope *has been* to Mexico already, he probably *will* not *go* again.

3 Sequence of verb tenses with infinitives

There are two kinds of infinitives: the **present infinitive** (*to* plus the base form of a verb) and the **perfect infinitive** (*to have* plus the past participle of a verb) (see 24a-8). Use the present infinitive for an action that occurs at the same time as or later than the action expressed by the main verb.

Samantha *wants* me *to pick up* the car.

Use the perfect infinitive for an action that occurs prior to the action expressed by the main verb.

Samantha *wants* me *to have picked up* the car.

Guidelines for Choosing the Correct Sequence of Tenses in a Complex Sentence

1. Consider the two adjacent clauses: Does the action in clause A occur at approximately the same time as the action in clause B? If so, use the same verb tense in both clauses.

2. If the action in clause A *precedes* the action in clause B, follow these guidelines:

   a. If clause B is in the *present* tense, put clause A in the *past* or *present perfect.*

   b. If clause B is in the *past* tense, put clause A in the *past perfect.*

   c. If clause B is in the *future* tense, put clause A in the *present* or *present perfect.*

4   Sequence of verb tenses with participles

The **present participle** (the *-ing* form of a verb) can be used to represent an action that occurs at the same time as that expressed by the main verb.

Walking into the house, Jim sensed that something was wrong.

The **past participle** is used to indicate that an action occurs before or during the action expressed by the main verb.

Stung by criticism of his latest film, Costner is working hard on a new one.

The **present perfect participle** (*having* plus the past participle) expresses an action occurring prior to the action of the main verb.

Having signed a contract, Deanna was afraid she had to go through with the deal.

EXERCISE 26.6

Correct any sequence-of-tense errors in the following sentences.

1. As soon as she entered the room, several people rush over to say hello.

2. He was disappointed when some of his sources are found to be fraudulent.

3. He believed that his thesis is credible.

4. We insisted on using pesticides, even though this is not proven to be the best solution to an insect problem.
5. Her eyesight has begun to fail, and she turned to the radio for information.
6. Who expected that old car to lasted all these years?
7. His roommate has expected him to have done the laundry by Friday.
8. Entering the workplace, they have understood the safety concerns of the employees.
9. Having fired the employees who reported the safety problem, the manager had faced a lawsuit.
10. Concerned that the number of beds in the emergency shelter would be inadequate, the city council votes to open another shelter during the winter.

26f   Use transitive and intransitive verbs correctly

A **transitive verb** is a verb that takes a direct object (see 24a-4). In other words, a transitive verb transfers an action from a subject to an object. The sentence "A virus damaged my hard drive" has a transitive verb (*damaged*) that transfers the action to the direct object (*hard drive*). Some typical transitive verbs are *see, hear, consult, kick, recognize,* and *mix.* Transitive verbs are usually marked in dictionaries with the abbreviation *vt* or *tr.*

An **intransitive verb** is one that does not take a direct object. Some typical intransitive verbs are *sleep, relax, die, go, fall, come,* and *walk.* Intransitive verbs are usually identified in dictionaries by the abbreviation *vi* or *intr.*

Many English verbs can be used either transitively or intransitively. For example, the verb *jump* is transitive in the sentence "Mike jumped the fence" but intransitive in the sentence "Mike jumped for joy." Some other common "two-way" verbs are *run, dream, write, eat, grow,* and *develop.*

Many speakers of English confuse *sit* and *set, lie* and *lay,* and *rise* and *raise.* The two verbs in each of these pairs sound somewhat alike and have related meanings, but they differ as to whether they can take an object (see 24b-3). The first member of each pair is intransitive and cannot take an object; the second member is transitive and does take an object.

INTRANSITIVE   Jorge *will sit* over there.   [The verb has no object.]

TRANSITIVE   Jorge *will set* the *flowers* over there.   [The verb has an object, *flowers.*]

| INTRANSITIVE | I think I *will lie* down.   [The verb has no object.] |
| TRANSITIVE | We *will lay* the *groundwork* for the project.   [The verb has an object, *groundwork*.] |

| INTRANSITIVE | The sun *rises* in the east.   [The verb has no object.] |
| TRANSITIVE | The senator always *raises* a lot of *money* for his re-election campaigns.   [The verb has an object, *money*.] |

EXERCISE 26.7

Identify the sentences that contain a transitive verb, and circle the direct object in each.

1. I have to do my homework.
2. I am too busy to go to the game.
3. You can send me an email message.
4. The store closes at 10 p.m.
5. Last night, somebody in our dorm set off the fire alarm.
6. My father plays tennis three times a week.
7. He hits the ball harder than I do.
8. Our club has six new members.
9. Some people like to have a watermark on their stationery.
10. Does your word processor automatically correct typos?

26g   Favor active over passive voice

Voice is the characteristic of a verb that indicates whether the subject of a sentence is acting or being acted upon. In the **active voice,** the subject of the sentence performs an action on a direct object (see 24b). In the **passive voice,** the subject of the sentence is acted upon. Only transitive verbs can be cast in active and passive voice (see 26f).

	Subject/actor	DO
ACTIVE	My friend Julie *handcrafted* this pin. [The subject acts upon an object.]	

	Subject	DO/actor
PASSIVE	This pin *was handcrafted* by my friend Julie. [The subject is acted upon by the object following the verb.]	

The passive voice consists of an appropriate form of the auxiliary verb *be* and the past participle of a main verb (see 26a). A passive-voice sentence may refer to the performer of the action in a *by* phrase following the verb. In practice, though, such a *by* phrase is often omitted, which has the effect of concealing or de-emphasizing the performer of the action.

PASSIVE   This pin *was handcrafted.*   [The phrase *by my friend Julie* is omitted.]

In general, good writers favor the active voice over the passive voice. The active voice is more concise and more direct—and thus more vigorous—than the passive. In some cases, however, the passive voice works better than the active voice. For example, when identifying the performer of an action is unimportant or difficult, using the passive voice allows you to write a grammatical sentence without mentioning the actor (see 34d).

Bacterial infections are usually treated with antibiotics.

Style/Grammar Checker Alert: If the style/grammar checker you use is preprogrammed to eliminate the passive voice, it will highlight most of the passive verbs in your writing and make a comment like "This main clause may contain a verb in the passive voice." If you decide to change some of the passive verbs to the active voice, you can do so by simply making the actor (whether stated or concealed) the subject of the sentence and changing the predicate. Note, however, that some passive-voice sentences are perfectly fine and should be left unchanged (see 34d).

WEB

http://webster.
commnet.edu/HP/
pages/darling/
grammar/verbs.htm
A fantastic resource
on verbs, including
quizzes and lots of
cute graphics

EXERCISE 26.8

Some of the following sentences are in the passive voice; others are in the active voice. For practice, change all passive-voice sentences to active-voice sentences (which may require inventing an actor) and all actives to passives (which may involve omitting the actor). (Note: Some sentences have intransitive verbs, which cannot be changed.)

1.   We can recycle most ordinary materials.
2.   Twelve protesters were arrested by the police.
3.   Cartilage serves as padding material in joints.
4.   It keeps bones from grinding on bones.
5.   You can use toolbar buttons instead of menu or keyboard commands.

6. A group of marine scientists and conservationists recently voted Palau, Micronesia's coral reef, one of the seven underwater wonders of the world.

7. *A Tale of Two Cities* by Charles Dickens should be reread by everyone who thinks reading it in high school was enough.

8. In the summer of 1996, scientific evidence pointing to the possible existence of life beyond Earth was announced by NASA.

9. The purported evidence was found in a 4.5 pound meteorite that landed in Antarctica 13,000 years ago.

10. Did someone switch off the copier?

26h Make sure verbs are in the proper mood

The **mood** of a verb indicates the type of statement being made by the sentence—an assertion, a question, a command, a wish, or a hypothetical condition. English verbs have three moods: indicative, imperative, and subjunctive.

The **indicative mood** is used to make assertions, state opinions, and ask questions (see 24d-1). It is the most commonly used mood in English.

> Washington *was* the first president of the United States.
> [Assertion]
>
> Citizens *should take* more interest in local government.   [Opinion]
>
> *Do* you *want* to vote?   [Question]

http://owl.english.purdue.edu/writers/by-topic.html#parts
Coverage of irregular verbs, auxiliary verbs, tense, sequence of tenses, voice, and mood

The **imperative mood** is used to express commands and give instructions. Commands are always addressed to a second person, although the explicit *you* is normally omitted. Instructions are often cast in the imperative mood (see 24b-1).

> *Insert* Setup Disk 1 in the floppy disk drive. Then *run* the program.

The **subjunctive mood** is used for hypothetical conditions, polite requests, wishes, and other uncertain statements. A verb in the subjunctive mood often appears in dependent clauses beginning with *if* or *that*. The present subjunctive is the same as the base form of the verb. The past subjunctive is identical to the past tense of the verb. The only exception is *were,* which is used for all subjunctive uses of *be* except after verbs of requesting, requiring, or recommending, where *be* is used.

I wish I *were* an A student!

The defense attorney requested that her client *be* given probation.

The past perfect subjunctive has the same form as the ordinary past perfect.

1 Hypothetical *if* constructions

When an *if* clause expresses a contrary-to-fact or unreal condition, the verb of the clause should be in the past subjunctive or past perfect subjunctive mood. The main clause verb should include the modal auxiliary *would, could,* or *might.*

If I *were* you, I *would* make up my Incompletes as soon as possible. [Expresses a hypothetical future condition.]

If John *had been* there, he *might* have been able to help.   [Expresses a hypothetical past condition.]

Do not use *would, could,* or *might* in a hypothetical *if* clause. In contrary-to-fact sentences, modal auxiliaries such as *would* and *could* belong in the main clause, not in the conditional (subordinate) clause. Use the subjunctive in the conditional clause.

SUBJUNCTIVE FORM REVISED

lived
If we ~~would live~~ closer to San Francisco, we would go there more often.

2 Dependent clauses expressing a wish

In a dependent clause following the verb *wish,* use the past subjunctive for present contrary-to-fact conditions and the past perfect subjunctive for past contrary-to-fact conditions.

I wish [that] he *were* here.

I wish [that] he *had stayed.*

3 Dependent clauses expressing a request, suggestion, or demand

Verbs like *require, demand, suggest,* and *insist* are usually followed by a dependent clause beginning with *that*. The verb in the *that* clause should be in the subjunctive mood. (Note: Sometimes *that* is omitted.)

The police require that all pets *be* kept on a leash.

They suggested that he *go* to the emergency room.

EXERCISE 26.9

Correct any errors in mood in the following sentences.

1. If I was rich, I would go on a world tour.
2. If Denju would get a job, he could move out of his parents' house.
3. If she would have been more careful, the accident might never have occurred.
4. I might believe you if you would have been more honest with me in the past.
5. Rahim knew that if he was to eat less, he would lose weight.
6. I wish that Shu-Chuan was still my roommate.
7. Nedra might be able to leave town for the weekend if she would finish her history research paper before Friday night.
8. Was he to actually consider Joanne's stock-option offer, he might take more interest in the future of the company.
9. If Josh was any better a dancer, he could probably be in an MTV video.
10. If he could have gone to the store, I am sure he would have remembered to buy the strawberries.

Agreement

Which is correct: "Athletics *are* . . ." or "Athletics *is* . . ."? (27a)

Should I say "The jury took *its* time" or "The jury took *their* time"? (27b)

How can I avoid using *he, him,* or *his* to refer to people in general? (27b)

?

Agreement refers to two related facts about standard English. First, subjects and verbs should agree in number; that is, they must both be either singular or plural. "He go to work at nine o'clock" is ungrammatical because *he* is singular and *go* is plural. Second, pronouns should agree in number and in gender with their antecedents. "An athlete should always do his best" is unacceptable to many people because this use of *his* implies that all athletes are male.

27a Make verbs agree in number with their grammatical subjects

Here are some rules on subject-verb agreement.

1. *Plural subjects require plural verbs; singular subjects require singular verbs.*

He goes to work at nine o'clock.

We see each other later in the day.

With a modified subject, be sure to make the verb agree with the simple subject (see 24b-1).

Meg's circle of friends gives her a lot of support.   [*Circle* is the simple subject of the phrase *Meg's circle of friends.*]

When a singular subject is followed by a phrase beginning with *as well as, along with, in addition to,* or *together with,* the verb should be in the singular.

Meg, as well as her friends, usually votes for the more liberal candidate.

If this seems awkward to you, you can restructure the sentence to create a compound subject (which takes a plural verb):

Meg and her friends usually vote for the more liberal candidate.

ESL Note: Speakers of languages that do not mark nouns and verbs for number (for example, Chinese and Japanese) often have trouble with subject-verb agreement in English, as in this example:

There are times when we experience or witness events that disturb us.

2. *Compound subjects usually require plural verbs.* Compound subjects refer to two or more people, places, or things and are formed with the conjunction *and.* In most cases, compound subjects have a plural sense and thus require plural verbs.

Geography and history are my favorite subjects.

In some cases, a compound subject has a singular sense and requires a singular verb.

Law and order is a desirable feature for all modern societies.

Rock 'n' roll has remained popular for decades.

> **WEB**
>
> http://webster.
> commnet.edu/
> hp/pages/
> darling/grammar/
> sv_agr.htm
> A great guide to
> subject/verb agreement, complete
> with quizzes
> and exercises

3. *With a disjunctive subject, the verb should agree in number with the part of the subject closest to it.* A **disjunctive subject** consists of two nouns or pronouns joined by *or* or *nor*. The verb in a sentence with such a subject agrees with the second part of the subject.

Either my sister or my parents are coming.

Neither my parents nor my sister is coming.

If the singular verb sounds awkward to you with such a mixed subject, you can switch the two parts of the subject and use the plural form of the verb:

Neither my sister nor my parents are coming.

4. *Indefinite pronouns with a singular sense take singular verbs; those with a plural sense take plural verbs.* Indefinite pronouns include *anybody, everyone, nothing, each,* and *much.* Unlike regular pronouns, they do not necessarily refer to any particular person or thing. Most indefinite pronouns are grammatically singular. Therefore, when used as subjects, they should have singular verbs.

No one is here.

Something needs to be done about this.

Each of the candidates is giving a short speech.

A few indefinite pronouns, including *both* and *others,* are plural and therefore require plural verbs. Other indefinite pronouns, such as *some, all, any, more,* and *none,* can be used with either singular or plural verb forms, depending on what they refer to.

All of the committee members were at the meeting.

All of their attention was directed at the speaker.

In the first example sentence, *all* is plural because it refers to the plural noun *members; all of the committee members* could be replaced by the pronoun *they.* In the second example sentence, *all* is singular because it refers to the singular noun *attention; all of their attention* could be replaced by *it.*

5. *Collective nouns typically take singular verbs.* Collective nouns are words such as *team, faculty, jury,* and *committee,* which can have either a singular or a plural sense depending on whether they refer to the group or to the individuals within the group (see 24a-1). These nouns usually take singular verbs.

The team is doing better than expected.

The band seems to be road-weary.

To emphasize the plural sense of collective nouns, simply insert an appropriate plural noun.

The band members seem to be road-weary.

OR

The members of the band seem to be road-weary.

6. *Nouns that are plural in form but singular in sense require singular verbs.* Words such as *mathematics, athletics, politics, economics, physics,* and *news* look like plural nouns because of the *s* ending. However, these nouns are usually singular in meaning and thus require singular verbs.

Economics is my favorite subject.

The news from Lake Wobegon always interests me.

Likewise, titles of creative works and names of companies that look plural in form but actually refer to a singular entity take a singular verb.

The Brothers Karamazov was probably Dostoevsky's best novel.

Allyn & Bacon publishes this handbook and others.

In some cases, however, a word may take either a singular or a plural verb depending on whether it refers to an entire field (singular) or to a set of activities or properties (plural).

The physics of fiber-optic technology are pretty complicated.

[Here, *physics* refers to properties.]

At our school, physics is required for all college-bound seniors.

[Here, *physics* refers to a field of study.]

7. *A linking verb always agrees with its subject.* Sometimes you may find yourself faced with a sentence of the form "X is Y," in which the subject X is singular and the subject complement Y is plural, or vice versa. In such cases, the linking verb should agree in number with the subject, not with the subject complement (see 24b-3).

Her main interest is boys.

Boys are her main interest.

8. *In a sentence beginning with the expletive* here *or* there *and some form of the verb* be, *the verb should agree with its true subject.* The true (grammatical) subject of such a sentence is usually the noun that immediately follows the *be* verb form.

There are some people at the door.

Here is the address you were looking for.

ESL Note: Many languages besides English have expletive constructions (for example, *hay* in Spanish, *il y a* in French, *es gibt* in German), but number agreement between the verb and the noun following the verb generally is not required.

EXERCISE 27.1

In each of the following sentences, select the correct verb form and draw an arrow to its grammatical subject. The first one has been done for you.

1. The clocks in this building [run, runs] slow.
2. Basketball and football [is, are] Lucy's favorite sports.
3. Either my brother or my cousins [is, are] coming to babysit the children.
4. Neither my sisters nor Todd [is, are] interested in going to college.
5. Each of the Spanish club members [is, are] going to bring an authentic Hispanic dish to share.
6. All of the Norwegians studying in the United States [celebrates, celebrate] Norwegian Independence Day on May 17.
7. All of her love [was, were] manifest in the poem she wrote him.
8. The faculty of the English department [decides, decide] how many fellowships are granted each year.
9. Many Americans believe that White House politics [is, are] corrupt.
10. There [is, are] several different dresses you can try on that are in your size.

27b Make pronouns agree in number and gender with their antecedents

A **pronoun** substitutes for a noun (or noun equivalent), which is called the **antecedent** of the pronoun (see 24a-2). Pronouns and their antecedents must agree in number and gender.

Antecedent   Pronoun
Bad luck can happen to anyone, and *it* can happen at any time.

In this sentence, *bad luck* and *it* are both singular; therefore, they agree in **number.** They also agree in **gender** because *bad luck* is neuter (neither masculine nor feminine) and *it* can serve as a pronoun for neuter antecedents.

Be especially careful about agreement when the pronoun is far away from its antecedent:

Each of the graduating football players was asked to say a few words about what ~~they~~ he thought was the highlight of the season.

Here are some rules on pronoun-antecedent agreement.

1. *A compound antecedent usually is plural and thus requires a plural pronoun.* A **compound antecedent** is a noun phrase containing two or more terms joined by *and*.

Mr. and Mrs. Kwan are here for *their* appointment.

2. *With disjunctive antecedents, the pronoun should agree in number with the nearest part.* A **disjunctive antecedent** is a noun phrase consisting of two or more terms joined by *or* or *nor*. When a disjunctive antecedent contains both a singular and a plural part, this rule works well if the singular noun precedes the plural one.

Either Tamara Wilson or *the Changs* will bring *their* barbeque set to the next picnic.

Neither the President nor *the Republicans* will give *their* support to this bill.

http://webster.
commnet.edu/hp/
pages/darling/
grammar/pronouns.
htm
A fun guide to pronoun agreement, with quizzes and exercises

If the plural noun precedes the singular one, however, following the rule usually leads to an awkward-sounding sentence:

Neither the Republicans nor *the President* will give *his* support to this bill.

In such cases, it is best to reword the sentence so as to either get rid of the pronoun or put the singular noun before the plural one.

3. *As an antecedent, a collective noun can be either singular or plural, depending on its sense.* Both of these sentences are correct:

The jury took only two hours to reach *its* verdict.

The jury took only two hours to reach *their* verdict.

The first sentence emphasizes the singularity of the jury as a body, while the second puts more emphasis on the jury as a group of individuals.

4. *Pronouns must agree with antecedents that are indefinite pronouns.* Most indefinite pronouns (such as *everybody, anyone,* and *each*) are singular. When an indefinite pronoun serves as the antecedent for another pronoun, that pronoun should also be singular.

Everything was in *its* place.

Each of the women had *her* reasons for opposing the plan.

Some indefinite pronouns (*some, all, more*) can have either a singular or a plural sense. When one of these indefinite pronouns is used as the antecedent for another pronoun, the other pronoun can be either singular or plural, depending on the sense of the sentence.

Some of the *news* was as bad as we thought *it* would be.

Some of the team's *players* have lost *their* motivation.

5. *Sexist use of pronouns should be avoided.* Which one of the following sentences is correct?

A doctor should listen carefully to his patients.

A doctor should listen carefully to her patients.

In the past, the first sentence was the accepted way to make this general statement about the behavior of doctors. Since *his (he, him)* was used as the all-purpose, or generic, pronoun, readers understood the sentence as referring to doctors in general, both male and female. Today, however, the gender bias of such constructions is no longer acceptable to many writers and readers. Singling out one gender at the expense of the other is unfair, inaccurate, and unnecessary. Thus, both sentences are incorrect. There are better ways to make generic statements.

The three most effective techniques for avoiding sexist pronoun usage are (1) making the pronoun and its antecedent plural, (2) rewording the sentence, and (3) using an occasional disjunctive pronoun like *he or she.*

> **WEB**
>
> http://www.wisc.edu/
> writetest/Handbook/
> SubjectVerb.html
> Hypertext discussion
> of a variety of agree-
> ment issues, including
> subject-verb and pro-
> noun agreement

Doctors should listen carefully to *their* patients.   [Plural]

An important part of medical practice is listening carefully to patients.   [Rewording]

A doctor should listen carefully to *his or her* patients.   [Disjunctive pronoun]

As you can see, these three revisions of the unacceptable sentence have subtle differences in tone and meaning. One version might work best in a certain context; another might be best in a different context. Knowing this, good writers do not rely exclusively on any single technique for avoiding sexism but instead use whichever they deem most appropriate in the given situation. (See also 41a.)

EXERCISE 27.2

Select the correct pronoun in each of the following sentences, and draw an arrow to its antecedent.

1. Earthquakes most often occur near a fault line, and [it, they] are usually impossible to predict.

2. Tony and Michiyo are here to pick up [his, their] final research projects.

3. Some of the coaches have lost [its, their] faith in the team.

4. Drinking and driving can cause fatal automobile accidents, but [it, they] can easily be prevented.

5. Everything in the office was in [its, their] proper place.

6. The members of the committee took three hours to make [its, their] decision.

7. Choong was required to take physics during his undergraduate course of study, and he was sure that [it, they] would be a very difficult subject.

8. The NBA imposes fines on [its, their] athletes if they break the rules.

9. Neither the former owners nor the current owner could find [his, their] signature on any of the documents.

10. A lawyer should always treat [his or her, his/her] clients with respect.

Adjectives and Adverbs

What is the difference between an adjective and an
    adverb? (28a, 28c)
Should I say "I feel bad" or "I feel badly"? (28d)
What is wrong with the phrase "most unique"? (28e)

?

Using adjectives and adverbs allows writers to add details to their work, making it more precise and colorful. But adjectives and adverbs have their proper uses, and it is important not to confuse them or use them incorrectly.

28a Use adjectives to modify nouns

An **adjective** is a word that modifies a noun (see 24a-3). Typically, adjectives answer one of the following questions: which? what kind? how many? Sometimes an adjective is placed next to the noun it modifies, either directly before the noun (an *ancient* building, the *first* page) or directly after (a dream *forsaken*, his curiosity *satisfied*). Other times an adjective is separated from the noun it modifies, as in the sentence "The movie was *exciting*." In these cases, a linking verb (such as *is*, *was*, or *seemed*) connects the noun and its modifier.

Some adjectives have "pure" forms; others are derived from nouns or verbs by adding a suffix. Examples of pure adjectives include *small, hot, blue, quick, correct, ambiguous, ornery,* and *sharp.* Examples of derived adjectives are *beautiful, annoying, suitable, restless, foolish, supportive,* and *perilous.*

Base form	Suffix	Adjective
harm	-ful	harmful
interest	-ing	interesting
desire	-able	desirable
biology	-ical	biological
worth	-while	worthwhile
fool	-proof	foolproof
sweat	-y	sweaty

Many adjectives have the same form as the present and past participles of verbs (a *roaring* lion, a *deserted* island). There also are many pronoun-like adjectives: **possessive adjectives** (*her* guitar), **demonstrative adjectives** (*that* tree), **interrogative adjectives** (*Which* way do I go?), and **indefinite adjectives** (*some* ideas).

28b   Avoid overuse of nouns as modifiers

A noun can modify another noun and thus function as an adjective. Some examples are *park* bench, *soda* pop, *letter* opener, *telephone* book, *fender* bender, *tape* player, and *movie* theater. Indeed, this **noun compounding** is such a common occurrence in English that some noun-noun combinations eventually become single words (*windshield, placekicker, flowerpot, dishrag, sideshow, screwdriver*). And it is not uncommon to find three nouns in a row, with the first two serving as adjectival modifiers of the third (*soda pop dispenser, brass letter opener, tape player cabinet, movie theater lobby*). In principle, there is no limit to the number of nouns that can be stacked up as adjectives before another noun. (Here is an example from a cookbook: *rose-hip jam dessert ideas.* Can you figure out what it means?)

> http://www.edunet. com/english/grammar/ adjectiv.html
> A complete discussion of adjectives

Noun compounding can help you save a few words—*windshield* is more concise than *shield against the wind*—but it can be confusing for readers, especially if you use more than three nouns in a row. To avoid long noun strings like *the picnic table cross brace,* use a prepositional phrase: *the cross brace under the picnic table.* Such phrasing may take a few more words, but the meaning will be clearer.

28c   Use adverbs to modify verbs, adjectives, other adverbs, and clauses

An **adverb** is a word that modifies a verb, an adjective, another adverb, or a clause (see 24a-5). Adverbs modify verbs by answering one of the following questions: when? how? how often? where?

Bob *quickly* raised his hand.

Linda *often* goes to the gym to work out.

In the following examples, the adverb modifies a clause, an adjective, or another adverb.

Luckily, I was able to find a backup disk.   [Modifies the entire clause]

They made a *very* bad mistake.   [Modifies the adjective *bad*]

The car was turned *almost* upside down.   [Modifies the adverb *upside down*]

28d   Be aware of some commonly confused adjectives and adverbs

The pairs of words *good/well* and *bad/badly* are misused by many writers who fail to recognize that *good* and *bad* are adjectives while *well* and *badly* are adverbs. The sentence "Fielder runs *good* for a man his size" is ungrammatical. The correct version is

http://www.edunet.
com/english/grammar/
adverbs.html
A complete discussion
of adverbs

Fielder runs *well* for a man his size.   [The adverb *well* modifies the verb *runs.*]

The adjective *good* is appropriate when the word being modified is a noun.

He has a *good,* long stride.   [The adjective *good* modifies the noun *stride.*]

When the main verb expresses a feeling or a perception (such verbs include *look, appear, feel, seem, taste,* and *smell*), the correct modifier is an adjective complement.

I feel *bad* about what I did.   [Not *badly; bad* modifies *I*]

This gazpacho tastes *good*.   [Not *well; good* modifies *gazpacho*]

You look *wonderful*.   [Not *wonderfully; wonderful* modifies *You*]

EXERCISE 28.1

Circle the correct adjective or adverb in each sentence.

1.   Although David played [good, well] for the audition, he did not get the job.
2.   Many students study long hours, sleep [bad, badly], and have trouble concentrating in class.
3.   Mariko looked [good, well] in her new school uniform.
4.   The senator felt [bad, badly] about his involvement in the scandal.
5.   It seems like a [good, well] idea to refrigerate the leftovers.
6.   Whenever I do too much heavy lifting, I ache [bad, badly] the next day.
7.   After the sultry heat of the afternoon sun, it feels [good, well] to sleep in the shade.
8.   After eating garlic, Tom's breath smells [bad, badly].
9.   The athlete swam [good, well] in spite of her injured knee.
10.   Teresa got off to a [bad, badly] start in the fourth race.

28e   Use comparative and superlative forms of adjectives and adverbs correctly

Most adjectives and a few adverbs can be used to make comparisons.

Ted works *hard*. He is *determined* to get ahead.

Ted works *harder* than I do. He is *more determined* than I am.   [Comparative forms]

Ted works the *hardest* of anybody I know. He is the *most determined* person I have ever met.   [Superlative forms]

Using both *more* and a comparative form of an adjective (with the *-er* ending) is incorrect:

Ted works ~~more~~ harder than I do.

Likewise, using both *most* and a superlative form of an adjective (with the *-est* ending) is incorrect:

Ted is the ~~most~~ hardest working person I know.

Adjectives of one or two syllables usually add *-er* and *-est* in their comparative and superlative forms. For adjectives with more than two syllables, the comparative and superlative forms typically consist of the positive form with *more* and *most*.

	Comparative	*Superlative*
smart	smarter	smartest
tasty	tastier	tastiest
beautiful	more beautiful	most beautiful
interesting	more interesting	most interesting

A few common adjectives have irregular comparative and superlative forms:

good	better	best
bad	worse	worst
far	farther/further	farthest/furthest

Only a few adverbs—those that are similar in form to adjectives—have regular comparative and superlative forms. Some of these regular adverbs are

early	earlier	earliest
fast	faster	fastest
hard	harder	hardest
late	later	latest
long	longer	longest
near	nearer	nearest
quick	quicker	quickest
short	shorter	shortest
slow	slower	slowest

Several other adverbs have irregular forms:

badly	worse	worst
far	farther/further	farthest/furthest
little	less	least
much	more	most
well	better	best

When making comparisons, be accurate, complete, and logical. When comparing two items, use the comparative form. When comparing three or more items, use the superlative form.

Of the two candidates, I like Johnson *better.*

Of the three candidates, I like Johnson *best.*

Use *few, fewer,* or *fewest* with count nouns (such as *books, calories, flowers,* and *dollars*). Use *little, less,* or *least* with noncount nouns (such as *water, understanding,* and *progress*).

The team has *fewer* fans that it used to have.

The new package contains *less* rice.

Make sure the terms of a comparison are complete. Do not write a sentence like "This headache remedy works better." Many readers will wonder, "Better than what?" Including a *than* phrase as part of the comparison makes it clear:

This headache remedy works better *than any other.*

Occasionally, the context allows you to omit the *than* phrase. For example, if you have been discussing the movies *Star Wars* and *The Empire Strikes Back,* you could say, "I think *Star Wars* is better."

Certain adjectives, by definition, express an absolute condition or quality and thus logically cannot have different degrees. Words such as *unique, dead, pregnant, final,* and *incomparable* belong in this category. It makes no sense to say that something or someone is *more unique* or *less dead.*

              talented
Michael Jordan is the most ~~unique~~ basketball player in the world.

EXERCISE 28.2

Correct the errors of comparative or superlative form in the following sentences.

1. Chris is the most smartest friend I have.

2. I went to the grocery checkout line marked "Twelve Items or Less."

3. The morning paper will give us recenter news on the situation in the Middle East.

4. The farest AAA recommends driving in a single day is 200 miles.

5. My grandmother's chocolate cheesecake is my most favorite dessert.

6. The store manager told the cashiers that they had to dress less casual for work than they had been dressing.

7. A 1990 study by the Federal Reserve Board showed that African Americans and Latinos were 60 percent likelier than European Americans to be rejected for home mortgages.

8. There are experts who believe that in some more early societies women and men may have been social equals.

9. These societies had much littler gender discrimination than does the contemporary world.

10. Forced to choose among several appealing options on the menu, I opted for the one that intrigued me more.

28f   Avoid double negatives

A **double negative** is a sentence or phrase containing two negative modifiers (typically adverbs such as *never, no, not, hardly, barely,* and *scarcely*) that carry the same meaning. Double negatives are considered nonstandard in modern English and should be avoided in formal writing and speaking.

The city buses do not have ~~no~~ *any* lifts for disabled passengers.

The passengers ~~can't~~ *can* hardly get on board.

Unfortunately, the drivers could not do ~~nothing~~ *anything* about it.

PART 7

CORRECT SENTENCES

CHAPTER 29

Sentence Fragments

What is a "sentence fragment"?
How can I identify fragments in my writing? (29a)
How can I fix a fragment? (29b, 29c)

?

A **fragment** is a grammatically incomplete sentence. Here are some examples:

The one in the corner.

Runs like the wind.

Because we had no choice.

Whichever film you prefer.

In ordinary conversation, people say things like the above. But these are not complete sentences, and formal English requires that complete sentences be used to convey meaning. Complete sentences (1) have a complete predicate, (2) have a grammatical subject, and (3) do not begin with a subordinating conjunction or relative pronoun unless they are connected to a main clause (see 24c-3). In the four examples of fragments, the first has no predicate, the second has no subject, the third begins with an unattached subordinating conjunction (*Because*), and the fourth begins with an unattached relative pronoun (*Whichever*).

Sometimes writers produce fragments because they write an idea the way they would talk about it. But formal writing and casual speech are two different things. In casual speech, conversational interactions usually fill in the meaning of brief phrases. Therefore, people do not always need to follow all the rules of standard English grammar—and often do not. When you are writing a college paper or some other piece that requires a formal style, employing the casual speech you use when talking with friends will leave your meaning vague and unclear.

More often, writers produce fragments through mispunctuation. This chapter provides many examples of how to correct sentence fragments with proper punctuation. (You may want to consult Part 10, Punctuation, while reading this chapter, especially 45a, 46a, 46e, 47a, 48b, 51a, and 51d.)

29a   Make sentences grammatically complete

If you have a good style/grammar checker in your computer, it should identify most of the sentence fragments in your writing. But it will not be able to tell you how to fix them. When we ran a grammar check on this chapter, our word processor flagged only three of the fragments listed at the beginning. For the first two, it only said "This does not seem to be a complete sentence"; for the third, it said, "This sentence does not seem to contain a main clause." So, even with a good style/grammar checker, you will need to solve these problems on your own.

1   Does the sentence have a complete predicate?

In standard English, all sentences must have a complete predicate—that is, a main verb plus any necessary helping verbs and complements. The main verb must be a *finite* verb, not an infinitive (*to* form) or a gerund (*-ing* form).

The second part of the following example has been incorrectly set off as a separate sentence; it does not have a finite verb and so cannot be a full sentence:

> Seven is a very symbolic number in Judeo-Christian culture. *Appearing often in the Bible and other sacred texts.*

Simply replacing the period with a comma will correct the problem:

Seven is a very symbolic number in Judeo-Christian culture, appearing often in the Bible and other sacred texts.

2 | Does the sentence have a subject?

In standard English, all sentences (except commands) must have a grammatical subject (see 24b).

Sometimes, a fragment can be corrected by simply inserting an appropriate subject and making other related changes:

> Most of today's sitcoms are not about families in suburbia. ~~But~~
> Rather, they are
> ~~rather~~ about young adults in the big city.

Sometimes, simply changing the punctuation and making the fragment part of the previous sentence will correct the error:

> but
> Most of today's sitcoms are not about families in suburbia. ~~But~~
>
> rather about young adults in the big city.

By removing the period after *suburbia*, you enable *most of today's sitcoms* to serve as the subject for the rest of the sentence, thereby eliminating the fragment.

3 | Are the subordinating phrases or clauses connected to a main clause?

Check to be sure that word clusters beginning with a subordinating conjunction (such as *because, although,* or *if*) or a relative pronoun (such as *which, who,* or *that*) are connected or subordinated to a main subject and predicate (see 29b).

29b | Connect dependent clauses

Dependent clauses have a subject and a predicate but are linked to a main clause with a subordinating conjunction (such as *because, although,* or *if*) or a relative pronoun (such as *which, who,* or *that*). Because

How do I locate sentence fragments?

1. Open the SEARCH function of your word-processing program.

2. Launch a search to locate each period in your document.

3. Look carefully at the group of words preceding each period located. Determine whether each group is indeed a complete sentence, using the questions raised in 29a.

dependent clauses depend for their meaning on their connection to a main clause, they cannot stand alone. Therefore, if you begin a clause with a subordinating conjunction or relative pronoun and then end it with a period or semicolon before connecting it to a main clause, you have produced a fragment, not a sentence. In the following sentence, changing the period to a comma allows the *Before* clause to serve as a dependent clause:

> *Before I delve into critically analyzing the characters͵* I must first
>
> discuss the opening sequence.   [Changing the period to a comma allows the *Before* clause to serve as a dependent clause linked to *I must first discuss . . . ,* the main clause.]

Likewise, relative clauses also need to be connected to a main clause. In the following sentence, the solution is simply to eliminate the period, joining the two clauses:

> *may*
> What seems annoying to me, ~~May~~ not bother you at all.

29c   Connect phrases

Phrases are similar to clauses except that they lack full verbs (see 24c-2). Phrases can be used as modifiers, subjects, objects, or complements—but never as sentences. Make sure that all of your phrases are connected to main clauses.

To prevent powerful foreign corporations from gaining too much influence. ~~Some~~ ^some^ African governments insisted on owning 51 percent of
key national industries.   [Putting a comma after *influence* connects the
modifying phrase (*To . . . influence*) to the main clause.]

Many nations began to process
their own food, minerals, and
other raw materials. ~~Using~~ ^using^
foreign aid and investments to
back their efforts.

http://owl.english.
purdue.edu/Files/
67.html
A basic discussion of
fragments, with exercises

Checklist for Fixing Fragments

1. Can I connect the fragment to an independent clause by changing
   the punctuation?

FRAGMENT   Some African nations emphasized the growing of
             export crops. *Which provided badly needed capital for*
             development.

REVISED   Some African nations emphasized the growing of
             export crops, which provided badly needed capital for
             development.   [Inserting a comma after *crops* connects the
             relative clause (*which . . . development*) to the main clause.]

FRAGMENT   Agricultural development was hampered by natural
             disasters. *Such as locust plagues and cattle diseases.*

REVISED   Agricultural development was hampered by natural
             disasters, such as locust plagues and cattle diseases.
             [The phrase beginning with *such* has been attached to the
             main clause with a comma.]

2. Can I turn the fragment into an independent sentence?

FRAGMENT   Some of the problems facing African nations can be
             traced to colonialism. *Some European nations doing*
             little to prepare their colonies for independence.

REVISED   Some of the problems facing African nations can be
             traced to colonialism. Some European nations did
             little to prepare their colonies for independence.
             [Changing the verb of the fragment into a full verb turns
             the fragment into an independent sentence.]

EXERCISE 29.1

Correct the fragments in the following sentences.

1. John Lennon was killed in 1980. By a deranged young man.

2. Were it not for the dynamics of racism in US society. Chuck Berry probably would have been crowned king of rock 'n' roll.

3. It was the phenomenal success of "Rapper's Delight." That first alerted the mainstream media to the existence of hip hop.

4. Roger Maris hit sixty-one home runs in one year. Setting a new record.

5. Mauritania is an Islamic country. Which is located in northwest Africa.

6. Lamarck thought that acquired traits could be passed on to one's offspring. His ideas being challenged much later by Charles Darwin.

7. Having thought about our situation. I have decided I should take a second job.

8. This is a good economic arrangement. For working and taking care of the children.

9. Two years after his disastrous invasion of Russia in 1812. Napoleon was exiled to the island of Elba.

10. He regained power the following year. But was defeated at Waterloo.

29d Use sentence fragments only for special effect

Occasionally sentence fragments can be used for special effect, such as to add emphasis or to make writing sound conversational. Here is an example from the writing of Molly Ivins:

http://www.english.uiuc.edu/cws/wworkshop/fragments.htm
A full review of sentence fragments, with exercises

Shrub's proposal to cut property taxes, on which our public schools depend, by $1 billion merely shifts the tax burden even more dramatically to the folks with the least money. *Nice work, Shrub.*

—Molly Ivins, "Truly Happy News"

In this editorial column, Ivins is criticizing a state politician. After giving her interpretation of the politician's proposal in the first sentence, she uses a common conversational expression, in the form of a fragment, to make a sarcastic comment.

Be cautious about using fragments in any kind of formal writing you do. Since they are rarely found in such writing, readers might see them only as grammatical mistakes, not as "special effects."

EXERCISE 29.2

Fragments are commonly seen in advertisements. Find a magazine ad or Internet ad containing at least three sentence fragments.

1. Underline all the fragments in the ad.
2. Rewrite the ad, turning the fragments into complete sentences.
3. Explain why you think the writers of the ad chose to include the fragments.

Comma Splices
and Run-on Sentences

What is a "comma splice"?
How do I know when I have written a run-on sentence?
How do I correct a comma splice or run-on sentence?
(30a, 30b, 30c, 30d)

?

Joining two independent clauses with a comma creates a **comma splice:**

The best keyboard for one-handed users is the Dvorak keyboard, it has a more convenient layout than the standard Qwerty keyboard.

Although comma splices are acceptable in casual English, they are *not* acceptable in formal written English (see 46j).

http://webster.
commnet.edu/
HP/pages/darling/
grammar/runons.htm
All you need to know
about comma splices
and run-on sentences,
with exercises

Putting two independent clauses together without a conjunction or any punctuation creates a **run-on sentence** (or *fused sentence*):

Dvorak keyboards put the most frequently typed characters within easy reach they are often used in speed-typing competitions.

Grammar Checker Alert: When looking for comma splices and run-on

How do I identify comma splices and run-on sentences?

1. Open your style/grammar checker.
2. Click on the OPTIONS feature.
3. Select a CUSTOM file.
4. Open the customization feature.
5. Deselect all the grammar and style features except the one called something like CLAUSE ERRORS or COMMA SPLICE OR FUSED SENTENCE.
6. For extra speed, turn off the spell checker.
7. Run the program on your document.

sentences with a style/grammar checker, remember that style/ grammar checkers are not always reliable. You should look carefully at each case the checker identifies to see if it is really a comma splice or a run-on sentence.

Run-on sentences are incorrect in standard English and are often confusing to readers. There are four main ways to correct comma splices and run-on sentences:

- Turn one clause into a subordinate clause.
- Add a comma and a coordinating conjunction.
- Separate the clauses with a semicolon.
- Separate the clauses with a period.

30a   Turn one clause into a subordinate clause

Often the best way to correct a comma splice or run-on sentence is to convert one of the two clauses into a subordinate clause. This can be done by using either a subordinating conjunction (such as *while, although, because,* or *if*) or a relative pronoun (such as *which, that,* or *who).*

The best keyboard for one-handed users is the Dvorak keyboard, ~~it~~ ^{*which*} has a more convenient layout than the standard Qwerty keyboard.

^{*Because*} ⌃Dvorak keyboards put the most frequently typed characters within easy reach⌃they are often used in speed-typing competitions.

Sometimes this technique may require switching the two clauses around:

Because it has a more convenient layout than the standard Qwerty keyboard, the best keyboard for one-handed users is the Dvorak keyboard.

30b Separate clauses with a comma and a coordinating conjunction

If the two parts of a comma splice or run-on sentence are of equal importance, you can put a comma and a coordinating conjunction (such as *and, or, but, nor,* or *yet*) between them:

An eagle once flew past our house⌃I only got a brief glimpse of it. ^{⌃*but*}

Simply inserting a comma in a run-on sentence is not enough, for that only produces another error (a comma splice); you must also insert a conjunction.

30c Separate independent clauses with a semicolon

If the two parts of a comma splice or run-on sentence are of equal importance, you can insert a semicolon between them.

Desktop computers usually have bigger screens than laptops do⌃[;] laptops are easier to carry around.

If you use a conjunctive adverb like *however, therefore,* or *for example,* place the semicolon before it:

Laptops are coming down in price⌃*therefore,* more people are buying them.[;]

30d   Separate independent clauses with a period

Often the easiest way to correct a comma splice or run-on sentence is by inserting a period between the two independent clauses:

The best keyboard for one-handed users is the Dvorak keyboard. It has a more convenient layout than the standard Qwerty keyboard.

Dvorak keyboards put the most frequently typed characters within easy reach. They are often used in speed-typing competitions.

> http://www.wisc.edu/ writetest/Handbook/ CommonErrors.html An essential checklist that covers all sorts of common writing problems, including comma splices

Although adding a period is the easiest way to correct these errors, it is not usually the best way. Inserting a period between the two clauses turns them into two separate sentences, thereby making it more difficult for the reader to see the relationship between them. As a general rule, try to use one of the other three methods before settling on this one.

EXERCISE 30.1

Correct the following comma splices and run-on sentences.

1. Ritchie Valens was the first Chicano rock 'n' roll star, he recorded a string of hits before his fatal plane crash in February 1959.
2. In order to access the Internet via modem you must install the Dial-Up Networking option click here to start.
3. I started reading Russian literature when I was young, though I did not know that it was Russian, in fact I was not even aware that I lived in a country with any distinct existence of its own.
4. We always ate dinner at eight o'clock we spent the whole day anticipating the time we could talk and eat together as a family.
5. Mine is a Spanish-speaking household we use Spanish exclusively.

6. The side pockets of her jacket were always bulging they were filled with rocks, candy, chewing gum, and other trinkets only a child could appreciate.

7. Some people seem to be able to eat everything they want they do not gain weight.

8. The VCR was not a popular piece of equipment with movie moguls, the studios quickly adapted.

9. Some magazines survive without advertising, they are supported by readers who pay for subscriptions.

10. A multimillion-dollar diet industry has developed, they sell liquid diets, freeze-dried foods, artificial sweeteners, and diet books by the hundreds.

Pronoun Reference

FAQs

Can my computer help me spot pronoun problems? (31b)
Is there anything wrong with beginning a sentence with
  This? (31b)
When should I use *that* and when should I use *which*?
  (31d)

Sometimes using pronouns in place of nouns can make writing more concise and readable. But pronouns can be confusing to readers if they are not used correctly.

31a   Refer to a specific noun antecedent

Pronouns (such as *she, it,* and *that*) work best when they refer back to a particular noun, called the **antecedent.**

The conductor announced to the orchestra members that *she* was resigning.

Only one of the new hockey players knew what *his* position would be.

1 Avoiding use of generalized *they* or *you*

In casual speech, people often use pronouns in vague ways, without explicit antecedents (*"They* say that television is dulling our brains"). In formal writing, however, such vagueness can sabotage meaning and must be avoided.

VAGUE *THEY* REVISED
> *Some people*
> ~~They~~ say that television is dulling our brains.

Similarly, avoid using the pronoun *you* unless you are addressing the reader directly.

VAGUE *YOU* REVISED
> *One never knows*
> ~~You never know~~ when calamity will strike.

2 Avoiding use of implied antecedents

Pronouns should refer back to specific antecedents, not implied ones.

IMPLIED REFERENCE REVISED
> *the notes*
> Notetaking is very helpful in doing research, especially if ~~they~~ are well organized.

3 Clarifying references with more than one possible antecedent

Writers sometimes get into trouble by using a pronoun that could refer to more than one noun. Usually it is necessary to rewrite the sentence so that the antecedent is named, whether or not it has been mentioned previously in the sentence.

VAGUE REFERENCE REVISED
> *Fred*
> Neither Bill nor Fred knew what ~~he~~ should do.

> OR

> *their friend*
> Neither Bill nor Fred knew what ~~he~~ should do.

If *he* refers to "Neither Bill nor Fred," the sentence is correct as originally written (though you might want to revise it to avoid confusion). However, if *he* refers either to Fred or to a mutual friend mentioned in a previous sentence, it is important to say so.

31b   Avoid vague use of *this, that, which,* and *it*

The pronouns *this, that, which,* and *it* may be used with care to refer broadly to an entire statement:

> According to the linguistic school currently on top, human beings are all born with a genetic endowment for recognizing and formulating language. *This* must mean that we possess genes for all kinds of information, with strands of special, peculiarly human DNA for the discernment of meaning in syntax.
>
> —Lewis Thomas, *Lives of a Cell*

In this excerpt, the word *this* leading off the second sentence refers clearly to the main clause of the first sentence ("human beings . . . language").

In many cases, though, using pronouns for broad reference may confuse the reader. What does *it* refer to in the following paragraph?

> Watching Monday Night Football on ABC has become a ritual for countless American sports lovers. *It* is symbolic of contemporary American life.

It could refer to (1) Monday Night Football, (2) watching Monday Night Football, or (3) watching Monday Night Football has become a

HELP

How do I identify possible pronoun reference problems?

1. Open the SEARCH feature of your word-processing program.
2. Enter *it* in the SEARCH field.
3. Run the search.
4. Whenever the program highlights an *it,* use the guidelines in this chapter to determine if you have used the word correctly.
5. Do a similar search for *this, that,* and *which.*

ritual for countless American sports lovers. One way to resolve this ambiguity is to replace the pronoun with a full noun phrase:

VAGUE REFERENCE REVISED

> Watching Monday Night Football on ABC has become a ritual for
> countless American sports lovers. ~~It~~ *Monday Night Football* is symbolic of contemporary
> American life.

31c Avoid mixed uses of *it*

The word *it* can function either as a pronoun or as an expletive. Do not use the word both ways in the same sentence (see 31b):

> ~~In the manual it~~ *The manual* says that it is important to turn off all other applications before installing a new program.

31d Be consistent with use of *that, which,* and *who*

The relative pronoun *that* is used only with essential (restrictive) relative clauses—clauses that are essential to identify the nouns they modify:

http://www.uottawa.ca/
academic/arts/writcent/
hypergrammar/pronref.
html
All you need to know
about pronoun reference issues

ESSENTIAL CLAUSE

> First prize went to the longhaired collie *that came all the way from Hartford.* [There were other longhaired collies in the competition.]

Although many people prefer using *which* only for nonessential relative clauses, the relative pronoun *which* can be used either with essential relative clauses or with nonessential (nonrestrictive) relative clauses—clauses that merely add extra information (see 46e, 46j):

NONESSENTIAL CLAUSE

> First prize went to the longhaired collie, *which came all the way from Hartford.* [It was the only longhaired collie in the competition.]

ESSENTIAL CLAUSE

First prize went to the longhaired collie *which came all the way from Hartford.* [There were other longhaired collies in the competition.]

The style/grammar checker on your computer will probably suggest that you use *that* for essential clauses, but this is not a strict rule. Many expert writers use either *that* or *which* for essential relative clauses, depending on how formal they want to sound. (*Which* is slightly more formal than *that.*)

It is conventional to use the personal relative pronouns *who, whose,* and *whom,* rather than *which,* when referring to people.

PERSONAL REFERENCE REVISED

who

This is the ambulance driver ~~which~~ rescued me.

Note: In reference to objects and nonspecific or unnamed animals, it is conventional to use *that, which,* and *whose,* not *who.*

EXERCISE 31.1

Correct the pronoun errors in the following sentences.

1. *Sesame Street* is a valuable children's program. Not only is one able to learn from a show like this, one also is able to fall in love with your favorite character who has the ability to become your friend and teacher.
2. Then there is the Disney book club, that provides short-story versions of the animated films.
3. The most popular sitcoms today are set in big cities and do not have anything to do with family, which is a change from the sitcoms of old.
4. We do not tear your clothing with machinery. We do it carefully by hand.
5. Every student must bring their books to class tomorrow and be prepared to discuss Chapter 6. It is important for you to do this.
6. Only one of the members of the House of Representatives decided that they would vote against the proposed bill.
7. They say that drinking and driving kills more people each year than cancer. They should not drink and drive.
8. Filling out college applications and worrying about SAT scores are annual rituals for many high school seniors. It is a part of the admissions process.
9. In the annual report it says it has been a disappointing year for the company.
10. The dog which chases my cat lives in the house across the street.

CHAPTER

32

Misplaced and Dangling Modifiers

What is a modifier?
How can I tell when I have misused a modifier? (32b, 32c, 32d)
What is a "split infinitive"? (32d-2)
What is a "dangling modifier"? (32e)

?

Modifiers are words, phrases, or clauses that qualify other words, phrases, or clauses. Used properly, modifiers can make writing richer and more precise.

32a   Position modifiers close to the words they modify

For maximum clarity, modifiers should be placed as close as possible to (ideally, right next to) the words they modify.

Unlike George,
ₐKramer does not need the approval of anyoneₐ ~~unlike George.~~

frequently
Businessesₐpublish the URLs for their Web sites ~~frequently~~ in advertisements.

Take special care with limiting modifiers like *only, just, even, not,* and *almost,* which are often used imprecisely in ordinary speech. In formal writing, they should generally be positioned directly before the word or phrase they modify.

The yucca plant ~~only~~ grows well *only* in full sunlight.

England ~~did not win~~ *won* the battle *not* because of superior firepower but because of better tactics.

32b   Avoid ambiguity

A modifier that is not carefully positioned may present the reader with two or more possible interpretations.

> Bound, gagged, and trussed up nude in a denim bag with plugs in her ears and tape over her eyes, Cleveland teacher Brenda P. Noonan told yesterday how she was kidnapped and taken to Florida without knowing where she was going or why.
>   —Quoted in Richard Lederer, *Anguished English*

http://www.uottawa.ca/ academic/arts/writcent/ hypergrammar/ msplmod.html
How not to use misplaced and dangling modifiers in your writing

It must have been quite a trick to describe these things while being bound and gagged! This sentence recounts three main actions (telling, being kidnapped, and being taken to Florida); the writer should have positioned the modifier closer to the third action:

> Cleveland teacher Brenda P. Noonan told yesterday how she was kidnapped and taken to Florida bound, gagged, and trussed up nude in a denim bag with plugs in her ears and tape over her eyes, without knowing where she was going or why.

Adverbs like *happily, quickly,* and *easily* are often ambiguous if they are positioned between two verb phrases.

Most people who responded to the ad *quickly* decided not to look at the car.

In this sentence, does *quickly* modify *responded* or *decided?* The ambiguity can be resolved by repositioning the modifier:

Most people who *quickly* responded to the ad decided not to look at the car.

OR

Most people who responded to the ad decided *quickly* not to look at the car.

Shifting the position of certain limiting adverbs can alter the meaning or emphasis in a sentence (see 32a). The following sentences differ in meaning because of the different locations of *only*:

Only Martha crammed for the exam.   [Other students did not cram.]

Martha *only* crammed for the exam.   [She did not prepare in any other way.]

Martha crammed for the exam *only*.   [She did not cram for quizzes and other assignments.]

32c   Try to put lengthy modifiers at the beginning or end

When a lengthy modifier is placed in the middle of a sentence, it tends to disrupt the basic structure (subject–verb–complement) of the sentence. By moving such modifiers to the beginning or end of the sentence, you preserve the basic structure and make the sentence more readable.

MODIFIER IN THE MIDDLE OF THE SENTENCE

A television network usually, after it airs a documentary, makes the film available to groups for a nominal rental fee.

REVISED

After it airs a documentary, a television network usually makes the film available to groups for a nominal rental fee.

32d   Avoid disruptive modifiers

English sentences are made up of subgroupings of words, such as the verb and its object or the word *to* and the rest of the infinitive construction. When modifiers are inserted into these subgroupings, there is a risk of interrupting and obscuring the vital connections between key words.

 1 Modifiers between the verb and its object

Readers like to be able to move easily through the main predicate of a sentence, going from verb to object without interruption. For this reason, it is best to avoid inserting any interupting modifiers between the verb and its object.

The magician shuffled ~~quickly~~ the cards. [*quickly* inserted above after "magician"]

Sometimes, in following this advice, you may also be heeding the guideline that recommends moving a lengthy modifier to the beginning or end of the sentence (see 32c).

~~Several~~ customers decided, *after reading the news reports*, to boycott the store. [*After reading the news report, several* inserted at beginning]

2 Split infinitives

Some readers prefer to see both parts of an infinitive construction (*to escape*) together, as in "He hoped *to escape* easily." Other readers will accept a one-word interruption between parts, or **split infinitive,** as in "He hoped *to* easily *escape.*" Almost all readers have difficulty comprehending an infinitive construction when its parts are split with a longer phrase, as in "He hoped *to* easily and quickly *escape.*" As a writer, you need to make a decision about the infinitive style that is appropriate for you, your readers, and the occasion for writing. If the occasion is suited to a formal style, you may need to rewrite sentences to avoid splitting infinitives.

SPLIT INFINITIVES REVISED

Star Trekkers hope to *boldly, loyally, and optimistically* ~~go~~ where *go* none have gone before. [With all due respect for the original motto, too many modifiers splitting the infinitive here interrupt the sense of the sentence.]

Style/Grammar Checker Alert: Many style/grammar checkers allow a range of choices regarding split infinitives. The checker for Microsoft Word 6.0, for example, offers five different warning options on split infinitives to suit readers and situations: no warning (allowing any split to go unnoticed); warning against splits of any length; or warning against splits of one, two, or three words between *to* and the base form. Look at the options on your checker to see what choices are available for different writing occasions.

32e Avoid dangling modifiers

A mistake that plagues many writers is the use of the **dangling modifier,** an introductory verbal phrase that does not have a clear referent.

> Breaking in through the window of the girls' dormitory, the dean of men surprised ten members of the football team.
>
> —Quoted in Richard Lederer, *Anguished English*

Did the dean break into the girls' dormitory? To prevent this misinterpretation, the writer should have put the real culprits in the subject position of the main clause.

> Breaking in through the window of the girls' dormitory, *ten members of the football team* were surprised by the dean of men.

It will not do simply to mention the missing agent somewhere in the main clause; the referent must be in the subject position.

WEB

http://owl.english.
purdue.edu/Files/
24.html
Another site on using
modifiers correctly

Plunging 1,000 feet into the gorge, we saw Yosemite Falls.

—Quoted in Richard Lederer,
Anguished English

(But it was only a hurried glimpse, as we soon smashed into the ground!) Of course, the reader can figure out that it was Yosemite Falls that was plunging, not the writer. But why force the reader to make this kind of mental correction? A better version puts the modifier next to what it modifies:

We saw Yosemite Falls plunging 1,000 feet into the gorge.

EXERCISE 32.1

Correct the modifier errors in the following sentences.

1. Politicians who run for office frequently need to raise a lot of money.

2. Two cars were reported stolen by the Groveton police yesterday.

3. To get the job, his résumé had to be completely revised.

4. Please take time to look over the brochure that is enclosed with your family.

5. Before installing a new program, all other applications should be turned off.

6. Having missed class four times in three weeks, Professor Kateb decided that Melissa should be penalized.

7. Yoko Ono will talk about her husband, John Lennon, who was killed in an interview with Barbara Walters.

8. The patient was referred to a psychiatrist with a severe emotional problem.

9. A former scout leader will plead guilty to two counts of sexually assaulting two boys in a New Hampshire court.

10. The judge sentenced the killer to die in the electric chair for the second time.

(Sentences 2, 4, 7, 8, 9, and 10 are courtesy of Richard Lederer, *Anguished English*.)

Consistency

What does it mean to say that writing is "inconsistent"?
(33a, 33b, 33c)

What is a "mixed construction," and how can I avoid it? (33d)

Readers expect a certain consistency in what they read. They expect writers to use a consistent tone, time frame, and point of view. Writers should try to satisfy this expectation by avoiding unnecessary shifts.

33a   Avoid unnecessary shifts in person and number

Person, which indicates to whom a discourse refers, is denoted mainly by pronouns. The first-person pronouns *I, me, we,* and *us* refer to the writer or speaker. The second-person pronoun *you* refers to the reader or listener. The third-person pronouns *he, him, she, her, they,* and *them* refer to people being written or spoken about. Use care when making shifts in person.

You should start writing a paper well before the deadline; otherwise, ~~one~~ *you* may end up doing it at the last minute, with no chance to revise it.

We were hoping to get tickets to the Smashing Pumpkins' concert.
                                         we
But the line was so long ~~you~~ had no chance.

Number refers to whether a noun, pronoun, or verb is singular or plural. If you use two or more words to refer to the same thing, make sure that they are consistently singular or consistently plural (see Chapter 27).

                                                              his or her
Anyone who weaves in and out of traffic is endangering ~~their~~

fellow drivers.

OR

 People
~~Anyone~~ who weave~~s~~ in and out of traffic ~~is~~ *are* endangering their

fellow drivers.

33b   Avoid unnecessary shifts in verb tense, mood, and subject

Verb tense indicates the time frame of an action (see 26e). Readers will be confused by arbitrary shifts in time frame. Unless you are describing a situation where there is a natural or logical difference in time frames, it is best to use the same verb tense throughout.

In 1995, the median pay for full-time female workers in the United States was $22,497, while the median pay for males was $31,496. In other words, women *made* ~~make~~ 71 cents to a man's dollar.

http://owl.english.
purdue.edu/Files/
72.html
How to avoid inappropriate shifts of verb tense

Accounts of literary narratives are usually written consistently in the present tense:

Huxley's *Brave New World* depicts a nightmare utopia in
                     is
which there ~~was~~ no passion, no frustration, and no deviation
from normalcy.

There are three **moods** in English: indicative, imperative, and subjunctive. The **indicative mood** is used for facts and assertions, the **imperative mood** for commands, and the **subjunctive mood** for conditions that are contrary to fact (see 26h). If you mix moods in the same sentence, you may confuse your readers:

INCONSISTENT MOOD

> If China were a democracy, it will have elections at periodic intervals.

Is China a democracy? Does it have regular elections? Or is the writer just posing a hypothetical idea? The mixing of subjunctive mood (in the first clause) and indicative mood (in the second clause) makes it impossible to know. Either of the following revisions would clarify the meaning:

REVISED

> If China *is* a democracy, it *will have* elections at periodic intervals. [Both verbs are in the indicative, suggesting a factual assertion.]

> If China *were* a democracy, it *would have* elections at periodic intervals.   [Both verbs are in the subjunctive, indicating a contrary-to-fact condition.]

The grammatical **subject** of a sentence serves as a focal point for the reader (see 24b-1). It usually indicates what the sentence is about and who is performing the verb's action. By repeating the same subject from one sentence to the next, the writer helps readers maintain focus on it. Conversely, by shifting from one subject to another in sentence after sentence, the writer may disorient readers.

INCONSISTENT SUBJECT

> When people try to move an accident victim, they should use proper lifting techniques. The legs should be used, not the back. The body should be bent at the knees and hips, and all twisting should be avoided.

Notice how the grammatical subjects change from one clause to another:

> people
> they
> the legs
> the body
> all twisting

A better version would retain the focus on *people* by keeping it in the subject position:

REVISED

> When *people* try to move an accident victim, *they* should use proper lifting techniques. *They* should use their legs, not their back. *They* should bend their body at the knees and hips and avoid all twisting.

33c   Avoid shifts in tone

Tone refers to the writer's attitude toward the subject matter or the audience (see 40c). It can be formal or informal, ironic or direct, friendly or hostile, and so on. Since readers need to get a clear sense of what the writer's attitude is, a writer should strive to maintain a consistent authorial tone.

INCONSISTENT TONE

> The world of folklore and fairy tales is one that attracts adults and children alike. As adults, we look back fondly on childhood cartoons and still get a kick out of 'em.

Because most of this passage is written in a fairly formal tone, the colloquial "still get a kick out of 'em" is jarring. The following revision has a more consistent tone:

REVISED

> The world of folklore and fairy tales is one that attracts adults and children alike. As adults, we look back fondly on childhood cartoons and find them as enjoyable as ever.

EXERCISE 33.1

Correct the shifts in the following sentences.

1. One should do some type of physical activity at least three times a week for thirty minutes. Regular exercise is good for your heart and lungs.
2. We wanted to go to the U2 concert. However, the tickets sold out before I even got there, and there was no chance that you could buy them from scalpers for less than $100.
3. Someone who does not love themselves can never hope to love anyone else.
4. We hike up in the mountains every Saturday morning. We love the feeling of sheer exhilaration. We were happy to be tired.

5. Elizabeth Bishop's *A First Death in Nova Scotia* discusses death from the point of view of a child. It painted a picture of a young girl's emotional reaction to the death of her cousin.

6. If she were rich, she will buy all her clothes at Nordstrom and Lord and Taylor.

7. If you want to learn to speed-read, you have to first learn to concentrate. We need to focus on the words on the page. It is important not to let the attention wander. The eyes should always catch the center of each page.

8. If our goal is educational and economic equity and parity, then we need affirmative action to catch up. We are behind as a result of discrimination and denial of opportunity, and that is totally not fair.

9. Married couples make a deep commitment to one another and to society; in exchange, society extends certain benefits to them, which really helps them out with money and other stuff.

10. There can be no excuse for what you did. The act is shameful, and one should not be forgiven for it.

33d Avoid mixed constructions

Mixed constructions are those that result when a writer starts a sentence in a certain way but then changes track and finishes it differently. The two parts of the sentence end up being incompatible—and confusing to the reader.

WEB
http://webster.
commnet.edu/
hp/pages/darling/
grammar/
consistency.htm
Upbeat advice on maintaining consistency—
even includes a quiz

MIXED   In the world created by movies and television makes fiction seem like reality.

Where is the grammatical subject in this sentence? The writer began with a prepositional phrase but then apparently got sidetracked and failed to create a complete main clause. One way of revising this sentence would be to turn the prepositional phrase into a noun phrase, which could then serve as the grammatical subject.

REVISED   The world created by movies and television makes fiction seem like reality.

Another option would be to set off the prepositional phrase with a comma and then reconstruct the rest of the sentence to form a main clause.

REVISED   In the world created by movies and television, fiction seems like reality.

Subordinating adverbs like *although, since, because,* and *if* are used only in subordinate clauses. Thus, if you start a sentence with such an adverb, you must finish the subordinate clause and then construct a main clause.

MIXED   Since the campus parking situation makes you want to take the bus.

REVISED   Since the campus parking situation is so bad, you will want to take the bus.

Alternatively, you can omit the subordinating adverb and reconstruct the entire sentence.

REVISED   The campus parking situation makes you want to take the bus.

33e   Create consistency between subjects and predicates

Subjects and predicates should always harmonize, both logically and grammatically. When they do not, the result is **faulty predication.**

FAULTY   Writer's block is when you cannot get started writing.

In this sentence, a noun (*writer's block*) is compared to an adverb of time (*when . . .*). This is ungrammatical and illogical. In a sentence of the form *A is B,* the *A* and *B* terms must be of the same grammatical type (see 24b).

                 N   N
REVISED   *Writer's block* is *a condition* in which you cannot get started writing.

Make sure the predicate fits logically with the subject.

FAULTY   Shaw's *Pygmalion* wins out over the snobbish aristocrat, Henry Higgins.

Pygmalion is the name of a play, so it cannot "win out" over one of its characters.

REVISED   In Shaw's *Pygmalion,* the lowborn Eliza Doolittle wins out over the snobbish aristocrat, Henry Higgins.

33f   Avoid unmarked shifts between direct and indirect discourse

Direct discourse is language that is taken word for word from another source and thus is enclosed in quotation marks. **Indirect discourse** is language that is paraphrased and therefore is *not* enclosed in quotation marks. If you shift from one mode to the other, you may have to alter not only punctuation but also pronouns and verb tenses so as not to confuse your readers.

CONFUSING   Agassiz, the legendary Swiss scientist and teacher, once said I cannot afford to waste my time making money. [Without quotation marks, this statement seems to refer to two different people: Agassiz and the writer.]

REVISED   Agassiz, the legendary Swiss scientist and teacher, once said, "I cannot afford to waste my time making money." [By signaling direct discourse, the quotation marks make it clear that Agassiz is talking only about himself.]

REVISED   Agassiz, the legendary Swiss scientist and teacher, once said that he could not afford to waste his time making money. [By signaling indirect discourse, the change of pronouns and verb tense also makes it clear that Agassiz is referring only to himself.]

EXERCISE 33.2

Correct the mixed constructions and faulty predications in the following sentences.

1. By using the terms *alligator* and *crocodile* to refer to the same reptile misleads many people.
2. A foot is when you can measure twelve inches.
3. The job of all UPS drivers delivered packages from its city of origin to their final destinations.
4. She asked did you like the concert?
5. One reason the Slavic Festival was so popular was because they had a band play polka music.
6. To creative writers, such as Lita, romanticized her adventures.
7. The reason why strawberries are picked while slightly green is because if left to ripen they rot before they are picked.
8. When the homecoming parade included William Smith and Ted Jackson became school heroes.
9. In processing caramel at high heat softens their centers.
10. The Great Salt Lake is a lake that is easy to swim in where there is a high salt content to make the water more buoyant.

PART 8

EFFECTIVE SENTENCES

CHAPTER 34

Clarity and Conciseness

FAQs

> What is a passive sentence? (34d)
> How can I tighten up my writing so that it is not so wordy? (34e)
> How can I be sure that readers will understand my meaning? (34g, 34h, 34i, 34j)

?

Readers today often are under time pressure and are not willing to spend valuable minutes trying to decode a piece of writing. Writers must accommodate their readers by making their writing as clear and concise as possible.

34a Avoid excessively long sentences

Sentences that are more than about twenty-five words long sometimes can be difficult for a reader, especially if the sentences are complicated.

Despite their significance in contemporary society, social movements seldom solve social problems, because in order to mobilize resources a movement must appeal to a broad constituency, which

How do I guard against using long sentences?

1. Open your style/grammar checker.
2. Select the CUSTOMIZE SETTINGS feature. (It may be under OPTIONS.)
3. If there is a sentence length entry, use it to set a maximum word limit of twenty-five words.
4. Thereafter, whenever you write, use your style/grammar checker to flag all sentences longer than twenty-five words.

means that the group must focus on large-scale issues which are deeply embedded in society.

This sentence is forty-two words long. The following three shorter sentences say the same thing and are much easier for the reader to understand:

Despite their significance in contemporary society, social movements seldom solve social problems. To mobilize resources, a movement must appeal to a broad constituency. This means that the group must focus on large-scale issues which are deeply embedded in society.

34b   Avoid unnecessary repetition and redundancy

A certain amount of repetition is necessary, both for emphasis and to maintain focus. Repetition is especially useful for linking one sentence to another (see 6c). However, unnecessary repetition will only clutter your writing and irritate readers.

Life offers many lessons ^about life.

People seem to learn things best when they ~~learn~~ *experience* them firsthand.

If you repeat nouns too often, you will end up with a dull, heavy style of writing. The best way to avoid repetition of nouns is to use pronouns (see 24a-2). Pronouns can establish and maintain coherence in paragraphs just as repeated nouns do, but with a lighter touch.

Redundancy is the use of words that could be left out without changing the meaning of the sentence. Saying that something is *blue in color* is redundant, because readers already know that blue *is* a color. Some other redundant phrases are *repeat again, combine together, end result, true fact,* and *basic essentials.* Such phrases should always be pruned.

I was caught ~~unexpectedly~~ off guard by the boss's telling me I had ~~successfully~~ made the grade in my new job.

34c Use expletives only where appropriate

An **expletive** is an "empty" phrase, like *there* or *it,* that occupies the subject position in a sentence but is not its grammatical subject (see 24a-9). Expletives have useful functions. The construction *there is (are, was, were)* typically introduces a new topic for discussion, whereas *it is (was)* typically creates special emphasis. Because expletives can be overused, look for opportunities to convert expletive constructions into more direct expressions.

My computer has many new features.
~~There are many new features that can be found in my computer.~~

~~It is recommended that~~ All candidates be on time for their interviews.
(A) (should)

34d Use passive voice only where appropriate

In passive-voice constructions, the subject position is occupied not by the agent of the verb's action but by the recipient (see 26g). Since passive-voice constructions tend to be wordier and less direct than active-voice constructions, try to write most of your sentences in the active voice.

PASSIVE Flexible songs, containing a variety of motifs arranged to its liking, are sung by the robin.

ACTIVE The robin sings flexible songs, containing a variety of motifs arranged to its liking.

http://webster.
commnet.edu/
hp/pages/
darling/grammar/
concise.htm
A helpful guide to
concise writing

The passive version of this sentence is wordy and confusing, whereas the active version is direct and clear.

Passive sentences are appropriate when the recipient of the verb action is the topic of discussion or when the agent can be omitted without loss of clarity.

> Over the past ten years, more than three million white-collar jobs have been eliminated in the United States.

Using the active voice would force the writer to mention the agent of this job elimination (presumably management), taking the focus of the sentence off the loss of jobs.

> Over the past ten years, management has eliminated more than three million white-collar jobs in the United States.

34e   Eliminate wordy phrases

Many commonly used phrases are unnecessarily long. If you can replace them with no loss of meaning, you should do so.

~~In a very real sense,~~ *T*rickle-down economics ~~exhibits a tendency~~ *tends* to trickle up, benefiting only the rich.

Wordy phrases	Concise phrases
as a matter of fact	in fact
at the present time	today, presently
at this point in time	now
due to the fact that	because
in spite of the fact that	although, even though
in the event that	if
in the final analysis	finally, ultimately
until such time as	until

EXERCISE 34.1

Revise the following sentences to make them as clear and concise as possible.

1. The lunar mission was going to the moon.

2. She did the daily paperwork every day.

3. I experienced a frightening experience when my teenage daughter took me out for a drive.

4. The quarterback who had been injured early in the season and had undergone extensive knee surgery to repair the damage had been conscientious about his rehabilitation exercises and was therefore feeling ready to play again only four months after the surgery.

5. The lack of a warm pair of mittens and a hat on that very cold morning led to the trumpeter's inability to play well during the halftime show at the Thanksgiving game.

6. Several unusual songs were sung by the Girl Scouts during their annual awards ceremony.

7. The Boy Scout Eagle rank was achieved by a boy who works with my son during the summer.

8. Hundreds of items were marked down by the store management for the annual August clearance sale.

9. There are many people in this society who do not have enough leisure time.

10. It is often that students find their work piling up at finals time.

34f   Avoid a noun-heavy style

A noun-heavy style is a writing style characterized by many more nouns than verbs. It tends to make excessive use of the verb *be* (*am, are, is, was, were*) and have strings of prepositional phrases. A noun-heavy style results partly from the use of **nominalizations**— that is, nouns derived from verbs. For example, *determination* is a nominalization derived from the verb *determine*. Other examples include *remove/removal, insist/insistence, develop/development,* and *jog/jogging*. Although nominalizations can be useful for certain purposes, using too many of them will make your style ponderous and dull. Turning some of your nominalizations into verbs will give your writing a more active, concise flair.

> WEB
>
> http://www.wisc.edu/
> writetest/Handbook/
> ClearConciseSentences.
> html
> A resource for writing clear and concise sentences

| NOUN-HEAVY | The preference of most writers is for an understanding of their composing as a species of fine frenzy. |
| MORE VERBAL | Most writers prefer having it understood that they compose in a species of fine frenzy. |

NOUN-HEAVY   Thomas Jefferson was not a believer in the divinity of Jesus Christ and indeed was the author of a version of the Four Gospels that included the removal of all references to "miraculous" events.

MORE VERBAL   Thomas Jefferson did not believe in the divinity of Jesus Christ and indeed wrote a version of the Four Gospels from which he removed all references to "miraculous" events.

Noun-heavy writing also is created through the use of phrasal expressions like *perform an examination* instead of simple verbs like *examine.*

Before ~~making the purchase of~~ ^{purchasing} a used car, one should always ~~perform an examination on~~ ^{examine} it.

EXERCISE 34.2

The following phrasal expressions are characteristic of a wordy, noun-heavy style. Convert them into simpler verb forms. (The first one has already been done.)

1. create an improvement in   *improve*
2. give a summary of   _____
3. put emphasis on   _____
4. perform an operation on   _____
5. do an analysis of   _____
6. make an estimate of   _____
7. come to the realization that   _____
8. provide an explanation for   _____
9. have a lot of sympathy for   _____
10. conduct an inspection of   _____

EXERCISE 34.3

Revise the following sentences to make them less noun-heavy.

1. The scientist came to the conclusion that she had made an important discovery.
2. The United Nations wanted to conduct an inspection of the country's weapons storage facilities.

3. The committee reached a decision to hire the man it had interviewed.

4. The stance of the institution in regard to the question of affirmative action was unclear.

5. The group held the belief that disaster was coming at the close of the century.

6. The opinion of my mechanic is that there is nothing wrong with the transmission of my car.

7. Their press release gave an explanation for the behavior of the demonstrators.

8. The education reform law passed by the legislature demands that schools make improvements in their ways of teaching.

9. The composition of a piece of music is a requirement of the music theory course.

10. The man was justifiably proud of the achievement of his goal.

34g   Choose words that express your meaning precisely

Good writing conveys its meaning efficiently, with precision. Such precision is achieved largely through the careful selection of words. Minimize your use of vague nouns like *area, aspect, factor, kind, nature, situation, sort, thing,* and *type,* as well as your use of vague adjectives like *bad, good, interesting, nice,* and *weird* and vague adverbs like *basically, completely, definitely, really,* and *very.*

> Democracy   an
> ~~A democratic type of government basically~~ requires ~~a pretty~~ informed citizenry.

Word use is discussed in more detail in Part 9.

34h   Use *that* to clarify sentence structure

Clear sentence structure helps the reader see how the pieces of a sentence fit together. In sentences with a main clause–*that* clause structure, it usually helps to include the *that.*

>   that
> It is important we understand the instructions before we proceed.

Sometimes, failure to include *that* can cause the reader to misinterpret the sentence initially.

> Some people are claiming their rights have been violated by the government.

By beginning with a string of words that looks like a sentence in itself ("Some people are claiming their rights . . ."), the writer of this sentence risks misleading the reader. Inserting *that* after *claiming* helps to clarify the sentence structure.

> Some people are claiming *that* their rights have been violated by the government.

34i   Make comparisons complete and clear

Comparative constructions inherently involve two terms: "*A* is _____er than *B*." In casual conversation, speakers sometimes omit the *B* term on the assumption that listeners can easily figure out what it is. In writing, however, you should make both terms of the comparison explicit.

INCOMPLETE   Talk radio has become a popular form of entertainment because it gets people more involved.   [More involved than what?]

COMPLETE   Talk radio has become a popular form of entertainment because it gets people more involved than most other media do.

Comparative constructions sometimes are open to two possible interpretations. In such cases, add a few words to help the reader know which interpretation is meant.

AMBIGUOUS   Abstract expressionism was more influenced by cubism than surrealism.

CLEAR   Abstract expressionism was more influenced by cubism than surrealism *was.*

CLEAR   Abstract expressionism was more influenced by cubism than *it was by* surrealism.

(See 28e on comparative and superlative forms.)

34j   Avoid multiple negation

A single negative word, such as *no, not, never, nobody, unhappy,* or *unpleasant,* can change the entire meaning of a sentence. If you put two or more negative words in the same sentence, therefore, you may change the meaning in multiple ways and confuse the reader.

CONFUSING   Not many of the assignments were left unfinished, but none of the students did all of them.

By rewriting the first part of the sentence in positive rather than negative terms, you can make its meaning much clearer:

CLEAR   Most of the assignments were finished, but none of the students did all of them.

EXERCISE 34.4

Make the following sentences clearer and more concise.

1. I think that people learn the most from personal experience and hard work, not from memorizing dates or facts, and that hard times or failure is a success if you learn something from it and improve.

2. In our natural childbirth class, I planned a calm and relaxing natural childbirth plan for my own pregnancy.

3. This book contains a significant amount of information on art in history because without a knowledge of art history, one may find it difficult to discern the principles of art which are clearly crucial to an understanding of the aspects of art today.

4. I have come to conclude that to serve the purpose of conveying the overall benefit of chemical weapons incineration, the report should maintain an argumentative tone while clarifying the success of chemical weapons incineration and the safety standards followed by those who carry it out, and through this, to contradict any negative views.

5. Although she was in a family way, she continued in the fulfillment of her familial and employment responsibilities.

6. In recent months, research has come to light that bright red, green, yellow, and other colored fruits and vegetables may be instrumental in preventing lung cancer.

7. The weather, which was hostile, and the native inhabitants, the Indians, led to the death of most of the expedition members, who died.

8. The grassy area, which contains grass and trees, will be turned into a parking lot, so that students can park their cars there.

9. During that time period, many people who were car buyers preferred cars that were large in size and bright in color but not of a cheap quality.

10. Truly, for all intents and purposes, the industrial productivity in America generally depends on various and certain factors which are really usually more psychological in kind than of any true given technological aspect.

35

Coordination and Subordination

What is the best way to avoid "choppy" writing? (35a)
How can I emphasize some ideas and de-emphasize others? (35c)

?

In any piece of writing, readers will instinctively look for the most important points. By emphasizing these points and de-emphasizing others, writers make their main points easier to locate in the text and thereby make their writing more readable.

Two important ways to create emphasis are through coordination and subordination of sentence elements. Remember, *form should reflect content*. If two related ideas are equally important, *coordinate* them by putting them on the same grammatical level. If they are not equally important, put the less important idea in a grammatically *subordinate* form. (For other ways to create emphasis, see Chapter 37.)

35a   Look for a way to combine closely related sentences

Writing that contains one short sentence after another not only is unpleasantly choppy but also fails to emphasize some sentences more than others.

TOO CHOPPY

> I was born and raised in a small midwestern town. It was easy to make friends. I got to know a lot of people. I was able to achieve almost all of my goals. I could do almost anything I wanted to. School and sports were a challenge. But I could always make my way to where I wanted to be.

This paragraph is so choppy that it is hard to get a sense of what the writer's main point is. You can solve this problem by noticing that several pairs of sentences are closely related and combining these sentences.

REVISED VERSION

> I was born and raised in a small midwestern town. It was easy to make friends, *and so* I got to know a lot of people. *Since* I could do almost anything I wanted to, I was able to achieve almost all of my goals. School and sports were a challenge, *but* I could always make my way to where I wanted to be.

http://leo.stcloud.
msus.edu/style/
sentencev.html
How to combine sentences using coordination or subordination

Instead of seven sentences, there are now four sentences, each conveying a single idea. This reorganization helps readers get a sense of the writer's main point—that growing up in a small town made it easy for him to be popular and successful.

The revised paragraph has three instances of sentence combining. In two of these cases, the sentences seemed to be of equal value and so *coordination* was used.

> It was easy to make friends, *and so* I got to know a lot of people.

> School and sports were a challenge, *but* I could always make my way to where I wanted to be.

In the third case, one sentence seemed to be more important than the other, so *subordination* was used.

> *Since* I could do almost anything I wanted to, I was able to achieve almost all of my goals.

Whenever you have written two closely related sentences, you should consider combining them into one, with either a conjunction, an adverb, or punctuation.

35b Coordinate related sentences of equal value

Coordination is the pairing of sentences or sentence elements by putting them in the same grammatical form and linking them via a coordinating conjunction, conjunctive adverb, or semicolon. The coordinating conjunctions include *and, but, or, nor, for, so,* and *yet.*

USE OF A COORDINATING CONJUNCTION

A high-fiber diet appears to lower the risk of certain cancers, *so* the National Cancer Institute recommends consuming 25–35 grams of fiber a day.

Conjunctive adverbs provide another way of giving equal emphasis to two conjoined sentences. The conjunctive adverbs include *however, consequently, therefore, thus, hence, furthermore, moreover, afterward, indeed,* and *otherwise.* They often are preceded by a semicolon.

USE OF A CONJUNCTIVE ADVERB

The 1928 Pact of Paris offended nobody, since it included no compulsory machinery of enforcement; *hence,* the European nations rushed to sign it.

A coordinate relationship also can be created between two sentences simply by using a semicolon.

USE OF A SEMICOLON

People are affected by social forces sometimes far removed from their immediate perceptions; they perceive only a relatively small portion of the influences that play upon them.

For further discussion of semicolon use, see Chapter 47.

35c Subordinate less important ideas

To combine two closely related but unequal ideas, use **subordination;** put the more important idea in a main clause and the lesser one in a subordinate clause. Subordinate clauses are typically set off by subordinating conjunctions (such as *although, because, if, since,* *though, unless, until,* and *while*) or by relative pronouns (such as *that, which, who, whom,* and *whose*).

Consider these two sentences:

We know that advertisers are "out to get us."

We do not make much of an attempt to refute advertising messages.

These two statements are closely related, so they could be combined. Since the author's point is that people allow themselves to be seduced by advertising, the second statement is more important (that is, more topic-oriented) than the first. Therefore, the second statement should become the main clause and the first statement should become the subordinate clause.

USE OF A SUBORDINATING CONJUNCTION

Even though we know that advertisers are "out to get us," we do not make much of an attempt to refute their messages.

Here is another example of how a subordinating conjunction can be used to set off a subordinate clause:

Using hands-on experience is one of the best ways of learning. It helps the student learn on a more interactive level.

USE OF A SUBORDINATING CONJUNCTION

Using hands-on experience is one of the best ways of learning, *as* it helps the student learn on a more interactive level.

When one sentence adds information to the entire preceding sentence, it is often possible to convert the second sentence to a relative clause.

The Great Lakes cool the hot winds of summer and warm the cold winds of winter. This gives the state of Michigan a milder climate than some of the other north central states.

USE OF A RELATIVE CLAUSE

The Great Lakes cool the hot winds of summer and warm the cold winds of winter, *which gives* the state of Michigan a milder climate than some of the other north central states.

Relative clauses can sometimes be shortened by getting rid of the relative pronoun.

The Great Lakes cool the hot winds of summer and warm the cold winds of winter, *giving* the state of Michigan a milder climate than some of the other north central states.

When two sentences modify the same noun, you can sometimes embed one into the other as an **appositive** (see 24c-2).

Julia Cameron was a British photographer. She is considered one of the most important portraitists of the 19th century.

USE OF AN APPOSITIVE

Julia Cameron, *a British photographer,* is considered one of the most important portraitists of the 19th century.

EXERCISE 35.1

Each of the following items contains two or more sentences that can be combined into one. Use coordination or subordination, as appropriate, to do the combining. (You may rearrange the order of the information any way you like.)

1. In a Molière comedy, the central character is a type, only slightly individualized.
   Tartuffe, for example, is a great artistic creation.
   He is not a living human being.

2. In his youth, Watergate burglar G. Gordon Liddy listened to Hitler's speeches in German on the radio.
   Liddy knew only a few German phrases.
   Liddy often found these speeches very persuasive.

3. In 1848, the Treaty of Guadalupe Hidalgo was signed.
   This treaty ended the Mexican War.
   About half the territory of Mexico was incorporated into the United States.

4. With the land came its inhabitants.
   Many of these inhabitants were Mexican citizens of Spanish or Spanish-Indian descent.
   The majority were Indians.

5. Under the terms of the treaty, former Mexican citizens were granted US citizenship.
   The Indians were treated in the traditional American fashion.
   The subsequent history of the Mexican-American has been one of dispossession and discrimination.

6. There are many ways to form opinions about current events.
   First, you have to gather information.
   You can gather information from a variety of sources, such as newspapers, magazines, and television.

7. When you write a paper, the statements should be your own. You should never claim a statement as your own if it is not. That is called plagiarism.

8. You can help shape your audience. You can send your writing to a particular person or persons. You can also send your writing to a publication chosen for its readership.

9. Spoken conversation is different from written conversation. In spoken conversation, you have limited control over whom you will talk with. In written conversation, you have many more options and wider-ranging possibilities in determining the conversation's participants.

10. Margaret Mead was an anthropologist. She communicated with many different groups of people, from Samoan tribe people to international political leaders. Her writing reflects her unique sense of audience.

Parallelism

FAQs

What does it mean to make sentences "parallel"?

If I want to set two or more sentences up in parallel, how can I make sure that they match each other? (36a)

How do parallel sentence elements work to make comparisons? (36d)

Why is a set of parallel elements sometimes considered "incomplete"? (36e)

?

Whenever a writer links two or more words or phrases that have similar roles in a sentence, readers expect to see them in the same grammatical form. When the linked similar words or phrases are balanced and in the same form, the result is called **parallelism** (or *parallel structure* or *parallel form*). When Benjamin Franklin wrote "A penny saved is a penny earned," he was using parallelism. The adjective *saved* parallels in content and form the adjective *earned*. If he had written "A penny saved is a penny that someone has earned," his sentence would have been out of balance (and would not have been so memorable!).

Parallelism not only can make writing more elegant; it also can direct the reader's attention to important structural relationships among ideas within sentences. Putting two elements in parallel form makes it easy for the reader to compare them.

36a   Put parallel content in parallel form

Words and phrases that are linked by the coordinating conjunctions *and, but, or,* or *nor* often are parallel in content. In such cases, they also should be parallel in form.

cease and *desist*   [Both verbs]

hook, line, and *sinker*   [All nouns]

of the people, by the people, [and] *for the people*   [All prepositional phrases]

Sometimes parallel structures are quite complicated, as in this famous sentence from Abraham Lincoln's Gettysburg Address, contrasting politicians' speeches with soldiers' bravery:

$$\begin{bmatrix} \text{The world will} \\ \text{it can} \end{bmatrix} \begin{bmatrix} \text{little note,} \\ \text{long remember,} \\ \text{never forget} \end{bmatrix} nor \begin{bmatrix} \text{what we say here,} \\ \text{what they did here.} \end{bmatrix} but$$

To make sure that you use parallelism appropriately, follow this three-step procedure:

1. Whenever you write a sentence that has words or phrases joined by *and, but, or,* or *nor,* ask yourself if there is comparable content somewhere on each side of the conjunction. If so, identify exactly what that comparable content is. In the Gettysburg Address, for example, "what we say here" is compared with "what they did here."

    > **WEB**
    > http://owl.english.
    > purdue.edu/Files/
    > 68.html
    > A definition of parallelism, accompanied by examples and proofreading strategies

2. Check to see if the comparable parts are in the same grammatical form. The two parts cited from the Gettysburg Address are both relative clauses, beginning with the same relative pronoun (*what*), followed by a personal pronoun (*we/they*), a verb (*say/did*), and the same adverb (*here*).

3. If the comparable parts are not in the same grammatical form— but should be—use the elements in one part of the sentence as a model and put the elements in the other parts in the same grammatical form.

    The world will little note *nor* ~~remember forever~~ *long remember* . . .

All of this may seem quite complicated—and indeed it is—but it is worth learning because parallelism is one of the most powerful tools a writer has for presenting ideas clearly and memorably.

In the following sentence, the conjunction *and* alerts the reader to the possibility that there is comparable content in the two parts of the sentence. The writer seems to be saying that creativity has two identifying characteristics of a similar kind, and the sentence seems to have this kind of structure: Creativity = $X + Y$.

FAULTY   Creativity is being able to identify a situation or problem and the knowledge of how to solve it.

Are X and Y in the same grammatical form? No; "being able to identify a situation or problem" is a gerund (*-ing*) phrase, whereas "the knowledge of how to solve it" is a noun phrase.

To fix this problem, use the first part of the sentence as a model for the second part. The first part is a gerund phrase, so you can create parallelism by turning the second part into a gerund phrase as well: "knowing how to solve it."

REVISED   Creativity is *being* able to identify a situation or problem and *knowing* how to solve it.

Consider these additional examples of similar sentence elements that can be confusing if their elements are not made parallel:

FAULTY   An expert is someone who knows more and more about increasingly little.

REVISED   An expert is someone who knows *more and more* about *less and less.*

FAULTY   The young talk about what they are doing; old people reminisce about the past; fools only tell what their plans are.

REVISED   The young talk about what they are doing; the old about what they have done; fools about what they plan to do.
[Old French proverb]

EXERCISE 36.1

Correct the faulty parallelism in the following sentences.

1.   Her interests include skiing, running, and bike rides.

2.   We must either turn left on Martin Luther King Drive or take a right turn on Main Street.

3.   Nothing in the world can take the place of persistence: talent will not, genius will not, being educated won't.

4. My present occupation is repairing appliances, VCRs, and refinishing floors.

5. Mark Twain claimed that a friend is one who will side with you when you are wrong, since when you are right anyone is willing to be on your side.

6. Prejudice is the real robber, and vice murders us.

7. What we call the beginning is often the end, and what we referred to as an ending was a place to begin.

8. Destiny is not a matter of chance. It is a matter to be chosen. It is not a thing to be waited for. It is a thing you should try to be achieving.

9. Ask not what your country can do for you; ask what can be done by you for your country.

10. The television commercial is not at all about the character of the products to be consumed. It is about the product consumers' character.

EXERCISE 36.2

Select a sample of your own writing. Following the instructions in the Help box below, identify all phrases that should be parallel. Where necessary, make appropriate corrections.

HELP

How do I find places where I should be using parallelism?

1. Open the SEARCH (or FIND) feature of your word-processing program.

2. Enter the word *and* in the search field, and run the program.

3. Whenever the program highlights an *and*, examine the phrases linked by it to see if they represent comparable or equivalent content. If they do, they should be in parallel form.

4. Follow the same procedure with *but*, *or*, and *nor*.

36b · Make all items in a list or series parallel

Whenever you present any kind of listing in formal or academic writing, whether it is a formatted list such as an outline or just a series of items in a sentence, all of the items should be in the same grammatical form. They are, in effect, being lined up for comparison on an "apples with apples" basis, and readers expect each item to be in similar form. For example, the headings in this chapter constitute a formatted list, with each item set off with a number (36a, 36b, 36c). Notice how each heading is in the form of an imperative verb phrase ("Put parallel content in . . . ," "Make all items in . . . ," "Use parallelism with . . . "). This parallel structure helps the reader approach each guideline for writing in a similar way; phrasing that goes off in different directions is likely to distract the reader.

NONPARALLEL SERIES REVISED

The last decades of the 19th century through the early decades of our present century marked a period when Americans confronted rapid industrialization, a communications revolution,
the growth of big business.
and ~~big business was growing~~. [A third noun phrase is put into the series to replace the distracting clause.]

All addictions are characterized by compulsion, loss of control, ~~there are~~ negative consequences, and
denial.
~~people deny they're addicted~~. [Turning the last two items into noun phrases makes it clear that the sentence contains a series of four items.]

36c · Use parallelism with correlative conjunctions

Whenever you use correlative conjunctions like *both/and, either/ or, neither/nor,* or *not only/but,* you are lining up two sentence elements for comparison. Thus, those elements require parallel grammatical form.

Either *we go full speed ahead* or *we stop right here.*

Making verb phrases parallel usually involves having the verbs in the same tense:

Not only *have* these three books by Twain *received* high critical acclaim, but they *have been* more widely *read* than any other American books with any claim to literary standing.

HELP

How do I keep track of elements that need to be parallel?

If your paragraphs are so dense with potentially parallel elements that you cannot keep track of them all, try using the word processor's LIST function to help you keep things straight.

1. Reduce or minimize your main document, and focus its window on the paragraph you want to analyze.
2. Make a new blank working document, and reduce or minimize it so that it fits on the screen alongside the key portion of your main document.
3. In the new working document, pull down the FORMATTING OPTIONS menu and go to the LISTING, or NUMBERING, format. Choose a numbered or lettered listing format for each sentence you want to analyze.
4. From the main document, copy the first element that precedes an *and, or, nor,* or *but,* and then insert it into your working document as the first list item.
5. Find the other elements linked by that *and, or, nor,* or *but;* copy them into your working document as the second and ensuing list items.
6. As you line up elements in the list, change the wording to create a balanced sentence structure, matching the structure of each element in the list with that of the corresponding element immediately above it. Make sure that each item in the list has a similar balanced construction.
7. Once the new structure is clear in your working document, either revise the main document to match or copy key portions from the working document and insert them as revisions into the main document.

While the verb phrases remain parallel here, note the inverted auxiliary (*have*) and subject (*these three books*) in the first part of the sentence—a formation that is peculiar to an introductory *not only.*

36d · Use parallelism for comparisons or contrasts

A comparison or contrast involves two statements or terms that are seen as somehow equivalent; indeed, it is this equivalence that allows them to be compared. These two statements or terms therefore should be parallel. Abraham Lincoln's use of parallelism in the Gettysburg Address excerpt is a good example. Another good example of contrasting parallelism occurs in Shakespeare's *Julius Caesar,* where Brutus tries to justify, before the citizens of Rome, his assassination of Caesar:

> Not that I loved Caesar less, but that I loved Rome more. Had you rather Caesar were living, and die all slaves, than that Caesar were dead, to live all free men?
>
> —*Julius Caesar,* 3.2.21–24

36e   Make parallel constructions complete and clear

In addition to similar grammatical form, parallelism generally involves one or more words that appear in both parts of the construction. In the Gettysburg Address example, the words *what* and *here* are found in both parts of the sentence; *world* is referred to again with the pronoun *it*. Usually only a few matching words are needed. As writers create parallel sentences, they sometimes forget to pull all the grammatical elements together to make the comparison complete. Sometimes an extra word or two is all that is needed to complete the parallelism and clarify the connection for the reader.

> http://webster.
> commnet.edu/hp/
> pages/darling/grammar/
> parallelism.htm
> Full coverage of parallelism, with good examples and quizzes

INCOMPLETE PARALLELISM REVISED

It seems apparent to even the casual observer that all people crave some form of recognition,∧*that* no one lives in total isolation, and∧*that* any healthy society will find some way to meet this human imperative.   [Inserting *that* makes it clearer that there are three things "that seem apparent."]

In other cases, a rearrangement of words or phrases is called for.

MISLEADING   Speculation leads to learning, in the same way that science is supported by theory.

In this sentence, the conceptual analogy between the first part of the sentence and the second part is not clear. Rearranging the words of the mixed comparison solves the problem.

CLEARER   Speculation leads to learning, just as theory leads to science.   [The revision puts the second part of the sentence into the active voice, matching the first part and enabling the reader to line up *speculation* and *theory* on the one hand and *learning* and *science* on the other.]

36f   Use parallelism to enhance coherence

As mentioned in Chapter 6, parallelism promotes coherence within paragraphs (see 6e). If two related sentences are equivalent in function and content, show their relatedness by putting both in the same grammatical form. In the following example from a psychology text, two similar *If . . .* constructions are used to create parallel explanations.

> The distinction between formative and summative assessment is based on how the results are used. The same assessment procedure can be used for either purpose. *If the goal is to obtain information about student learning for planning purposes, the assessment is formative. If the purpose is to determine final achievement (and help determine a course grade), the assessment is summative.*
>
> —Anita E. Woolfolk, *Educational Psychology*

Checking for Parallelism with Grouped Elements

1. How many of your sentences have words or phrases joined by *and, but, or,* or *nor?* (You can use the SEARCH, or FIND, feature to identify them. See the Help box on page 614.) *Example:* "She liked apples, but pears were what she always preferred."

2. Do your sentences have equivalent content linked by these conjunctions—elements that might be compared or contrasted? If so, identify exactly what those equivalent elements are. *Example:* "... liked apples" and "pears . . . preferred."

3. Are these comparable sentence elements in the same grammatical form? If not, use the elements in one part of the sentence as a model, and arrange the other parts in the same grammatical form, so that all parts are consistent. *Example:* "She liked apples but always preferred pears."

EXERCISE 36.3

Correct the faulty parallelism in the following sentences.

1. We live in a time when people seem afraid to be themselves, when a hard, shiny exterior is preferred to the genuineness of deeply felt emotion.

2. Most people prefer to watch others exercise rather than participate because exercise is so difficult and it is so easy to lie on a couch.

3. The responsibilities of a stagehand include keeping track of props, changing scenery, and they sometimes help out with special effects.

4. Two complaints being investigated by the task force were lack of promotions for women and writing company memos that were not gender inclusive.

5. Just a generation ago, people would not have dreamed of eating strawberries in September, nor would corn have been available in May.

6. Objectivity is assumed to be fundamental to news reporting, but public relations and advertising personnel are not assumed to be objective.

7. The history of television is a history of technology and policy, economics and sociology, and entertainment and news are part of it, too.

8. More than twenty-five years after the Beatles disbanded and one member died fifteen years ago, the group reunited in 1995.

9. Good therapists will assess a client's general problem fairly early, and provisional goals will be set for the client.

10. Minor hassles—losing your keys, the grocery bag rips on the way to the door, you slipped and fell in front of everyone in a new class, finding that you went through the whole afternoon with a big chunk of spinach stuck in your front teeth—may seem unimportant, but the cumulative effect of these minor hassles may be stressful enough to be harmful.

EXERCISE 36.4

Proverbs often use parallelism. Complete each of the following proverbs by putting the words in parentheses into a form that parallels the first part of the sentence.

1. A wise man knows his own ignorance; (fool, thinks, knows, everything).

2. Love is a furnace, but (does not cook, the stew).

3. If a man steals gold, he is put in prison; (if, land, made, king).

4. You can hardly make a friend in a year, but (easily offend, an hour).

5. Perspective continues to be our greatest shortage, just as (our ironies, most abundant product).

6. We promise according to our hopes, and (perform, fears).

7. She who leaves nothing to chance will do few things ill, but (she, very few things).

8. Fear less, hope more (eat, chew; whine, breathe; talk, say; hate, love); and all good things are yours.

9. The harder the conflict, (glorious, triumph). What we obtain too cheap, (esteem, lightly).

10. Live your own life, for (you, die, death).

CHAPTER

37

Emphasis

FAQs

How can I make my main ideas stand out more? (37a, 37b, 37c)

Why should I avoid using underlined words or fancy typography to create emphasis? (37e)

?

In any writing, some ideas are more important than others. It is helpful to readers if those ideas stand out. This is where emphasis comes in. Emphasis can be created in various ways. Emphatic writing is clear and concise (see Chapter 34), employs coordination and subordination (see Chapter 35), and uses parallelism (see Chapter 36). This chapter discusses some other ways of creating emphasis.

37a   Create emphasis through end-weight

All other things being equal, the most emphatic part of a sentence is its ending. This explains the power of Franklin Roosevelt's famous line "The only thing we have to fear is fear itself." If you read that sentence aloud, you can hear your voice rising naturally at the end before abruptly falling. This natural intonation pattern underlies **end-weight.** Using end-weight means putting a key word or phrase where intonation naturally gives it emphasis—at the end of the sen-

Create emphasis through end-weight   **621**

tence. If FDR had said "Fear itself is the only thing we have to fear," he would have missed out on a good opportunity to use this principle.

As you edit your writing, look for opportunities to give end-weight to key concepts. In this example, note how the writer made the phrase *better and wiser* more prominent by shifting it toward the end of the sentence:

FIRST DRAFT We all muddle through life, falling along the way. But we will become better and wiser people if we pick ourselves up and keep moving on.

REVISION We all muddle through life, falling along the way. But if we pick ourselves up and keep moving on, we will become better and wiser for it.

EXERCISE 37.1

The following are email tag lines, rewritten in a form less elegant than their original form. Using the end-weight principle, try to restore them to their original form. (Suggestion: First identify a key concept, then try to move the phrase related to that concept to the end of the sentence.)

1. Television is very educational: I go to the library and read a book the minute someone turns it on.
2. Recycled electrons were used to print this message.
3. The tree of liberty grows only when the blood of tyrants waters it.
4. Where ignorance is bliss, to be wise is folly.
5. The heart has its reasons which are not known by reason.
6. You risk even more if you do not risk anything is the trouble.
7. Life is nothing if it is not a daring adventure.
8. Time is the stuff life is made of. Do not squander time if you love life.
9. To gain your heart's desire and to lose it are the two tragedies in life.
10. Courage is the mastery of fear. It is not the absence of it.

37b Create emphasis through selective repetition

Another powerful way of emphasizing important ideas is through repetition—especially combined with some form of grammatical parallelism. Notice how Studs Terkel uses the repetition of the simple pronoun *my* to emphasize the personal significance of his work:

A further personal note. I find some delight in *my* job as a radio broadcaster. I'm able to set *my* own pace, *my* own standards, and determine for myself the substance of each program. Some days are more sunny than others, some hours less astonishing than I'd hoped for; *my* occasional slovenliness infuriates me . . . but it is, for better or worse, in *my* hands.

—Studs Terkel, *Working*

Repetition is effective only if used judiciously. Overdoing repetition will make your writing boring and wordy (see 34b).

37c   Create emphasis through contrast

You can create emphasis through attention-getting contrasts. One approach is to set up opposing words or phrases within a sentence. As with repetition, this technique benefits from the use of parallelism (see 36d).

The democratic faith is based not as much upon the assumption of leadership by the few as upon the wisdom and conscience of the many.

—Norman Cousins, *Human Options*

In this sentence, the author uses the contrast between *few* and *many* to emphasize the broad-based nature of democratic governance. Note the parallelism between *leadership by the few* and *wisdom and conscience of the many*. If the author had written "The democratic faith is based mainly upon the wisdom and conscience of many people," the statement would have been less emphatic.

Another way of creating emphasis through contrast is by using transitional expressions like *however, though, while, yet,* or *but* (see 6c-1) to "trump" one idea with another. In this example from a discussion of investigative journalism, note how the writer uses *though* and *while* to emphasize her main point:

While most newspapers carry on a continuous series of investigations of local and often national or international issues, these investigations are limited in their scope. In particular, local journalistic investigations tend to be focused on the illegal, unethical, or personally extravagant activities of public officials or the harmful actions of private individuals or business firms acting against the public interest. *Though* there is often great value to these investigations in keeping both public officials and private interests from plundering the commonweal, they too infrequently address questions like the efficacy or wisdom of the public proposals and plans.

—Phyllis Kaniss, *Making Local News*

37d   Create emphasis through careful word choice

You can often produce emphatic writing simply by using vivid, powerful words (see Chapter 40). Even a single carefully chosen word can have a powerful effect. Note the effect Antonio Ramirez achieves by using the word *bombarded* in the opening sentence of his essay (see Chapter 7):

In the past few weeks, the media have bombarded us with information about

a Finn Dorset ewe named Dolly.

Antonio could have chosen a milder expression like *exposed* or *subjected*, but neither of these verbs would have had the power of *bombarded*. This more emphatic expression not only draws the reader's attention; it also allows the reader to anticipate an important theme that the rest of the essay will develop.

Even simple adverbs can make a difference in how emphatic a statement is. Which of the following sentences seems more emphatic to you?

Robert's GPA is 3.79.

Robert's GPA is *just under* 3.8.

Robert's GPA is *nearly* 3.8.

All three sentences say essentially the same thing, but the second and especially the third subtly imply that Robert's GPA is very high. For readers who already know about GPAs, the extra wording simply adds emphasis.

In using emphatic vocabulary, be sure to be accurate. If you use powerful words just for shock effect without regard for accuracy, you will be accused of *hyperbole* (exaggeration for effect) and will lose your credibility (see Chapter 7). To find appropriate powerful replacements for dull expressions, consult your online thesaurus and dictionary (see Chapter 43).

EXERCISE 37.2

Review your most recent piece of writing to determine where you can make it more emphatic.

37e   Create emphasis through punctuation or typography

With all the style options available on today's word processors, it is tempting to create emphasis simply through punctuation, formatting, or typography. You can use <u>underlining,</u> **boldface,** *italics,* ALL CAPS, or a special font to draw attention to certain words or phrases. You can use exclamation points (see 45g) and dashes (see 51e). (Note that quotation marks are *not* used for emphasis.) You can use white space, bulleted lists, boxes, and other formatting devices (see 17b). In email, you can even use emoticons, such as :-) to represent ☺ (see 21b-4).

> http://owl.english.
> purdue.edu/Files/
> 89.html
> Five techniques for
> adding emphasis to
> your prose
>
> WEB

These are all effective techniques, but only if they are used sparingly. Readers quickly become irritated if these kinds of visual devices are used excessively. In general, the more formal the writing, the less you should use such devices. Learn to rely instead on end-weight, parallelism, selective repetition, contrast, and other sentence-construction techniques to add emphasis to your writing.

EXERCISE 37.3

Restructure the following sentences so that emphasis is created not by punctuation and typography but by sentence structure.

1. Gravity is the <u>law</u> (and it is also a good idea).
2. Truth can set you free, and it is the only thing that can.
3. A hero is braver than an ordinary man by only five minutes!
4. It was <u>Polish</u> that was Joseph Conrad's first language not English, and most people do not understand that.
5. It would be a LIE if I said that I did not want to see you again.
6. George is looking for a woman who is athletic, romantic, and adventurous and who looks like a super model :-)
7. Capital punishment is one of the most controversial issues discussed in the United States today. The reason why it is such a controversial issue is that it raises many questions— political questions and moral questions. It is an *immensely* difficult issue to deal with!

8. It was **Emily** Bronte who wrote *Wuthering Heights,* not her sister Charlotte.

9. The <u>family</u> cannot be replaced when it comes to keeping children away from drugs. Schools, religious institutions, the police—they all can help.

10. <u>Either</u> passage A or reading passage B, *not both,* should be chosen to be summarized!

Variety

How can I jazz up my writing style? (38a, 38b, 38c)
How much variety should I aim for in my writing? Are
   there some situations that call for more variety than
   others? (38d)

?

Good writers always try to make their writing interesting, not only in content but also in style. This is where variety comes in. By varying your style, you change the rhythm of your writing and keep your readers interested. If you write the same kind of sentence over and over again, you are likely to put your readers to sleep.

38a   Vary sentence length

One of the easiest and most effective ways to alter the rhythm of your writing is to vary the length of your sentences. Readers usually process one sentence at a time. If sentences are all of similar length, the result will be a monotonous tempo that will bore readers. A mixture of sentences—long, short, and something in between—is much more interesting. You do not have to change length with every sentence, but you certainly should do so from time to time.

Note how Barbara Kingsolver does it in the opening paragraph of *The Bean Trees:*

> I have been afraid of putting air in a tire ever since I saw a tractor tire blow up and throw Newt Hardbine's father over the top of the Standard Oil sign. I'm not lying. He got stuck up there. About nineteen people congregated during the time it took for Norman Strick to walk up to the Courthouse and blow the whistle for the volunteer fire department. They eventually did come with the ladder and haul him down, and he wasn't dead but lost his hearing and in many other ways was never the same afterward. They said he overfilled the tire.

> —Barbara Kingsolver, *The Bean Trees*

There are six sentences in this paragraph, varying in number of words as follows: 32-3-5-27-29-6. Not only is this kind of variety pleasing for variety's sake; it also allows the author to emphasize the three short sentences and spin out details in the three long sentences.

Of course, creative writers like Barbara Kingsolver are supposed to do whatever they can to make their writing interesting. But does this principle apply to the kind of ordinary, everyday writing the rest of us do? Yes, it does. Varying the length of your sentences will make your writing more interesting—more readable—no matter what kind of writing it is. Believe it or not, even textbooks can benefit from varied sentence length. Here is an example from the opening paragraph of *Fundamentals of Anatomy and Physiology:*

> The world around us contains a staggering number of living organisms with very different appearances and lifestyles. Despite the diversity of sizes and habits, all living things perform the same basic functions. They respond to changes in their immediate environment. You move your hand away from a hot stove, dogs bark at approaching strangers, fish are scared by loud noises, and tiny amoebas glide toward potential prey. Living things also show adaptability, and their internal operations and responses to stimulation can vary from moment to moment.

> —Frederic Martini, *Fundamentals of Anatomy and Physiology*

The sentences in this passage vary in length as follows: 17-15-8-27-19. There is not as much sentence-length variation as in the Kingsolver piece, but it adds to the writing style nonetheless. Notice in particular how the short third sentence makes the main point, while the long fourth sentence provides supporting details. As well as being pleasing to the ear, varying sentence length also helps the reader distinguish between main points and details.

EXERCISE 38.1

Examine a sample of your own writing. Do your sentences vary in length? (Use your word count program to check.) If not, try to revise them so that they do.

38b Vary sentence structure

Another way to alter the rhythm and cadence of your writing is by varying the structure of your sentences. Based on clause structure (see 24c-3), sentences can be divided into four basic types (see 24d-2):

A **simple sentence** contains one independent clause and no other clauses.

A **compound sentence** contains two independent clauses.

A **complex sentence** contains one independent clause and one or more subordinate clauses.

A **compound-complex sentence** contains two independent clauses and at least one subordinate clause.

All four sentence types are found in the following paragraph.

Complex	One of the great paradoxes in history is that the truest expression of Christianity is to be found not in the West but
Complex	in the East. In India countless millions of people are living out the ideas of Christ, though they do not call themselves Christians and are unfamiliar with Christian theology. They
Simple	are the poor, the meek, the merciful, and the pure in heart.
Compound	They regard life as sacred and they will not harm it in any
Simple	of its forms. They practice renunciation. They believe in
Compound-complex	nonviolence and they worship the memory of a human being who perhaps has come closer to enacting Christianity than anyone in modern history. Interestingly enough,
Simple	Gandhi's struggle was directed against a Western Christian nation.

—Norman Cousins, *Human Options*

Notice how pleasing this paragraph is to the ear. By using a variety of sentence structures, Cousins changes the tempo of the writing, avoiding monotony. Notice, too, how the changes in tempo lead to sentences of different length, ranging from three to twenty-six words. Thus, the two strategies—varying sentence length and varying sentence structure—work together.

38c   Avoid excessive repetition

Repetition always draws attention. If you use it deliberately to create parallelism (see Chapter 36) or emphasis (see 37b), that is fine. But if you use it for no particular reason, you will only draw attention to your repetitiveness—not a good way to liven up your style! This problem of excessive repetition can occur in a number of ways. Following are some typical sources of excessive repetition:

http://owl.english.
purdue.edu/Files/
113.html
How to create variety
by combining, restruc-
turing, or varying the
length of sentences

1. Continual use of sentences of the same length
2. Continual use of the same sentence type
3. Overuse of a special grammatical form (for example, passive voice, *there is,* or *it is*)
4. Continual use of the same grammatical subject
5. Frequent use of the same kind of sentence opener (for example, a subordinate clause, transitional phrase, or adverbial phrase)
6. Frequent use of the same word

Here is how to avoid these problems: After you have written a draft or two and are ready to edit for style, read the text aloud. Listen especially for rhythm and cadence—the tempo of the writing. Do you notice a consistent tempo from one sentence to the next, creating a sing-song rhythm? If so, revise your writing, using one or more of the Strategies for Increasing Sentence Variety.

Let us try this procedure on the following short essay:

ORIGINAL

Out of all the experiences I've had throughout my life, I've learned the most through real-life experiences. Working with people, how a hospital system works, and the value of health are a few of the skills I've gained through volunteer work at Rosewood Hospital.

First, working with people has been one of the greatest joys I've had the opportunity to learn. For example, in the hospital there are many patients who need special attention. I am often asked to get them supplies, help them

with reading, or just be there for someone to talk to. Through volunteering to
help with patients, I've learned how to work easily with others.

Next, gaining knowledge about how the hospital system works is
something else I've learned. Watching nurses care for patients and running
errands for them to other areas of the hospital has given me this knowledge.
Observing the hospital system has also helped me realize that I want to
study for a health career in the future.

Finally, the principle of the value of health is the skill I hold most
valuable. Taking care of sick patients has made me realize how valuable
health is. For instance, . . .

If you read this essay aloud, you will notice that it suffers from a monotonous rhythm, which almost lulls you to sleep. This is because
the sentences are similar in length, type, and structure. Except for the
second one, the sentences vary in length from only thirteen to
twenty-one words. Most are complex sentences and many start with
a gerund phrase (*First, working with people; Next, gaining knowledge
about*). It seems that the writer is trying overly hard to categorize the
different things she has done and learned.

The following revision incorporates many changes that contribute
to sentence variety.

REVISED

Of all the experiences I've had throughout my life, I've learned the most
through real-life ones. By doing volunteer work at Rosewood Hospital, for
example, I've learned how to work with people, how a hospital system
operates, and how important health is.

Learning how to work with people has been a particular joy. Many
patients need special attention, and I am often asked to get them supplies,
help them with reading, or just be there for someone to talk to. In this way,
I've learned how to interact easily with others.

Something else I've learned is how the hospital system works. By
watching nurses care for patients and running errands for them to other
areas of the hospital, I've learned enough about the hospital system to know
that I want to begin studying for a future career in healthcare.

Finally, and most importantly, taking care of sick patients has made me

realize how valuable health is. For instance, . . .

What changes have been made? First, deleting unnecessary verbiage has reduced the total number of words by 19 percent (from 196 to 159). Second, sentence-combining has created eight sentences from the original eleven. The result is sentences of varying length—some as short as 10 words, others as long as 38. Third, the types of sentences vary more; now only half the sentences are complex. Furthermore, putting the writer (*I*) more frequently into the grammatical subject position has broken up the heavy pattern of starting sentences with a gerund phrase.

Caution: In making stylistic changes, be careful not to violate any of the guidelines discussed in Chapters 29 through 37. For example, do not create an excessively long sentence (see 34a); if you decide to move a modifier, do not misplace it (see Chapter 32).

EXERCISE 38.2

Test a sample of your own writing for sentence variety. Read it aloud, and then revise it as necessary, following the Strategies for Increasing Sentence Variety.

Strategies for Increasing Sentence Variety

1. Revise for clarity and conciseness (see Chapter 34).
2. If sentences sound short and choppy, try forming an occasional long sentence by combining two shorter ones.
3. If sentences are so long that you have to take a deep breath after each one, create some shorter sentences by dividing a few of the long ones.
4. Move some transitional expressions; they do not always have to be at the beginning of the sentence.
5. Move some modifiers. They often can either precede or follow what they are modifying.
6. Restructure some sentences.
7. Eliminate excessive repetition of words and phrases.

38d Respect different standards and purposes

In seeking to make your writing more varied and interesting, be sensitive to the kind of writing you are doing and who your audience is. In technical and business writing (see Chapter 22), for example, stylistic variety is not valued as highly as it is in, say, literary or magazine writing (see Chapter 14). Your biology or accounting instructor will probably be less concerned about variety than your English or history instructor. In this respect, different academic fields are likely to hold you to different standards. The guidelines offered in this chapter will be especially useful in those classes where the instructor pays close attention to the quality of students' writing.

> **WEB**
>
> http://webster.
> commnet.edu/hp/
> pages/darling/
> grammar/
> sentences.htm
> Dazzling advice for
> spicing up your writing,
> with great examples
> and a quiz

In nonacademic situations, such as when writing email to friends, you will probably want to use sentence variety for the same reason—to spice up your writing and make it more interesting. But in this case, you can do it in different ways—with sentence fragments, quick shifts of topic, jokes, or digressions (see 21b). In this type of writing, you can punctuate your sentences any way you like—even with emoticons.

Another issue of concern is correctness, especially when you are writing in formal (Standard Edited) English. Dictionaries, grammar books, and handbooks have long included rules about what constitutes "correct" usage and what does not. In general, it is best to observe such rules. However, some "rules" are actually only guidelines, meant to be observed in some cases but not in others. For example, there is a longstanding rule against splitting infinitives, or putting anything between *to* and the base form of the verb. According to this rule, the sentence "We wanted to more than double our production" would be ungrammatical because *more than* comes between, or splits, the infinitive *to double*. But most expert writers would readily use such a sentence, and so should you, as rewording the sentence to avoid splitting the infinitive would make the sentence more convoluted. The following split infinitive is more problematic: "We wanted to quickly and without any complications double our production." Here, the intervening words *quickly and without any complications* disrupt the flow of the sentence. It would be better to write "We wanted to

double our production quickly and without any complications."
Moving the long modifying adverbial to the end of the sentence (see
32c) makes it easier for readers to process the verb phrase. (For advice on how to use a style/grammar checker to deal with the split
infinitive problem, see 32d-2.)

Word-Processing Tools and Online Resources for Improving Sentences

FAQs

Should I change everything my style/grammar checker
points out in my writing? (39a-1)

What is a good readability score? (39a-2)

I have to write a résumé. Should I use the résumé
template in my computer? (39b)

Are there some Internet sites that can help me with my
writing? (39d)

?

Among the conveniences of using a computer for writing is the ready access to editing and formatting tools, which are found in any standard word-processing program. But these tools must be used with care. This chapter discusses such word-processing tools as style/grammar checkers and style templates. (Other tools, including thesauruses and spell checkers, are discussed in Chapters 43 and 44.)

This chapter concludes with a brief discussion of the kinds of Internet sites that can be helpful in sentence revision. In addition to facilitating searching and computer networking (see Chapters 9 and 21), the Internet can provide help at the sentence and paragraph level, with tips on evaluating and improving writing habits, as well as useful and sometimes amusing information about the writing and revision process.

39a Use a style/grammar checker

A typical style/grammar checker will scan your document and apply whatever rules it has been programmed to observe. Since the rules reflected in the programs are taken from traditional grammar and style books, computerized style/grammar checkers are similar in the kinds of things they flag, such as long sentences, archaic words, sexist expressions, double negatives, sentence fragments, and passive verbs.

http://www.writepage.com/writing/gramchek.htm
"Grammar Checkers, Reading Ease and Other Faery Tales"

You may be able to get a full listing of the rules observed by your style/grammar checker, along with an explanation of each, by clicking on the customization feature. You can then select which rules you want to apply to your writing. Some word processors allow you to choose a particular set of rules appropriate to a particular style—formal or informal, for example.

Note: For extra speed when using a style/grammar checker, turn off the spell checker.

1 Understanding the limitations of style/grammar checkers

Style/grammar checkers can be useful in pointing out potential trouble spots, but they have serious shortcomings. First, *they overlook many potential problems.* Of all the stylistic and grammatical problems illustrated in the examples in Part 7 of this book, for example, our style/grammar checker could identify only a third. It was unable to identify any of the pronoun reference problems in Chapter 31, or any of the modifier problems in Chapter 32, or any of the consistency problems in Chapter 33.

Second, *style/grammar checkers flag many things that are not problematic.* In some cases, the computer misreads the sentence. In other cases, it applies a rule too simplistically. For example, if your style/grammar checker flags a passive-voice verb, you may decide that you should change it to active voice. But using the passive voice is not always wrong; indeed, sometimes it is the best choice (see 34d).

Typical Rules Found in Style/Grammar Checkers

Cross-references to sections in this book appear in parentheses.

1. Correct ungrammatical expressions. (Parts 6 and 7)
2. Use correct pronoun case. (Chapter 25)
3. Make subjects and verbs agree in number. (27a)
4. Use proper agreement with *here* and *there*. (27a)
5. Use complete sentences. (29a)
6. Avoid run-on sentences. (Chapter 30)
7. Make nouns and adjectives agree in number. (33a)
8. Avoid excessively long sentences. (34a)
9. Avoid redundant expressions. (34b)
10. Use passive verbs sparingly. (34d)
11. Avoid wordy expressions. (34e)
12. Avoid strings of three or more nouns. (34f, 57b)
13. Avoid multiple negatives. (34j)
14. Avoid excessive repetition. (38c)
15. Avoid split infinitives. (38d)
16. Do not misuse words. (Chapter 40)
17. Avoid common word confusions. (40a)
18. Avoid informal expressions in formal writing. (40c)
19. Use contractions only in informal writing. (40c, 49b)
20. Avoid jargon. (40d)
21. Avoid pretentious words. (40e)
22. Avoid overused phrases and clichés. (40g)
23. Avoid sexist expressions. (41a)
24. Avoid misspellings. (Chapter 44)
25. Use homophones correctly. (44b)
26. Avoid punctuation errors. (Part 10)
27. Use noncount and count nouns correctly. (55a)
28. Use appropriate prepositions, especially with phrasal verbs. (56a)

Many stylistic choices depend on things that a computer cannot assess —such as purpose, tone, coherence, ambiguity, pronoun reference, consistency, emphasis, and variety. When we ran our grammar/style checker on this paragraph, we received eight suggestions, none of which were constructive and all of which we chose to ignore.

E X E R C I S E   3 9 . 1

Select a professionally written paragraph from an Internet site, copy it, and save it as a document. Then run your style/grammar checker on it. Look at each "error" that the computer identifies, and make a guess as to why the writer might have chosen to write the offending item that way.

E X E R C I S E   3 9 . 2

Run your style/grammar checker on a paragraph of your own writing. Analyze each "error" the computer identifies, referring to the corresponding section in this book (see the Typical Rules on page 637). Make whatever changes you think appropriate.

2 Using readability scores

A style/grammar checker gives a "readability" score, which is supposed to correlate with a school-grade reading level. A score of 7.0, for example, means that an average seventh-grade student supposedly would be able to understand the document. But readability measures, like style/grammar checks, can give you only a very rough idea, at best, of how simple or complex your writing is. They were designed not for college writing but for primary and secondary school texts. The formulas on which readability scores are based are extremely simplistic, measuring only those things that are easiest for a computer to calculate: average sentence length and average word length. They ignore more important factors like word meaning, sentence structure, and paragraph cohesion and coherence.

Readability formulas do not give consistent scores, even though they measure similar things. Our word-processing program, for example, uses the Flesch-Kincaid formula, the Coleman-Liau formula, and the Bormuth formula, all of which measure only word length and sentence length. When we ran it on the paragraph above, the formulas gave us scores of 9.6, 12.1, and 9.8, respectively.

Readability scores clearly do not measure readability in anything but the most superficial sense. For example, in the paragraph just cited, we lowered the scores a full grade level by re-punctuating—namely, by dividing the first, third, and fifth sentences into two sentences each. But these changes hardly made the paragraph more readable. In fact, they had just the opposite effect—the more staccato, choppy pacing disrupted the flow of ideas.

Nevertheless, you can take advantage of readability formulas to obtain at least a crude idea of how readable your writing is. Research has shown that longer words and sentences make for more difficult reading. Continual use of long sentences and big words throughout a paper is likely to make it complex and difficult for readers to follow. If you compare the readability ratings for different portions of your paper, you may find some interesting contrasts. Portions with a higher grade level than the paper as a whole may be more dense than they need to be. Portions with abnormally low readability scores may be dominated by brief sentences and short, simplistic words or have too much repetition. Once you have detected such problems through a readability score, you can then find ways to make your writing more emphatic and varied (see Chapters 34–38).

EXERCISE 39.3

Check the readability scores on a paragraph of your own writing. Try revising the paragraph in order to lower the score. Then compare the "before" and "after" versions. Does the "after" version seem more readable to you? Show the two versions to some friends, and ask them for their opinions.

39b   Use style templates

Style **templates** are preset formats for common types of documents, such as business letters, memos, résumés, and reports. Whenever you need to write these types of documents, you can get off to a quick start by just opening the template (usually in the FILE menu).

Style templates are handy tools, especially if you frequently write the same kind of document. But do not hesitate to modify any template that is preset in your computer. Most word-processing programs do not offer much variety in the way of templates, and the templates they do provide are not always the best. As noted in Chapter 22, even standard types of documents such as business letters, résumés, memos, and reports have variable formats. Learn how to create and modify the templates on your word processor so that you can tailor them to your tastes and needs.

EXERCISE 39.4

Is there a certain type of document that you write frequently? If so, set up a style template for it, and then learn how to modify the template. (For example, you could set up an email template complete with tag line and learn how to substitute other tag lines.)

39c   Use other applications for sentence revision

In addition to style/grammar checkers and style templates, professional word-processing applications offer a number of special functions that can be used in revising sentences or paragraphs. For example, a revisions program allows you to insert changes in a draft and then compare what the draft looks like with and without the changes. There are a variety of options with such a program. For example, the revisions can appear on the screen and/or on the printed document; the changes can be marked by underlining, boldface, or italics in the left or the right margin; and the deletions can be marked by different-colored strikethroughs. We recommend that you familiarize yourself with the revisions program on your computer.

http://webster.
commnet.edu/hp/
pages/darling/
grammar.htm
A fabulous guide to
grammar and writing

There are also window display options, including split-screen windows that allow you to modify one section of a document while keeping another in view. A number of word-processing programs let you keep two or more files open simultaneously, thereby allowing you to modify one document while viewing or copying material from another document.

You also may want to take advantage of bookmarks, or placement markers, that allow you to flag key passages in the document to which you may want to return as you revise. Once you give the key location a tag name, it appears in a menu of bookmark items from which you may choose when selecting key passages for comparison or revision.

One of the most common word-processing applications is the SEARCH, or FIND, feature (often located in the EDIT menu). This feature can help you locate any word or word configuration in a text. Most applications allow you to specify the context in which you want to find a specific word or letter combination. For example, if you want to track each instance of *the* in your text (but not *them, theater,* or *there*), you might simply type SPACE-*t-h-e*-SPACE in the SEARCH box. To replace all instances of a certain form, just use the SEARCH and RE-PLACE features. For instance, if you have made a mistake repeatedly throughout a paper—for example, writing *it's* when you meant *its*—just enter *it's* in the SEARCH box and *its* in the REPLACE box and then run the program; the problem will be taken care of in a flash. Of course, if you correctly used the contraction *it's* anywhere to stand for *it is,* it too will be replaced by *its,* creating an error. In general, it is a good idea to learn what you can about the SEARCH function on your computer. The Help boxes in Parts 6–12 offer many suggestions for using this function to locate key items likely to need revision.

Help Boxes in Parts 6–12

- How do I locate expletives in my writing? (Chapter 24)
- How do I customize a style/grammar checker to search for pronoun case problems? (Chapter 25)
- How do I locate sentence fragments? (Chapter 29)
- How do I identify comma splices and run-on sentences? (Chapter 30)
- How do I identify possible pronoun reference problems? (Chapter 31)
- How do I guard against using long sentences? (Chapter 34)
- How do I find places where I should be using parallelism? (Chapter 36)
- How do I keep track of elements that need to be parallel? (Chapter 36)
- How can I speed up spell checking? (Chapter 44)
- How do I identify punctuation errors in my writing? (Chapter 46)
- How can I spot places where I need a semicolon with a conjunctive adverb? (Chapter 47)
- How do I identify possible apostrophe problems? (Chapter 49)
- How do I find out whether I have a "parenthesis habit"? (Chapter 51)
- How do I check my placement of adverbs? (Chapter 57)

39d   Consult Internet resources for writing help

Chapters 9 and 21 describe how to use the Internet and networking resources for research and for peer exchanges or collaborative work associated with the composition process. In addition, the Internet can provide you with help in writing and revising sentences and in developing stronger word usage. Some of this help can come from useful and entertaining Web sites that offer advice on all kinds of grammar, usage, and vocabulary topics (see the WWW boxes found throughout this book). Some of these sites will answer questions put to the Webmaster by email. Other links can be set up through Usenet so that you can post bulletin board questions. Finally, a number of colleges and universities and some college publishers have set up Web pages on sentence writing and word choice, providing instructional material—and sometimes even feedback—to supplement what you get from textbooks or classes. From some of the university Web sites, you can gain access to extensive samples of student writing, which may spark ideas or give you a model or point of comparison for writing projects of your own.

http://www.tc.cc.va.
us/vabeach/writcent/
hotline.html
A state-by-state
directory of grammar
hotlines

http://www.clearcf.
uvic.ca/writersguide/
Pages/StartHere.html
The most complete
online writing guide
around

PART 9

EFFECTIVE WORDS

CHAPTER 40

Choosing the Right Words

FAQs

What is the difference between "denotation" and
"connotation"? (40a, 40b)
Is there anything I can do to make my writing more
colorful? Should I try using figures of speech?
(40g-1, 40g-2)
What are "clichés"? What is wrong with using them?
(40g-3)

?

Since meaning is conveyed through words, a writer's choice of
words, or **diction,** is crucial. Choose your words carefully, and you
will make your writing clearer and more interesting; choose your
words carelessly, and you may leave your readers frustrated.

40a Choose the right denotation

The **denotation** of a word is its basic dictionary meaning. The
verbs *walk, stroll, hobble, saunter, promenade, hike, march,* and *tramp* all
have the same basic meaning, or denotation—"to move by alter-

nately putting one foot in front of the other, always having at least one foot on the ground." Unlike these words, the verbs *run, walk,* and *crawl* differ in denotation:

http://webster.
commnet.edu/hp/
pages/darling/
grammar/notorious/
notorious_list2.htm
An extensive list
of commonly
confused words

Immediately after the accident, Julie *ran* to the nearest house.

Immediately after the accident, Julie *walked* to the nearest house.

Immediately after the accident, Julie *crawled* to the nearest house.

Your first obligation in choosing words is to select ones that accurately denote whatever idea you are trying to convey. If Julie *crawled* to the nearest house, it would be a misrepresentation to say that she either *walked* or *ran.*

By choosing among the various words denoting an event, activity, idea, or object, you can make your focus general or specific, abstract or concrete.

1   General statements vs. specific details

As noted in Chapter 6, all good writing involves a mixture of general statements and specific details. General statements establish main points, while specific details make these points precise, vivid, and memorable. Good writers thus continually make choices among words whose denotations range from general to specific. For example, instead of deciding whether Julie *ran, walked,* or *crawled,* the writer could have chosen to use a verb with a more general meaning, such as *go:*

Immediately after the accident, Julie *went* to the nearest house.

This would be an accurate statement regardless of whether Julie crawled, walked, or ran. But it would lack the specificity of the three earlier versions and could mislead the reader, since the manner in which Julie moved tells us something about the seriousness of the accident.

Always look for ways to add specific details to your generalizations. As you do, take care to choose the words that most accurately depict those details.

E X E R C I S E   4 0 . 1

Rearrange the words in each of the following sets in order of increasing specificity. The first one has been done for you.

1. vegetation, tree, small tree, small fir tree, small subalpine fir tree
2. pollution, smog, air pollution, dense urban smog, urban smog
3. decoration, plants, ferns, potted plants, interior decoration
4. log cabin, dwelling, old log cabin, building, cabin
5. animal, cow, organism, grazing animal, Guernsey cow
6. wood, building material, hardwood, oak, material
7. casserole, food, shrimp creole, main dish, rice casserole
8. sport, tennis, recreational activity, racquet sport, mixed-doubles tennis
9. garment, men's suit, clothing, tuxedo, suit
10. ceremony, baptism, religious ceremony, baptism by immersion, ritual

2   Abstract vs. concrete nouns

Abstract nouns are those that have broad, often vague denotations, like *power, romance,* and *democracy.* Such words refer to concepts rather than to tangible objects. **Concrete nouns** refer to things that are available to the senses—things that we can see, touch, hear, smell, or taste. For example, *raccoon, Statue of Liberty,* and *radishes* all bring to mind tangible, concrete objects. As with general statements and specific details, you should aim for a mixture of the abstract and the concrete. Abstractions state ideas, while concrete expressions make those ideas more vivid and real.

In the following example, Norman Cousins defines and describes an abstract concept (despair) by means of a series of vivid concrete images: *calling out to one another, frozen faces, clouds racing across the sky.* He even talks about the "breaking up" of words!

> Human despair or default can reach a point where even the most stirring visions lose their regenerating and radiating powers. It will be reached only when human beings are no longer capable of calling out to one another, when words in their poetry break up before their eyes, when their faces become frozen toward their young, and when they fail to make pictures out of clouds racing across the sky.
>
> —Norman Cousins, *Human Options*

40b   Choose the right connotation

Connotations are the extra nuances of meaning that distinguish otherwise synonymous words. *Walk, stroll, hobble, saunter, promenade, hike, march,* and *tramp* all are considered synonyms, yet each brings to mind a somewhat different image. Make sure that you are aware of a word's connotations before you use the word; otherwise, the message you convey to your readers may be very different from the one you intended, as in this excerpt from an annual Christmas letter to family and friends.

http://www.uottawa.ca/academic/arts/writcent/hypergrammar/diction.html
A hyperlinked discussion of denotation, connotation, catch phrases, and clichés

MISLEADING   It was another interesting year on the social scene. People say we have the most *contrived* parties in town.

The writer meant to say that their parties reflect ingenuity and cleverness. But *contrived* connotes a phoniness and artificiality that the author did not mean to convey.

EXERCISE 40.2

The synonyms in each of the following sets can be used to describe people. But some of the terms have more favorable connotations than others do. Rearrange each set to order the terms from most favorable to least favorable. If you are unsure of the synonyms' connotations, choose the most common term in the group and look it up in a dictionary. You may find usage notes there to help you.

1.   apt, intelligent, clever, bright, smart, shrewd
2.   gaunt, skinny, slender, thin, slim, lanky
3.   aggressive, domineering, dynamic, assertive, pushy, forceful
4.   funny, silly, humorous, comical, amusing, ridiculous
5.   poor, insolvent, destitute, broke, penniless, indigent
6.   clique, circle, clan, faction, gang
7.   solitary, independent, self-reliant, separate, autonomous

8.   immature, childlike, innocent, green, callow
9.   animalistic, bestial, wild, untamed, unbroken
10. unkempt, sloppy, disheveled, messy, untidy

40C   Find the right level of formality

Sometime in the course of growing up, children learn that they should speak more formally, or "correctly," to adults than to their peers. In other words, they learn to shift **registers,** or levels of formality. People continue to adjust registers naturally, if imperfectly, throughout their lives, in part through their selection of words. Words vary in their level of formality, from very formal to colloquial. Always listen to what you are writing, to make sure that you consistently use words in the appropriate register.

1   Formal, academic vocabulary

Virtually all writing you do for school and college assignments (except for special cases such as creative writing or personal narratives) should be in a fairly formal register, as is this handbook. Formal, academic vocabulary consists largely of words derived from Latin and Greek—words like *inevitable, hypothesis, perception, theory,* and *superfluous*—which is why you are tested on such words when you take the SAT or ACT exam. The formal register excludes contractions (such as *can't, they'll,* and *you're*) and colloquialisms (such as *uptight, get movin',* and *dig up*).

Try to learn as many Greco-Latinate words as you can (see Chapter 42). And once you have learned them well, feel free to use them wherever they seem appropriate. *Appropriate* is the key word here; simply using as many "big words" as possible will not impress anyone. If you overdo it, you will likely misuse some of the words; in any case, your writing will sound stuffy and pretentious.

2   Informal vocabulary

Informal words are those you might use in ordinary, everyday contexts such as talking with friends and sending email messages. The informal register consists mainly of words derived from the Germanic roots of English—words like *keep, laugh, throw, kitchen,* and *hassle.* Such words tend to be shorter than their Latinate equivalents, but they are often used with prepositions to form longer **idiomatic expressions.** For example, the formal Latinate words *inspect* and *examine* have as their equivalent the informal idiomatic phrase *take a close look at.* The informal register also contains many **contractions,** such as *can't, she's,* and *they'll.*

ESL Note: The difficulties of idiomatic phrases for non-English speakers are discussed in 58c.

Although informal vocabulary is sometimes acceptable in formal writing, you should generally try to use the more formal equivalents where possible.

Informal	Formal	Informal	Formal
friendly	amicable	do again	repeat
worn out	exhausted	go faster	accelerate
hard-working	industrious	take apart	dismantle
funny	amusing	get hold of	seize

EXERCISE 40.3

Give a formal equivalent for each of the following informal terms.

1. cheap
2. put up with
3. take into account
4. under the weather
5. a lot of clapping
6. kind of like
7. put down
8. get something straight
9. take grief from
10. a bunch of

EXERCISE 40.4

Translate each of the following sentences into a more formal register.

1. If you turn up any glitches in the program, let me know.
2. Ahab was so hung up on tracking down the white whale, he went out of his mind.

3. When the savings and loans started going belly up in the 1980s, many small investors found themselves up a river without a paddle.
4. Right now, good workers are hard to come by.
5. Too often the blame for all the ills of welfare is put on the backs of social workers.
6. The guy next door got taken by a con artist selling vinyl siding.
7. My kid brother fixes cars at the garage downtown.
8. The food at the new restaurant is cheap but good.
9. Customers shouldn't have to put up with crappy service.
10. Government waste makes me sick.

40d Avoid jargon, slang, or dialect

There are many versions of English, only one of which—Standard Edited English—is represented in this book. Standard Edited English is the version most widely used in academic and professional contexts and most widely understood around the world. Other versions, including jargon, slang, and dialect, are valuable in their own right. However, they are less widely understood, and thus you should refrain from using them except with audiences composed of "insiders" or members of special interest groups.

Jargon is any technical language used by professionals, sports enthusiasts, hobbyists, or other special interest groups. By naming objects and concepts that are unique to a group's special interests, jargon facilitates communication among members of the group. (Imagine computer engineers trying to get by without terms like *buffer, cache, serial port, CPU,* and *configuration.*) But it has the opposite effect when used with outsiders. Unless you are addressing an audience of fellow insiders, avoid using jargon.

Used by teenagers and other subcultures, **slang** is a deliberately colorful form of speech, whose appeal depends on novelty and freshness. For this reason, slang terms tend to be short-lived, quickly giving way to newer, fresher replacements. At the time this book was written, student slang included terms like *bro', dweeb, ditsy, tweak,* and *rad,* and hacker slang included *obviosity, fritterware, hackification, frob,* and *cruft* (all of which are now probably outdated). Like jargon, slang is understood and appreciated only by insiders. If you are trying to reach a broad audience, avoid using it.

ESL Note: A good Web site for learning American slang and idiomatic expressions is Weekly Words at *www.students.uiuc.edu*.

A **dialect** is the type of speech used by a specific social, ethnic, or regional group. Dialects typically have a distinctive accent, many unique words and expressions, and even some grammatical patterns that differ from those of Standard Edited English. For example, in some dialects you might hear a sentence like "She be working hard" or "They might could of done it." While perfectly logical and correct within that dialect, such sentences are likely to confuse outsiders— that is, people who do not speak that dialect. Thus, if you are addressing a broad audience, avoid using dialect in your writing.

EXERCISE 40.5

Log on to a chat group, newsgroup, or other Internet site where slang, jargon, or dialect is being used. Print out several sentences, and translate them into Standard Edited English.

40e   Avoid pretentiousness

College students are continually exposed to the discourse of academics—professors, scholars, textbook writers—who have spent most of their adult lives developing a large vocabulary and an embellished style of writing. If you find yourself tempted to imitate this style of discourse, do so with great caution. You are at risk of sounding pretentious.

PRETENTIOUS   By virtue of their immersion in a heterogeneity of subcultures, the majority of individuals have internalized an extensive repository of collective aphorisms about a multitude of quotidian concerns.

The following rewritten version says essentially the same thing but in clearer, simpler language:

BETTER   Because of their participation in a variety of subcultures, most people know a large number of common sayings about many everyday issues.

There are basically two paths to pretentiousness, both of which can get you into trouble:

1. *Using literary language in nonliterary writing.* When you are reading a great work of literature like *Moby Dick*, you may become enthralled with such words as *doleful, naught,* and *convivial.* But such words have very restricted conditions of usage; indeed, that is one reason why poets and other creative writers like to use them. Unless you know exactly how these words should be used, do not use them—you will only sound foolish.

2. *Using big words just because they are big.* Academic vocabulary has many long, Latinate-sounding words like *recalcitrant, egalitarian,* and *indissoluble.* Unless you know exactly what these words mean and how to use them, however, you are likely to misuse them.

EXERCISE 40.6

Common sayings and proverbs usually use simple words so that children can easily learn them. Notice how silly they sound when reworded below with pretentious vocabulary. Restore these sentences to their normal form.

1. In locales displaying visible fumes, one can expect to find combustion.

2. A dyad of uppermost anatomical extremities outperforms a single such entity.

3. Genetically similar members of the aviary realm manifest a pronounced desire to congregate.

4. The greater the number of alterations in whatever is perceived to have a separate existence, the greater the amount of equivalency in those entities.

5. The fruit of any of the various trees of the genus *Quercus,* after moving under the influence of gravity, does not come to rest at any considerable distance from the parent plant.

6. Irrespective of the direction in which one moves, one finds oneself in that particular place.

7. Your harsh, abrupt canine utterance is directed upward at the incorrect tall, woody plant.

8. A single complete movement of a threaded needle when accomplished within a certain amount of passing time prevents nine such movements.

9. Human beings who inhabit dwellings fashioned from transparent material ought not to hurl projectiles consisting of earthy or mineral matter.

10. It is futile to make inarticulate sobbing sounds after whitish liquid falls out of its container.

40f Try to please the ear

Although most writing is meant to be read silently, many readers sound out words as they read. Such readers will respond unconsciously to the sound pattern of your writing and will appreciate sentences with a nice rhythm, without heavy rhyming, repetition, or alliteration (repetition of an initial sound).

UNRHYTHMIC A ban on cloning would be a poor plan, mollifying maybe those whom cloning horrifies but not doing anything else, I think.

BETTER A ban on cloning would do little, I think, but reassure those who fear it.

The first version of this sentence suffers from distracting attempts at rhyme (*ban/plan, mollifying/horrifies*), alliteration (*poor plan, mollifying maybe*), and repetition (*cloning/cloning*). The revised version avoids these problems, making the sentence easier to read.

40g Use figurative language

Figurative language uses words in nonliteral, creative ways to enhance the reader's understanding. Such nonliteral uses of words are called **figures of speech.** Two of the most common figures of speech are simile and metaphor, both of which attempt to explain the unfamiliar by comparing it to the familiar.

Similes

A **simile** is the explicit use of one thing (called the *vehicle*) to describe another (the *tenor*). In the following example, scientist Carl Sagan uses similes to explain how the two hemispheres of the brain work:

> The left hemisphere processes information sequentially; the right hemisphere simultaneously, accessing several inputs at once. The left hemisphere works in series; the right in parallel. *The left hemisphere is something like a digital computer; the right like an analog computer.*
>
> —Carl Sagan, *The Dragons of Eden*

Assuming that readers are more familiar with computer technology than with neuroscience, Sagan uses the former to explain the latter.

Similes are created in the space of a single sentence, normally using the word *like* or *as* to make a simple, straightforward comparison. When a simile extends beyond one sentence, it is called an **analogy**.

2 Metaphors

A **metaphor** is an implicit simile. It draws the reader's attention to a surprising similarity between otherwise dissimilar things, but it does so without using *like, as,* or other explicit markers. Metaphors are much more common than similes. In fact, some scholars claim that most of our everyday language is metaphorical in nature. When you say "Her ideas *cast some light* on the subject" or "I *fell* into a deep depression," you are speaking metaphorically. Feel free to use metaphors in your writing, as Gretel Ehrlich does in this passage describing springtime in the Wyoming plains:

> Spring weather is capricious and mean. It snows, then blisters with heat. There have been tornadoes. They lay their elephant trunks out in the sage until they find houses, then slurp everything up and leave. I've noticed that melting snowbanks hiss and rot, viperous, then drip into calm pools where ducklings hatch and livestock, being trailed to summer range, drink. With the ice cover gone, rivers churn a milkshake brown, taking culverts and small bridges with them. . . .

—Gretel Ehrlich, *The Solace of Open Spaces*

Ehrlich's use of metaphor gives us a vivid picture of Wyoming spring weather. She describes tornadoes in terms of elephants, melting snowbanks in terms of snakes (*viperous*), and rivers in terms of milkshakes. In using words like *capricious* and *mean,* she gives the weather a distinct human personality. This is an example of the use of **personification,** in which inanimate objects or abstractions are described as having human traits.

You can use different metaphors in a single piece of writing, as Ehrlich does, so long as you do not put them too close together. Otherwise, you will have what is called a **mixed metaphor.**

MIXED METAPHOR   The idea was hatched two years ago, but it didn't catch fire until last month, when the school principal decided to jump on board.

—Adapted from Richard Lederer, *Anguished English*

This sentence mixes three incompatible metaphors: newborn chicks, fires, and boats.

3   Clichés

When they are still fresh, metaphors add sparkle to writing. But over time, if they are used heavily, they become worn out and lose their charm. An overused metaphor is called a **cliché**. Clichés are especially common in political discourse, because when politicians discover a catchy phrase that scores well with the public, they like to use it over and over. In a 1996 television appearance, presidential candidate Ross Perot used the term "a giant sucking sound" to describe the thousands of American jobs being transferred to Mexico via the North American Free Trade Agreement. It went over so well with the viewing audience that other politicians and media figures began using it. Soon it had lost its freshness and was just another hackneyed expression.

http://webster.
commnet.edu/hp/
pages/darling/
grammar/concise.htm
Good advice on
avoiding clichés
and euphemisms

How do clichés differ from ordinary idiomatic expressions like *take a close look at, take someone for a ride,* and *learn the nuts and bolts of something,* which are also used frequently (see 40c-2, 58c)? Clichés are simply more noticeable, either because they evoke extremely vivid images (*white as a ghost, climbing the ladder of success*) or because they are repeated so frequently (*It's the real thing, Just do it*). They draw attention, which makes them more effective at first but also causes them to wear out quickly.

Clichés, like other kinds of metaphors, have two levels of meaning: figurative and literal. If you describe someone as *a snake in the grass,* people will understand you to mean that the person cannot be trusted—that is the figurative meaning of the expression. But the literal meaning, that of a snake lurking in grass, is never entirely lost. Likewise, the cliché *bark up the wrong tree* has both a figurative meaning ("choose the wrong course of action") and a literal one. In using figurative language, stay alert to both the figurative and the literal levels of meaning. Otherwise, you may inadvertently say something silly like "That snake in the grass is barking up the wrong tree."

Clichés are generally less irritating in conversation than they are in writing because, like idiomatic expressions, they help speakers cope with the moment-to-moment pressure of putting ideas into words. When you have time to *plan* your thoughts—as you do when writing—you should make an effort to be original or at least use less hackneyed expressions.

If you want to use an occasional cliché, be sure to use it correctly. Like any idiomatic expression, clichés have a fixed form. Do not say "It's time to swallow the bullet" if you mean "It's time to bite the bullet."

EXERCISE 40.7

Think of five clichés and write them down. Where have you heard them? What does this tell you about your customary sources of information? Just for fun, imagine that you are a subversive graffiti artist. How would you alter these clichés to make them interesting or truthful? (For example, instead of the advertising slogan "Come to where the flavor is," you might write "Come to where the *cancer* is.")

EXERCISE 40.8

Revise the following sentences (from Richard Lederer, *Anguished English*) to get rid of the clichés and mixed metaphors.

1. I wouldn't be caught dead in that movie with a ten-foot pole.
2. In our school, freshmen are on the lowest rung of the totem pole.
3. Flexibility is one of the cornerstones of program budgeting.
4. He was a very astute politician with both ears glued to the ground.
5. Many cities and towns have community gardening programs that need a little more help to get off the ground.
6. The slowdown is accelerating.
7. The sacred cows have come home to roost with a vengeance.
8. The bankers' pockets are bulging with the sweat of the honest working man.
9. When we get to that bridge, we'll jump.
10. It's time to grab the bull by the tail and look it in the eye.

Avoiding Biased Language

FAQs

What is sexist about a sentence like "Everyone should pay
attention to his spelling"? (41a-2)
How can I avoid stereotyping? (41a-3, 41d)
Why do I have to check my writing for bias? (41b)

?

The power of language can be used negatively as well as posi-
tively. One of the main ways in which language can cause harm is
through bias, the one-sided (usually negative) characterization of an
entire group. Bias can be either direct ("All Catholics are _____") or
indirect ("Jody's Southern, so she tends to _____"). It can arise from
a single discriminatory term, an ill-conceived sentence, or a poorly
chosen example or illustration. Bias is so endemic to all human societies that people often are not even conscious of it. That, however,
does not make it acceptable. Writers should try at all times to avoid
bias in their writing.

41a   Avoid biased gender references

In the past, men and women had distinctly different roles in society. The tasks performed primarily by men were considered high-
status jobs, and the work done mostly by women was considered

low-status. Language developed accordingly. The head of a committee was called a chair*man*, the work done by the labor force was known as *man*power, and humanity itself was referred to as *man*kind or just *Man*. A doctor was presumed to be male; in the relatively few cases where a woman happened to be a doctor, she was referred to as a *woman doctor*. A nurse, on the other hand, was presumed to be female; gender was indicated only in those relatively few cases involving a *male nurse*. And whenever one talked about secretaries or elementary school teachers or flight attendants, the default pronoun was *she*.

> **WEB**
>
> http://www.udel.edu/ apa/publications/ texts/nonsexist.html
> An excellent discussion of nonsexist language from the APA
>
> http://owl.english. purdue.edu/Files/ 26.html
> Guidelines from the National Council of Teachers of English on avoiding sexist language

Today, women are pursuing career paths long dominated by men, participating in what were once considered male sports, and challenging the myth of male superiority in other ways. To acknowledge and encourage this trend, we all need to rethink our use of gender references. Since language is our primary means of communicating, we need to be more conscious about how we use it.

1 Gender-specific nouns

Many nouns in the English language implicitly discriminate against women because they emphasize one gender over another. If you use a word like *chairmen* to refer to a group of men and women, you are discriminating against the women in the group; a better choice would be *chairperson* or just *chair*. Likewise, female-marked terms such as *poetess* and *hostess* unnecessarily highlight the gender of the person involved; unless you think the person prefers such a term, use *poet* and *host* instead. In general, do not use gender-marked terms in situations where a person's gender should not be of any relevance. Fortunately, it is relatively easy to find nonsexist equivalents for such words. Your style/grammar checker should be helpful.

Sexist	*Gender-neutral*
businessmen	businesspersons
chairmen	chairs, chairpersons
congressmen	representatives

Sexist	Gender-neutral
foremen	supervisors
mankind	humanity, humankind
manpower	personnel, staff
policemen	police officers
salesmen	salesclerks, salespersons
stewardesses	flight attendants
workmen	workers

2 Generic pronouns

Pronouns are more of a challenge, because the English language lacks a gender-neutral pronoun in the third-person singular. Traditionally, *he, him,* and *his* were used as **generic pronouns** to refer to all members of a group, regardless of sex. A sentence such as "Everyone should pay attention to his spelling" would (in theory) apply to both males and females. But studies have shown that when people are asked to visualize the meaning of such a sentence, they usually think of a male. Thus, the so-called generic pronoun is actually discriminatory in its psychological effects.

There is no simple way around this problem. But "How to Avoid the Generic Pronoun Problem" lists four techniques, all of which are employed by expert writers.

How to Avoid the Generic Pronoun Problem

1. *Pluralize the antecedent and use* they/their: "All writers should pay attention to their spelling."
2. *Restructure the entire sentence to get rid of the pronoun:* "Spelling deserves careful attention." This often works, but it lacks the vividness of the personal pronoun.
3. *Keep the singular antecedent and use* he or she (*or* his or her, *or* him or her): "Everyone should pay attention to his or her spelling." This is a cumbersome solution and should be used sparingly.
4. *Use the passive voice to get rid of an antecedent subject:* "Spelling should be paid close attention to." This solution produces an indirect statement that is less forceful than an active-voice statement; it too should be used sparingly.

3 Stereotyping in examples

Stereotyping can arise unwittingly through the careless use of examples and illustrations. If you use examples that consistently portray women as homemakers and men as breadwinners, you will be reinforcing a longstanding stereotype. Try to vary the roles of men and women in your examples, thereby broadening the spectrum of possibilities for both sexes. Of course, you should attempt to keep examples within reason; using a woman to exemplify professional boxers, for example, is likely to be seen as either heavy-handed or silly.

41b Avoid biased language about race and ethnicity

Just as offensive as gender stereotyping is language that either intentionally or unintentionally discriminates against people because of their race or ethnicity. Obviously this type of language includes slurs, which are clearly a form of deliberate verbal aggression. But it also includes the sort of disparaging stereotyping evident in ethnic jokes and in statements like "African Americans would do better if they just worked harder."

Terms such as *inner-city residents* and *illegal immigrants* also can be discriminatory if they are consistently linked to a specific ethnic or racial group. Although such terms do have legitimate uses, they are often used as indirect labels or "code words," to refer only to certain kinds of inner-city residents or illegal immigrants. Do not let yourself be drawn into this kind of stereotyping.

Like sexism, ethnic and racial stereotypes can be reinforced by poorly chosen examples and illustrations. If you are writing about welfare recipients, for instance, and you use a single, teenaged African American mother as your main example, you will be perpetuating a longstanding, discriminatory myth. (Most welfare recipients in the United States are, in fact, white.)

Understandably, people are sensitive about the names used to describe their ethnic or racial identity because of the connotations that invariably attach to them. Since ethnic and racial labels often change over time, the issue can be confusing: should you use *American Indian* or *Native American? Hispanic* or *Latino? African American* or *black?* The best rule of thumb is to call people by whatever term they prefer, just as you should pronounce their personal name however they want it pronounced. If you are unsure of what name to use to describe a certain group of people, just ask members of that group.

41c   Avoid biased language about age

In our youth-oriented culture, it is not uncommon to hear demeaning references to age. Indeed, the adjective *old* often is used gratuitously as a way of denigrating others, as in "When Bush lost the election, people said that was the end of the line for old George." (This is the same man who, five years later, took up skydiving!) Although it is true that people undergo certain changes as they age and that some of these changes are undesirable, other changes are for the better. Avoid focusing on the negative aspects of aging and assuming that anyone beyond a certain age is unworthy of respect. Do not use expressions like *old fogey, one foot in the grave,* and *over the hill,* and avoid age-related stereotypes in examples and jokes.

41d   Avoid biased language about other differences

Occupational, religious, political, regional, socioeconomic, and disability-related groups are among the many other groupings in our society that are subject to stereotyping. As with ethnic groups, it is generally best to refer to such groups in ways that they themselves prefer. For example, most people with physical disabilities prefer to be called *physically disabled* rather than *handicapped,* and most people who clean buildings prefer the title of *custodian* rather than that of *janitor.* Political *conservatives* usually do not like being called *right-wingers,* nor do *Pentecostals* appreciate the label *holy rollers.* Sometimes people invent new labels just to exalt themselves, as in the case of one airline's flight attendants who decided to call themselves *personal service managers.* Most of the time, however, relabeling is driven by a desire to cast off undesirable connotations. This is a legitimate desire, worthy of respect.

EXERCISE 41.1

Remove the biased language from the following sentences, and replace it with more acceptable terminology.

1. The newly revised cookbook would be a welcome addition to any woman's library.
2. Orientals are good at math.

3. A professional nurse has a responsibility to keep up with developments in her field.

4. The old man must be pretty senile to believe that!

5. The church held a food drive to make sure that no little black children went hungry.

6. We await the day when man discovers a cure for the common cold.

7. Old people are not able to look after themselves.

8. The physical education teacher told the two boys not to speak Puerto Rican in her class.

9. We must pay attention to the needs of the deaf and dumb.

10. The shrewd Jewish businessman made a handsome profit.

EXERCISE 41.2

Revise the following passage to make it bias-free.

The clear superiority of the Anglo-American culture placed great pressure on the wretched immigrants to blend into this better way of life. Poor immigrant urchins learned more quickly than the old people to drop their backward ways and language for the more progressive customs of English-speaking Americans. In fact, just a few short years after their forefathers had arrived poverty-stricken, illiterate, and disease-ridden from the slums of Europe, the grandsons of immigrants had embraced a new American identity and way of life.

Building a Powerful Vocabulary

How can I improve the vocabulary in my writing?
Word definitions are always referring to meanings
from ancient languages like Latin and Greek.
Why should I pay attention to those meanings?
(42a)

?

Writing, in its simplest definition, is "putting words on paper" (or on a computer screen). Words are the nuts and bolts, the essential ingredient, of the entire enterprise. In order to write well, writers need to know lots of words—a large vocabulary means more tools to work with.

In general, the best way to learn the sort of vocabulary needed for academic and professional writing is through reading. Reading exposes one to a greater variety of words than does television, radio, conversation, or any other form of communication. Reading—whether of course textbooks, news magazines, a Toni Morrison novel, or online discussions—is the best way to develop a strong vocabulary.

As you come across new words in your reading, you can accelerate your learning of them by employing some basic strategies. This chapter describes those strategies.

42a   Learn roots, prefixes, and suffixes

Sometimes when you encounter an unfamiliar word, you can make an educated guess at its meaning by looking closely at its parts—its root and whatever prefixes or suffixes it may have. The **root** (or **stem**) of a word is its core, the part to which prefixes and suffixes are attached. A **prefix** is a word part that precedes the root; a **suffix** is one that follows it. Thus, in the word *renewal, -new-* is the root, *re-* is the prefix, and *-al* is the suffix. By recognizing that *re-* sometimes means "again," *-new-* means "new," and *-al* marks a noun form, you can guess that *renewal* is a noun meaning something like "making new again."

This kind of educated guesswork can be very productive in enlarging your vocabulary, especially the vocabulary needed for academic and professional writing and reading. Most of the specialized terms found in academic and professional discourse were created from Latin and Greek roots, prefixes, and suffixes. *Introvert, counterintuitive, antibiotic,* and *hypothesis* are typical of words formed from Latin and Greek parts. By recognizing the parts and then noting the context in which the words are found, you can narrow down the possible meanings. With multiple exposures to a word—and perhaps some help from a dictionary—you can gradually learn the exact meaning of the word and how it should be used.

> **WEB**
> http://webster.
> commnet.edu/hp/
> pages/darling/
> grammar/
> vocabulary.htm
> An excellent guide
> to building a better
> vocabulary, with links
> to online resources
> and activities

Some Common Roots

Root	Meaning	Examples of words
-audi- (L)	to hear	audible, audience, auditorium
-bene- (L)	good, well	benefit, benevolent, benefactor
-bio- (G)	life	biology, biography, biosphere
-chrono- (G)	time	chronological, chronometer, synchronic
-cogni- (L)	know	cognition, recognize, incognito
-dict- (L)	say, speak	diction, dictaphone, predictable

Root	Meaning	Examples of words
-duc- (L)	lead, make	ductile, production, reduce
-fac- (L)	make, do	factory, facsimile, manufacture
-gen- (L)	kind, class	gene, generalization, genesis
-graph- (G)	write	graphic, photography, geography
-jur-, -jus- (L)	law	jury, perjure, justice
-log- (G)	reason, speech	logic, sociology, dialog
-luc- (L)	light	lucid, elucidate, translucent
-manu- (L)	hand	manuscript, manual, manufacture
-mis-, -mit- (L)	send	mission, transmit, emit
-path- (G)	feel, suffer	pathetic, pathology, sympathy
-phon- (G)	voice, sound	phonetics, phonograph, telephone
-port- (L)	carry	port, portable, transport
-prim- (L)	first	prime, primary, primitive
-scient- (L)	know	scientific, science, omniscient
-scrib-, -script- (L)	write	scribble, prescribe, description
-sens-, -sent- (L)	feel	sense, sensation, sentiment
-spect- (L)	see	spectacle, inspect, circumspect
-terr- (L)	earth	terrain, territory, inter
-therm- (G)	heat	thermal, thermometer, thermodynamics
-vert- (L)	turn	convert, diversion, versatile
-vid-, -vis- (L)	see	video, visible, envision
-voca- (L)	call	vocal, vocation, provoke

Some Common Prefixes

Prefix	Meaning	Examples of words
anti-	against, opposite	antibiotic, anticommunist, antithesis
co-, con-	together, with	cooperate, collaborate, conspire
dis-	do the reverse	disagree, disable, disappear
e-, ex-	out of	emit, evoke, export
hyper-	excessive(ly)	hypercorrect, hypersensitive, hyperbole

il-, im-, in-	not	illegal, immoral, inactive
im-, in-	in	immigrate, inaugurate, invade
inter-	between	intermission, intercept, international
intra-	within	intramural, intravenous, intracellular
intro-	inside	introduce, introverted, introspection
mono-	one	monologue, mononucleosis, monotony
neo-	new	neo-Nazi, neocolonialism, neoconservative
omni-	all	omnipresent, omniscient, omnivorous
out-	to surpass	outshine, outperform, outclass
over-	excessive	overworked, overexcited, overenthusiastic
re-	again	redesign, renew, reload
syn-	same	synonym, synchronize, syndrome
trans-	across	transmit, translate, transcontinental
uni-	one	uniform, unicycle, unisex

Some Common Suffixes

Suffix used to create a noun	Meaning	Examples of words
-al	act of	portrayal, dismissal
-ance	process of	acceptance, maintenance
-ism	practice of, belief	Taoism, activism
-ment	process of	government, atonement
-ness	state of being	kindness, dampness
-ship	condition	hardship, fellowship
-tion	action of	pollution, abstraction

Suffix used to create a verb	Meaning	Examples of words
-ate	cause to become	activate, irritate
-en	cause to become	strengthen, lessen
-ize	cause to become	memorialize, minimize

vocab

42a

Suffix used to create an adjective	Meaning	Examples of words
-able, -ible	capable of being	desirable, edible
-al	relating to	national, political
-ful	having or promoting	powerful, useful
-ous, -ious	characterized by	monstrous, fictitious

Suffix used to create an adverb	Meaning	Examples of words
-ly	in this manner	quickly, suddenly

EXERCISE 42.1

Using the roots, prefixes, and suffixes listed in this section (and others that you know), try to determine what the following words mean. Keep in mind that the task is not simply a matter of decoding, as word meanings often change over time.

1. transcribe
2. synchronize
3. convocation
4. omnipotent
5. hyperconscientiousness
6. inducement
7. vertex
8. audiologist
9. omniscient
10. remission

EXERCISE 42.2

Identify the common root in each of the following sets of words, and try to determine its meaning. Also try to determine the meanings of any of the words you do not already know.

1. paternal, paternalism, patriot
2. congregate, gregarious, integration
3. fluid, effluent, confluence
4. emerge, immersion, merger
5. distend, tensile, extensive
6. agitate, agenda, action
7. astronaut, astrology, disaster
8. unicorn, cornea, cornet

9.   pedal, pedestal, pedigree
10. sedentary, reside, session

42b   Learn denotations and connotations

As you develop your vocabulary, try to learn both the exact dictionary meanings of words and the associations attached to them. The **denotation** of a word is its standard dictionary meaning—that is, what it means to anyone who knows the word (see 40a). Many words have more than one denotation. For example, *sanitize* means "to make sanitary" or "to make more acceptable by removing undesired features (as in a document)." The **connotations** of a word are the additional, often emotive, meanings it has for some people due to its association with certain contexts (see 40b). For example, the word *lawyer* denotes a person whose profession involves advising clients on legal rights and obligations and representing them in a court of law. However, for some, *lawyer* may connote someone who files inappropriate lawsuits or otherwise abuses the legal system. Such negative connotations have led many legal practitioners to call themselves *attorneys*.

Using words accurately is a vital part of writing. The best way to learn how to use words correctly is through extensive reading, because reading allows you to encounter words in their natural contexts. You will find that two words like *heinous* and *infamous,* though they have similar basic meanings, differ somewhat in nuance and usage. If you encounter such words often enough, you will figure out how they should be used, primarily by using other nearby words and phrases as *context clues* to the meaning and usage of the target word. Common types of context clues include informal definitions, synonyms, contrasts, and examples. The following passage from a medical guide illustrates three of these.

Allergic rhinitis, commonly called hay fever, is similar to asthma except in one respect. In asthma, an airborne substance causes an allergic, or hypersensitive, reaction in your lungs and chest. In allergic rhinitis, the reaction occurs in your eyes, nose, and throat.

—*American Medical Association Family Medical Guide*

This passage twice uses synonyms to clarify the meaning of less common terms (*hay fever* for *allergic rhinitis* and *hypersensitive* for *allergic*), it contrasts allergic rhinitis to asthma, and it contains an informal definition: "Allergic rhinitis [is a disease in which] an airborne substance causes an allergic reaction in your eyes, nose, and throat."

Be aware, however, that context clues are not always reliable. If you are not certain about the meaning or usage of a word, consult a good dictionary (see Chapter 43).

42c   Learn related words

Although a word can be seen in isolation, as a thing unto itself, readers normally experience words in relation to other words, as part of a word system. All words are related to certain other words. Knowing these relationships helps you as a writer, because it allows you to choose just the right word to express your meaning. There are three important ways in which words are related: in collocations, as synonyms, and as antonyms.

http://www.linguarama.com/ps/392-7.htm
A variety of strategies for learning new words

1   Collocations

Words often occur in combination with certain other words. These word relationships are called **collocations.** Some collocations, such as *bread and butter, cease and desist,* and *reinvent the wheel,* are so common as to be formulaic. Just hearing the first part of such a collocation allows you to fill in the rest: *beat around the _____, make a mountain out of a _____, leave someone holding the _____.* Other collocations are less predictable. The word *rumor,* for example, is commonly used with at least five different verbs: *spread, circulate, deny, confirm,* and *hear.* The sentence "I heard a rumor the other day" sounds like normal everyday English; "I absorbed a rumor the other day" does not. So, the words *hear* and *rumor* commonly go together, or collocate, whereas *absorb* and *rumor* do not. To learn to speak and write well, you should familiarize yourself with as many collocations as possible. Such knowledge will make it easier for you to construct idiomatic, or natural-sounding, sentences. It also will serve you well on those occasions when you want to create a humorous or stylish twist on a timeworn expression.

http://www.quizmaster.com/cotd.htm
Crossword puzzle of the day—a great way to build up your vocabulary

Be careful, though, not to overuse collocations. If you depend exclusively on common word combinations, your writing will lack originality and may be laden with clichés (see 40g-3).

ESL Note: Collocations are especially troublesome for non-English speakers (see 58b).

EXERCISE 42.3

Each of the following sentences contains a word that does not quite fit. Replace it with a suitable collocating word.

1. My family is probably one of the closest families anyone could come around.
2. The best way to learn is by doing mistakes and learning from them.
3. Education is important to me because it is my only hope to gain my goals.
4. To be creative in the food industry you need to have an open mind and a feeling of adventure.
5. Children aren't born knowing how to decipher right from wrong, so they must be taught by their parents.
6. Traffic was stalled because of a mishap involving several cars.
7. Contrary to myth, the Pilgrims did not solemnize Thanksgiving.
8. Many latent supporters are watching the gubernatorial candidate as she campaigns.
9. The referee called far fewer infractions in last night's game than he has called in previous games.
10. The pirate distinguished the spot where the treasure was buried.

2 Synonyms

Synonyms are words that mean essentially the same thing: *dreary/gloomy, fury/rage,* and *injure/damage* are all synonymous pairs. If you know lots of synonyms, you can use them to avoid the sort of heavy repetition that makes for an irritatingly dull style. Bear in mind, though, that there are almost no perfect synonyms in English (or in any other language). That is, there are very few cases where two words can be freely substituted for each other with exactly the same meaning in all possible contexts. Consider the words *injure* and *damage.* Although they have similar meanings, *injure* is used only with reference to humans and animals while *damage* can refer to inanimate objects. It would sound odd to say "I injured my computer." An important part of building your vocabulary is learning these subtle differences among synonyms. Consulting a thesaurus, or book of synonyms, can be a big help in this respect. Remember, however, to choose carefully among the synonyms listed; each one has its own particular uses and nuances of meaning. Better dictionaries often contain cross references and usage notes that explain the differences among common synonyms (see Chapter 43).

3 Antonyms

Antonyms are words that have opposite meanings: *wrong/right, tall/short,* and *hate/love* are examples. Antonyms are useful in creating irony, sarcasm, and other special effects. For example, a well-chosen antonym can be used effectively in tongue-in-cheek fashion to ridicule someone you do not want to accuse directly: "Senator _____ is the most *undefiled* [read *corrupt*] public servant we are privileged to know." Antonyms also can help you learn new words. By knowing the opposite of a word, you can get a better sense of what the word itself means.

EXERCISE 42.4

Each of the following sentences contains an italicized word or phrase that is not quite right for the context. Consult your thesaurus, and then substitute an appropriate synonym.

1. Efforts to *fulfill* economic growth in Latin America have been hindered by overpopulation.

2. Political *confusion* in Latin America, as elsewhere, has often led to violations of human rights.

3. The United States strongly opposed the *diffusion* of communism in the Western Hemisphere.

4. For several decades, Brazil *has fantasized* about entering the twenty-first century as one of the world's industrial giants.

5. Relations between the United States and Latin America have been *branded* both by friendship and by tension.

6. He *infracted* the city's ordinance that bans the feeding of birds on public property.

7. She *conveyed* her application in plenty of time to meet the deadline.

8. The rotten meat *issued* a sickening odor, which could be smelled throughout the house.

9. I made a list of ten *intentions* on New Year's Day.

10. The body of the *inanimate* president lay in state for three days.

Using a Thesaurus and Dictionary

Do I really need a thesaurus? (43a)

How can I get help if I am thinking of a certain concept but cannot remember the word for it? (43a-1)

If a dictionary gives several different meanings for a word, how can I tell which one is the most common? (43b-4)

A writer needs tools, and two of the best are a good thesaurus and a good dictionary. A thesaurus such as *Roget's International Thesaurus*, 5th ed. (New York: HarperCollins, 1992), *Bartlett's Roget's Thesaurus* (Boston: Little Brown, 1996), or *Random House Webster's College Thesaurus*, revised ed. (New York: Random House, 1997) can be of great use in selecting appropriate words. A dictionary such as *The American Heritage College Dictionary*, 3rd ed. (Boston: Houghton Mifflin, 1997), *The Random House Webster's College Dictionary*, 2nd ed. (New York: Random House, 1997), *Merriam-Webster's Collegiate Dictionary*, 10th ed. (Springfield: Merriam-Webster, 1996), or *Webster's New World College Dictionary*, 3rd ed. (New York: Macmillan, 1997) can provide indispensable information about spelling, pronunciation, meaning, usage, word division, and etymology (word origin). These reference works are especially useful in describing Standard Edited English, the kind of English you are expected to use in college and in most professional careers (see 38d).

ESL Note: If you are a non-English speaker, consider getting one of the specialized dictionaries that contain information about count and noncount nouns (see 55a), phrasal verbs (see 56a), verb complements (see 56b), and collocations (see 58b) and offer many sample sentences. (See Chapter 57 for specific references.)

43a   Use a thesaurus to find the exact word

Part of being a good writer is choosing words that accurately express your thoughts (see Chapter 40). Do you ever find yourself thinking of a concept and knowing that there is a word to describe it, yet not being able to come up with the word? Do you find yourself wanting to vary your word choices to avoid excessive repetition (see 38c), yet not knowing exactly which substitute words to use?

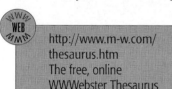

http://www.m-w.com/
thesaurus.htm
The free, online
WWWebster Thesaurus

These are situations in which a thesaurus is of great help. A **thesaurus** is a book of synonyms and antonyms that allows you to zero in on the exact word you are looking for.

A word of advice: Do not use a thesaurus just to find fancy words with which to dress up your writing. As synonyms often have special conditions of use and are not freely interchangeable (see 40b, 42c-2), substituting fancy synonyms for more common words just to impress your readers is likely to have the opposite effect.

1   Electronic thesaurus

Today, most word-processing programs have a built-in thesaurus, which you can use as you write. (It is usually on the same menu as the spell checker.) You can also find thesauruses on the Internet. Use *thesaurus* as your search term, and bookmark whatever good sites you find. One such site can be found at *http://ecco.bsee.swin. edu.au/text/roget/search.html*. Or, you can buy a thesaurus on a CD-ROM, either by itself or as a supplement to a dictionary.

With an electronic thesaurus, you have a great writing tool that is quick and easy to use. If you notice that a word you have written is not quite the word you want to use, all you have to do is select the word with your mouse and then click on THESAURUS. You will get a listing of synonyms and, in some cases, antonyms and related words.

Sometimes, you quickly find the word you need; other times, the exact word does not pop up immediately. In these cases, you will have to be a little more inventive.

For example, Jennie Lee used the thesaurus a number of times when she was writing an essay called "Ride the Bus!" At one point, she wanted to criticize students who think they have to own a car to get around.

Many people have been seduced into believing that owning a vehicle is the

best means of meeting personal transportation needs.

At first this sentence seemed okay, but when Jennie was revising her draft she decided that the word *seduced* was not quite right. It had a sexual connotation that she wanted to avoid. So she selected it with her mouse and clicked on THESAURUS. Figure 43.1 shows the computer screen that came up.

Jennie examined all the synonyms listed (*captivated* through *fascinated*) and decided that none of them was what she was looking for. This confirmed her suspicions about the inappropriateness of using *seduced*, but she still needed the right word. Thinking that maybe one of these synonyms would lead her to the right word, Jennie settled on *beguiled* as the best possibility. Unfortunately, when she clicked on *beguiled*, she only got the same set of words as before.

Persisting, Jennie decided that *attracted* might be worth trying. It was not the word she was looking for, but it was more general than either *seduced* or *beguiled* and thus might yield a broader set of synonyms

Figure 43.1   Thesaurus Screen for *seduced*

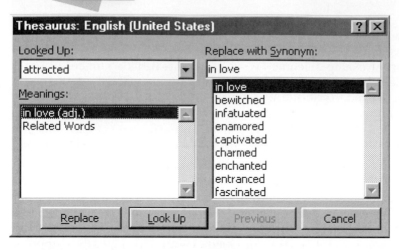

Figure 43.2   Thesaurus Screen for *attracted*

(see 40a). After clicking on *attracted,* she got the synonyms shown in Figure 43.2, all connoting love and romance.

Not giving up, Jennie decided to click on RELATED WORDS just to see what was there. At first, the results did not seem promising: only *attract,* as a verb. But Jennie persevered. She selected *attract* and then clicked on LOOK UP—and that did the trick.

As Figure 43.3 shows, a new set of terms popped up, including the verb *entice.* "Yes!" she thought. "That's it. People are being *enticed*

Thesaurus: English (United States)   [?] [X]

Looked Up:
attract ▼

Replace with Synonym:
draw towards

draw towards	▲
draw	
pull	
pull in	
bring in	
magnetize	
drag	
	▼

Meanings:

draw towards (verb) ▲
entice (verb)
Antonyms
▼

[Replace] [Look Up] [Previous] [Cancel]

Figure 43.3   Thesaurus Screen for *attract*

into buying cars." And when she clicked on *entice* and LOOK UP, she got the synonyms *lure, coax,* and *cajole.* Like *seduce,* all of these words suggest deception, but without the strong sexual, romantic connotations. In the end, Jennie decided that *lured* captured the exact meaning she had been looking for.

What is the moral of this story?

- *Take advantage of your electronic thesaurus.* It will let you quickly search for the word you want. (Her entire search took Jennie less than a minute.)
- *Be persistent.* If at first you do not succeed, do some exploring.

Some of the newer electronic thesauruses offer special features that make it easier to find the word you are looking for. For example, one feature provides help when you have a certain concept in mind but cannot think of the exact word for it. It works as a "reverse dictionary": you enter a combination of key words or concepts, and it suggests possible words. Jennie Lee could have benefited from this feature by entering the combination *seduce* NOT *sexual* or *attract* AND *tempt.* Either would have produced the word *lure.* (See 9c-1 for tips on using the Boolean operators AND and NOT.)

Another program allows you to find words when you can think of only part of the word. For example, say you know that the word you are looking for starts with *for-* but you cannot remember how it ends. With this special program, you enter *for** and get a list of words all beginning with *for-,* including *forsake, forgo,* and *forget.* Or, if you are writing a poem and want to know all words that end in *-ette,* you just type **ette* and receive a list including *etiquette, diskette, corvette,* and *sermonette.*

2   Traditional thesaurus

You should also feel comfortable using a thesaurus in traditional book form. The pocket-size versions are handy for carrying around; larger, desk-size thesauruses are found in all libraries and many offices. In many pocket-size thesauruses, the words are arranged alphabetically, as in a dictionary. With most desk-size thesauruses, you first look up the word in an index at the back of the book and then turn to the most relevant sections indicated.

Whereas multiple clicks and extended searching are often required to find the word you are looking for in an electronic thesaurus, traditional thesauruses typically present a number of words in one place, allowing you to get a comprehensive look at the full set of synonyms for a word. For example, when we used our electronic thesaurus to look up the word *succinct,* we were presented with a screen containing nine synonyms. But when we checked in a modest traditional thesaurus, we were given seventeen: *concise, terse, short, brief, curt, laconic, pithy, trenchant, pointed, crisp, neat, compact, summary, condensed, shortened, abbreviated,* and *compressed.* Furthermore, unlike the electronic thesaurus, the traditional thesaurus gave us five antonyms: *verbose, prolix, loquacious, long-winded,* and *garrulous.* In short, the traditional thesaurus offered an immediate, more comprehensive sense of what the word *succinct* means.

EXERCISE 43.1

Each of the following sentences contains an italicized word that does not quite fit with the rest of the sentence. Use a thesaurus to find a synonym that sounds better.

1. When I am bored, I like to go *observe* a movie.
2. A true New Englander enjoys a *segment* of pie for breakfast.
3. The Brothers Grimm were collectors of German fairy *narratives.*
4. The man playing third base is a very promising *neophyte.*
5. The couple went to the market to buy *comestibles.*
6. Most of us love to *vocalize* along with the radio.
7. Before starting the job, the teacher signed an employee *pact.*
8. We will need to measure the *girth* of the piano to see if it will fit through the door.
9. Ron and Sylvia have an *assignation* on Friday.
10. The board should *convoke* a special meeting of the leadership to review the current situation.

43b   Use a dictionary to learn about words

Do you sometimes come across a new word in your reading and wonder what it means? Have you ever argued with a classmate about how a word should be pronounced? Have you ever had an instructor circle a word in one of your papers and write *usage* in the margin? Are you curious about where a word like *maverick* comes from? In using your thesaurus, do you find yourself trying to decide how the various words listed as synonyms differ? A good dictionary will help you out in all of these situations and more.

WEB

http://www.m-w.com/
dictionary.htm
The free, online
WWWebster Dictionary

1 Kinds of dictionaries

Traditional, hardbound dictionaries come in two types: pocket size and desk size. The pocket size is handy, but the desk size contains more complete information. Electronic dictionaries usually have as much information as desk-size types.

There are two kinds of electronic dictionaries: those on CD-ROM and those on the Internet. Although the preferred method of using the CD-ROM type is to download it to your hard drive, you can play it directly from your CD-ROM drive. To use the Internet type of electronic dictionary, you log on to a Web site like WWWebster Dictionary (*http://www.m-w.com/dictionary.htm*), the Oxford English Dictionary (*http://www.oed.com*), or OneLook Dictionaries (*http://www.onelook.com*). In some cases, you may have to pay a subscription fee.

A typical entry from a comprehensive dictionary, whether hardbound or electronic, will look something like the one in Figure 43.4, on page 678, from *The American Heritage College Dictionary*, 3rd ed.

2 Spelling, word division, and pronunciation

A typical dictionary entry begins with the main word, correctly spelled and divided into syllables: *ha·rass*. Knowing where to divide a word is helpful for typing if you do not use automatic hyphenation on your computer (see 54a). If a word has two correct spellings, they are both listed, with the preferred spelling first. A compound word is spelled according to its preferred usage, either hyphenated (*black-and-blue*), separated (*black magic*), or fused (*blackjack*).

> **WEB**
>
> http://www.
> colostate.edu/
> Depts/WritingCenter/
> resources/page1.htm
> Direct access to the
> best online dictionaries
> and thesauruses

The word's pronunciation is indicated next, in parentheses: (hăr′əs, hə-răs′). Most modern dictionaries have a pronunciation key at the bottom of the page to help you decipher the pronunciation. For words of more than one syllable, a heavy accent mark (′) indicates which syllable should receive primary stress; some words have a secondary accent (′) as well. Some electronic dictionaries allow you to click on a button and get a voice recording of the correct pronunciation of the word.

Pronunciation   Part of speech   Word endings

Spelling — **ha•rass** (hăr'əs, hə-răs') *tr.v.* **ha•rassed, ha•rass•ing,**
and word   **ha•rass•es. 1.** To irritate or torment persistently. **2.** To wear
division   out; exhaust. **3.** To impede and exhaust (an enemy) by repeated
                 attacks or raids. [French *harasser,* possibly from Old French
Word   *harer,* to set a dog on, from *hare,* interjection used to set a dog — Etymology
senses   on, of Germanic origin.] —**ha•rass'er** *n.* —**ha•rass'ment** *n.*—Related
(definitions)   words

Words   *SYNONYMS: harass, harry, hound, badger, pester, plague, bait.*
having   These verbs are compared as they mean to trouble persistently
similar —   or incessantly. *Harass* and *harry* imply systematic persecution
meanings,   by besieging with repeated annoyances, threats, demands, or
with   misfortunes: *The landlord harassed tenants who were behind in
examples   their rent.* "*Of all the griefs that harass the distress'd*" (Samuel John-
                 son). *A gang of delinquents harried the storekeeper. Hound* suggests
                 unrelenting pursuit to gain a desired end: *Reporters hounded the
                 celebrity for an interview.* To *badger* is to nag or tease persistently:
                 The child badgered his parents to buy him a new bicycle. To *pester* is
                 to inflict a succession of petty annoyances: "*How she would have
                 pursued and pestered me with questions and surmises*" (Charlotte
                 Brontë). *Plague* refers to the infliction of tribulations, such as
                 worry or vexation, likened to an epidemic disease: "*As I have
                 no estate, I am plagued with no tenants or stewards*" (Henry Field-
                 ing). To *bait* is to torment by or as if by taunting, insulting, or
                 ridiculing: *Hecklers baited the speaker mercilessly.*

USAGE NOTE: Educated usage appears to be evenly divided — Authoritative
on the pronunciation of *harass.* In a recent survey 50 percent of   opinions
the Usage Panel preferred a pronunciation with stress on the   about
first syllable, while 50 percent preferred stress on the second   correct
syllable. Curiously, the Panelists' comments appear to indicate   usage
that each side regards itself as an embattled minority.

Figure 43.4   **Entry from *The American Heritage College Dictionary***

3 Parts of speech and word endings

Next come symbols describing some aspect of the word—for example, what part of speech it is (such as a noun, verb, or adjective)
or whether it is singular or plural. (See Chapter 24 for an introduction to the parts of speech.) The most common abbreviations follow:

adj.	adjective	*intr.*	intransitive	*pron.*	pronoun
adv.	adverb	*n.*	noun	*sing.*	singular
aux.	auxiliary	*pl.*	plural	*suff.*	suffix
conj.	conjunction	*pref.*	prefix	*tr.*	transitive
interj.	interjection	*prep.*	preposition	*v.*	verb

Often an entry will include variants of the main word, showing different word endings. For verbs, for example, a comprehensive dictionary will give the principal tenses (see 26a). In the example shown in Figure 43.4, *The American Heritage College Dictionary* gives the past tense (*harassed*), the present participle (*harassing*), and the simple present tense (*harasses*). For other word types, you can expect to find other kinds of word endings. Adjectives, for example, will usually have their comparative and superlative forms listed. Nouns with irregular plural forms will have those listed.

4 Word senses

Many words have more than one meaning, or **sense.** Each sense has a separate listing, generally preceded by a boldfaced number. In some dictionaries, these senses are arranged historically, according to when they entered the language; in other dictionaries, senses are listed according to current popularity, with the most commonly used sense appearing first. (It is a good idea to consult the front of your dictionary to see which system it uses.) Sometimes the main senses are further divided into subsenses, generally indicated by a boldface lowercase letter.

5 Etymology and related words and expressions

Information about a word's origin, or **etymology,** is given in square brackets. This information can help you to learn the word and use it accurately. Sometimes, **related words**—words derived from the same root—are given as well. These might include related expressions such as phrasal verbs (see 56a) and idioms (see 58c).

6 Synonyms and usage notes

Some dictionaries list synonyms for certain words, along with explanations of the differences among them and examples. Also, some dictionaries provide **usage notes,** which typically represent the judgments of a panel of authorities about "correct" usage (see 38d). In many dictionaries, particular senses of a word may be given **usage labels** such as *Informal, Colloquial, Non-Standard, Slang, Vulgar, Obscene, Offensive, Archaic,* or *Obsolete.* You may want to check the front of your dictionary to see how the different kinds of usage are defined.

7 Field labels

If a word sense typically is used only in a certain field of study or activity, most dictionaries will label it accordingly. For example, a *genoa* is a type of sail on a sailboat, so it is labeled *Naut.* (for nautical). Some other common field labels are *Anat.* (for anatomy), *Biochem.* (for biochemistry,) *Comp. Sci.* (for computer science), *Gk. Myth* (for Greek mythology), *Mus.* (for music), and *Phys.* (for physics). A full listing of field labels can usually be found in the dictionary's front matter.

EXERCISE 43.2

Select two interesting new words from your course readings. Go to a library or bookstore and look them up in three of the newest dictionaries. Take note of the differences among them. Write a two-page report describing these differences and recommending one dictionary over the other two.

Spelling

FAQs

My spell checker is too slow. Can I make it go faster? (44a)

Are there certain times when I should not depend on a
spell checker for help? (44b)

What are the most helpful spelling rules? (44d)

?

Modern English is a product of many other languages, including German, French, Latin, Greek, Scandinavian, and Spanish. One unfortunate result of this hybridization is an irregular system of spelling that causes problems for many users of the language. If you are one of those people, be assured that you are not alone. However, it is important that you work on your spelling and keep trying to improve it. Many readers have little tolerance for bad spelling.

44a   Use a spell checker

A computerized spell checker makes it easy to review for spelling errors. If you are not already doing so, you should routinely run a final spell check on any important document you write. Some word processors allow you to set the spell checker so that it will identify possible misspellings either while you are typing or after

HELP

How can I speed up spell checking?

1. If you have already checked part of your document for spelling errors, you can set the spell checker so that it skips that part the next time you run it. (See the HELP menu in your word-processing program.)

2. If you are using a lot of specialized terms, consider customizing the spell checker by installing one or more specialized dictionaries. (The HELP menu in your word-processing program will explain how.)

you have finished. Although spell checking can be frustratingly slow, there are things you can do to speed it up (see the Help box).

Spell checkers are far from perfect. Sometimes they flag words that are spelled correctly (especially names), and sometimes they fail to flag words that are spelled incorrectly. The first problem is particularly annoying, but it can be resolved. For example, suppose you are writing a paper on Hemingway and your spell checker keeps flagging the name *Hemingway*. Instead of clicking IGNORE every time, you can customize the spell checker so that it will recognize the name. With most spell checkers, you can customize as you write. You also can add special dictionaries to the one on your word-processing program. (Web sites such as OneLook Dictionaries at *http://www.onelook.com* and CSEN Global List of Special Dictionaries at *http://www.csen.com/special-dictionaries* allow you to download a special dictionary—as long as you are using it for educational purposes and do not publish it anywhere as though it were your own work.)

Identifying misspellings that the spell checker missed is a more difficult problem. Spell checkers will accept any word that happens to match a word form in its dictionary, even if the word is misused. For example, if you write *golf coarse,* the spell checker will not rec-

> WEB
> http://owl.english.
> purdue.edu/writers/
> by-topic.html#spell
> Spelling rules and
> advice

ognize the misspelling of *course* because the word *coarse* is in its dictionary. Thus, even with a spell checker, you must have the knowledge to prevent or correct misspellings. The most effective ways to gain such knowledge are by (1) mastering troublesome homophones, (2) guarding against common spelling errors, and (3) learning some general spelling rules and patterns. The remainder of this chapter is devoted to these topics.

EXERCISE 44.1

Create a document called "Personal Spelling Demons" on your word processor, and enter any words that you have trouble spelling.

44b   Master troublesome homophones

Homophones are words that sound alike but are spelled differently and have different meanings. They are one of the most common causes of misspelling in English and cannot be detected by a spell checker. For this reason, you should study them and learn their differences, especially those listed here:

affect	verb: "to have an influence on"
effect	verb: "to bring about"; noun: "result"
its	possessive pronoun
it's	contraction of *it is*
loose	adjective: "free, not tightly secured"
lose	verb: "to fail to keep"
their	possessive form of *they*
there	adverb: "in that place"
they're	contraction of *they are*
to	preposition
too	adverb: "also"
two	adjective and noun: "2"
who's	contraction of *who is*
whose	possessive form of *who*
your	possessive form of *you*
you're	contraction of *you are*

Some other frequently confused homophones and near homophones include the following:

advice	recommendation
advise	to recommend
all ready	fully prepared
already	by now
all together	everyone or everything in one place
altogether	completely
allude	to refer to
elude	to avoid or escape
allusion	reference to
illusion	misleading appearance
brake	to stop
break	to reduce to pieces, destroy
breath	air inhaled and exhaled
breathe	to inhale and exhale air
choose	to select
chose	past tense of *choose*
cite	to quote as an authority
sight	vision
site	place, location
clothes	garments
cloths	pieces of fabric
coarse	rough
course	path, track; academic class
conscience	sense of right and wrong
conscious	aware
dairy	place where milk is produced
diary	personal daily journal
desert	dry, barren area
dessert	sweet food at the end of a meal
device	apparatus, tool
devise	to plan or invent
dominant	controlling, ruling
dominate	to control, govern
elicit	to call forth, evoke
illicit	illegal

eminent	distinguished
immanent	existing within, inherent
imminent	about to happen
envelop	to surround
envelope	flat paper container
fair	equitable, permissible, acceptable
fare	transportation charge
formally	in a formal manner
formerly	previously
forth	forward or onward
fourth	in position 4 in a countable series
gorilla	ape
guerrilla	irregular soldier
heard	past tense of *hear*
herd	group of animals
hole	opening
whole	entire, complete
human	referring to people
humane	compassionate
lead	to guide or direct
led	past tense of *lead*
may be	might be
maybe	perhaps
miner	someone who works in a mine
minor	underage person
patience	perseverance, endurance
patients	doctor's clients
peace	absence of war
piece	fragment, part
personal	individual, private
personnel	employees
plain	ordinary, simple, clear
plane	flat surface; airplane
presence	being in attendance
presents	gifts
principal	leading person; a capital sum; most important
principle	rule or guideline

quiet	silent
quite	completely; somewhat
rain	water drops falling to earth
reign	period of rule
rein	strap to control a horse
respectfully	with respect
respectively	in that order
right	correct; opposite of left
rite	ceremony
write	to put words on paper
sense	reason, feeling
since	because, subsequently
stationary	standing still
stationery	writing paper
than	in comparison with
then	at that time
threw	past tense of *throw*
through	in one side and out another
thorough	complete
waist	midsection of body
waste	useless byproduct; to use needlessly
weak	opposite of strong
week	seven days
weather	atmospheric conditions
whether	if it is the case that
were	past tense of *are*
where	at or in what place

EXERCISE 44.2

In the following sentences, choose the correct spelling from each pair of words in brackets. Add any words you get wrong to your Personal Spelling Demons document. (See Exercise 44.1.)

1. The doctor [who's, whose] license was revoked by the medical [bored, board] is no longer allowed to treat [patients, patience].

2. The television [diary, dairy] is one of the [devices, devises] used by A. C. Nielsen to research the programs people choose.

3. The [peace, piece] of [advice, advise] Ann Landers gave was simple, practical, and [fare, fair].

4. The poster [sighted, cited] Jesse Jackson, who said, "Your children need your [presents, presence] more than your [presents, presence]."

5. Because he is an excellent magician, he always allows the audience a [through, thorough] inspection of his props before he creates his wonderful [allusions, illusions].

6. More than once last [weak, week], the tardy student managed to [allude, elude] the [principal, principle] as she entered the building.

7. At a gorgeous [site, sight] atop a hill, the women gathered for a bonding [right, rite], calling forth the [immanent, eminent] wisdom from each person present.

8. The [personal, personnel] department's intense search for a [principle, principal] engineer to [led, lead] the department [led, lead] to the promotion of a woman [who's, whose] talent had [formally, formerly] gone unrecognized.

9. When the camouflaged [gorilla, guerrilla] [herd, heard] something moving in the underbrush, he tried to determine [weather, whether] it was an enemy soldier.

10. The small craft carrying [elicit, illicit] drugs encountered bad [whether, weather] that night and traveled far from [it's, its] intended [coarse, course].

44c   Guard against common spelling errors

Although a spell checker can flag many spelling errors for you, it is still worth learning the correct spelling of the most commonly misspelled words. Some of these words follow.

Commonly Misspelled Words

accidentally	develops	occasionally
accommodate	environment	occurred
achieved	exaggerate	parallel
address	exceed	quantity
apparent	February	receive
appropriate	government	recommend
argument	heroes	seize
basically	lose	separate
beneficial	maintenance	success
calendar	manageable	therefore
committee	misspell	truly
definitely	necessary	until
dependent	noticeable	without

If you find your spell checker flagging the same misspelled words over and over, add them to your Personal Spelling Demons document and study them from time to time. Most spell checkers will allow you to enter such words into a file with just a single mouse click.

Many words include letters or syllables that are not pronounced in casual speech (or even, in some cases, in careful speech). Here are examples of such words; try to "see" the silent letters or syllables as you visualize these words.

address	government	quantity
candidate	interest	recognize
different	library	restaurant
dumb	parallel	surprise
environment	pneumonia	therefore
February	privilege	tomatoes
foreign	probably	Wednesday

If you are unsure about a certain letter in a word, try to think of a related word; it may provide a clue. For example, suppose you are wondering whether *grammar* or *grammer* is correct. If you think of *grammatical*, you will spell *grammar* correctly. Here are some other examples:

	Think of
competition or compitition?	compete
democracy or democricy?	democrat
mystery or mystry?	mysterious
relative or relitive?	relate

EXERCISE 44.3

In the following paragraph, choose the correct spelling from each pair of words in brackets. Add any words you get wrong to your Personal Spelling Demons document.

On the second [Wensday, Wednesday] in [Febuary, February], those running for various positions in town [government, goverment] gathered for a [Candidates', Canidates'] Night. At the event, the two [canidates, candidates] for school [comittee, committee] expressed [diffrent, different] opinions about how to [accomodate, accommodate] the new state education standards without having to [excede, exceed] the available amount of money. Mr. Smith believes that the state legislature is right to make [forein, foreign] language a required course. He also pointed out that an up-to-date school [libary, library] is [neccessary, necessary] for student [sucess, success]. Ms. Jones, on the other hand, [basically, basicly] believes that, although beneficial, both [forein, foreign] language courses and school [libaries, libraries] are less important than other things, such as regular school building [maintainance, maintenance]. The [canidates, candidates] then had an [arguement, argument] about building [maintainance, maintenance], Ms. Jones [reccomending, recommending] that the town [seize, sieze] the opportunity to repair current buildings and Mr. Smith stating that the [maintainance, maintenance] budget is [exagerated, exaggerated] and proposing that the town defer some of the repairs in order to spend more on educational programming. Because the debate highlighted [noticeable, noticable] [diffrences, differences] between the [canidates, candidates], the voters who attended the event were well served.

44d Learn general spelling rules and patterns

Although English is not the simplest language in the world to learn when it comes to spelling, it does have a number of general rules and patterns that make things easier.

1 Prefixes

Prefixes are small word parts, like *re-*, *anti-*, and *pre-*, placed at the beginnings of words (see 42a). Prefixes do not change the spelling of the root word: *anti-* added to *-freeze* becomes *antifreeze*. In some cases, though, a hyphen is required: *anti-* plus *-intellectual* is spelled *anti-intellectual* (see 54a).

http://webster.commnet.edu/hp/pages/darling/grammar/spelling.htm
Rules and advice about spelling, along with many quizzes

mis + spell = misspell

un + necessary = unnecessary

re + entry = reentry

dis + service = disservice

2 Suffixes

Suffixes are small word parts, like *-age*, *-ence*, *-ing*, and *-tion*, placed at the ends of words (see 42a). By adding suffixes to a root word such as *sense-*, you can create different meanings: *sensitive, sensual,* *sensory, senseless.* In doing so, however, you must observe the follow-ing spelling rules.

1. If the word ends in a silent *e* and the suffix starts with a vowel, drop the *e.*

imagine + ation = imagination

debate + able = debatable

pure + ist = purist

perspire + ing = perspiring

There are some exceptions. Some words need to retain the *e* in order to be distinguished from similar words (*dyeing/dying*), to prevent mispronunciation (*mileage, being*), or to keep a soft *c* or *g* sound (*noticeable, courageous*).

2. If the word ends in a silent *e* and the suffix starts with a con-sonant, do not drop the *e.*

require + ment = requirement

spine + less = spineless

hate + ful = hateful

definite + ly = definitely

Some exceptions are *argument, awful, ninth, truly,* and *wholly.*

EXERCISE 44.4

Combine the following words and suffixes, keeping or dropping the silent *e* as necessary. Add any words that you spell incorrectly to your Personal Spelling Demons document.

1. complete + ly
2. grace + ious
3. grieve + ance
4. wholesome + ness
5. exercise + ing
6. trace + able
7. continue + ous
8. sole + ly
9. argue + ment
10. sedate + ive

3. When adding a suffix to a word that ends in *y,* change the *y* to *i* if the letter preceding the *y* is a consonant.

study + ous = studious

joy + ous = joyous

comply + ance = compliance

pay + ment = payment

Exceptions are words with the suffix -*ing*, which keep the *y* in all cases: *studying, carrying, drying, paying*.

4. In creating adverbs from adjectives, add -*ly* to the adjective unless the adjective ends in -*ic*, in which case use -*ally*.

silent + ly = silently

hopeful + ly = hopefully

vile + ly = vilely

wild + ly = wildly

terrific + ally = terrifically

basic + ally = basically

An exception is *publicly*.

5. In choosing between -*able* and -*ible*, use -*able* if the root word can stand alone; otherwise, use -*ible*.

understand + able = understandable

change + able = changeable

agree + able = agreeable

vis + ible = visible

ed + ible = edible

aud + ible = audible

Some exceptions are *resistible, probable,* and *culpable*.

6. Double the final consonant of the root word if (a) the root word ends with a single accented vowel and a single consonant and (b) the suffix begins with a vowel.

drop + ed = dropped

slim + er = slimmer

occur + ence = occurrence

begin + ing = beginning

laugh + ed = laughed   [Root word does not end with a single consonant.]

sleep + ing = sleeping   [Root word has two vowels.]

commit + ment = commitment   [Suffix does not start with a vowel.]

happen + ing = happening   [Root word does not end with an accented vowel.]

EXERCISE 44.5

In each case, combine the root word and the suffix so as to form a single, correctly spelled word. Add any words you get wrong to your Personal Spelling Demons document.

1. room + mate =
2. hesitant + ly =
3. shop + ing =
4. control + (able or ible?) =
5. plaus + (able or ible?) =
6. cool + er =
7. drastic + (ly or ally?) =
8. quiet + est =
9. thin + ness =
10. public + (ly or ally?) =

3   Plurals

English has several different ways of forming plurals from singular nouns. Following are some rules for forming plurals.

1. For most words, add *s*.

tool, tools   minute, minutes

window, windows

2. For words ending with *s, sh, ch, x,* or *z*, add *es*.

bus, buses   sandwich, sandwiches

crash, crashes   fox, foxes

quiz, quizzes   [Note the doubled final consonant.]

3. For words ending with a consonant followed by *y*, change the *y* to *i* and add *es*.

enemy, enemies   strawberry, strawberries

mystery, mysteries   theory, theories

4. For some words ending with *f* or *fe*, change the *f* or *fe* to *v* and add *es*.

calf, calves   life, lives

half, halves   thief, thieves

knife, knives   yourself, yourselves

Some exceptions are *belief, beliefs; chief, chiefs; proof, proofs;* and *motif, motifs.*

5. For compound nouns written as single words, add the plural ending as you would to an ordinary noun.

    laptop, laptops   database, databases

    workstation, workstations

6. For compound nouns written as two or more words or hyphenated, add the plural ending to the noun being modified.

    video game, video games [The noun being modified is *game.*]

    word processor, word processors [The noun being modified is *processor.*]

    sister-in-law, sisters-in-law [The noun being modified is *sister.*]

Irregular plurals must be learned individually. Sometimes, an internal vowel must be changed to make a noun plural:

    woman, women   mouse, mice

    tooth, teeth

With some nouns derived from Latin or Greek, a final *us, um,* or *on* must be changed to *i* or *a:*

    syllabus, syllabi   curriculum, curricula

    alumnus, alumni   medium, media

    stimulus, stimuli   criterion, criteria

Some nouns have the same form for both singular and plural:

    deer, deer   species, species

    sheep, sheep

EXERCISE 44.6

Make the following words plural. If necessary, check your dictionary.

    1. device   6. kiss

    2. memorandum   7. sky

    3. church   8. syllabus

    4. goose   9. mailbox

    5. moose   10. mouse

4 The "*i* before *e*" rule

The rule you had to memorize in elementary school is worth keeping in mind: "*i* before *e* except after *c* or when sounded like *ay*, as in *neighbor* or *weigh*."

I BEFORE *E*

achieve	field
believe	friend
brief	piece

EXCEPT AFTER C

ceiling	deceive
conceive	receive

OR WHEN SOUNDED LIKE AY

eight	vein
neighbor	weigh

Some exceptions are *ancient, caffeine, conscience, counterfeit, either, foreign, height, leisure, neither, seize, science,* and *weird.*

EXERCISE 44.7

Insert the correct form (*ei* or *ie*) in the following words:

1. exper___nce
2. perc___ve
3. h___ght
4. ch___f
5. v___n
6. dec___t
7. for___gn
8. th___f
9. b___ge
10. anc___nt

PART 10

PUNCTUATION

End Punctuation

Which is correct, *FBI* or *F.B.I.*? (45d)

Should the question mark go inside or outside quotation marks? (45e-1)

What is an "indirect question," and how do you punctuate it? (45f)

It is important to end sentences with proper punctuation so that readers know what types of statements are being made and what kinds of silent intonation to give each one. There are three ways to punctuate a sentence: with a period, a question mark, or an exclamation point.

The Period

The period is used for several purposes: to indicate the end of a statement, to punctuate initials and abbreviations, and to mark basic divisions in units and computer names.

45a Use a period to mark the end of a statement

Sometimes called a "full stop," the period is most commonly used to mark the end of a sentence. Just make sure before you place the period that the words form a *complete grammatical sentence,* or else you will be creating a sentence fragment (see Chapter 29).

If the sentence ends with a quotation mark, place the period *inside* the quotation mark (see also 50e):

> One commentator said that "rainforest destruction, overpopulation, and the global arms trade are problems for the entire world."

If the sentence ends with a parenthesis, place the period *outside* the parenthesis unless the entire sentence is a parenthetical comment (see also 51a, 51b, 51c):

> Mexicans voted Sunday in elections that could weaken the power of the world's longest ruling political party, the Institutional Revolutionary Party (PRI).

45b Use periods to punctuate initials and many abbreviations

Initials that stand for middle names or first names take periods:

Mary W. Shelley   O. J. Simpson   F. Scott Fitzgerald

Leave one space after each period when punctuating initials in names.

Most abbreviations ending in lowercase letters take periods. Some such abbreviations are

Ms.	a.m.	St.	Jan.
Mrs.	p.m.	Ave.	i.e.
Mr.	etc.	Rd.	Jr.
Dr.	e.g.	apt.	Inc.

For further discussion of abbreviations, see Chapter 53.

45c Use periods to mark basic divisions in units and computer names

Basic divisions in money, measurements, email addresses, and filenames all take periods:

$99.50   3.2 meters   13.5 gallons
English.paper.doc   michael.okiwara@u.cc.utah.edu

45d Avoid common misuses of periods

1. *Do not use a period to mark just any pause.* If you insert a period whenever you want readers to pause, you run the risk of creating sentence fragments. Consider this example:

> Attempts to challenge reactionary political views are often branded as "politically correct" by those same reactionaries. Who support only their own versions of "free speech."

http://sti.larc.nasa.gov/html/Chapt3/Chapt3-TOC.html
A description of all uses of the period and the question mark

The second statement is a fragment (see Chapter 29), because the writer has incorrectly set it off as a separate sentence. The correct way to signal a pause is to insert a comma (see Chapter 46), thus turning the fragment into a relative clause:

> Attempts to challenge reactionary political views are often branded as "politically correct" by those same reactionaries, who support only their own versions of "free speech."

2. *Do not use periods with acronyms and other all uppercase abbreviations.* The recent trend is not to use periods with common abbreviations for states, countries, organizations, computer programs, famous people, and other entities, such as

CA	NJ	USA	UN	FBI
NOW	NAACP	MS-DOS	CD-ROM	COBOL
MIT	NBA	JFK	FDR	AAA

3. *Do not use periods at the end of stand-alone titles or headings.* The title of this chapter and its numbered headings are examples of stand-alone titles and headings, respectively.

4. *Do not use periods at the end of sentences within sentences.* Here is an example of a sentence within a sentence:

> The famous statement "I think, therefore I am" originated in an essay by the French philosopher Descartes.

5. *Do not use periods after items in a formatted list (except for full sentences).* The table of contents for this handbook is an example of a formatted list. Only when the items in the list are full sentences is it acceptable to have periods after the individual items.

The Question Mark

Question marks are placed after direct questions, whereas periods follow indirect questions. Do not use a comma or a period after a question mark.

45e   Use a question mark after a direct request

REQUESTING INFORMATION	Who wrote *Jesus Christ, Superstar*?
ASKING FOR CONFIRMATION	It's a complicated situation, isn't it?
MAKING A POLITE REQUEST	Could you please be a little quieter?

1   Using question marks with quotation marks

If the quotation is a question and it is at the end of the sentence, put the question mark inside the quotation marks.

The police officer asked me, "Do you live here?"

If the quotation is a statement embedded within a question and it comes at the end of the sentence, put the question mark outside the quotation marks.

Who said, "Those who forget history are condemned to repeat it"?

(See Chapter 50 for more on question marks.)

2   Using question marks in a series

It is acceptable to put a question mark after each independent item, even if it is not a full sentence.

Will our homeless population continue to grow? Stay about the same? Get smaller?

If the question is an either/or type, put a question mark only at the end of the sentence.

Are you coming with us or staying here?

45f   Do not use a question mark after an indirect question

An indirect question is the writer's rewording of a question posed by someone else.

A tourist asked me where the Lincoln Memorial was.

The Exclamation Point

Exclamation points are used to show strong emotion, including amazement and sarcasm. Do not use a comma or a period after an exclamation point.

45g   Use an exclamation point to signal a strong statement

The statement marked with an exclamation point does not have to be a full sentence.

http://www.uottawa.ca/
academic/arts/writcent/
hypergrammar/
endpunct.html
All about end
punctuation

AN OUTCRY OR COMMAND	Oh! Watch out!
STRONG EMPHASIS	People before profits!
ASTONISHMENT	Imagine reading this news report and not getting upset!
SARCASM	And the cigarette companies claim that smoking is not addictive!

1   Using exclamation points with quotation marks

If the quotation itself is an exclamation, put the exclamation point inside the quotation marks.

It is not a good idea to go into a crowded movie theater and shout "Fire!"

Otherwise, the exclamation point should be placed outside the quotation marks.

Can you believe that he said, "Alice doesn't live here"!

2 Avoiding overuse of exclamation points

Exclamation points are rarely used in college papers, essays, and other kinds of formal writing. Try not use them except in highly unusual circumstances. Any kind of writing—even informal writing—that has too many exclamations sounds juvenile. There are better ways to express your enthusiasm (see Chapter 37).

EXERCISE 45.1

The following email message contains a number of errors in end punctuation. Make the appropriate corrections.

Guess what

I just found the Web site for NoF.X. Which I have been meaning to search out. It's NoF.X.@anyservercom.

I just got their new C.D. it was a real deal At WEJones Music downtown—$12 99 I'm listening to it now—it rules.

That's it for now I have to write a paper (yuck) due Tues It's on F.D.R. and W.W.II Got to go

Later :)

EXERCISE 45.2

The end punctuation marks have been deleted from the following paragraphs. Supply the appropriate punctuation marks.

1. How long have human beings been concerned about population growth If you believe the warnings, we have long been on the verge of overpopulating the earth In a warning written around 200 AD, a Roman writer named Tertullian lamented that "we are burdensome to the world and the resources are scarcely adequate to us" The population at the time is believed to have been 200 million, barely 3 percent of today's 5.8 billion He thought *he* had reason for concern

2. Can a program ever be believed once it stages an incident Sometimes it can NBC's *Dateline* was not the first network to fake a car crash when it used igniters in its dramatization of

the hazards of GM trucks; all three networks had done the same Unfortunately, the public was not told that program personnel "helped" ignite the fire Why did the network do it They did it because of competition for viewers The line between entertainment and news was badly blurred What was the reason for the media error *Dateline* anchor Jane Pauley replied, "Because on one side of the line is an Emmy; the other, the abyss"

The Comma

The comma is the most common and most useful punctuation mark in the English language—and also perhaps the most difficult to master. Commas are used essentially to interrupt the flow of a sentence, to set off certain parts of it and thereby enhance the sentence's readability. This chapter provides some *guidelines* (not rules) for the use of commas. In most cases, these guidelines will help you clarify meaning and follow conventions for separating confusing elements. But there are occasional situations where it is helpful to look beyond the guidelines to see what separations may be needed to clarify meaning. Practice (and reading lots of expert writing) will give you the intuition and confidence required to use commas appropriately and effectively.

46a   Use a comma to set off an introductory phrase or clause

When readers start to read a sentence, one of the first things they do (unconsciously) is try to locate the grammatical subject. Help them do this by setting off with a comma any potentially distracting words that *precede* the subject. In the following excerpt, note how the commas allow the reader to identify easily the sentence subjects that follow them: *cultural relativism, most US citizens,* and *bullfighting.*

> http://owl.english.
> purdue.edu/
> writers/by-topic.
> html#Punctuation
> A discussion of the
> main uses of the
> comma, accompanied
> by good proofreading
> strategies and exercises

> *Because we tend to use our own culture to judge others,* cultural relativism presents a challenge to ordinary thinking. *For example,* most US citizens appear to have strong feelings against raising bulls for the sole purpose of stabbing them to death in front of crowds shouting "Olé!" *According to cultural relativism, however,* bullfighting must be viewed strictly within the context of the culture in which it takes place—its history, its folklore, its ideas of bravery, and its ideas of sex roles.

The writer has put a comma after an introductory subordinate clause (*Because we tend to use our own culture to judge others*), an appositive phrase (*For example*), and a prepositional phrase and conjunctive adverb (*According to cultural relativism, however*). In each of these sentences, the comma marks off everything preceding the subject, allowing the reader to locate the subject easily.

Using a comma after an introductory element is especially important in cases where it is needed to prevent possible confusion.

CONFUSING   Soon after starting the car began making funny noises.

CLEAR   Soon after starting, the car began making funny noises.

Exception: If the introductory element is short and unemphatic, you do not need to insert a comma.

Today I have class from 9:00 a.m. to 1:00 p.m.

Sometimes the mail does not get here until late afternoon.

46b   Use a comma before a coordinating conjunction to separate independent clauses

The combination of a comma and a coordinating conjunction (*and, but, or, nor, for, so, yet*) is one of the most common ways of connecting independent clauses.

> Members of a mainstream culture often feel threatened by a counterculture, *and* they sometimes move against it in the attempt to affirm their own values.

> Conflict theorists acknowledge that social institutions were originally designed to meet basic survival needs, *but* they do not see social institutions as working harmoniously for the common good.

Using a comma before a coordinating conjunction to separate independent clauses, as in these examples, clarifies for the reader that each clause is making a separate statement.

When the two clauses are closely linked, however, you may want to omit the comma, as in this example from a short story.

> It was very hot and the men had marched a long way. They slumped under the weight of their packs and the curiously black faces were glistening with sweat.

> —George Orwell, "Marrakech"

When you are using a coordinating conjunction to link phrases rather than clauses, you generally do not insert a comma.

> Acupuncture has proved effective for treating chronic pain/ and for blocking acute pain briefly. [The simple parallel phrases need no separation; a revision removes the unnecessary comma.]

However, writers sometimes insert a comma to create more separation between the two parts.

> Acupressure is similar to acupuncture ˄but does not use needles. [The contrastive phrase is separated with a comma.]

Here the writer has put a comma between the two verb phrases in order to emphasize the contrast in meaning between them. (See 24d, 29b, and Chapter 30 for more on using phrases and clauses in sentences.)

46c   Use commas between items in a series

A series of three or more items should have commas—called **serial commas**—after all but the last item.

My super-patriotic neighbor says *red, white, and blue* are his favorite colors.

Each day, cigarettes contribute to over 1,000 deaths from *cancer, heart disease, and respiratory diseases.*

Occasionally in journalistic writing or in company names composed of three or more personal names, the last comma in the series omitted.

My uncle used to work for *Pierce, Fenner and Smith.*

Usually lists are easier to read when all the serial commas are included. Note that a comma should never be used to lead off a list (see 46j, 48a).

46d   Use commas to separate coordinate adjectives

When the adjectives in a series could be arranged in any order or could be (but are not) strung together with the use of *and*, they are termed **coordinate adjectives.** To show their loose relationship and also to avoid confusion with adjectives that cumulate in a particular order to modify each other, separate coordinate adjectives with commas (see 46j).

A *rusty, dented, broken-down* car was left behind.

In this example, each adjective modifies the word *car*, and the string of adjectives could be rearranged:

A *broken-down, dented, rusty* car . . .

(See Chapter 57 for more on word order.)

46e   Use commas to set off nonessential phrases or clauses

A **nonessential element**, or **nonrestrictive element**, provides an extra piece of information that can be left out without changing the basic meaning of the sentence. Always use punctuation to set off nonessential or nonrestrictive elements from the rest of the sentence. (By contrast, elements that are essential or restrictive are always integrated into the sentence without separating punctuation; see 46j.) Nonessential elements are most commonly set off with commas; however, dashes (51d) or parentheses (51a) may also be used.

> Lung cancer, *the leading cause of cancer deaths in the United States,* kills more than 153,000 Americans each year. [A nonessential appositive is set off with commas.]

> Many other illnesses, *like the common cold and even back strain,* are self-limiting and will improve in time. [A nonessential phrase is set off with commas.]

> Universal health care, *which guarantees every citizen at least basic medical benefits,* is found in every industrialized country in the world except the United States and South Africa. [A nonessential clause is set off with commas.]

In each of these sentences, the writer could have omitted the italicized elements without affecting the basic meaning of the sentence. She could have said,

> Lung cancer . . . kills more than 153,000 Americans each year.

> Many other illnesses . . . are self-limiting and will improve in time.

> Universal healthcare . . . is found in every industrialized country in the world except the United States and South Africa.

Instead, she chose to insert extra information to help the reader.

Unless the nonessential element ends the sentence, be sure to use *two* commas to set if off, not just one.

FAULTY SINGLE COMMA REVISED

> Alzheimer's disease, *a progressive impairment of the brain,*strikes
>
> over 4 million older Americans every year.

When should you use commas instead of dashes or parentheses to set off nonrestrictive elements? Commas represent less of a break in the flow of thought, so the elements they enclose are a bit more closely attached to the main part of the sentence. Dashes (see 51d) give more emphasis to the nonrestrictive element, while parentheses (see 51a) can make the nonrestrictive element seem almost like an afterthought.

How do I identify punctuation errors in my writing?

1. Open the style/grammar checker.
2. Click on the OPTIONS feature.
3. Select the CUSTOM setting.
4. Open the customization feature.
5. Deselect all grammar and style features except the one called something like PUNCTUATION ERRORS.
6. Run the program on your document. For extra speed, turn off the spell checker.

EXERCISE 46.1

Correct the comma errors in the following sentences.

1. The anti-tax group collected 65,202 signatures, on a petition, in support of an immediate tax cut.
2. Although this is more than the required 64,928 signatures it still may not be enough.
3. Because of duplications, illegible signatures and people improperly signing for other family members a minimum margin of at least 2,000 is usually needed, to withstand challenges experts say.
4. At one time many states often barred the sale of contraceptives to minors prohibited the display of contraceptives or, even, banned their sale altogether.
5. Today condoms are sold in the grocery store and some television stations, even air ads for them.
6. The capital campaign which was off to a great start, hoped to net $1.2 million.
7. When we shop we want to get the most for our money.
8. Herbalists practice herbal medicine which is based on the medicinal qualities of plants or herbs.

9. Economically and culturally overshadowed by the United States Canada has nonetheless managed to carve out a feisty independent identity since World War II.
10. The participants who had been carefully chosen by Akron's political and community establishment expressed a range of views.

46f Use commas to set off conjunctive adverbs

Conjunctive adverbs include the words and phrases *however, therefore, consequently, thus, furthermore, on the other hand, in general,* and *in other words* (see 35b). They serve as useful transitional devices, helping the reader to follow the flow of the writer's thinking. By enclosing conjunctive adverbs in commas, you give them more prominence, clearly marking a shift in thinking.

Over eighty million people in the United States suffer from chronic health conditions. Their access to health care, *however,* is largely determined by whether or not they have health insurance.

Resistance training exercises cause microscopic damage to muscle fibers, which take twenty-four to forty-eight hours to heal; *therefore,* resistance training programs require at least one day of rest between workouts.

46g Use commas with dates, place names and addresses, titles and degrees, and numbers

1 Using commas with dates

When writing a date in the traditional American format of month, day, and year, set off the year by placing a comma after the day.

John F. Kennedy died on November 22, 1963.

Do not use a comma if only the month and year are given.

John F. Kennedy died in November 1963.

Do not use a comma when writing the date in inverse order (day, month, year).

John F. Kennedy died on 22 November 1963.

2   Using commas in place names and addresses

Use commas after all major elements in a place name or address. However, do not put a comma before a zip code.

Aretha Franklin was born in Memphis, Tennessee, on March 25, 1942.

Alfredo's new address is 112 Ivy Lane, Englewood, NJ 07631.

3   Using commas with titles and degrees

Use commas to set off a title or degree following a person's name (see 53a).

Stella Martinez, MD, was the attending physician.

Ken Griffey, Jr., may someday break the major league home run record set by Mark McGwire.

4   Using commas in numbers

Use a comma in numbers of five digits or more, to form three-digit groups. In a number of four digits, the comma is optional.

     2,400 OR 2400

    56,397

1,000,000

Exceptions: Do not use commas in street numbers, zip codes, telephone numbers, account numbers, model numbers, or years.

46h   Use commas with speaker tags

If you are quoting someone and using a speaker tag (such as *he said, according to Freud,* or *notes Laurel Stuart*), put a comma between the tag and the quotation.

Thomas Edison said, "Genius is 1 percent inspiration and 99 percent perspiration."

"The only thing about the fishing industry that has not changed much," *she writes,* "is the fishermen themselves."

Note that if a quote ends in a comma, the comma goes *inside* the quotation mark (see 50e).

A comma is not used if the quote ends in another punctuation mark.

> "What a marvelous performance!" exclaimed the Queen.

A comma is not used if the quotation is introduced with *that*.

> Rush Limbaugh claims that "the poorest people in America are better off than the mainstream families in Europe."

46i   Use commas with markers of direct address

Put commas around words that indicate that you are talking directly to the reader: words such as *yes* or *no*, the reader's name (*Bob*), question tags (*don't you agree?*), or mild initiators (*Well, Oh*).

> *Yes*, the stock market is likely to turn around.

> Do you really think, *Grace*, that Professor Wilson will postpone the test?

> Intelligence is impossible to measure with just one type of test, *don't you think?*

> Some people say we should all have guns to protect ourselves. *Well*, I do not agree.

EXERCISE 46.2

Correct the comma errors in the following sentences.

1. One fictitious address used by advertisers is John and Mary Jones 100 Main Street Anytown USA 12345
2. We are a nation of shoppers aren't we?
3. Easy access to birth control however, was not always the case.
4. "It would be good to have this question on the ballot" the governor said.
5. Dr. Martin Luther King Jr. often quoted lines from the Bible.
6. For example, he would sometimes say "Let justice roll down like the waters."
7. A Renoir exhibition organized and first shown by the National Gallery of Canada in Ottawa Ontario opened at the Art Institute of Chicago, on October 21 1997 and ran through January 4th, of the next year.

8. Much to the irritation of its neighbor, for instance Canada keeps friendly ties with Fidel Castro's Cuba.

9. Lee surrendered to Grant at Appomattox Court House Virginia on April 9 1865.

10. On December 4, 1997 President Clinton hosted his first town meeting on race relations at the University of Akron.

46j   Avoid misuse of commas

1. *Never use a single comma between the subject and predicate.* When a complex subject begins a sentence, writers sometimes feel inclined to add an inappropriate comma that splits the subject and predicate.

FAULTY COMMA REVISED

Numerous psychological and social factors/have a strong influence on how people age.

This mistake arises only if you insert a *single* comma between subject and predicate. A nonrestrictive element between the subject and the predicate may be set off by two commas.

http://webster. commnet.edu/ hp/pages/ darling/grammar/ commas.htm
An excellent illustrated guide to commas, with quizzes

Police discretion, the decision as to whether to arrest someone or even to ignore a matter, is a routine part of police work.

2. *Never use commas with restrictive elements.* **Restrictive elements** are phrases or clauses that are essential to defining the meaning of the sentence. They should not be set off with commas.

Consumers/who are considering using a hospital or clinic/should scrutinize the facility's accreditation. [In this sentence, the writer is referring not to all consumers but only to those who are considering using a hospital or clinic.]

3. *Avoid using commas with cumulative adjectives.* Adjectives that accumulate before a noun, each one modifying those that follow, are called **cumulative adjectives.** Their modifying relationships, which depend on their order, are likely to be confused by the separating commas that are common with adjectives in a coordinate series (see 46d).

Guidelines for Comma Use

Use commas to separate	*Do not use commas to separate*
Introductory phrases or clauses, especially if they tend to obscure the subject (46a)	Subjects and predicates that would be split with a single comma
Independent clauses connected with a coordinating conjunction (46b)	Restrictive phrases or clauses that are essential to a sentence's basic meaning
Three or more items in a series (46c)	Adjectives that depend on their order to show modification in meaning
A string of adjectives that could be rearranged or linked by *and* (46d)	Items in a series of only two items
Nonessential phrases or clauses that add to but do not restrict the sentence's basic meaning (46e)	Phrases beginning with *than*
	Subordinating conjunctions
Conjunctive adverbs used as transitional devices (46f)	Items in a series of only two items
Speaker tags (46h)	Independent clauses that are not connected with a coordinating conjunction (30b, 46b)
Markers of direct address (46i)	

CONFUSING COMMAS REVISED

The suspect was seen driving a *small/ new/ Italian/ luxury/* car.

Cumulative adjectives follow a certain order (see 57a). Therefore, one way of identifying cumulative adjectives is to see if they can be re-ordered. If the result sounds awkward (*a luxury Italian new small car*), the original ordering is cumulative.

Coordinate adjectives are different. Instead of modifying the following adjectives, they each modify the head noun directly. Therefore, it is appropriate to separate them with commas (see 46d).

4. *Avoid putting a comma before* than. Resist the urge to heighten a comparison or contrast by using commas to separate the *than* clause from the rest of the sentence.

FAULTY COMMA REVISED

Beating our arch-rival was more important/than getting to the state playoffs.

5. *Avoid using a comma after a subordinating conjunction.* A comma should not be used to separate a subordinating conjunction from its own clause; it should be used before the conjunction to separate the entire clause from the rest of the sentence.

FAULTY COMMA REVISED

Although/the car is fifteen years old, it seems to be in good shape.

ALTERNATIVE REVISED SENTENCE

The car seems to be in good shape, although it is fifteen years old.

6. *Never use a comma before parentheses or after a question mark or exclamation point.* A comma is superfluous with an opening parenthesis, question mark, or exclamation point.

UNNECESSARY COMMAS REVISED

Muhammad was born in Mecca/(now in Saudi Arabia) and founded the religion of Islam around AD 610.

"Where are you going?," he asked.

7. *Do not insert a comma before a list.* Resist the urge to punctuate before a listed series. (For suggestions on rewriting sentences to handle a list, see 48a.)

UNNECESSARY COMMAS REVISED

Some countries, such as/Holland, Sweden, and Denmark, have very compassionate welfare systems.

My toughest subjects are/math, biology, and physics.

8. *Do not use a comma in a two-item series.* While commas are needed to separate three or more items in series, separating two items with a comma is unnecessary and distracting.

UNNECESSARY COMMA REVISED

Her outfit used strong contrasts between red/and blue.

EXERCISE 46.3

Insert or remove commas where appropriate in the following sentences.

1. Length area and volume, are properties that can be measured.
2. Many plants are poisonous and others can be toxic if used in high doses.
3. We spend more on health care than does any other nation yet, unlike the rest of the industrialized world we do not provide access to health care for our entire population.
4. Stereotypes concerning inevitable intellectual decline among the elderly, have largely been refuted.
5. Classified advertisements are lists of ads set in small, type sizes, that advertise jobs items for sale and garage sales.
6. Long detailed explanations, can put a listener to sleep.
7. People, who are good shoppers, spend many hours planning their purchases.
8. They check sale circulars, from the newspaper and use the telephone to compare prices.
9. When they, finally, find an item at the best possible price they make their purchase.
10. Celebrations, marking the year 2000, will be held in cities and towns across the continent.

CHAPTER

47

The Semicolon

FAQs

When should I use a semicolon? (47a, 47b, 47c)

Do semicolons go inside or outside quotation
marks? (47d)

?

There are three ways to show a close relationship between independent clauses: with a *comma* and coordinating conjunction (see
46b), a *colon* (see 48b), or a *semicolon.*
A semicolon is used when the two
clauses have a coordinate relationship
—that is, when they convey equally
important ideas (see 35b)—but do
not have a coordinating conjunction
(*and, but, or, nor, for, so, yet*) between
them.

http://sti.larc.nasa.gov/
html/Chapt3/Semicolon.
html#Semicolon
A thorough descrip-
tion of all uses of
the semicolon

47a Use a semicolon to separate independent clauses
not linked by a coordinating conjunction

When there is no coordinating conjunction, related independent
clauses should be connected with a semicolon rather than a comma.

http://www.wisc.edu/ writetest/Handbook/ Semicolons.html A complete guide to semicolons

The first panacea for a misman- aged nation is inflation of the currency; the second is war. Both bring a temporary prosper- ity; both bring a permanent ruin.

—Ernest Hemingway, *Notes on the Next War*

47b   Use a semicolon to separate independent clauses linked by a conjunctive adverb

If you separate two independent clauses with a conjunctive adverb like *however, therefore,* or *nevertheless,* you must use a semi- colon (see 30c):

More than 185 countries belong to the United Nations; *however,* only five of them have veto power.

Japan and Germany are now among the five most powerful nations in the world; *therefore,* they would like to have veto power, too.

47c   Use semicolons in a series with internal punctuation

A **complex series** is one that has internal punctuation. Normally, commas are used to separate items in a series (see 46c); however, if the individual items contain commas, it can be difficult for readers to determine which commas are internal to the items and which commas separate the items. In these cases, semicolons are used to separate the items.

I have lived in Boulder, Colorado; Corpus Christi, Texas; and Vero Beach, Florida.

47d   Place semicolons outside quotation marks

Semicolons are always positioned outside quotation marks.

Those who feel abortion is not a woman's prerogative say they are "pro-life"; those who feel it is say they are "pro-choice."

How can I spot places where I need a semicolon with a conjunctive adverb?

1. Open the SEARCH (or FIND) program in your computer.
2. Enter *however* in the SEARCH field, and run the search.
3. Wherever your computer flags the word *however*, see whether there are independent clauses on both sides of the word.
4. If there are, insert a semicolon before *however* and a comma after it (see 30c).
5. Do the same with *therefore, for example, nevertheless,* and other conjunctive adverbs.

47e   Avoid common semicolon errors

Most errors with semicolons occur as a result of confusing semicolons with commas (see Chapter 46) or with colons (see Chapter 48).

1. *Do not use a semicolon between an independent clause and a dependent clause or phrase.* Dependent clauses or phrases are linked to independent clauses most often by commas, not semicolons (see Chapter 46).

> http://www.uottawa.
> ca/academic/
> arts/writcent/
> hypergrammar/
> semicoln.html
> **Abbreviated help with use of semicolons**

When we say that a country is "underdeveloped", we imply that it is backward in some way. [The introductory clause should be linked by a comma, not a semicolon (see 46a).]

In MS Word, you can remove several items from a document and then insert them as a group into another document by using the Spike, a scrapbook-like feature.

2. *Do not use a semicolon to introduce a list.* Use a colon instead of a semicolon to introduce a list (see 48a).

Utah has five national parks⌃Arches, Bryce, Canyonlands, Capitol Reef, and Zion.

EXERCISE 47.1

Correct the punctuation errors in the following sentences.

1. Socrates disliked being called a "teacher," he preferred to think of himself as an intellectual midwife.
2. Tests will be given on the following dates; Monday, November 2, Friday, November 20, and Monday, December 7.
3. The scientific naming and classification of all organisms is known as *taxonomy*, both living and extinct organisms are taxonomically classified.
4. A single category of a species is called a *taxon*, multiple categories are *taxa*.
5. Since laughter seems to help the body heal; many doctors and hospitals are prescribing humor for their patients.
6. Beethoven was deaf when he wrote his final symphonies, nevertheless, they are considered musical masterpieces.
7. Some people think that watching a video at home is more fun than going to a movie, movie theaters are often crowded and noisy.
8. The lifeguards closed the beach when a shark was spotted, a few hours later some fishermen reported seeing the shark leave; so the beach was reopened.
9. The feeling of balance is controlled by the ears, inside each ear are three small tubes filled with fluid.
10. Since its opening in 1955; Disneyland has been an important part of American culture, it has the ability to reflect and reinforce American beliefs, values, and ideals.

The Colon

FAQs

How does the colon differ from the semicolon? (48b)

What punctuation mark should I use to introduce a quotation? (48c)

?

In formal writing, the colon is used mainly after a general statement to announce details related in some way to the statement. These details may be a list of items, a quotation, an appositive, or an explanatory statement.

48a   Use a colon to introduce a list or appositive

In creating a macro, you can assign it to any one of three places: the toolbar, the keyboard, or a menu.

One principle should govern your choice: which one is most convenient?

In using a colon to introduce a list or appositive, be sure that the introductory part of the sentence is a grammatically complete clause.

> **WEB**
>
> http://www.uottawa.
> ca/academic/arts/
> writcent/hypergrammar/
> colon.html
> An introduction to
> using the colon

FAULTY COLON USE

The four main parts of a memo are: header, introduction, summary, and details.

FAULTY COLON USE REVISED

A memo has four main parts: header, introduction, summary, and details.

OR

There are four main parts to a memo: header, introduction, summary, and details.

In academic writing, the phrase *as follows* is often used. It directly precedes the colon.

There are four main parts to a memo, as follows: header, introduction, summary, and details.

48b Use a colon to set off a second independent clause that explains the first

Rock climbing is like vertical chess: in making each move up the wall, you should have a broad strategy in mind.

Note: You may begin the clause after the colon with either an uppercase letter or a lowercase letter.

Although both the colon and the semicolon can be used to searate independent clauses, they cannot be used interchangeably. A semicolon is used when the two clauses are balanced (see 47a); a colon is used when the second clause is a specification of the first.

COLON   Blessed are the pure in heart: for they shall see God.

SEMICOLON   And the earth was without form and void; and darkness was upon the face of the deep.

48c Use a colon to introduce a quotation

When a colon is used to introduce a quotation, the part of the sentence that precedes the colon should be grammatically independent (see 48a).

In *Against Empire*, Michael Parenti states his concern about American foreign policy: "We should pay less attention to what US policymakers profess as their motives—for anyone can avouch dedication to noble causes—and give more attention to what they actually do."

If the part introducing the quotation is not an independent clause, use a comma instead of a colon.

In *Against Empire*, Michael Parenti states, "We should pay less attention . . . ."

48d   Use colons in titles

Colons are often used in the titles of academic papers and reports. The part of the title that follows the colon is called the subtitle. It usually provides a more explicit description of the topic than does the title.

Nature and the Poetic Imagination: Death and Rebirth in "Ode to the West Wind"

48e   Use colons in business letters and memos

In business letters and memos, colons are used in salutations (*Dear Ms. Townsend:*), to separate the writer's initials from the typist's initials (*TH:ab*), and in memo headings (*To:, From:, Date:, Subject:, Dist:*). (See Chapter 22 for more on business writing.)

48f   Use colons in numbers and addresses

Colons are used in Biblical citations to distinguish chapter from verse (*Matthew 4:11, Genesis 3:9*), in clock times to separate hours from minutes and minutes from seconds (*5:44 p.m.*), in ratios (*3:1*), and in Web site addresses (*http://www.fray.com*).

http://leo.stcloud.msus.edu/punct/colon.html
A comprehensive discussion of all uses of the colon

EXERCISE 48.1

Correct the punctuation errors in the following sentences.

1. There are several steps involved in writing an effective summary; read the original carefully, choose the material for your summary rewrite the material in a concise matter, identify the source of the original text.

2. We need to buy several ingredients in order to bake the cookies, brown sugar, chocolate chips eggs, and milk.

3. In *Becoming a Critical Thinker,* Ruggiero states, "Truth is not something we create to fit our desires. Rather, it is a reality to be discovered."

4. There are three important characteristics that all critical thinkers possess; the ability to be honest with themselves, the ability to resist manipulation, and the ability to ask questions.

5. Experts say swimming is one of the best forms of exercise, it burns as many calories as running but is low-impact.

6. The hacker apparently logged on to *http//www.au.org* at 9.03 a.m.

7. There are four qualities of a diamond that a prospective buyer should be aware of, color, clarity, cut, and carat weight.

8. In *The Language Instinct,* Steven Pinker discusses the inherent nature of language, "We are all born with the instinct to learn, speak, and understand language."

9. There are six major speech organs which are used to articulate sounds; the larynx, soft palate, tongue body, tongue tip, tongue root, and lips.

10. Denise titled her paper "Howls of Delight; Reintroduction of the Wolf into Yellowstone National Park."

The Apostrophe

FAQs

What is the difference between *it's* and *its*? (49a-1)
How do I show possession with two names, like *Maria and Roberto*? (49a-2)
Should I write *1990's* or *1990s*? (49c-2)

?

The apostrophe is used to indicate possession, to alert the reader to contractions and omitted letters, and to form certain plurals.

49a Use apostrophes with nouns to indicate possession

In its grammatical sense, *possession* refers to ownership, amounts, or some other special relationship between two nouns. With singular nouns, possession is usually indicated by attaching *'s* to the end of the noun.

Sue Ellen's jacket   everyone's dream
my mother's photo   yesterday's bad weather
the club's treasurer   Gandhi's place in history
Ahmad's smile   a week's worth of work
Mr. Linder's class

There are two exceptions to this rule:

http://www.
researchpaper.com/
writing_center/13.html
An excellent guide
to apostrophes, includ-
ing exercises

1. If the rule would lead to awkward pronunciation, the extra *s* may be omitted: *Euripides' plays, Moses' laws, Mister Rogers' Neighborhood.*

2. In names of places, companies, and institutions, the apostrophe is often omitted: *Robbers Roost, Kings County, Starbucks, Peoples Republic.*

For plural nouns ending in *s*, form the possessive by just adding an apostrophe at the end:

the Browns' car   the Yankees' star pitcher   my parents' friends

For plural nouns not ending in *s*, form the possessive by adding *'s:*

women's rights   children's section   sheep's wool

1 Avoiding apostrophes with possessive pronouns

Pronouns never take apostrophes to indicate possession. They have their own possessive forms: *its, his, her/hers, your/yours, their/theirs, our/ours, my/mine* (see 25e).

Be careful not to confuse *its* and *it's*. The former is possessive; the latter is a contraction for *it is.*

FAULTY CONTRACTED POSSESSIVE REVISED

The university has revised i̶t̶'s̶ policy on hate speech.
(its)

FAULTY CONTRACTION REVISED

If you fall way behind in your studies, i̶t̶s̶ hard to catch up.
(it's)

2 Showing possession with multiple nouns

With multiple nouns, use apostrophes according to your intended meaning. If you want to indicate joint possession, add an apostrophe only to the last of the nouns:

Bill and Hillary's wedding

Siskel and Ebert's recommendations

How do I identify possible apostrophe problems?

1. Open the SEARCH (or FIND) feature of your word-processing program.
2. Enter an apostrophe (') in the SEARCH field.
3. Run the search.
4. Whenever the program flags an apostrophe, use the guidelines discussed in this chapter to determine whether you have used it correctly.

If you want to show *separate* possession, put an apostrophe after each of the nouns:

Julie's and Kathy's weddings

Omar's, Gretchen's, and Mike's birthdays

49b Use apostrophes to indicate contractions and omitted letters

In casual speech, syllables are sometimes omitted from common word combinations. For example, *cannot* becomes *can't*. In formal writing, such contractions are generally inappropriate. In much informal writing, however, such as email messages and personal letters, contractions are quite common. Just be sure to punctuate them correctly with an apostrophe.

will not → won't	should not → shouldn't	it is → it's
I am → I'm	you have → you've	they are → they're

The apostrophe also can be used for less common contractions, especially if you are trying to create a colloquial, slangy tone.

the 1990s → the '90s	magazine → 'zine
underneath → 'neath	neighborhood → 'hood

49c   Use apostrophes to mark certain plural forms

When a letter or symbol is used as a noun, the usual way of pluralizing nouns (adding an *s* or *es*) does not work well: "There are three *ss* in *sassafras.*" In such cases, an apostrophe can help out.

1   Forming the plurals of letters, symbols, and words referred to as words

http://owl.english.
purdue.edu/Files/
13.html
A discussion of all uses of
the apostrophe, accompa-
nied by proofreading
strategies and exercises

Adding *'s* instead of *s* clarifies the plural forms of unusual nouns.

There are three *s's* in *sassafras.*

How can she have two *@'s* in her email address?

My instructor said I have too many *there's* in my paper.

2   Forming the plurals of numbers and abbreviations

Both the Modern Language Association and the American Psychological Association recommend omitting the apostrophe in forming plurals like the following:

the 1990s   several IOUs
a pair of 6s   a shipment of PCs

49d   Avoid misusing the apostrophe

Be careful not to use apostrophes where they do not belong. The following box lists some of the most common apostrophe errors.

Common Apostrophe Errors

1. Do not use an apostrophe for the possessive form of *it*.

   NO   Her dog lost *it's* collar.

   YES   Her dog lost *its* collar.

2. Do not use an apostrophe with nonpossessive nouns.

   NO   This report discusses four major *features'* of modern mass media.

   NO   This report discusses four major *feature's* of modern mass media.

   YES   This report discusses four major *features* of modern mass media.

3. Do not use an apostrophe with present-tense verbs.

   NO   TV news reporting *seem's* like yet another form of entertainment.

   YES   TV news reporting *seems* like yet another form of entertainment.

EXERCISE 49.1

Each of the following sentences contains at least one error involving apostrophes. Make the appropriate correction(s).

1. Its unfortunate that Bobs' birthday falls on February 29.
2. I wanted to go to Maria's and Roberto's party, but I wasnt able to.
3. The snake sheds it's skin many times during its life.
4. Does the mens' group meet here?
5. No, its a womens' group that meets in this room on Thursdays.
6. I can't wait til my vacation comes!
7. Im taking my lawyers advice on such matter's.
8. All of the orchestra member's instruments seemed to be out of tune.
9. The driver and passenger's airbags both deployed after the accident.
10. Kevin's and Lauren's older sister is in high school now.

Quotation Marks

FAQs

Should I use quotation marks if I am only paraphrasing someone's words? (50a-1)

Should a comma go inside or outside the quotation mark? (50e)

How do I introduce a quotation? (50e)

The primary use of quotation marks is to acknowledge other people's words and statements. Using quotation marks is especially important in academic writing, which puts a premium on the ownership of ideas.

50a Use quotation marks for exact direct quotations

Quotation marks should be placed around any words, phrases, or sentences that you have borrowed from someone else (unless the quotations are so lengthy that you prefer to set them off as an indented block).

In *The End of Work,* Jeremy Rifkin said, "In the years ahead, more than 90 million jobs in a labor force of 124 million are potentially vulnerable to replacement by machines."

One reviewer called it "a very readable and timely book."

A few years ago, a group of artists designed a "space bridge" between Los Angeles and New York. Two windows in major department stores, one in New York and one in Los Angeles, were converted into giant TV screens. Each TV screen projected images from the opposite city. The effect was as if one were looking through a window a continent away.

1 Paraphrasing or quoting indirectly

A summarization, restatement, or paraphrase of a statement made by someone else is a form of **indirect discourse,** and quotation marks are not used. Putting quotation marks around words that were not those of the speaker or writer would be extremely misleading.

MISLEADING QUOTATION MARKS REVISED

Rifkin argues that /in the future more than two-thirds of the American workforce could be displaced by automation./

2 Setting off long quotations in block form

A long quotation (more than about four lines) should be set off as an indented block without quotation marks.

Rifkin sees this reduction of the workforce as having profound social effects:

> The wholesale substitution of machines for workers is going to force every nation to rethink the role of human beings in the social process. Redefining opportunities and responsibilities for millions of people in a society absent of mass formal employment is likely to be the single most pressing social issue of the coming century.

(For an example of such indentation in a student paper, see 14c.)

50b Use quotation marks to suggest skepticism about a term

Sometimes you may find yourself writing about a concept that you think does not deserve the respect other people are giving it. In such cases, you can convey your skepticism by putting the concept name in quotation marks.

> Although many people consider the family the foundation of American society and talk about a return to "family values" as a desirable objective, it is clear that the modern American family looks quite different from families of previous generations.

In this example, the quotation marks around *family values* suggest that the writer has a skeptical view of the term.

This application of quotation marks should be reserved for cases where you believe that a term is being misused by others. In a sense, you are quoting others (see 50a), though not directly. Only on rare occasions should you use quotation marks simply to make ironic or sarcastic comments.

MISUSED QUOTATION MARKS

> Action films are very "intellectual," aren't they?

MISUSED QUOTATION MARKS REVISED

> Action films are not very intellectual, are they?

50c   Use quotation marks to indicate shifts of register

Quotation marks can be used occasionally to set off a colloquial term from the more formal discourse surrounding it.

> One should always try to avoid an inflexible, "cookie-cutter" approach to rhetorical criticism.

Note: Colloquialisms should be used sparingly in formal writing, even when punctuated with quotation marks.

50d   Use quotation marks when citing titles of short works

When referring by title to short stories, book chapters, poems, essays, songs, and other brief works, enclose the titles in quotation marks.

> I will never forget the first time I read Shirley Jackson's short story "The Lottery."

"Smells Like Teen Spirit" has become a '90s classic.

Chapter 17, "Design Principles and Graphics," talks about the functionality and aesthetics of formatting.

Titles of longer or more encompassing works are italicized or underlined (see 52e).

50e   Follow standard practice in using other punctuation with quotations

Quoted material is commonly combined and mixed with a writer's original material. Here are common guidelines for using other punctuation with quotations.

1. *Put commas and periods inside the end quotation mark.* Standard American editorial practice calls for commas and periods to be placed as shown in the following passage:

> "The definition of community implicit in the market model," argues Patricia Hill Collins, "sees community as arbitrary and fragile, structured fundamentally by competition and domination. In contrast, Afrocentric models of community stress connections, caring, and personal accountability."

> http://owl.english.purdue.edu/Files/14.html
> A description of all uses of quotation marks, with links to exercises and related topics

Note: Readers of British publications may see exceptions to this rule, as the British style is to place commas and periods outside quotation marks. When quoting from British sources, you should standardize punctuation for consistency with modern American usage, placing periods and commas inside quotation marks.

2. *Put colons and semicolons outside the end quotation mark.*

One critic called 1990 "the year in which rock & roll was reborn": the fusing of metal and rap by groups like Living Colour and Faith No More broke down racial barriers in a way reminiscent of early rock & roll.

One of the things that distinguished Snoop Doggy Dogg from other rappers was his style, which was described in the *New York Times* as "gentle"; "where many rappers scream," said *Times* reporter Touré, "he speaks softly."

3. *Put other punctuation marks inside the end quotation mark if they are part of the quotation; otherwise, put them outside the end quotation mark.* Question marks, exclamation points, dashes, parentheses, and other punctuation marks should be positioned according to meaning.

PART OF QUOTED TITLE

Whitney Houston's "How Will I Know?" entered the pop charts at number one.

PART OF SENTENCE

What do you think of controversial songs like "Deep Cover" and "Cop Killer"?

4. *Use single quotation marks (' ') for quotation marks within quotation marks.*

Garofalo notes that "on cuts like 'JC' and 'Swimsuit Issue,' Sonic Youth combined an overt sexuality with uncompromisingly feminist lyrics about women's issues."

5. *Introduce quotations with the punctuation standard grammar calls for.* The sentence or phrase you use to introduce a quotation should be punctuated according to the grammatical relationship between the introduction and the quotation. If the introduction is not a grammatically complete sentence, do not use any punctuation.

The conservative Parents Music Resource Center maintained that heavy metal was "the most disturbing element in contemporary music."

If the introduction is a quotation tag like *she said* or *he notes,* use a comma.

As *Rolling Stone* noted, "Beneath the 'save the children' rhetoric is an attempt by a politically powerful minority to impose its morality on the rest of us."

If the introduction is a grammatically independent clause, use a colon.

Nelson Mandela indicated his understanding of the power of mega-concerts when he thanked the performing artists backstage for their efforts: "Over the years in prison I have tried to follow the developments in progressive music. . . . Your contribution has given us tremendous inspiration. . . . Your message can reach quarters not necessarily interested in politics, so that the message can go further than we politicians can push it."

Common Quotation Mark Errors

1. Do not use quotation marks just to call attention to something.

   NO   Pete Sampras has won the Wimbledon championship "five" times.

   YES   Pete Sampras has won the Wimbledon championship five times.

2. Do not use quotation marks for indirect discourse (see 33f).

   NO   President Clinton said "he was sorry about the Monica Lewinsky affair."

   YES   President Clinton said he was sorry about the Monica Lewinsky affair.

3. When presenting the title of your paper on a title page or at the head of the paper, do not put quotation marks around it. If your title contains within it the title of *another* short work, that work's title should be enclosed in quotation marks. (See 17a for an example.)

50f   Avoid misusing quotation marks

Be careful not to use quotation marks where they do not belong. The box above lists some common errors to avoid.

EXERCISE 50.1

Correct the punctuation errors in the following sentences.

1. The question is not "why some rappers are so offensive, but rather, why do so many fans find offensive rappers appealing"?

2. "When you hear your record company has been sold for 20 or 30 times its earnings", said Tim Collins, Aerosmith's manager, "you think, "I want a piece of that"."

3. According to critic Anthony Kiedis, the 1992 Lollapalooza summer tour was, "way too male and way too guitar-oriented."

"

4. Garth Brooks's songs challenged some of country music's most "sacred cows." In 1991, TNN refused to air the video of The Thunder Rolls, which ends with a woman shooting her abusive husband. We Shall Be Free was written as a response to the Rodney King beating and includes lines supportive of gay rights.

5. PMRC's Pam Howar expressed the concern that Madonna was teaching young girls: "how to be porn queens in heat".

6. In announcing that US superskier Picabo Street will miss the World Cup races because of a knee injury, her coach told the press", When the mind is ready but the body is not . . . there is danger of another injury".

7. The citation for the 1986 Nobel Peace Prize given to Elie Wiesel reads, in part: From the abyss of the death camps he has come as a messenger to mankind—not with a message of hate and revenge, but with one of brotherhood and atonement.

8. There are people who really enjoy line dances like "YMCA" and "The Electric Slide", although there are others who think those dances are silly.

9. Older people are often labeled "old and sick", "old and helpless", old and useless, or old and dependent:" in fact, the general image of old age is negative.

10. The Celtic tune "Greensleeves" is the melody used for the carol "What Child Is This"?

Other Punctuation Marks

When should I use dashes instead of parentheses? (51d, 51e)

How should I use brackets and ellipses in quotations? (51g, 51h, 51i, 51k)

?

Parentheses, dashes, brackets, ellipses, and slashes can all be used, in moderation and in proper contexts, to clarify meaning and add interest to writing. (See 21b-4 for a discussion of punctuating with email diacritics.)

WEB

http://sti.larc.nasa.gov/html/Chapt3/Chapt3-TOC.html
A full discussion of parentheses, dashes, brackets, ellipses, and slashes

Parentheses

Parentheses are indispensable to formal writing. Be sure, though, not to overuse them.

51a   Use parentheses to insert parenthetical comments

Usually, parenthetical comments—clarifications, asides, examples, or other extra pieces of information—are embedded within sentences. They can be as short as a single word or as long as an entire clause.

> Many components of biological diversity (biodiversity) are dwindling, and attempts to conserve them in the United States through the Endangered Species Act (ESA) and other policies affecting land use and aquatic resources sometimes conflict with the short-term economic goals of individuals, firms, industries, or political entities.

> For most right-handed people, the left hemisphere of the brain controls manual skills and language (and vice versa for most left-handed people). . . . The fact that manual skill (i.e., the skill associated with tool-making and tool-using) is usually localized in the same hemisphere as speech has led some anthropologists to speculate that tool-making either necessarily preceded or developed concurrently with language.

Sometimes parenthetical comments comprise one or more sentences.

> The worst release of radioactive substances in US history was during a deliberate experiment in 1949. . . . The experiment, called "green run," released into the atmosphere some 5,500 curies of iodine 131 and a still-classified inventory of other fission products, secretly measured by the AEC, in a 200-by-40 mile plume. There was no public health warning. (By contrast, when the 1979 Three Mile Island nuclear accident released 15 to 24 curies of radioactive iodine into the countryside, people around Harrisburg were evacuated and milk was impounded.)

Another common use of parentheses is in documentation. The scientific reference style calls for inserting reference citations in parentheses within sentences (see 13a, 13b, 13d). This parenthetical style is the preferred method of the MLA, APA, and CBE.

HELP

How do I find out whether I have a "parenthesis habit"?

1. Select several pages of your writing.
2. Open the SEARCH (or FIND) feature of your word-processing program.
3. Enter a left parenthesis in the SEARCH field, and have the program search your document.
4. Record how many times you have to click FIND NEXT.
5. Using your style/grammar checker, determine how many sentences are in your document.
6. If you have more than one parenthesis for every four or five sentences, you may have a parenthesis habit.

51b Do not overuse parentheses

Parentheses are so handy that you may be tempted to overuse them. Resist the temptation. Too many parentheses can make it difficult for readers to follow the main train of thought. If you find yourself developing a "parenthesis habit" (see the Help box), look for ways to rewrite some of the parenthetical comments as modifiers (see 24c) or as subordinate clauses (see 35c).

51c Use parentheses around letters or numbers to set off embedded lists

Listed phrases or clauses embedded in a longer sentence may be itemized with numbers or letters placed within parentheses.

Socialism has three essential components: (1) the public ownership of the means of production, (2) central planning, and (3) distribution of goods without a profit motive.

EXERCISE 51.1

The following passage has too many parentheses. Rewrite it, using the suggestions given in 24c and 35c.

Abatement of water pollution in the United States (like that of air pollution) has been largely a success story. It also is one of the longest running (its legislative origins go back to the turn of the century). Until the 1970s, most legislation addressed public health issues and included provisions for helping communities build treatment plants (specifically, for water and sewage). With passage of the Water Pollution Control Act in 1972 (later called the Clean Water Act), the federal government turned its attention to cleaning up the nation's waterways (they had become badly polluted from industrial effluents and inadequately treated sewage).

Dashes

Dashes are an informal kind of punctuation, with several uses and some misuses. You can create a dash either by typing two hyphens, which some word processors will then convert into a solid dash, or by opening the special character or symbol feature on your word-processing program and selecting the full-length dash (called the "em dash").

51d Use dashes to highlight extra informational comments

Dashes set off internal, informational comments in a more emphatic way than parentheses do.

Public decision makers have a tendency to focus mostly on the more obvious and immediate environmental problems—usually described as "pollution"—rather than on the deterioration of natural ecosystems upon whose continued functioning global civilization depends.

Dashes are particularly useful for setting off an internal list of items:

As costs have climbed, resistance to increased pollution controls by some business and industry groups has also risen, contributing to the environmental backlash. Particularly hard hit have been small businesses in California—paint dealers, gas stations, and dry-cleaning establishments—which the state began regulating in 1990.

51e Use dashes to set off important or surprising points

If not overused, dashes can be a dramatic way to set off an inserted comment.

While the Marshall Islanders continue to wrestle with the consequences of nuclear testing, a new proposal is on the table that will make the islands a dumping ground for American garbage—literally. An American waste disposal company, Admiralty Pacific, proposes to ship household waste from the west coast of the US to the Pacific islands—an estimated 34 billion pounds of waste in the first five years of the program alone.

51f Confine yourself to one pair of dashes per sentence

Dashes, like parentheses, can be overused. If you need to add more than one informational comment to a sentence, use commas (see 46e) or parentheses around the other comments. Too many dashes in a paragraph are a sign of poorly integrated ideas.

Style/Grammar Checker Alert: If you suspect that you have a "dash habit," check your writing for dashes, using the SEARCH process described for parentheses.

EXERCISE 51.2

Insert appropriate punctuation if needed (parentheses, dashes, or commas) in the places marked in the following sentences.

1. In 1987, officials in the Guatemalan government and the US Drug Enforcement Agency __DEA__ entered into an agreement to defoliate vast areas of Guatemala's north and northwest__a region that contains a wildlife refuge and the largest area of unplundered rainforest remaining in Central America.

2. On the Internet are thousands of Usenet newsgroups, made up of people who communicate about almost any conceivable topic __ from donkey racing and bird watching to sociology and quantum physics__.

3. People look forward to communicating almost daily with others in their newsgroup, with whom they share personal, sometimes intimate, matters about themselves __even though they have "met" only electronically __.

4. There is no theory that would have led anyone to expect that after World War II, Japan __ with a religion that stressed fatalism, with two major cities destroyed by atomic bombs, and stripped of its colonies__ would become an economic powerhouse able to turn the Western world on its head.

5. Although the distinction between race and ethnicity is clear__ one is biological, the other cultural__ people often confuse the two.

6. The United Nations defines seven basic types of families, including single-parent families, communal families __unrelated people living together for ideological, economic, or other reasons__, extended families, and others.

7. By the late 1980s, the proportion of adult Americans who were single by choice or by chance__ often after failed marriages__ had increased to slightly over 25 percent of adult men and over 20 percent of adult women.

8. If you were to go on a survival trip, which would you take with you__ food or water__?

9. The key to a successful exercise program is to begin at a very low intensity, progress slowly__ and stay with it__!

10. The three branches of the US government__the executive, the legislative, and the judicial__ are roughly equal in power and authority.

Brackets

Brackets are an important editorial device for providing proper context for the quoted or cited material used in research writing.

51g

Use brackets to insert editorial comments or clarifications into quotations

Quotations represent someone's exact words. If you choose to alter those words (because of a misspelling in the original quotation or to add explanatory information, for example), you must indicate that you have done so by putting brackets around the alterations.

> "One of the things that will produce a stalemate in Rio [the site of the 1992 UN conference on the environment] is the failure of the chief negotiators, from both the north and the south, to recognize the contradictions between the free market and environmental protection."

The reference to "Rio" in this quotation might not be understood out of context, so the author has inserted a brief clarification between brackets.

Whenever you insert a quotation from your reading into your writing, be aware that you may need to give the reader important information that was located in the sentences immediately preceding or following it in the original. Any necessary clarification may be added either outside the actual quotation or within it, in which case it should be in brackets. Say, for example, that you have come across this passage in your reading and want to quote the final sentence:

http://webster.
commnet.edu/
hp/pages/
darling/grammar/
marks.htm
Excellent coverage
of a range of punctuation marks, from
the common to
the rarely used,
with illustrations
and exercises

> Sea snails are the source of highly refined painkilling chemicals now being tested for human use. One scientist describes these as "little chemical factories" that are in essence doing what drug companies are trying to do. They have created thousands of chemical compounds and refined them to be exquisitely sensitive and potent.

If you just quoted the final sentence word for word, readers would not know what *They* referred to. Therefore, you should write the sentence in one of the following two ways:

> Sea snails "have created thousands of chemical compounds and refined them to be exquisitely sensitive and potent."

OR

> "[Sea snails] have created thousands of chemical compounds and refined them to be exquisitely sensitive and potent."

51h   Use brackets with the word *sic*

The Latin word *sic* (meaning "so" or "thus") indicates a mechanical error—for example, an error of grammar, usage, or spelling—in a quotation. You may want to use it to show both that you recognize an error in a quote and that you did not introduce the error when transposing the quote into your writing. Place it in brackets in the quotation, immediately following the error.

> "Any government that wants to more and more restrict freedoms will do it by financial means, by creating financial vacums [*sic*]."

If you frequently quote Internet messages like this one, you may have many opportunities to use *sic*. Overusing it, though, may make your writing sound snobbish.

51i   Use brackets to acknowledge editorial emphasis within a quotation

When you quote a passage, you may want to emphasize a certain part of it that is not emphasized in the original. You can do so by underlining or italicizing that part and then, at the end of the passage, acknowledging the change by writing *emphasis added* or *italics mine* between brackets.

> Brown states,
> > Whereas in the past the world has relied primarily on fishers and farmers to achieve a balance between food and people, it now depends more on family planners to achieve this goal. *In a world where both the seafood catch and the grain harvest per person are declining, it may be time to reassess population policy.* For

example, in such a world, is there any moral justification for couples having more than two children, the number needed to replace themselves? If not, then political leaders everywhere should be urging couples to limit themselves to two surviving children. [Emphasis added.]

51j Use brackets for parenthetical comments within parentheses

If one parenthetical comment is nested within another, the inner one should be punctuated with brackets to distinguish it from the outer one.

The spectacular palace that King Louis XIV built at Versailles (which is located 19 kilometers [12 miles] west of Paris) required 35,000 workers and 27 years to construct.

Ellipses

An **ellipsis** (plural: **ellipses**) is a series of three periods, used to indicate a deletion from a quotation or a pause in a sentence. An ellipsis consists of three *spaced* periods (. . .), not three bunched ones (...). If you end a quoted sentence with an ellipsis, use a fourth period to indicate the end of the sentence.

"The notion of literature as a secular scripture extends roughly from Matthew Arnold to Northrop Frye . . . ."

51k Use an ellipsis to indicate a deletion from a quotation

The sentence with an ellipsis should not be significantly different in meaning from the original sentence, nor should it be ungrammatical.

"Practically any region on earth will harbor some insect species—native or exotic—that are functioning near the limits of their temperature or moisture tolerance."

An ellipsis can be used to mark a deletion from either the middle or the end of a sentence, but not the beginning of a sentence.

51l　Use an ellipsis to indicate a pause in a sentence

To mark a pause for dramatic emphasis in your own writing, use an ellipsis.

I was ready to trash the whole thing . . . but then I thought better of it.

Beware, however, of overusing ellipses to indicate pauses.

EXERCISE 51.3

Reduce the following passage to a two-sentence quotation, using at least one set of brackets and one ellipsis.

Preserving the planet's remaining natural areas is one of our most urgent responsibilities. Such places are fundamental to every economy in the world, no matter how divorced from "nature" it might appear to be, and no conceivable development will lessen that dependence. There is no substitute for a stable hydrological cycle, healthy pollinator populations, or the general ecological stability that only natural areas can confer. We need these places in ways that are direct enough to satisfy even the most hard-nosed economist, but we also need them for reasons that are harder to quantify.

Slashes

Slashes serve a variety of purposes in both formal and informal writing.

51m　Use slashes to separate lines of poetry quoted within a sentence

If you are quoting lines of poetry without setting them off in separate lines as they appear in the poem, put a slash (surrounded by spaces) between the lines.

Gerard Manley Hopkins's poetry features what he called "sprung rhythms," as can be heard in these lines from "The Windhover": "No wonder of it: sheer plod makes plow down sillion / Shine, and blue-bleak embers, ah my dear, / Fall, gall themselves, and gash gold-vermilion."

51n Use a slash to show alternatives

Slashes are used in expressions like *either/or, pass/fail, on/off, win/ win,* and *writer/editor.* Readers may object, though, if you overuse them. The expressions *he/she, his/her,* and *s/he* are admirable attempts at gender neutrality, but many people dislike their phonetic clumsiness. We suggest you use *he or she* and *his or her* or find other ways of avoiding sexist pronouns (see 41a-2).

51o Use a slash to indicate a fraction

Fractions that would be set in formal mathematics on separate lines also can be shown on one line, with a slash dividing the numerator from the denominator:

1/3   3/8   2-2/5

Your word-processing program may automatically convert fractions into more elegant versions like ½ and ¼, but first you have to type them with slashes. (Check under AUTOFORMAT to see whether your program will format fractions for you.)

51p Use slashes in Internet addresses

Slashes are indispensable components of URLs (Web site addresses) like *http://www.abacon.com/compsite/.* Include the last slash if it brackets a directory, but not if it brackets an actual HTML file. (Tip: If your browser automatically adds a final slash to the address, that tells you the final term names a directory, not a file.)

51q   Use slashes in writing dates informally

Instead of writing out a date like June 16, 1999, you can write the date informally: 6/16/99. (Note: In many other countries, this date would be written 16/06/99.)

MECHANICS

Capital Letters and Italics

Should I capitalize the first word of a sentence in
parentheses? (52a)
Should I capitalize directions like *east* and *northwest?* (52b)
Do I need to capitalize email addresses? (52d)
If I cite a URL, should I put it in italics? (52f)
Should all foreign words be italicized? (52h)

Capital Letters

Capital (uppercase) letters are used to indicate the start of a new sentence. They also are used for proper names, proper adjectives, and some abbreviations.

52a   Capitalize the first word of all free-standing sentences

Sentences like the one you are now reading should always start with a capital letter. Sentences that are embedded in other sentences, however, may or may not start with a capital letter, depending on the situation.

If a sentence follows a colon or dash, capitalization is optional:

http://sti.larc.nasa.
gov/html/Chapt4/
Chapt4-TOC.html
A discussion of almost
all uses of capital letters

Some employees have strong objections to mandatory drug testing in the workplace: They believe that their civil liberties are being violated.

OR

Some employees have strong objections to mandatory drug testing in the workplace: they believe that their civil liberties are being violated.

You should be sure to pick one capitalization style for this situation, however, and use it consistently throughout your writing.

If a sentence occurs in parentheses within another sentence, the first word of the parenthetical sentence should not be capitalized:

Major league baseball no longer seems to enjoy the civic loyalty
                        for
it used to (~~For~~ example, several teams have threatened to leave
their cities if new facilities are not built).

If, however, the parenthesized sentence is set off as a separate sentence, the first word should be capitalized:

Major league baseball no longer seems to enjoy the civic loyalty it used to. (For example, several teams have threatened to leave their cities if new facilities are not built.)

If a sentence occurs as a quotation within another sentence and is set off by a colon, comma, or dash, the first word should be capitalized:

                            Vegetarians
Rush Limbaugh once said, "~~vegetarians~~ are a bunch of weaklings
who wouldn't be able to bench press 50 pounds after one of their
meals."

However, if the quotation is not set off by a colon, comma, or dash, the first word should be lowercase:

                          vegetarians
Rush Limbaugh once said that "~~Vegetarians~~ are a bunch of weaklings who wouldn't be able to bench press 50 pounds after one of
their meals."

Question fragments can also be capitalized.

Will the stock market keep booming? Level off? Take a dive?

If you are quoting a poem, capitalize the first letter of each line (if the original did so).

Long as the heart beats life within her breast
   Thy child will bless thee, guardian mother mild,
And far away thy memory will be blest
   By children of the children of thy child.

—Alfred, Lord Tennyson, 1864

52b   Capitalize all names, associated titles, and proper adjectives

Capitalize the first letter of any name, title, or proper adjective referring to a particular person, place, or thing.

1. *Capitalize names and associated titles of people.*

Ralph Nader	Aunt May
Ruth Bader Ginsburg	Dr. Harris
Professor Mixco	Ken Griffey, Jr.

Note: Professional titles and family relationships are *not* capitalized if they are not used as part of the person's name:

My aunt is a doctor specializing in internal medicine.

2. *Capitalize place names.*

San Diego, California	the Rockies
Lake Michigan	Maple Street
the Great Northwest	Apartment 34
Long Island	Yellowstone National Park
the Mississippi River	Africa

Note: Compass points (*north, southwest*) are capitalized only when they are incorporated into a name (*North Carolina*) or when they function as nouns denoting a particular region (*the Southwest*).

3. *Capitalize the names of historic events.*

World War II	the Boston Tea Party
Reconstruction	the My Lai Massacre
the Middle Ages	the Cold War

4. *Capitalize the names of days, months, holidays, and eras.*

Monday	the Reagan Era
April	Thanksgiving
the Gilded Age	Veteran's Day

Note: Seasons of the year usually are not capitalized:

last fall   winter sports   spring semester

5. *Capitalize the names of organizations, companies, and institutions.*

Common Cause	the Central Intelligence Agency
the National Rifle Association	Digital Equipment Corporation
Time-Warner, Inc.	New York University
the United Nations	Alameda Community College

6. *Capitalize the names of certain objects and products.* In most cases, only the first letter of each word in an object or product name is capitalized:

the Power Mac	the *Titanic*
the Plymouth Voyager	the North Star
the Hope Diamond	the Boeing 767

Some manufacturers, however, especially in the computer industry, use intercaps:

WordPerfect	QuarkXPress
HotJava	GlobalFax

Many objects and products have abbreviated names in all uppercase letters: *MS-DOS, AOL, RISC* (see 53d).

7. *Capitalize religious, national, and ethnic names.*

Catholicism	Passover
the Koran	the Prophet
Buddha	Holy Communion
the Bible	the Ten Commandments
Korean	African American
Chicana	Polynesian

8. *Capitalize adjectives based on proper nouns.*

American football	Jewish literature
French history	Southern hospitality
Newtonian physics	Islamic tradition

52c   Capitalize all significant words in titles

In titles of books, poems, articles, plays, films, and other cultural works, every word except articles (*a, an, the*), conjunctions, and short prepositions should be capitalized. The first word of the title and of the subtitle should be capitalized, even if it is an article, conjunction, or short preposition.

http://webster.
commnet.edu/
hp/pages/
darling/grammar/
capitals.htm
A brief guide to
capitalization

For Whom the Bell Tolls   "Ode to the West Wind"
The Joy Luck Club   "Learning in Context:
Death of a Salesman   A Qualitative Study"
Pulp Fiction

Note: The APA reference style calls for capitalizing only the first word of the title and of the subtitle and any proper nouns (see 13c).

52d   Follow the owner's preferences in capitalizing email addresses and URLs

Although most of the Internet is not case-sensitive, there are two important reasons for writing email and Internet addresses exactly as the owners do. First, some parts of Net addresses, such as the URL pathnames that follow the first single slash, *are* case-sensitive. Second, some Netizens use uppercase and lowercase letters to make important distinctions in their addresses. For example, Joe Opiela at Allyn & Bacon uses uppercase and lowercase letters to help users make sense out of his email name: Instead of *jopielaab*, he writes *JOpielaAB*.

EXERCISE 52.1

Correct the capitalization errors in the following sentences.

1. On july 17, 1996, a Trans World airlines passenger plane crashed into the atlantic ocean, killing all 230 people aboard.
2. Bound for paris, france, the boeing 747 disappeared from Radar screens at 8:48 p.m.

3. The plane was about fifty miles East of the Airport when it plunged into the Ocean about ten miles South of East Moriches, long island.

4. The US coast guard conducted a futile rescue effort, and the national transportation safety board carried out a long investigation.

5. Meanwhile, rumors circulated on the internet and a well-known Politician claimed, "the plane was shot down by a US navy missile."

6. I logged on to *HTTP://WWW.cbpp.org/pa-1.htm* and found a report called "Pulling apart: a State-by-state analysis of income Trends."

7. The report, published by the center on Budget and policy priorities, says that "in 48 States, the gap between the incomes of the richest 20 percent of families with children and the incomes of the poorest 20 percent of families with children is significantly wider than it was two Decades ago." (only Alaska and north Dakota bucked the trend.)

8. Individual states could counteract this National trend (Few, however, have done so).

9. My Nephew, Julius Evans, jr., is a Junior at San Francisco state university.

10. A key section in T. S. Eliot's "the Love song of J. Alfred Prufrock" starts like this:
    No! I am not prince Hamlet, nor was meant to be;
    am an attendant Lord, one that will do
    to swell a progress, start a scene or two . . .

Italics

   In published documents, *italic* typeface is used for a number of purposes, which will be described in the sections that follow. Although most word processors permit the selection of an italic typeface, many instructors prefer that students use <u>underlining</u> instead of italics in their papers, as underlined letters and words stand out more than italicized ones. If you are a student and wish to use italics rather than underlining, we suggest that you check with your instructor first.

52e   Italicize titles of independent creative works

Titles of books, magazines, digital magazines ("e-zines"), newspapers, and other creative products that are independently packaged and distributed to a public audience should be written with italics or underlining (see Chapter 13). Here are some examples:

> http://webster.
> commnet.edu/hp/
> pages/darling/
> grammar/italics.htm
> A brief guide to using
> italics and underlining

BOOKS	*The Scarlet Letter* or <u>The Scarlet Letter</u>
MAGAZINES	*National Geographic* or <u>National Geographic</u>
E-ZINES	*Salon* or <u>Salon</u>
NEWSPAPERS	*Los Angeles Times* or <u>Los Angeles Times</u>
LONG POEMS	*Paradise Lost* or <u>Paradise Lost</u>
MOVIES	*Dead Man Walking* or <u>Dead Man Walking</u>
PLAYS	*The Iceman Cometh* or <u>The Iceman Cometh</u>
TV PROGRAMS	*The X-Files* or <u>The X-Files</u>
PAINTINGS	*Nude Descending a Staircase* or <u>Nude Descending a Staircase</u>
SCULPTURES	Rodin's *The Kiss* or Rodin's <u>The Kiss</u>
CDS	*Cracked Rear View* or <u>Cracked Rear View</u>
MUSIC VIDEOS	*Binge & Purge* or <u>Binge & Purge</u>
COMPUTER GAMES	*Mortal Kombat* or <u>Mortal Kombat</u>
ONLINE WORKS	*Encarta* or <u>Encarta</u>

Note: The names of personal or commercial homepages should not be underlined or italicized.

52f   Italicize URLs and email addresses

When writing an Internet or email address in the body of a text, use underlining or italics.

Helpful information about current Congressional legislation can be found at *http://thomas.loc.gov/*. The email address is *thomas@loc.gov*.

52g   Italicize names of vehicles

Names of particular vehicles, not types of vehicles, should be underlined or italicized. These include the names of spacecraft, airplanes, ships, and trains.

Voyager 2 or <u>Voyager 2</u>

Spirit of St. Louis or <u>Spirit of St. Louis</u>

Titanic or <u>Titanic</u>

Wabash Cannonball or <u>Wabash Cannonball</u>

52h   Italicize foreign words and phrases

In general, it is best to avoid using foreign words and phrases when writing in English. However, if you need to use a foreign expression (for example, because there is no good English equivalent), write it with underlining or italics and, if possible, provide a brief English explanation.

One of the nice things about Brazilian culture is the custom of giving a *jeitinho,* or helping someone work things out.

My Dutch friends say they like being in a *gezellig* environment, one that has a lot of human warmth.

Latin names for plants, animals, and diseases should be underlined or italicized.

The sandwich tern (*Sterna sandvicensis*) is slightly larger than the common tern.

If foreign words and phrases have been so thoroughly assimilated, or Anglicized, that they are commonly recognized, however, they do not need underlining. Here are some examples:

machete (Spanish)	judo (Japanese)
sauerkraut (German)	coffee (Arabic)
pasta (Italian)	data (Latin)
cologne (French)	criteria (Greek)

The richness of the English language comes from borrowings like these, and they can all be found in a standard English dictionary. The best rule of thumb is to underline or italicize only truly foreign expressions. If the expression can be found in a standard English dictionary, do not underline or italicize it.

52i Italicize words, letters, and numbers referred to as such

When you write a word, letter, or number so as to talk about it as a word, letter, or number, use underlining or italics.

Many people misspell the word *misspell;* they write it with only one *s.*

The witness said the license plate had two *5*'s in it.

Underlining or italics is also appropriate for a word you are about to define. (Alternatively, boldface type can be used.)

Before starting up a cliff, rock climbers sometimes like to get *beta*—advice from someone who has already done the climb.

52j Italicize words for emphasis

You can use underlining or italics to emphasize a certain word or phrase (see 37e).

According to a US Senate hearing, $13 billion the Pentagon handed out to weapons contractors between 1985 and 1995 was simply "lost." Another $15 billion remains unaccounted for because of "financial management troubles." That's *$28 billion*—right off the top— that has simply *disappeared.*

—Mark Zepezauer and Arthur Naiman,
Take the Rich off Welfare

http://sti.larc.nasa.
gov/html/Chapt3/
Italics-TOC.
html#italics
A thorough description
of the different uses
of italics

But be sure that you do not overdo it. If you use this kind of underlining too often, you may irritate your readers. It is better to rely on word choice and syntactic structuring to create emphasis (see Chapter 37).

ital

EXERCISE 52.2

In each of the following sentences, add underlining to those words and phrases that need it.

1. My favorite poem in Robert Creeley's book For Love is "A Wicker Basket."
2. Juan says the new drama teacher is very simpático.
3. Of the fifty people interviewed, twenty-two said that 13 is an unlucky number.
4. You can keep track of the spaceship NEAR's progress at http://spacelink.nasa.gov/.
5. Smoking also contributes to platelet adhesiveness, or the sticking together of red blood cells that is associated with blood clots.
6. She's an easy teacher—she gives all A's and B's.
7. For me, the best track on Fleetwood Mac's Greatest Hits is Rhiannon.
8. The flower that does best under these conditions is the prairie zinnia (Zinnia grandiflora).
9. For further information, email us at johnsonco@waterworks.com.
10. The term dementia implies deficits in memory, spatial orientation, language, or personality. This definition sets it apart from delirium, which usually involves changing levels of consciousness, restlessness, confusion, and hallucinations.

Abbreviations and Numbers

FAQs

Is it okay to use acronyms in formal writing? (53d)

When should I spell out numbers? (53f, 53g, 53h, 53i, 53j)

?

Abbreviations

Abbreviations include shortened versions of words (*Mr., Rev., fig.*), initialisms formed from the first letters of a series of words (*FBI, NBC, IBM*), and acronyms, or initialisms that are pronounced as words (*OPEC, NASA, RAM*). In formal writing, abbreviations should be used sparingly. If you are not sure that readers will know what a certain abbreviation stands for, spell out the word the first time it is used and put the abbreviation in parentheses right after it:

The Internet uses a domain name system (DNS) for all its servers worldwide.

53a   Abbreviate titles, ranks, and degrees only before or after full names

Title before full name	*Degree or rank after full name*
Ms. Yuko Shinoda	Jan Stankowski, DDS
Mr. Steven D. Gold	Derek Rudick, CPA
Dr. Teresa Rivera	Teresa Rivera, MD
Prof. Jamie Smith-Weber	Young-Sook Kim, PhD
Rev. Martin Luther King, Jr.	James Norton, PFC
Rep. Richard A. Gephardt	Chris L. Miller, DSW

When titles or ranks are followed by only a surname, they should be spelled out:

General Powell   Senator Wellstone   Professor Davis

53b   Use abbreviations after numerical dates and times

The following abbreviations are commonly used in writing dates and times:

124 BC ("before Christ") OR 124 BCE ("before the common era")

AD 567 (*anno Domini,* or "year of our Lord") OR 567 CE ("common era")

9:40 a.m. (*ante meridiem*) OR 0940 hrs (military or international twenty-four-hour time)

4:23 p.m. (*post meridiem*) OR 1623 hrs

Avoid using *a.m.* or *p.m.* unless it is adjoined to a specific number:

The package arrived late in the ~~a.m.~~ *morning.*

Avoid abbreviating the names of months, days, and holidays in formal writing:

This year ~~Xmas~~ *Christmas* fell on a ~~Thurs.~~ *Thursday.*

53c Use Latin abbreviations sparingly

The following abbreviations, derived from Latin, are appropriate in academic writing. Be careful, however, not to overuse them.

Abbreviation	Latin term	English meaning
cf.	*confer*	compare
e.g.	*exempli gratia*	for example
et al.	*et alii*	and others
etc.	*et cetera*	and so forth
i.e.	*id est*	that is
N.B.	*nota bene*	note well

53d Use acronyms and initialisms only if their meaning is clear

An **initialism** is an abbreviation formed from the first letters of a name—for example, *FBI* (for *Federal Bureau of Investigation*). Usually the letters are all capitalized. An **acronym** is an initialism that is pronounced as a word—for example, *ASCII, PAC, AIDS*. Some abbreviations, such as *JPEG, MS-DOS,* and *DRAM,* are **semi-acronyms:** part of the term is pronounced as one or more letters, the rest as a word (for example, "jay-peg"). Some initialisms and acronyms have "morphed" into verbs, gerunds, and participles. In such cases, use uppercase letters only for the abbreviated part: *ID'd, MUDding, CCing, BBSes, ATMs, AOLer.*

Because they are so convenient and economical to use, initialisms and acronyms tend to be overused. But in many cases, especially in the computer world, they are virtually indispensable. As long as your audience knows what they mean and as long as you do not overdo it, there is nothing wrong with using such abbreviations where appropriate.

> WEB
> http://webster.
> commnet.edu/hp/
> pages/darling/grammar/
> abbreviations.htm
> A superb guide to
> abbreviation

53e   Avoid most other abbreviations in formal writing

Place names, including the names of states, countries, provinces, continents, and other localities, should not be abbreviated except in addresses and occasionally when used as adjectives (for example, in *US government*). Organization and company names should not be abbreviated unless they are extremely familiar: *IBM, CBS, UPS, UCLA, NYU.* Many official company names, however, include one or more abbreviations, which should be kept as is: *Canon, Inc.; Braun AG; Mac Pro.* Fields of study should not be abbreviated. Write *political science* (not *poli sci*) and *psychology* (not *psych*).

http://www.ucc.ie/
info/net/acronyms/
index.html
The Abbreviation and
Acronym Server

In formal, nontechnical writing, most units of measure should be spelled out: *inches, yards, meters, square feet, gallons.* In technical and scientific writing, abbreviations are standard: *m, kg, bps, dpi, mips, GB, rpm.* Symbols such as @, #, &, +, and = should not be used in the body of a paper. They can be used, though, in graphs, tables, and email addresses and for other similar purposes.

EXERCISE 53.1

In the following sentences, correct any abbreviations that are not in the proper form and write out any expressions that are not appropriately abbreviated in academic writing.

1. Dr. Ernesto Garcia, M.D, is a specialist in the treatment of A.I.D.S.

2. There has always been a friendly rivalry between people who live in N.H. and those who live in Mass.

3. The Girl Scouts of Tr. 76 visited Representative Harriet Stanley at the Mass. State House.

4. Among the questions the girls asked Rep. Stanley were several about a proposal to extend the school year into July and Aug.

5. The G.O.P. and the Dems have very different positions on that bill.

6. Many colleges have a phys. ed. requirement.

7. When I drive to work in the a.m., my usual radio station is 1030 a.m.

8. The unit of blood one gives at a blood drive measures 450 ml.
9. It was a dramatic advance in science when DNA was 1st used to clone a sheep.
10. HTML is the fundamental language of the WWW.

Numbers

When you are writing text and need to cite a number, keep in mind the following guidelines.

53f Use figures with abbreviations and conventionally numerical references

Time

7:00 a.m.	0700 hrs	seven o'clock in the morning
2:45 p.m.	1445 hrs	two forty-five in the afternoon

Dates

65 BC (or BCE)	AD 126 (or 126 CE)	the 1890s	May 15, 1996
from 1996 to 1998	1996–1998	1996–98	

Money

$23.4 billion $12,566 $7.99   45¢   forty-five cents   one dollar

Rates of speed

55 mph   33.6 bps
200 MHz   3000 rpm

Decimals and percentages

.05   5 percent (or 5%)

Telephone numbers

617-555-1284 [US]   +1 (617) 555 1284 [International]

Addresses

233 East 19th Street   PO Box 45   Route 66
New York, NY 10011

WWW
WEB

http://webster.commnet.
edu/hp/pages/darling/
grammar/numbers.htm
An excellent guide to the
use of numbers

Divisions of books and plays

volume 2, chapter 11, pages 346–55
King Lear, act II, scene i, lines 5–7 OR *King Lear* II.i.5–7
The Alchemist, act 2, scene 1, lines 5–7 OR *The Alchemist* 2.1.5–7

53g Write out other numbers that can be expressed in one or two words

One to ninety-nine

fifteen   twenty-two   eighty-four

Fractions

two-thirds   one-fourth   five-sixteenths

Large round numbers

thirteen hundred   four thousand   thirty million

Decades and centuries

the eighties (or the '80s)

the twenty-first century (or the 21st century)

53h Write out numbers that begin sentences

FAULTY   18% of Americans believe that career preparation should begin in elementary school.

REVISED   Eighteen percent of Americans believe that career preparation should begin in elementary school.

When a number is too large to write out (more than two words), keep the numerical form but rearrange the sentence so as to avoid beginning with a number.

FAULTY   240,183 people could be fed for one year with the food we Americans waste in one day.

REVISED   We Americans waste enough food in one day to feed 240,183 people for one year.

53i When one number modifies another, write one as a figure and the other as a word

We bought fourteen $25 tickets.

There were 75 twelfth-graders at the dance.

53j Write related numbers alike

When comparing two or more numbers in the same sentence or paragraph, make the comparison easy to see by putting the numbers in the same form, as either words or figures.

It takes ~~nine hundred~~ ^900^ hours of training to become a licensed hair braider in New York City but only 117 hours to become an emergency medical technician.

EXERCISE 53.2

Correct the use of numbers in the following sentences.

1. 200 prayers are sent to the Wailing Wall each day by email.
2. 1998 is the year in which Hong Kong was turned back to the Chinese government.
3. Some workers now work two eight-hour jobs back to back.
4. In 1582, Pope Gregory the 13th instituted the calendar we still use today.
5. At one time, mathematicians were able to work only with the 3 dimensions they can visualize, but now they have analytic methods which allow them to deal with 4, 5, or more dimensions.
6. Much has changed over the years, but the price of Boardwalk remains $200 Monopoly.
7. The long passage of 16th notes in that piece makes it a difficult one for a beginner to play.
8. Abraham, patriarch of Christianity, Judaism, and Islam, probably lived in about 1800 B.C.E.
9. The university hopes to increase its endowment by 50% over the next 5 years.
10. In the early 80's, home mortgage interest rates were as high as 16 or 17%.

The Hyphen

FAQs

> Should I hyphenate a term like *third grader*? (54a)
> What are the rules for hyphenating a word at the end of
>   a line? (54e)

?

The hyphen (-) is typed as a single keystroke, with no space before or after. It differs from a dash, which is typed as two consecutive hyphens (--) and then usually converted by the computer into what looks like a long hyphen (—). The hyphen has two main functions: punctuating certain compound words and names (*self-destruct, fifty-fifty, Coca-Cola*) and dividing a word at the end of a line.

54a Consult your dictionary on hyphenating compounds

A **compound** is a word made up of two smaller words. Sometimes these smaller words are connected by a hyphen (*screen-test*), sometimes they are separated by a space (*screen pass*), and sometimes

they are fused (*screensaver*). Many compounds start out as two separate words (*data base*), become hyphenated for a while (*data-base*),
and then, if they are widely used, evolve into a single word (*database*).
There are no firm rules for determining how to write a particular
compound, so it is best to check your dictionary. *Wired Style* says,
"When in doubt, close it up," giving examples like *email, homepage,
offline,* and *userid.*

54b Hyphenate compounds acting as adjectives before nouns

When you place a compound in front of a noun to act as a modifier, you usually hyphenate the compound.

> I teach *seventh-grade* algebra.

Notice that the same compound,
when *not* put before a noun, is *not*
hyphenated.

http://owl.english.
purdue.edu/Files/
18.html
All about hyphens

> I teach algebra to the *seventh
> grade.*

Hyphenate only compounds that *precede* nouns, not those that follow.

> She goes to a *little-known* college. The college is *little known.*

Exceptions to this rule include everyday compounds like *science fiction, long distance,* and *zip code,* which can be used as modifiers without hyphens.

> Do you have a *zip code directory?*

> There's something wrong with my *floppy disk drive.*

Complex compounds are compounds made up of three or more
words, like *cut-and-paste, ultra-high-density,* and *up-to-date.* When you
hyphenate a complex compound, be sure to hyphenate all its parts—
put hyphens between all the terms.

> I do a lot of *cut-and-paste* revising.

> My boyfriend needs a more *up-to-date* computer.

54c   Hyphenate spelled-out fractions and numbers from twenty-one through ninety-nine

one-half	three-eighths	forty-four
two-fifths	twenty-six	seventy-nine

54d   Hyphenate to avoid ambiguity and awkward spellings

Some words, especially those with the prefix *re-*, *pre-*, or *anti-*, require hyphens to prevent misreadings, mispronunciations, and awkward-looking spellings:

> Now that Professor Muller has complicated the problem, we will
> have to ~~resolve~~ it. [Without the hyphen, *re-solve*, "to solve again," would
> *re-solve*
> be read as *resolve*, "to deal with successfully."]

> *Pre-emergent*
> ~~Preemergent~~ weedkillers are best used in springtime. [Without
> the hyphen, some readers might see *preem* as a single, unrecognizable
> syllable.]

Hyphens can be used in series to indicate the omission of repeated words.

> My neighbor has both first- and second-generation satellite dishes
> for his TV. [The hyphen after *first* helps the reader understand that the
> writer is referring to *first-generation*.]

54e   Use hyphens for end-of-line word division

In general, it is best to avoid dividing a word at the end of a line. But there are situations where word division is desirable. For example, if you are trying to arrange text in columns (in a brochure or résumé, for instance), end-of-line hyphenation may provide valuable extra space. (Note: You should be able to turn your hyphen-

Checklist for Using Automatic Hyphenation

1. Can the document have a ragged right margin?

   a. If so, you can disable your word-processing program's automatic end-of-line hyphenation without running the risk of having large gaps, or "rivers," in the middle of lines. Rivers reduce readability (see 17b-4).

   b. If the document is a brochure or newsletter, for example, and requires block-justified text, activate the hyphenation program so as to avoid internal rivers.

2. Does the justified text have too many hyphenated lines? If so, further steps are needed, as excessive hyphenation can interfere with readability.

   a. You may want to adjust some of the hyphenated lines manually.

   b. You might consider changing the width of your columns.

ation program on or off.) General principles for end-of-line word division follow.

1 Dividing words only between syllables

If you are using a computer, you can have the hyphenation program divide words for you. Otherwise, consult a dictionary to find out where the syllable breaks are. In most dictionaries, a dot indicates a syllable break). For example, the entry **den • si • ty** means that the word can be hyphenated as either *den-sity* or *densi-ty*.

2 Avoiding a second hyphen in a hyphenated word

Words with prefixes like *self-*, *ex-*, and *all-* and complex compounds should not be hyphenated anywhere else.

Jimmy Carter has set a new standard for civic activism by ex-~~Presi-~~
Presidents.
~~dents.~~

3   Leaving at least two letters on a line

Do not divide a word so that a single letter is left hanging either on the first line or on the second line.

Stress management requires an examination of one's ~~e-~~ ^{emo-}
~~motional~~ _{tional} responses to others.

If you have to divide a name that includes two or more initials, keep the initials together.

In the movement for racial equality, few stand taller than ~~W. E.~~ ^{W. E. B.}

~~B.~~ Dubois.

4   Avoiding consecutive lines ending in hyphens

Ending three or more lines in a row with hyphens draws attention and looks ungainly.

Admitting to your feelings and allowing them to be expressed through either communication or action is a stress-
management technique that can help you through many difficult situations.

On a word processor, you can prevent such situations by clicking on the LIMIT CONSECUTIVE HYPHENS feature in the hyphenation program and setting the maximum number of hyphens in a row at two. Alternatively, you can widen the hyphenation zone (which determines the range in the width of the characters on the line).

Either way, however, you run the risk of creating another problem—extreme raggedness in left-justified text or large internal gaps in block-justified text. One of the main reasons for using end-of-line hyphenation is to have attractively filled-out paragraphs and blocks of text. If you are using a ragged right (left-justified) text style, you do not want the text to look *too* ragged. If you are using block justification, you do not want to have large gaps in the middle of lines (see 17b-4). Although you can avoid these extremes by making the hyphenation zone narrower, you then are increasing the odds of producing an excessive number of hyphens. You may have to experiment with your word-processing program until you get the right balance.

EXERCISE 54.1

Correct the hyphenation errors in the following paragraphs.

1. Stress-management calls for the development of positive self esteem, which can help you cope with stressful situations. Selfesteem skills are instilled through learned habits. Stress management also requires that you learn to see stressors not as adversaries but as exercises in life. These skills, along with other stress management techniques, can help you get through many difficult situations.

2. Smoke-less tobacco is used by approximately 12-million Americans, one fourth of whom are under the age of twenty one. Most users are teen-age and young adult males, who are often emulating a professional sports-figure or a family-member.

3. In a consumer oriented environment, many hospitals are making efforts to improve patient care. Many are now designated as trauma-centers. They have helicopters to transport victims, they have in house specialty physicians available around-the clock, and they have specialized-diagnostic equipment. Though very expensive to run, trauma-centers have dramatically reduced mortality-rates for trauma-patients.

4. Hispanics made up the fastest growing segment of the US-population during the 1990s. However, Hispanics constitute diverse groups, having come from a variety of Spanish speaking countries at different times in the nation's history-Because the United States at one time seized large amounts of land from Mexico- the largest group of Hispanics are of Mexican-descent. Newspapers serving these descendants are called the Chicano-press and are printed in Spanish, English, or sometimes both languages.

5. Felice Schwartz (1989) suggested that corporations offer women a choice of two parallel career paths. The "fast-track" consists of high powered, demanding positions that

require sixty-or-seventy hours of work per week, regular responsibilities, emergencies, out of town meetings, and a briefcase jammed with work on week-ends. The second track, the "mommy-track," would stress both career and family. Less would be expected of a woman on the mommy-track, for her commitment to the firm would be lower and her commitment to her family higher.

PART 12

ESL ISSUES

Tips on Nouns and Articles

FAQs

Why is it necessary to use articles?

How do I know whether to use *a* or *the*? (55a, 55b, 55c)

When is it okay to use no article at all? (55e)

?

Articles (*a, an, the*) are important in the English language because they clarify what nouns refer to. There is a significant difference in meaning between "I found *a* new Web site" and "I found *the* new Web site." The first sentence introduces new information, while the second sentence implies that the new Web site is something the reader or listener already knew about. Articles can be used to mark other subtleties as well. Because many other languages do not use articles in this way, though, many nonnative speakers of English have trouble with articles.

55a   Use the plural only with count nouns

To use articles correctly, you first need a clear understanding of the difference between count nouns and noncount nouns. **Count nouns** refer to things that have a distinct physical or mental form and thus can be counted, like *book, apple, diskette, scientist,* and *idea.*

Common Examples of Two-Way Nouns

As *a count noun*	As *a noncount noun*
a wine (a type of wine)	*wine* (the fermented juice of grapes)
a cloth (a piece of cloth)	*cloth* (fabric made by weaving or knitting)
a thought (an idea)	*thought* (mental activity, cogitation)
a beauty (a lovely person or thing)	*beauty* (loveliness)
a hair (a single strand of hair)	*hair* (filamentous mass growing out of the skin)

Count nouns can be enumerated and pluralized—for example, *eight books, three apples, several diskettes, two scientists,* and *many ideas.*

Noncount (or **mass**) **nouns** are words like *air, rice, electricity, excitement,* and *coverage* that do not have a distinct form as a whole. (Though each grain of rice may have a distinct form, rice as a mass quantity is variable in form.) Noncount nouns are neither enumerated nor pluralized. No one would say *eight airs, three rices, several electricities, two excitements,* or *many coverages.* Noncount nouns can be quantified with expressions like *a lot of, much, some,* and *a cup of*—for example, *some air, a cup of rice, much excitement,* and *a lot of coverage.*

http://leo.stcloud.
msus.edu/grammar/
countnon.html
Help with count and
noncount nouns

Some nouns can be used as either count or noncount nouns. In such cases, the countable sense is more specific than the uncountable sense. For example, *reading* as a noncount noun refers to the general activity ("I enjoy *reading*"), while *reading* as a count noun refers to a particular type of reading—for example, a text ("We were assigned a collection of *readings*"), an interpretation ("I made several *readings* of the data"), or a performance ("We were invited to a public *reading*"). See the Common Examples of Two-Way Nouns. (See also 24a-1 for more on count and noncount nouns.)

E X E R C I S E 5 5 . 1

Decide whether each of the nouns listed below is countable, non-countable, or both (depending on context). If the noun is countable, write its plural counterpart next to it. If the noun can be either countable or noncountable, explain in what context it would be appropriate to pluralize the noun.

1. idea
2. money
3. math problem
4. government
5. party
6. memorization
7. computer program
8. silence
9. tobacco
10. movie

55b   Use *the* for specific references

In deciding whether to use *the, a, an,* or no article at all, keep in mind the concept of specificity. Does the noun refer to some particular thing or set of things, or does it refer to something general? As mentioned in the introduction to this chapter, "*the* Web site" refers to a specific, unique Web site, whereas "*a* Web site" refers to any Web site.

There are many different types of situations in which nouns refer to specific things and must be preceded by *the* (see Situations Requiring the Use of *the* on page 775). In all these cases, the writer assumes that the reader knows *which* thing or set of things is being referred to. If you are using a noun that names something unique and specific, use the definite article *the* with the noun, whether or not the noun is countable. (Note: This guideline applies to common nouns only, not to most proper nouns.)

http://owl.english.
purdue.edu/Files/
25.html
A discussion of the use
of articles, with links to
count vs. noncount
nouns and exercises

WWW
WEB

1 Using *the* with superlative adjectives

Adjectives like *best, worst,* and *most interesting* single out one particular thing among many.

Pete Sampras is *the best tennis player* in the world.

2 Using *the* with unique things

The past, the present, the sun, and *the solar system* all have unique identities. There is only one past, only one present, only one sun (in our solar system anyway).

Thirty minutes after boarding, the plane was still on *the ground.*

3 Using *the* with nouns followed by a modifier

Many nouns are followed by a phrase or clause that restricts the noun's identity.

The theory of relativity was developed by Einstein.

The girl in the corner is in my physics class.

4 Using *the* to refer to a previous mention

Once something has been mentioned, it becomes part of the reader's knowledge. When you refer to it again, use *the* so that the reader knows that you are talking about the same thing.

I went shopping today and bought some beans, rice, and *chicken.*
We can cook *the chicken* for dinner.

Note: For clarity or emphasis, the demonstrative adjective *this, that, those,* or *these* may be used instead of *the.*

5 Using *the* to draw on shared knowledge

If you and your reader can draw on shared experience to identify something in particular, use *the* to mark it.

Please shut down *the computer* when you are done with it.

Situations Requiring the Use of *the*

	Examples
Superlative adjectives	*the best, the worst, the strongest, the most valuable*
Unique things	*the past, the future, the earth, the moon*
Nouns followed by a modifier	*the book* on the table, *the number* of the course
Previous mention	A man and a woman dropped by to see you. *The man's* name was . . . .
Shared knowledge	I can meet you at *the fountain.*
Contextual specificity	At last week's game, *the fans* were pretty rowdy.
An entire class of things	*The handheld computer* may replace *the laptop.*

6   Using *the* for contextual specificity

Sometimes the context of a situation allows you and your reader to identify something as unique. Consider, for example, the word *printer*. There are many printers in the world, but if you are writing about a computer and you want to mention the printer attached to it, use *the* to indicate that it is the only printer in this particular context.

I was using my friend's computer and could not get *the printer* to work.

7   Using *the* to denote an entire class of things

The can be used with a singular count noun to denote an entire class or genre of things.

The earthworm is one of nature's most valuable creatures.

The personal computer has revolutionized modern life.

Note: This generic use of *the* to refer to an entire class of things applies only to singular count nouns, not to plural count nouns or noncount nouns.

EXERCISE 55.2

Study the following paragraph, and insert *the* where appropriate.

_____ physical fatigue is _____ result of overworking our muscles to _____ point where _____ metabolic waste products—carbon dioxide and lactic acid—accumulate in _____ blood and sap our strength. Our muscles cannot continue to work efficiently in _____ bath of these chemicals. _____ physical fatigue is usually a pleasant tiredness, such as that which we might expect after playing a hard set of _____ tennis, chopping _____ wood, or climbing a mountain. _____ cure is simple and fast: we rest, giving _____ body a chance to get rid of _____ accumulated wastes and restore _____ muscle fuel.

55c Use *the* with most proper nouns derived from common nouns

Proper nouns are names of things such as persons, places, holidays, religions, companies, and organizations. Most proper nouns, even though they uniquely identify somebody or something, do not take the definite article:

Muhammad Ali	Mother Theresa	New York	China
Christmas	Ramadan	Catholicism	Microsoft
September	Greenpeace	*Hamlet*	

Many proper nouns, though, do take the definite article:

the Rolling Stones	the United States
the Panama Canal	the International Red Cross
the Vietnam War	the Golden Gate Bridge
the Himalaya Mountains	the University of Chicago
the Fourth of July	*The Grapes of Wrath*

Do you see a general pattern that distinguishes these two kinds of proper nouns? Those that take the definite article have a head noun derived from a common English noun: *stones, states, canal, cross, war, bridge, mountains, university, fourth,* and *grapes.*

There are many exceptions, however, to this pattern. Many common-noun names do not take the definite article: *Elm Street, Salt Lake City, Carleton College, Princeton University, Lookout Mountain, Pine*

Creek, Walden Pond, Capitol Hill, Burger King. And a few names not derived from a common noun nonetheless do take the definite article: *the Vatican, the Amazon, the Congo, the Hague.* In general, major landmarks tend to take the definite article, while lesser ones do not: *the Pacific Ocean* vs. *Walden Pond, the United Kingdom* vs. *Burger King.* This is not an absolute rule, however: Michigan State University and the University of Michigan are of comparable size, yet only one is referred to with the definite article. We suggest that you pay close attention to each proper name you encounter and note whether it is used with *the.*

> http://www.
> researchpaper.com/
> writing.html#ESL
> More help with count
> and noncount nouns and
> articles, plus exercises

55d Use *a* or *an* in nonspecific references to singular count nouns

Nonspecific nouns refer to *types* of things rather than to specific things. With nonspecific singular count nouns, such as *shirt, jacket, belt,* and *hat,* you must use an indefinite article (either *a* or, if the next sound is a vowel sound, *an*) or some other determiner (for example, *my, your, this,* or *each*).

I bought *a shirt* and *an overcoat.*

55e Use no article in nonspecific references to plural count nouns or noncount nouns

With nonspecific plural count nouns, such as *shirts, jackets, belts,* and *hats,* no article is used. You may use, however, determiners like *our, some, these,* and *no.*

> There were *socks* and *shorts* on sale, but *no belts.*

> http://www.aitech.
> ac.jp/~iteslj/quizzes/
> grammar.html
> A great collection of
> self-study quizzes for
> ESL students

Nonspecific noncount nouns, such as *clothing, apparel,* and *merchandise,* do not take articles either. They can, however, take determiners like *some, much, enough, your, their, this,* and *no.*

> *People* were buying *lots of clothing,* but I did not have *enough money* to get everything I needed.

EXERCISE 55.3

Study the following sentences, and insert *a, an,* or *the* where appropriate.

1. Sarah used to play _____ soccer for her high school team, and she was _____ star player.
2. He gave me _____ good advice.
3. _____ anecdote is _____ type of illustration.
4. You should give credit to _____ people who did _____ work.
5. _____ professor surprised _____ students with _____ quiz.
6. All of _____ dogs in _____ neighborhood started to bark when _____ power went out.
7. Vera bought _____ new pink dress for graduation, but, unfortunately, _____ dress was too big.
8. We need to go to _____ grocery store; I need _____ loaf of bread.
9. _____ people who do not eat _____ meat are generally healthy.
10. All _____ children have _____ need for _____ love.

EXERCISE 55.4

Study the following paragraphs, and insert *a, an,* or *the* where appropriate.

1. In _____ different societies, _____ gift giving is usually ritualized. _____ ritual is _____ set of multiple, symbolic behaviors that occurs in _____ fixed sequence. Gift-giving rituals in our society usually involve the choosing of _____ proper gift by _____ giver, _____ removing of _____ price tag, wrapping of _____ gift, timing _____ gift giving, and waiting for _____ reaction (either positive or negative) from _____ recipient.

2. In _____ latter part of _____ nineteenth century, _____ capitalism was characterized by _____ growth of _____ giant corporations. Control of most of _____ important industries became more and more concentrated. Accompanying this concentration of industry was _____ equally striking concentration of _____ income in _____ hands of a small percentage of _____ population. There was _____ increase in _____ amount of influence that _____ large corporations had on _____ government.

Tips on Verbs

I have a lot of trouble with verbs like *look out for* and *look over.* Do I need to learn them? (56a)

If it is okay to say "I like to read," what's wrong with "I dislike to read"? (56b, 56c)

What is wrong with "The program is consisting of four parts"? (56f)

What are the correct verb tenses for *if* sentences? (56i, 56j, 56k)

?

If you are having trouble with English verbs, take heart: verbs often pose a problem for speakers of English, both native and nonnative. The main features of the English verb system are discussed in Chapter 26, subject-verb agreement in 27a, and tense, mood, and voice in 33b. This chapter addresses aspects of the verb system that may give nonnative speakers of English special difficulties: phrasal verbs, verb complements, verbs of state, modal auxiliary verbs, and conditional sentences.

Phrasal Verbs

Phrasal verbs are made up of a verb and one or two particles (prepositions or adverbs)—for example, *pick over, look into, get away with*. For this reason, they are sometimes called **two-word verbs** or **three-word verbs.** Phrasal verbs are common in English, especially in informal speech. Some phrasal verbs mean something quite different from their associated simple verbs. For example, if a friend of yours says, "I just *ran into* Nguyen in the library," the encounter probably had nothing to do with running. *To run into* means "to encounter unintentionally." Other phrasal verbs are used merely to intensify the meaning of the simple verb. For example, *fill up* is a more emphatic version of *fill.*

http://www.gsu.
edu/~wwwesl/
egw/three.htm
Three rules for distin-
guishing phrasal verbs
from verb + preposi-
tion combinations

Some phrasal verbs are **transitive** (that is, they have direct objects), while others are **intransitive.** For example, *dig up* (meaning "find") is transitive ("I *dig up* some information for my paper"), but *speak up* (meaning "speak louder") is intransitive ("Please *speak up*"). Some phrasal verbs have both transitive and intransitive meanings. For example, *show up* can mean either "expose or embarrass (someone)" or "appear," depending on whether it is used transitively or intransitively: "He tried to *show up* the teacher" (transitive) versus "He never *shows up* on time" (intransitive). (See 24a-4 and 26f for more on transitive and intransitive verbs.)

Some transitive phrasal verbs are separable, meaning that the particle may be placed after the object of the verb: "I quickly *looked over* my paper" or "I quickly *looked* my paper *over*." Other transitive phrasal verbs are inseparable, meaning that the verb and the particle must be kept together: "I quickly *went over* my paper," not "I quickly *went* my paper *over*."

56a Note phrasal verbs as you listen and read

The list of Common Phrasal Verbs represents only a small fraction of all the phrasal verbs in the English language. To master idiomatic English, you must learn hundreds of such verbs.

Some Common Phrasal Verbs

Phrasal verb	Formal equivalent	Example
bring up	raise	He *brought up* the issue of salaries.
brush up on	refresh one's knowledge of	I need to *brush up on* my German.
check up on	investigate	The police are *checking up on* him.
check with	consult	You should *check with* your advisor.
come across	discover, encounter	I *came across* a new bug in the program.
come through	satisfy a need	My family *came through* with the money.
come up with	develop, find	He *came up with* a solution to the problem.
fall back on	have recourse to	We can always *fall back on* our original plan.
fall through	not happen, fail	I hope the car deal does not *fall through*.
go over	review, examine	We should *go over* our notes before the exam.
hang on	persist	If you *hang on*, I am sure things will work out.
keep on	continue	It is important to *keep on* trying.
look for	seek	She went to *look for* her sweater.
look over	review, examine	Do you want to *look over* the practice test?
pick out	identify, choose	He finally *picked out* the flowers he wanted.
put off	postpone	We should *put off* our meeting until tomorrow.
put up with	tolerate	No teacher should *put up with* cheating.
run out of	exhaust, deplete	My printer seems to be *running out of* ink.

The best way to do so is by listening to and reading as much informal English as you can and noting the phrasal verbs. Also consult a good pocket dictionary of phrasal verbs, such as *Handbook of Commonly Used American Idioms*, 3rd ed., by A. Makkai, M. Boatner, and J. Gates (New York: Barron's, 1995). A good Web site to visit is Dave Sperling's Phrasal Verb Page (*http://www.eslcafe.com/pv/*).

WEB
http://www.aitech.
ac.jp/~iteslj/quizzes/
idioms.html
Fun quizzes on idioms,
phrasal verbs, and slang

EXERCISE 56.1

Using at least six of the phrasal verbs given in the list of Common Phrasal Verbs, write a short, coherent passage on a topic of your choice.

Verb Complements

Verb complements include gerunds (*swimming*), *to* infinitives (*to swim*), and unmarked infinitives (*swim*). English verbs differ in the kinds of verb complements they can take.

WEB
http://owl.english.
purdue.edu/writers/
by-topic.html#ESL
Thorough coverage of
verb complements and
verb tenses

    V   Comp
I *dislike* *swimming*. [Not "I dislike to swim" or "I dislike swim"]

    V   Comp
I *want* *to swim*. [Not "I want swimming" or "I want swim"]

   V Comp   V Comp
I *like* *swimming*. OR I *like* *to swim*. [Not "I like swim"]

    V   Comp
I *made* her *swim*. [Not "I made her swimming" or "I made her to swim"]

56b   Learn which verbs take gerunds as complements

The following verbs take gerunds (verbals ending in *ing*), but not infinitives, as complements, as in "Maria *acknowledged skipping* class."

acknowledge	deny	give up	put off
admit	depend on	have trouble	quit
advise	detest	imagine	recommend
anticipate	discuss	insist on	regret
appreciate	dislike	keep	resist
avoid	dream about	miss	result in
cannot (can't) help	enjoy	object to	risk
consider	escape	plan on	succeed in
consist of	evade	postpone	suggest
delay	finish	practice	talk about

56c Learn which verbs take *to* infinitives as complements

The following verbs take *to* infinitives, but not participles, as complements, as in "Kim cannot *afford to buy* a car."

afford	decide	intend	offer	seem
agree	demand	learn	plan	struggle
ask	expect	like	prepare	tend
attempt	fail	manage	pretend	threaten
claim	hesitate	mean	promise	wait
consent	hope	need	refuse	want

56d Learn which verbs take both gerunds and *to* infinitives as complements

The following verbs can take either a gerund or a *to* infinitive as a complement: "He *began learning* English as a small child" or "He *began to learn* English as a small child."

begin	dread	like	stop*
cannot (can't) stand	forget*	love	try
continue	hate	remember*	

For those verbs marked with an asterisk, the meaning of the sentence depends on the type of complement: "He *forgot to go* to the store" means that he did not go to the store, while "He *forgot going* to the store" means that he did go to the store but then did not remember going there.

56e   Learn which verbs take only unmarked infinitives as complements

There are four verbs that, when followed by a noun or pronoun, take an infinitive without *to*, as in "She let *him pay* for dinner." These verbs are

have   help   let   make

(Note that *help* can also take a *to* infinitive as a complement.)

EXERCISE 56.2

In the following sentences, fill each blank with the correct form of the verb in parentheses.

1. Professor Adams refused (change) _____ the student's grade.

2. The student believed that (change) _____ the grade was the only fair course of action.

3. The student also insisted on (discuss) _____ the matter with the dean of the college.

4. The student hoped (convince) _____ the dean that the professor was being unjust in her refusal to change the grade.

5. The dean, however, decided (side) _____ with the professor, so the student's grade was never changed from a B to an A.

6. The famous scientist offered (speak) _____ at the university graduation ceremony.

7. Most students dislike (study) _____ for final examinations.

8. She suggested (walk) _____ to the birthday party instead of (drive) _____ in the car.

9. She offered (help) _____ him study for his mid-term exam.

10. The professor helped the student (understand) _____ the importance of coherence and unity in academic writing.

Verbs of State

Many English verbs depict states or conditions rather than events or actions. These verbs are called **verbs of state.**

56f Do not use the progressive tense with verbs of state

Verbs of state generally cannot occur in the progressive tense. For example, *consist of* is a verb of state and therefore cannot occur in the progressive tense (see 26d).

The program ~~is consisting~~ ^{consists} of four parts.

The program is consisting of four parts. *(consists)*

The following verbs do not occur in the progressive tense:

appear	contain	know	result in
believe	correspond	mean	seem
belong	differ from	need	suppose
consist of	exist	possess	understand
constitute	involve	represent	want

Modal Auxiliary Verbs

The **modal auxiliary verbs** include *can, could, may, might, must, will, would,* and *should* (see 24a-4, 26c). They are used to express a variety of conditions including possibility, necessity, ability, permission, and obligation. Each modal auxiliary has at least two principal meanings, one relating to social interaction and the other to logical probability. For example, the word *may* in a sentence like "*May* I sit down?" requests permission, an aspect of social interaction, while the word *may* in a sentence like "It *may* rain today" denotes logical possibility. Within these two general categories, the modal auxiliaries

Modal Auxiliaries Ranked by Strength

Modal verb	Social interaction meaning	Logical probability meaning	Strength
will	intention	certainty	**Strong**
must	obligation	logical necessity	
would	conditionality	conditional certainty	
should	advisability	probability	
may	permission, possibility	possibility	
can	permission	possibility	
might/could	very polite permission, possibility	low possibility	**Weak**

carry different degrees of strength, as shown in the box. Modal auxiliary verbs have certain distinct grammatical features that can cause problems for nonnative speakers.

56g Use only a base verb form immediately after a modal auxiliary

Any verb immediately following a modal auxiliary must be in the base, or simple, form (for example, *teach, have, go, run*), not in the *to* infinitive or gerund form.

NO   History *can to teach* us many good lessons.

YES   History *can teach* us many good lessons.

NO   The UN *should done* more to help stop the Rwandan civil war.

YES   The UN *should have done* more to help stop the Rwandan civil war.

56h   Do not use more than one modal at a time

NO   If I study hard, I *might could* get an A.

YES   If I study hard, I *might* get an A.

YES   If I study hard, I *could* get an A.

If you want to combine a modal auxiliary verb with some other modal meaning, use a modal phrase such as *be able to, be allowed to,* or *have to.*

YES   If I study hard, I *might be able to* get an A.

EXERCISE 56.3

Some of the following sentences have verb tense errors. Make the appropriate corrections.

1. A formal academic essay usually is containing an introduction, the main discussion, and a conclusion.
2. My parents must will send me some money.
3. A thesis statement should to present the main idea of the essay.
4. Right now, Marinela studies in the library for a test in her 1:00 class.
5. Yuka could not imagining to miss even a day of her ESL conversation class.
6. Many students enjoy to study in small groups.
7. Many students are not understanding that the organization of an essay is as important as its content.
8. Manuel resisted to sleep in late, because he needed finishing his math assignment.
9. Serena hopes to buy a new car, but first she might should save money for a down payment.
10. The teacher planned waiting until next week to begin the unit to deal with the American Revolution.

Conditional Sentences

Conditional sentences have two parts: a subordinate clause beginning with *if* (or *when* or *unless*) that sets a condition and a main clause that expresses a result. The tense and mood of the verb in the subordinate clause depend on the tense and mood of the verb in the main clause. There are three main types of conditional sentences: factual, predictive, and hypothetical.

56i · In factual conditionals, use the same verb tense in both parts

Factual conditional sentences depict factual relationships. The conditional clause begins with *if, when, whenever,* or some other condition-setting expression; the conditional clause verb is cast in the same tense as the result clause verb.

If you don't *get* enough rest, you *get* tired.

When we *had* a day off, we *went* hiking in the mountains.

56j · In predictive conditionals, use a present-tense verb in the *if* clause and an appropriate modal in the result clause

Predictive conditional sentences express future possible conditions and results. The conditional clause starts with *if* or *unless* and has a present-tense verb; the result clause verb is formed with a modal (*will, can, should, may,* or *might*) and the base form of the verb.

If we *leave* now, we *can be* there by 5 o'clock.

She *will lose* her place in class unless she *registers* today.

56k · In hypothetical conditionals, use a past-tense verb in the *if* clause and *would, could,* or *might* in the result clause

Hypothetical conditional sentences depict situations that are unlikely to happen or are contrary to fact (see 25h). For hypothetical past situations, the verb in the conditional clause should be in the past perfect tense and the verb in the main clause should be formed from *would have, could have,* or *might have* and the past participle.

If we *had invested* our money in stocks instead of bonds, we *would have gained* a lot more.

For hypothetical present or future situations, the verb in the conditional clause should be in the past tense and the verb in the main clause should be formed from *would, could,* or *might* and the base form.

> If we *invested* our money in stocks instead of bonds, we *would gain* a lot more.

EXERCISE 56.4

Construct one example of each of the three main types of conditional sentences: factual, predictive, and hypothetical.

CHAPTER

57

Tips on Word Order

If I have several adjectives in a row, what order should
they go in? (57a)
How can I create new terms by stringing nouns together?
(57b)
Where should adverbs be placed? (57c, 57d, 57e, 57f)

?

Unlike many other languages, English depends on word order to convey meaning. A change in word order often produces a different meaning. For example, "Kevin likes Maria" means something quite different from "Maria likes Kevin." Basic sentence patterns like these are discussed in 24b. This chapter discusses some other word-order patterns involving strings of adjectives, compound nouns, and adverb placement.

57a   String adjectives in the order preferred in English

Usually, adjectives either directly precede the nouns they modify or follow a linking verb (see 24b, Chapter 28).

The fence is *broken*. The *broken* fence will be repaired.

In general, adjectives should be used only one at a time, as in these examples. Occasionally, though, you may want to string two or more adjectives together; in such cases, you will have to put them in the appropriate order.

FAULTY   The *wood broken* fence will be repaired.

REVISED   The *broken wood* fence will be repaired.

http://webster.
commnet.edu/
hp/pages/
darling/grammar/
adjectives.htm
Good stuff on
ordering adjectives,
with exercises

The following list shows the preferred ordering of adjectives in English:

1. Article or determiner: *the, a, an, my, our, Carla's, this, that, those*
2. Ordinal expression: *first, second, last, next, final*
3. Quantity: *one, two, few, many, some*
4. Evaluation: *beautiful, delicious, interesting, unfortunate, ugly*
5. Size: *tiny, small, short, tall, large, big*
6. Shape: *square, oval, cylindrical, round*
7. Condition: *shiny, clean, dirty, broken*
8. Age: *new, young, old, ancient*
9. Color: *black, red, yellow, green, white*
10. Nationality: *Mexican, Chinese, Vietnamese, Japanese*
11. Religion: *Catholic, Confucian, Buddhist, Muslim*
12. Material: *cotton, stone, plastic, gold*
13. Special use or purpose (may be a noun used as an adjective): *carving, carrying, sports, medical, computer*
14. The noun being modified

Here are some expressions created by following the preferred ordering:

1	2	3	4	5	6	7	8	9	10	11	12	13	14
The	first			small		shiny	new		Japanese			sports	car
A		few					young			Buddhist			monks
Her			favorite		long			yellow			silk		flowers

EXERCISE 57.1

Create three strings of your own, using at least three adjectives in each.

57b   String nouns for easiest recognition

Stringing nouns together to form **noun compounds** is common in English (see 28b). Terms like *bike lock, keyboard, houseboat, picnic table,* and *bookmark* were formed by putting two ordinary nouns together. And it is easy to add a third noun to make them more descriptive: *combination bike lock, keyboard cover, houseboat community, picnic table leg,* and *bookmark program.* In theory, you can make noun strings as long as you want. However, if you use more than three nouns in a row, you will make it difficult for the reader to figure out what you are trying to say.

In all noun compounds, the rightmost noun is the **head noun** and the nouns preceding it serve as modifiers. These modifier nouns can modify either the head noun or another modifier noun.

Modifier noun	Head noun		Modifier noun	Head noun
combination	bike lock		mountain bike	lock

When you create a noun compound, be sure to build it from familiar parts. For example, say you wanted to buy for your bicycle a lock that included a cable. If you were calling a local store to ask if the store carried such a lock, what name would you give it? Three nouns are needed—*bike, lock,* and *cable.* The head noun, *lock,* should go at the end. But what about the other two nouns? Should you call the lock a *bike cable lock* or a *cable bike lock?* The latter term is better. Because *bike lock* is a more recognizable term than *cable lock,* you should use *cable* as a modifier of *bike lock.* In effect, you are talking about a *bike lock* with a *cable.*

In creating noun compounds, bear in mind that nouns used as modifiers typically lose any plural endings they might have. Someone who loves movies is a *movie lover,* not a *movies lover;* the juice from cranberries is *cranberry juice,* not *cranberries juice.* (Exceptions to this pattern include *claims adjuster* and *weapons manufacturer.*)

EXERCISE 57.2

Convert the following expressions into noun compounds. The first one has been done for you.

1. An institute that does research in marketing is called a market-ing research institute.

2. A car that uses fuel generated in cells is called a
_____.

3. A computer device that uses a touchpad for pointing (instead of a mouse) is called a _____.

4. An electronic program for taking notes is called an
_____.

5. A program feature that allows you to send attachments with email is called an _____.

6. A baseball player who is designated to hit for the pitcher is called a _____.

7. Someone who provides daycare in his or her home is called a _____.

8. A service that prepares tax returns is called a
_____.

9. Someone whose job it is to control airplane traffic is called an _____.

10. A module designed to land on the moon is called a
_____.

57c   Use meaning to place adverbs that modify verbs

Adverbs can modify verbs, adjectives, other adverbs, or entire sentences (see 28c). Adverbs that modify verbs can be placed at either the beginning, the middle, or the end of a clause, depending on their meaning.

1   Placing adverbs of frequency

Adverbs of frequency (*usually, seldom, always, never*) are usually placed directly before the main verb (and after the auxiliary verb, if there is one).

Tim says he *usually* writes his papers on time, yet he is *always* turning them in late.

Some adverbs of frequency (*often, twice, many times*) can also be placed at the end of the clause.

He has missed class *quite often.*

> http://webster.
> commnet.edu/hp/
> pages/darling/grammar/
> adverbs.htm
> Fun discussion of adverb placement, with exercises

2 Placing adverbs of time when

Adverbs of time when (*yesterday, at eight o'clock, last year*) are normally placed at the end of the clause.

The exhibit will open *next month.*

Will they be there *after dinner?*

3 Placing adverbs of place

Adverbs of place (*upstairs, in the park, under a tree*) usually follow the verb. However, they should not intervene between the verb and an object.

Mike went *inside* to escape the heat.

She took her dog for a walk *in the park.*

57d Place adverbs directly before adjectives or adverbs that they modify

An adverb that modifies an adjective or another adverb should be placed directly before the word it modifies.

Jose is an *unusually quick* learner. He concentrates *very intensely* on his studies.

57e Place adverbs before sentences or clauses that they modify

An adverb that modifies a whole sentence or clause is usually placed at the beginning of the sentence or clause.

Unfortunately, his younger brother Ramon does not follow his example.

Less commonly, it is placed after the grammatical subject or at the end of the sentence.

His younger brother Ramon, *unfortunately,* does not follow his example.

His younger brother Ramon does not follow his example, *unfortunately.*

How do I check my placement of adverbs?

Using the fact that most adverbs end in -*ly*, you can often have your word-processing program flag the majority of the adverbs in a passage.

1. Open the SEARCH (or FIND) feature of your word-processing program.
2. Type *ly* in the SEARCH FOR (or FIND WHAT) field, and then have your program do the search.
3. Inspect each word. If it is an adverb, use the guidelines given in this chapter to determine whether it has been properly placed.

57f Do not put an adverb between a verb and its object

Nonnative speakers sometimes make the mistake of positioning an adverb between the verb and its object or objects.

FAULTY   Javier writes *often* letters to his family.

REVISED   Javier *often* writes letters to his family.

EXERCISE 57.3

The following sentences contain adverbs that have been incorrectly placed. Make the appropriate corrections.

1. Hanna has seen twice the movie *The Lost World*.
2. Princess Diana was only thirty-seven when she died sadly.
3. She swims usually laps in the afternoon.
4. I twice sent the fax before my brother received it.
5. Never Guillermo stops working.
6. Downstairs he went to do the week's laundry.
7. The sponge cake recipe is difficult quite to follow.
8. The string orchestra played last night a very difficult program.
9. The skater misses seldom her required jumps.
10. Around the curve coasted smoothly the car.

Tips on Vocabulary

Are there Internet resources that would help me expand
   my vocabulary? (58b)
Can I use idiomatic expressions in academic writing? (58c)

?

Many nonnative speakers of English feel that they just do not know enough words to express their thoughts as fully as they would like. Knowing enough words, and knowing them well, is a challenge for almost all nonnative speakers of English; indeed, it is a challenge for many native speakers, too. This chapter covers some of the most common vocabulary problems for nonnative speakers—those related to cognates, collocations, and idioms.

58a Look for cognates, but watch out for "false friends"

Cognates are words that have a formal relation to similar words in another language. They are usually quite recognizable. For example, the English *telephone* and Spanish *teléfono* are cognates, and it is easy for speakers of either language to recognize this word when learning the other language. Cognates are either derived from a common ancestor language or borrowed by one language from another. Sometimes the borrowing process involves minor alterations, as in *telephone/teléfono;* sometimes it involves more significant changes, as in the English *northwest* and Spanish *noroeste.*

If your native language is closely related to English, cognate recognition is a good strategy for learning new words. In most cases, you can trust a cognate to carry more or less the same meaning in your second language as it has in your first language. Of course, there are often subtle differences that you should pay attention to. For example, although the word *collar* is used in both English and Spanish to refer to the band around the neck of an animal, in Spanish it is also used to mean "necklace."

Sometimes, however, words that look similar in two different languages have entirely different meanings. These words are called **false cognates.** An example of a false cognate is the English *jubilation* and Spanish *jubilación.* The English word means "happiness," while the Spanish one means "retirement, pension (money)." You should always be on the alert for false cognates. Never assume that two words mean the same thing just because they look similar.

EXERCISE 58.1

If your native language is related to English, create a special document on your word processor called "False Cognates." Set up a table like the one above, and enter as many false cognates as you can think of. Use this document as an ongoing resource for vocabulary building.

Some Spanish/English False Cognates

Spanish	Meaning	English	Meaning
bonanza	fair weather	*bonanza*	a treasure
coraje	anger, rage	*courage*	bravery, valor
desgracia	misfortune	*disgrace*	dishonor
eventual	possible	*eventual*	final, ultimate
falacia	deceit, fraud	*fallacy*	false reasoning
informal	unreliable	*informal*	casual
lunático	temperamental	*lunatic*	insane
particular	private, personal	*particular*	specific
sensible	sensitive	*sensible*	reasonable
voluble	moody, fickle	*voluble*	talkative

58b   Try to get a feel for collocations

Collocations are words that commonly occur together (see 42c-1). For example, the word *advice* commonly occurs with the verbs *give*, *get*, and *receive* and with the adjectives *good*, *bad*, and *sound*. This is why the sentence "She gave me some good advice" sounds like normal American English, while the sentence "She presented me some nice advice" does not.

An intermission allows theatergoers to ~~extend~~ *stretch* their legs.

A steep ~~upshoot~~ *rise* in grain prices could topple many governments in the Third World.

On Christmas Day, the children were bubbling ~~up~~ *over* with excitement.

Lazy thinkers tend to make ~~wide~~ *broad* generalizations about things.

The best way to develop your knowledge of collocations is to pay attention to them in the English you see and hear around you. In this way, you will develop a feel for which words go with which. Another good strategy is to consult collocational dictionaries like the *COBUILD English Language Dictionary,* 2nd ed. (New York: Harper-Collins, 1996), which is based on a fifty-million-word corpus of actual written and spoken English. By logging on to the Web site at *http://titania.cobuild.collins.co.uk*, you can access the corpus directly and take advantage of the concordance program, which will give you forty random samples of actual usage for any word in contemporary English.

You can also get help with collocations through a specialized English learner's dictionary that provides plenty of example sentences. Good choices include the *Longman Dictionary of Contemporary English,* 3rd ed. (London: Longman, 1996), the *Longman Dictionary of American English,* 2nd ed. (Reading: Addison-Wesley, 1997), and the *Oxford Advanced Learner's Dictionary,* 5th ed. (New York: Oxford University Press, 1995). On the Internet, try OneLook Dictionaries at *http://www.onelook.com* and CSEN Global List of Special Dictionaries at *http://www.csen.com/special-dictionaries.*

EXERCISE 58.2

In each of the following sentences, replace the underlined word to form a collocation. You may want to consult an appropriate dictionary for help. The first sentence has already been done.

1. *highest*
   Kenya has one of the <u>tallest</u> standards of living in sub-Saharan Africa.
2. Gone are the days when a doctor would make <u>house visits</u>.
3. Let's all give the winner a <u>volley</u> of applause.
4. The students were on their <u>promise</u> not to cheat.
5. She was the first woman to <u>achieve</u> the finish line at the Boston Marathon.
6. The young actor had to learn his lines <u>to</u> heart.
7. I just got an A on my English paper, and things are <u>seeing</u> up.
8. He told the waiter that he would <u>eat</u> the specialty of the house.
9. He asked the bus driver if she knew the <u>hour</u>.
10. Today is the day the company will <u>propel</u> its new advertising campaign.

58c   Learn idioms in their entirety

A special type of collocation, an **idiomatic expression**, or **idiom**, is a fixed phrase whose meaning cannot be deduced from the meanings of its parts. For example, even if you know the words *kick* and *bucket*, you may not know what the idiom *kick the bucket* means (it means "die"). The same holds true for other idioms like *beat around the bush, have a screw loose*, or *lip service*. Because of their unpredictability, you have to learn idioms in their entirety, one at a time. And you have to use them in exactly the right form. If you said *kick a bucket* or *kick the pail*, many listeners would not understand what you meant. Many idioms involve phrasal verbs (see 56a).

http://www.eslcafe.com/idioms/
An interactive site for learning colloquial idioms

http://www.aitech.ac.jp/~iteslj/quizzes/grammar.html
A great collection of self-study quizzes for ESL students

The best way to learn a language's idioms is by listening to native speakers. Some good Web sites can also be of help: Dave Sperling's

Idioms That Can Be Used in Academic Writing

Idiom	Meaning	Example
allow for	take into consideration	My calculations failed to *allow for* random errors.
by and large	more often than not	*By and large,* women can bear pain better than men.
catch up on	do what was postponed earlier	Now that exams are over, I want to *catch up on* my sleep.
dwell on	be overly concerned with	Why *dwell on* problems that we cannot control?
enlarge upon	explain in more detail	The instructor said I should *enlarge upon* this idea.
keep abreast of	be up to date with	It is important to *keep abreast of* the latest developments in the field.
out of the question	impossible	Getting new funding for this project is *out of the question.*
play on	influence	Many television shows *play on* the viewer's emotions.
to the letter	precisely	He followed the professor's instructions *to the letter.*

Idiom Page at *http://www.pacificnet.net/~sperling/idioms.cgi*, The Weekly Idiom at *http://www.comenius.com/idiom/index.html*, and Vocabulary on the Internet at *http://www.hku.hk/engctr/vec/vocint.html*.

Because most idioms are colloquial, you should generally avoid them in formal written English (see 40c). They are most often used for casual communication, as in ordinary conversation, email correspondence, or chat groups. Some idioms, though, are quite acceptable in more formal uses.

EXERCISE 58.3

Log on to the three Web sites recommended for learning about idioms, and learn one new idiom from each site. Then try using the idiom in conversation or email communication with an acquaintance, preferably one who is a native speaker of English. If possible, ask the native speaker to evaluate your usage of each idiom.

Glossary of Computer Terms

address The identifying code (usually a sequence of letters, sometimes combined with numbers) assigned to an email account or to a document on the World Wide Web. (21b-2). *See also* URL.

alias *See* login name.

anchor A specific section within a Web page that is linked to another point within the same Web page. (20b-3)

appearance tag HTML code that tells a browser how the text in a document should look—for example, which phrases should appear as headings and which words should be in italics. (20b-2)

applet A small application written in the Java programming language and embedded in a Web site to perform a single function.

ASCII American Standard Code for Information Interchange; a generic code used for writing text without any formatting specific to a particular word-processing program. Most word processors allow text to be saved as ASCII (or text only) so that it can be read by other word-processing programs.

asterisk (*) A "wild card" symbol used by some operating systems to mean "all." For example, if you wanted to delete all your backup files at once in DOS, you might use the asterisk in the command delete *.bak.

asynchronous communication Correspondence or communication that takes place over a period of time. The sender transmits the message at one point in time; the recipient listens to or reads it at some later time. Email and voice mail are both forms of asynchronous communication.

attachment A document sent along with an email message but not incorporated into the body of the message. The receiver of the email must open the message in order to read it. An attachment can be saved to a folder or disk. (21b-5)

bit   A binary digit; the smallest amount of information that can be transmitted electronically. *See also* byte.

block-justify   To begin lines of text even with the left margin and end them even with the right margin. (17b-4)

bookmark   (*v*) To keep a record in one's computer of the location of a site on the Internet. (*n*) An Internet address that has been saved in the browser's bookmark directory for future reference. (9c-3)

Boolean operator   A connecting word with which users can combine terms in order to customize a key word search. The main Boolean operators are AND, OR, and NOT. (8e-2, 9c-1)

box   A ruled element, of fixed size, that is placed around a text or graphic. This formatting tool is useful for highlighting a part of a document. (17b-5)

browser   Software that allows users to navigate the Internet. (9b, 21a-2)

bulleted list   An itemized list that uses bullets, diamonds, dashes, or some other symbol to organize an unordered set of items. (17b-2)

bulletin board   A discussion forum where messages are posted electronically for anyone to access and read. (21a-2)

byte   A combination of eight binary digits, or bits. Bytes are combined to make larger units of data, such as words. A kilobyte is about 1,000 bytes, so a 19 K file contains about 19,000 bytes. A megabyte is about 1,000,000 bytes, so a 2 MB program is about 2,000,000 bytes.

CD-ROM   Compact disk–read only memory; a type of disk on which large databases may be stored. Data stored on CD-ROM must be accessed through a CD disk drive. (8f-4)

chat   An informal term referring to conversation in real-time on the Internet. (21a-3)

client/server   A term used to describe a network in which clients give instructions to a powerful, remote central computer (server).

client software   A program that allows a computer to share an interface with, or connection to, the Internet. For example, there are mail clients, newsreader clients, and Web browser clients.

clip art   Ready-made images, designed to be easily incorporated into electronic documents. (17c-5)

code   The combination of letters, numbers, and symbols in which software programs are written. *See also* source code, tags. (20b)

computerized catalog   A listing, on a computer database, of the materials in a library's collection. Computerized catalogs can be searched by author, title, subject, and key word. (8f-1)

container   A pair of HTML tags that bracket the text they affect. (20b-2)

CPU   Central processing unit; the electronic elements responsible for the internal workings of the computer's memory and operating system.

cyberspace A term coined by William Gibson to describe the Internet and other virtual environments.

database A collection of digital information organized for ease of storage and retrieval.

descriptor *See* key word.

desktop publishing The creation and printing of documents of near-professional quality on a desktop computer.

digital A term used to describe a device or method in which electrical variations are used to carry binary code.

directory A unit for organizing files on a computer disk drive or disk. Some operating systems use the equivalent term *folder.* (19b-1)

disk drive The hardware in a computer that stores data on magnetically sensitive disks. In general, if the disk is permanent, it is called a *hard disk,* and if it is removable, it is called a *floppy disk,* although removable hard disks are becoming more common.

DNS Domain name system; a method for identifying Internet host computers and their Internet addresses. The domain ending provides information about the type of site—for example, .edu stands for education, and .mil stands for military. (21b-1)

document source *See* source code.

document tag HTML code that identifies major elements in a document, such as head, title, body, background, and comments. (20b-2)

download To transfer documents (files) from another database or the Internet to a disk or to your local computer. (8a-2, 9b-5)

e-form An electronic application form, such as a job application form found at a Web site. (22c)

electronic thesaurus Software that provides users with alternative words to use. (43a-1)

email Electronic mail; the major form of communication via the Internet, allowing users to exchange messages with anyone who is also connected to the Internet. (Chapter 21)

email diacritics Asterisks, emoticons, and other characters used to add creative emphasis to email messages. (21b-4)

email discussion list A method of distributing a single email message to large numbers of subscribers at once. Also called a *listserv,* after the popular software program designed to perform this distribution. (21a-1)

emote Command used in an Internet chat room or MOO to cause the action specified next to be viewed by the other participants.

emoticons A collection of characters used to indicate emotions in an email message—for example, :-) stands for a smile. (21b-4)

FAQs Frequently asked questions; a collection of the questions most commonly asked about a topic. FAQs, along with relevant answers, are often presented in the form of an online archive as part of a Web site. Looking at a site's FAQs can help visitors better understand the site's audience and purpose.

file   A document on a computer disk drive or disk.

flame   (*v*) To send a personal attack message via email. (*n*) A personal attack sent via email message or posted in a newsgroup discussion.

folder   A collection of related documents, or files, placed in a common directory on a computer disk drive or disk.

font style   A particular variant of a typeface, such as regular or italic. Also called *font weight*. (17b-7)

font type   The distinctive design of a typeface. (17b-7)

font weight   *See* font style.

format   (*v*) To configure a blank disk for a particular operating system; to change the appearance of text. (*n*) The particular style of a document. (12e-2, 17b)

frame   (1) In desktop publishing, a ruled element around which text flows. A formatting tool useful for highlighting a part of a document, it is more dynamic and flexible than a box. (2) In Internet viewing, a division of a browser window allowing multiple Web pages to be displayed simultaneously. (17b-5, 20b-8)

FTP   File transfer protocol; a method for transferring files between computers over the Internet. (19b-1)

full block format   Format for a business letter in which every line of text starts at the left margin. (22a)

GIF   Graphics interchange format; a standard format for graphics or image files used on the Web.

gopher site   A location on the Internet where a menu-based protocol is used to access information. Gopher sites were precursors of Web sites and have largely been replaced by those sites.

grammar checker   *See* style/grammar checker.

hanging indent   A style of indentation in which the first line of text begins at the left margin and subsequent lines are indented. (17b-3)

hard disk drive   *See* disk drive.

hardware   The electronic elements that compose a computer system, including the CPU (central processing unit), the disk drives, and the monitor.

heading   A title given to a portion of a document and set off typographically from the rest of the document through font type, font style, or white space. This formatting tool is useful for drawing readers' attention, marking off parts of a text, and giving readers an immediate sense of what those parts are about. (17b-1)

history   A record of links visited while navigating the Web. A history can be recalled at any time during a search. However, once the browser is closed, that history will no longer be saved. Also called *search history*. (9c-2)

hit   A successful return on a key word search—an occurrence in the database of the specified search terms.

home   *See* homepage.

homepage   The starting page for a Web site. Also called *home*. (19b-4)

hot spot   A location on an Internet page that activates a hypertext link when the mouse is used to click on it. (19a-2)

hot text   A highlighted word or phrase on an Internet page that activates a hypertext link when the mouse is used to click on it. (19a-2)

HTML   Hypertext markup language; the system for embedding codes that tell a Web browser how to display the text. (20b)

HTML editor   A software program designed to help writers insert the appropriate HTML codes into their documents. (20b-1)

HTTP   Hypertext transfer protocol; the system of rules used for linking files in a hypertext format.

hyperlink   *See* link.

hypermedia   Hypertext along with other media, such as audio and video. (19a-2)

hypertext   Web text that is broken down into discrete pieces, which are then connected through electronic links. (19a-2)

identifier   *See* key word.

image source tag   HTML code inserted in a Web document to tell the browser where to locate a particular graphical image. (20b-5)

imagemap   A Web image with hot spots that activate hypertext links. Clicking on different sections of the image takes the user to different Web locations.

Internet   A worldwide network of computers. (9b)

Internet directory   An index of Internet sites, catalogued by subject.

invisible writing   Freewriting on the computer without seeing the results on the screen. The purpose is to avoid the interruptions in thought that often result from the writer's seeing errors in his or her typing. (3b-3)

IP   Internet protocol; the system of rules that determines how information travels on the Internet.

IRC   Internet relay chat; a location on the Internet where users can have real-time conversations with each other. (21a-3)

itemized list   A device for setting apart the individual elements in a set. This formatting tool is useful for drawing attention to details in a text. (17b-2)

Java   An object-oriented programming language used for special applications on Web pages.

JPEG   Joint photographic experts group; a method used to compress graphic images for use on the Web.

key word   A word used to identify the subject one is searching for in an electronic database. Also called *descriptor* or *identifier*. (8e-2)

key word search   A computer search that locates descriptors, or identifiers, specified by the user. (8e-2, 9c-1, 22c, 23a)

kilobyte   Loosely, 1,000 bytes; precisely, 1,024 bytes.

LAN   Local area network; a network linking computers in a specific geographic area, such as a building or a campus.

launch   To start up a software program.

left-justify   To begin lines of text at the left margin, leaving the right margin ragged. (17b-4)

lettered list   An itemized list that uses ordered letters to suggest either a ranking of items or a step-by-step procedure. (17b-2)

link   (*v*) To connect pieces of information in a hypertext. (*n*) A connection that allows readers to get from one location to another within a Web document or to move from one Web document to another by clicking on a hot spot. Also called a *hyperlink*. (19b-4, 20b-3). *See also* relative link, remote link.

linked graphic   An image that activates a hypertext link when the mouse is used to click on it.

listserv   Widely used email software that creates a mailing list of subscribers and then distributes messages to all the subscribers simultaneously; the email discussion list itself. (21a-1)

load   To place a particular piece of software on a computer and prepare it for use.

login name   A name that identifies the user to a computer system or network. Also called *alias, user ID, user name*. (21b-1)

lurk   To read messages posted on a listserv or newsgroup without posting messages oneself. (21a-1)

lurker   One who lurks.

mail client   Email program. (21b)

mailing list   A collection of email addresses of subscribers, to whom messages are sent simultaneously. (21a-1)

megabyte   Loosely, 1,000,000 bytes; precisely, 1,048,576 bytes (1,024 kilobytes).

modem   A device that allows a computer to be connected to other computers or to the Internet via a phone line. (21a)

moderated group   An email discussion group or newsgroup with a moderator, who screens messages for appropriateness. (21a-1)

moderator   An individual who screens email or newsgroup messages. (21a-1)

MOO   MUD, object-oriented; a special version of a MUD that allows for text-based descriptions and manipulations of objects. In a

MOO, for example, a participant may virtually sit on a virtual chair. (21a-3)

MUD Multiple-user dimension; a text-based Internet space where multiple users can talk to each other, play games, and otherwise interact electronically. (21a-3)

multimedia The combination of two or more media, such as sound, graphics, and video. (19a-1)

navigational button Graphical icon at a Web site that, when clicked on, will take visitors in a particular direction or to a particular location. (19b-4)

Net, the *See* Internet.

netiquette The customs of polite behavior recognized in Internet forums. (21b-3)

network Two or more computers that are connected and can share resources and programs. (Chapter 21)

newbie A colloquial expression used to describe a newcomer to an Internet forum.

news host An Internet server that stores and distributes newsgroup messages. Also called a *news server.*

news server *See* news host.

newsgroup An Internet discussion forum centered on a particular topic or interest group. (21a-2)

newspaper column A way of clustering information in which the text is continuous, flowing down the first column and then continuing at the top of the next column to the right. (17b-6)

newsreader client Software that allows users to read and to post messages to newsgroups.

nickname The persona chosen by a user when logging on to an IRC channel.

node A single unit of a hypertext—a text document, graphic, sound file, or anything else linked in a hypertext; a component of a network to which data can be sent.

numbered list An itemized list that uses ordered numbers to suggest either a ranking of items or a step-by-step procedure. (17b-2)

online Having access to the Internet.

OS Operating system; the software that controls how a computer operates. Common operating systems include DOS, Windows 98, and MacOS.

page *See* Web page.

password A sequence of characters a user must enter in order to access certain accounts or information. It protects against unauthorized use. A random combination of letters and numbers is generally considered to be the most secure password.

platform   An inclusive term encompassing the operating system, hardware, and software that a computer is designed to use. For example, some computers use DOS platforms, whereas others use Mac platforms.

plug-in   An extension to a Web browser that allows the browser to display files created with other applications.

port   A physical socket on the back of the computer; the port number in many MOO addresses.

post   (*v*) To send a message to a mailing list or newsgroup. (*n*) The message that has been sent to such a mailing list or newsgroup.

query   A question composed of key words and posted to an Internet search engine.

real-time communication   Correspondence or communication in which there is no delay between when the sender transmits the message and when the recipient listens to or reads it. Also called *synchronous communication*. (21a-3)

relative link   In HTML, a connection to another Web page on the same site or another section of the same page. Unlike an absolute link, it will not be broken when a document is moved from one server or directory to another. (19b-4, Chapter 20)

remote link   A connection that allows readers to get to other Web sites on the Internet by clicking on a hot spot. (Chapter 20)

script   A complete segment of code, written in computer programming language, that can be inserted as a whole in other programs.

search engine   A program that searches the Internet for occurrences of key words. (9c-1)

search history   *See* history.

server   The hardware and software used to store and run files and to share information with network clients.

shareware   Software written and distributed with the expectation that payments will be made on the honor system.

signature   Information automatically appended to the end of each email message telling something about the message's sender.

site   The location of a server on the Internet. *See also* Web site.

software   Programs that direct the operations of a computer.

source code   The combination of HTML tags and text that tells a Web browser what to display on the screen. Also called *document source*. (20b)

spam   (*v*) To post unsolicited messages and advertisements to a large number of users or newsgroups at once. (*n*) Electronic junk mail.

spell checker   Software that checks for correct spelling and suggests alternatives. (44a)

style/grammar checker   Software that verifies some aspects of the writer's grammar and indicates areas where revisions might be needed. (Chapter 24, 39a)

subject tree   A topical, hierarchical structure that many search engines use to search by subject on the Internet. (9c-1)

surfing the Net   Browsing through various Web sites found on the Internet. (3d-3)

synchronous communication   *See* real-time communication.

table   A cellular layout that allows authors of Web pages to present information in rows and columns. (17c-1, 20b-8)

tabular columns   A way of clustering information in which independent cells of text are placed side by side. Tabular columns are useful for presenting data. (17b-6)

tag   A basic HTML code that tells the browser something about how to format a Web page. (20b-2). *See also* appearance tag, document tag.

TCP/IP   Transmission control protocol/Internet protocol; the standard network communications protocol (system of rules) used to connect computers across the Internet.

telnet   A protocol (system of rules) for connecting to another computer and accessing information from that computer.

template   In word-processing programs, a preformatted file used as a model for other, similar files. (Chapter 18, 20b-9, 39b)

thread   The collection of an initial posting to a newsgroup or listserv and all its accompanying responses.

typography   All the design features associated with individual letters, numbers, and other symbols. (17b-7)

UNIX   The most common operating system for servers on the Internet.

URL   Uniform resource locator; the unique Internet address of a document on the World Wide Web. (Chapter 20)

Usenet   A collection of public newsgroups. Many colleges and universities subscribe to Usenet in order to provide students and faculty with access to newsgroups. (21a-2)

user ID   *See* login name.

user name   *See* login name.

virus   Damaging code, within a program, that can be transferred between computers and then can destroy data. Virus-protection software, designed to identify and delete problem viruses, is widely available.

WAN   Wide area network; any network that extends beyond a single building or campus.

Web, the   *See* World Wide Web.

Web page   A single document, of any length, on a Web site. (19b-4)

Web site   A location on the World Wide Web where someone has published a hypertext document. *See also* site.

window   The view of a document on a computer screen. Several windows can be open simultaneously. (4a-2)

word processing   Using a computer to type and format written documents. (1b-1)

World Wide Web (WWW)   Internet medium through which hypertexts can be posted and read by users around the world. Also called *the Web*. (9b)

WYSIWYG   What You See Is What You Get. It describes software that shows exactly what something will look like, without embedded codes. Most word-processing programs are WYSIWYG—that is, the underlying word-processing codes are not visible unless the user specifically selects VIEW CODES.

Glossary of Grammatical and Rhetorical Terms

absolute phrase   A subject and an adjective phrase (often a participial phrase) used to modify an entire clause—for example, *"Her curiosity satisfied,* she left the meeting." (24c-2)

abstract   A concise synopsis (usually 100–150 words) of a report. (22d-3)

abstract noun   A word that names an idea, emotion, quality, or other intangible concept—for example, *beauty, passion, despair.* (24a-1, 40a-2)

acronym   A pronounceable word formed from the first letters of a multi-word name and usually written in uppercase letters—for example, *UNESCO, ASCII, RAM.* (53d)

active voice   The form a transitive verb takes to indicate that the subject is performing the action on the direct object. Also called the *active form.* (24a-2, 26g)

adjective   A word that modifies a noun by qualifying or describing it—for example, *new, interesting.* (24a-3, Chapter 28). *See also specific types of adjectives.*

adjective clause   A dependent clause, usually introduced by a relative pronoun, that modifies a noun or pronoun. Also called a *relative clause.* (24c-3)

adverb   A word that modifies a verb, adjective, clause, sentence, or other adverb—for example, *quickly, well.* (24a-5, Chapter 28, 57c, 57d, 57e, 57f). *See also specific types of adverbs.*

adverb clause   A dependent clause that begins with a subordinating conjunction and answers the question when, where, how, or why. (24c-3)

agreement   The grammatical requirement that a verb and its subject have the same number (either plural or singular) and that a pronoun and its antecedent have the same number and gender. (Chapter 27)

analogy   A simile that extends beyond one sentence. (40g-2)

analytical writing   Writing that examines the whole of a work in relationship to its component parts. (14a-2)

annotating   Making summary notes in the margin, as well as underlining or highlighting important words and passages. (2a-2)

antecedent   The noun that precedes and is replaced by a pronoun. For example, in the sentence "David is proud of himself," *David* is the antecedent of *himself*. A pronoun should agree in number and gender with its antecedent. (24a-2, 27b, 31a)

antonyms   Two words having opposite meanings—for example, *love* and *hate*. (42c-3)

appositive   A special type of pronoun-noun pairing in which a pronoun is conjoined with a noun—for example, *we students*. Also, a noun that is placed next to the subject to give it extra characterization. *See also* appositive phrase. (25c)

appositive phrase   A noun phrase, placed next to another noun, that describes or defines the other noun and is usually set off by commas—for example, "Ken Griffey, Jr., *my favorite baseball player,* may someday break the home run record." Also called an *appositive*. (24c-2, 25c)

article   A word that precedes a noun and indicates definiteness or indefiniteness. Standard Edited English has three articles: *a, an, the*. (24a-1, Chapter 55)

aspect   *See* verbal aspect.

attributive possessive pronoun   A possessive pronoun used directly before a noun. (25e)

auxiliary verb   A verb, such as *has, be,* or *do,* that combines with a main verb to form a simple predicate—for example, "The guests *have* left." Also called a *helping verb*. (24a-4, 26c)

base form   The main form of a verb, given as the headword in the dictionary—for example, *run, ask, consider*. Also called *simple form*. (26a)

brainstorming   Generating random ideas or fragments of thought about a topic. (3b-1)

case   The form a pronoun takes to indicate its grammatical relation to other words in the sentence. (Chapter 25). *See also* objective case, possessive case, subjective case.

clause   A group of words that has a subject and a predicate. (24c-3). *See also specific types of clauses.*

cliché   An overused expression—for example, *sick and tired, climbing the ladder of success*. (40g-3)

clustering   A prewriting technique that helps a writer to see relationships among ideas. (3b-4, 17a-1)

cognates   Two words, from different languages, that are similar in form and meaning—for example, the English *disaster* and the Spanish *desastre*. (58a)

collective noun   A singular word that names a group—for example, *team, band, trio*. (24a-1)

collocation The relationship between two or more words that frequently occur together—for example, *write* and *check*. (42c-1, 58b)

comma splice Two independent clauses joined only by a comma. Comma splices are not acceptable in formal English. (Chapter 30)

common noun A word that names one or more persons, places, things, concepts, or qualities as a general category—for example, *flowers, telephone, determination*. Common nouns are lowercased. (24a-1)

complement *See* object complement, subject complement, verb complement.

complete predicate The simple predicate plus any objects, complements, or adverbial modifiers. (24b-2)

complete subject The simple subject of a sentence, plus all modifiers. (24b-1)

complex compound A word made up of three or more words. (54b)

complex sentence A sentence that has a single independent clause and one or more dependent clauses. (24d-2)

complex series A series in which individual items contain internal commas, necessitating the use of semicolons to separate the items. (47c)

compound A word made up of two smaller words. (54a)

compound antecedent A noun phrase consisting of two or more terms joined by *and*—for example, *Kim and her brother*. It is usually considered plural; therefore, if it is referred to later by a pronoun, the pronoun should be plural. (27b)

compound-complex sentence A sentence that has two or more independent clauses and one or more dependent clauses. (24d-2)

compound predicate A predicate containing two or more verbs with the same subject. (24b-2)

compound sentence A sentence that has two or more independent clauses and no dependent clauses. (24d-2)

compound subject A sentence subject consisting of two or more simple subjects. (24b-1)

concrete noun A word that names something that can be touched, seen, heard, smelled, or tasted—for example, *automobile, music, cloud*. (24a-1, 40a-2)

conjunction A word that joins two sentences, clauses, phrases, or words—for example, *and, or, but*. (24a-7). *See also specific types of conjunctions.*

conjunctive adverb An adverb that modifies an entire sentence or clause while linking it to the preceding sentence or clause—for example, *however, therefore*. (24a-5, 35b, 46f)

connotation Extra meaning that a word has, beyond its basic meaning. (40b, 42b)

contraction A reduced form of a word or pair of words—for example, *can't* for *cannot, I'll* for *I will*. (40c-2)

coordinate adjectives   A series of adjectives, separated by commas, that could be arranged in any order—for example, a *rusty, dented, broken-down* car. (46d)

coordinating conjunction   A conjunction used to connect sentences, clauses, phrases, or words that are parallel in meaning—for example, *and, but, or, nor, yet.* (24a-7, 35b)

coordination   The pairing of equivalent sentences or sentence elements by putting them in the same grammatical form and linking them via a coordinating conjunction, conjunctive adverb, or semicolon. (35b)

correlative conjunctions   Conjunctions that are used in pairs—for example, *both/and, either/or, neither/nor.* The two elements connected by such conjunctions should be in parallel grammatical form. (24a-7, 36c)

count noun   A word that names something that can be counted and pluralized—for example, a *book,* some *friends,* three *dollars.* (24a-1, 55a)

cumulative adjectives   A series of adjectives, each one modifying those following it—for example, *a small new Italian luxury* car. These adjectives must follow a certain order, and commas are not used to separate them. (46i-3, 46j)

dangling modifier   An introductory verbal phrase that does not refer to the subject of the sentence. Dangling modifiers are unacceptable in formal English. (32e)

debating   A prewriting technique that helps writers to examine arguments for and against a controversial issue. (3b-5)

declarative sentence   A sentence that makes a statement about something. In most writing, declarative sentences predominate. (24d-1)

deductive arrangement   A pattern in which the writer states the main claim for an argument near the beginning of the work. This pattern is appropriately used with a supportive audience. (7f-5)

demonstrative adjective   An adjective that singles out a specific noun—for example, *this* book, *those* promises. (24a-3, 28a)

demonstrative pronoun   A pronoun that points to its antecedent noun—for example, *this, those.* (24a-2)

denotation   The basic dictionary meaning of a word. Compare with *connotation.* (40a, 42b)

dependent clause   A clause that cannot stand alone as a sentence but must be attached to a main clause. A dependent clause typically begins with a subordinating conjunction or relative pronoun. The three types of dependent clauses are adjective, adverb, and noun clauses. Also called a *subordinate clause.* (24c-2, 29b, 35c)

dialect   Speech that is identified with a particular social, ethnic, or regional group. (40d)

diction   A writer's choice of words. (Chapter 40)

direct discourse   Language that is taken word for word from another source and is enclosed in quotation marks. (33f)

direct object   A noun, pronoun, or noun phrase that completes the action of the verb in an active sentence—for example, "Our neighbor plays *the piano.*" (24b-2)

disjunctive antecedent   A noun phrase consisting of two or more terms joined by *or* or *nor*—for example, *the wife or the husband.* If the disjunctive antecedent is referred to later by a pronoun, the pronoun should agree in number with the last term in the phrase. (27b)

disjunctive subject   A sentence subject consisting of two nouns or pronouns joined by *or* or *nor.* (27a)

double negative   Sentence or phrase containing two negative modifiers that carry the same meaning. (28f)

ellipsis   Three spaced periods marking the omission of a word or phrase. (11b-2, 51k, 51l)

end-weight   The emphasis that falls naturally on the words located at the end of a clause or sentence. (37a)

etymology   Information about a word's historical development. (43b-5)

exclamatory sentence   A sentence that expresses strong emotion and is punctuated with an exclamation point. (24d-1)

exemplification   The use of examples to make difficult concepts understandable. (6b-7)

expletive   An introductory word (*it*, *there*) that opens a sentence but carries little meaning. Expletives are sometimes overused. (24a-9, 34c)

false cognates   Two words, from different languages, that resemble each other but have different meanings—for example, the Spanish *compromiso* and the English *compromise.* Also called *false friends.* (58a)

false friends   *See* false cognates.

faulty predication   An ungrammatical sentence in which the subject and the predicate are not consistent with each other. (33e)

figure of speech   A figurative, or nonliteral, use of language such as a metaphor or simile. (40g)

fragment   *See* sentence fragment.

freewriting   Writing down thoughts in connected sentences as they come to mind. (3b-2)

functional classification   Categorization of a sentence according to the function it performs. Also called *rhetorical classification.* (24d-1). *See also* declarative sentence, exclamatory sentence, imperative sentence, interrogative sentence.

functional résumé   A résumé in which certain skills are emphasized through the use of categories such as "Computer Skills" and "Language Skills." (22c)

fused sentence   *See* run-on sentence.

future perfect progressive tense   A verb tense formed by combining *will have been* and the *-ing* form of the main verb. It emphasizes the continuous or repetitive nature of the action—for example, "Next month, my father *will have been teaching* for 30 years." (26d-3)

future perfect tense   A verb tense formed by combining *will have* and the past participle of the main verb. It describes an action that will occur in the future but before some specified time—for example, "Soon I *will have completed* all the requirements." (26d-3)

future progressive tense   A verb tense formed by combining *will be* and the *-ing* form of the main verb. It expresses action that will be continuing or repeated in the future—for example, "My daughter is on vacation now, but she *will be going* back to school in the fall." (26d-3)

future tense   A verb tense formed by combining the modal auxiliary *will* and the base form of the main verb. It expresses actions or conditions that will occur in the future—for example, "The final exam *will be* hard." Also called *simple future tense*. (26d-3)

gender   Classification of a noun or pronoun as masculine, feminine, or neuter. (27b)

generic pronoun   A pronoun used to refer to all people regardless of gender. (41a-2)

gerund   A verb form that ends in *ing* and functions as a noun—for example, "My favorite sports are *skiing* and tennis." (24a-8)

gerund phrase   A phrase consisting of a gerund and any modifiers, objects, and/or complements—for example, "*Running a business* can be difficult." (24c-2)

head noun   The rightmost noun in a noun compound. (57b)

helping verb   *See* auxiliary verb.

homophones   Words that sound alike but are spelled differently and have different meanings—for example, *brake* and *break*. (44b)

idiom   *See* idiomatic expression.

idiomatic expression   A phrase whose meaning differs from that of its individual words—for example, *kick the bucket*. Also called an *idiom*. (40c-2, 58c)

imperative mood   A grammatical form of a verb used to express a command or a strong request and give instructions. Imperative sentences are always addressed to an understood subject *you*, which is usually omitted. (24a-4, 26h, 33b)

imperative sentence   A sentence that expresses a command, a request, or a suggestion, usually with an understood subject *you*—for example, "Don't fret!" "Try using the toolbar buttons." (24d-1)

indefinite adjective   A nonspecific adjective—for example, *some* people. (24a-3, 28a)

indefinite pronoun   A pronoun that refers to one or more nonspecific persons, places, or things and does not require an antecedent—for example, *anybody, anything*. (24a-2)

independent clause   A group of words that includes a subject and predicate and can stand alone as a sentence. Also called a *main clause*. (24c-3)

indicative mood A grammatical form of a verb used to make assertions, state opinions, and ask questions. (24a-4, 26h, 33b)

indirect discourse A summarization, restatement, or paraphrase of a statement made by someone else. (33f, 50b-1)

indirect object A noun, pronoun, or noun phrase that is indirectly affected by the action of the verb—for example, "My boyfriend gave *me* a present." (24b-2)

inductive arrangement A pattern in which the writer states the main claim for an argument late in the work, in order to first present a skeptical audience with supporting evidence. (7f-5)

infinitive The base form of a verb preceded by *to*. It can function as a noun, adjective, or adverb. (24a-8). *See also* perfect infinitive, present infinitive.

infinitive phrase A phrase consisting of an infinitive and any modifiers, objects, and/or complements—for example, "Kevin said he wanted *to make his own way.*" (24c-2)

initialism An unpronounceable abbreviation formed from the first letters of a multiword name and usually written in uppercase letters—for example, *FBI, CPU.* (53d)

inseparable verb A transitive phrasal verb whose particle must be kept together with the verb—for example, "I quickly *went over* my paper." Compare with *separable verb.* (56a)

intensive pronoun A pronoun that consists of a personal pronoun plus *-self* or *-selves* and is used for emphasis—for example, "They did it *themselves.*" (24a-2)

interpretive writing Writing that discusses another person's intended meaning or the impact of a work on an audience. (14a-2)

interrogative adjective An adjective that raises a question about a noun—for example, "*Which* way do I go?" "*Whose* hat is this?" (24a-3, 28a)

interrogative pronoun A pronoun that introduces a question—for example, *who, what, whose.* (24a-2, 25d)

interrogative sentence A sentence that raises a question and is punctuated with a question mark. (24d-1)

intransitive verb A verb that does not take a direct object—for example, "My driver's license *has expired.*" (24a-4, 26f, Chapter 56)

irregular verb A verb whose past tense and past participle are not formed through the standard pattern of adding *d* or *ed* to the base form—for example, *run (ran, run); know (knew, known).* (24a-4, 26b)

jargon Specialized, technical language used by a professional or special interest group. (40d)

linking verb A verb that joins a sentence subject to a subject complement, indicating a condition, quality, or state of being—for example, "They *will be* late."

literary genre Type of literature, such as poetry, fiction, or drama. (14a-1)

main clause   *See* independent clause.

mass noun   *See* noncount noun.

metaphor   A figure of speech in which the writer describes something in a way normally reserved for something else, thus presenting it in a new light. (40g-2)

mixed construction   An ungrammatical sentence that starts out one way but finishes in another. (33d)

mixed metaphors   Two different metaphors put close together in a piece of writing—for example, "Milwaukee is the golden egg that the rest of the state wants to milk." Mixed metaphors should be avoided. (40g-2)

modal auxiliary verb   A special type of verb that indicates necessity, probability, or permission—for example, *may, might, should, can*. Also called a *modal verb*. (24a-4, 26c, 56g, 56h). *See also* auxiliary verb.

modal verb   *See* modal auxiliary verb.

modifier   A word, phrase, or clause that adds detail to another word, phrase, or clause. (24c, Chapter 32). *See also* dangling modifier, split infinitive.

mood   Classification of a verb according to the type of statement made—indicative, imperative, or subjunctive. (24a-4, 26h, 33b)

narrative   A type of writing that tells a story in a time-ordered sequence. (6b-6)

nominal possessive pronoun   A possessive pronoun that is used with a linking verb—for example, "This book is *yours*." (25e)

nominalization   A noun derived from a verb—for example, *removal* (derived from *remove*) and *fascination* (derived from *fascinate*). The frequent use of nominalizations results in a noun-heavy style. (34f)

noncount noun   A word that names something that typically is not counted or pluralized—for example, *milk, generosity, rain*. Also called a *mass noun*. (24a-1, 55a)

nonessential element   *See* nonrestrictive element.

nonrestrictive element   A phrase or clause that provides extra information in a sentence. A nonrestrictive element can be omitted without changing the basic meaning of the sentence; it is set off with commas, dashes, or parentheses. Also called a *nonessential element*. (46e)

noun   A word that names a person, place, thing, quality, idea, or action. (24a-1). *See also specific types of nouns.*

noun clause   A dependent clause that begins with a relative pronoun and functions as a sentence subject, object, complement, or appositive. (24c-3)

noun compound   A sequence of two or more nouns, with the rightmost noun being the head noun and the other noun(s) serving to modify it—for example, *income tax form*. (28b, 57b)

number   Classification of a noun, pronoun, or verb as singular or plural. (27b, 33a)

object   *See* direct object, indirect object, object of the preposition.

object complement A noun, noun phrase, adjective, or adjective phrase that elaborates on or describes the direct object of a sentence—for example, "The film made me *angry.*" (24b-2)

object of the preposition A noun or pronoun in a prepositional phrase—for example, "He was on the *boat.*"(24a-6)

objective case The form a pronoun takes when it is used as a grammatical object. (Chapter 25)

paragraph A sentence or group of sentences, presented in a text as a unit, that develops a main idea. (Chapter 6)

parallel form *See* parallelism.

parallel structure *See* parallelism.

parallelism The use of similar grammatical form for words or phrases that have a coordinate relationship. Also called *parallel structure* or *parallel form*. (6e, Chapter 36)

participial phrase A phrase consisting of a present or past participle plus any objects, modifiers, and/or complements—for example, "I saw someone *running down the street.*" (24c-2)

participle A verb form that can serve as an adjective—for example, *earned* income or *earning* power. (24a-8). *See also* past participle, present participle, present perfect participle.

particle A preposition or adverb that, when attached to a verb, creates a phrasal verb—for example, look *into*, see *through*, knock *out*. (24a-6)

parts of speech The different categories in which words can be classified according to their grammatical function: nouns, verbs, adjectives, adverbs, pronouns, prepositions, conjunctions, verbals, and expletives. (24a)

passive voice The form a transitive verb takes to indicate that the subject is being acted upon. Also called the *passive form*. (24a-4, 26g)

past participle A verb form that can be used by itself as an adjective or can be combined with some form of the auxiliary *have* to form perfect tenses or with some form of the verb *be* to create passive-voice sentences. With regular verbs, it is similar in form to the past tense—for example, *picked, opened*. (24a-8, 26a, 26e-4)

past perfect progressive tense A verb tense formed by combining *had been* and the present participle of the main verb. It puts emphasis on the continuing or repetitive nature of a past action—for example, "By the time he crossed the bridge, Roy *had been running* for two hours." (26d-2)

past perfect tense A verb tense created by combining *had* and the past participle of the main verb. It is used to describe a past action that preceded another past activity—for example, "Before she injured her knee, Beth *had hoped* to become a top ski racer." (26d-2)

past progressive tense A verb tense formed by combining the auxiliary verb *was* or *were* and the present participle of the main verb—for example, "I *was* just *starting* to cook when our guest arrived." (26d-2)

past tense A verb tense that indicates past action—for example, "World War I *started* in 1914." With regular verbs, the past tense is formed by adding *d* or *ed* to the base form. Also called *simple past tense*. (26a, 26d-2)

perfect infinitive A verb form consisting of *to have* plus the past participle of the verb—for example, *to have changed, to have stopped*. It is used for an action that occurs prior to the action expressed by the main verb. (26e-3)

person Classification of a pronoun based on whether it refers to the speaker (first person: *I, me, us*), the person spoken to (second person: *you*), or someone or something spoken about (third person: *she, him, it, they*). (33a)

persona A writer's presentation of himself or herself through a piece of writing. (3a-2, 19b-2)

personal pronoun A pronoun that refers to one or more specific persons, places, or things—for example, *she, it, they*. (24a-2)

personification A type of metaphor in which an inanimate object or abstraction is described as having human traits. (40g-2)

phrasal verb A verb consisting of a verb and one or two particles—for example, *pick over, look into, get away with*. Also called a *two-word verb* or *three-word verb*. (24a-6, 56a)

phrase A group of related words that does not have both a subject and a complete predicate (compare with *clause*). Phrases can function as nouns, verbs, or modifiers. (24c-2). *See also specific types of phrases*.

plagiarism Unauthorized or misleading use of the language and thoughts of another author. (11a-3)

possessive adjective An adjective that indicates possession—for example, *my* coat, *their* country. (24a-3, 28a)

possessive case The form a pronoun takes when it is used as a grammatical possessive. (Chapter 25)

predicate The part of a sentence that contains the verb and makes a statement about the subject. (24b-2)

predicate adjective An adjective that follows a linking verb and refers back to the noun subject. (24a-3)

predicate nominative *See* predicate noun.

predicate noun A noun serving as subject or object complement. Also called a *predicate nominative*.

prefix A word part, such as *anti-, re-*, or *dis-*, that is attached to the beginning of a word—for example, *anti*freeze, *re*new, *dis*cover. (42a, 44d-1)

preposition A word that indicates a relationship between a noun or pronoun and some other part of the sentence—for example, *to, in, at, from, on*. Also called a *particle* in phrasal verbs. (24a-6)

prepositional phrase A group of words consisting of a preposition plus a noun or pronoun and its modifiers. (24a-6, 24c-2)

present infinitive A verb form consisting of *to* plus the base form of the verb—for example, *to go, to hesitate*. It is used for an action that occurs at the same time as or later than the action expressed by the main verb. (26e-3)

present participle   A verb form created by adding *ing* to the base form—for example, *sewing, writing*. It can be used by itself as an adjective or noun or can be combined with some form of the verb *be* to form the progressive tenses. (24a-8, 26a, 26e-4)

present perfect participle   A verb form consisting of *having* plus the past participle of the verb. It is used to express an action occurring prior to the action of the main verb—for example, *"Having changed* my PIN number, I cannot remember it."* (26e-4)

present perfect progressive tense   A verb tense formed by combining *have been* or *has been* and the present participle of the main verb. It typically emphasizes the ongoing nature of the activity—for example, "People *have been complaining* about the working conditions for years." (26d-1)

present perfect tense   A verb tense formed by combining the auxiliary verb *have* or *has* and the past participle of the main verb. It is used to indicate action that began in the past and either is continuing or has continuing effects in the present—for example, "The United Nations *has served* many purposes." (26d-1)

present progressive tense   A verb tense formed by combining the auxiliary verb *am, is,* or *are* and the *-ing* form of a main verb. It is typically used to indicate present action—for example, "Mike *is taking* a heavy load of classes this term." (26d-1)

present tense   The verb tense used to express a general statement, make an observation, or describe an habitual activity—for example, "Geese *fly* south in autumn." Also called *simple present tense*. (26a, 26d-1)

primary research   Generating information or data through processes such as interviewing, administering questionnaires, and observing. (8a-1, 8f-6)

principal parts   The major forms of a verb: base form, present tense, past tense, past participle, and present participle. (26a)

process description   A type of writing that depicts a step-by-step procedure. (6b-6)

pronoun   A word that substitutes for a noun and always refers to a noun. (24a-2, 27b). *See also specific types of pronouns.*

proper noun   A word that names a particular person, place, institution, organization, month, or day—for example, *Anne, New York City, Monday.* Proper nouns are almost always capitalized. (24a-1)

reciprocal pronoun   A pronoun that refers to the separate parts of a plural antecedent—for example, "They made promises to *one another.*" (24a-2)

redundancy   The use of words that could be left out without changing the meaning of a sentence. (34b)

reflexive pronoun　A pronoun that consists of a personal pronoun plus *-self* or *-selves*. It refers back to the subject to show that the subject is the object of an action—for example, "Katy cut *herself.*" (24a-2)

register　The overall degree of formality of a piece of writing, including its identification with a particular field or community of users. (40c)

regular verb　A verb that forms the third-person singular present tense by adding *s* or *es* to the base form, forms the present participle by adding *ing* to the base form, and forms the past tense and past participle by adding *d* or *ed* to the base form. (24a-4, 26a)

related words　Words derived from the same root. (43b-5)

relative clause　*See* adjective clause.

relative pronoun　A pronoun that introduces a dependent clause—for example, *that, which, whom.* (24a-2, 25d)

restrictive element　Information essential to the precise meaning of a sentence and thus not set off with commas. Compare with *nonrestrictive element.* (46j)

résumé　A concise summary of an individual's accomplishments, skills, experience, and personal interests. (22c). *See also* functional résumé.

rhetorical classification　*See* functional classification.

rhetorical stance　A writer's approach to his or her topic, encompassing purpose, persona, and audience. (3a-2)

root　The main part of a word, to which prefixes and suffixes can be attached—for example, the root of *telephonic* is *phon. Also called a *stem.* (42a)

run-on sentence　Two independent clauses fused together without any intervening conjunction or punctuation. Run-on sentences are not acceptable in formal English. Also called a *fused sentence.* (Chapter 30)

secondary research　Finding information in secondary, or previously published, sources. (8a-1)

sense　The meaning of a word. (43b-4)

sentence　The basic unit of written language for expressing a thought. All sentences except commands have a stated grammatical subject and a predicate. (24b). *See also specific types of sentences.*

sentence fragment　A grammatically incomplete sentence. (Chapter 29)

sentence subject　*See* subject.

separable verb　A transitive phrasal verb whose particle may be placed after the object of the verb—for example, "I quickly *looked* my paper *over.*" Compare with *inseparable verb.* (56a)

sequence of tenses　The time relationship among verbs in a block of text, expressed by verb tenses. (26e)

serial comma　In a series of items, the comma that separates the items. (46c)

simile　A figure of speech in which the writer uses one thing to describe another. Similes typically employ the word *like* or *as*—for example, "The brain is somewhat like a computer." (40g-1)

simple form　*See* base form.

simple future tense   *See* future tense.

simple past tense   *See* past tense.

simple predicate   A main verb plus any auxiliary verbs. Also called a *verb phrase*. (24b-2). *See also* predicate.

simple present tense   *See* present tense.

simple sentence   A sentence that has a single independent clause and no dependent clauses. (24d-1)

simple subject   The noun or pronoun that constitutes the heart of a sentence subject. (24b-1)

slang   Nonstandard language characterized by short-lived, colorful expressions. It is most commonly used by teenagers and tight-knit subcultures. (40d)

split infinitive   A *to* infinitive with one or more words between *to* and the verb—for example, *to quickly retreat*. (32d-2)

stative verb   *See* verb of state.

stem   *See* root.

structural classification   Categorization of a sentence according to its overall grammatical construction. *See also* complex sentence, compound sentence, compound-complex sentence, simple sentence. (24d-2)

subject   A noun, pronoun, or noun phrase that indicates what a sentence is about and typically precedes the main verb of the sentence. (24b-1, 33b). *See also specific types of subjects.*

subject complement   A noun, noun phrase, adjective, or adjective phrase that elaborates on the subject of a sentence and usually follows a linking verb—for example, "Joanne was elected *student body president.*"

subjective case   The form a pronoun takes when it is used as a grammatical subject. (Chapter 25)

subjunctive mood   A grammatical form of a verb used to express hypothetical conditions, wishes, and other uncertain statements. Verbs in subjunctive mood often appear in dependent clauses beginning with *if* or *that*. (24a-4, 26h, 33b)

subordinate clause   *See* dependent clause.

subordinating conjunction   A conjunction that is used to introduce a dependent clause and connect it to an independent clause—for example, *although, because, if, since*. (24a-7)

subordination   In a sentence containing two ideas that are not equal in importance, making the lesser idea into a subordinate, or dependent, clause. (35c)

suffix   A word part, such as *-ful, -ship,* or *-ness,* that is attached to the end of a word—for example, boast*ful,* fellow*ship,* kind*ness.* (42a, 44d-2)

synonyms   Words that are similar in meaning—for example, *desire* and *want.* (42c-2)

tense   *See* verb tense.

theoretical writing   Writing that examines individual works or events to determine how they exemplify broader trends. (14a-3)

thesaurus   A collection of synonyms and antonyms. (43a)

three-word verb   *See* phrasal verb.

topic sentence   A sentence, usually at the beginning of a paragraph, that gives readers an overview of the paragraph. (6a-1)

transitive verb   A verb that acts upon an object—for example, *carry, show*. In the active voice, a transitive verb acts upon the direct object of the sentence. In the passive voice, it acts upon the subject. (24a-4, 26f, Chapter 56)

two-word verb   *See* phrasal verb.

unified paragraph   A paragraph that focuses on and develops a single main idea. (6a)

usage label   In dictionaries, a notation indicating a particular sense of a word—for example, *Informal, Archaic*. (43b-6)

usage note   In dictionaries, an expert judgment about the "correct" use of a word. (43b-6)

verb   A word that expresses action, occurrence, or existence. (24a-4, Chapter 26). *See also specific types of verbs.*

verb complement   A participial or infinitive phrase attached to a verb—for example, in the sentence "I like to swim," *to swim* is the complement of the verb *like*. (56b, 56c, 56d, 56e)

verb of state   A verb that expresses a condition or state, rather than an action or event—for example, *involve, need, consist of*. Verbs of state do not have progressive tense forms. Also called a *stative verb*. (26d-1, 56f)

verb phrase   A main verb plus any auxiliary verbs. Also called a *simple predicate*. (26c)

verb tense   The form a verb takes to indicate the time of the action or the state of being. (26d, 33b)

verbal   A verb form that functions in a sentence as a noun, adverb, or adjective. There are three types of verbals: participles, gerunds, and infinitives. (24a-8, 24c-2)

verbal aspect   The particular form a verb takes, within its tense, to indicate duration or completion of the verb's action or state of being. Standard Edited English has three verbal aspects: perfect, progressive, and perfect progressive. Also called *aspect*. (26d)

voice   The form a transitive verb takes to indicate whether the subject is acting (*active voice*) or being acted upon (*passive voice*). (26g)

warrant   An explanation in the form of a general statement or rule (often unstated) that logically connects the evidence or data a writer is using to the point he or she is making. (7d-2)

Glossary of Usage

a, an Use *a* before words beginning with a consonant sound: *a* program, *a* uniform. Use *an* before words beginning with a vowel sound: *an* open book, *an* uncle.

accept, except *Accept* is a verb meaning "to receive gladly." *Except* is usually a preposition meaning "with the exclusion of." "The restaurant *accepts* any form of payment *except* credit cards."

advice, advise *Advice* is a noun meaning "guidance." *Advise* is a verb meaning "to guide." "I *advised* her to take my *advice.*"

affect, effect Most commonly, *affect* is used as a verb meaning "to influence": "Bad weather seems to *affect* my mood." *Effect* is generally used as a noun meaning "result." As a verb, *effect* means "to bring about": "The new policy will *effect* important changes."

ain't Nonstandard. *Am not, is not, are not,* and *have not* are preferred in Standard Edited English; the contractions *isn't, aren't,* and *haven't* are acceptable in casual discourse.

all ready, already *All ready* is an adjective phrase meaning "all prepared": "They were *all ready* to go." *Already* is an adverb meaning "by this time": "They have *already* left."

allusion, illusion An *allusion* is an indirect reference. An *illusion* is a false perception of reality.

amongst British equivalent of *among.*

an See *a.*

as See *like.*

awful, awfully Avoid using these terms to mean "very," except in informal communication.

bad, badly *Bad* is an adjective: "I feel *bad.*" *Badly* is an adverb: "He plays *badly.*"

because of, due to   Use *because of* when a clause describes the situation to which you are attributing a cause: "She had a headache *because of* stress." Use *due to* when a noun describes the situation to which you are attributing a cause: "Her headache was *due to* stress."

can't hardly, can't scarcely   Nonstandard for *can hardly* or *can scarcely*. "Even accountants *can hardly* make sense of the tax code."

center around   In formal writing, *center on* is preferred. "My paper will *center on* hate speech."

cite, site   *Cite* is a verb meaning "to quote." *Site* is a noun meaning "place."

complement, compliment   To *complement* is to complete so as to make a whole: "The flowers beautifully *complemented* the table setting." To *compliment* is to express praise: "She *complimented* me on my dancing."

conscience, conscious   *Conscience* is a noun meaning "a sense of right and wrong." *Conscious* is an adjective meaning "aware" or "intentional." "Todd made a *conscious* decision to clear his guilty *conscience*."

could of   Nonstandard for *could have*. "He *could have* tried harder."

criterion, criteria   *Criterion* is a singular noun, meaning "standard of judgment." *Criteria* is the plural form.

data   Traditionally, *data* was used only as the plural form of *datum*. However, it is now commonly used as a singular form to mean "numerical information."

different from, different than   In formal writing, use *different from* when the comparison is between two persons or things: "My opinion is *different from* hers." Use *different than* when the object of comparison is a full clause: "The party turned out *different than* I wanted it to be."

discreet, discrete   *Discreet* mean "tactful" or "modest." *Discrete* means "distinct" or "separate."

due to   See *because of*.

effect   See *affect*.

elicit, illicit   *Elicit* is a verb meaning "to call forth." *Illicit* is an adjective meaning "illegal."

emigrate, immigrate, migrate   *Emigrate* means "to move permanently away from." *Immigrate* means "to move permanently to." *Migrate* means "to move temporarily from one place to another."

eminent, immanent, imminent   *Eminent* means "distinguished": "She is an *eminent* scholar." *Immanent* means "inherent": "God's spirit is *immanent* in nature." *Imminent* means "about to occur": "A stock market crash is *imminent*."

except   See *accept*.

farther, further   *Farther* refers to distance: "She hit the ball *farther* than anyone else." *Further* refers to time or degree: "Should we go *further* with our research?"

fewer, less Use *fewer* with items that can be counted. Use *less* with general amounts associated with noncount nouns. "He had *fewer* problems and *less* anxiety than I did."

firstly, secondly, thirdly Common in British English. In American English, *first*, *second*, and *third* are preferred.

further See *farther*.

good, well *Good* is an adjective. *Well* is an adverb. "When I feel *good*, I write *well*."

gorilla, guerrilla A *gorilla* is a large ape. A *guerrilla* is a member of a rebel army.

he/she, him/her, his/her Although these forms can be used to avoid the sexism of the generic *he, him,* or *his,* use them sparingly (see 41a).

heard, herd *Heard* is the past tense of the verb *to hear. Herd* is a group of animals.

hisself Nonstandard for *himself.* "He shot *himself* in the foot."

hole, whole *Hole* is a noun meaning "gap" or "cavity." *Whole* is an adjective meaning "complete" or "entire."

hopefully Technically, *hopefully* may be used as a sentence adverb: "*Hopefully,* the war will soon be over." However, many critics object to this usage because there is no subject to be full of hope. You can replace *hopefully* with *I hope that.*

illicit See *elicit.*

illusion See *allusion.*

immanent See *eminent.*

immigrate See *emigrate.*

imminent See *eminent.*

imply, infer *Imply* means "to suggest indirectly." *Infer* means "to draw a conclusion from what someone else has said." "The owner *implied* that I did not have enough experience; I *inferred* that she would not offer me the job."

incredible, incredulous *Incredible* means "unbelievable": "His performance was *incredible.*" *Incredulous* means "disbelieving": "He was *incredulous* when he heard the news."

infer See *imply.*

irregardless Nonstandard for *regardless.*

its, it's *Its* is the possessive form of *it. It's* is the contracted form of *it is.* "*It's* important that a company give *its* employees a sense of security."

lay, lie *Lay* takes a direct object and means "to place": "They want to *lay* a wreath at his grave." *Lie* does not take a direct object and means "to recline": "I think I'll *lie* down for a while." (Note, however, that *lay* is also the past tense of *lie.*)

lead, led *Led* is the past tense of the verb *to lead:* "Our efforts have *led* to nothing." *Lead,* pronounced the same way as *led,* is a noun referring to a certain type of metal.

leave, let   *Leave* means "to go away": "She plans to *leave* tomorrow." *Let* means "to allow": "*Let* me pay for this."

lend, loan   Both verbs mean "to give something temporarily." But *loan* is used only for physical transactions, such as *loaning money,* while *lend* can be used more figuratively as in *lending someone a hand.*

less   See *fewer.*

lie   See *lay.*

like, as   In formal writing, use *like* as a preposition before a noun phrase: "She looked *like* her mother." Use *as* as a conjunction before a clause: "She looked *as* I thought she would."

loan   See *lend.*

lose, loose   *Lose* is a verb meaning "to fail to keep." *Loose* is an adjective meaning "not fastened."

man, mankind   Avoid these terms in situations where gender-inclusive terms, such as *people, humanity, humans, humankind,* or *men and women,* can be used instead.

migrate   See *emigrate.*

moral, morale   A *moral* is a lesson taught in a story. *Morale* is a state of mind reflecting levels of confidence and cheerfulness.

must of   Nonstandard for *must have.* "They *must have* [not *must of*] lost their way."

okay, OK, O.K.   Informal. In formal writing, use more precise terms like *enjoyable, acceptable,* or *pleasing.*

patience, patients   *Patience* is the quality of being tolerant and steadfast. *Patients* are people who receive medical treatment.

peace, piece   *Peace* is the opposite of war. A *piece* is a segment or part.

personal, personnel   *Personal* is an adjective meaning "private" or "individual." *Personnel* is a noun meaning "the people employed by an organization."

piece   See *peace.*

plain, plane   *Plain* is a noun meaning "flat area of land" or an adjective meaning "obvious," "clear," or "ordinary in appearance." *Plane* is the short form of the noun *airplane.*

presence, presents   *Presence* is the opposite of absence. *Presents* are gifts.

pretty   In formal writing, avoid using *pretty* as an adverb. "JFK was a rather [not *pretty*] good writer."

principal, principle   *Principal* is an adjective meaning "foremost." *Principle* is a noun meaning "rule" or "standard." "Our *principal* concern is to maintain our high *principles.*"

raise, rise   *Raise* is a transitive verb meaning "to lift" or "to build": "He *raises* his hand." *Rise* is an intransitive verb meaning "to stand up" or "to ascend": "She *rises* from her chair."

real, really   *Real* is an adjective; *really* is an adverb. In most cases, both of these terms should be avoided in formal writing. "The economy is doing extremely [not *real* or *really*] well."

respectfully, respectively   *Respectfully* means "with respect." *Respectively* means "in the order given": "The teacher called on Bart and Juana, *respectively*."

rise   See *raise*.

secondly   See *firstly*.

set, sit   *Set* is used most often as a transitive verb meaning "to place" or "to arrange": "*Set* the table." *Sit* is an intransitive verb meaning "to take a seat": "*Sit* down over here."

shall, will   Use *shall* for polite questions in the first person: "*Shall* we sit down?" Otherwise, use *will*.

should of   Nonstandard for *should have*.

sit   See *set*.

site   See *cite*.

stationary, stationery   *Stationary* is an adjective meaning "not moving." *Stationery* is a noun meaning "writing materials."

than, then   *Than* is a conjunction used to introduce the second part of a comparison: "Donna is taller *than* Jo." *Then* is an adverb meaning "at that time."

that, which   As a relative pronoun, *that* is used only in restrictive clauses: "The storm *that* [or *which*] everyone talks about occurred ten years ago." *Which* can be used with either restrictive or nonrestrictive clauses: "The storm of 1989, *which* I will never forget, destroyed part of our roof."

their, there, they're   *Their* is the possessive form of *they*: "They retrieved *their* car." *There* is an adverb of place; it is also used in expletive constructions: "*There* is someone at the door." *They're* is a contraction for *they are*: "*They're* too young to drive."

theirselves   Nonstandard for *themselves*.

then   See *than*.

thirdly   See *firstly*.

threw, through/thru   *Threw* is the past tense of the verb *to throw*. *Through* is a preposition: "Walk *through* the house." Do not use *thru* in formal writing.

till, until, 'til   *Till* and *until* are both acceptable in formal writing; *'til* is informal.

use, utilize   In most cases, *use* is the better choice. *Utilize* should be used specifically to mean "to make practical use of."

weak, week   *Weak* is the opposite of strong. *Week* is a period of seven days.

weather, whether   *Weather* is a noun meaning "atmospheric conditions." *Whether* is a conjunction meaning "if" or "either."

well   See *good.*

which   See *that.*

who, whom   *Who* and *whom* are used as interrogative or relative pronouns (see Chapter 25). *Who* stands for a grammatical subject: "*Who* is calling?" *Whom* stands for a grammatical object: "*Whom* are you calling?"

whole   See *hole.*

who's, whose   *Who's* is a contraction for *who is. Whose* is the possessive form of *who.*

will   See *shall.*

would of   Nonstandard for *would have.*

your, you're   *Your* is the possessive form of *you. You're* is a contraction for *you are.* "*You're* loyal to *your* friends."

Credits

Allyn & Bacon Homepage. 12 Nov. 1997 <http://www.abacon.com>.

American Heritage College Dictionary, The. 3rd ed. Boston: Houghton, 1993. Copyright © 1997 by Houghton Mifflin Company. Reproduced by permission from *The American Heritage College Dictionary, Third Edition.*

American Medical Association Family Medical Guide, The. New York: Random, 1987. 350.

Barlow, John Perry. "Crime and Puzzlement." *CyberReader.* Ed. Victor Vitanza. Boston: Allyn, 1996. 92–115.

Beebe, Steven A., and Susan J. Beebe. *Public Speaking: An Audience-Centered Approach.* Boston: Allyn, 1997.

Bishop, Elizabeth. "One Art." THE COMPLETE POEMS 1927–1979 by Elizabeth Bishop. Copyright © 1979, 1983 by Alice Helen Methfessel. Reprinted by permission of Farrar, Straus & Giroux, Inc.

Briggs, Barrett M. "Resuscitating Trigger." Online posting. Writing Program Administration Listserv. 1 Dec. 1997.

Cassity, Jeri. *Brochure Writing: Examining the Rhetorical Situation.* Logan: Utah State University, 1993. 6–7.

Cole, K. C. *The Scientific Aesthetic.* New York: Discover, 1983. From K. C. Cole/© 1983. Reprinted with permission of Discover Magazine.

Corel® WordPerfect® Suite 8.

Cousins, Norman. *Human Options.* New York: Berkley, 1981. 41–42, 63, 90.

Deja News. 3 Aug. 1997 <http://www.dejanews.com>.

Donatelle, Rebecca J., and Lorraine G. Davis. *Access to Health.* 4th ed. Boston: Allyn, 1996. Copyright © 1996 by Allyn & Bacon. Reprinted by permission.

Ehrlich, Gretel. *The Solace of Open Spaces.* New York: Viking, 1985. 7.

Environmental Periodicals Bibliography. Citation taken from *Environmental Periodicals Bibliography* database (copyright, International Academy at Santa Barbara). This database is available on CD-ROM and on the Internet. Subscription information is available on the Academy's Website at http://www.iasb.org.

Excite [Online]. 5 Nov. 1997 <http://www.excite.com>. Excite and the Excite Logo are trademarks of Excite, Inc. and may be registered in various jurisdictions. Excite screen display copyright 1995–1998 Excite, Inc.

Farb, Peter. *Living Earth.* New York: Harper & Row, 1959.

Garofalo, Reebee. *Rockin' Out: Popular Music in the USA.* Boston: Allyn, 1997. Copyright © 1997 by Allyn & Bacon. Reprinted by permission.

Hacker, Andrew. *Money.* New York: Scribner, 1997. 11. Reprinted with the permission of Scribner, a Division of Simon & Schuster from MONEY by Andrew Hacker. Copyright © 1997 by Andrew Hacker.

Hemingway, Ernest. "Notes on the Next War: A Serious Topical Letter." *By-Line: Ernest Hemingway.* Ed. William White. New York: Scribner's, 1967. 206.

Henslin, James M. *Sociology: A Down-to-Earth Approach.* 3rd ed. Boston: Allyn, 1997. Copyright © 1997 by Allyn & Bacon. Reprinted by permission.

Homesite, Vers. 2.0. Allaire Corporation. 10 March 1998 <http://www.allaire.com/homesite>.

Hopper, Vincent F., and Bernard D. N. Grebanier. *Essentials of European Literature.* Vol. 2. Great Neck, NY: Barron's, 1952.

Hult, C. *HETI Final Report.* 2 Sept. 1997. 7 Oct. 1997 <http://english.usu.edu>.

Hult, C. *Syllabus, Honors 204.* 21 Jan. 1998 <http://english.usu.edu/w98/204 honors>.

Internaut Capt. Jack. "A 'Livable Minimum Wage' Is a Bad Idea." 8 Nov. 1997 <www.mindspring.com/~bumpy1/page4.htm>.

Ivins, Molly. "Truly Happy News to Look For: Better 'Doug Jones' Average," syndicated column, published by Creators Syndicate; appeared in *Salt Lake Tribune,* 2/20/97.

Kaniss, Phyllis. *Making Local News.* Chicago: U of Chicago P, 1991. 88–89.

Kantrowitz, Barbara. "Men, Women, Computers." *Newsweek,* May 16, 1994.

Kingsolver, Barbara. *The Bean Trees.* New York: Harper, 1988. 1.

Lederer, Richard. *Anguished English.* New York: Wyrick, 1987. 115, 150–153. Excerpts from *Anguished English,* copyright 1987 by Richard Lederer. Published by Wyrick & Company.

Lycos [Online]. 7 Oct. 1997 <http://www.lycos.com>. © 1998 Lycos, Inc. Lycos® is a registered trademark of Carnegie Mellon University. All rights reserved.

Martini, Frederic. *Fundamentals of Anatomy and Physiology.* Englewood Cliffs, NJ: Prentice, 1989. 3.

Meyer, Michael, with Anne Underwood. "Crimes of the 'Net.' " *CyberReader.* Ed. Victor Vitanza. Boston: Allyn, 1996. 63–65.

Microsoft Corporation. Screen shots reprinted by permission from Microsoft Corporation.

My Virtual Reference Desk. Ed. B. Drudge. 1985–1998. 10 Jan. 1998 <http://www.refdesk.com>.

Netscape. Copyright Netscape Communications Corporation, 1997. All Rights Reserved. Netscape, Netscape Navigator and the Netscape N logo are registered trademarks of Netscape in the United States and other countries.

New Book of Knowledge, The. New York: Grolier, 1998.

Orwell, George. "Marrakech."*A Collection of Essays.* Garden City, NY: Doubleday, 1957. 186–192.

Readers' Guide to Periodical Literature, February 1997. Reprinted with permission by H. W. Wilson Company.

Rifkin, Jeremy. *The End of Work.* New York: Putnam, 1995.

Sagan, Carl. *The Dragons of Eden.* New York: Ballantine, 1977. 177.

Salt Lake Community College's Virtual Writing Center. 20 Jan. 1998 <http://www.slcc.edu/wc>. Used by permission.

Social Sciences Index. November 1997. Reprinted with permission by H. W. Wilson Company.

Tannen, Deborah. *That's Not What I Mean.* New York: Morrow, 1986.

Taylor, Todd. "The Persistence of *Difference* in Networked Classrooms: *Non-Negotiable Difference* and the African American Student Body." *Computers and Composition* 14 (1997): 169–178.

Terkel, Studs. *Working.* New York: Avon, 1972. xix.

Thomas, Lewis. *Lives of a Cell.* New York: Viking, 1974. 107.

Woolfolk, Anita E. *Educational Psychology.* 6th ed. Boston: Allyn, 1995. 551. Copyright © 1995 by Allyn & Bacon. Reprinted by permission.

Yahoo! [Online]. Oct. 1997 <http://www.yahoo.com>. Text and artwork copyright © 1998 by Yahoo! Inc. All rights reserved. YAHOO! and the YAHOO! logo are trademarks of YAHOO! Inc.

Zepezauer, Mark, and Arthur Naiman. *Take the Rich off Welfare.* Monroe, ME: Odonian, 1996.

Index

a

a/an, 502, 777, 825
Abbreviations, 470, 757–761
   forming plurals of, 726
   periods with, 696–697
ABI-INFORM, 162
-able/-ible, 691
Absolute phrases, 516–517
Abstract nouns, 503, 645
Abstracts
   citation of, 267, 274, 294
   humanities, 337–339
   natural science, 361–365
   in reports, 342, 372, 486
   social science, 384–386
Academic discourse, 26. *See also*
   Academic writing
Academic writing, 26, 27, 71, 130
   idioms used in, 800
   vocabulary in, 647, 651
accept/except, 825
Access-mode identifier, 271
Acknowledging sources, 199. *See*
   also Documentation
Acronyms, 470, 757, 759
   periods with, 697
Active voice, 506, 545–546,
   597–598

Ad hominem fallacy, 132
Address. *See also* URL
   commas in, 709
   email, 467–468, 801
   figures for, 761
   inserting into Web site, 452
Adjacent sentences, verb tenses in,
   541–542
Adjective clause, 517
Adjectives, 505, 558–559
   commonly confused, 560–561
   comparative, 505, 561–564
   coordinate, 705
   cumulative, 711–712
   demonstrative, 505, 559
   derived, 559
   indefinite, 505, 559
   interrogative, 505, 559
   irregular, 562
   ordering of, 790–791
   possessive, 505, 559
   predicate, 505
   proper, 749
   pure, 559
   superlative, 505, 561–564, 774
Adverb clause, 518
Adverbs, 506–507, 560
   ambiguity in, 583–584
   commonly confused, 560–561

Revision Symbols

Boldface letters and numbers refer to sections in the handbook.

ab	abbreviation	**53a**
ad	form of adjective/adverb	**28**
agr	agreement	**27**
awk	awkward diction or construction	**32, 40**
ca	case form	**25**
cap	capitalization	**52**
coh	coherence	**6c**
coord	coordination	**35b**
cs	comma splice	**30**
d	diction, word choice	**40, 42, 43**
dev	development needed	**3, 4, 5, 6f**
dm	dangling modifier	**32**
doc	check documentation	**13**
emph	emphasis needed	**37**
frag	sentence fragment	**29**
fs	fused sentence	**30**
hyph	hyphen	**54**
inc	incomplete construction	**24b, 33**
ital	italics	**52e–j**
lc	lowercase letter	**52**
log	logic	**7g**
mm	misplaced modifier	**32**
ms	manuscript form	**12f**
mix	mixed construction	**33d**
no ¶	no paragraph needed	**5**
num	number	**53b**
¶	paragraph	**6**
¶ dev	paragraph development needed	**6**

ref	unclear pronoun reference	**31**
rep	unnecessary repetition	**34b**
search	check research or citation	**10, 11, 13**
sp	spelling error	**44**
shift	inconsistent, shifted construction	**33a–c**
sub	sentence subordination	**35c**
t	verb tense error	**26d–e**
trans	transition needed	**5b, 6c**
var	sentence variety	**38**
vb	verb form error	**26**
w	wordy	**34e**
ww/wc	wrong word; word choice	**40, 41**
//	faulty parallelism	**36**
.?!	end punctuation	**45**
:	colon	**48**
ᵥ	apostrophe	**49**
—	dash	**51b**
( )	parentheses	**51a**
[ ]	brackets	**51c**
. . .	ellipses	**51d**
/	slash	**51e**
;	semicolon	**47**
ᵥ ᵥ	quotation marks	**50**
⋏	comma	**46**
⌒	close up	
⋀	insert a missing element	
⨞	delete	
∿	transpose order	

Useful Boxes

Help Boxes